Exploring Autodesk Revit 2017 for MEP

(4th Revised and Updated Edition)

Sham Tickoo
Professor
Purdue University Northwest
Hammond, Indiana, USA

Contributing Authors
Tickoo Institute of Emerging Technologies (TIET)
Gurgaon, India

CADCIM Technologies
Indiana, USA

ISBN: 978-93-86551-07-8
4th Revised and Updated Edition
(For Distribution in SAARC countries only)

Limits of Liability and Disclaimer of Warranty

The information contained in this book is the best of Author's & Publisher's knowledge. We are committed to serve students with best of our knowledge and resources. We have taken utmost care and attention while editing and printing of this book but Author and Publisher should not be held responsible for errors, omissions and any other unintentional mistake that might have crept in. However, errors brought to our notice shall be gratefully acknowledged and attended to.

All trademarks referred to in the book are acknowledged as properties of their respective owners. This book is written solely for the benefit and guidance of the students.

Distributors

COMPUTER BOOK CENTRE
12, Shrungar Shopping Centre
M.G. Road
BENGALURU–560001
Ph: 25587923/25584641

DECCAN AGENCIES
4-3-329, Bank Street
HYDERABAD-500195
Ph: 24756967/24756400

MICRO MEDIA
Shop No. 5, Mahendra Chambers
150 DN Rd. Next to Capital Cinema
V.T (C.S.T.) Station
MUMBAI-400001

BPB BOOK CENTRE
376 Old Lajpat Rai Market
DELHI-110006
Ph: 23861747

INFOTECH
G-2, Sidhartha Building, 96 Nehru Place
NEW DELHI-110019
Ph: 26438245

BPB PUBLICATIONS
20, Ansari Road, Darya Ganj
New Delhi-110002
Ph: 23254990/23254991

Published by Manish Jain for BPB Publications, 20 Ansari Road, Darya Ganj
New Delhi-110002 and Printed Repro India Pvt. Ltd, Mumbai

DEDICATION

To teachers, who make it possible to disseminate knowledge to enlighten the young and curious minds of our future generations

To students, who are dedicated to learning new technologies and making the world a better place to live in

SPECIAL RECOGNITION

A special thanks to Mr. Denis Cadu and the ADN team of Autodesk Inc. for their valuable support and professional guidance to procure the software for writing this textbook

THANKS

To employees of CADCIM Technologies and Tickoo Institute of Emerging Technologies (TIET) for their valuable help

Note

If you are a faculty member, you can register by clicking on the following link to access the teaching resources: ***http://www.cadcim.com/Registration.aspx***. The student resources are available at ***http://www.cadcim.com***.

Table of Contents

Dedication iii
Preface xiii

Chapter 1: Introduction to Autodesk Revit 2017 for MEP

Introduction to Autodesk Revit for MEP Enhanced 1-2
Mechanical Discipline 1-2
Electrical Discipline 1-2
Plumbing Discipline 1-2
Autodesk Revit as a Building Information Modeler (BIM) 1-3
Basic Concepts and Principles 1-3
Understanding the Parametric Building Modeling Technology 1-4
Terms Used in Autodesk Revit for MEP 1-5
Creating an MEP Model Using Parametric Elements 1-7
Visibility/Graphics Overrides, Scale, and Detail Level 1-8
Extracting Project Information 1-8
Creating an MEP Drawing Set 1-9
Creating an Unusual Building Geometry 1-9
Flexibility of Creating Special Elements 1-9
Creating Services Layouts 1-9
Working on Large Projects 1-9
Working in Large Teams and Coordinating with Consultants 1-10
Starting Autodesk Revit 2017 Enhanced 1-10
User Interface 1-12
Title Bar 1-12
Ribbon 1-12
Application Frame 1-15
Status Bar 1-16
View Control Bar 1-16
Options Bar 1-17
Type Selector 1-17
Drawing Area 1-17
Project Browser 1-17
Keyboard Accelerators 1-18
Properties Palette 1-18

Dialog Boxes 1-19
Multiple Document Environment 1-20
Interoperability of Autodesk Revit 1-21
Building Information Modeling and Autodesk Revit 2017 1-21
Worksharing using Revit Server 1-21
Autodesk Revit Help Enhanced 1-23
Self-Evaluation Test 1-23
Review Questions 1-24

Chapter 2: Getting Started with an MEP Project

Overview of an MEP Project 2-2
Essentials for an MEP Project 2-2
Starting a New Project 2-3
Project Units 2-4
Common Unit Type 2-5
HVAC Unit Type 2-8
Electrical Unit Type 2-9
Piping Unit Type 2-10
Project Templates 2-11
Creating a Custom Project Template 2-11
Settings for the Project Template 2-12
Linking Revit Models and Sharing Coordinates 2-20
Linked Revit Models in the Project Browser 2-21
Converting Linked Models to Groups - Binding Links 2-21
Controlling the Visibility of Linked Models 2-22
Managing Links 2-23
Including Elements of Linked Models in Schedules 2-24
Copying Linked Model Elements 2-24
Copying and Monitoring Linked Model Elements 2-24
Snaps Tool 2-25
Dimension Snaps Area 2-26
Object Snaps Area 2-26
The Temporary Overrides Area 2-27
Saving an MEP project 2-27
Using the Save As Tool 2-27
Using the Save Tool 2-28
The Options Dialog Box 2-28
General Tab 2-29
Graphics Tab 2-30
File Locations Tab 2-31
Rendering Tab 2-32
Check Spelling Tab 2-33
SteeringWheels Tab 2-34
ViewCube Tab 2-35
User Interface Tab Enhanced 2-36

Closing an MEP Project 2-37
Exiting an MEP Project 2-37
Opening an Existing MEP Project 2-37
Opening an Existing Project Using the Open Tool 2-37
Using the Windows Explorer to Open an Existing Project 2-39
Tutorial 1 - Office Space 2-39
Self-Evaluation Test 2-49
Review Questions 2-50
Exercise 1 - Power Plant 2-51

Chapter 3: Creating Building Envelopes

Introduction 3-2
Levels 3-2
Understanding Level Properties 3-3
Adding Levels 3-7
Modifying Level Parameters 3-9
Controlling the Visibility of Levels 3-9
Working with Grids 3-10
Creating Grids 3-10
Modifying Grids 3-13
Grid Properties 3-14
Reference Planes 3-15
Work Planes 3-16
Setting a Work Plane 3-16
Controlling the Visibility of Work Planes 3-16
Working with Project Views 3-17
Viewing a Building Envelope 3-17
Overriding the Visibility/Graphic of an Element 3-18
Overriding the Visibility/Graphic of Element Category 3-19
Making Elements Transparent 3-20
Using the Temporary Hide/Isolate Tool 3-20
Plan Views 3-21
Elevation Views 3-23
Section Views 3-25
Using the Scope Box Tool 3-28
Understanding Wall Types 3-29
Exterior Wall Type 3-30
Creating Architectural Walls 3-30
Specifying Architectural Wall Properties 3-30
Sketching Walls 3-35
Using Doors in a Building Model 3-39
Adding Doors 3-39
Understanding Door Properties 3-41

Adding a Door to a Wall 3-43
Adding Windows in a Building Model 3-45
Adding Windows 3-45
Understanding Window Properties 3-45
Adding a Window to a Wall 3-47
Doors and Windows as Wall Openings 3-48
Openings in the Wall 3-49
Creating Architectural Floors 3-49
Sketching the Floor Boundary 3-50
Placing Ceilings 3-52
Creating an Automatic Ceiling 3-52
Sketching a Ceiling 3-53
Using the Pick Walls Method 3-54
Modifying a Ceiling 3-54
Creating Rooms 3-55
Adding Rooms 3-55
Calculating Room Volumes 3-59
Cutting Openings in a Wall, Floor, and Ceiling 3-60
Creating Openings Using the By Face Tool 3-60
Creating Openings Using the Vertical Tool 3-61
Creating Openings Using the Wall Tool 3-61
Creating Openings Using the Dormer Tool 3-62
Creating Openings Using the Shaft Tool 3-62
Tutorial 1 - Office Building I 3-62
Tutorial 2 - Office Building II 3-76
Self-Evaluation Test 3-88
Review Questions 3-88
Exercise 1 - Residential Building 3-89

Chapter 4: Creating Spaces and Zones and Performing Load Analysis

Introduction 4-2
Space Modeling for Building Analysis 4-2
Creating Spaces 4-2
Modifying Spaces 4-8
Color Schemes 4-15
Creating and Editing Color Schemes 4-16
Applying a Color Scheme to the Spaces 4-19
Adding Color Scheme Legends 4-19
Modifying a Color Scheme 4-20
Modifying a Color Scheme Legend 4-20
Creating Zones from Spaces 4-20
Adding and Modifying HVAC Zones 4-21
Performing Heating and Cooling Load Analysis 4-24
Tutorial 1 - Placing Spaces- Office Space 4-28
Tutorial 2 - Creating Zones- Office Space 4-39
Tutorial 3 - Heating and Cooling Load Analysis 4-43

Self-Evaluation Test 4-51
Review Questions 4-51
Exercise 1 - Creating Spaces 4-51

Chapter 5: Creating an HVAC System

Introduction 5-2
Creating an HVAC System 5-2
Adding Supply Air Terminals 5-2
Adding Air Equipments 5-3
Creating Air Supply System 5-4
Creating Return Air Terminals, Air System, and Air Ductwork 5-5
Inspecting the Duct System 5-6
Checking the Duct System 5-7
Creating Duct Legend 5-7
Different Components of an HVAC System 5-7
Recommended Practices for Creating HVAC Systems 5-11
Generating HVAC System Layouts 5-11
Creating Ducts and Duct Fittings 5-15
Creating Ducts 5-15
Fabrication Details in Revit Enhanced 5-18
Configuring the Fabrication and Loading Services 5-18
Placing the Fabrication Parts 5-21
Tutorial 1 - Placing Air Terminals 5-24
Tutorial 2 - Creating Schedules-Air Terminals 5-31
Self-Evaluation Test 5-36
Review Questions 5-37
Exercise 1- HVAC System 5-37

Chapter 6: Creating an Electrical System

Introduction 6-2
Adding Electrical Equipment 6-2
Adding Transformers 6-2
Placing Switchboard Components 6-5
Placing the Panel Board or Distribution Board 6-7
Adding Power and System Devices 6-9
Adding Electrical Fixtures 6-9
Adding Lighting Devices 6-11
Adding Communication Devices 6-13
Adding Lighting Fixtures 6-14
Type Properties of a Lighting Fixture 6-16
Specifying the Electrical Settings 6-18
Setting the Wires 6-19
Setting the Voltage Definition 6-23
Setting the Distribution System 6-24
Setting the Load Calculations 6-25
Setting the Panel Schedules 6-26

Creating Power Distribution System 6-27
Performing Lighting Analysis 6-28
Creating Circuits 6-29
Adding Wires to the Circuit 6-29
Tutorial 1 - Planning the Electrical Systems 6-30
Tutorial 2 - Analyzing the Illumination Requirement 6-35
Tutorial 3 - Adding the Lighting Fixtures and Switches 6-47
Self-Evaluation Test 6-54
Review Questions 6-54
Exercise 1 - Placing Lighting Fixtures and Switches 6-55

Chapter 7: Creating Plumbing Systems

Introduction 7-2
Creating a Plumbing System 7-2
Adding Plumbing Fixtures 7-2
Specifying the Pipe Settings 7-6
Routing Pipes in the Pipe System Enhanced 7-13
Modifying a Pipe Segment 7-20
Placing Fittings 7-21
Placing Pipe Accessories 7-22
Tutorial 1 - Office-Space 7-23
Self-Evaluation Test 7-36
Review Questions 7-37
Exercise 1 - Community-Center 7-37

Chapter 8: Creating Fire Protection System

Introduction 8-2
Fire Protection Systems 8-2
Sprinkler Libraries 8-3
Piping Tools 8-3
Wet and Dry Fire Protection Systems 8-4
Designing the Fire Protection System 8-5
Setting Up a Fire Protection System Project 8-5
Creating the Space Schedule 8-8
Placing Sprinkler Heads 8-8
Connecting the Sprinklers 8-10
Tutorial 1 - Office Space- Fire Suppression 8-11
Self-Evaluation Test 8-19
Review Questions 8-19
Exercise 1- Fire Protection System 8-20

Chapter 9: Creating Construction Documents

Introduction 9-2
Dimensioning 9-2
Types of Dimensions 9-2

- Using Temporary Dimensions 9-3
- Entities in a Dimension 9-4
- Adding Permanent Dimensions 9-6
- Modifying Dimension Parameters 9-12
- Locking Permanent Dimensions 9-13
- Converting Temporary Dimensions into Permanent Dimensions 9-13

Text Notes 9-14
- Adding Text Notes 9-14
- Editing Text Notes 9-17

Adding Tags 9-18
- Tagging Elements by Category 9-18
- Tagging All Elements in a View 9-21

Callout Views 9-22
- Creating a Callout Using the Rectangle Tool 9-23
- Creating a Callout Using the Sketch Tool 9-23
- Displaying Callout View 9-24
- Modifying the Properties of a Callout View 9-24
- Creating Details in a Callout View 9-25

Drafting Details 9-25
- Creating a Drafting View 9-26
- Drafting a Detail 9-26

Duplicating Views 9-27
- Creating Duplicate View as Dependent View 9-27

Sheets 9-28
- Adding a Drawing Sheet to a Project 9-28
- Adding Views to a Drawing Sheet 9-29
- Modifying a Building Model in Sheets 9-32
- Adding Schedules to a Drawing Sheet 9-32
- Adding Guide Grids to a Sheet 9-33

Tutorial 1 - Office Space-Tags 9-33

Tutorial 2 - Office Space- Sheet 9-38

Self-Evaluation Test 9-44

Review Questions 9-44

Exercise 1 - Conference Hall 9-45

Chapter 10: Creating Families and Worksharing

Introduction to Massing 10-2

Understanding Massing Concepts 10-2

Creating the Massing Geometry 10-3
- Creating a Massing Geometry in the Family Editor 10-4
- Editing a Massing Geometry in the Family Editor 10-12
- Creating Cuts in a Massing Geometry Using the Family Editor 10-13
- Loading Massing Geometry into a Project 10-14
- Placing the Massing Geometry in a Project 10-15
- Creating the In-Place Mass in a Project 10-16

Massing in Conceptual Design Environment 10-17
- Interface of the Conceptual Design Environment 10-17

Creating Masses in the Conceptual Design Environment 10-18
Worksharing Concepts 10-23
Worksharing Using Workset Tools 10-23
Process of Worksharing 10-23
Saving Methodology in Worksharing 10-29
Element Ownership Concepts 10-30
Tutorial 1 - Dual Duct VAV box 10-31
Self-Evaluation Test 10-49
Review Questions 10-49
Exercise 1 - Supply Diffusers 10-50

Index **I-1**

Preface

Autodesk Revit 2017

Autodesk Revit is a Building Information Modeling software designed for Architects, Structural Engineers, MEP Engineers, Designers, and Contractors. The software has the capability to design the 3D model of a building with its various components, annotate the model with 2D drafting elements, and access building information from the building model's database.

Autodesk Revit also has the capabilty of executing 4D BIM with tools to plan and track various stages in the building's lifecycle, from concept to construction and later demolition.

Revit was developed by Charles River Software, in Newton, Massachusetts, on October 31, 1997. Leonid Raiz and Irwin Jungreis were the key developers of Revit, which was designed specifically with Architecture in mind. The Charles River Software company was later renamed to Revit Technology Corporation. In 2002, Autodesk purchased Revit from Revit Technology Corporation for their building solutions and infrastructure group.

The MEP discipline of Revit was introduced to the users in 2006 as Revit MEP. This software is primarily used in designing the Mechanical, Electrical, Plumbing, and Piping system, which are the three disciplines of building services. In Revit, you can create the plans, elevations, sections, schedules, and 3D models of a building project that can be easily accessed and shared between different users.

The **Exploring Autodesk Revit 2017 for MEP** textbook explains the concepts and principles of MEP in Revit through practical examples, tutorials, and exercises. This enables the users to harness the power of BIM with Autodesk Revit for their specific use. In this textbook, the author explains in details the procedure of evaluating HVAC cooling and heating loads and the usage of tools required for designing HVAC, electrical, and plumbing design. In addition, in this textbook, you will learn tools and concepts for creating families and process to document the final drawings.

In this textbook, special emphasis has been laid on the concepts of space modeling and tools to create systems for all disciplines (MEP). Each concept in this textbook is explained using the detailed description and relevant graphical examples and illustrations. The accompanying tutorials and exercises, which relate to the real world projects, help you understand the usage and abilities of the tools available in Autodesk Revit. Along with the main text, the chapters have been punctuated with tips and notes to make the concepts clear, thereby enabling you to create your own innovative projects.

The main features of this textbook are as follows:

- **Project-based Approach**
  The author has adopted the project-based approach and the learn-by-doing theme throughout the textbook. This approach guides the users through the process of creating the designs given in the tutorials.

- **Real-World Designs as Projects**
  The author has used real-world building designs and architectural examples as projects in this textbook so that the users can correlate them to the real-time designs.

- **Tips and Notes**
  Additional information related to various topics is provided to the users in the form of tips and notes.

- **Learning Objectives**
  The first page of every chapter summarizes the topics that are covered in that chapter.

- **Self-Evaluation Test, Review Questions, and Exercises**
  The chapters ends with a Self-Evaluation Test so that the users can assess their knowledge of the chapter. The answers to Self-Evaluation Test are given at the end of the chapter. Also, the Review Questions and Exercises are given at the end of chapter and they can be used by the instructors as test questions and exercises.

- **Heavily Illustrated Text**
  The text in this book is heavily illustrated with about 200 line diagrams and screen capture images.

Symbols Used in the Textbook

Note

The author has provided additional information to the users about the topic being discussed in the form of notes.

Tip

Special information and techniques are provided in the form of tips that help in increasing the efficiency of the users.

Enhanced

This symbol indicates that the command or tool being discussed has been enhanced in Autodesk Revit 2017.

Formatting Conventions Used in the Textbook

Please refer to the following list for the formatting conventions used in this textbook.

- Names of tools, buttons, options, browser, palette, panels, and tabs are written in boldface.

  Example: The **Duct** tool, the **Modify** button, the **HVAC** panel, the **Systems** tab, **Properties** palette, **Project Browser**, and so on.

- Names of dialog boxes, drop-downs, drop-down lists, list boxes, areas, edit boxes, check boxes, and radio buttons are written in boldface.

  Example: The **Options** dialog box, the **Wire** drop-down in the **Electrical** panel of the **Systems** tab, the **Name** edit box in the **Name** dialog box, the **Chain** check box in the **Options Bar**, and so on.

- Values entered in edit boxes are written in boldface.

  Example: Enter **4" (100mm)** in the **Offset** edit box.

- Names of the files saved are italicized.

  Example: *c03_Office-Space_tut2.rvt*

- The methods of invoking a tool/option from the ribbon, Application Menu, or the shortcut keys are given in a shaded box.

  Ribbon: Systems > Electrical > Wire drop-down > Arc Wire
  Application Menu: New
  Shortcut Keys: CTRL+N

- When you select an element or a component, a contextual tab is displayed depending upon the entity selected. For example: **Modify | (Elements / Components)**.

Naming Conventions Used in the Textbook

Tool

If you click on an item in a panel of the ribbon and a command is invoked to create/edit an object or perform some action, then that item is termed as **tool**.

For example:
Duct tool, **Air Terminal** tool, **Isolated** tool
Filled Region tool, **Trim/Extend to Corner** tool, **Rotate** tool

If you click on an item in a panel of the ribbon and a dialog box is invoked wherein you can set the properties to create/edit an object, then that item is also termed as **tool**, refer to Figure 1.
For example:
Load Family tool, **Duct** tool, **Wall** tool
Plumbing Fixture tool, **Visibility/Graphics** tool

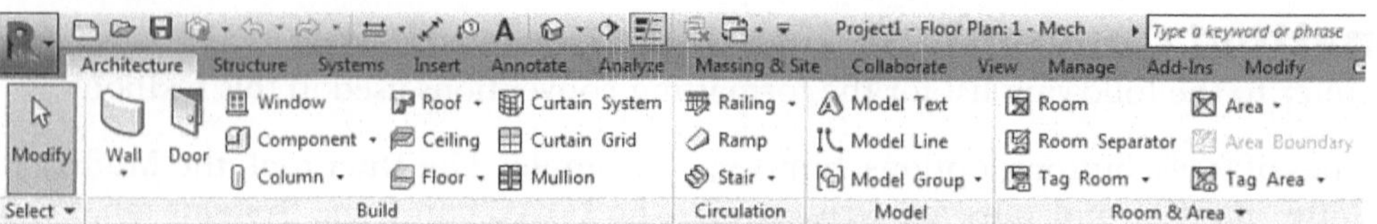

***Figure 1** Tools in the ribbon*

Button

The item in a dialog box that has a 3d shape like a button is termed as **button**. For example, **OK** button, **Cancel** button, **Apply** button, and so on. If the item in a ribbon is used to exit a tool or a mode, it is also termed as button. For example, **Modify** button, **Finish Editing System** button, **Cancel Editing System** button, and so on; refer to Figure 2.

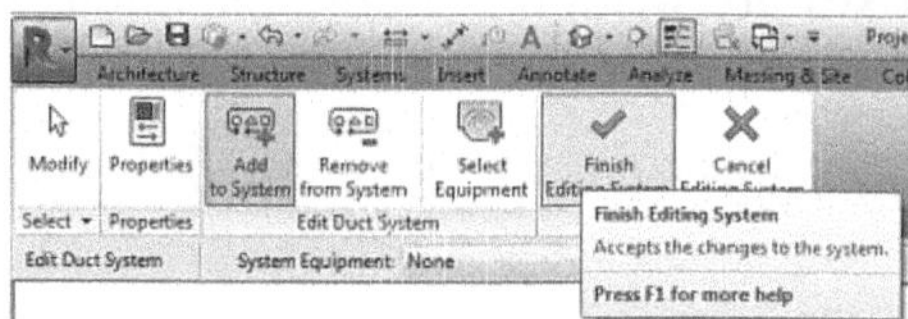

***Figure 2** Choosing the **Finish Editing System** button*

Dialog Box

In this textbook, different terms are used for referring to the components of a dialog box. Refer to Figure 3 for the terminology used.

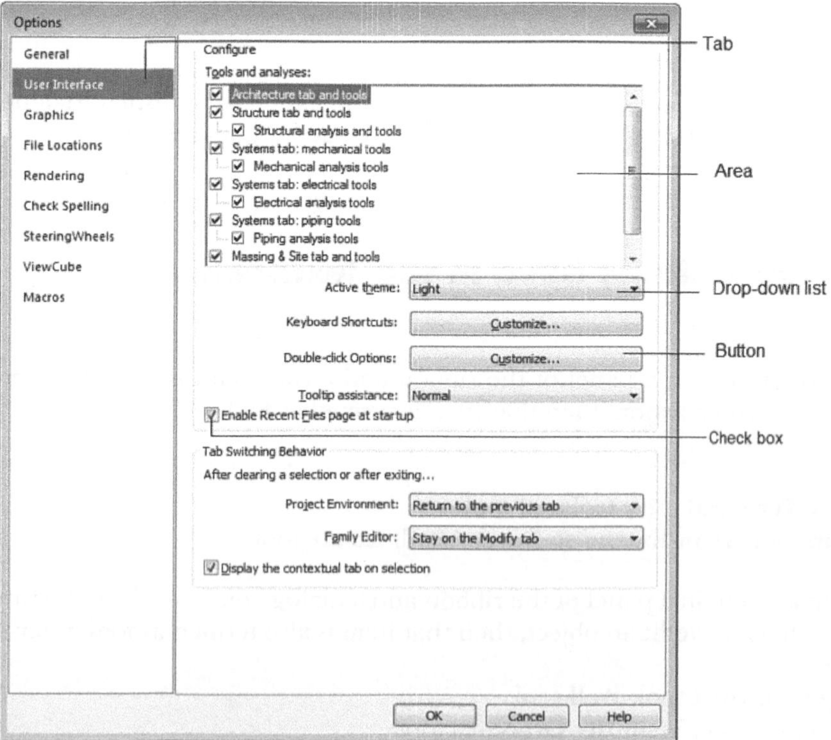

***Figure 3** Components of a dialog box*

Drop-down

A drop-down is the one in which a set of common tools are grouped together for creating an object. You can identify a drop-down with a down arrow on it. These drop-downs are given a name based on the tools grouped in them. For example, **Wall** drop-down, **Component** drop-down, **Region** drop-down, and so on; refer to Figure 4.

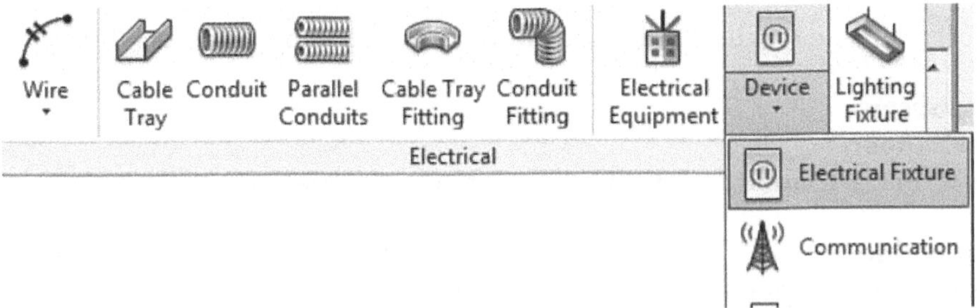

***Figure 4** Choosing a tool from the drop-down*

Drop-down List

A drop-down list is the one in which a set of options are grouped together. You can set various parameters using these options. You can identify a drop-down list with a down arrow on it. For example, **Type Selector** drop-down list, **Units** drop-down list, and so on; refer to Figure 5.

Options

Options are the items that are available in shortcut menus, drop-down lists, dialog boxes, and so on. For example, choose the **Zoom In Region** option from the shortcut menu displayed on right-clicking in the drawing area; refer to Figure 6.

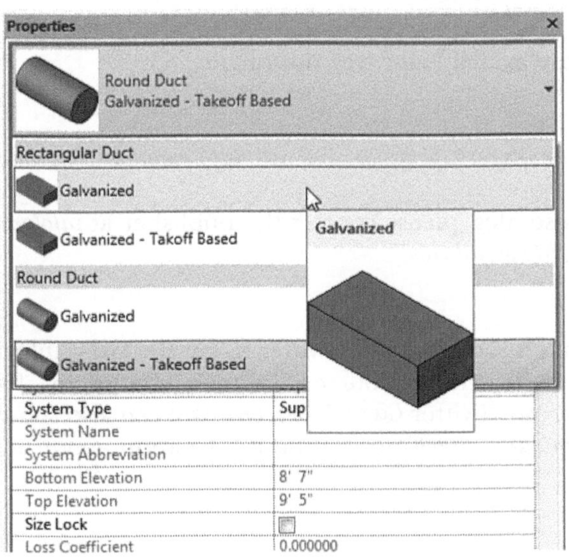

***Figure 5** Selecting an option from the **Type Selector** drop-down list*

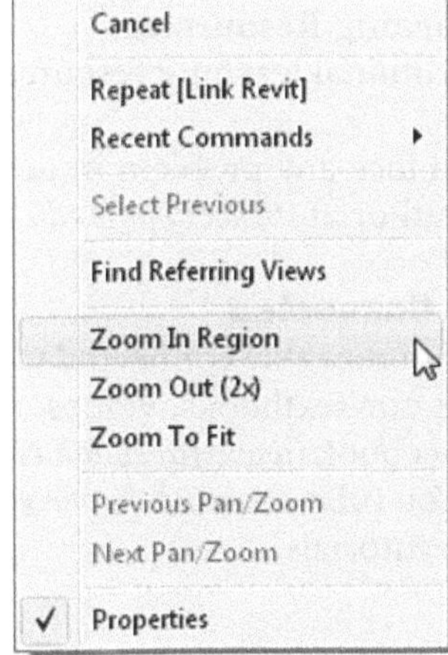

***Figure 6** Choosing an option from the shortcut menu*

Free Companion Website

It has been our constant endeavor to provide you the best textbooks and services at affordable price. In this endeavor, we have come out with a Free Companion website that will facilitate the process of teaching and learning of Autodesk Revit 2017. If you purchase this textbook, you will get access to the files on the Companion website.

The resources available for the faculty and students in this website are as follows:

Faculty Resources

- **Technical Support**
  You can get online technical support by contacting ***info@tiet.in***.

- **Instructor Guide**
  Solutions to all review questions and exercises in the textbook are provided in this guide to help the faculty members test the skills of the students.

- **PowerPoint Presentations**
  The contents of the book are arranged in PowerPoint slides that can be used by the faculty for their lectures.

- **Revit Files**
  The Revit files (*.rvt*) used in tutorials and exercises are available for free download.

Student Resources

- **Technical Support**
  You can get online technical support by contacting ***info@tiet.in***.

- **Revit Files**
  The Revit files (*.rvt*) used in tutorials are available for free download.

- **Learning Resources**
  Additional learning resources at *http://revitxperts.blogspot.com* and *http://youtube.com/cadcimtech*.

If you face any problem in accessing these files, please contact the publisher at *info@tiet.in* or the author at *stickoo@pnw.edu* or *tickoo525@gmail.com*.

Stay Connected

You can now stay connected with us through Facebook and Twitter to get the latest information about our textbooks, videos, and teaching/learning resources. To get such updates, follow us on Facebook (***www.facebook.com/cadcim***) and Twitter (***@cadcimtech***). You can also subscribe to our YouTube channel (***www.youtube.com/cadcimtech***) to get the information about our latest video tutorials.

Chapter 1

Introduction to Autodesk Revit 2017 for MEP

Learning Objectives

After completing this chapter, you will be able to:

- *Understand the basic concepts and principles of Revit for MEP*
- *Understand various terms used in Revit for MEP*
- *Describe the parametric behavior of Revit*
- *Start the Revit 2017 program*
- *Understand the interface of Revit 2017*
- *Access the Revit 2017 Help*

INTRODUCTION TO Autodesk Revit FOR MEP

Enhanced

Autodesk Revit is a Building Information Modeling software, which is developed for professionals in the AEC (Architecture, Engineering, and Construction) industry. Revit is used by Architects, Structural Engineers, MEP Engineers, Designers and Contractors for a building project.

The MEP functionality in Revit was introduced in 2006 as a separate software, Revit MEP. It was specifically built for MEP engineers and designers. Since then, it has become very popular in the Building Information Modeling (BIM) workflow. This software provides engineers and designers with tools for the analysis, modeling, and design of various building elements and systems for MEP (Mechanical, Electrical, and Plumbing) services. In 2017 release of Autodesk Revit, Revit MEP has been discontinued as an individual software and the MEP functionality of this software is now available in the Revit 2017 suite.

Revit is a BIM software that helps users to coordinate the documentation of MEP designs with other engineering disciplines. Its integrated parametric modeling technology is used to create the information model of a project and to collect and coordinate information across all its representations. In Autodesk Revit, drawing sheets, 2D views, 3D views, sectional view, callout details, and schedules directly represent the same building information model (BIM) as the real one does. Autodesk Revit (for MEP) is developed with an approach to bring the Mechanical, Electrical, and Plumbing engineers together under the BIM framework and make the building services system efficient and interoperable with other systems. In Revit, a designer can not only work with various pre-designed elements of different MEP disciplines but can also model customized elements and add parameters to them. This helps in modeling complex designs with various permutations. Different disciplines of Revit (for MEP) are briefly described next.

Mechanical Discipline

In the Mechanical discipline, you can develop an HVAC (Heating, Ventilation and Air Conditioning) system, keeping in view the energy requirements of that building. The study of the energy requirements of the building is very essential for developing an efficient and cost effective design. In mechanical discipline, you can design the whole ducting network with the ventilation layout plan. You can also route the piping or ducting networks manually or generate routing solutions by using various tools in this software. In this discipline, you can also develop a Fire Suppression System.

Electrical Discipline

While working with the electrical discipline, you can design an electrical system. In this system, you can add various lighting fixtures, switches, alarms, communication devices, and more as per the requirement of the project. You can also add panels and prepare panel schedules and perform the load analysis. Further, you can connect the devices and fixtures through logical circuits.

Plumbing Discipline

In this discipline, you can design a plumbing system for a project. In the plumbing system, you can add plumbing fittings, accessories, and fixtures as per the requirement of a project. In addition, you can also design fire fighting system for a building and add fire safety components to the system.

Autodesk Revit AS A BUILDING INFORMATION MODELER (BIM)

The history of computer aided design and documentation dates back to the early 1980s when architects and engineers began using this technology for documenting their projects. Realizing its advantages, information sharing capabilities were developed, especially to share data with other consultants. This led to the development of object-based CAD systems in the early 1990s. Before the development of these systems, objects such as HVAC components, pipes, plumbing fixtures, electrical fixture, and more were stored as a non-graphical data with the assigned graphics. These systems arranged the information logically but were unable to optimize its usage in a building project. Realizing the advantages of the solid modeling tools, the mechanical and manufacturing industry professionals began using the information modeling CAD technology. This technology enabled them to extract data based on the relationship between model elements.

The Building Information Modeling (BIM) provided an alternative approach to building design, construction, and management. This approach, however, required a suitable technology to implement and reap its benefits. In such a situation, the use of parametric technology with the Building Information Modeling approach was envisaged as an ideal combination. In 1997, a group of mechanical CAD technologists began working on a new software dedicated to the building industry. They developed a software that was suitable for creating MEP projects. This led to the development of Autodesk Revit.

Autodesk Revit is a design and documentation platform in which a digital MEP model is created using the parametric elements such as HVAC system, mechanical equipment, plumbing network, fire fighting, and so on. All MEP elements have inherent characteristics, and therefore, they can be tracked, managed, and maintained by using computer.

BASIC CONCEPTS AND PRINCIPLES

Autodesk Revit enables you to envisage and develop an MEP model with actual 3D parametric elements. It provides a new approach to MEP design and implementation process. It replicates the way MEP engineers conceive the structure of an MEP system. For example, the 2D CAD platforms mostly use lines to represent all elements, as shown in Figure 1-1. However, in Autodesk Revit, you can create the MEP model of a building project using 3D elements, such as HVAC components, pipes, plumbing fixtures, electrical fixtures, as shown in Figure 1-2.

Using these 3D elements, you can visualize the MEP project with respect to its scale, volume, and proportions. This enables you to study design alternatives and develop superior quality design solutions. Autodesk Revit automates routine drafting and coordination tasks and helps in reducing errors in documentation. This, in turn, saves time, improves the speed of documentation, and lowers the cost for the users.

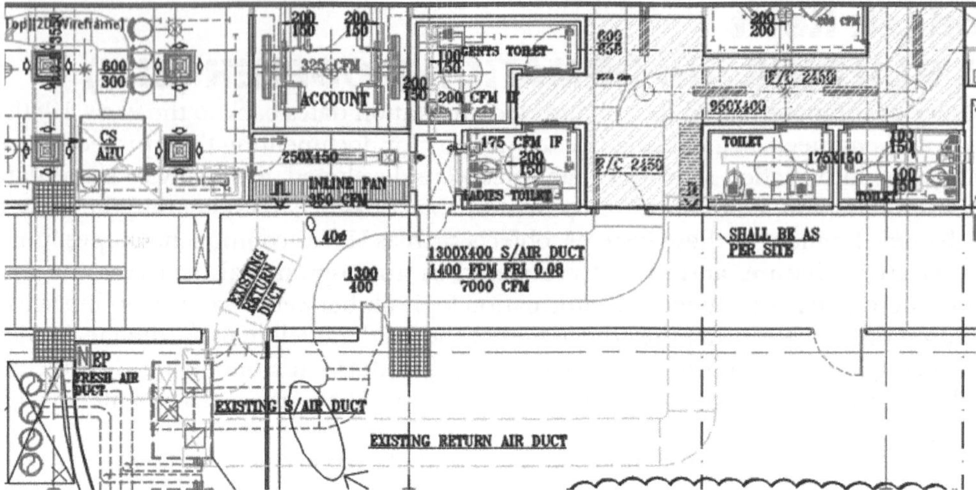

Figure 1-1 *CAD project created using 2D lines*

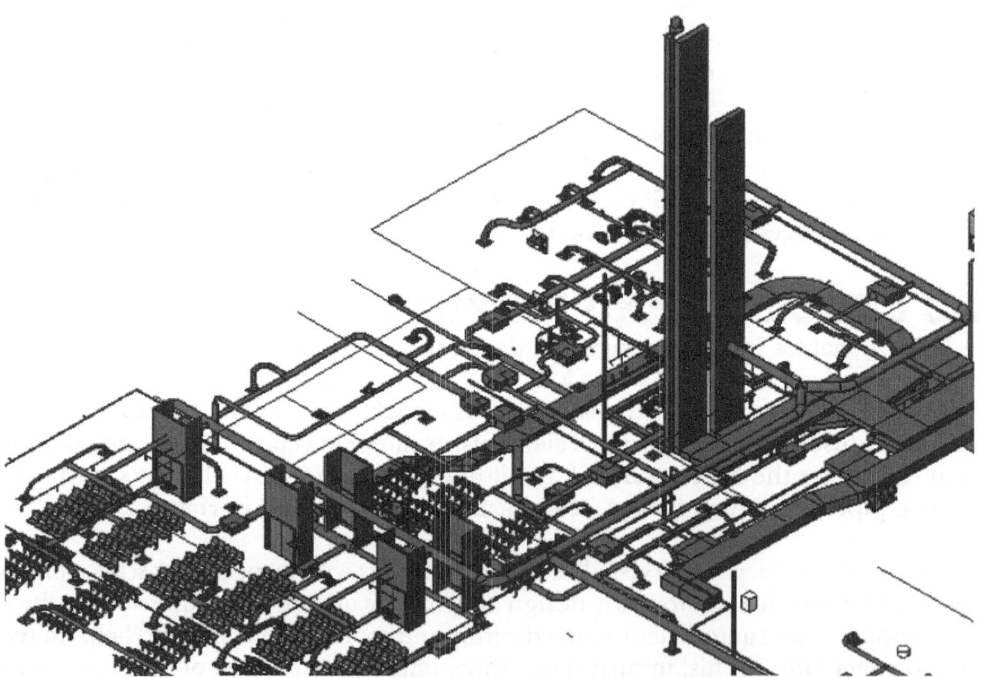

Figure 1-2 *An MEP project created using parametric elements*

Understanding the Parametric Building Modeling Technology

A project in Autodesk Revit is created using the inbuilt parametric building elements. The term 'parametric' refers to parameters that define relationship between various building elements. Some of these relationships are defined by Autodesk Revit itself and others by the users. For example, the relationship between air terminals and ceilings are defined by MEP and the relationship between connectors and ducts are defined by the users.

In an MEP project, each element has inbuilt bidirectional associativity with many other elements. These elements together form an integrated building information model. This model contains all data needed for the design and development of the project. You can then use this data to create project presentation views such as ceiling plans, sections, elevations, and so on for documentation. As you modify the model while working in certain views, Autodesk Revit's parametric change engine automatically updates other views. This capability is, therefore, the underlying concept in Autodesk Revit.

Autodesk Revit's parametric change engine enables you to modify design elements at any stage of the project development. As changes in the model are reflected immediately and automatically in the project, the time and effort required in coordinating the changes in other views is saved. This feature provides immense flexibility in the design and development process along with an error-free documentation.

Autodesk Revit also provides a variety of in-built parametric element libraries that can be selected and used to create a building model. It also provides you with the flexibility to modify the properties of these elements or to create your own parametric elements, based on the project requirement.

Terms Used in Autodesk Revit for MEP

Before working with Autodesk Revit, it is important to understand the basic terms used for creating a building model. Various terms in Autodesk Revit such as project, level, category, family, type, and instance are described next.

Autodesk Revit Project

A project in Autodesk Revit is similar to an actual project. In an actual project, the entire documentation such as drawings, 3D views, specifications, schedules, cost estimates, and so on are inherently linked and read together. Similarly, in Autodesk Revit, a project not only includes the digital 3D MEP model but also its parametrically associated documentation. Thus, all the components such as the building model and its standard views, MEP drawings, and schedules together form a complete project. A project file contains all the project information such as building and MEP elements used in a project, drawing sheets, schedules, cost estimates, 3D views, renderings, and so on. A project file also stores various settings such as environment, lighting, and so on. As the entire data is stored in the same file, so it becomes easier for Autodesk Revit to coordinate the database.

Levels in a Building Model

In Autodesk Revit, a building model is divided into different levels. These levels may be understood as infinite horizontal planes that act as hosts for different elements such as roof, floor, ceiling, and so on. Each element that you create belongs to a particular level.

Subdivisions of Elements into Categories and Subcategories

Apart from MEP elements, an Autodesk Revit project also contains other associated elements such as annotations, imported files, links, and so on. These elements have been divided into the following categories:

Model Category : Consists of various MEP elements such as HVAC elements, ducts, air terminals, diffusers, pipes, plumbing fixtures, electrical conduits, and others used in creating systems

Annotation Category : Consists of annotations such as dimensions, text notes, tags, symbols, and so on

Datum Category : Consists of datums such as levels, grids, reference planes, and so on

View Category : Consists of interactive project views such as the architectural, mechanical, and plumbing floor plans, elevations, sections, 3D views, and renderings

In addition to these four categories, other categories such as **Imported**, **Workset**, **Filter**, and **Revit Categories** can also exist if the project has imported files, enabled worksets, or linked Autodesk Revit projects, respectively.

Families in Autodesk Revit

Another powerful concept in Autodesk Revit is family. A family is described as a set of elements of the same category that are grouped together based on certain common parameters or characteristics. Elements of the same family may have different properties, but they all have common characteristics. For example, **Rectangular Diffuser - Round Connection** is an air diffuser family and it contains different sizes of air diffusers. Family files have the *.rfa* extension. You can load additional MEP component families from the libraries provided in Autodesk Revit package.

Families are further divided into certain types. A type or family type, as it is called, is a specific size or style of a family. For example, **Rectangular Diffuser - Round Connection 24x24 - 10 Neck** in Metric (**M_Rectangular Diffuser - Round Connection 600x600- 230 Neck)** is an air diffuser type. Family and family types can also be used to create new families using the **Family Editor**.

Instances are the actual usage of model elements in an MEP model or annotations in a drawing sheet. A family type, created at a new location, is identified as an instance of the family type. All the instances of the same family type have the same properties. Therefore, when you modify the properties of a family type, the properties of all its instances also get modified. The family categorization of Revit elements is given below:

Model Category : Air diffuser
Family : **Rectangular Diffuser - Round Connection**
Family type : **Rectangular Diffuser - Round Connection 24x24 - 10 Neck**
Instance : Particular usage of a family type

The hierarchy of service elements in Autodesk Revit plays an important role in providing flexibility and ease in managing a change in a building model. Figure 1-3 shows the hierarchy of categories and families in a typical Autodesk Revit project.

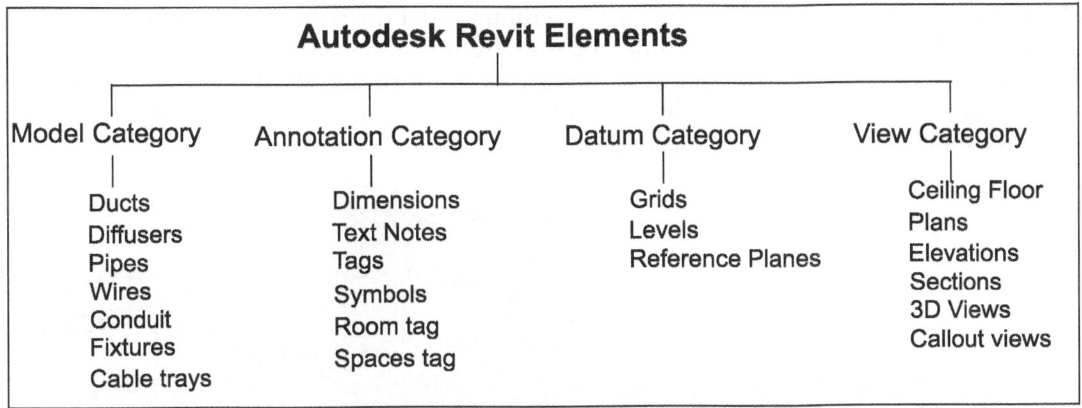

Figure 1-3 *Hierarchy of Autodesk Revit MEP categories and families*

Creating an MEP Model Using Parametric Elements

Another classification of categories of elements followed in Autodesk Revit is based on their usage. Autodesk Revit uses five classes of elements: Host, component, annotation, view, and datum. Hosts are the element categories that form the basic system of an MEP model and include model elements such as ducts, pipes, cables, and more. Components are the elements that are added to host elements or act as stand-alone elements such as air terminals, diffusers, and conduits. Annotations are the 2D, view-specific elements such as dimensions, tags, text notes, and so on that add content to the project documentation. Views represent various orientations of a building model such as plans, elevations, sections, 3D views, and so on. Datum refers to the reference elements that assist you in creating a building model, which include grids, levels, reference planes, and so on.

There is no specific methodology available for creating a services model in Autodesk Revit. It provides you with the flexibility of generating the MEP model based on the project requirement, design complexity, and other factors. However, the following steps describe a general procedure that may be followed for creating an MEP model using the built-in parametric elements provided in Autodesk Revit.

In Revit, you can start designing a project for individual discipline (Mechanical, Electrical, or Plumbing) by selecting the specific template. For example, to design a project for a mechanical discipline, you can select the *Mechanical-Default.rte* (*Mechanical-Default_Metric.rte*) template file. Alternatively, you can start a project to work in all the disciplines by selecting the *Systems-Default.rte* (*System-Default_Metric.rte*) template file.

Once you have started a project, you need to copy the levels of the architectural model to the current project or create additional levels as per the requirement. Next, you can start with any of the disciplines by activating the specific view from the **Project Browser**. For example, to start with mechanical discipline, activate the desired mechanical plan view under **Views (Discipline) > Mechanical** node from the **Project Browser**.

In Revit, there are specific workflows for each discipline as per the requirement of the project. The workflow for disciplines generally includes analysis, design, and documentation. For mechanical discipline, you need to analyze spaces to design an appropriate HVAC system. Then, based on the analysis, you need to place air terminals, equipment, and design ducts for the system. Figure 1-4 shows an example of a mechanical system.

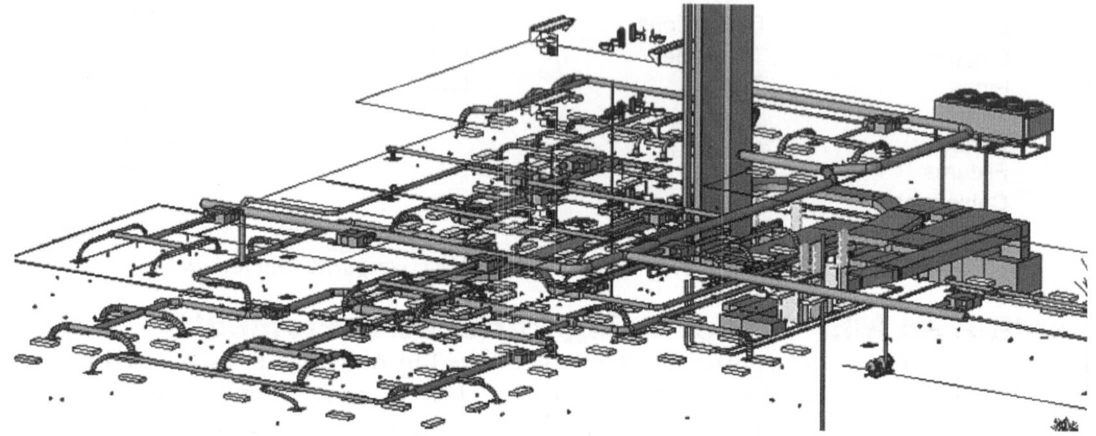

Figure 1-4 *Mechanical system with its elements*

Visibility/Graphics Overrides, Scale, and Detail Level

Autodesk Revit enables you to control the display and graphic representation of a single element or the element category of various elements in the project views. This is done by using the visibility and graphics overrides tools. You can select a model category and modify its linetype and detail level. This can also be done for various annotation category elements and imported files. These settings can be done for each project view based on its desired representation. You can also hide an element or an element category in a view using the **Hide in view** and **Isolate** tools. You can override the graphic representation of an element or an element category in any view using the **Visibility/Graphics** tool.

The scale is another important concept in an Autodesk Revit project. You can set the scale for each project view by selecting it from the available list of standard scales such as **1/16"=1'0"**, **1/4"=1'0"**, **1"=1'0"**, **1/2"=1'0"** for Imperial system or **1: 50**, **1: 100**, **1: 200**, **1: 500** for Metric system. As you set a scale, Autodesk Revit automatically sets the detail level that is appropriate for it. There are three detail levels provided in an Autodesk Revit project: **Coarse**, **Medium**, and **Fine**. You can also set the detail level manually for each project view. Each detail level has an associated linetype and the detail lines associated with it. The details of annotations, such as dimensions, tags, and so on, are also defined by the selected scale.

Extracting Project Information

A single integrated building information is used to create and represent a building project. You can extract project information from a building model and create area schemes, schedule, and cost estimates, and then add them to the project presentation.

Autodesk Revit also enables you to export the extracted database to the industry standard Open Database Connectivity (ODBC) compliant relational database tables. The use of the building information model to extract database information eliminates the error-prone method of measuring building spaces individually.

Creating an MEP Drawing Set

After creating the building model, you can easily arrange the project views by plotting them on the drawing sheets. The drawing sheets can also be organized in a project file based on the established CAD standards followed by the firm. In this manner, the project documentation can easily be transformed from the conceptual design stage to the design development stage and finally to the construction document stage. The project view on a drawing sheet is only a graphical representation of the building information model. Therefore, any modification in it is immediately made in all associated project views, keeping the drawing set always updated.

Creating an Unusual Building Geometry

Autodesk Revit also helps you conceptualize a building project in terms of its volume, shape, and proportions before working with actual building elements. This is done by using the **Massing** tool, which enables you to create quick 3D models of buildings and conduct volumetric and proportion study on overall masses. It also enables you to visualize and create an unusual building geometry. The same massing model can then be converted into a building model with individual parametric building elements. It provides continuity to the generation of building model right from sketch design to its development. You can also create various custom MEP elements as per the project requirement and then load them to the project.

Flexibility of Creating Special Elements

Autodesk Revit provides a large number of in-built family types of various model elements and annotations. Each parametric element has the associated properties that can be modified based on the project requirement.

Autodesk Revit also enables you to create the elements that are designed specifically for a particular location. The in-built family editor enables you to create new elements using family templates. This provides you with the flexibility of using in-built elements for creating your own elements. For example, using the furniture template, you can create a reception desk that is suitable for a particular location in the design.

Creating Services Layouts

Autodesk Revit provides you with an extensive in-built library of MEP elements that can be used to add elements such as ducts, air terminals, diffusers, conduits, and so on to a project. This helps MEP consultants to include these service elements in the basic architectural building model and check for inconsistency, if any.

Working on Large Projects

In Autodesk Revit, you can work on large projects by linking different building projects together. For a large project that comprises of a number of buildings, you can create individual buildings as separate projects and then link all of them into a single base file. The database recognizes the linked projects and includes them in the project representation of the base file.

For example, while working on a large educational institution campus, you can create separate project files for academic building, administration area, gymnasium, cafeteria, computer centre, and so on, and then link them into the base site plan file. In this manner, large projects can be subdivided and worked upon simultaneously.

Working in Large Teams and Coordinating with Consultants

In Autodesk Revit, worksets enable the division of the MEP model into small editable sets of disciplines such as Mechanical, Electrical, and Plumbing. The worksets can be assigned to different teams working on the same project and then their work can easily be coordinated by sharing the files in the central file location. The effort required to coordinate, collaborate, and communicate the changes between various worksets is taken care of by the computer. Various consultants working on a project can be assigned a workset with a set of editable elements. They can then incorporate their services and modify the associated elements.

For example, a high rise commercial building project can be divided into different worksets with independent teams working on different disciplines such as Mechanical, Electrical, Plumbing, Architecture, Structure, and so on. The structural consultants can be assigned to the exterior skin and the core workset, in which they can incorporate structural elements. Similarly, the rest of the teams can work independently on different worksets.

STARTING Autodesk Revit 2017

You can start Autodesk Revit by double-clicking on the **Revit 2017** icon on the desktop. Alternatively, you can choose the **Start** button at the lower left corner of the screen (default position) in the taskbar for Windows 7 and then choose **All Programs > Autodesk > Revit 2017 > Revit 2017**, as shown in Figure 1-5, to display the interface, as shown in Figure 1-6. Note that this path is for the Windows 7 operating system.

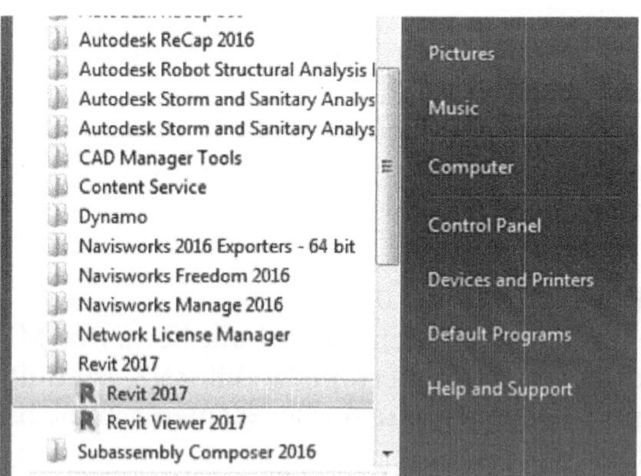

Figure 1-5 *Starting Autodesk Revit 2017 from the taskbar*

Note

The path for starting Autodesk Revit depends on the operating system being used.

The screen interface has three sections: **Projects**, **Families**, and **Resources**. The options in the **Projects** section are used to open a new or an existing project. The options in the **Families** section are used to open a new or an existing family. You can also invoke the Conceptual Mass environment from this section to create a conceptual mass model. If you choose the

Autodesk Seek option from the **Families** section, you will be directed to *http://seek.autodesk.com/localeTaxBrowse.htm?category=en_us:adsk:revit-mep&locale=en-us&globaldd=globaldropdown.option.b* and the **AUTODESK® Revit WEB LIBRARY - US EDITION** page will open. From this page, you can download various components for your project.

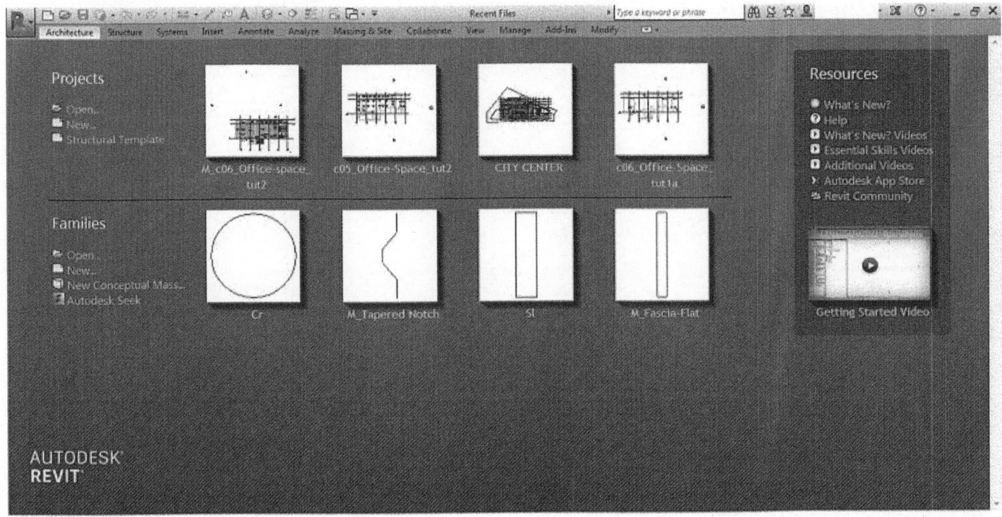

Figure 1-6 *The interface of Autodesk Revit 2017*

In the **Resources** section, you can choose the **What's New?** option to get information about the new tools and features in Autodesk Revit 2017. In addition, you can choose the **Help** option from the **Resources** section. On doing so, you will be directed to the link *http://help.autodesk.com/view/RVT/2017/ENU/*. In this section, you can choose the **Additional Videos** option to view additional video tutorials other than essential videos of working in Revit. On choosing this option, the **Autodesk Revit 2017** page will be displayed. In right section of this page, the various videos related to Revit workflow are listed with headings mentioning the title of the video. You can choose any of the headings and watch the video tutorial related to the topic mentioned in it. In the **Resources** section, you can choose the **Autodesk App Store** option to launch the Autodesk App Store website for Revit. The App Store will provide access to add-ins that will allow you to more efficiently author information-rich Building Information Models in Revit. In the **Resources** section, you can also choose the **Getting Started Video** option to view the videos related to basic and advanced concepts in Autodesk Revit 2017. You can also choose the **Revit Community** option from the **Resources** section to view various online communities related to Autodesk Revit. Various articles on the basic and advanced topics of Revit 2017 posted by members of these communities can also be viewed in this section.

In the **Projects** section, choose the **Open** option; the **Open** dialog box will be displayed. Browse to the desired location in the dialog box and select the file. Now, choose the **Open** button to open the file.

To open a new project file, choose the **New** option from the **Projects** section. Alternatively, choose **New > Project** from the **Application Menu**; the **New Project** dialog box will be displayed. In this dialog box, make sure that the **Project** radio button is selected, and then choose the **OK** button; a new project file will open and the interface screen is activated.

USER INTERFACE

In Autodesk Revit, the user interface consists of the Ribbon, Drawing area, Properties palette, Status Bar, and the View Control Bar, as shown in Figure 1-7. In Autodesk Revit, all the tools are grouped in several panels in the ribbon.

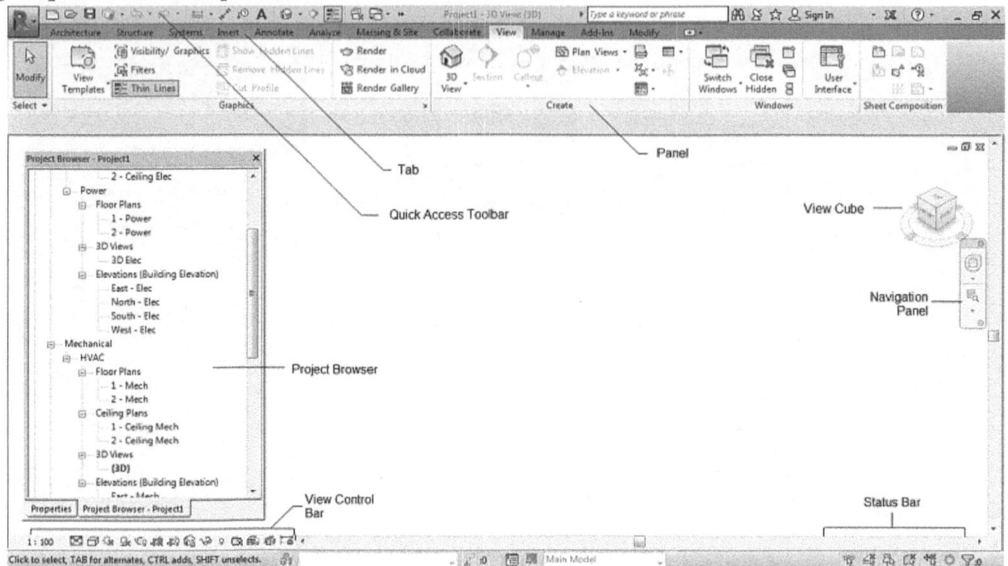

Figure 1-7 The Autodesk Revit 2017 user interface screen

The ribbon, which contains task-based tabs and panels, streamlines the structural workflow and optimizes the project delivery time. In Autodesk Revit, when you select an element in the drawing area, the ribbon displays a contextual tab that comprises of tools corresponding to the selected element. The interface of Autodesk Revit is similar to the interfaces of many other Microsoft Windows-based programs. The main components in the Revit interface are discussed next.

Title Bar

The Title Bar, docked on the top portion of the user interface, displays the program's logo, name of the current project, and the view opened in the viewing area. **Project 1- Floor Plan: Level 1** is the default project name and view displayed.

Ribbon

The ribbon, as shown in Figure 1-8, is an interface that is used to invoke tools. When you open a file, the ribbon is displayed at the top in the screen. It comprises of task-based tabs and panels, refer to Figure 1-8, which provide all the tools necessary for creating a project. The tabs and panels in the ribbon can be customized according to the need of the user. This can be done by moving the panels and changing the view states of the ribbon (the method of changing the ribbon view state is discussed later in this chapter). The ribbon has three types of buttons: general, drop-down, and split. These buttons can be used from the panels.

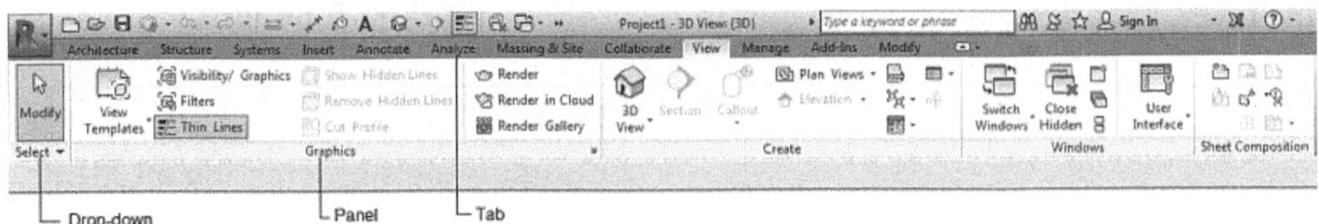

Figure 1-8 Different components of a ribbon

In the ribbon, you can move a panel and place it anywhere on the screen. To do so, press and hold the left mouse button on the panel label in the ribbon, and then drag the panel to a desired place on the screen. After using the tools of the moved panel, place the panel back to the ribbon. To do so, place the cursor on the moved panel and choose the **Return Panels to Ribbon** button from the upper right corner of this panel, as shown in Figure 1-9; the panel will return to the ribbon.

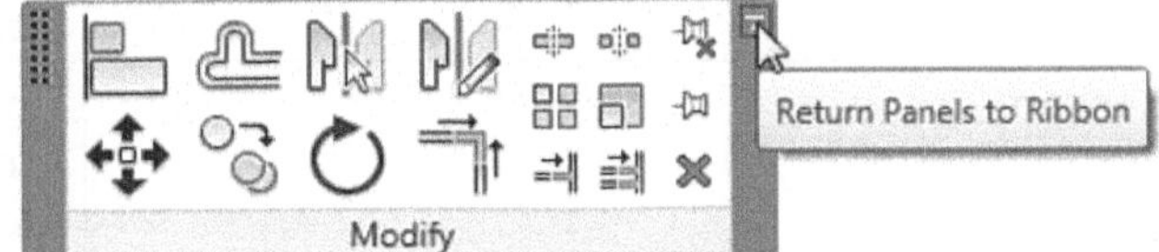

*Figure 1-9 Choosing the **Return Panels to Ribbon** button*

Tip

Tooltips appear when you place the cursor over any tool icon in the ribbon. The name of the tool appears in the box, assisting you in identifying each tool icon.

Changing the View States of the Ribbon

The ribbon can be displayed in three view states by selecting any of the following four options: **Minimize to Tabs**, **Minimize to Panel Titles**, **Minimize to Panel Buttons**, and **Cycle through All**. To use these options, click on the down arrow located on the right of the **Modify** panel, refer to Figure 1-10; the arrow will be highlighted. Next, click on the down arrow; a flyout will be displayed, as shown in Figure 1-10.

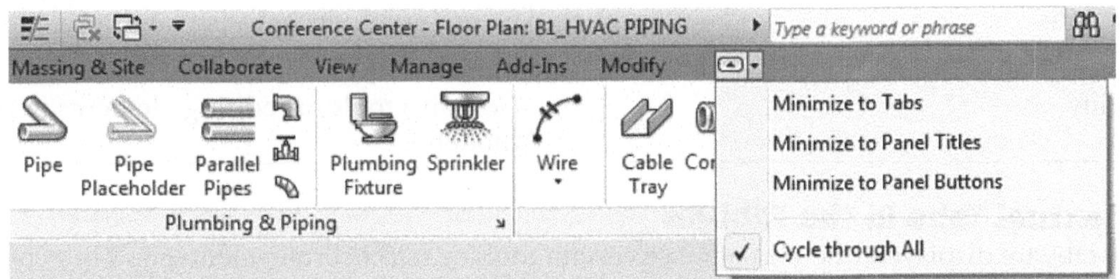

Figure 1-10 Various options in the flyout for changing the view state of the ribbon

From this flyout, you can choose the **Minimize to Tabs** option to display only the tabs in the ribbon. If you choose the **Minimize to Panel Titles** option, the ribbon will display the titles of the panels along with the tabs. You can choose the **Minimize to Panel Buttons** option to display panels as buttons along with tabs in the ribbon.

Note

*If the ribbon is changed to a different view state, then on placing the cursor over the first arrow on the right of the **Modify** tab, the **Show Full Ribbon** tooltip will be displayed. Click on the arrow; the full ribbon will be displayed.*

The table given next describes various tabs in the ribbon and their functions.

Tab	**Description**
Systems	Contains tools for creating an MEP model
Architecture	Contains tools for creating an architectural model
Annotate	Contains tools for documenting a building model such as adding texts and dimensions
Insert	Contains tools for inserting or managing secondary files such as raster image files and CAD files
Analyze	Contains tools for analyzing the structural model
Massing & Site	Contains tools for creating massing and site elements
Collaborate	Contains tools for collaborating the project with other team members (internal and external)
View	Contains tools for managing and modifying the current views, switching views, and so on.
Manage	Contains tools for specifying the project and system parameters and settings
Add - Ins	Contains add in links for interoperability of BIM software
Modify	Contains tools for editing elements in the model

Contextual Tabs in the Ribbon

These tabs are displayed when you choose certain tools or select certain elements. They contain a set of tools or buttons that relate only to a particular tool or element.

For example, when you invoke the **Duct** tool, the **Modify | Place Duct** contextual tab is displayed. This tab has the following panels: **Select**, **Properties**, **View**, **Measure**, **Geometry**, **Clipboard**, **Create**, **Modify**, **Tag**, and **Placement Tools**. The **Select** panel contains the **Modify** tool. The **Properties** panel contains the **Properties** button and the **Type Properties** tool. The **Mode** panel has some necessary tools that are used to load model families or to create the model of a window in a drawing. The other panels, apart from those discussed above, contain the tools that are contextual and are used to edit elements when placed in a drawing or selected from a drawing for modification.

Application Frame

The application frame helps you manage projects in Autodesk Revit. It consists of **Application** button, **Application Menu**, **Quick Access Toolbar**, **InfoCenter**, and **Status Bar**. These are discussed next.

Application Button

The **Application** button is displayed at the top-left corner of the Autodesk Revit 2017 interface. This button is used to display as well as close the **Application Menu**.

Application Menu

The **Application Menu** contains the tools that provide access to tools such as **Open**, **Close**, and **Save**. Click on the down arrow on the **Application** button to display the **Application Menu**, as shown in Figure 1-11. Alternatively, press ALT+F to display tools in the **Application Menu**.

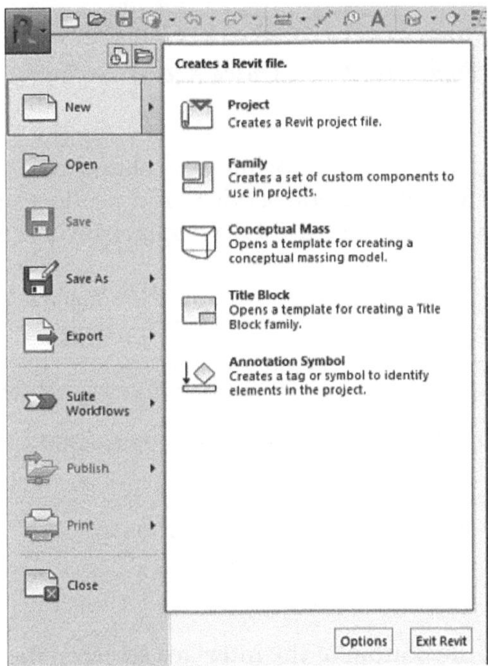

Figure 1-11** The **Application Menu

Quick Access Toolbar

The **Quick Access Toolbar**, shown in Figure 1-12, contains the options to undo and redo changes, open and save a file, create a new file, and so on.

By default, the **Quick Access Toolbar** contains the options such as **Open**, **Save**, **Redo**, **Undo**, and so on. You can customize the display of the **Quick Access Toolbar** by adding more tools and removing the unwanted tools. To add a tool or a button from the panel of the ribbon to the **Quick Access Toolbar**, place the cursor over the button; the button will be highlighted. Next, right-click; a flyout will be displayed. Choose **Add Quick Access Toolbar** from the flyout displayed; the highlighted button will be added to the **Quick Access Toolbar**. The **Quick Access Toolbar** can be customized to reorder the tools displayed in it. To do so, choose the down arrow next to the **Switch Windows** drop-down, refer to Figure 1-12; a flyout will be displayed. Choose the **Customize Quick Access Toolbar** option located at the bottom of the flyout; the **Customize Quick Access Toolbar** dialog box will be displayed. Use various options in this dialog box to customize the display of toolbar and choose the **OK** button; the **Customize Quick Access Toolbar** dialog box will close and the tools in the **Quick Access Toolbar** will be reordered.

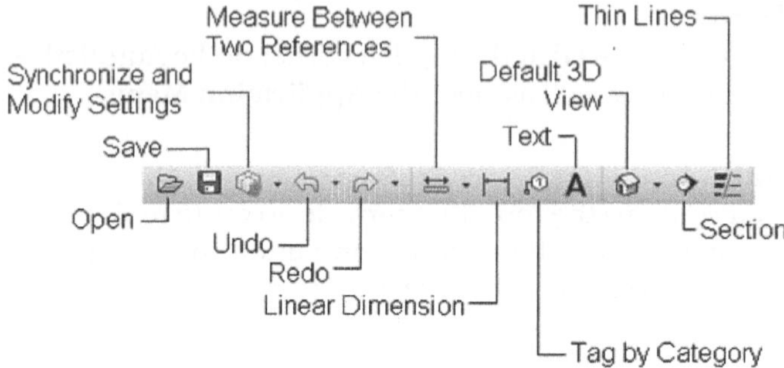

Figure 1-12 The Quick Access Toolbar

InfoCenter

You can use **InfoCenter** to search for information related to Revit (Help) to display the **Subscription Center** panel for subscription services and product updates, and to display the **Favorites** panel to access saved topics. Figure 1-13 displays various tools in **InfoCenter**.

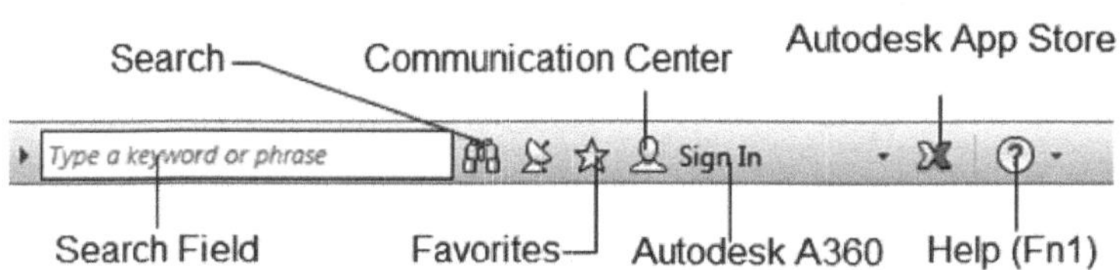

Figure 1-13 The InfoCenter

Status Bar

The **Status Bar** is located at the bottom of the interface screen. When the cursor is placed over an element or a component, the **Status Bar** displays the name of the family and the type of the corresponding element or components. It also displays prompts and messages to help you use the selected tools.

View Control Bar

The **View Control Bar** is located at the lower left corner of the drawing window, as shown in Figure 1-14. It can be used to access various view-related tools. The **Scale** button shows the scale of the current view. When you can choose this button, a flyout containing standard drawing scales is displayed. From this flyout, you can then select the scale for the current view. The **Detail Level** button is used to set the detail level of a view. You can select the required detail level as **Coarse**, **Medium**, and **Fine**. Similarly, the **Visual Style** button enables you to set the display style. The options for setting the display style are: **Wireframe, Hidden Line, Shaded, Consistent Colors, Shaded**, and **Raytrace**.

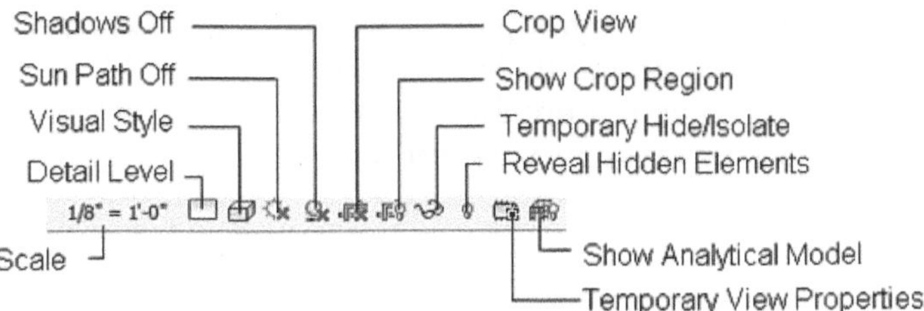

***Figure 1-14** The View Control Bar*

Options Bar

The **Options Bar** provides information about the common parameters of a component type. It also displays options for creating or editing them. The options displayed in the **Options Bar** change according to the type of component being created and selected for editing. Figure 1-15 displays the options in the **Options Bar** to create a structural column.

***Figure 1-15** The **Options Bar** with different options to create a structural column*

Type Selector

The **Type Selector** drop-down list is located in the **Properties** palette for the currently invoked tool. On invoking the **Duct** tool, the properties of the duct will be displayed in the **Properties** palette. In this palette, you can use the **Type Selector** drop-down list to select the required type of the beam. The options in the **Type Selector** drop-down list keep changing, depending upon the current function of the tool or the elements selected. The **Type Selector** drop-down list can also be used to specify the type of an element or component while placing that element or the component in a drawing by using the **Place a Component** tool. You can also use this drop-down list to change the type of a selected element.

Drawing Area

The Drawing Area is the actual modeling area where you can create and view the building model. It covers the major portion of the interface screen. You can draw building components in this area. The position of the pointing device is represented by the cursor. The Drawing Area also has the standard Microsoft Windows functions and buttons such as close, minimize, maximize, scroll bar, and so on. These buttons have the same function as that of the other Microsoft Windows-based programs.

PROJECT BROWSER

The **Project Browser** is located below the ribbon. It displays project views, schedules, sheets, families, and groups in a logical, tree-like structure, as shown in Figure 1-16 and helps you to open and manage them. To open a view, double-click on the name of the view, or drag and drop the view in the Drawing Area. You can close the **Project Browser** or dock it anywhere in the Drawing Area.

Note

*If the **Project Browser** is not displayed on the screen, choose the **View** tab from the ribbon and then select the **Project Browser** check box from **View > Windows > User Interface** drop-down.*

The **Project Browser** can be organized to group the views and sheets based on the project requirement. For example, while working on a large project with a number of sheets, you can organize the **Project Browser** to view and access specific sheets.

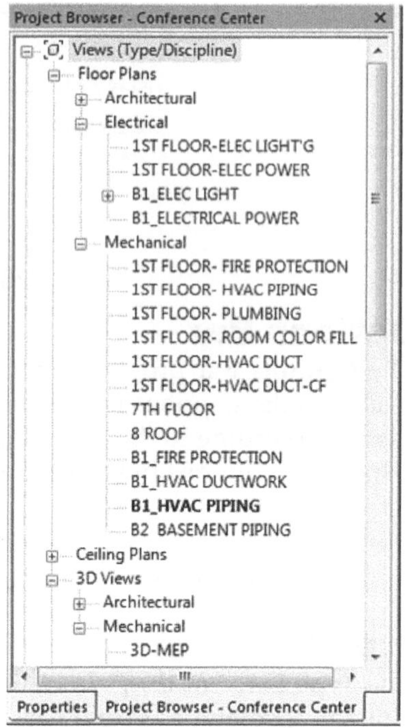

*Figure 1-16 The **Project Browser***

Note

*In the **Project Browser**, you can expand or contract the view listing by selecting the '+' or '-' sign, respectively. The current view in the drawing window is highlighted in bold letters. The default project file has a set of preloaded views.*

Keyboard Accelerators

In Autodesk Revit, accelerator keys have been assigned to some of the frequently used tools. These keys are shortcuts that you can type from the keyboard to invoke the corresponding tool. The accelerator key corresponding to a tool appears as a tooltip when you move the cursor over the tool.

Properties Palette

The **Properties** palette, as shown in Figure 1-17, is an interface without model, which displays the type and element properties of various elements and views in a drawing.

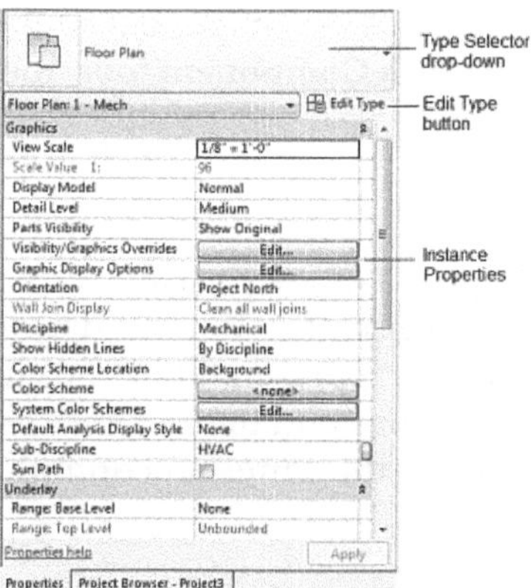

*Figure 1-17 The **Properties** Palette*

The **Properties** palette is dockable and resizable, and it supports multiple monitor configurations. The **Properties** palette is displayed in the Revit interface by default and it shows the instance properties of the active view.

Tip

As you become accustomed to use Autodesk Revit, you will find these Keyboard Accelerators quite useful because they save the effort of browsing through the menus.

When you select an element from a drawing, the **Properties** palette displays its instance properties. You can also access the type properties of the selected element from the **Properties** palette. To do so, choose the **Edit Type** button from the palette; the **Type Properties** dialog box will be displayed. In this dialog box, you can change the type properties of the selected element.

In the **Properties** palette, you can assign a type to the selected element in a drawing using the options from the **Type Selector** drop-down list. In Revit, you can toggle the display of the **Properties** palette in its interface. Choose the **Properties** button in the **Properties** panel of the **Modify** tab to hide it. Similarly, you can choose the **Properties** button to display the palette if it is not visible in the interface.

DIALOG BOXES

Some Autodesk Revit tools, when invoked, display a dialog box. A dialog box is an interface for accessing, specifying, and modifying the parameters related to that tool. For example, when you choose **Save As > Project** from the **Application Menu**, the **Save As** dialog box is displayed, as shown in Figure 1-18.

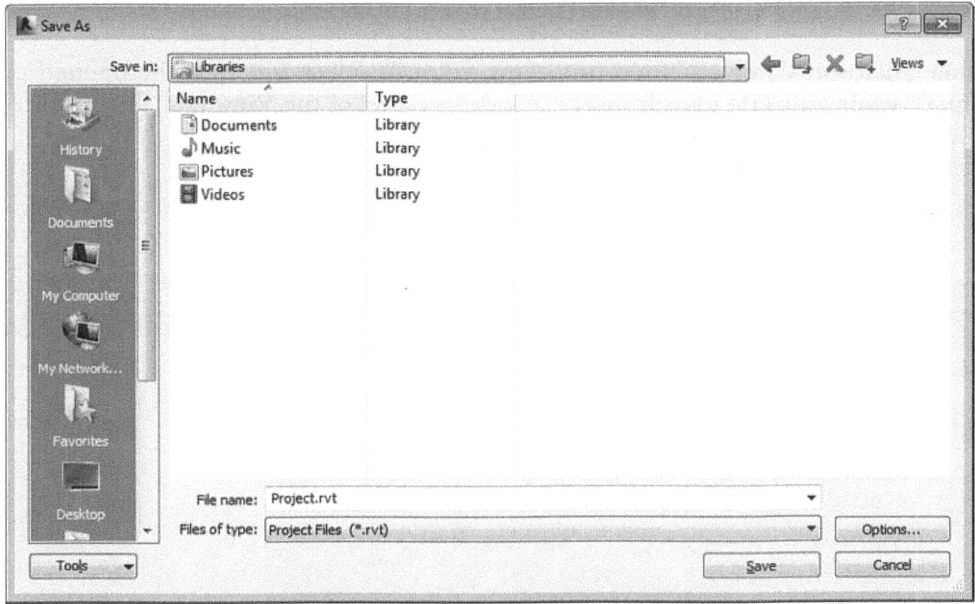

***Figure 1-18** The **Save As** dialog box*

A dialog box consists of various parts such as dialog label, radio buttons, text or edit boxes, check boxes, slider bars, image box, buttons, and tools, which are similar to other windows-based programs. Some dialog boxes contain the **Browse** button, which displays another related dialog box. There are certain buttons such as **OK**, **Cancel**, and **Help**, which appear at the bottom of most of the dialog boxes. The names of the buttons imply their respective functions.

MULTIPLE DOCUMENT ENVIRONMENT

The multiple document environment feature allows you to open more than one project at a time in a single Autodesk Revit session. This is very useful when you want to work on different projects simultaneously and make changes with reference to each other.

Sometimes, you may need to incorporate certain features from one project into the other. With the help of multiple document environment feature, you can open multiple projects and then use the **Cut**, **Copy**, and **Paste** tools from the **Clipboard** panel of the **Modify (type of element)** tab to transfer the required components from one project to another. These editing tools can also be invoked by using the CTRL+C and CTRL+V keyboard shortcuts.

To access the opened projects, click on the **Switch Windows** drop-down in the **Windows** panel of the **View** tab; the options for the names of different opened project files will be displayed, as shown in Figure 1-19.

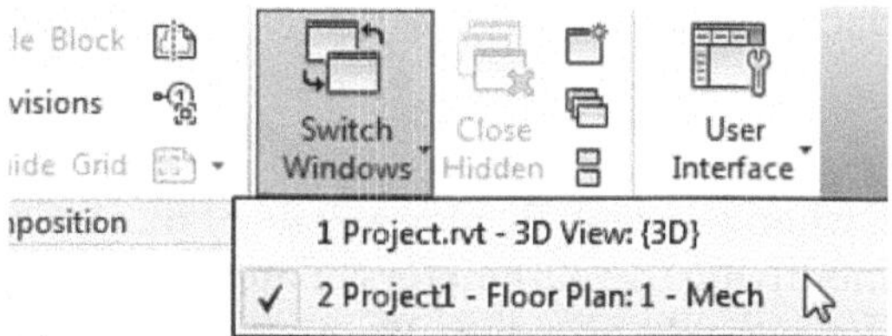

***Figure 1-19** Selecting an option from the **Switch Windows** drop-down*

Like other Microsoft Windows-based programs, you can select and view the opened projects using the **Cascade** and **Tile** tools from the **Windows** panel of the **View** tab. The cascaded view of projects is shown in Figure 1-20.

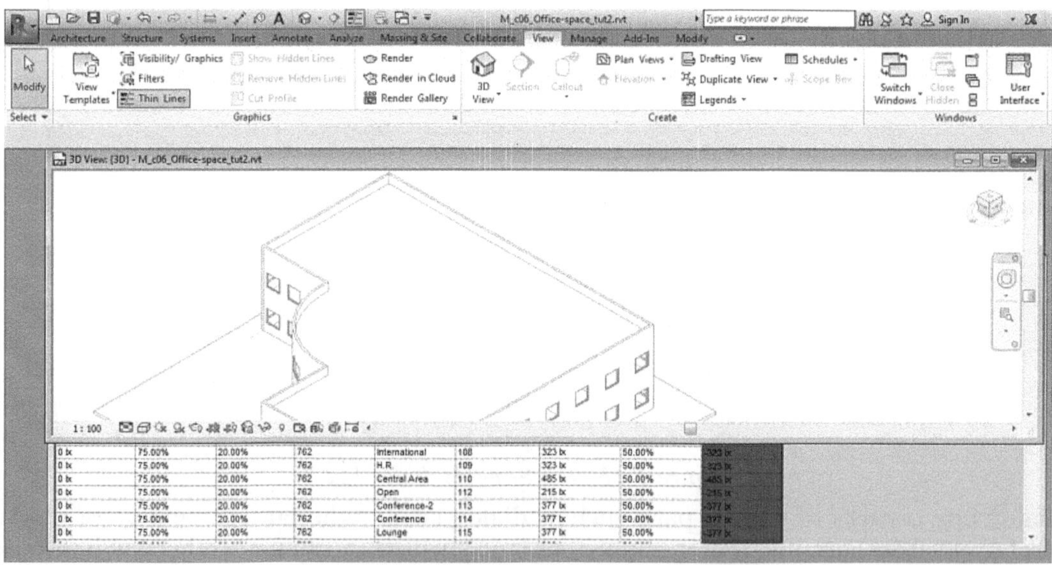

***Figure 1-20** The cascaded view of projects*

INTEROPERABILITY OF Autodesk Revit

The models or geometries created in Autodesk Revit can be easily exported to AutoCAD and AutoCAD Architecture in the DWG file format. This enables structural engineers to collaborate with Architects. One of the important aspects of the job of a structural engineer is to collaborate and share information with the rest of the design team including the architect. To facilitate this requirement, Revit 2017 follows a wide range of industry standards and supports various CAD file formats such as *DWF*, *DGN*, *DWG*, *DGN*, *IFC*, *SKP*, and *SAT*. For image files, it supports

JPG, *TIFF*, *BMP*, *PNG*, *AVI*, *PAN*, *IVR*, and *TGA* file formats. Besides these, the formats that are supported by Revit include *ODBC*, *HTML*, *TXT*, *XML*, *XLS*, and *MDB*. Autodesk Revit is compatible with any CAD system that supports the DWG, DXF, or DGN file format. Revit can import the models and geometries as ACIS solids. This enables engineers to import models from AutoCAD Architecture and AutoCAD MEP (Mechanical, Electrical, and Plumbing) software and to link the 3D information to Revit. This feature makes Autodesk Revit 2017 an efficient, user-friendly, and compatible software.

BUILDING INFORMATION MODELING AND Autodesk Revit 2017

Building Information Modeling (BIM) is defined as a design technology that involves the creation and use of coordinated, internally consistent, and computable information about a building project in design and construction.

Using BIM, you can demonstrate the entire life cycle of a building project starting from the process of construction, facility operation, and information about quantities and shared properties of elements. BIM enables the circulation of virtual information model from the design team to contractors and then to the owner, thereby updating them about the changes made in the model at each stage. The ability to keep information up-to-date and make it available in an integrated digital environment enables the architects, owners, builders, and engineers to have a clear vision of the project before the commencement of actual construction. It also enables them to make better and faster decisions to improve the quality and profitability of projects. Autodesk Revit 2017 is a specially designed platform based on BIM.

In Revit, the analytical and physical representations of an MEP model are created simultaneously. These representations are different views of a computable building model that contains necessary information for a third-party analysis application which is done with the help of a common modeling interface. You can use Revit API to move data directly from the Revit building information model to the analysis software. Further, you can bring back the analysis reports while keeping the analysis, design, and documentation synchronized.

Revit's parametric model represents a building as an integrated database of coordinated information. In Revit, a change anywhere is a change everywhere. A change made in your project at any stage is reflected in the entire project, and also due to the parametric behavior of elements, the project is updated automatically. Also, the integration of Revit with the available in-built commercial tools such as solar studies, material takeoffs, and so on greatly simplifies the project design and reduces the time consumed for analysis, thereby enabling faster decision making.

WORKSHARING USING REVIT SERVER

Worksharing is a method of distributing work among people involved in a project to accomplish it within the stipulated period of time. In worksharing, each person involved in the project is assigned a task that has to be accomplished through proper planning and coordination with the other members of the team.

In a large scale building project, worksharing helps in finishing a project in time and meeting the quality requirements that are set during the process. Generally, in a large scale building project, the professionals such as structural engineers, architects, interior architects, and MEP engineers are involved in their respective fields to accomplish the project. So, the distribution of work at the primary stage is made on the basis of the area of specialization. Each professional has his own set of work to perform for the accomplishment of the project. Therefore, worksharing is an important process that is required to be implemented efficiently to complete the project in time.

In Autodesk Revit, you can apply server-based worksharing with the help of Revit Server which is a server application. Revit Server uses a central server and multiple local servers for collaborating across a Wide Area Network (WAN). The central server hosts the central model of a workshared project and remains accessible to all the team members over the Wide Area Network. Similarly, the local server is accessible to all team members in a Local Area Network (LAN). The local server hosts a local updated copy of the central model. In the Worksharing environment, the team members are not aware of the local server, as it is transparent in their daily operations. Refer to Figure 1-21 for the network model of Revit Server.

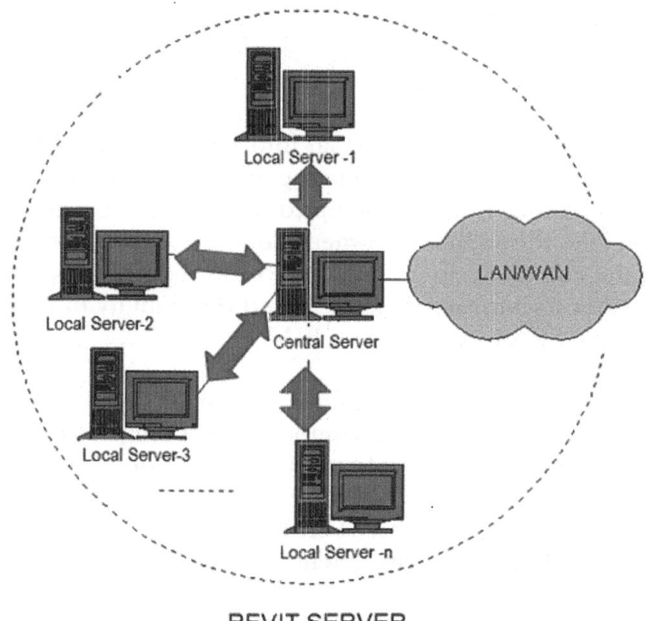

Figure 1-21 *The Network Model of Revit Server*

In Worksharing environment, a team member starts working on the local model of the central model. The local model will be saved in the computer of the team member. As the team member works, the local server requests updated information from the central model on the central server, using available network capacity to transfer the data over the WAN. The updated version of the model is stored on the local server, so the updates are readily available when a team member requests for them.

Autodesk Revit HELP

In Autodesk Revit, **Autodesk Revit 2017** help page has been introduced to access various help topics online. You can access the help topics in Revit 2017 by choosing the **Help** tool from the **InfoCenter**. On doing so, the **Autodesk Revit 2017** page will be displayed, as shown in Figure 1-22. In this page, different areas such as **Learn about Revit**, **Resources**, and others are displayed. You can click on the required link from these areas to get the related information. In the **Learn about Revit** area, various help options related to Autodesk Revit are available. You can click on the required option to display the help page corresponding to the option. The **Resources** area contains various learning resources. You can click on the desired option in this area to get the information related to it.

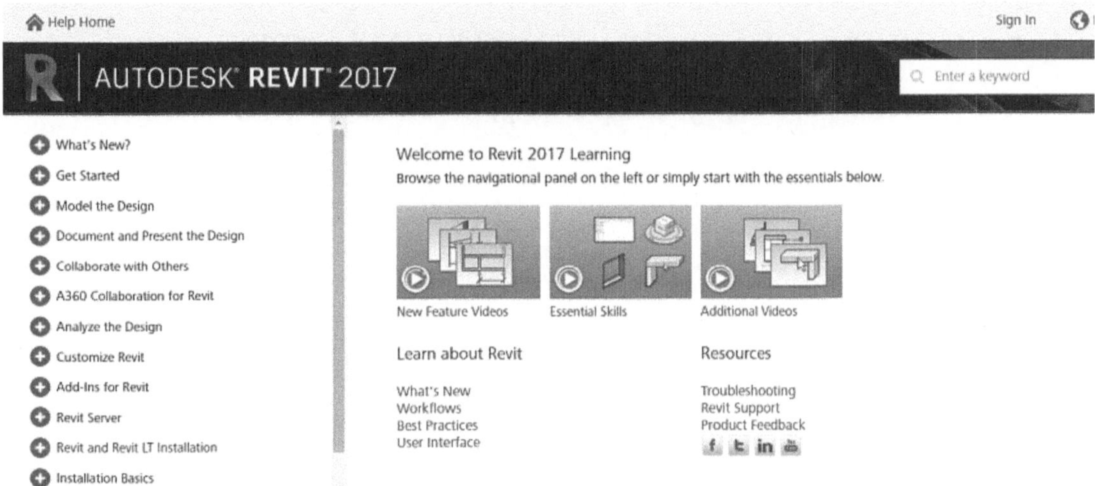

Figure 1-22 The AUTODESK REVIT 2017 page

Self-Evaluation Test

Answer the following questions and then compare them to those given at the end of this chapter:

1. MEP is the acronym for__________.

2. BIM is the acronym for__________.

3. In the Mechanical discipline, you can develop an HVAC (Heating, Ventilation and Air Conditioning) system. (T/F)

4. The **View Control Bar** is located at the lower right corner of the drawing window. (T/F)

5. The **Autodesk App Store** option is located in the **Status Bar**. (T/F)

Review Questions

Answer the following questions:

1. The__________enable the division of the MEP model into small editable sets of disciplines such as Mechanical, Electrical, and Plumbing.

2. The__________displays the name of the current project.

3. In Revit, the analytical and physical representations of an MEP model are created simultaneously. (T/F)

4. In Autodesk Revit, you cannot apply server-based worksharing. (T/F)

5. You can press ALT+F to display tools in the **Application Menu**. (T/F)

Answers to Self-Evaluation Test

1. Mechanical, Electrical, and Plumbing, **2.** Building Information Modeling, **3.** T, **4.** F, **5.** F

Chapter 2

Getting Started with an MEP Project

Learning Objectives

After completing this chapter, you will be able to:

- *Understand the essentials of an MEP Project*
- *Start a new project*
- *Set the units of various measurement parameters in a project*
- *Understand the use of Project Templates*
- *Learn the concept of snaps, dimensions, and object snaps*
- *Use the Options dialog box*
- *Save a project*
- *Close and exit an MEP Project*
- *Open an existing project*

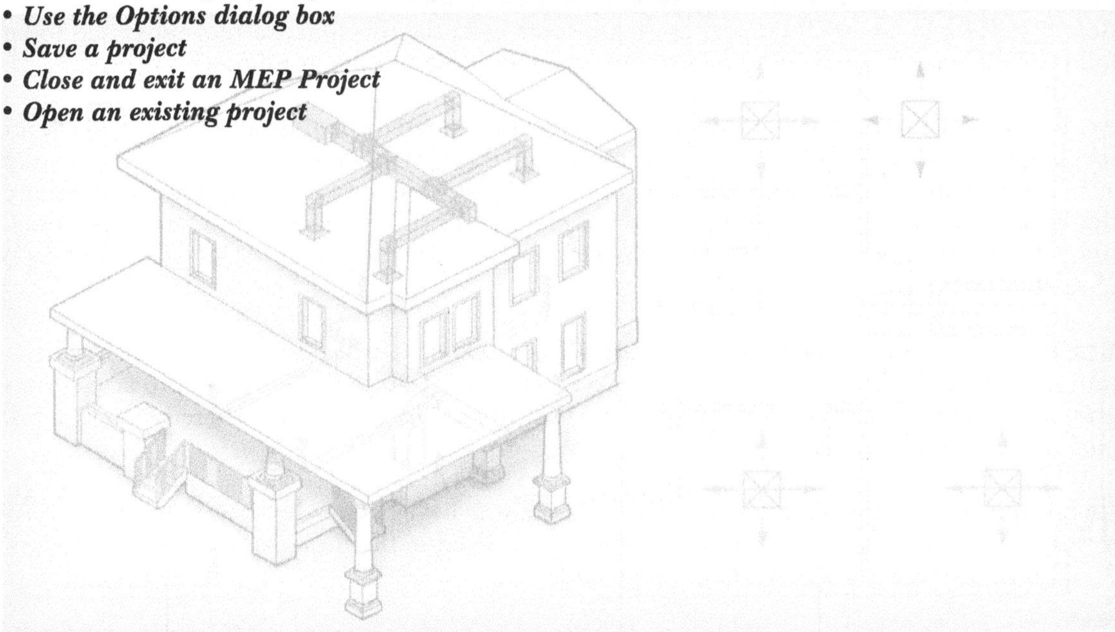

OVERVIEW OF AN MEP PROJECT

In Revit, a project is delivered as a single model with an integration of various disciplines such as Architecture, MEP, and Structure. This means that the project file that you create will contain all the information related to building design from geometry to various construction documentations such as schedules and legends. Generally, this information includes the details of the building elements like walls, doors, windows, beams, columns, ducts, pipes, equipment, fixtures, and others. The information in the project also includes different views of the project, working drawings created from the building elements, and the documentation related to design of the model.

In Revit, you can generate different views such as plan, elevation, and sections from a 3D building project. These views are associative in nature which means when you change the building design in one view, it is propagated throughout the project.

In Revit, the project file in which you will create the MEP project is based on a Revit Template File (*.rte*). This template provides initial settings for the project such as its units, material used, and display settings. You can customize the default settings of a project as required. The basic template file has predefined information and settings for a project.

Generally, each organization has its own standard of working in a building project. Based on the standard, a user can customize the template and then save it for further use.

Tip

It is recommended to follow a slower approach to set up a project and give more time to create the standard template for practice and to organize the structure of the required components in a project. This helps in carrying out the project smoothly and efficiently.

ESSENTIALS FOR AN MEP PROJECT

Before starting up an MEP Project, there are some essential tips that are recommended to be followed for smooth functioning of a project. The essential tips are as follows:

Arrange a BIM Project Kick-off Meeting. It is recommended to arrange a BIM Project kick-off meeting for the people involved in all disciplines and the BIM modeler. This meeting is essential as it brings all the people involved in the project and provides everyone an opportunity to share the information about the expectation of the clients and the firms from the building model. Also, the information is shared on the expected Level of Development (AIA Document E202) of the building model.

Establish a common Project Settings and Project Goal. It is required to establish project settings and goals before starting up a new project in Revit. Following are the project settings and goals that you need to establish for the MEP project: File Structure, Shared Coordinates, and the Project milestones.

Communicate with the Architects. Since the architects have been using Revit for a long time, it is required to communicate with those who are involved in the project regarding the design.

STARTING A NEW PROJECT

Application Menu: New > Project
Shortcut Key: CTRL+N

To start a new project in Revit 2017, first you need to open the software. To open the software, choose **All Programs > Autodesk > Revit 2017 > Revit 2017** from the **Start** menu for Windows 7; the **Autodesk Revit** interface will be displayed. From this interface, choose the **Application** button; the **Application Menu** will be displayed. From the **Application Menu**, choose **New > Project**, as shown in Figure 2-1; the **New Project** dialog box will be displayed, as shown in Figure 2-2.

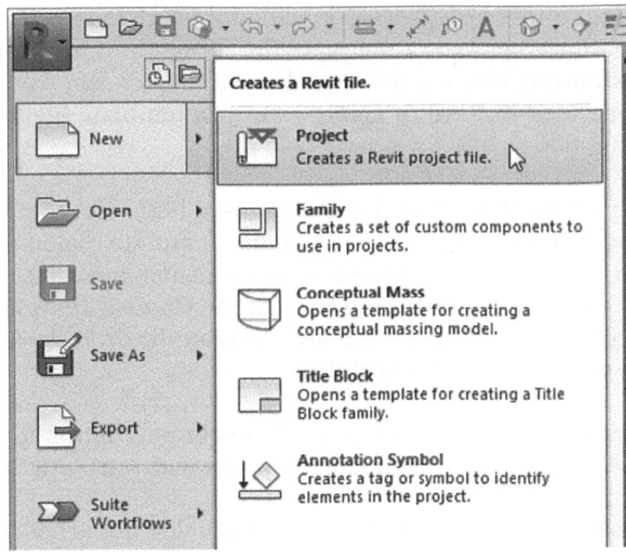

*Figure 2-1 Choosing the **Project** option from the **Application Menu***

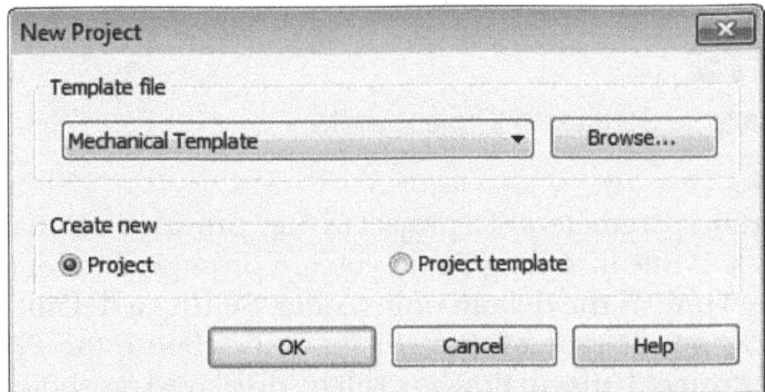

*Figure 2-2 The **New Project** dialog box*

In this dialog box, the **Mechanical Template** option is selected by default in the drop-down list in the **Template file** area. As a result, the new project will adopt the settings of the *Mechanical-Default* template file. Alternatively, you can select any of the following options from the drop-down list in the **Template file** area: **Electrical Template, Plumbing Template, Systems Template**, and **<None>**.

Note

The selection of the option from the drop-down list depends on the MEP discipline that you are going to work within the project.

Tip

For an MEP project, it is recommended to start with the ***Systems.rte*** *template file. To use this file, you need to select the* ***Systems Template*** *option from the drop-down list in the* ***Template file*** *area of the* ***New Project*** *dialog box. The* ***Systems.rte*** *template file provides a useful set up for all the disciplines such as Mechanical, Electrical, and Plumbing.*

A template file has various project parameters saved in it such as units, views, and so on. When you apply the template file to a new project, it will adopt the same parameters as that of the template file. The difference between a template file format and a project file format is that the former has a *.rte* extension, whereas the latter has a *.rvt* extension. You can either select any of the template files provided in Revit or create your own template file. You can also save any project file as a template file.

You can select a file as template by choosing the **Browse** button in the **Template file** area of the **New Project** dialog box. On doing so, the **Choose Template** dialog box will be displayed. In this dialog box, you can browse to the specified file location and select the desired template file of your choice and then choose the **Open** button; the **Choose Template** dialog box will be closed and the selected file will be displayed as an option in the drop-down list that is displayed in the **Template file** area of the **New Project** dialog box.

In the **New Project** dialog box, you can select the **Project** radio button to create a new project. Alternatively, you can select the **Project template** radio button to start with a new project template.

After specifying the various options in the **New Project** dialog box, choose the **OK** button; the **New Project** dialog box will be closed and the Revit project interface will be displayed with the applied settings.

PROJECT UNITS

Ribbon: Manage > Settings > Project Units
Shortcut Key: UN

Units are important parameters of a project as they provide a standard of measurement for different entities. While installing Revit, you are prompted to set the Imperial (feet and inches) or Metric (meter) unit as the default unit system. Setting a default unit system helps you start your project with a specific type of unit. To set units, choose the **Project Units** tool from the **Settings** panel; the **Project Units** dialog box will be displayed, as shown in Figure 2-3. Under the **Units** column in this dialog box, you can specify various units that are relevant to the building project.

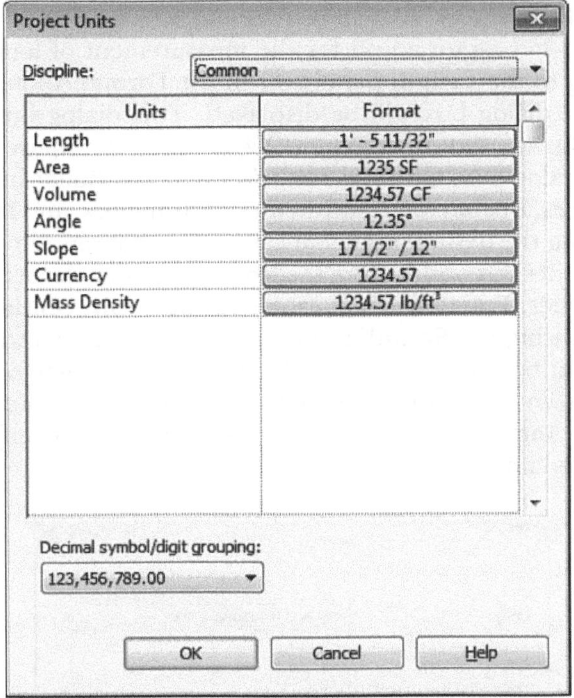

*Figure 2-3 The **Project Units** dialog box*

In the **Project Units** dialog box, units are grouped into six disciplines: **Common**, **Structural**, **HVAC**, **Electrical**, **Piping**, and **Energy**. Each discipline has a set of measurement parameters. You can select any of these disciplines from the **Discipline** drop-down list in the **Project Units** dialog box. The **Format** column in this dialog box displays the current unit format for the corresponding parameter in the **Units** column. You can preview and select the possible digit grouping and decimal separators from the **Decimal symbol/digit grouping** drop-down list, which is at the lower left corner of the dialog box. Some of the disciplines that are used in MEP projects are discussed next.

Note

*The values for different parameters displayed in the **Format** column of the **Project Units** dialog box may differ depending upon the type of unit system, Imperial or Metric, selected for the project. In this textbook, the Imperial unit system has been used in the tutorials and illustrations.*

Common Unit Type

The **Common** unit type used in an MEP project includes the parameters such as length, volume, angle, slope, and so on. In the **Project Units** dialog box, the **Common** option is selected by default in the **Discipline** drop-down list, refer to Figure 2-3. The **Common** unit type used in Revit is similar to that used in other Revit platforms. Moreover, the settings of the parameters of common units are similar to those used in other CAD programs. The methods of setting various parameters under the **Common** unit type are discussed next.

Setting Length Units

In an MEP project, you can assign a unit for the measurement of length. To do so, click on the field corresponding to the **Length** parameter in the **Format** column of the **Project Units** dialog box; the **Format** dialog box will be displayed. This dialog box displays the units of length and their settings, as shown in Figure 2-4. Select the required unit from the **Units** drop-down list in the dialog box: **Decimal feet, Feet and fractional inches, Decimal inches, Fractional inches, Meters, Decimeter, Centimeters, Millimeters,** and **Meters and centimeters** and so on. After selecting the desired unit, you can specify the rounding value for the selected unit. To do so, select the desired option from the **Rounding** drop-down list. For units other than **Feet and fractional inches, Fractional inches,** and **Meters and centimeters,** you can specify custom rounding value using the **Rounding increment** edit box placed next to the **Rounding** drop-down list. This edit box is inactive by default. To make it active, first select any option from the **Units** drop-down list and then the **Custom** option from the **Rounding** drop-down list. Once the **Rounding increment** edit box is activated, you can specify the desired rounding value in it for the selected unit.

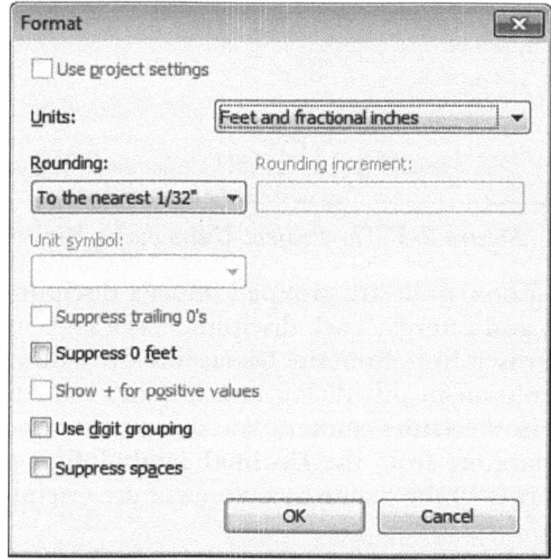

*Figure 2-4 The **Format** dialog box*

The **Unit symbol** drop-down list will be inactive if the **Feet and fractional inches, Fractional inches,** or **Meters and centimeters** option is selected from the **Units** drop-down list. Once you make the **Unit symbol** drop-down list active, you can select the desired option from it to specify the measurement symbol to be used along with the unit of length in a project. For example, to use the symbol 'm' after you select the **Meters** option from the **Units** drop-down list, select **m** from the **Unit symbol** drop-down list as the measurement symbol. You can select the **Suppress spaces** check box for the **Feet and fractional inches** option to remove all spaces around the dash from the length strings.

Setting Area Units

In the **Project Units** dialog box, you can assign a unit to the measurements of areas. To do so, click on the field corresponding to the **Area** parameter in the **Format** column of the **Project Units** dialog box; the **Format** dialog box will be displayed. In this dialog box, you can set the unit for measuring the area by using the options in the **Units** drop-down list. This drop-down list contains various options for the units of area such as **Square feet**, **Square meters**, **Acres**, and so on. By default, the **Square feet** option is selected in this drop-down list, if the **Imperial** units system is selected at the time of installing Revit. The settings for rounding, rounding increment, and unit symbol for the area units can be made from their respective drop-down lists and edit box.

Tip
*While selecting a rounding value from the **Rounding** drop-down list in the **Format** dialog box, you should consider the extent of detailing required for the project. For projects that require too much detailing, a lower rounding value may be set. This parameter, however, can be modified at any time during the project development.*

Setting the Volume Units

Similar to setting the units for the length and area, you can set units for volume. To set unit for the volume measurement, click in the field of the **Format** column corresponding to the **Volume** parameter in the **Project Units** dialog box; the **Format** dialog box will be displayed. In this dialog box, click in the **Units** drop-down list and select any of the following options: **Cubic yards**, **Cubic feet**, **Cubic meters**, **Liters** and so on. After selecting a suitable option from the **Units** drop-down list, choose the **OK** button; the **Format** dialog box will be closed and the selected unit for the volume measurement will be displayed in the field of the **Format** column corresponding to the **Volume** parameter in the **Project Units** dialog box.

Setting the Angle Units

You can specify the unit for the angle measurement by selecting the required option from the **Units** drop-down list in the **Format** dialog box for the **Angle** parameter.

Setting the Slope Units

To specify the unit for the slope measurement, click on the field corresponding to the **Slope** parameter in the **Project Units** dialog box; the **Format** dialog box will be displayed. In this dialog box, you can specify the desired unit by selecting it from the **Units** drop-down list. The **Units** drop-down list contains options such as **Ratio : 12**, **Ratio : 10**, **Rise / 12"**, **Rise / 1'-0"**, **Rise / 1000mm**, **Decimal degrees**, and **Percentage**. By default, **Rise / 12"** is selected as unit for the slope measurement, if the **Imperial** unit system is set while installing Revit.

Setting the Currency Units

In Revit, you can set the unit for currency as well. To do so, click on the field corresponding to the **Currency** parameter in the **Project Units** dialog box; the **Format** dialog box will be displayed. In this dialog box, select the required currency symbol and rounding value from the **Unit symbol** and **Rounding** drop-down lists, respectively.

Setting the Mass Density Units

In Revit, you can set the unit for mass density. To do so, click on the field corresponding to the **Mass Density** parameter in the **Project Units** dialog box; the **Format** dialog box will be displayed. In this dialog box, you can specify the desired unit by selecting it from the **Units** drop-down list. The **Unit** drop-down list contains options such as **Kilogram per cubic meter** and **Pound per cubic foot** for mass density measurement. By default, the **Pound per cubic meter** option is selected in this drop-down list, if you had selected the **Imperial** unit system at the time of Revit installation. The settings for the parameters of the rounding, rounding increment, and units symbol can be set by selecting the required option from the respective drop-down lists.

Note

You can format only the display of units on the screen or in the printout using the ***Project Units*** *dialog box. The actual values for these units in the project may be different. For example, if you set the wall length rounding to the nearest value 1', the wall may show this rounded value, but the actual length of the wall might be in fractional feet.*

HVAC Unit Type

HVAC units are commonly used while working in the Mechanical discipline of an MEP Project. Some of the frequently used HVAC units are Density, Power, Pressure, Velocity, Air Flow, and more. In Revit, you can set the HVAC units in the **Project Units** dialog box. To do so, select the **HVAC** option from the **Discipline** drop-down list in the **Project Units** dialog box, as shown in Figure 2-5. Some of the important HVAC units are discussed next.

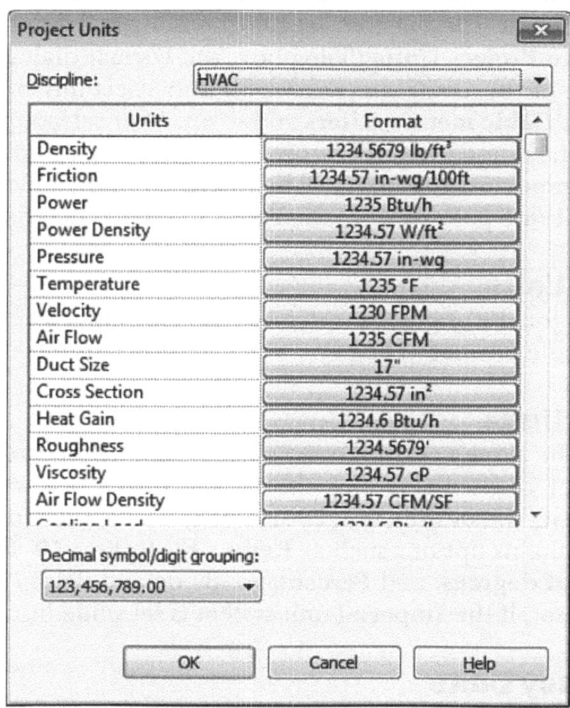

Figure 2-5 *The* ***Project Units*** *dialog box with the* ***HVAC*** *option selected in the* ***Discipline*** *drop-down list*

Setting the Unit for Power

To specify the unit for the power used for various HVAC units, click on the field corresponding to the **Power** parameter in the **Format** column; the **Format** dialog box will be displayed. In this dialog box, specify a unit by selecting the required option from the **Units** drop-down list. The **Units** drop-down list contains the options such as **Watts, Kilowatts, BTU (British Thermal Units) per second**, **BTU (British Thermal Units) per hour**, and so on. For the **Imperial** unit setting, **BTU (British Thermal Units) per hour** is the default option selected in the drop-down list. For the **Metric** unit setting, **Watts** is the default option selected in the drop-down list.

Setting the Unit for Pressure

The pressure in an HVAC system implies the static pressure of the system and of the air flowing inside the duct. To specify unit for the pressure, click on the field corresponding to the **Pressure** parameter in the **Format** column of the **Project Units** dialog box; the **Format** dialog box will be displayed. In this dialog box, specify the desired unit by selecting an option from the **Units** drop-down list. The **Units** drop-down list contains options such as **Inches of water(60 °F)**, **Pascals**, **Kilopascals**, **Megapascals**, **Bars**, and so on. The default unit selected for the **Imperial** unit setting in the drop-down list is **Inches of water(60 °F)**. The default unit selected for the **Metric** unit setting in the drop-down list is **Pascals**.

Setting the Unit for Air Flow

The **Air Flow** parameter specifies the flow rate of the air flowing in the ducts in an HVAC system. In Autodesk Revit, to set the unit for the **Air Flow** parameter, choose the button corresponding to this parameter in the **Project Units** dialog box; the **Format** dialog box will be displayed. In this dialog box, you can select various options such as **Cubic feet per minute**, **Liters per second**, **Cubic meters per second**, and so on. The default unit selected for the **Imperial** unit system for this parameter is **Cubic feet per minute**. The default unit selected for the **Metric** unit setting in the drop-down list is **Liters per second**.

Setting the Unit for Heating Load

The **Heating Load** parameter specifies the heating load of the space for which the HVAC system has to be designed. To set the unit for the **Heating Load** parameter, choose the button corresponding to this parameter in the **Project Units** dialog box; the **Format** dialog box will be displayed. In this dialog box, you can select any option such as **Watts**, **Kilowatts**, **BTU (British Thermal Units) per second**, **BTU (British Thermal Units) per hour**. The default unit selected in the imperial unit system for this parameter is **BTU (British Thermal Units) per hour**. For the **Metric** unit setting, **Watts** is the default option selected in the drop-down list.

Electrical Unit Type

Electrical units are commonly used while working in the Electrical discipline of an MEP Project. Some of the frequently used Electrical units are Current, Electrical Potential, Frequency, Illuminance, and more. To specify these units, invoke the **Project Units** dialog box and then select the **Electrical** option from the **Discipline** drop-down list. Some of the frequently used Electrical units are discussed next.

Setting the Unit for Illuminance

The Illuminance in an Electrical system refers to the measurement of the illumination of the surface. To specify unit for the illuminance, click on the field corresponding to the **Illuminance** parameter in the **Format** column of the **Project Units** dialog box; the **Format** dialog box will be displayed. In this dialog box, specify the desired unit for the illuminance by selecting an option from the **Units** drop-down list. The **Units** drop-down list contains two options **Footcandles** and **Lux**. The default unit selected for the **Imperial** unit setting in the drop-down list is **Footcandles**. For the **Metric** unit setting, **Lux** is the default option selected in the drop-down list.

Setting the Unit for Electrical Potential

In the Electrical discipline the Electrical Potential refers to the potential difference of two points in the distribution. Generally, it is the voltage of the electrical supply to the equipment.

In Autodesk Revit, to set the unit for the **Electrical Potential** parameter, choose the button corresponding to this parameter in the **Project Units** dialog box; the **Format** dialog box will be displayed. In this dialog box, you can select the required option from the various options provided such as **Volts, Kilovolts**, and **Millivolts**. The default unit selected in the **Imperial** and **Metric** unit systems is **Volts**.

Setting the Unit for Demand Factor

The Demand factor for an electrical system is the ratio of the maximum electrical load required in given time period to the maximum possible electrical load available. In Autodesk Revit, to set the unit for the **Demand Factor** parameter, choose the button corresponding to this parameter in the **Project Units** dialog box; the **Format** dialog box will be displayed. From this dialog box, you can select any of the two available options: **Percentage** and **Fixed**. The default unit selected for the **Imperial** and **Metric** unit systems is **Percentage**.

Piping Unit Type

Piping units include units for Density, Flow rate, Pressure, Velocity, and so on. In Revit, you can set the piping units in the **Project Units** dialog box. To do so, select the **Piping** option from the **Discipline** drop-down list in the **Project Units** dialog box. Some of the piping units are discussed next.

Setting the Unit for Flow

The flow in the piping system implies the flow rate of the water or fluids. To specify unit for flow, click on the field corresponding to the **Flow** parameter in the **Format** column of the **Project Units** dialog box; the **Format** dialog box will be displayed. In this dialog box, specify the desired unit for the flow by selecting an option from the **Units** drop-down list. The **Units** drop-down list contains options such as **US gallons per minute, US gallons per hour, Cubic meters per hour**, and so on. The default unit selected for the **Imperial** unit setting in the drop-down list is **US gallons per minute**. For the **Metric** unit setting, **Liters per second** is the default option selected in the drop-down list.

Tip
*In Revit, you can also select the piping flow unit as **Liters per minute**.*

Setting the Unit for Velocity

The velocity in the piping system implies the velocity of water or fluids. To specify unit for velocity, click on the field corresponding to the **Velocity** parameter in the **Format** column of the **Project Units** dialog box; the **Format** dialog box will be displayed. In this dialog box, specify the desired unit for the flow by selecting an option from the **Units** drop-down list. The **Units** drop-down list contains options such as **Feet per second** and **Meters per second**. The default unit selected for the **Imperial** unit setting in the drop-down list is **Feet per second**. For the **Metric** unit setting, **Meters per second** is the default option selected in the drop-down list.

Setting the Unit for Pipe Size

The pipe size in the piping system implies the size of the pipes used in the piping distribution system. To specify unit for pipe size, click on the field corresponding to the **Pipe Size** parameter in the **Format** column of the **Project Units** dialog box; the **Format** dialog box will be displayed.

In this dialog box, specify the desired unit for the pipe size by selecting an option from the **Units** drop-down list. The **Units** drop-down list contains options such as **Fractional inches, Decimal inches, Decimal feet**, and more. The default unit selected for the Imperial unit setting in the drop-down list is **Fractional inches**. For the **Metric** unit setting, **Millimeters** is the default option selected in the drop-down list.

PROJECT TEMPLATES

Project templates are commonly known as template files. These files contains predefined settings for projects for the display of annotations, graphics, and so on. In a project, these files contain predefined settings for units, mechanical components, electrical components, and piping components. Similarly, for the display of graphics, the template files contain predefined settings for materials, line styles, line weights, line patterns, and various symbols relevant to the MEP project.

When you install the Revit software you will find in-built templates that are saved with *.rte* as file extension. You can also create your own template based on the project requirement. In Revit, any new template-based project inherits all families, settings (such as units, fill patterns, line styles, line weights, and view scales), and geometry from the template.

The use of template file is quite extensive and it helps in reducing the cycle time of a project. In the following sections, you will learn to create custom templates and then to use them in a structural project.

Creating a Custom Project Template

In Revit, there are various methods to create a custom project template. The common method is to open an existing template file and modify its settings based on the project requirement and then save it as a different template file. You can also create a custom project template by starting a blank project file, defining all settings such as naming the viewports, creating levels, adding grids, and others, and then saving it as a template (.rte) file. For certain projects, you can create a template file which includes geometry that can be used repeatedly as a base for the new projects. For example, if you have defined geometry for a hospital project and want to include this geometry whenever you start a new project, you can save the file that includes this geometry as a template. Each time you open a project with this template, the geometry will be included.

Creating a New Template from a Blank Project File

In Revit, you can create a new template file from a blank project file or use any of the default template files (*Mechanical-Default.rte*, *Electrical-Default.rte*, *Plumbing-Default.rte*, and *Systems-Default.rte*). To create a template file from a blank project file, choose **New > Project** from the **Application Menu**; the **New Project** dialog box will be displayed. In the **Template file** area of this dialog box, select the **None** option from the drop-down list. Next, select the **Project template** radio button in the **Create New** area and choose the **OK** button; the **Undefined System of Measurement** message box will be displayed, prompting you to select the system of measurement that you want to use in your project, as shown in Figure 2-6. You can select the **Imperial** or **Metric** option from this message box. If you choose the **Imperial** option, a template file containing all default unit settings for the Imperial unit system will open. Similarly, if you select the **Metric** option, the template file containing default units for the **Metric** system will open. After opening the template file, you can modify its existing settings based on your project environment and then save the modified file as a template file. To do so, choose **Save As > Template** from the **Application Menu**; the **Save As** dialog box will be displayed. In this dialog box, select a folder from the **Save in** drop-down list and enter a name for the template file in the **File name** edit box. Note that the **Template Files (*.rte)** option is selected from the **File of type** drop-down list. After entering the file name, choose the **Save** button; the template file will be saved with the settings defined in the blank project file.

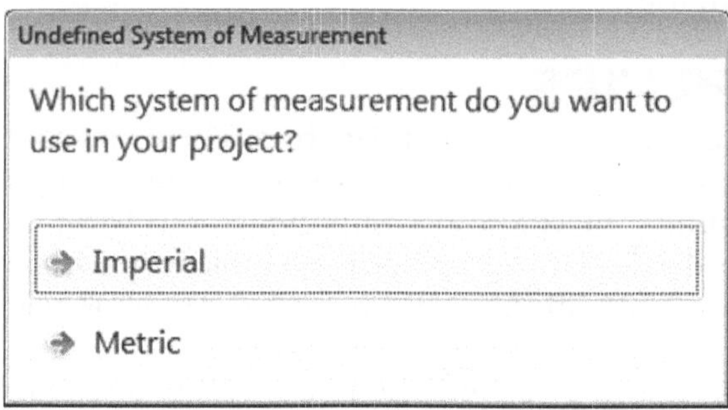

*Figure 2-6 The **Undefined System of Measurement** message box*

Note

*You can also select the default template file, **Systems-Default.rte**, to create a new template file for a blank project. To do so, select the **Systems Template** option from the drop-down list in the **Template file** area of the **New Project** dialog box, and then choose the **OK** button.*

Creating a New Project Template from an Existing Project Template

To speed up your project, you may be required to use predefined template files. These template files contain predefined information or settings pertaining to the project you need to start. To use these template files, choose **New > Project** from the **Application Menu**; the **New Project** dialog box will be displayed. In this dialog box, ensure that the **Project template** radio button in the **Create new** area is selected. Now, to select the desired template file for your project, choose the **Browse** button; the **Choose Template** dialog box will be displayed. In this dialog box, browse to the desired folder to locate the template file. Next, select the template file from the folder and choose the **Open** button; the **Choose Template** dialog box will close and the **New Project** dialog box will be displayed again. Choose the **OK** button; a new project file will open, which inherits all project settings from the selected template file.

Settings for the Project Template

While creating a project template, you can predefine certain settings based on your project requirement. To start a new project template, you need to fill in the information specific to the project. The information includes the name of the project, project number, client's name, and so on. This information is useful while publishing or plotting the drawing. Next, you need to enter the project settings. These settings include units, snaps, the line styles for components and lines, fill patterns for materials, and more.

After modifying the project settings, you can create settings for families. The families in a project template can be system families and loaded families. While defining the settings for the project template, you can modify or duplicate system families (for example, walls) as required for the project. You can also load the commonly used families, user-defined families, and title blocks.

After setting families in the project template, you can modify or create settings for project views. The other settings that can be made for the project template are visibility/graphics settings, and the plot (Print) settings. The settings for the project information are discussed in the next section.

Setting the Project Information

When you create a project template, you can also set the project information. To do so, choose the **Project Information** tool from the **Settings** panel of the **Manage** tab; the **Project Information** dialog box will be displayed, as shown in Figure 2-7.

Figure 2-7 *The **Project Information** dialog box*

In this dialog box, you can specify various settings related to the project information. To enter information regarding the **Organization Name**, **Organization Description**, **Building Name**, and **Author** of the project, click on the value fields of their corresponding parameters and enter appropriate values in them. Similarly, to edit the energy setting of the project, choose the **Edit** button in the **Value** field of the **Energy Settings** parameter; the **Energy Settings** dialog box will be displayed. In this dialog box, you can specify various settings related to the type of the building, site location of the building, and the level that will represent the ground plane of the site. To do so, click on the **Value** fields corresponding to the **Building Type**, **Location**, and **Ground Plane** parameters and specify the desired values in them. In the **Energy Settings** dialog box, you can specify various parameters under the **Detailed Model** heading to set the level of detail of the MEP model for the propose of exporting it to a third party software or use it for energy analysis. In the **Energy Settings** dialog box, you can also set various parameters under the **Energy Model** and **Energy Model - Building Services** headings to specify various parameters for the energy model of the MEP project. Next, choose the **OK** button; the **Energy Settings** dialog box will be closed and the **Project Information** dialog box will be displayed. In this dialog box, you can enter information regarding the start date or the issue date of the project. To do so, click on the **Value** field of the **Project Issue Date** parameter and enter a valid date. Similarly, to specify the status of the project, click on the **Value** field of the **Project Status** parameter and specify a valid status of the project.

To specify the location of the project, click in the **Value** field of the **Project Address** parameter; a browse button will be displayed. Choose the browse button; the **Edit Text** dialog box will be displayed. In the text area of this dialog box, specify the location and choose the **OK** button; the location of the project will be updated. Next, specify the name and number of the project in the **Value** fields of the **Project Name** and **Project Number** parameters, respectively. After specifying the appropriate information in the **Project Information** dialog box, choose the **OK** button; the **Project Information** dialog box will close and the specified project information will be updated. In addition to the parameters discussed in the **Project Information** dialog box, you can add more parameters for entering projėct information. These parameters can be a local parameter or a shared parameter. To add a local parameter, choose the **Project Parameters** tool from the **Settings** panel of the **Manage** tab; the **Project Parameters** dialog box will be displayed. Choose the **Add** button from this dialog box; the **Parameter Properties** dialog box will be displayed, as shown Figure 2-8.

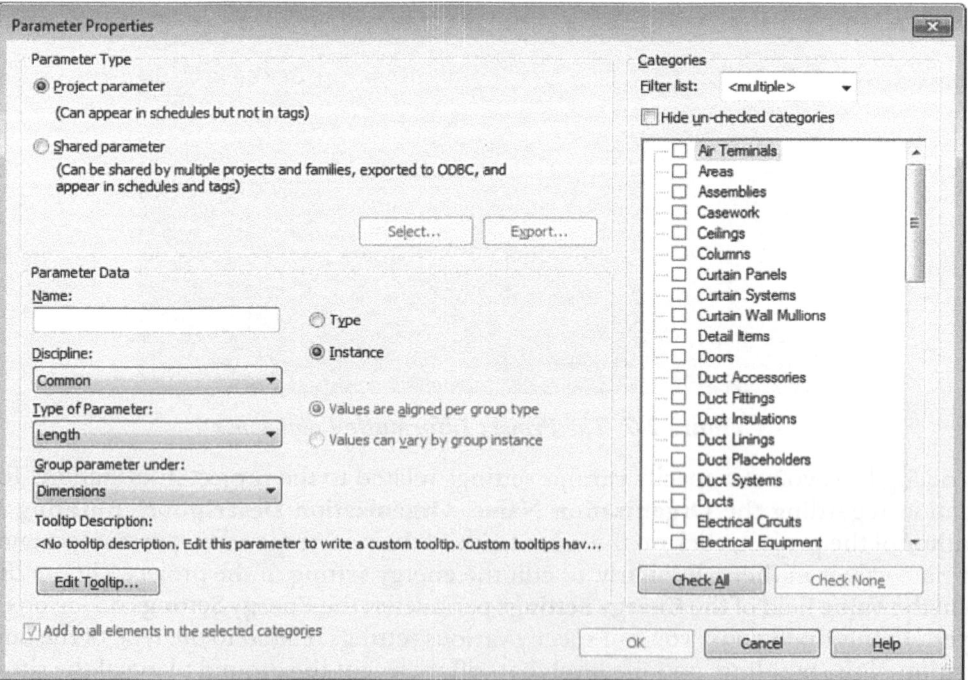

***Figure 2-8** The **Parameter Properties** dialog box*

In the dialog box, ensure that the **Project parameter** radio button is selected in the **Parameter Type** area of this dialog box. Next, in the **Categories** area, ensure that the **Architecture** option is selected in the **Filter list** drop-down list. Also in the list box of this area, select the **Project Information** check box. In the **Parameter Data** area, enter the name of the parameter data in the **Name** edit box. For example, you can specify **MEP Consultant** as the name of the parameter data. Next, you need to assign a discipline for the new parameter. To do so, select an appropriate option from the **Discipline** drop-down list. For example, to assign a discipline for the **MEP Consultant** parameter, ensure that the **Common** option is selected in the **Discipline** drop-down list. To assign type and group for the **MEP Consultant** parameter, select the **Text** and **Other** options from the **Type of Parameter** and **Group parameter under** drop-down lists. Next, choose the **OK** button twice; the **Parameter Properties** and the **Project Parameter** dialog boxes will be closed and the **MEP Consultant** parameter will be added in the **Project Information** dialog box. Figure 2-9 shows the **Project Information** dialog box for the project information with **MEP Consultant** as the added parameter.

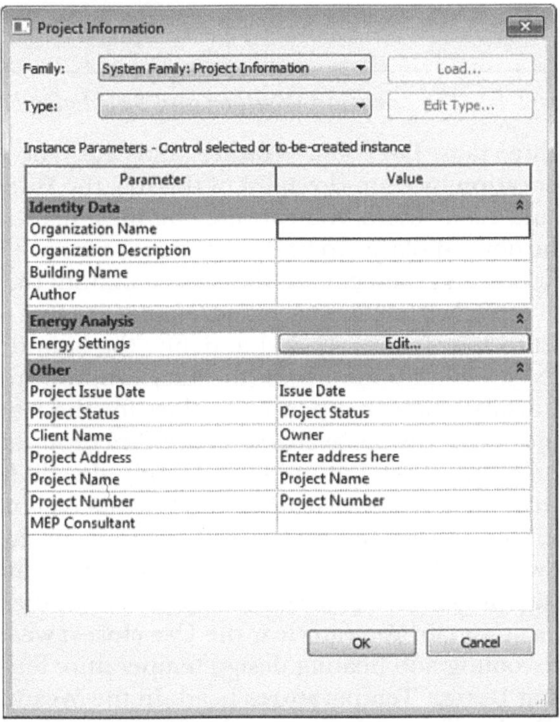

***Figure 2-9** The added parameter in the **Project Information** dialog box*

Setting the Project Location

For every project in MEP, you need to define its geographical location (azimuth), which includes the latitude and longitude of the nearest city and the coordinate system of the host model and the linked model (if present). To do so, choose the **Location** tool from the **Project Location** panel of the **Manage** tab; the **Location Weather and Site** dialog box will be displayed, as shown in Figure 2-10.

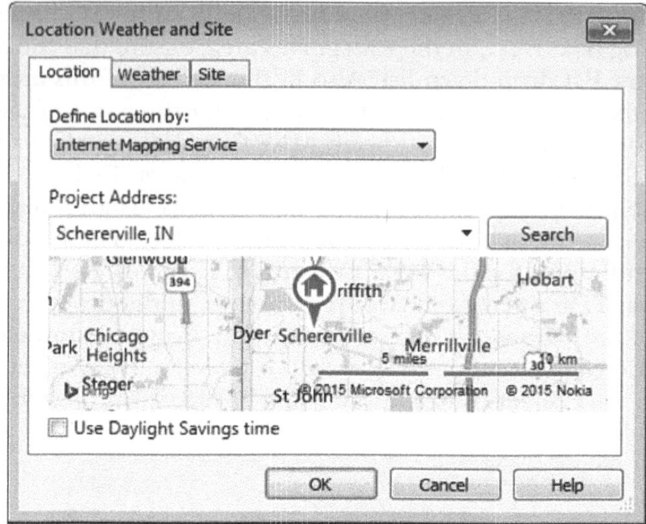

***Figure 2-10** The **Location Weather and Site** dialog box*

This dialog box contains three tabs: **Location**, **Weather**, and **Site**. The **Location** tab is chosen by default. In the **Define Location by** drop-down list of this tab, the **Internet Mapping Service** option is selected by default. As a result, you can use the **bing** map service to find out the geographical location of the desired place. To find out the geographical location, type its name in the **Project Address** edit box and then choose the **Search** button; the location searched will be displayed in a map. Alternatively, you can select the **Default City List** option from the **Define Location by** drop-down list to specify the city and to define the latitude and longitude of the location. To specify the city, select an option from the **City** drop-down list; the **Latitude** and **Longitude** edit boxes will display the corresponding values for the latitude and longitude of the selected city. If the name of a city is not available in the **City** drop-down list, then enter the values of its latitude and longitude in the **Latitude** and **Longitude** edit boxes, respectively. You can choose the **Weather** tab in the **Location Weather and Site** dialog box to specify the cooling and heating design temperature of the site throughout the year. In this tab, the **Use closest weather station** check box will be selected by default. As a result, the value of the cooling design temperature of the proposed project will be taken from the data of the weather station to the location specified in the **Location** tab. You can clear the **Use closest weather station** check box and specify the value of the cooling and heating design temperature for all months in the table displayed under the **Cooling Design Temperatures** head. In the **Weather** tab, you can specify the value for the **Heating Design Temperature** and the **Clearness Number** in their respective edit boxes.

You can choose the **Site** tab in the **Location Weather and Site** dialog box to name the current settings for the location. The options in the **Site** tab are shown in Figure 2-11. In this tab, the name(s) of location(s) is (are) displayed in the **Sites defined in this project** list box. By default, the **Internal (current)** location is listed and selected in the list box. To define a different location for the project, choose the **Duplicate** button; the **Name** dialog box will be displayed. Enter a name in the **Name** edit box and choose the **OK** button; the **Name** dialog box will be closed and the name of the new location will be listed in the **Sites defined in this project** list box. After you have added a location, you will notice that the **Delete** and **Make Current** buttons are active. You can choose the **Delete** button to delete location(s) apart from the current location. Current location is the location currently being used. To make a location current, select the location from the **Sites defined in this project** list box and choose the **Make Current** button. Note that after you have made a location current, the name of the location is suffixed with the word **(current)**.

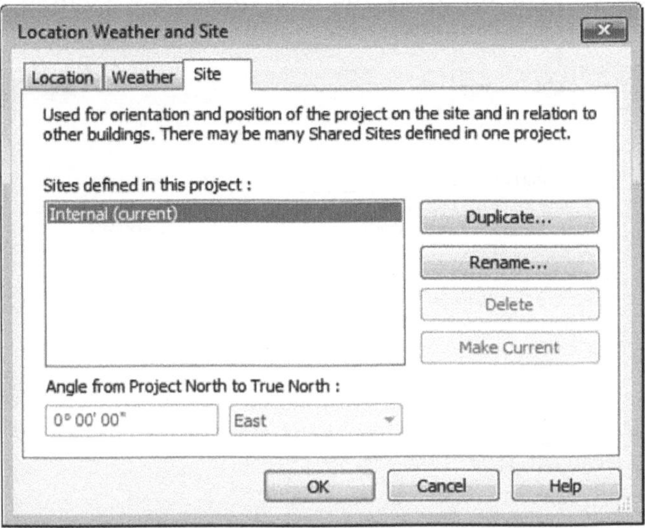

Figure 2-11 *The options in the* ***Site*** *tab of the* ***Location Weather and Site*** *dialog box*

Transferring Project Standards

When you create a template file, you can copy project standards from some other project to the current file. These standards include various project settings such as Family Types (only system families, not loaded families), line weight, line styles, line patterns, materials, view templates, and so on. To transfer project standards to the template file (target file), open the source file from which the standards are to be copied. Next, choose the **Transfer Project Standards** tool from the **Settings** panel of the **Manage** tab; the **Select Items To Copy** dialog box will be displayed, as shown in Figure 2-12.

Note

If you invoke the ***Transfer Project Standards*** *tool without any opened files in the current session, the* ***Revit*** *message box informing that there are no open projects to transfer project from will be displayed. Choose the* ***Close*** *button in this message box and then open a project in the current session from which you want to transfer the project standard to the current project.*

In the **Select Items To Copy** dialog box, click on the down arrow in the **Copy from** drop-down list; a list of opened projects will be displayed in the drop-down list. Next, select the project from which you want to copy the project standards. Note that when you select a source project from this list, the standards included in the project are displayed along with their respective check boxes. By default, all check boxes in the list box are selected. You can keep the check boxes selected corresponding to the standards to be copied to the template file and clear the rest of them. If you want to clear all check boxes for fresh selection, you can choose the **Check None** button located on the right of the list box. Similarly, to select all check boxes, you can choose the **Check All** button. After selecting the check boxes for the standards that you want to transfer, choose the **OK** button; the **Select Items To Copy** dialog box will be closed. Note that if the selected standards are already present in the template file, the **Duplicate Types** message box will appear, as shown in Figure 2-13. You can choose the **Overwrite** button from this message box to overwrite the common standards or choose the **New Only** button to transfer the standards that are present in the template file. After you have chosen the required options, the selected standards will be copied to the destination file.

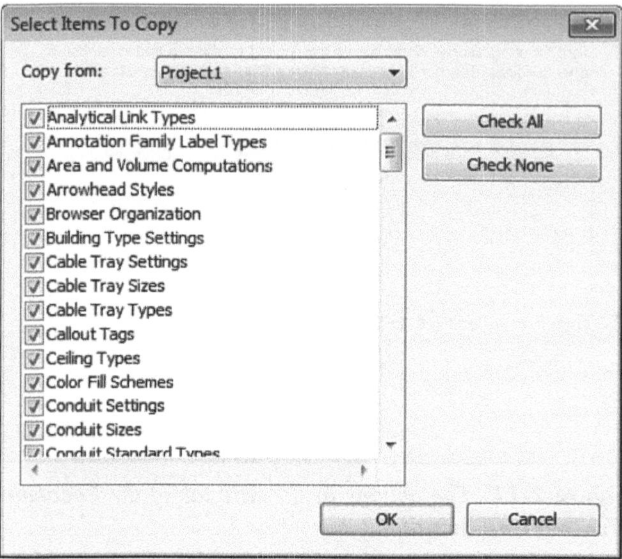

*Figure 2-12 The **Select Items To Copy** dialog box*

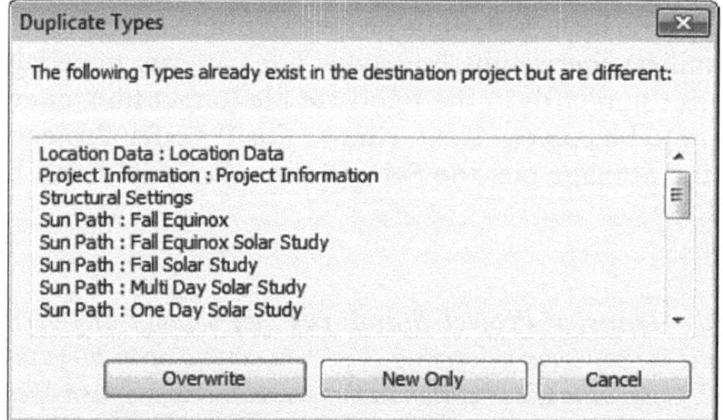

*Figure 2-13 The **Duplicate Types** message box*

Setting the Browser Organization

While creating a project template, you can organize the **Project Browser**. To do so, choose the **Browser Organization** tool from the **Windows** panel of the **View** tab; the **Browser Organization** dialog box will be displayed, as shown in Figure 2-14. This dialog box contains two tabs: **Views** and **Sheets**. The **Views** tab is chosen by default. The options in this tab are used to select, edit, or create a browser organization for the views present in the project. In the list box of the **Views** tab, a list of default browser organizations is displayed with their respective check boxes.

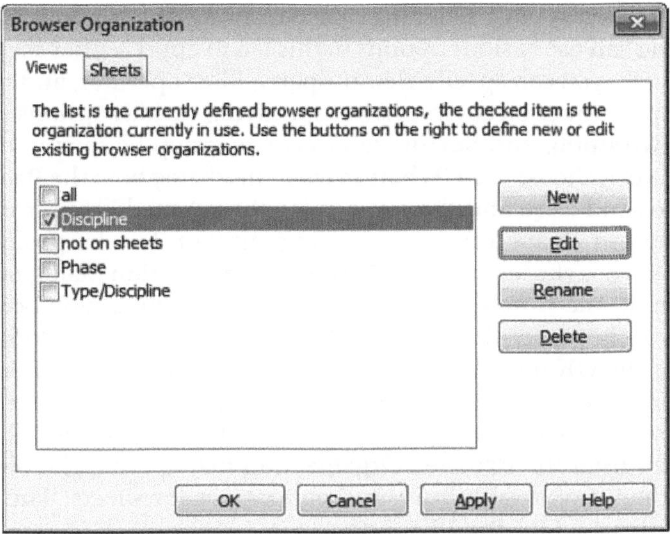

*Figure 2-14 The **Browser Organization** dialog box*

By default, the check box for all browser organization is selected. You can edit the settings of the check boxes displayed. To do so, click on the name of the browser organization whose settings you want to change, and then choose the **Edit** button; the **Browser Organization Properties** dialog box will be displayed, refer to Figure 2-15.

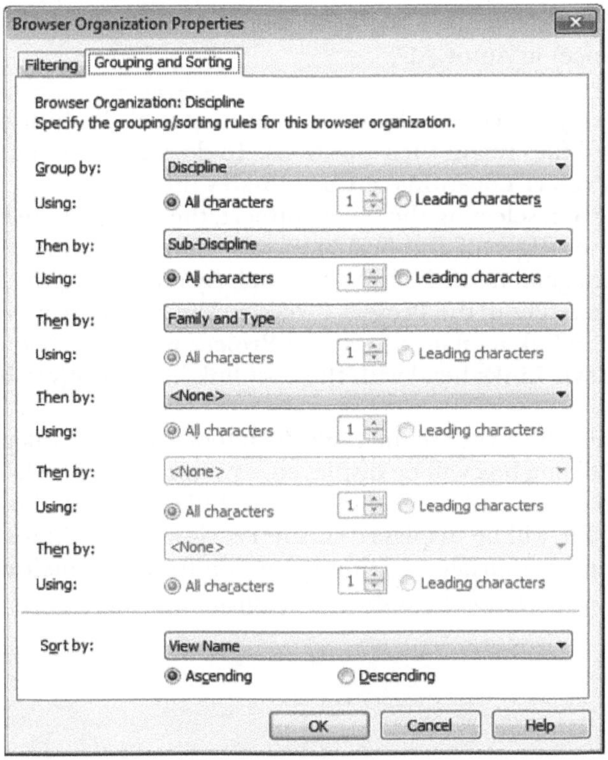

*Figure 2-15 The **Browser Organization Properties** dialog box*

This dialog box contains two tabs: **Filtering** and **Grouping and Sorting**. The **Filtering** tab is chosen by default. You can use various options in this tab to apply a filter to project views. In the **Filter by** area of this tab, you can specify view property, filter operator, and filter value required for sorting and grouping the project views. After specifying various options in the **Filtering** tab, you can choose the **Grouping and Sorting** tab to create group by sorting the project viewing, refer to Figure 2-15. Next, choose the **OK** button from this dialog box; the **Browser Organization Properties** dialog box will close and the settings for the selected browser organization will be edited. Similarly, you can create a new browser organization for the project views. To do so, ensure that the **Views** tab is chosen from the **Browser Organization** dialog box and then choose the **New** button from it; the **Create New Browser Organization** dialog box will be displayed. In this dialog box, you can enter the name of the new browser organization in the **Name** edit box and then choose the **OK** button; the **Browser Organization Properties** dialog box will be displayed. The options in this dialog box have already been discussed. Similar to creating browser organization for a project view, you can also create browser organization for sheets. To do so, choose the **Sheets** tab from the **Browser Organization** dialog box. The **Sheets** tab displays a list box containing the list of default browser organizations for sheets. The options in this tab are similar to those discussed for the **Views** tab.

LINKING REVIT MODELS AND SHARING COORDINATES

You can link a Revit Architecture and Revit Structure project file (.rvt) with a Revit project. After linking, you can use the project created in Revit to coordinate and monitor the changes in the architectural and structural model, respectively. In addition, you can use various tools in Revit to check for correct interference condition between the elements in the Architectural and Structural models and the elements in the MEP model. Linking Revit models is very similar to Xrefs (External Reference) in AutoCAD.

When you link a model, you need to share the coordinates of the host model with the linked model so that the linked files retain their positions. To do so, invoke the **Acquire Coordinates** tool from **Manage > Project Locations > Coordinates** drop-down and then select the linked project in your drawing. On selecting the linked project, the origin of the linked project's shared coordinate becomes the origin of the host project's shared coordinates. Revit provides the flexibility and easy management of the linked models by enhancing the linking of the models and organizing the linked files in the **Project Browser**. You can easily access the linked files, the nested link files, and the link manager from the **Project Browser**. The nested Revit links are also listed under the **Revit Links** head with the host link in the **Project Browser**.

To link or import the Revit files, choose the **Link Revit** tool from the **Link** panel of the **Insert** tab; the **Import/Link RVT** dialog box will be displayed, as shown in Figure 2-16. In this dialog box, navigate to the desired folder and select the file to be linked with the host project; the preview of the selected project file will be displayed in the **Preview** pane. Choose the **Open** button to open the file. Select the appropriate positioning option from the **Positioning** area to position the model automatically or manually in the host project.

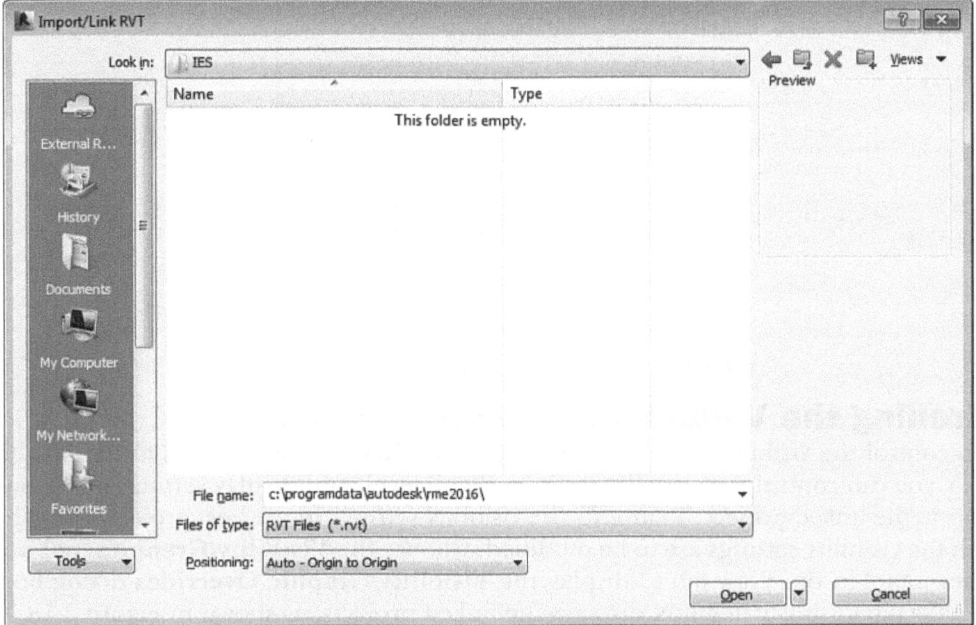

*Figure 2-16 The **Import/Link RVT** dialog box*

Linked Revit Models in the Project Browser

The linked Revit models are listed in the **Project Browser** under the **Revit Links** head. You can access the linked model files and also link a new file from the **Project Browser**. To do so, select the **Revit Links** sub-node in the **Project Browser** and right-click; a shortcut menu will be displayed. Choose **New Link** from the shortcut menu; the **Import/Link RVT** dialog box will be displayed. Select the file to be linked from this dialog box. Similarly, you can access the link manager by choosing **Manage Links** from the shortcut menu and manage the links. You can also open the linked model in the project by dragging it from the **Project Browser** and dropping it in the project view.

Converting Linked Models to Groups - Binding Links

You can convert the linked Revit models into groups in the host project. You can do so by binding the linked model with the host project, thereby making it a part of the host project. After binding the linked model, the model geometry will be transformed into a group, and therefore making changes in the host project will be easier for you. To bind and group a linked model, select the linked model in the drawing; the **Modify | RVT Links** tab will be displayed. Choose the **Bind Link** tool from the **Link** panel; the **Bind Link Options** dialog box will be displayed, as shown in Figure 2-17. In the dialog box, select the **Attached Details**, **Levels**, and **Grids** check boxes to include them in the group and then choose the **OK** button; the linked model will be converted into a group. If there is any group in the project with the same name as that of the linked Revit model, a dialog box with a message will be displayed propmting you whether or not you want to replace the group. Choose **Yes** to replace the existing group or choose **No** to rename the group. On choosing **Yes**, the **Autodesk Revit 2017** warning message box will be displayed. This message box will inform to remove the link from the current project. Choose the **Remove Link** button in the message box or choose the **OK** button to remove it later; the linked model will transform into a group and will be listed in the **Project Browser** under the **Groups** head.

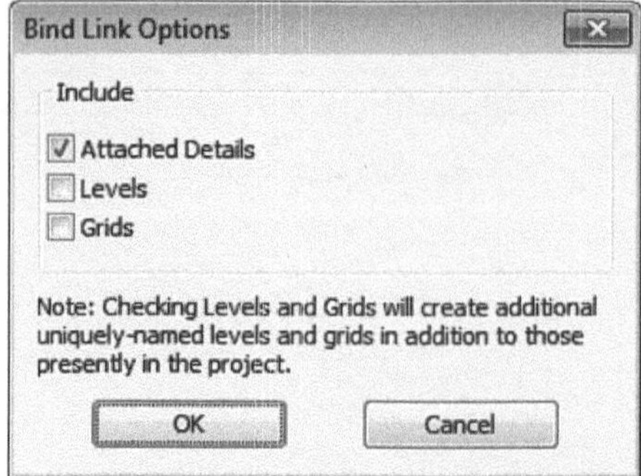

*Figure 2-17 The **Bind Link Options** dialog box*

Controlling the Visibility of Linked Models

You can control the visibility of the linked and nested Revit linked models in the host project file. Also, you can control the visibility settings, detail level, and display settings of the building elements in the linked project. To modify the visibility settings in the host project, open the view in which the visibility settings are to be modified. Choose the **Visibility/Graphics** tool from the **Graphics** panel in the **View** tab to display the **Visibility/Graphic Overrides** dialog box. The **Revit Links** tab in this dialog box displays the linked projects, as shown in Figure 2-18.

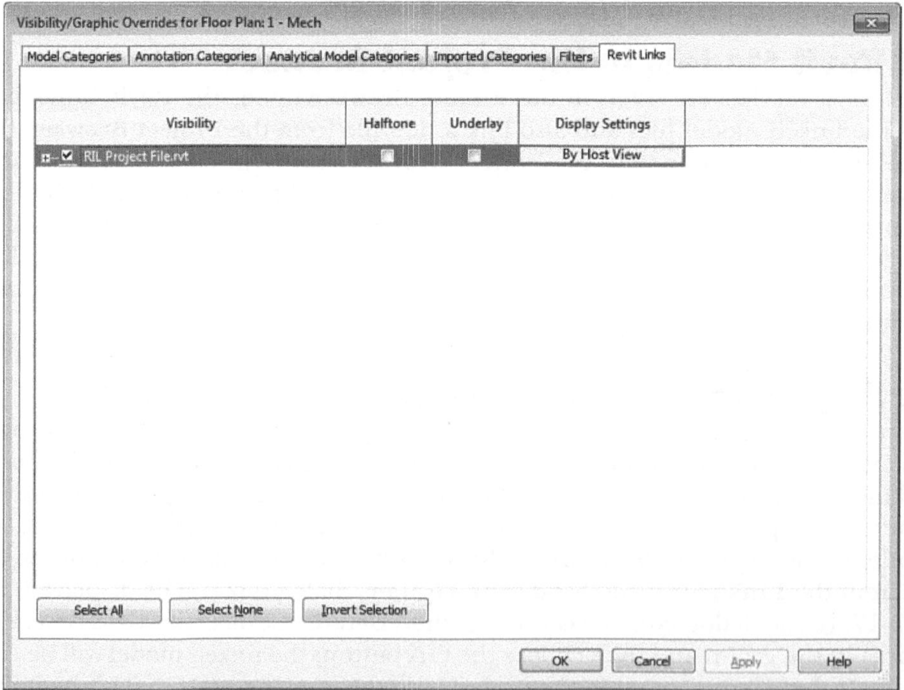

*Figure 2-18 The **Visibility/Graphic Overrides** dialog box with the **Revit Links** tab chosen*

Note that this tab will be displayed only when the files are linked in your project. Click on the project name to display the categories of components in the building model. Use the **Halftone** and **Display Settings** columns to modify the visibility settings and the filters of the components of each linked project. The **By Host View** button in the **Display Settings** column can be used to control the visibility of the nested links, phases, and phase filters.

Click in the **Display Settings** column; the **RVT Link Display Settings** dialog box will be displayed. Choose the **Basics** tab from the dialog box. If you select the **By host view** radio button in this tab, the nested linked model will be able to use the same visibility and graphics settings as in the host view. On selecting the **By linked view** radio button, the nested linked model adopt the visibility settings of the parent model to which it was linked originally. Also, the **Linked view** drop-down list will be enabled. You can select the view in which you want to display the linked model from this list. On selecting the **Custom** radio button, all the options in the **Basics** tab will be enabled. From the **Nested links** drop-down list, select the **By parent link** option to apply the visibility settings of the parent model to the nested link model. If you select the **By linked view** from the drop-down list, the visibility and graphics override settings of the top level nested model will be applied to the linked model. The top level model is the first nested linked model. In the example explained earlier, project A will be the top-level nested model. Choose the **Apply** button to view the changes in the project and then choose the **OK** button.

Managing Links

In a MEP project, you can manage links between the host and the linked projects. To do so, choose the **Manage Links** tool from the **Link** panel of the **Insert** tab; the **Manage Links** dialog box will be displayed with a list of linked projects, as shown in Figure 2-19.

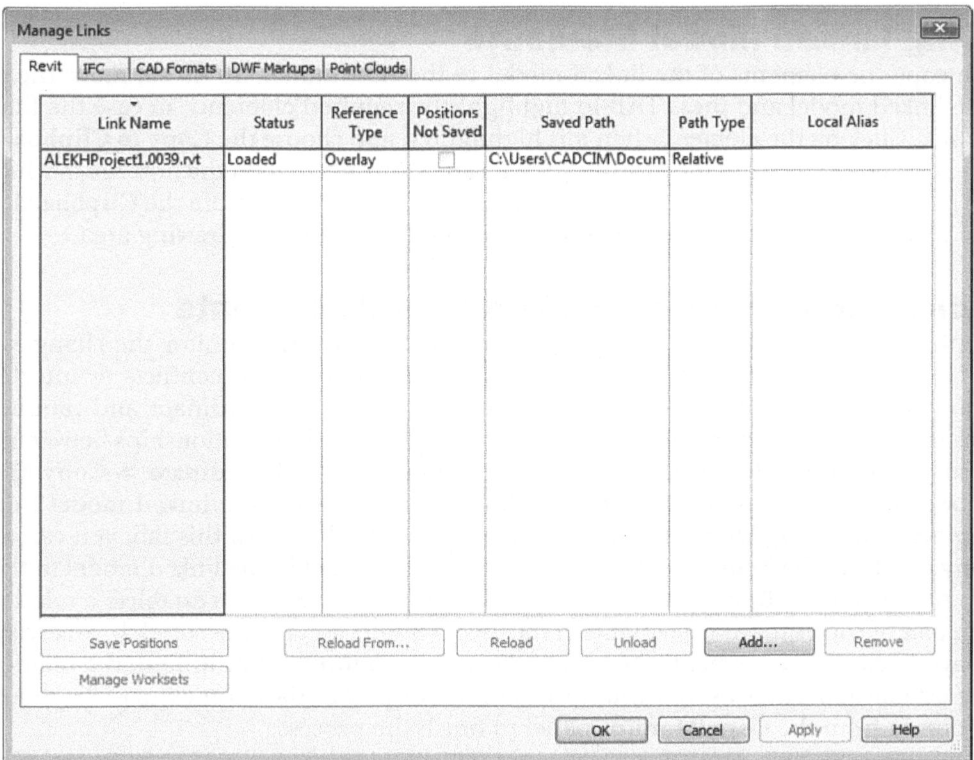

Figure 2-19 *The **Manage Links** dialog box*

The **Status** column in the **Manage Links** dialog box informs whether the linked project file is loaded in the host project. The **Reference Type** column in the dialog box provides you with the options to display or hide the nested linked Revit models. The default **Overlay** value in the **Reference Type** column restricts the loading and display of the nested linked models in the host project. The **Position Not Saved** column of the dialog box indicates whether or not the linked models location is saved in its shared coordinate system or not. The shared coordinates take care of the mutual positions of multiple interlinked files. The **Saved Path** column shows the path of the linked file on your computer. The **Path Type** column is used to specify whether the saved path of the linked file is relative or absolute. It is recommended to keep the linked path relative because it enables Autodesk Revit to trace and re-establish the link, if the host and linked projects are moved to a different folder.

Including Elements of Linked Models in Schedules

In Revit, you can include different model elements such as walls, doors, and windows from a linked file into a schedule. To do so, select the existing schedule of the current project from the **Schedules/Quantities** head in the **Project Browser**; the instance properties of the selected schedule will be displayed in the **Properties** Palette. In the value column of the Palette, choose **Edit** from the **Fields** parameter; the **Schedule Properties** dialog box will be displayed. Select the **Include elements in Linked files** check box to include the elements of a linked file, if required. To include project information from a linked file, select **Project Information** from the **Select available fields from** drop-down list. Choose the **Apply** button to view the changes in the project and then choose the **OK** button.

Copying Linked Model Elements

You can copy the elements of the linked model to the host model. To do so, move the cursor over the linked model and press TAB to highlight the required elements, in case the file has a nested link. Click on the element when it is highlighted and choose the **Copy to Clipboard** tool from the **Clipboard** panel of the **Modify | RVT Links** tab. Next, open the host file in which you want to paste the element and choose the **Paste from Clipboard** tool from the **Clipboard** panel. You can place the element by clicking at the required location in the drawing area.

Copying and Monitoring Linked Model Elements

After linking a Revit Architecture project, you need to constantly monitor the changes made to the elements in the Revit Project. This ensures that there are no conflicts or interference conditions between architectural and MEP elements. You can coordinate and monitor the changes made to Architectural and MEP elements by establishing relationships between them. To do so, choose the **Select Link** tool from the **Collaborate > Coordinate > Copy/Monitor** drop-down; you are prompted to select the linked model. Select the linked model from the drawing area; the **Copy/Monitor** contextual tab will be displayed. In this tab, you can choose the **Copy** tool from the **Tools** panel to copy the desired element in the linked model to the host project. Also, from the **Tools** panel, you can choose the **Monitor** tool to establish a relationship between pair of corresponding elements in the linked model and the host model. An eye symbol is displayed next to the element when an element is monitored, indicating that a relationship is being established. After using various tools in the **Copy/Monitor** contextual tab, choose the **Finish** button from the **Copy/Monitor** panel to finish the process.

SNAPS TOOL

Ribbon:	Manage > Settings > Snaps

The **Snaps** tool is one of the important tools used to snap elements in an MEP model. This tool is used to make the cursor snap or jump depending on the preset increments or on the specific object properties of elements such as endpoint and midpoint of elements. When you invoke the **Snaps** tool from the **Settings** panel of the **Manage** tab, the **Snaps** dialog box is displayed, as shown in Figure 2-20.

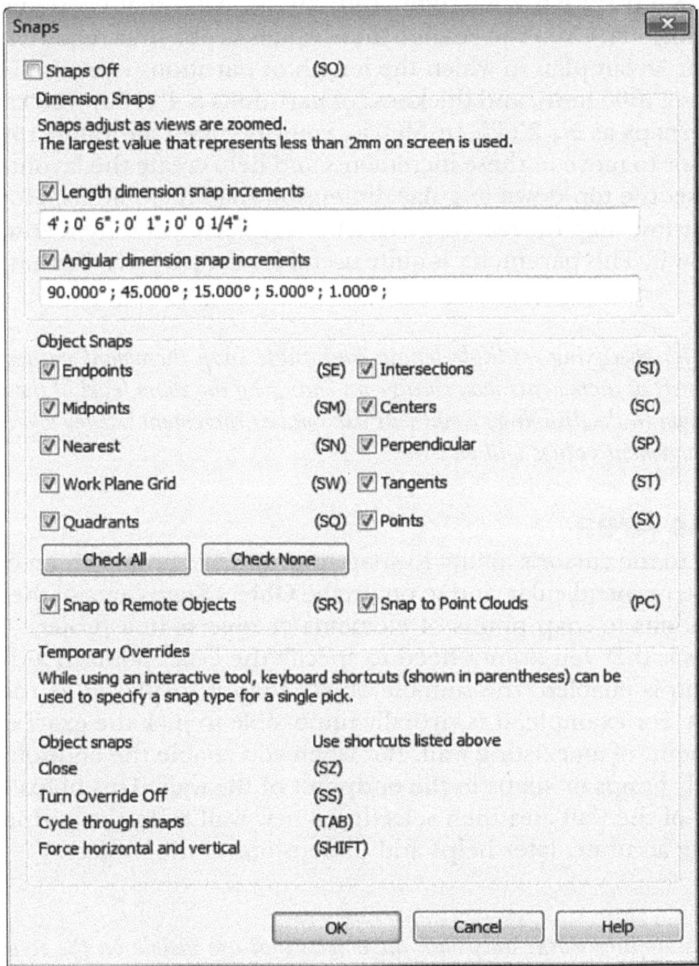

***Figure 2-20** The **Snaps** dialog box*

This dialog box has three areas, **Dimension Snaps**, **Object Snaps**, and **Temporary Overrides**. These areas are discussed next.

Note

The settings specified in this dialog box will be applied to all the projects opened in the session and will not be saved.

Dimension Snaps Area

In the **Dimension Snaps** area, you can set the length and angle dimension snap increments for placing the elements and components in a project. The dimension snap determines the increment, linear or angular, by which the cursor will jump/snap linearly or angularly while placing elements and components in a project.

The **Length dimension snap increments** check box is selected by default. As a result, you can set the snap increment value for the length in the edit box below it. The default values in this edit box are: **4'; 0'6"; 0'1"; 0'0 1/4"(1000; 100; 20; 5)**. Note that every incremental value is separated by a semicolon (;). You can change these values as per your requirement. For example, to create an interior layout plan in which the length of partitions is in 5' (1500 mm) modules, counter top width is 2'(600 mm), and thickness of partitions is 4"(100), you can enter the values for the dimension snaps as **5'; 2';4"**. In Metric, you can enter the value **1500; 600;100**. This will enable the cursor to move in these increments and help create the layout with relative ease. Similarly, you can set the top-down angular dimension snap increments. However, ensure that the **Angular dimension snap increments** check box is selected and then enter suitable value(s) in the edit box below it. This parameter is quite useful for the projects that have radial geometry.

Note

The reason for specifying multiple length and angle snap increment values in the edit boxes is that the priority of increments may change on changing the zoom level of the drawing. Therefore, when you zoom in the drawing, Revit will use smaller increment values whereas on zooming out, the larger increment values will be used.

Object Snaps Area

Object Snaps refer to the cursor's ability to snap to geometric points on an element such as its endpoint, midpoint, perpendicular, and so on. In the **Object Snaps** area of the **Snaps** dialog box, you can specify options to snap points of elements or objects in a project. The advantage of using these options is that you do not need to specify the exact point in a drawing. When the object snap function is enabled, the suitable object snap is displayed as the cursor is moved close to an element. For example, it is virtually impossible to pick the exact endpoint to start a wall from the endpoint of an existing wall. But when you enable the endpoint object snap, the cursor automatically jumps or snaps to the endpoint of the wall. This helps in identifying and selecting endpoint of the wall and then selecting a new wall from the endpoint. This, besides making the drawing accurate, later helps add dimensions to the project.

Note

The object snapping works only with the objects that are visible on the screen. A tooltip with a name as that of the object snap is also displayed when you bring the cursor close to a snap point.

In an MEP model, you can use various object snaps modes such as **Endpoints**, **Midpoints**, **Nearest**, **Work Plane Grid**, **Quadrants**, **Intersections**, **Centers**, **Perpendicular**, **Tangents**, **Points**, **Snap to Point Clouds**, and **Snap to Remote Objects**.

The name of each object snap option suggests its usage in the project. For example, the **Work Plane Grid** snap option helps you snap the intersection points of grid lines in a work plane grid that is displayed for the current work plane.

Each object snap mode is represented by a distinct geometrical shape to identify it from other object snaps. For example, the endpoint object snap is represented by a square cursor, midpoint by a triangular error, nearest by a cross, and so on. To use an object snap mode, move the cursor on the object. As you move it close to the snap point, a marker appears. To select the appropriate snap point, click when the corresponding marker or tooltip is displayed.

In Revit, all enabled object snaps work simultaneously. You can turn off all snap options, including dimension snaps and object snaps by selecting the **Snaps Off** check box located at the top of the **Snaps** dialog box. Alternatively, you can type **SO** on the keyboard to turn them off and on, while using a tool. The **Check All** and **Check None** buttons are used to select or clear all check boxes (except the **Snap to Remote Objects**) in the **Object Snaps** area.

The Temporary Overrides Area

The options in the **Temporary Overrides** area provide you with an alternative of overriding snaps setting for a single use only. For example, if you have not selected the **Endpoints** check box in the **Snaps** dialog box and you want to use this option while working with a tool, you do not need to open the **Snaps** dialog box to select this option. Instead, you can type the shortcut, **SE** in this case, to temporarily activate the endpoint object snap. Once you have used this object snap option, snapping to the endpoint is automatically turned off.

Using overrides, you can toggle between various object snap options available at the same location. To do so, press the TAB key while snapping the points in the drawing. You can also use other overrides like pressing the SHIFT key to create elements vertically or horizontally. This restricts the movement of the cursor in the orthogonal directions only. Once you release the SHIFT key, the cursor resumes its previous state. You can select the **Snaps Off** check box to disable all types of snapping.

SAVING AN MEP PROJECT

Before you close or exit a Revit session, it is recommended to save the project file. You can save a project file in a permanent storage device, such as a hard disk or a removable storage device like CD or USB. Also, you must save your work at regular intervals to avoid data loss due to any error in the computer's hardware or software.

Using the Save As Tool

In Revit, you can save your project file at the desired location by using the **Save As** tool. To do so, click the **Application** button and then choose **Save As > Project** from the **Application Menu**; the **Save As** dialog box will be displayed.

In the **Save As** dialog box, the **Save in** drop-down list displays the current drive and path in which the project file will be saved. The list box below the **Save in** drop-down list displays all folders available in the current directory. The **File name** edit box is used to specify the name to be assigned to the project or file. The **Places List** area on the left of the **Save As** dialog box contains shortcuts for the folders that are frequently used.

You can use different file saving features by choosing the **Options** button from the **Save As** dialog box. On choosing this button, the **File Save Options** dialog box will be displayed. In the

Maximum backups edit box of this dialog box, you can specify the maximum number of backup files that you need to store for a project. In Autodesk Revit, the non-workshared projects have three backup files and the workshared projects have twenty backup files by default. The options in the **Worksharing** area are inactive for non-workshared projects. You can use the options in this area to make the current workshared file central compact and select the default workset. The options in the **Thumbnail Preview** area enable you to specify the image to be used as the preview of the project file. This image is used at the time of opening a project file. You can specify a view of the model as a preview image by selecting the corresponding option from the **Source** drop-down list in the **Thumbnail Preview** area of the **File Save Options** dialog box. By default, the **Active view/sheet** option is selected in the **Source** drop-down list of the **Thumbnail Preview** area for the preview of a project file. For example, to make **Floor Plan 1-Mech** as the preview image, select it from the drop-down list. As a result, when you invoke the **Open** dialog box and select a file to open, the view displayed in the **Preview** area will correspond to the selection that is made in the **Source** drop-down list of the **File Save Options** dialog box. In the **File Save Options** dialog box, you can select the **Regenerate if view/sheet is not up-to-date** check box to see the preview with the latest modifications. On selecting this check box, the preview image will be updated when you close the project file.

Note

*Revit updates the preview image continuously. Therefore, selecting the **Regenerate if view/sheet is not up-to-date** check box can consume considerable resources.*

Using the Save Tool

Once a project has been saved using the **Save As** tool, you do not need to re-enter file parameters to save it again. To save a project to the hard disk, choose the **Application** button and then choose the **Save** option from **Application Menu**. If you are saving the project for the first time, the **Save As** dialog box will be displayed, even if you invoke the **Save** tool. Alternatively, you can save your project by choosing the **Save** button from the **Quick Access Toolbar**. As you save your project file, Revit updates it automatically without prompting you to re-enter the file name and path.

THE OPTIONS DIALOG BOX

In Autodesk Revit, you can configure global settings by using the **Options** dialog box. This dialog box can be invoked by choosing the **Options** button from the **Application Menu**. The **Options** dialog box, as shown in Figure 2-21, contains nine tabs: **General, Graphics, File Locations, Rendering, Check Spelling, SteeringWheels, ViewCube, User Interface,** and **Macros**. These tabs are discussed next.

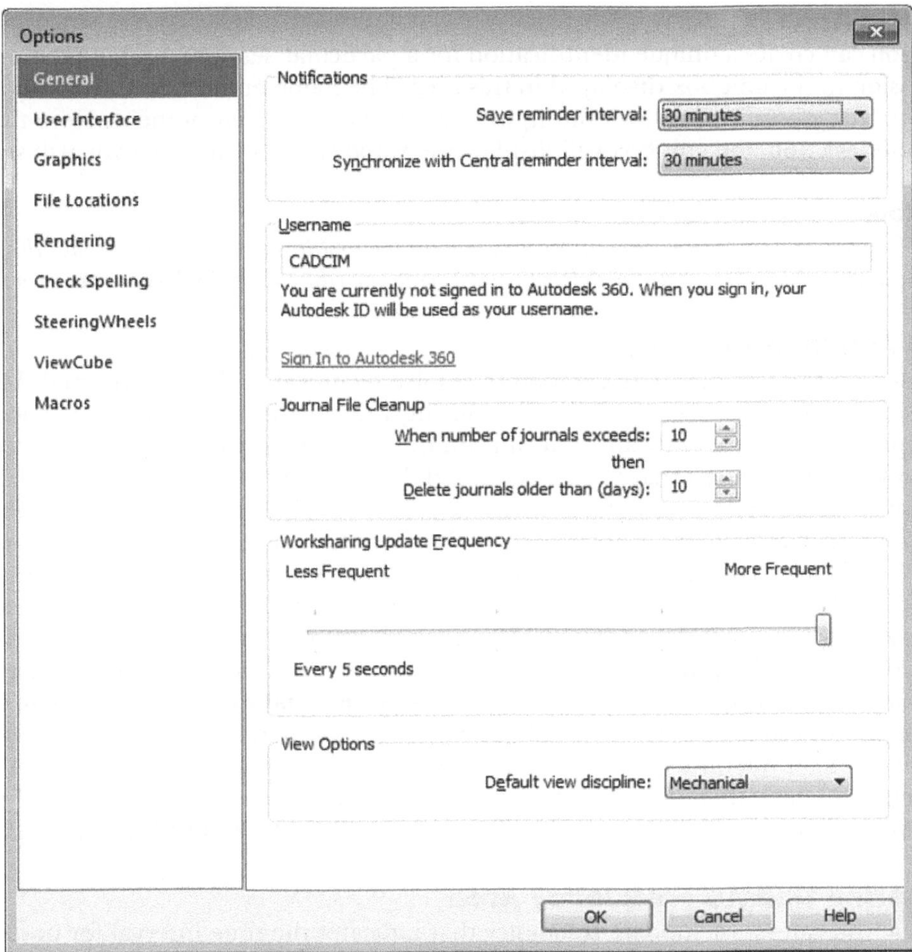

*Figure 2-21 The **Options** dialog box*

General Tab

The **General** tab is chosen by default and contains five areas: **Notifications, Username, Journal File Cleanup, Worksharing Update Frequency**, and **View Options**. These areas are discussed next.

Notifications Area

Revit provides an option for setting reminders to save the work at regular intervals. To do so, select the desired option from the **Save reminder interval** drop-down list in the **Notifications** area. By default, 30 minutes is selected in this drop-down list. If you do not want a reminder to save your work in the project, select the **No reminders** option from this drop-down list. Similarly, you can select a value from the **Synchronize with Central reminder interval** drop-down list. On doing so, you set the duration for the display of the reminder for synchronization of the local file with the central file.

Username Area

In Revit, you can create a unique identification for a particular session. To do so, enter a name for the session in the edit box displayed in this area. The name entered in this edit box will be used for granting permissions for editing in a multiuser Revit environment. Note that if you sign in **Autodesk 360,** the edit box will display the Autodesk ID with which you will sign in.

Note

*When you run Autodesk Revit in your system for the first time, you will notice that the Windows login name is displayed as the default username in the edit box in the **Username** area.*

Journal File Cleanup Area

Journal files are the text files that are used to resolve technical problems occurred during the Revit session. These files record every step during the session. Whenever you encounter a technical problem with the software, you can run this file to detect the problem or recover the lost files or to know the steps that may have caused the problem. In Autodesk Revit 2017, these files are saved at the following default location: *C:\Users\<Username>\AppData\Local\Autodesk\Revit\Autodesk Revit 2017\Journals* for Windows 7 or Window Vista users and *C:\Documents and Settings\<Username>\Local Settings\Application* for Windows XP users. These files are saved each time you close the Revit session. Therefore, the number of these files keeps on increasing until you remove these files from their location. However, to remove these files while retaining some of them, you can use the **Journal File Cleanup** area in the **General** tab of the **Options** dialog box. This area contains two spinners: **When number of journal exceeds** and **Delete journals older than (days)**. You can set the required values in these spinners to retain the recently created files. For example, if you want to delete journal files if their number exceeds 15 and if they were created before 30 days, then in such a situation, set the value in the **When number of journals exceeds** spinner to **15** and the value in the **Delete journals older than (days)** spinner to **30**.

Worksharing Update Frequency Area

In this area, you can set the update frequency that indicates the time interval for updating the project in a worksharing environment. To specify the limits for worksharing, you can set the slider between the **Less Frequent** and **More Frequent** limits.

View Options Area

In the **View Options** area, you can specify the default view discipline to be used in the Revit project. To do so, select an option from the **Default view discipline** drop-down list in this area. In this drop-down list, the **Mechanical** option is selected by default.

Graphics Tab

The options in the **Graphics** tab are used to configure the display card of your computer to improve the display performance. You can also use this tab to assign colors to selections, highlights and alerts, and enable anti-aliasing for 3D views. In the **Graphics Mode** area of this tab, the **Use Hardware Acceleration** check box is selected by default. As a result, the hardware accelerators are enabled. Hardware accelerators help in displaying the models of larger size faster on refreshing the views. In addition, the hardware accelerators help you speed up the process of switching between the views of windows. In Autodesk Revit 2017, the **Allow navigation during redraw** check box in the **Graphics Mode** area is selected by default. As a result, you will get the improved display while navigating a 2D view or a 3D view using the following methods of navigation: using the **ViewCube**, using the tools in the **Navigation Bar**, navigating by scrolling the mouse wheel, and while using the Keyboard shortcuts.

The table given next, shows the list of features barred for visual styles :

Feature	Visual Styles			
	Hidden Line	**Shaded**	**Consistent Colors**	**Realistic**
Edges	-----------	Barred	Barred	Barred
Fill Patterns	Barred	Barred	Barred	Barred
Shadows	Barred	Barred	Barred	Barred
Structural Hidden Lines	Barred	Barred	Barred	Barred
Mechanical Hidden Lines	Barred	Barred	Barred	Barred

Note

While navigating a camera view in the ***Wireframe*** *view style, the fill patterns are not displayed in the model.*

In the **Graphics Mode** area, the **Smooth lines with anti-aliasing** check box is selected by default. As a result, the options for controlling the smooth lines will be enabled. You can clear the check box to disable the options for controlling the smooth lines with antialiasing.

The buttons in the **Colors** area of the **Graphics** tab are used to toggle the color of the parameters. To specify the background color, click the button to the right of the **Background** parameter and select the desired color from the **Color** dialog box. Similarly, you can select the desired color for the **Selection**, **Pre-selection**, and **Alert** parameters. In the **Colors** area, the **Semi-transparent** check box is selected by default. As a result, you can make the selected elements semi-transparent and you can view the elements that are behind the selected elements. In the **Temporary Dimension Text Appearance** area, you can select an option from the **Size** drop-down list to specify the size of the text to be used in temporary dimensions. In this area, you can set the background of the text in the temporary dimensions. To do so, select the **Opaque** or **Transparent** option from the **Background** drop-down list.

File Locations Tab

The options in the **File Locations** tab are used to set the path for various files and directories that are accessed frequently, refer to Figure 2-22. The path for these files is set while installing Revit. However, you can modify the location of a file by choosing the corresponding **Browse** button and specify a new location. You can also change the default location of a template file, in case you wish to use a customized template file for your projects. In Revit, the default path to save or open a project can be specified in the **Default path for user files** edit box. You can also specify the default path for family template files and for the point clouds by using the corresponding **Browse** button.

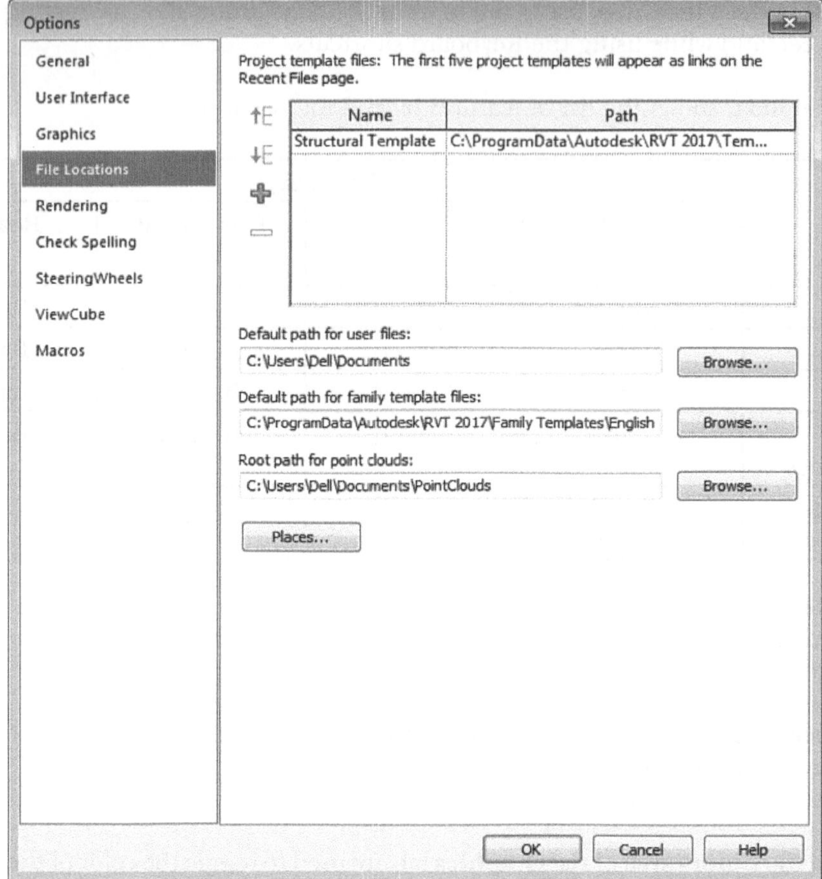

*Figure 2-22 The **Options** dialog box displaying the options in the **File Locations** tab*

Rendering Tab

Autodesk Revit uses the mental ray rendering engine for its rendering process. The mental ray has its own library, Render Appearance Library. This library stores information about render appearances for materials, default RPC contents in the software, and other information relevant to the rendering process. The Render Appearance Library is a read-only library and is loaded into the following default location while installing the Revit software: *C:\Program Files (x86)\Common Files|Autodesk Shared|Materials|2017\assetlibrary_base.fbm.* In addition to the default Render Appearance Library location, you can also specify paths for the additional image files defining texture, bump map, and custom color for the render appearance that you can use in the project. These image files are not present in the software and therefore, you need to specify their paths to use them. To do so, choose the **Add Value** button in the **Additional Render Appearance Paths** area and specify the required path in the displayed field or choose the browse button; the **Browse for Folder** dialog box will be displayed. In this dialog box, select the desired path and choose the **Open** button to add the path in the field.

Check Spelling Tab

Revit provides you with the option to run spell check to find out spelling errors in text and then rectify them. You can choose the **Check Spelling** tab from the **Options** dialog box to display its options. Figure 2-23 shows various options in the **Check Spelling** tab.

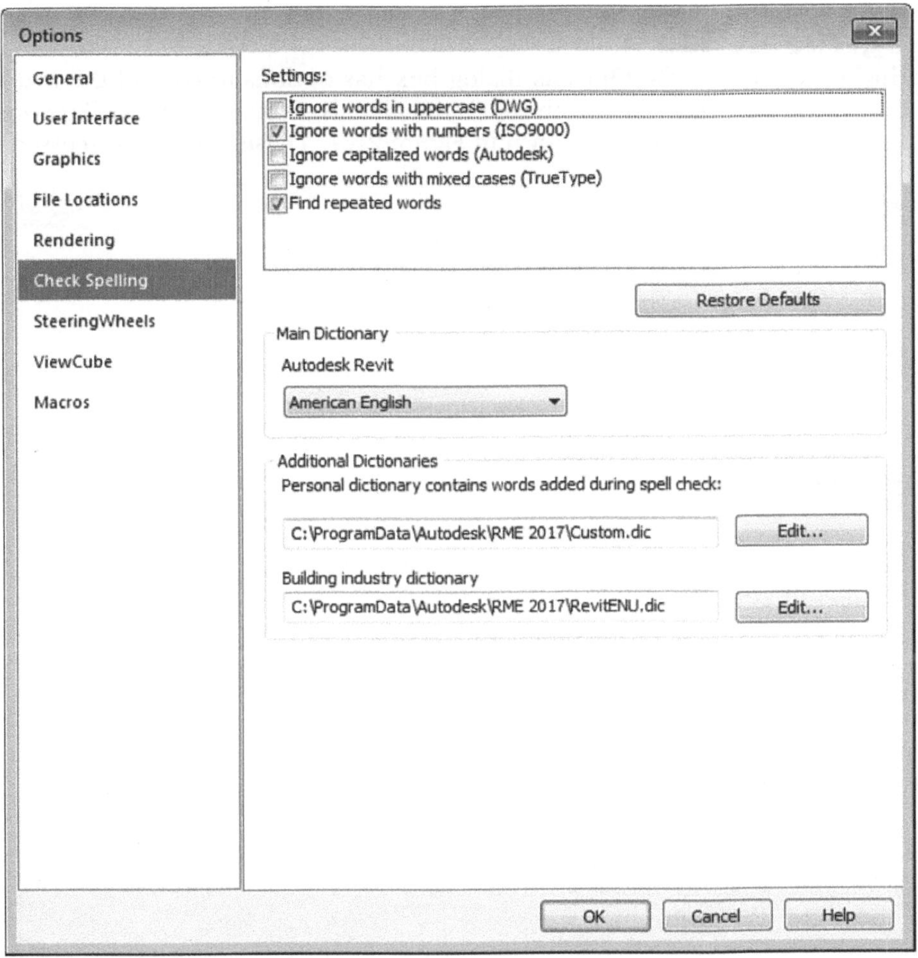

Figure 2-23 *The* ***Options*** *dialog box displaying the options in the* ***Check Spelling*** *tab*

In the **Settings** list box of this tab, you can specify various self-explanatory settings by selecting their respective check boxes. You can select the type of dictionary to be used as main dictionary for the spell check from the **Autodesk Revit** drop-down list in the **Main Dictionary** area. Apart from the main dictionary, you can also use additional dictionaries available in MEP such as the personal and building industry dictionaries. There are many words that are not included in the main dictionary but are frequently used in the building industry. For example, the abbreviation 'conc' for the word concrete is not available in the main dictionary. The additional building industry dictionary has many such words and abbreviations that can be used in the text of a project and therefore, you are not prompted for checking the spelling errors whenever such terms/words appear in the text. You can also add or remove words from your personal and building industry dictionary. To do so, choose the **Edit** button next to the option in the **Additional Dictionaries** area to view the list of words and then enter or remove any word from the lists by using the cursor and keyboard. To run spell check in your drawing, choose the **Check Spelling** tool from the **Text** panel of the **Annotate** tab; the **Spelling** dialog box will be displayed, wherein you can rectify spelling errors in the text by selecting the correct spelling and then choosing the **Change** button in the dialog box. Alternatively, you can press the F7 key to display the spelling dialog box.

SteeringWheels Tab

The **SteeringWheels** tab in the **Options** dialog box has options to control the text visibility, appearance of model, and behaviour of the operational tools of different types of SteeringWheels. This tab has seven different areas, as shown in Figure 2-24. These areas are discussed next.

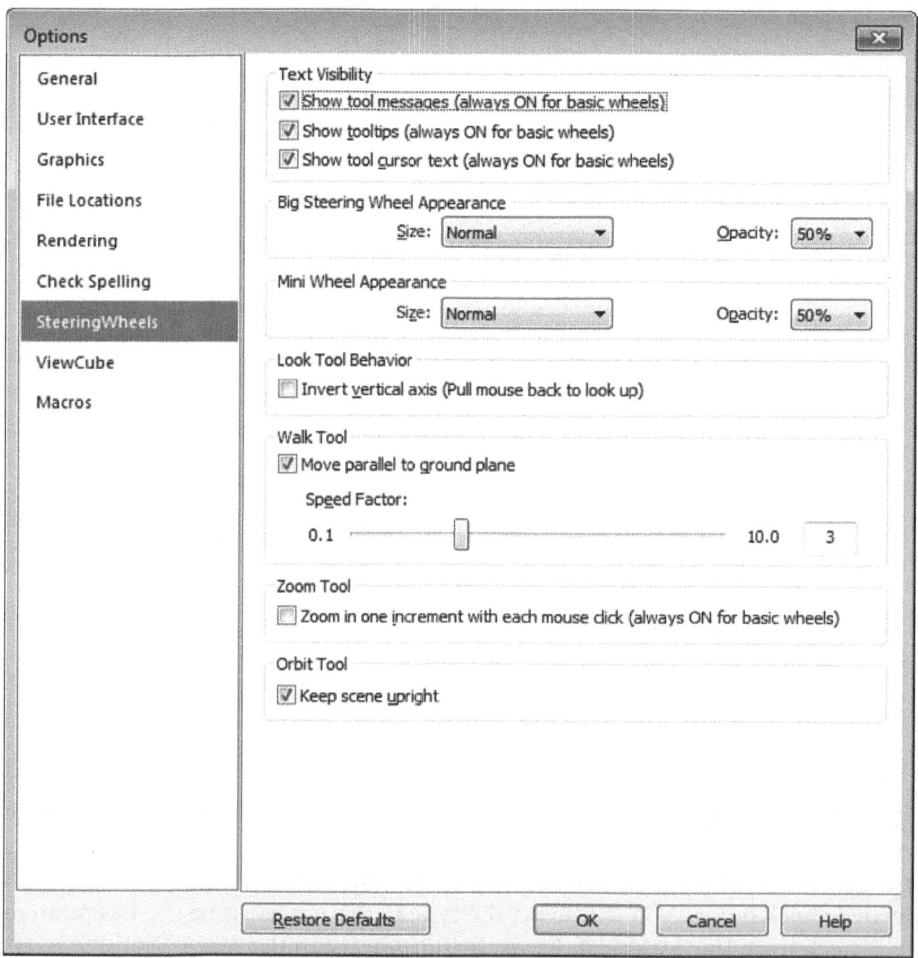

*Figure 2-24 The **Options** dialog box displaying the options in the **SteeringWheels** tab*

Text Visibility Area

You can control the display of tool messages, tooltips, and tool cursor of SteeringWheels by using the options in the **Text Visibility** area of the **SteeringWheels** tab. You need to select the **Show tool messages** check box to enable the visibility of tool messages in SteeringWheels. To display tooltips along with SteeringWheels, select the **Show tooltips** check box in this area. Similarly, to control the display of the cursor text when a tool is active, select the **Show tool cursor text** check box.

Big Steering Wheel Appearance and Mini Wheel Appearance Areas

The options in these areas are used to set the size and transparency of the SteeringWheels. To set the size of SteeringWheels, select the required option from the **Size** drop-down list in the corresponding areas and set its size to small, normal, or large. Similarly, you can set the transparency of SteeringWheels by selecting the required option from the **Opacity** drop-down list.

Look Tool Behavior and Walk Tool Areas

In the **Look Tool Behavior** area of the **SteeringWheels** tab, selecting the **Invert Vertical Axis** check box enables the view to move in the same direction as does the cursor.

The **Speed Factor** slider in the **Walk Tool** area is used to change the walk speed while using the **Walk** tool of the SteeringWheels. You can also select the **Move parallel to ground plane** check box in the **Walk Tool** area to constrain the angular movement of the walk to ground plane.

Zoom Tool and Orbit Tool Areas

Select the **Zoom in one increment with each mouse click** check box in the **Zoom Tool** area to enable the zooming operation with a single click.

In the **Orbit Tool** area, select the **Keep scene upright** check box to maintain perpendicularity between the sides of the model and the ground plane while using the **Orbit** tool.

ViewCube Tab

The **ViewCube** tab in the **Options** dialog box is used to edit the settings of the ViewCube. It has four different areas: **ViewCube Appearance, When Dragging the ViewCube, When Clicking on the ViewCube**, and **Compass**, as shown in Figure 2-25. These areas are discussed next.

ViewCube Appearance Area

This area is used to control the appearance and display of the ViewCube. In this area, the **Show the ViewCube** check box is selected by default. As a result, the ViewCube will be visible. If you clear this check box, the ViewCube will disappear and all options in the **ViewCube** tab will be deactivated. In the **ViewCube Appearance** area, you can use the options from drop-down lists to align, resize, and change the transparency of the ViewCube.

Select the options from the **On-screen position** drop-down list to align the ViewCube on the screen. Similarly, if you want to resize the ViewCube, select the required option from the **ViewCube size** drop-down list. You can also set the opacity of the inactive ViewCube by selecting an option from the **Inactive opacity** drop-down list.

When Dragging the ViewCube Area

Select the **Snap to closest view** check box in this area to enable the snap to select the closest view in the ViewCube.

When Clicking on the ViewCube Area

Select the **Fit-to-view on view change** check box in the **When Clicking on the ViewCube** area to fit the view on the screen while changing the viewing direction. In this area, the **Use animated transition when switching views** check box is selected by default. As a result, the animated transition occurs while switching the views. Clear this check box if you do not want the animated transition. Select the **Keep scene upright** check box to keep the sides of ViewCube and the sides of the view perpendicular to the ground plane. Clear the check box to turn around the model in full 360-degree swing. Clearing this check box can be useful when you are editing a family.

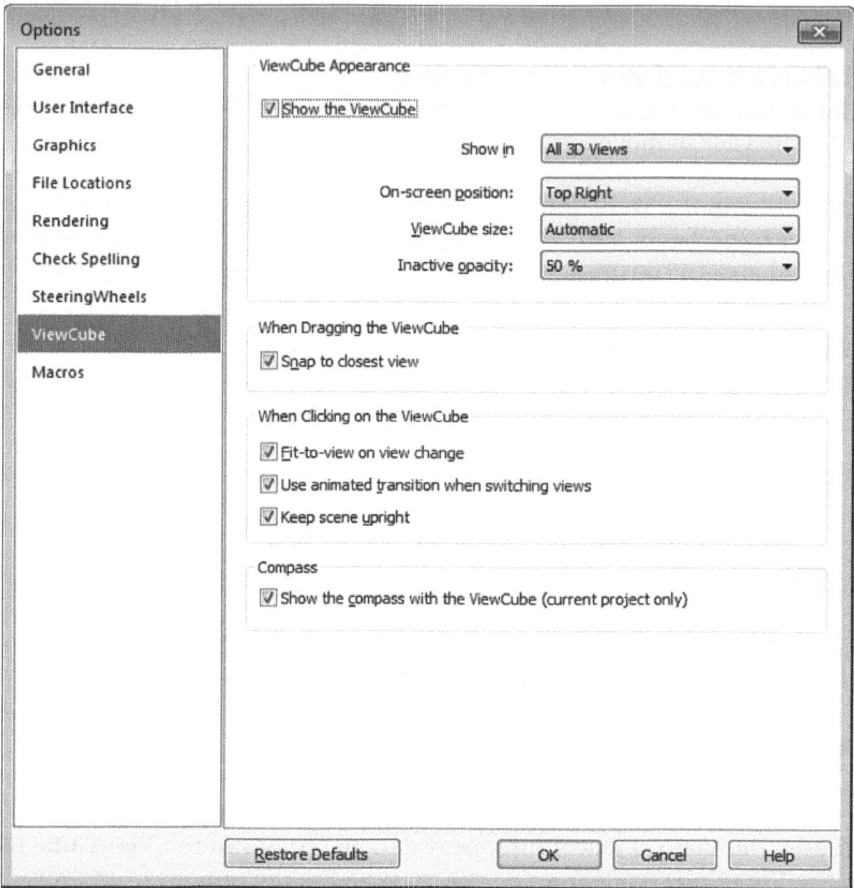

***Figure 2-25** The **Options** dialog box displaying the options in the **ViewCube** tab*

Compass Area

In this area, the **Show the compass with the ViewCube** check box is selected by default. As a result, the compass along with the ViewCube is visible in the drawing. In the **ViewCube** tab, you can choose the **Restore Defaults** button to restore the default settings that were changed in its different areas.

User Interface Tab

The **User Interface** tab contains tools and options that will help to configure the user interface of the Revit software. In this tab, you can access various tools and options from the **Configure** and **Tab Switching Behavior** areas. In the **Configure** area, you can customize the display of the tabs and tools available in the user interface of Revit. This can be achieved by using various options displayed in the **Tools and analyses** list box. For example, you can clear the **Architecture tab and tools** check box to hide the **Architecture** tab in the Revit interface. In the **Configure** area you can specify the options for the display of Revit user interface. You can do so by selecting the **Dark** or **Light** option from the **Active theme** drop-down list in this area. Also, you can choose the **Customize** button corresponding to the **Keyboard Shortcuts** parameter to customize the use of shortcut keys in a project. In the **Configure** area, you can select an option from the **Tooltip assistance** drop-down list to set the extent of the tip that will displayed with the cursor when it is close to a tool. The options in this drop-down list are **None, Minimal, Normal,** and **High**. By default, the **Normal** option is selected in this drop-down list. Note that the tooltip will appear more frequently in your drawing if you select **High** in the **Tooltip assistance** drop-down list. In the **Configure** area, the **Enable Recent Files page at startup** check box is selected by default. As a result, the recent files will be displayed on starting the Autodesk Revit software. You can clear this check box if you do not want to display the recent files at the startup. In the **Tab Switching Behavior** area, you can specify the tab to be displayed once you clear a selection or exit a tool. In this area, the **Project environment** drop-down list contains two options: **Stay on the Modify tab** and **Return to the previous tab**. Select the **Stay on the Modify tab** option to display the options in the **Modify** tab after exiting a tool or clearing a selection. Alternatively, you can select the **Return to the previous tab** option to display the last used tab after exiting a tool or clearing a selection. In the **Tab Switching Behavior** area, the **Display the contextual tab on selection** check box is selected by default. As a result, the contextual tab is displayed once you select a tool from the Autodesk Revit interface.

CLOSING AN MEP PROJECT

To close a project, choose the **Application** button and then select the **Close** option from the **Application Menu** displayed. If you have already saved the latest changes, the project file will be closed. Otherwise, Revit will prompt you to save the changes using the **Save File** dialog box. You can save the changes by choosing the **Yes** button or discard them by choosing the **No** button. You can also choose the **Cancel** button to return to the interface and continue working on the project file. You can also use the **Close** button (X) in the drawing window to close the project.

EXITING AN MEP PROJECT

To exit a Revit session, choose the **Exit Revit** button from **Application Menu**. Even if the project is open, you can choose the **Exit Revit** button to close the file and exit Revit. If the project has not been saved once, the **Save File** dialog box will be displayed on choosing the **Exit Revit** button. In this dialog box, if you choose the **No** button, all unsaved changes will be lost. You can also use the Close button (**X**) in the main Revit window (in the title bar) to end the Revit session.

OPENING AN EXISTING MEP PROJECT

In Autodesk Revit, there are several options available to open an existing project. These options are discussed next.

Opening an Existing Project Using the Open Tool

To open an existing project file, choose **Open > Project** from **Application Menu**. Alternatively, you can open the project file by choosing the **Open** button from **Quick Access Toolbar** or by pressing the CTRL+O keys. On invoking the **Open** tool, the **Open** dialog box will be displayed, as shown in Figure 2-26. Using the **Look in** drop-down list in this dialog box, you can access the desired folder and open the desired file.

The **Preview** area of the **Open** dialog box shows the preview of the selected project file. It helps you select a particular file by viewing its contents even if you are not sure about the name of the file. The window icons such as the **Views** menu, which is placed on the right of the **Look in** drop-down list, helps you select a project file based on its size, type, or date when it was last saved. On choosing the **Thumbnails** option from the **Views** menu, you can preview the contents of the project files inside the selected folder in the file list area. In the **Open** dialog box, you can browse to important locations from the **Places** list. The **Places** list is located on the left side of the **Open** dialog box. In this list, you can add or remove folders as per your requirement. To do so, choose the **Options** button from **Application Menu**; the **Options** dialog box will be displayed. In this dialog box, choose the **File Locations** tab and then the **Places** button from it; the **Places** dialog box will be displayed. The **Places** dialog box contains two columns: **Library Name** and **Library Path**.

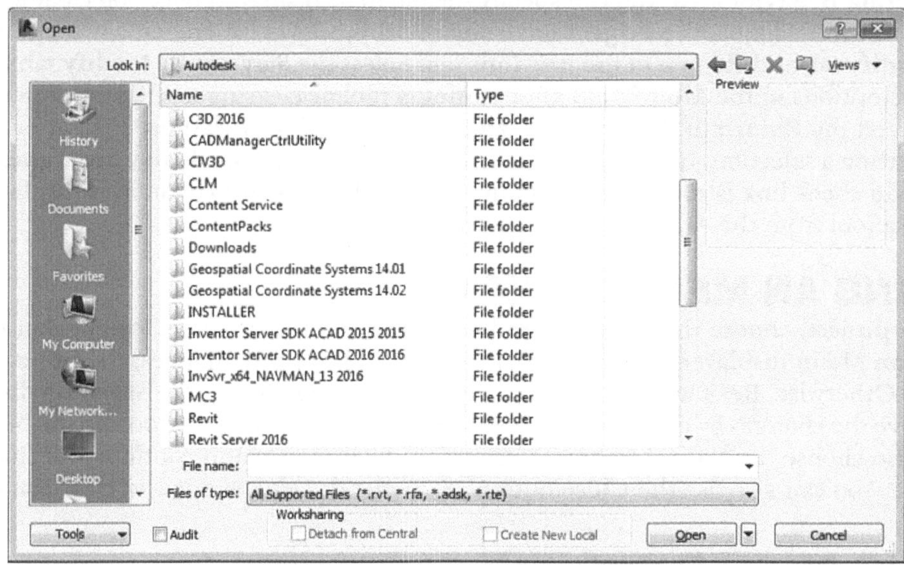

*Figure 2-26 The **Open** dialog box*

You can add or remove folders in the libraries list to create a list of frequently accessed folders. The four buttons on the left side of the **Places** dialog box can be used to create or delete a library, or move it up and down in the list. To create a new library, choose the **Add Value** button, which is the third button from the top; a new library will be added to the defined path. By default, the name of the new library in the **Library Name** section will be **NewLibrary2**. Change the name of the new library and then click in the **Library Path** column to display the **Browse** button. Choose the **Browse** button and select the folder to be added in the libraries list by using the **Browse for Folder** dialog box. Next, choose the **Open** button; the new folder will get added to the list. If required, choose the upward arrow button from the **Places** dialog box to move the folder up to the top of the list. Similarly, you can choose the down arrow button to move it down. To delete a library, select it and choose the **Remove Value** button. Choose the **OK** button in the **Places** dialog box to exit, and then close the **Options** dialog box. When you invoke the **Open** tool next time, the new folder icon will be displayed in the places list.

Once the file to be opened has been selected, its name will be displayed in the **File Name** edit box of the **Open** dialog box and its preview will be displayed in the **Preview** area.

Note

If you try opening an already opened file that has been modified in the Revit session, a message box will appear prompting you to close the file first and then reopen it. In case you open a file that has been created using an older version of Revit, the ***Program Upgrade*** *message box will be displayed. This message box informs that the file is being upgraded to the latest file format and that this is a onetime process. Once the file is opened, it gets upgraded to Autodesk Revit 2017 version.*

Using the Windows Explorer to Open an Existing Project

Apart from using the **Open** tool from the Revit interface to open a file, you can also open files directly from the **Windows Explorer** by using the methods discussed next.

A file can be opened by double-clicking on its icon in the Windows Explorer. It opens the project file in the latest Revit session. If Revit is not running, double-click on the file icon to start Revit and then open the file.

Another method of opening a project file is by dragging the project file icon from the Windows Explorer and dropping it in the drawing window of the Revit interface. You can also select, drag, and drop more than one file in the drawing window. In this case, Revit prompts you to open the files in separate windows. Choose the **OK** button to open all files in the same Revit session.

TUTORIAL

Tutorial 1 Office Space

In this tutorial, you will create a project setup for the *Office-Space* project using the following parameters and project specifications: **(Expected time: 45 min)**

1. Template file:
   For Imperial **US Imperial > Systems-Default**
   For Metric **US Metric > Systems-Default_Metric**
2. Project Units: Refer to Figure 2-29
3. File name to be assigned:
   For Imperial *c02_Office-Space_tut1.rvt*
   For Metric *M_c02_Office-Space_tut1.rvt*

The following steps are required to complete this tutorial:

a. Start the Revit 2017 session.
b. Use **Systems-Default** (Imperial) or **Systems-Default_Metric** (Metric) as the template file for the project, refer to Figure 2-27.
c. Specify the Project Units, refer to Figure 2-29.
d. Specify the Project Information, refer to Figure 2-30.
e. Create the Project Parameter, refer to Figure 2-31.
f. Add the Project Parameter to Project Information.

g. Set the Project Location.
h. Set the Browser Organization.
i. Save the project as *c02_Office-Space_tut1.rvt* by using the **Save As** tool.
j. Close the project by using the **Close** tool.

Starting Autodesk Revit 2017

1. Start Autodesk Revit 2017 by choosing **Start > All Programs > Autodesk > Revit 2017 > Revit 2017** from the taskbar. On doing so, the Revit interface window is displayed.

Opening a New Project

1. Click on the **Application** button; the **Application Menu** is displayed. Choose **New > Project** from this menu; the **New Project** dialog box is displayed, as shown in Figure 2-27.

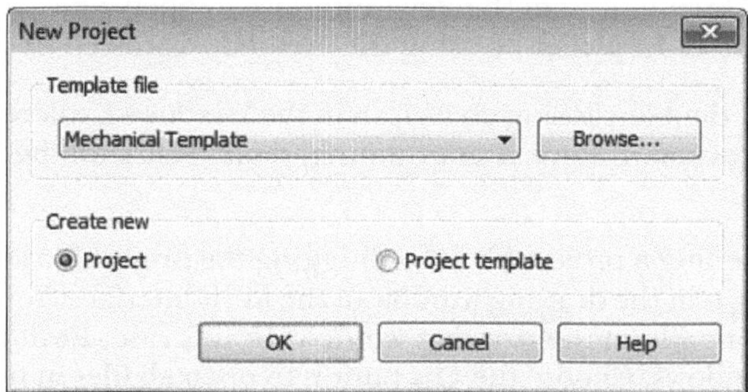

*Figure 2-27 The New **Project** dialog box*

Selecting the Template File

To select the template file for the project, you need to access the appropriate folder and select the required template file from it.

1. In the **New Project** dialog box, choose the **Browse** button from the **Template file** area; the **Choose Template** dialog box is displayed with a list of template files in the **US Imperial** folder. Note that for Metric system, the dialog box will display a list of template files in the **US Metric** folder.

2. In the **Choose Template** dialog box, select the **Systems-Default** template file from the list, as shown in Figure 2-28. For Metric system, select the **Systems-Default_Metric** template file from the list. Choose the **Open** button to assign the selected template file to the **New Project** dialog box.

3. In the **New Project** dialog box, ensure that the **Systems-Default.rte** (for Metric system **Systems-Default_Metric.rte)** option is selected in the drop-down list located in the **Template file** area and the **Project** radio button is selected in the **Create new** area. Now, choose the **OK** button; the **New Project** dialog box is closed and the *Systems-Default.rte* template file is loaded in the current file. For Metric system the *Systems-Default_Metric.rte* is loaded in the current file. Notice that the **Project Browser** now shows different levels and views that have already been created in the selected template file.

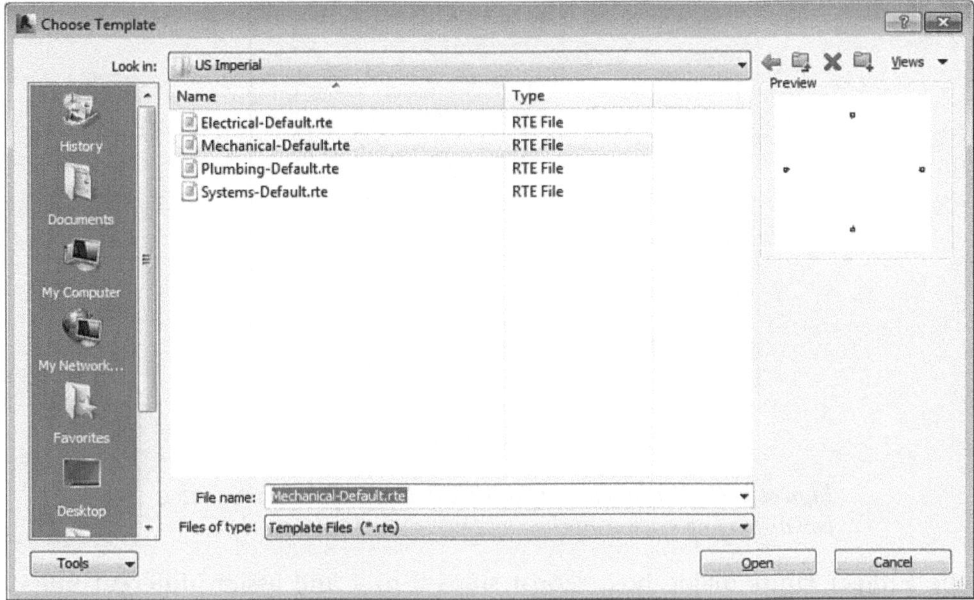

*Figure 2-28 The **Choose Template** dialog box*

Setting the MEP Units

1. To set units for the MEP project, choose the **Project Units** tool from the **Settings** panel of the **Manage** tab; the **Project Units** dialog box is displayed.

2. In the **Project Units** dialog box, select the **HVAC** option from the **Discipline** drop-down list; various units required in the HVAC workflow are displayed in a table located below the **Discipline** drop-down list, refer to Figure 2-29.

3. Next, choose the button in the **Format** column corresponding to the **Density** parameter; the **Format** dialog box is displayed.

4. In the **Format** dialog box, select the **Pounds per cubic inch** option (for Metric system, select the **kilograms per cubic meter** option) from the **Units** drop-down list and then choose the **OK** button; the **Format** dialog box is closed.

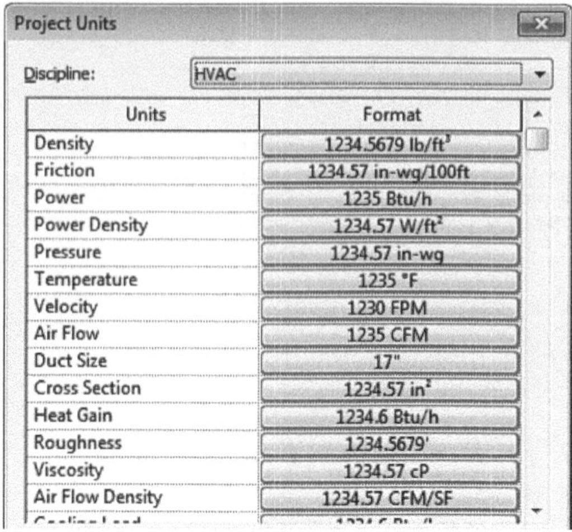

***Figure 2-29** Partial view of the table in the **Project Units** dialog box displaying various units required in the HVAC workflow*

5. In the **Project Units** dialog box, repeat steps 2 to 4 and assign different units to the **Electrical**, **Piping**, and **Energy** disciplines. Refer to the table given next for the formats and the discipline of different units needed to be specified.

Discipline	**Unit**	**Format (Imperial)**	**Format (Metric)**
HVAC	Pressure	Pounds per square inch	Pascals
Electrical	Illuminance	Footcandles	Lux
Electrical	Apparent Power	BTU (British Thermal Units) per seconds	Watts
Piping	Density	Pounds per cubic inch	kilograms per cubic meter
Energy	Coefficient of Heat Transfer	BTU (British Thermal Units) per hour square foot degree Farenheit	Watts per square meter kelvin

6. In the **Project Units** dialog box, after specifying the various formats for different units, choose the **OK** button; the **Project Units** dialog box is closed.

Setting the Project Information

In this section, you will add the project information to the *Office-Space* project file.

1. To set the project information, choose the **Project Information** tool from the **Settings** panel of the **Manage** tab; the **Project Information** dialog box is displayed.

2. In the **Project Information** dialog box, specify the project parameters as given in Figure 2-30.

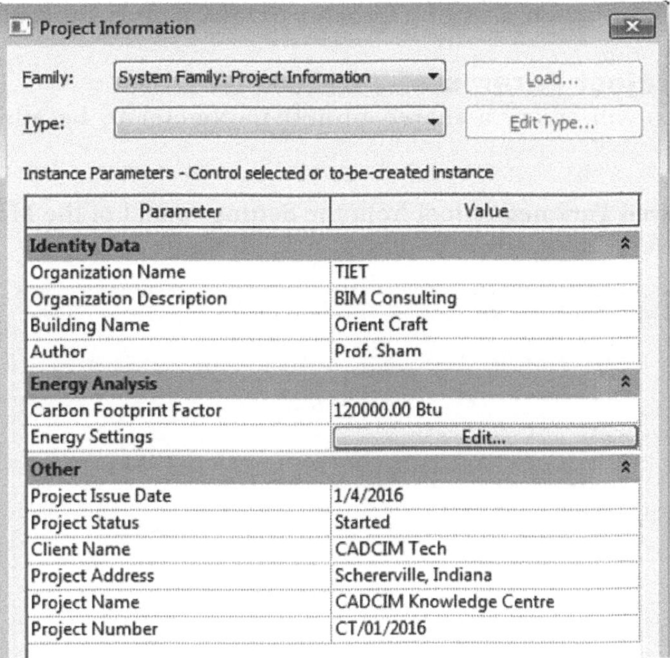

***Figure 2-30** Partial view of the **Project Information** dialog box displaying the specified project parameters*

3. In the **Project Information** dialog box, choose the **Edit** button displayed in the **Value** field corresponding to the **Energy Settings** parameter; the **Energy Settings** dialog box is displayed. In this dialog box, change the parameters as shown in the table given next and retain the other settings.

Parameter	**Value**
Export Category	Spaces
Building Infiltration Class	Tight
Report Type	Detailed
Building Service	VAV-Dual Duct
Sliver Space Tolerance	1'3" (381 mm)
Export Complexity	Complex with Shading Surfaces
Building Operating Schedule	24/7 Facility
HVAC System	Central VAV, HW Heat, Chiller 5.96 COP, Boilers 84.5 eff

4. In the **Energy Settings** dialog box, choose the **OK** button; the dialog box is closed and the specified values are assigned to the **Energy Settings** parameter in the **Project Information** dialog box.

5. In the **Project Information** dialog box, choose the **OK** button; the dialog box is closed.

Creating the Project Parameter

In this section, you will create a shared project parameter to be added to the project information.

1. Choose the **Shared Parameters** tool from the **Settings** panel of the **Manage** tab; the **Edit Shared Parameters** dialog box is displayed, refer to Figure 2-31.

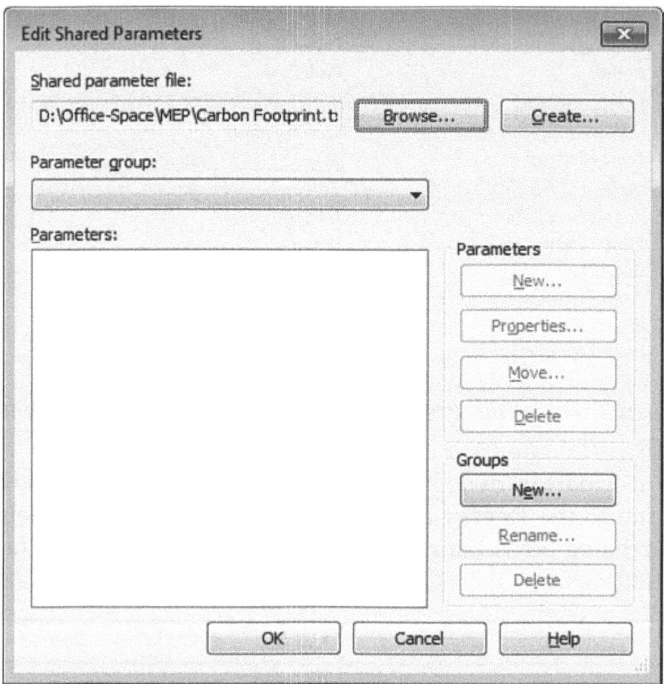

***Figure 2-31** The **Edit Shared Parameters** dialog box*

2. In the **Edit Shared Parameters** dialog box, choose the **Create** button; the **Create Shared Parameter File** dialog box is displayed.

3. In the **Create Shared Parameter File** dialog box, create a folder as per the following path *C:\Office-Space\MEP.*

4. Browse to the **MEP** folder and then enter the **Carbon Footprint** text in the **File name** edit box and then choose the **Save** button; the dialog box closes and the **Edit Shared Parameters** dialog box is displayed again.

5. In this dialog box, choose the **New** button in the **Groups** area; the **New Parameter Group** dialog box is displayed.

6. In the displayed dialog box, enter the **Green House Gas** text in the **Name** edit box and then choose the **OK** button; the **New Parameter Group** dialog box is closed and the new group is displayed in the **Parameter group** drop-down list of the **Edit Shared Parameters** dialog box.

7. Now, choose the **New** button in the **Parameters** area; the **Parameter Properties** dialog box is displayed.

8. In this dialog box, enter the **Carbon Footprint Factor** text in the **Name** edit box and then select the **Energy** option from the **Discipline** and **Type of Parameter** drop-down lists.

9. Now, in the **Parameter Properties** dialog box, choose the **OK** button; the dialog box is closed and the **Edit Shared Parameters** dialog box is displayed with the new parameter added.

10. In the **Edit Shared Parameters** dialog box, choose the **OK** button; the dialog box is closed.

Adding the Project Parameter to Project Information

In this section, you will add the project parameter to the project information.

1. Choose the **Project Parameters** tool from the **Settings** panel of the **Manage** tab; the **Project Parameters** dialog box is displayed.

2. In the **Project Parameters** dialog box, choose the **Add** button; the **Parameter Properties** dialog box is displayed.

3. In the **Parameter Type** area of the **Parameter Properties** dialog box, select the **Shared parameter** radio button and then choose the **Select** button; the **Shared Parameters** dialog box is displayed.

4. In this dialog box, ensure that the **Carbon Footprint Factor** parameter is selected in the **Parameters** area and then choose the **OK** button; the **Shared Parameters** dialog box is closed.

5. In the **Parameter Data** area of the **Parameter Properties** dialog box, ensure that the **Instance** and **Values are aligned per group type** radio buttons are selected. Also, ensure that the **Energy Analysis** option is selected from the **Group parameter under** drop-down list.

6. In the **Categories** area, select the **Project Information** check box from the list box displaying all categories.

7. Now, choose the **OK** button; the **Project Parameters** dialog box is displayed. Choose the **OK** button in the displayed dialog box to close it.

After assigning the shared parameter to the category of project information, now you need to specify a value to the added parameter in the **Project Information** dialog box.

8. Choose the **Project Information** tool from the **Settings** panel of the **Manage** tab; the **Project Information** dialog box is displayed.

9. In the **Project Information** dialog box, click in the **Value** field corresponding to the **Carbon Footprint Factor** parameter and enter **12000** in it.

10. Next, choose the **OK** button to close the **Project Information** dialog box.

Setting the Project Location

In this section, you will set the location of the project.

1. Choose the **Location** tool from the **Project Location** panel of the **Manage** tab; the **Location Weather and Site** dialog box is displayed.

2. In this dialog box, ensure that the **Location** tab is chosen by default. Now select the **Internet Mapping Service** option from the **Define Location by** drop-down list, if it is not selected by default.

Note

*On selecting the **Internet Mapping Service** option from the **Define Location by** drop-down list, the **Google Map** browser is activated for browsing the desired location. You should ensure that the internet connection is active at this stage.*

3. In the **Location** tab of the **Location Weather and Site** dialog box, enter **Schererville, IN** in the **Project Address** edit box and then choose the **Search** button; the **Bing Map** browser displayed under the **Project Address** edit box shows the desired location in the map, as shown in Figure 2-32.

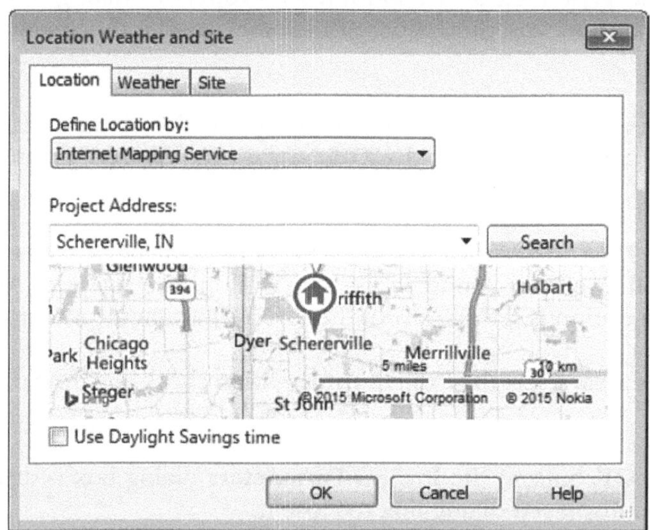

*Figure 2-32 The **Location Weather and Site** dialog box*

4. Now, choose the **OK** button to close the **Location Weather and Site** dialog box.

Setting the Browser Organization

In this section, you will set the **Project Browser** to display various views and information related to the project in the order of their discipline.

1. Choose the **Browser Organization** tool from **View > Windows > User Interface** drop-down; the **Browser Organization** dialog box is displayed.

2. In the displayed dialog box, ensure that the **Views** tab is chosen by default and then choose the **New** button; the **Create New Browser Organization** dialog box is displayed.

3. In the **Name** edit box of the displayed dialog box, enter **Office-Space-MEP** and then choose the **OK** button; the dialog box closes and the **Browser Organization Properties** dialog box is displayed.

4. In this dialog box, choose the **Grouping and Sorting** tab; various options in this tab are displayed.

5. Select the **Discipline** option from the **Group by** drop-down list.

6. Ensure that the **All characters** radio button located under the **Group by** drop-down list is selected. Now, select the **Family and Type** option from the **Then by** drop-down list.

7. Next, select the **View Name** option from the **Sort by** drop-down list located at the bottom in the **Browser Organization Properties** dialog box. Ensure that the **Ascending** radio button located below the **Sort by** drop-down list is selected.

8. Choose the **OK** button; the **Browser Organization Properties** dialog box is closed.

9. In the **View** tab of the **Browser Organization** dialog box, select the **Office-Space-MEP** check box. Now, choose the **Apply** button and then the **OK** button; the dialog box is closed and the specified settings are applied to the **Project Browser**, refer to Figure 2-33.

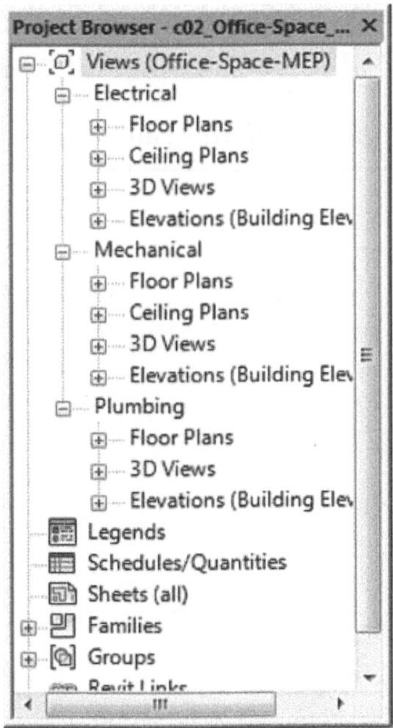

***Figure 2-33** The **Project Browser** displaying the settings specified in the **Office-Space-MEP** browser organization*

Saving the Project

In this section, you need to save the project and the settings using the **Save As** tool.

1. To save the project with the settings, choose **Save As > Project** from the **Application Menu**; the **Save As** dialog box is displayed.

2. In this dialog box, browse to the *C* drive and then create a folder with the name **rmp_2017.** Next, create a sub-folder with the name **c02_rmp_2017_tut** in it.

3. In the **File name** edit box, enter **c02_Office-Space_tut1** for Imperial or **M_c02_Office-Space_tut1** for Metric and then choose the **Options** button; the **File Save Options** dialog box is displayed.

4. In this dialog box, enter **5** in the **Maximum backups** edit box, and then in the **Thumbnail Preview** area, select the **3D View: {3D}** option from the **Source** drop-down list.

5. Select the **Regenerate if view/sheet is not up-to-date** check box in this dialog box.

6 Now, choose the **OK** button; the **File Save Options** dialog box is closed and the **Save As** dialog box is displayed.

7. In this dialog box, choose the **Save** button to save the current project file with the specified name and to close the **Save As** dialog box.

Closing the Project

1. To close the project, choose the **Close** option from the **Application Menu**.

   The file is closed and this completes the tutorial.

Self-Evaluation Test

Answer the following questions and then compare them to those given at the end of this chapter:

1. Which of the following tabs in the **Options** dialog box can be used to set the configuration of the fabrication application?

   a) **User Interface** b)**File Locations**
   c) **General** d) None of these

2. Which of the following tools can be used to set the **Project Browser** of a project?

   a) **Keyboard Shortcuts** b) **Project Browser**
   c) **Object Styles** d) **Browser Organization**

3. The__________tool can be used to set the disciplines in the **Project Browser**.

4. You can define the geographical location of a project by using the__________tool.

5. In an MEP project, you can inherit the project standard from another Revit project by using the___________ tool.

6. The __________ button in the **Save As** dialog box can be used to specify the maximum numbers of backup(s) for a project file.

7. The options in the __________ tab of the **Options** dialog box can be used to set the path for various frequently accessed files and directories.

8. You can choose the **Link Revit** tool from the ___________tab to link a Revit project to the current project.

9. You can open multiple Revit projects at a time. (T/F)

10. In Revit, you can enable all the object snap options at a time. (T/F)

11. The extension of a template file used in a Revit project is *.rft*. (T/F)

12. The **Options** dialog box is used to configure the global settings of the project. (T/F)

Review Questions

Answer the following questions:

1. Which of the following files are used to resolve technical problems occurred during a Revit session?

   a) Temporary　　b) History
   c) Journal　　d) Cookies

2. Which of the following options is not an object snap option?

   a) **Endpoints**　　b) **Work Plane Grid**
   c) **Dimension**　　d) **Centers**

3. Which of the following keys is used to toggle between the object snap options available at the same point?

   a) TAB　　b) CTRL
   c) ALT　　d) F3

4. You can specify the settings for **ViewCube** and **SteeringWheels** in the__________dialog box.

5. The __________tool can be used to share the coordinates of the host model with the linked model.

6. In Revit, you can create a unique identification for a particular session. (T/F)

7. The flow in the piping system implies the discharge rate of the water or fluids. (T/F)

8. You cannot control the visibility of an element in the linked model(s). (T/F)

9. The **Save reminder interval** drop-down list available in the **General** tab of the **Options** dialog box is used to specify the time interval between reminder prompts to save a project file. (T/F)

10. If you choose the **Close** button without saving the changes made in a project file, Revit will prompt you to save the changes before closing it. (T/F).

EXERCISE

Exercise 1 PowerPlant

In this exercise, you will create a new project file for the *Power Plant* project with the following parameters. **(Expected time: 15 min)**

1. Template file:
   For Imperial **US Imperial > Systems-Default**
   For Metric **US Metric > Systems-Default_Metric**

2. Project information to be added:
   Project Issue Date **10/05/2015**
   Project Status **Started**
   Client Name **CADCIM Technologies**
   MEP Consultant **CADCIM-Technologies**
   Mechanical Consultant **Sham Tickoo**
   Project Name **Power Plant**
   Commencement Date **20/09/2015**
   Documented Contract Completion Date **31/07/2017**
   Provisional Period Allowed in Contract **30 Days**

3. Project Units- Set the various units in the *Power Plant* project as shown in the table given next.

Discipline	Units	Format (Imperial)	Format (Metric)
HVAC	Power	Kilowatts	Kilowatts
HVAC	Heat Gain	Kilowatts	Kilowatts
HVAC	Duct Size	Decimal inches	Millimeters
HVAC	Factor	Fixed	Fixed
HVAC	Pressure	Pounds per square inches	Pascals
Electrical	Frequency	Cycles per second	Cycles per second
Electrical	Current	Kiloamperes	Kiloamperes
Electrical	Illuminance	Footcandles	Lux
Electrical	Electrical Potential	Kilovolts	Kilovolts
Piping	Velocity	Feet per second	Meters per second
Energy	Coefficient of Heat Transfer	BTU per hour	Joules

4. Energy Settings-Set it as specified in the table given next.

Parameter	Value
Export Category	Spaces
Building Infiltration Class	Tight
Project Phase	Existing
Location	Texas, USA
Building Services	Fan Coil System
Report Type	Simple
Sliver Space Tolerance	1'5" (432 mm)
Export Complexity	Complex with Shading Surfaces
Building Operating Schedule	24/7 Facility
HVAC System	Central VAV, HW Heat, Chiller 5.96 COP, Boilers 84.5 eff

5. File name to be assigned:
   For Imperial *c02_Power_Plant_exer1.rvt*
   For Metric *M_c02_Power_Plant_exer1.rvt*

Answers to Self-Evaluation Test

1. d, **2.** d, **3. Browser Organization, 4. Location, 5. Transfer Project Standards, 6. Options, 7. File Locations, 8. Insert, 9.** T, **10.** T, **11.** F, **12.** T

Chapter 3

Creating Building Envelopes

Learning Objectives

After completing this chapter, you will be able to:

- *Understand the concept of Levels*
- *Understand the concept of Grids*
- *Work with Project Views*
- *Understand walls*
- *Add doors and windows*
- *Create openings in walls*
- *Create ceilings*
- *Create floors*
- *Create rooms*

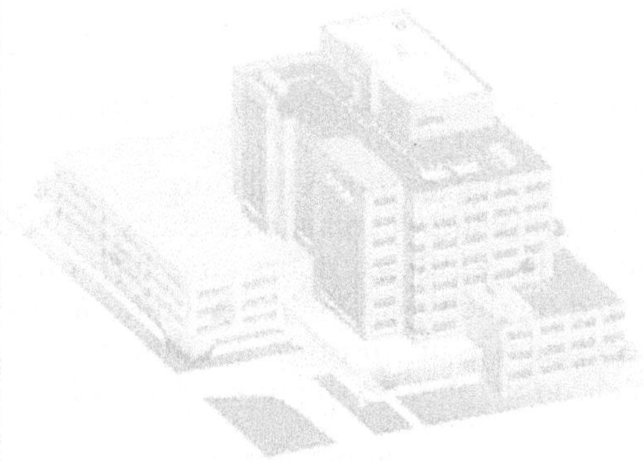

INTRODUCTION

In an MEP project "Building Envelope" comprises of all the architectural and structural elements that form the building. These include walls, doors, windows, floors, roofs, beams, columns, datum elements, and standard views.

Building Envelope is an integral part of a Revit model. Without a proper Building Envelope, you cannot design the MEP model in a project. In Autodesk Revit 2017, you can either create a building envelope in the current MEP project or link the architectural and structural models created in Revit to the current MEP project.

In this chapter, you will learn about various tools and options to create the Building Envelope for carrying out an MEP project.

LEVELS

Levels, in a multistory building, refer to the infinite horizontal planes that define each story of the structure. Autodesk Revit uses levels as references for level-hosted elements such as walls, ducts, AHUs, air terminals, pipes and pipe fixtures, sanitary fixtures, floor, roof, ceiling, and so on. The distance between levels can be used to define the story height of a building model, as shown in Figure 3-1. Autodesk Revit also provides flexibility to create a non-story level or a reference level such as sill level, parapet level, and so on.

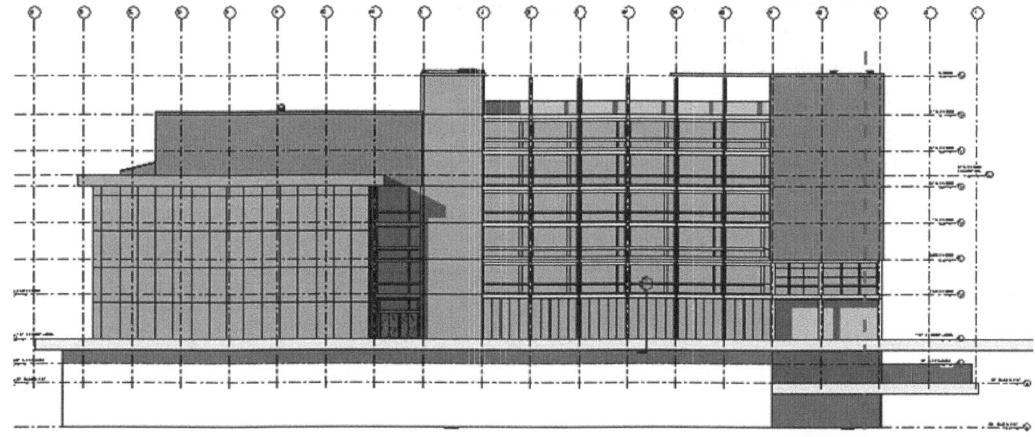

Figure 3-1 *The elevation view of a building model displaying different levels*

For example, a multistory office building, as shown in Figure 3-1, displays different story heights for each floor. MEP and architectural components such as ducts, pipes, fixtures, electrical wiring, fire fighting fixtures, exterior walls, windows, doors, and furniture may also differ on each floor. You can create levels based on the story height of a building. You can then create various building elements on each level such as an entrance door on the first floor level, bay windows on the second floor level, an elevator room on the roof level, and so on.

When you use the default template file for creating a new project file, two predefined levels, **Level 1** and **Level 2**, are displayed in the elevations or section views. You can view any of the elevation or section view using the **Project Browser**. Levels can be added, renamed, and modified at any time during the project development.

Tip

In an MEP project, it is recommended to create the levels and save them as a template. On doing so, you can save time while working on a project deadline. Also, the number of levels that you will create in the template will be based on the type of project your firm frequently works on. After you create the levels, you need to assign appropriate plans such as Lighting, Power, HVAC Piping, and more based on your requirement for each of the created levels.

Note

In Revit, you can view the levels in the elevations or section views displayed in the ***Project Browser*** *under each discipline such as Mechanical, Electrical, or Plumbing, refer to Figure 3-2.*

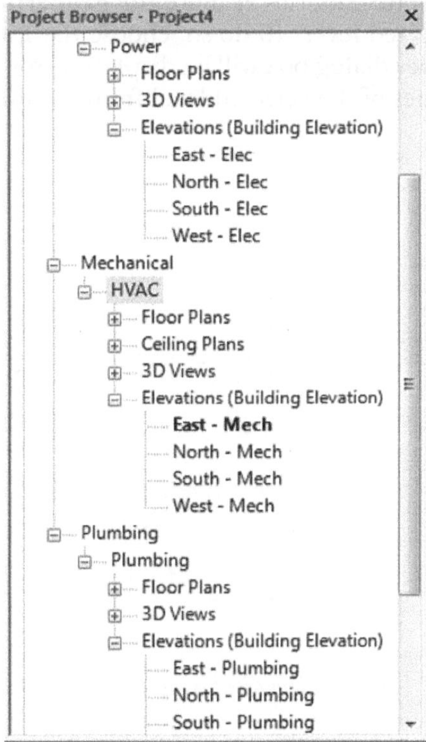

Figure 3-2 *The* ***Project Browser*** *displaying various elevation views for different disciplines*

Tip

If you are using a linked architectural model to create an MEP model, you can reuse the levels created in an architectural model for the current MEP model. To do so, choose the ***Select Link*** *tool from* ***Collaborate > Coordinate > Copy/Monitor*** *drop-down. The use of the* ***Copy/ Monitor*** *tool has already been discussed in Chapter 2 of this textbook.*

Understanding Level Properties

A typical level is represented by a level line, level bubble, level name, level elevation, and so on, refer to Figure 3-3. Using these parameters and controls, you can modify the appearance of a level. The level name is a modifiable parameter that is used to refer to each level. The level elevation is the distance of the level from the base level. The visibility of the level bubble on either side of the level line can be controlled by using the bubble display control. The length alignment control can be used to align level lines. Autodesk Revit provides the 2D or 3D extents control for datums when they are selected. This enables you to change their extents in one or multiple views in which they are visible. When a datum is in 3D mode, any modification made in the 3D view reflects in all views of the building model. Therefore, you cannot modify a specific view in the 3D mode. However, 2D mode can be used to modify a datum in a specific view, thereby making it view-specific.

Like other building and MEP elements used in an Autodesk Revit project, levels also have associated types and instance properties. You can view and modify instance properties of a level in the **Properties** palette. You can also use the **Properties** palette to view and modify the type properties of the selected level. To do so, choose the **Edit Type** button in the **Properties** palette; the **Type Properties** dialog box will be displayed. You can use this dialog box to modify and view the type properties of the selected level from the drawing. Various properties of level are described next.

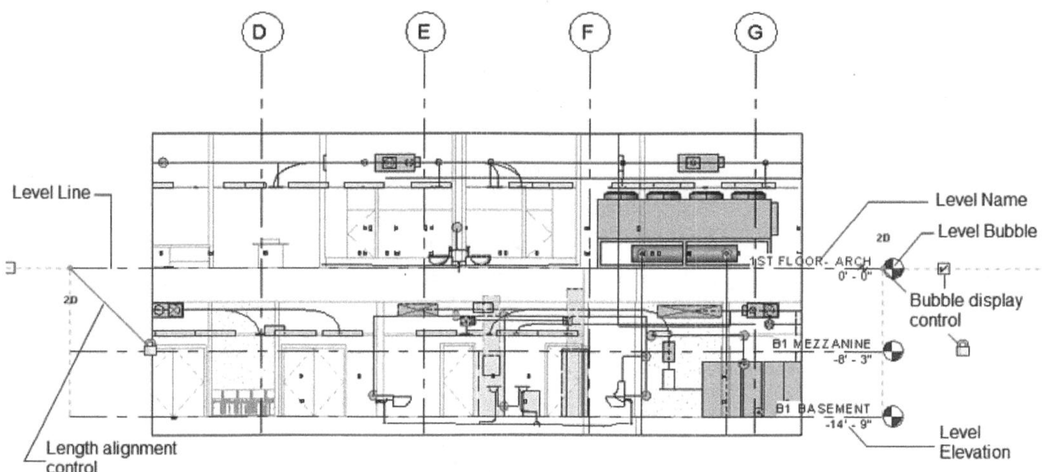

Figure 3-3 *A section view displaying levels with its various components*

Type Properties of Level

The type properties of a level can be viewed and modified in the **Type Properties** dialog box of a level, as shown in Figure 3-4. When you change the type properties of a level, all its instances are also modified. In the **Type Properties** dialog box of a level, you can modify the value of a parameter by clicking on its corresponding **Value** field and then selecting a new value from the drop-down list or entering a new value in the field. Different level type properties are described in the table given next.

Parameter Name	Value and Description
Elevation Base	Describes the elevation base value with respect to the project or the shared origin.

Line Weight	Refers to the line weight of the level. It can be specified by clicking in its **Value** field and selecting a desired option from the drop-down list displayed.
Color	Refers to the color of the level line and can be selected from the available colors. The default color is black.
Line Pattern	Used to set the linetype of the level line.
Symbol	Refers to the symbol indicating the level and can be chosen from the drop-down list. The **None** option can be specified if the level head is not required.
Symbol at End 1 Default	Check box is selected if a bubble is required at the left end of the level line.
Symbol at End 2 Default	Check box is selected if a bubble is required at the right end of the level line.

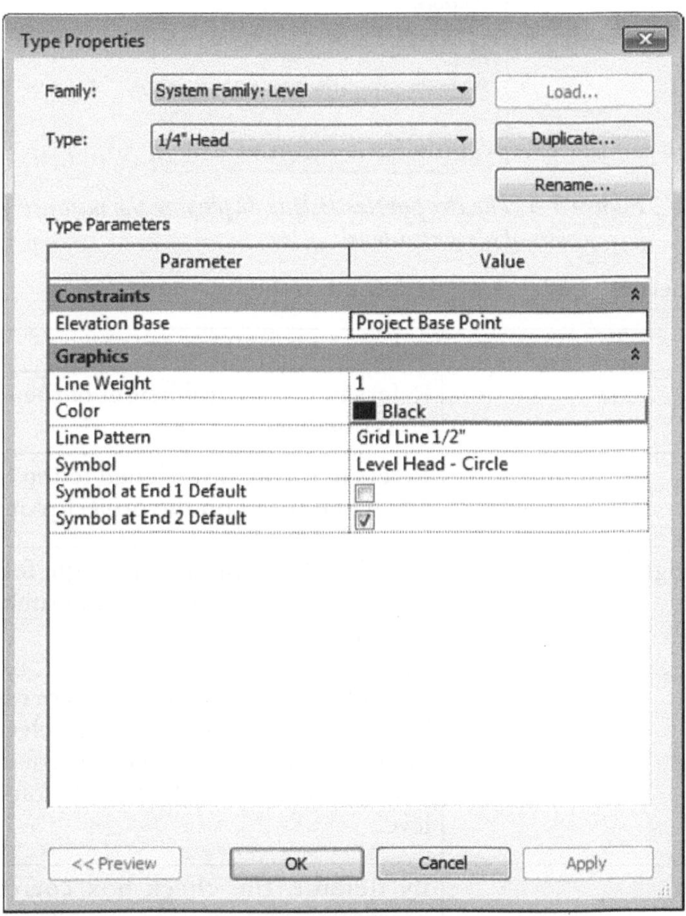

***Figure 3-4** The **Type Properties** dialog box displaying the type parameters of a selected level type*

Instance Properties of Level

You can change the instance properties of the selected level by using the **Properties** palette, refer to Figure 3-5. When you change the instance properties of a level, the properties of only the selected instance are changed.

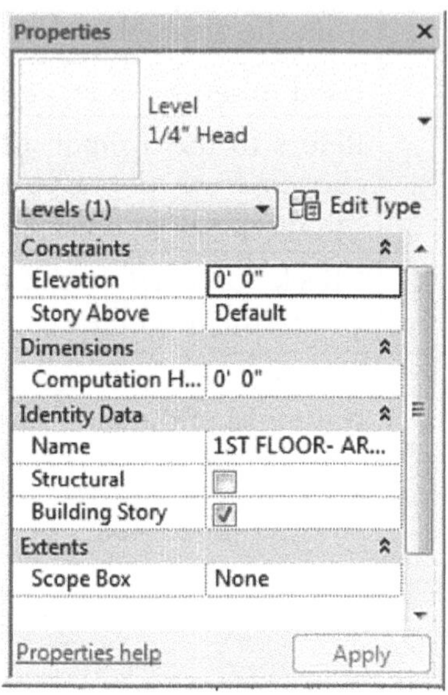

***Figure 3-5** The **Properties** Palette displaying the instance parameters of a selected level*

The instance properties of a level are described in the following table:

Parameter Name	**Value and Description**
Elevation	Refers to the vertical height of the level from the elevation base.
Name	Refers to the name assigned to the level. You can enter any name based on the project requirement.
Computation Height	Specifies the computation height for a level. This value is used to compute the area, perimeter, and volume of a room.
Structural	By default, the check box corresponding to this parameter is cleared. You can select the check box to define the level as structural. For example, the level defined for the top of a foundation can be a structural level.
Building Story	By default, the check box corresponding to this parameter is selected. As a result, you can define a level as a functional story or a floor in the project.

Story Above	Specifies the next building story for the level.
Scope Box	Refers to the scope box assigned to the level that controls its visibility in different views.

Adding Levels

In Autodesk Revit, you can create multiple levels based on your project requirements. Note that the **Level** tool remains inactive in the **Datum** panel for all the plan views. The **Level** tool will only be activated in an elevation or section view. To create a level, first select the desired section or elevation view on which you want to add the level. Next, invoke the **Level** tool from the **Datum** panel of the **Architecture** tab, as shown in Figure 3-6; the **Modify | Place Level** tab will be displayed. In this tab, choose any of the sketching options displayed in the **Draw** panel to create levels in your project. You can also invoke the **Level** tool by typing **LL**. In the displayed tab, you can select level type from the **Type Selector** drop-down list to modify an existing level. This drop-down list has three level types in Imperial unit system: **Level: 1/4" Head**, **Level: No Head**, and **Plenum**. In Metric unit system, the **Type Selector** drop-down list displays two types of levels: **Level: 8mm Head** and **Level: Plenum**. To make the level head visible, select the **Level: 1/4" Head** option for Imperial or **Level: 8mm Head** for Metric system. Else, select the **Level: No Head** or **Plenum** option.

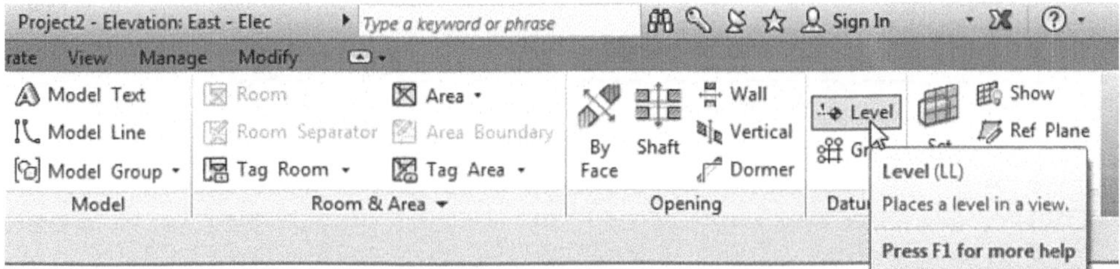

*Figure 3-6 Choosing the **Level** tool from the **Datum** panel*

Tip

*You can select the **Plenum** option from the **Type Selector** drop-down list when you are required to add a plenum level. The plenum level is generally added above the ceiling level. This level is used to generate a plan view in which you can add spaces to make the heating and cooling load analysis of a building accurate.*

In the **Draw** panel of the **Modify | Place Level** tab, you can use the **Line** (default selection) or **Pick Lines** tool to sketch a level line. In the **Options Bar**, the **Make Plan View** check box is selected by default. As a result, while adding a level in a project view, its associated plan view/s will be created. To specify the associated view/s to the level, choose the **Plan View Types** button displayed next to the **Make Plan View** check box; the **Plan View Types** dialog box will be displayed. In the **Select view types to create** area of this dialog box, two associated views will be displayed namely, **Ceiling Plan** and **Floor Plan**. You can select any one of them or both from the area and then choose **OK** to close the dialog box; the selected view/s will be associated with the level. If you clear the **Make Plan View** check box, the associated views will not be created. The **Offset** edit box in the **Options Bar** can be used to add a level at a specified distance from the selected point or element.

To add a level in the current project view(elevation/section), invoke the **Level** tool and move the cursor near the existing levels. On doing so, the temporary dimensions will be displayed, indicating the perpendicular distance between the nearest level and the cursor. To add a level at the specified distance from the existing level, specify the perpendicular distance value, as shown in Figure 3-7.

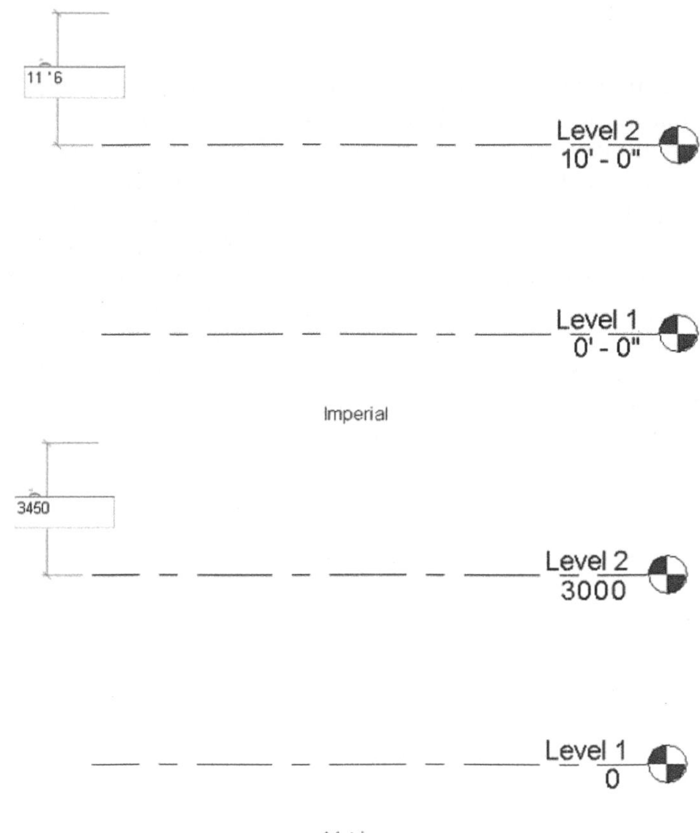

***Figure 3-7** Specifying the distance from the existing level*

To sketch a level line, specify its start point and endpoint. The level elevation and the level name will be specified simultaneously. Click to specify the first point and move the cursor to the left or the right. You will notice that the level line, level name, and elevation appear on the cursor and move along with it. Also, if you move the cursor above the endpoint of the existing level line, a dashed alignment line will appear, indicating its alignment with the existing level. When the alignment line appears, click to specify the endpoint of the level line. You can also specify the elevation of the level by entering the value before specifying the start point.

Note

Although you are required to specify the start point and the end point of level lines, the levels corresponding to these lines are infinite horizontal planes. However, the placement of the level line can be useful in the elevation and section views.

When you select a recently added level, it is highlighted and displays two square boxes, one each on either side of the level. These boxes are used to control the visibility of the level bubble. They can be selected or cleared to make the bubble visible or invisible at the desired side(s). The two small circles representing the drag controls for the level line can be used to increase or decrease the length of the level line by dragging. The padlocks act as the length alignment control for the alignment of all the level lines. When locked, the modification in the length reflects on all the level lines, simultaneously. To modify the length of a level line separately, unlock the control and then modify its length.

Modifying Level Parameters

You can change a level type by selecting the level from the drawing and then selecting the desired level type from the **Type Selector** drop-down list in the **Properties** palette. On doing so, the current level will be modified into the selected level. You can also specify the properties of the modified level using the **Properties** palette before adding it. Some of the parameters of the level can also be modified by clicking on the level in the drawing window and entering the new value.

For example, after selecting a level, you can click on its name and assign a new name to it. As you start typing the new name, an edit box appears with the new value. Also, Autodesk Revit prompts you to rename all the associated views such as the floor plan, ceiling plan, and so on, if required. If you choose to rename the views, the name of the associated views will change in the **Project Browser**. Similarly, you can modify the elevation of a level by selecting it and entering the new temporary dimension value. When you enter a new value, the level automatically moves to the specified elevation.

You can also move levels by simply dragging them to the desired location. Click to select a level(s) and drag it to the desired location. As you drag, the elevation level changes dynamically with respect to the cursor location. Hold the SHIFT key to move the cursor vertically. Next, release the mouse button at the appropriate location to complete the dragging process. When you move the cursor near a level, level will be highlighted. Right-click on the highlighted level line; a shortcut menu will be displayed with various options. You can choose the **Go to Floor Plan** option from the shortcut menu to open the corresponding floor plan for the level. On choosing the **Find Referring Views** option from the shortcut menu, the **Go To View** dialog box will be displayed. In this dialog box, select the desired view from the list of views and then choose the **Open View** button; the view in which the selected level is visible will be displayed.

For certain levels, you may want to move the level bubble to a different location. When you select a level, you will notice a break control, also known as **Add elbow**, appearing below the level name, next to the level bubble. This break control can be used to break the level line and move the level bubble away from it. On clicking this control, you will observe that the level name and the level bubble are also moved to the new location and an extension line is created. You can then use the displayed blue dots to place the level bubble at the appropriate location.

Controlling the Visibility of Levels

You can control the visibility of levels in any of the project views. To do so, select a level and right-click; a shortcut menu will be displayed, as shown in Figure 3-8. Choose **Hide in View > Category** from the shortcut menu; the level category will be hidden in the current view.

To hide a particular level, choose **Hide in View > Elements** from the shortcut menu; only the selected level will be hidden in the current view and will be displayed in all other views.

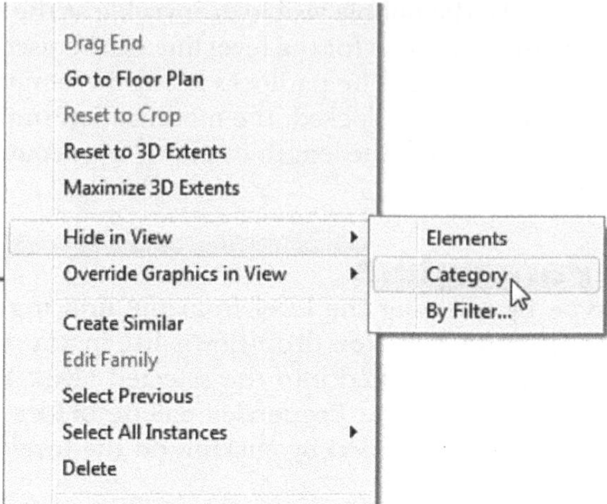

***Figure 3-8** Choosing the **Category** option from the shortcut menu*

To hide all the levels in a project view, select a level in the project view. Next, choose the **Override by Category** tool from **Modify| Levels > View > Override Graphics in View** drop-down; the **View-Specific Category Graphics** dialog box will be displayed. In this dialog box, clear the **Visible** check box and choose **OK**; all levels will be hidden from the current view. You can use the **Scope Boxes** feature to control the visibility of the levels. You will learn about this feature later in this chapter.

WORKING WITH GRIDS

Autodesk Revit provides you the option of creating rectangular or circular grids for your projects. Using these grids, you can create building envelopes easily and also place the MEP elements at desired locations and intersections.

Creating Grids

You can create grid patterns based on your project requirement. Grid patterns can be rectangular or radial, depending on the project geometry. A rectangular grid pattern can be created using straight grid lines, whereas a radial grid pattern can be formed using arc grids. The created grids are visible in all plan, elevation, and section views.

To create a grid line, invoke the view in which you want to create it and then choose the **Grid** tool from the **Datum** panel of the **Architecture** tab, as shown in Figure 3-9; the **Modify | Place Grid** tab will be displayed. Using this tab, you can modify the type and instance properties of grid. You can also change the grid type by selecting an option from the **Type Selector** drop-down list. The **Modify | Place Grid** tab, as shown in Figure 3-10, displays various options to draw and modify grids in a drawing. The **Draw** panel in the **Modify | Place Grid** tab displays various tools to draw grids as lines and curves or to convert existing model lines into grids. The methods of creating grids are discussed next.

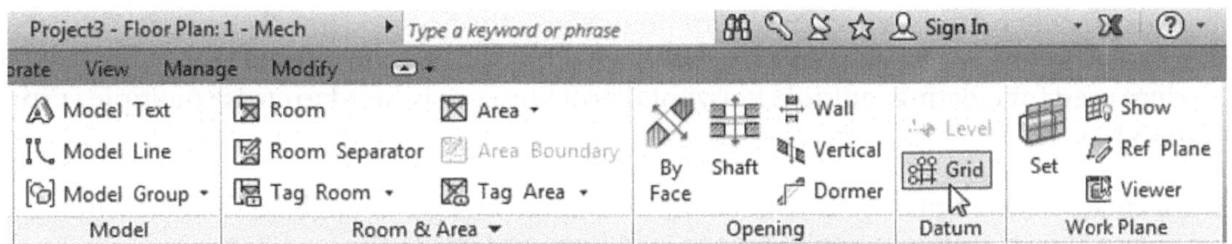

*Figure 3-9 Choosing the **Grid** tool from the **Datum** panel*

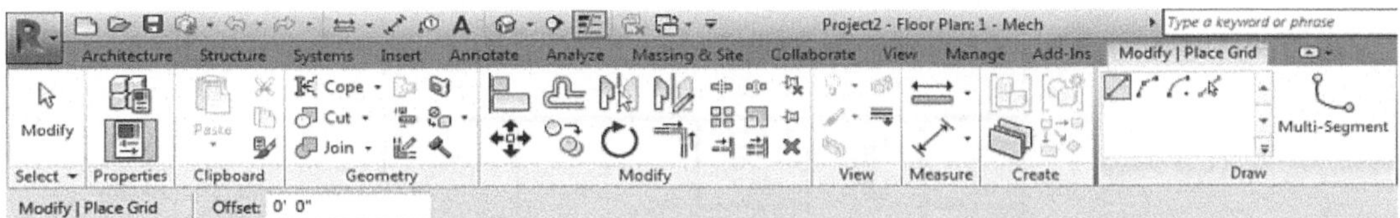

*Figure 3-10 Various options in the **Modify / Place Grid** contextual tab*

Creating Grids Using the Draw Tools

To create a straight grid line, select any floor plan view from the **Project Browser** and then choose the **Grid** tool from the **Datum** panel in the **Architecture** tab; the **Modify | Place Grid** tab will be displayed. The **Line** tool in the **Draw** panel is chosen by default. As a result, you can start sketching the grid line by clicking at the appropriate location to specify the start point and then moving the cursor to the desired direction. As you move the cursor, you will notice that a grid line is created with one end fixed at the specified point and the other end attached to the cursor. Also, a temporary angular dimension indicating the angle of the line with the horizontal axis is displayed. Click to specify the endpoint of the grid line when the appropriate angular dimension is displayed. You can also sketch an arbitrary inclined grid line and then click on the angular dimension to enter a new value of the angle. To draw orthogonal grids, hold the SHIFT key and restrict the movement of the cursor to the horizontal and vertical axes. When you click to specify the endpoint, a grid is created and its controls are highlighted. The grid thus created is highlighted and displays one square box on either side. These boxes are used to control the visibility of the grid bubble. They can be checked or cleared to make the grid bubble visible or invisible at the desired side(s). The two circles, on either corner, can be dragged to extend or reduce the extents of the grid line.

Similarly, when you sketch a new grid line near an existing one, a temporary dimension indicating the distance between the two grid lines is displayed. You can enter the value of distance in the displayed edit box. Alternatively, you can move the cursor to the desired distance using the temporary dimensions. Next, click to specify the start point of the second grid line. To do so, move the cursor horizontally to the right and click to specify the endpoint of the grid line when the alignment line is displayed. On doing so, the second grid line is created. Notice that the name of this grid is 2. Autodesk Revit automatically numbers the grid lines as they are created.

Similarly, you can draw other parallel grid lines as well. These lines will be numbered automatically as you draw them. The **Offset** edit box in the **Options Bar** can be used to create a grid line that starts at a specified offset distance from a point defined on an existing element. The offset distance can be specified in the **Offset** edit box in the **Options Bar**. The shape of the resulting grid line depends on the selected sketching tool.

To create vertical grid lines, specify the start point above the first grid line. Now, move the cursor vertically downward and click below the last horizontal grid line to specify the endpoint. The procedure used for creating multiple horizontal grid lines can be used to create multiple vertical grid lines too.

You can create a rectangular grid pattern that is aligned at a given angle to the horizontal axis. You can also specify different angles for the grid lines and create the grid patterns based on the project requirement. Figure 3-11 shows some other examples of the rectangular grid patterns.

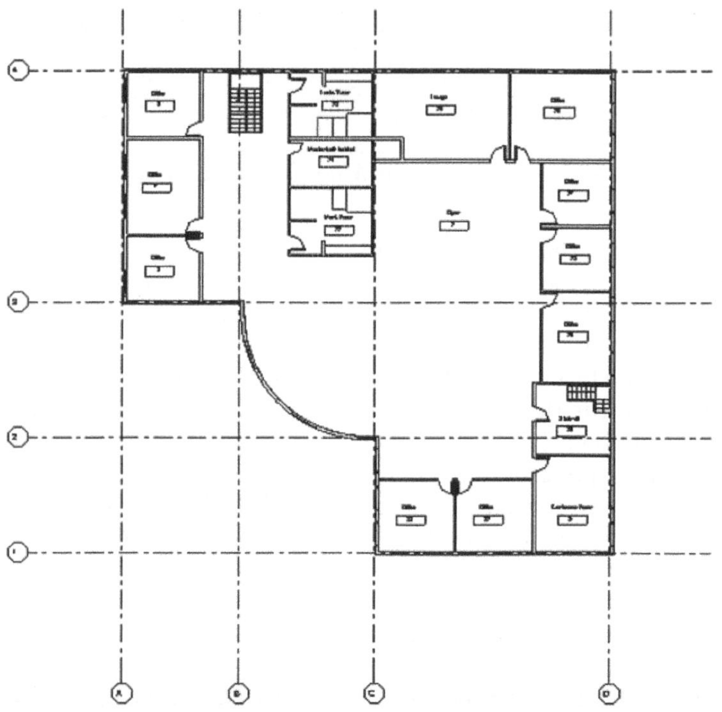

Figure 3-11 *Example of a rectangular grid pattern in an architectural layout*

In the **Draw** panel of the **Modify | Place Grid** tab, you can use the **Start-End-Radius Arc** and **Center-ends Arc** tools to create curved or radial grid patterns. The procedure of creating the curved grid lines using these options is similar to the sketching options for creating walls, which has been discussed later in this chapter. You can create multiple curved grids using the tools in the **Draw** panel and specifying their radius in the **Radius** edit box in the **Options Bar**. You can specify a value in the **Radius** edit box in the **Options Bar** only if you select the check box located before it.

Tip

*You can use the **Pick Lines** tool to create grid lines that are aligned to the existing elements. Invoke this tool from the **Draw** panel of the **Modify / Place Grid** tab and move the cursor near an existing element and click when the element is highlighted; a grid aligned to the highlighted element will be created.*

Creating Grids Using the Multi-Segment Tool

You can use the **Multi-Segment** tool to sketch a multi-segmented grid in the project. To do so, choose the **Grid** tool from the **Datum** panel of the **Architecture** tab; the **Modify | Place Grid** tab will be displayed. In this tab, choose the **Multi-Segment** tool from the **Draw** panel; the **Modify | Edit Sketch** tab will be displayed. In the **Draw** panel of the tab, you can choose any of the sketching tools, displayed in the list box, to sketch the multi-segmented gridline. After choosing the desired sketching tool, you need to use various options in the **Options Bar** to control the creation of the gridline in the project. After setting the options in the **Options Bar**, click in the drawing area; a magenta colored gridline with a temporary dimension will emerge from the point at which you have clicked. Next, click at the desired location to create the first segment of the grid. Similarly, you can click on multiple locations in the drawing area to create other segments. To finish the creation of the multi-segmented grids, choose the **Finish Edit Mode** button from the **Mode** panel of the **Modify | Edit Sketch** tab. Figure 3-12 shows a sketch with multi-segmented gridlines.

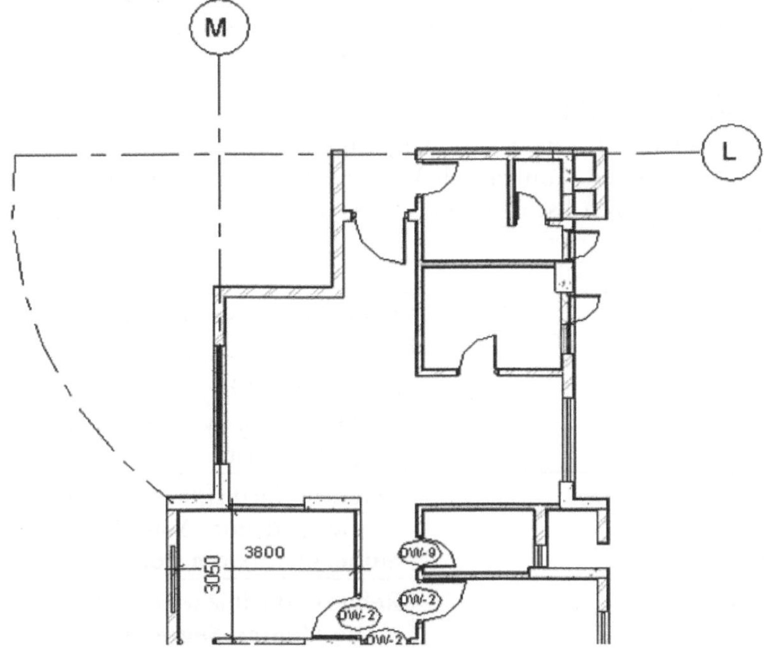

Figure 3-12 *A multi-segment grid pattern in an architectural layout*

Modifying Grids

As mentioned earlier, grids can be modified once they are created. To modify a grid, you need to select it and then modify its properties from the **Properties** palette. For example, after selecting a grid, you can click on its name and assign it a new name. Similarly, you can modify the distance between grids by selecting the temporary dimension and entering a new value. When you enter a new value, the grid automatically moves to the specified distance. You can also move the grids by simply dragging them to the desired location. To do so, click to select a single grid or click the multiple grids using the CTRL key to select multiple grids. You can now drag the grid(s) to the desired location. Hold the SHIFT key to restrain the movement of the cursor in the orthogonal direction. When you move the cursor near a grid, it gets highlighted. Now, right-click; a shortcut menu will be displayed with various options such as **Select Previous, Select All Instances, Create Similar, View Properties,** and so on.

For certain grids, you may need to move or offset the grid bubble to a different location. When you select a grid, a blue circle appears on each of its endpoints. The drag control, as mentioned earlier, controls the extents of the grid line. The grid line break control, which appears near the grid bubble, is used to create a grid bubble offset. You can click on this control and use the displayed drag controls to move the grid bubble to the desired location. While moving the grid bubble, the grid name also moves to the new location and an extension line is created.

Grid Properties

Like levels, grids too have associated properties. A typical grid consists of a grid line, grid bubble, grid name, and other controls. The usage of the controls such as grid bubble visibility, 2D or 3D extents, and grid bubble break is similar to the usage of controls described for levels.

To view and modify the properties of a grid, select it; the instance parameter of the selected grid will be displayed in the **Properties** palette. In this palette, choose the **Edit Type** button; the **Type Properties** dialog box will be displayed. You can use this dialog box to view and modify the type properties of the selected grid. The type properties of grids and their description are discussed next.

Type Properties of Grids

When the type properties of a grid are changed, the properties of all instance parameters related to it are also changed. You can click in the **Value** field and select a new value from the corresponding drop-down list or enter a new value in that field. The properties of grid types are described next.

Parameter Name	Value and Description
Symbol	Refers to the display of the symbol at the end of the grid line. You can control the display of the symbol by selecting an option from the drop-down list.
Center Segment	Refers to the display type of the center segment of the grid line. You can select **Continuous**, **None**, or **Custom** from the drop-down list.
Center Segment Weight	Refers to the line weight of the center segment, if the **Center Segment** parameter is set to **Custom**.
Center Segment Color	You can assign a color to the center segment if the **Center Segment** parameter is set to **Custom**.
Center Segment Pattern	Refers to the line type of the segment at the center if the **Center Segment** parameter is set to **Custom**. You can select various line patterns from the drop-down list.
End Segment Weight	Refers to the line weight of the grid line if the **Center Segment** parameter is set to **Continuous**. You can set the line weight of the end segments if the **Center Segment** parameter is set to **None** or **Custom**.

End Segment Color	Refers to the color assigned to the grid line if the **Center Segment** parameter is set to **Continuous**. You can set the color of the end segments if the **Center Segment** parameter is set to **None** or **Custom**.
End Segment Pattern	Refers to the line type of the grid line if the **Center Segment** parameter is set to **Continuous**. You can set the line type of the end segments if the **Center Segment** parameter is set to **None** or **Custom**.
End Segments Length	Refers to the length of each end segment as measured in the sheet if the **Center Segment** parameter is set to **None** or **Custom**.
Plan View Symbols End 1(Default)	Refers to the default status for the visibility of the symbol at end 1 of the grid line in plan views. By default, the check box is cleared. If you select the check box, the visibility of the symbol at end 1 in the plan view will be turned on.
Plan View Symbols End 2(Default)	Refers to the default status for the visibility of the symbol at end 2 of the grid line in the plan views. By default, the check box is selected. If you clear the check box, the visibility of the symbol at end 2 in the plan view will be turned off.
Non-Plan View Symbols (Default)	Refers to the default status for the visibility of the grid line in the sections and elevations, other than in the plan views. You can control the visibility of the symbol at the top and bottom of the grid line by selecting the desired option from the drop-down list.

Instance Properties of Grids

The instance properties of grids are given next.

Parameter Name	Value and Description
Name	Refers to the name assigned to the grid. You can enter any name, based on the project requirement.
Scope Box	Refers to the scope box assigned to the grid that controls its visibility in different views.

REFERENCE PLANES

Reference planes are useful while sketching and adding building elements to a design. They can be used as datum planes that act as a guideline for creating elements. They can also be used effectively for creating new family elements. To create a reference plane, choose the **Ref Plane** tool from the **Work Plane** panel of the **Architecture** tab; the **Modify | Place Reference Plane** tab will be displayed. Select the tools from the **Draw** panel and start drawing the reference plane in the drawing. Alternatively, you can type **RP** to invoke the **Ref Plane** tool.

After invoking the tool, click at the desired location in the drawing window to start a line that defines the reference plane. Now, move the cursor to the new location and release the left button to specify the endpoint of the reference line; the reference plane will be created. To assign a name to the reference plane, select it from the drawing. Next, in the **Properties** palette, enter the desired name of the selected reference plane in the value field of the **Name** instance parameter.

WORK PLANES

As the name suggests, the work plane is a plane that can be used for sketching elements. In Autodesk Revit, you can create and edit only those elements that lie in the current work plane. The work plane can be horizontal, vertical, or inclined at any specified angle. Each generated view has an associated work plane. This workplane is automatically defined for some standard views such as floor plans. For other views such as sections, elevations, and 3D views, you can set the work plane based on the location of the elements that are to be created or edited. The concept of work planes is quite useful for creating elements in elevations, sections, or inclined planes.

Setting a Work Plane

You can set a work plane based on your project requirement. To set a work plane, choose the **Set** tool from the **Work Plane** panel in the **Architecture** tab; the **Work Plane** dialog box will be displayed. It shows the current work plane and assists you in specifying the parameters to set a new work plane. A drop-down list of available views is displayed corresponding to the **Name** radio button. Select the required work plane from the drop-down list, which contains the names of levels, grids, and reference planes. You can select the **Pick a plane** radio button in the **Work Plane** dialog box to set a work plane along an existing plane. On selecting this radio button and choosing the **OK** button in this dialog box, you will be prompted to select an existing plane in the drawing with which you want to align the new work plane. The existing plane can be a face of a wall, floor, or roof. You can also select the **Pick a line and use the work plane it was sketched in** radio button from this dialog box to create a work plane that is coplanar with the plane on which the selected line was created.

Note

*In the project environment of Autodesk Revit, you can choose the **Viewer** tool from the **Work Plane** panel of the **Architecture** tab to display the **Workplane Viewer** window. In this window, you can modify the workplane dependent element with an ease.*

Controlling the Visibility of Work Planes

You can control the visibility of the current work plane by using the **Show** button from the **Architecture** tab. This button is used to toggle the display of grids in the workplane.

You can also set the grid spacing for a work plane. To do so, select the workplane in the drawing, the work plane will be highlighted. Specify the spacing by entering the new value in the **Spacing** edit box in **Options Bar**. You can snap to the work plane grid using the object snap tools.

WORKING WITH PROJECT VIEWS

While working on the building envelope and MEP models, you may need to view its different exterior and interior portions in order to add or edit the elements in the design. Revit provides various features and techniques that can be used to view the building model.

Viewing a Building Envelope

In Revit, the default template file (Mechanical, Electrical, Plumbing, or Systems) has certain predefined standard project views. These views are displayed under the **Views** head of the **Project Browser**, as shown in Figure 3-13.

These include floor plans (Mechanical, Electrical, and Plumbing), ceiling plans (Mechanical, Electrical, and Plumbing), elevations, sections, and 3D Views. To open any of these views, double-click on the name; the corresponding view will be displayed in the viewing area. You can control the visibility of the **Project Browser** by selecting the **Project Browser** check box from the **View > Windows > User Interface** drop-down.

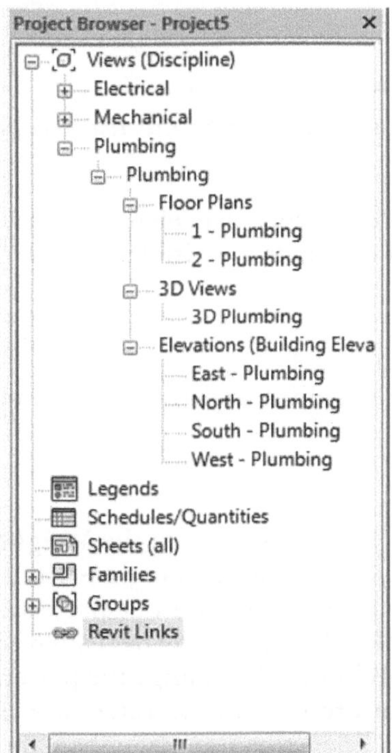

***Figure 3-13 Project Browser** displaying various project views*

When you open a new project, the viewing area displays four inward arrow symbols in the floor plan view, which indicate the four side elevations: North, East, South, and West. You can use these symbols to view the appropriate building elevation by double-clicking on them.

Apart from these standard building views, you can use different viewing tools to view the building model from various angles. To restrict the visibility of certain categories of elements, choose the **Visibility/Graphics** tool from the **Graphics** panel of the **View** tab; the **Visibility/Graphic Overrides** dialog box will be displayed. The **Model Categories** tab of this dialog box contains a list of model elements such as Air Terminal, HVAC Zones, doors, windows, and so on. The **Annotation Categories** tab contains annotations such as duct tags, flex pipe tags, wire tags dimensions, door tags, and so on. You can clear the category of elements that you want to hide from the current view using this dialog box.

Overriding the Visibility/Graphic of an Element

You can override the visibility and graphics of any element in a view. To do so, select an element and right-click; a shortcut menu will be displayed. Choose **Override Graphics in View > By Element** from the shortcut menu; the **View-Specific Element Graphics** dialog box will be displayed, as shown in Figure 3-14. The options in this dialog box are discussed next.

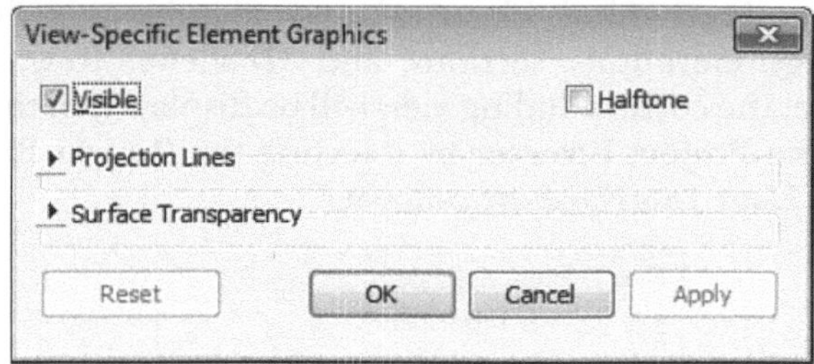

*Figure 3-14 The **View-Specific Element Graphics** dialog box*

Visible

The **Visible** check box controls the visibility of an element in a view. This check box is selected by default. As a result, the selected elements are visible in view. Clear the check box to hide the selected element in the view.

Halftone

Select the **Halftone** check box to adjust and blend the line color of an element with the background color.

Projection Lines

Choose the arrow button on the left of this option; the **Weight**, **Color**, and **Pattern** options of the projection lines will be displayed. Set the line weight of the projection lines using the options in the **Weight** drop-down list. To change the color of a projection line, choose the button at the right of the **Color** option; the **Color** dialog box will be displayed. Select the required color from the dialog box and choose the **OK** button. To change the pattern of the projection lines, choose the button at the right of the **Pattern** option; the **Line Patterns** dialog box will be displayed. Select a pattern of the projection lines from the dialog box and choose the **OK** button.

Surface Patterns

Choose the arrow button on the left of the **Surface Patterns** option to expand it. You can change the visibility of the surface pattern by clearing the **Visible** check box. Select the color and pattern of the surface in the same way as explained earlier for the projection lines.

Surface Transparency

Choose the arrow button on the left of the **Surface Transparency** option to expand it. In this area, you can change the transparency of the selected element by moving the **Transparency** slider or by entering a suitable value in the edit box displayed next to the slider. Note that higher the value you enter in the edit box, more transparent will be the object.

Cut Lines/Cut Patterns

Choose the arrow button on the left of these options to expand them. Change the visibility, weight and pattern of the cut lines or cut patterns, as explained earlier for the **Projection Lines** option. Once you have edited the graphics and visibility settings of an element in the **View Specific Element Graphics** dialog box, choose the **Apply** button to view the changes in the selected element. Choose the **OK** button to retain the settings and close the dialog box.

Overriding the Visibility/Graphic of Element Category

To edit the visibility and graphics of an element category in a project view, open the project view. Next, select an element of the required category and right-click; a shortcut menu will be displayed. Choose **Override Graphics in View > By Category** from the shortcut menu; the **View -Specific Category Graphics** dialog box will be displayed. Choose the **Open the Visibility Graphics dialog** button; the **Visibility/Graphic Overrides for Floor Plans** dialog box for the loaded view will be displayed, refer to Figure 3-15.

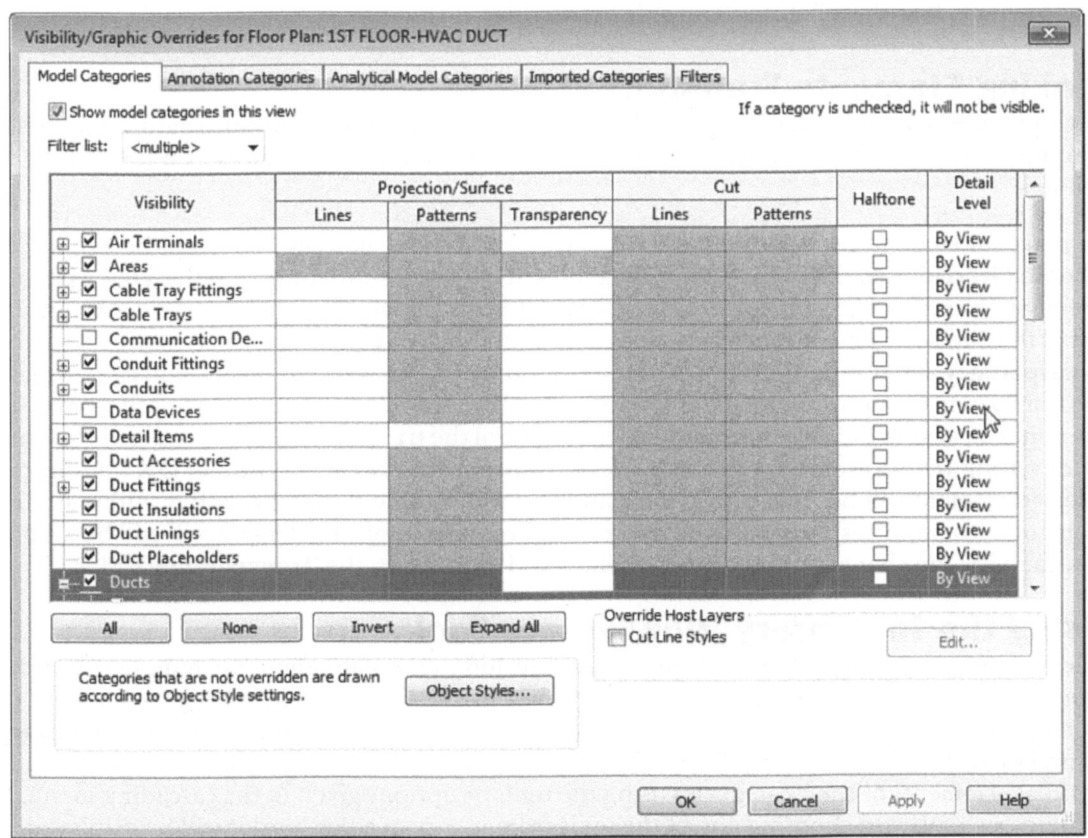

***Figure 3-15** The **Visibility/Graphics Overrides for Floor Plan** dialog box*

The dialog box contains various tabs. The options in these tabs are used to edit the settings for the visibility and graphic display of the models, annotations, and imported elements. Choose a tab to edit the visibility and graphics of the selected category. To edit the visibility in the view, clear or select the visibility check box available on the left of the category name in the **Visibility** column. To specify overrides to a category, click on the name of the category in the **Visibility** column; the **Overrides** button will be displayed for the respective column in the specified tab. To override patterns for the selected category, choose the **Override** button displayed in the **Patterns** column corresponding to the selected category; the **Fill Pattern Graphic** dialog box will be displayed. Set the visibility, color, and pattern by using the **Visible**, **Color**, and **Pattern** options, respectively in the dialog box and choose the **OK** button. Similarly, to override the transparency of the selected object, choose the **Override** button displayed in the **Transparency** column; the **Surfaces** dialog box will be displayed. In this dialog box, you can use the **Transparency** slider to control the transparency of the selected element.

Similarly, click in the required columns in the **Visibility/Overrides** dialog box to edit the graphic display of the category. Select the check boxes in the **Halftone** column, if required. You can set the detail level of the selected category in the **Detail level** column. To do so, click in the **Detail Level** column and choose the down arrow displayed on the left. Select the detail level from the **Detail Level** drop-down list displayed. Choose the **Apply** button to view the changes in the visibility and graphic display of the selected category. Choose the **OK** button to retain the changes and close the **Visibility/Graphics Overrides** dialog box.

Making Elements Transparent

Revit provides you with a tool to make elements transparent so that you can see through them. This tool can be used to view the interior of a building from the top even after adding roofs or ceilings.

To make an element transparent, select it and right-click; a shortcut menu will be displayed. Choose **Override Graphics in View > By Element** from the shortcut menu; the **View Specific Element Graphics** dialog box will be displayed. In this dialog box, click on the arrow on the left of the **Surface Transparency** area; the options in this area will be displayed. In this area, the **Transparency** slider is used to control the transparency of the selected object. You can increase the transparency by moving the slider toward right. Alternatively, you can enter a desired value in the edit box, next to the **Transparency** slider, to control the transparency of the selected element. After setting the transparency in the **Surface Transparency** area, choose the **OK** button; the selected element will become transparent and you will be able to see through it. Although the element becomes transparent, the edges and surface pattern of the element will still be visible. You can view the change in the element before and after using the **Transparency** slider.

Using the Temporary Hide/Isolate Tool

The **Temporary Hide/Isolate** tool can be used to hide or isolate elements temporarily from a project view. This tool will be available only after a selection is made. Select the element or elements that you need to hide or isolate in the project view and then choose the **Temporary Hide/Isolate** tool from the **View Control Bar**; a cascading menu will be displayed. You can hide or isolate elements or their categories using the tools or options given in the cascading menu. It contains six tools. On choosing any of the tools from it, a cyan color border will be displayed in the drawing area, indicating that the elements in the drawing are in the **Temporary Hide/Isolate** mode. You can choose the **Hide Element** tool from the cascading menu, refer to Figure 3-16, to hide the selected element in a view. On choosing the **Isolate Element** tool, only the selected elements will be displayed in the view while the rest will be hidden. The **Hide Category** tool is used to hide all the elements of the category of the selected element. The **Isolate Category** is used to display only the elements belonging to the category of the selected element in the view.

The **Reset Temporary Hide/Isolate** tool is used to revert to the original view without saving the temporary or isolate changes in the view. The **Apply Hide/Isolate to view** option is used to hide or isolate the temporary hidden or isolated elements permanently in the view. On choosing this tool, the blue boundary around the screen becomes invisible and the temporarily hidden or isolated elements and categories are permanently hidden or isolated. On hiding or isolating an element or category, the sunglasses symbol of the **Temporary Hide/Isolate** tool in the **View Control Bar** is highlighted in the same color as that of the boundary, indicating that certain elements have been hidden temporarily. When you choose the **Reset Temporary Hide/ Isolate** option, the sunglasses symbol is no longer highlighted.

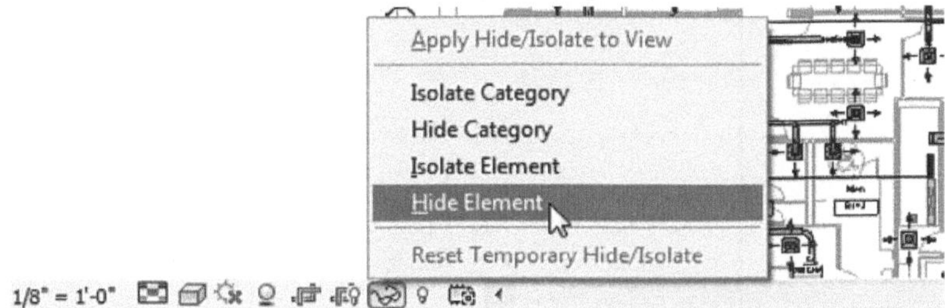

*Figure 3-16 Choosing the **Hide Element** tool from the **View Control Bar***

Revealing and Unhiding Elements

To reveal and unhide the hidden elements in the view, choose the bulb icon from the **View Control** bar to invoke the **Reveal Hidden Elements** tool. On doing so, a magenta color border will be displayed and the hidden elements will be highlighted in the same color. Select the required elements and choose the **Unhide Element** or the **Unhide Category** button from the **Reveal Hidden Elements** panel in the **Architecture** tab. Now, again you need to click on the bulb icon to invoke the **Exit Reveal Hidden Elements** mode. You will notice that all the hidden elements and categories will be displayed in the view.

Plan Views

In Autodesk Revit, you can use the floor and ceiling views to view the building plan of the respective discipline. If you are using the *Systems-Default.rte* template file to start a new project, by default Autodesk Revit opens the **1-Mech** floor plan view. The *Systems-Default.rte* template file contains floor plans for the Electrical, Mechanical, and Plumbing disciplines and ceiling plans for Electrical and Mechanical discipline.

Adding a Plan View

To create a new plan view for the added levels that do not contain associated plans in the **Project Browser**, choose the **Floor Plan** tool from **View > Create > Plan Views** drop-down; the **New Floor Plan** dialog box will be displayed, as shown in Figure 3-17. In the **New Floor Plan** dialog box, the **Floor Plan** option is selected in the **Type** drop-down list, refer to Figure 3-17. You can edit the existing type or create a new type by choosing the **Edit Type** button. On choosing the **Edit Type** button; the **Type Properties** dialog box will be displayed. In this dialog box, you can edit various type parameters for the existing view type or choose the **Duplicate** button and create a new type. Choose the **OK** button to return to the **New Floor Plan** dialog box. In this dialog box, you can select the appropriate level to create the plan view in the list box displayed. You can also select multiple levels by holding the SHIFT key. The **Do not duplicate existing views** check box can be cleared to create a plan view for a level that has an already existing plan view. The duplicate view is created and added in the **Project Browser** with the suffix (1). The number in the brackets increases as more copies of the plan view are added.

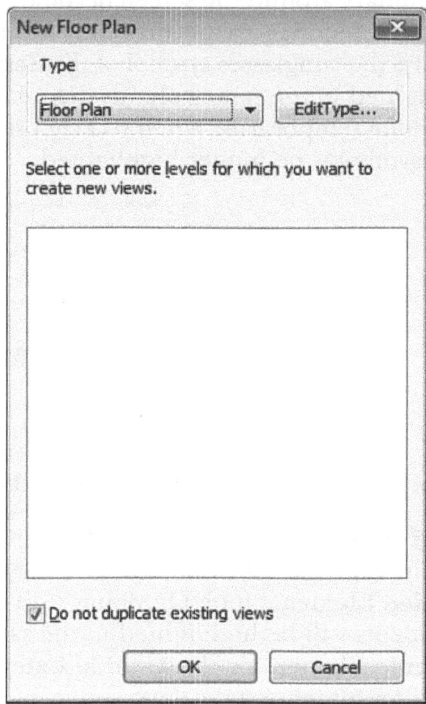

***Figure 3-17** The **New Floor Plan** dialog box*

Note

*While creating a level, if you have cleared the **Make Plan View** check box in the **Options Bar**, then its corresponding plan view will not be created.*

Modifying the Plan View Properties

To modify the view properties of a plan view or any other project view, select the view from the **Project Browser**; the properties of the selected view will be displayed in the **Properties** palette. Using this palette, you can modify the parameters related to the current view such as **View Scale**, **Display Model**, **Detail Level**, **View Name**, and so on. The **View Range** parameter in the **Extents** category controls the visibility and appearance of the elements in the view by defining the extent of horizontal plane of the view. The crop region parameter defines the boundary of a view and can be turned on or off using the **Crop Region Visible** check box. You can also access the tools related to the visibility settings of the view using the **View Control Bar** available near the bottom left corner of the drawing window.

Elevation Views

An elevation view refers to the view of the building model from the four sides, North, East, South, and West. If you are using the default template file, the four sided elevation views are created automatically by Autodesk Revit when the default template file is used. Using the elevation view, you cannot only visualize the building from its exterior but also create the views of the interior walls of various internal spaces.

Creating an Elevation View

To create an elevation view, invoke the **Elevation** tool from **View > Create > Elevation** drop-down; the **Properties** palette for the elevation will be displayed. In this palette, select the elevation type from the **Type Selector** drop-down list. On moving the cursor near the exterior walls, you will notice that the arrow head of the elevation symbol has changed its alignment and become perpendicular to the wall, as shown in Figure 3-18.

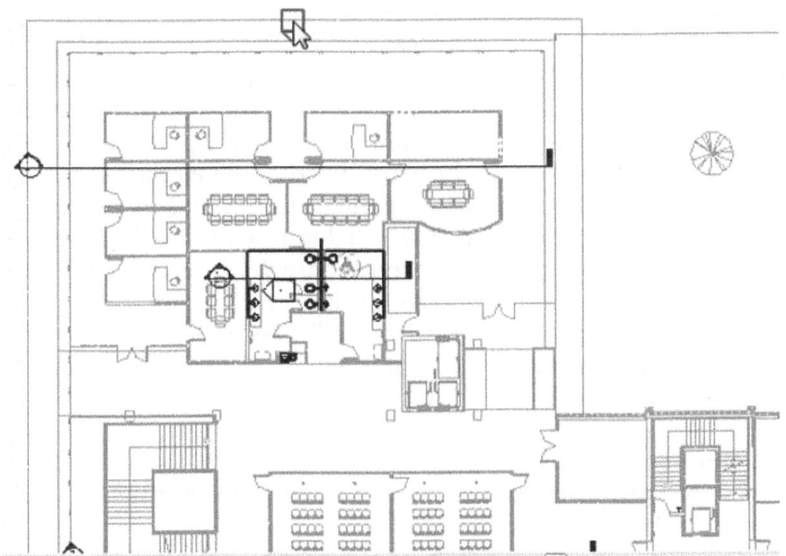

Figure 3-18 *The elevation symbol aligned perpendicular to the wall*

Now, click when the elevation arrow head symbol points toward the desired direction; the new elevation view will be created and added to the list of elevations in the **Project Browser**. Revit automatically numbers the elevation names. Note that if you add the elevation symbol in any of the floor plan view specific to the Mechanical discipline, the elevation corresponding to the added elevation symbol will be displayed under the **Mechanical** discipline of the **Elevations (Building Elevation)** head in the **Project Browser**, refer to Figure 3-19.

You can also set the width of the elevation view using the clip plane control. When you click on the arrow head of the elevation symbol, the clip plane is displayed as a blue line with the drag control dots on its two ends. You can drag them to resize the width of the elevation view. For the interior elevation views, Autodesk Revit automatically extends the clip plane to the extents of the room. You can drag the blue dots to increase or decrease the extents of the elevation view. To rename an elevation view, right-click on the view name in the **Project Browser**; a shortcut menu will be displayed. Choose the **Rename** option from the shortcut menu; the **Rename View** dialog box will be displayed. In this dialog box, enter a desired name in the **Name** edit box and choose the **OK** button; the elevation view will be renamed.

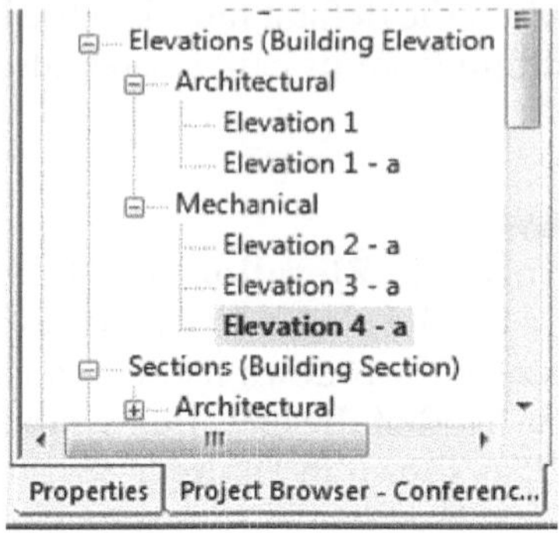

***Figure 3-19** Partial view of the **Project Browser** with the added elevation*

There are several methods to display an elevation view. To display an elevation view in the drawing area, double-click on the name of the elevation in the **Project Browser**; the corresponding elevation view is displayed in the drawing window, as shown in Figure 3-20. You can also display the elevation view by double-clicking on the arrow head of the elevation symbol. Alternatively, right-click on the elevation symbol; a shortcut menu is displayed. Next, choose **Find Referring Views** from the shortcut menu; the **Go To View** dialog box will be displayed. Next, select the view to be displayed from this dialog box and then choose the **Open View** button or double-click on the name of the view. The other method to display the elevation view is to select the arrow head of the elevation symbol and then right-click to display a shortcut menu. Next, choose the **Go to Elevation View** option from the shortcut menu displayed; the corresponding elevation will be displayed in the drawing area.

You can modify the properties associated with elevation views by using the **Properties** palette. This palette is displayed with instance parameters when you select the required view or when the required view is displayed in the drawing area.

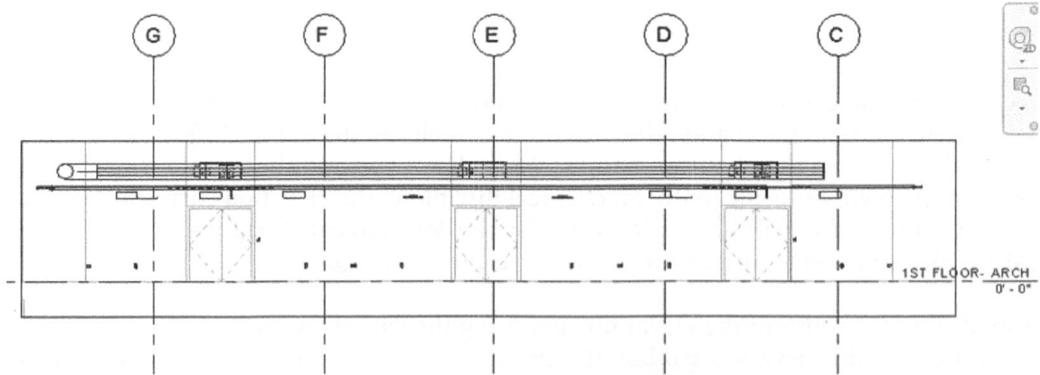

***Figure 3-20** The elevation view of the building model*

Note

While working on the floor plan, if the created building model extends beyond the clip planes of the four sided elevation views, the corresponding elevations no longer show the complete exterior views. Instead, an elevation view that is cut through the building model is displayed. You can drag the clip plane control symbol beyond the extent of the building profile to retain the view as a complete exterior elevation view.

Section Views

Section views are generated by cutting sections through the building model. These views are created to display various wall elevations, floor heights, and special vertical features of the project. They are also useful in creating and editing elements added to the interior spaces of the building model.

For example, in an office building, to emphasize the salient features of the central atrium, you may need to show a section through the central atrium. Autodesk Revit enables you to create it with relative ease. You can also modify the sectional view to create a section that displays the interior spaces.

Creating a Section View

To create a section view, invoke the **Section** tool from the **Create** panel of the **View** tab; the **Modify | Section** tab will be displayed. The options in the **Modify | Section** tab are used to specify the section type to be created and to specify the instance and its type properties. The section can be created in the plan, elevation, and section views. You can create different types of section views such as the building section, wall section, and detail section. You can choose the section view type to be created from the **Type Selector** drop-down list in the **Properties** palette. In the **Options Bar**, you can use the **Reference Other View** check box to create a reference section that acts as a reference for another view. Notice that the reference sections are not added as an additional section in the list of section views in the **Project Browser**.

To create a section, invoke the **Section** tool from the **Create** panel and move the cursor to the viewing area; the cursor will change into a cross symbol and you will be prompted to draw the section line in the current view. Click at the desired location to specify the start point. To create a section through a specific length of an area, click at desired point in the area. As you move the cursor, a section line will appear with one end fixed at the specified point and the other end attached to the cursor. You can even create a section line at any angle. To create a horizontal or vertical section view, move the cursor horizontally or vertically across the area, as shown in Figure 3-21 and click to specify the endpoint. The section line along with its controls is shown in Figure 3-22. It is represented by a section head and a line. The section head indicates the direction toward which the section will be created. Note that, the methods used for displaying the section views are similar to the ones described for the elevation views.

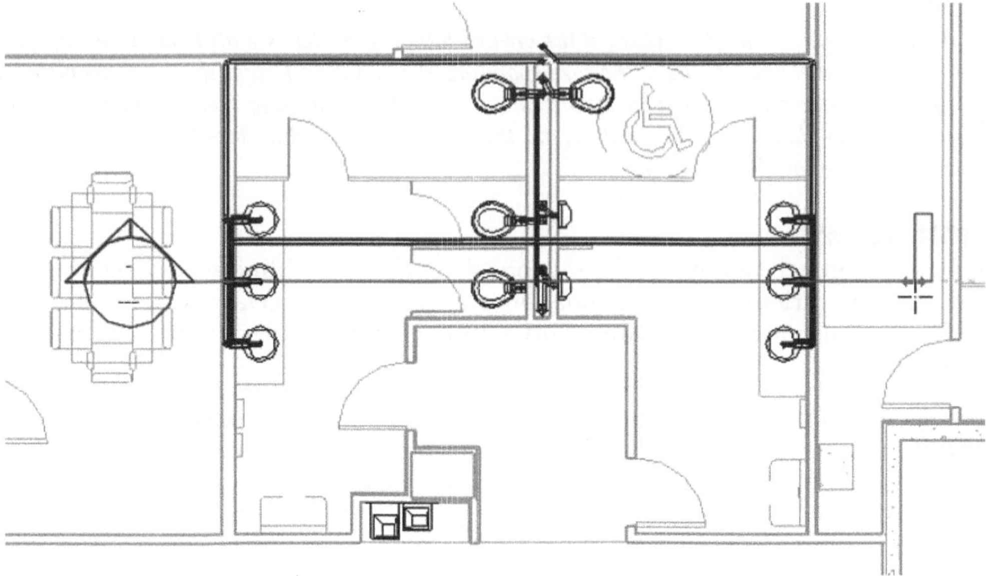

***Figure 3-21** The section line drawn horizontally across the plumbing layout*

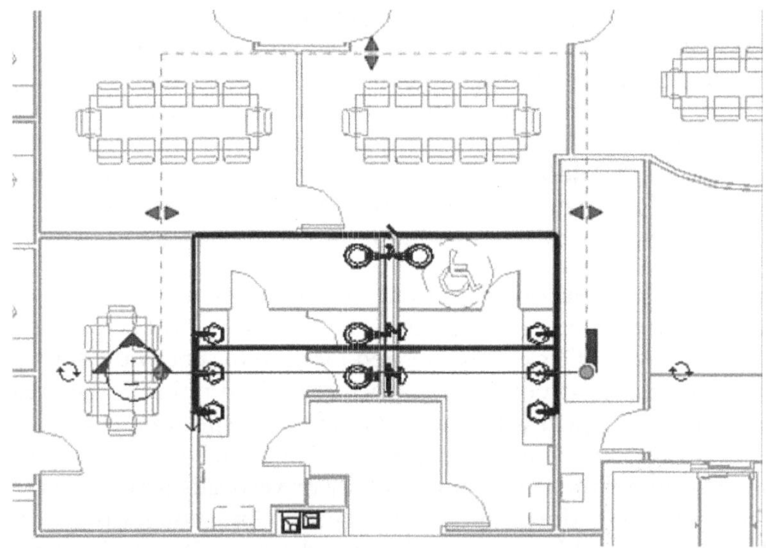

***Figure 3-22** The section line displayed along with its controls*

Modifying a Section View

After creating a section view, you can modify the location of the section line of the section view by dragging it. When you drag a section line, the corresponding section view is updated immediately. You can modify the parameters of the section view by using the controls available on the section view line. When you select the section line, the controls are displayed in it. The twin arrow symbol represents the flip tool that can be used to flip the viewing side of the section view. By default, the section head appears on one side. The cyclic control on both the ends of the section line can be used to change the visibility of the section head and tail at the respective ends. You can click on the symbol to hide or display them. Click on the break line symbol, which appears in the middle of the section line, to break it. You can then resize the two section lines to the required extent of the view. To rejoin the section line, click on the break line control again.

When you create a section view, Autodesk Revit intuitively creates its view depth, which is the extent of the view in the current view. It is represented by a dashed line and the blue arrows as drag controls. To modify the view depth, drag the arrows to the desired location. The section view shows only those elements that are within the view depth. To modify the properties of a section view, select its section line; the **Properties** palette will be displayed with the instance parameters of the section view. Using this palette, you can modify various instance properties such as **View Name**, **View Scale**, **Crop Region Visible**, and so on. To do so, click in the corresponding field in the **Value** column and select a new value from the drop-down list if available, or enter a new value in that field.

You can choose the **Edit Type** button to display the **Type Properties** dialog box and modify the type properties of the section view such as **Callout Tag**, **Section Tag**, and **Reference Label** from it.

Creating a Segmented Section

Autodesk Revit enables you to split the section into segments that are orthogonal to the direction of the section view. This enables you to show different parts of the building model in the same section view.

To create a segmented section, create a straight section line in the drawing area and then choose the **Split Segments** tool from the **Section** panel of the **Modify | Views** tab. On doing so, a split symbol will be attached to the cursor. Move it over the section line and click at the point from where you want to split it. Move the cursor perpendicular to the section line; it will break from the specified point. Next, you can move the cursor in the desired direction to split the section line along the head or tail side. Click again to specify the location of the split segment.

Controlling the Visibility of a Section Line

The section line is visible in plan, section, and elevation views, if the view range of the created views intersects the crop region of the current view. The section line created in any view is visible and is created simultaneously in all the other views.

You can also control the visibility of the section line in the views. To do so, select the section line, right-click, and choose the **Hide in View > Element** option from the shortcut menu displayed. The selection line becomes hidden in the current view.

Note

The section of elements is displayed when a section is cut through them. Sections through in-place elements are not available; therefore they are not displayed in the section view.

Creating a Detail and a Wall Section View

In Autodesk Revit, you can create different types of section views. There are three different types of section views such as detail, building, or wall section view in both the Imperial and the Metric systems. These section views can be selected from the **Type Selector** drop-down list in the **Properties** palette.

To create a detail section view from the building model, select the **Detail View : Detail** option from the **Type Selector** drop-down list of the **Properties** palette. Similarly, to create a building section or a wall section of the building model, select the **Section : Building Section** or **Section : Wall Section** option from the **Type Selector** drop-down list. After creating a wall section using the **Section : Wall Section** type, you will notice that its section view has been added to the list of sections under the subhead **Sections (Wall Sections)** in the **Project Browser** and you can display it by double-clicking on the section name. Similarly, a section view created as a building section or a detail section will be displayed in the subhead **Sections (Building Sections)** or **Detail Views (Detail)**, respectively. You will learn more about these views in the later chapters.

Using the Scope Box Tool

Autodesk Revit provides you the option of controlling the visibility of the datum elements in the project views using the **Scope Box** tool. As described earlier in this chapter, the datum planes have an infinite scope and extend throughout the project. Using the **Scope Box** tool, you can limit the boundary for the visibility of the datum planes. You can also specify the views in which these datum planes become visible.

Creating a Scope Box

The Scope box can be created in the plan view by invoking the **Scope Box** tool. You can invoke this tool from the **Create** panel of the **View** tab; the **Options Bar** displays the **Name** and **Height** edit boxes. You can enter the name and height of the scope box in these edit boxes. To create a scope box, move the cursor in the viewing area. It changes into a cross symbol, that prompts you to draw the scope box in the plan view. To draw the scope box, click on its upper left corner, move the cursor to the lower right corner, and then click to specify the diagonally opposite ends to draw a rectangle. The rectangle should be drawn in such a way that the elements that need to be visible are enclosed in it. The scope box with the assigned name is created. When it is selected, the drag controls are visible on it, as shown in Figure 3-23. These drag controls can be used to resize the scope box.

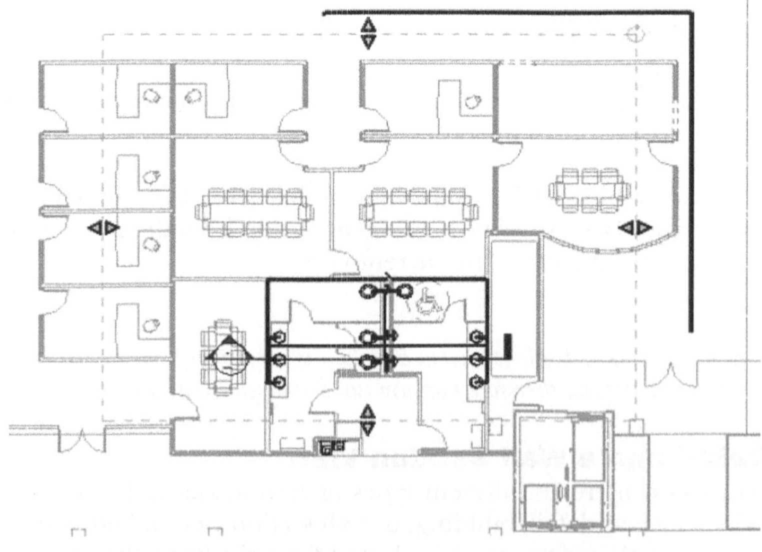

Figure 3-23 The selected scope box in a plumbing layout

Applying the Scope Box

The visibility of datum planes can be controlled by associating them with the scope box. You can select a datum such as a grid, a level, or a reference plane, and then in the **Properties** palette, click in the value column for the **Scope Box** parameter and select the name of the scope box from the drop-down list displayed. Now, choose the **Apply** button to apply the property to the selected datum. The datum will now appear only in those views whose cutting planes intersect the scope box.

Controlling the Visibility of the Scope Box

The scope box can be resized to limit its visibility for certain views. Its visibility can also be controlled for each view. To control the visibility of the scope box, select it; the instance properties of the selected scope box will be displayed in the **Properties** palette. In the **Parameters** area of the palette, choose the **Edit** button displayed in the value field for the **Views Visible** parameter; the **Scope Box Views Visible** dialog box will be displayed. This dialog box lists all view types and view names available in the project. In the **Scope Box Views Visible** dialog box, the **Automatic Visibility** column displays the current visibility of scope boxes. You can click in the value field in the **Override** column for a specific view. On doing so, a drop-down list will be displayed, as shown in Figure 3-24. The drop-down list has three options: **None**, **Visible**, and **Invisible**. You can select any of the options from the drop-down list displayed to override the automatic visibility setting.

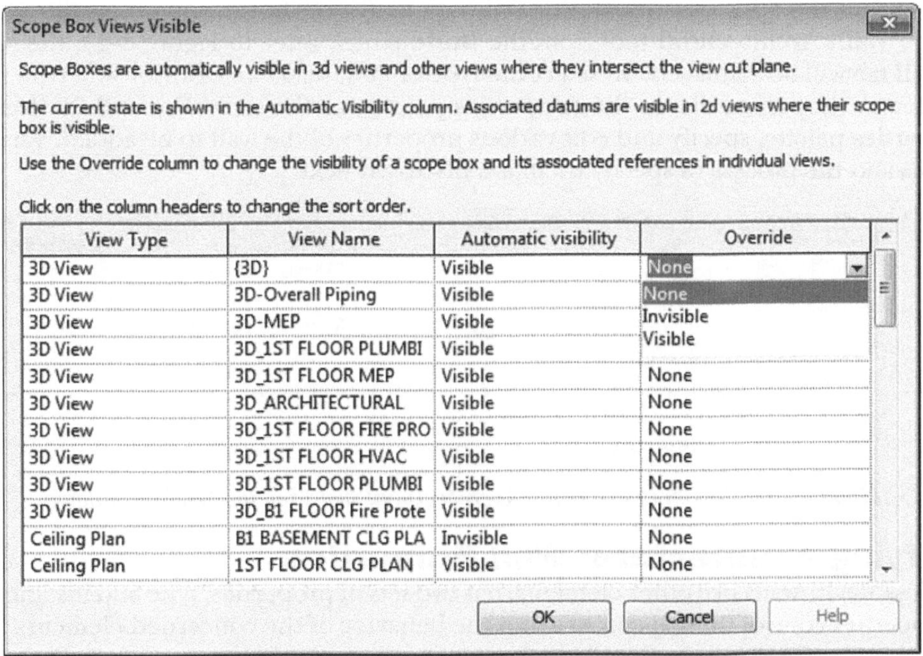

*Figure 3-24 The drop-down list displayed in the **Scope Box Views Visible** dialog box*

UNDERSTANDING WALL TYPES

Autodesk Revit provides you with several predefined wall types based on their usage. These wall types are discussed next

Exterior Wall Type

This is the wall type that is primarily used for generating the exterior of the building model. It has predefined wall types, such as **Brick on CMU**, **Brick on Mtl. Stud**, **CMU Insulated**, and so on.

Curtain Wall Type

Apart from the above discussed wall types, Autodesk Revit also has predefined curtain walls or screen walls that consist of panels and mullions.

Autodesk Revit also provides you with the flexibility of creating your own wall type. The walls that you will create can have different functions, which can be modified, depending on their functional usage. In Autodesk Revit, you can create both architectural and structural walls. An architectural wall does not contain analytical properties as the structural walls do. In the next section, various techniques to create and modify architectural walls are discussed.

CREATING ARCHITECTURAL WALLS

In Autodesk Revit, each wall type has specific predefined properties such as composition, material, characteristics, finish, height, and so on. You can select the wall type based on its specific usage in the project. Walls, like most other model elements, can be created in a plan view or a 3D view.

To create an exterior architectural wall, first you need to invoke the **Wall: Architectural** tool and then select the appropriate exterior wall type and specify various properties. To do so, invoke the **Wall: Architectural** tool from the **Build** panel, refer to Figure 3-25; the **Modify | Place Wall** tab will be displayed. To select the type of wall, select an exterior wall type from the **Type Selector** drop-down list in the **Properties** palette, as shown in Figure 3-26. Next, from the **Properties** palette, specify and edit various properties of the wall to be added. Various wall properties and the process to specify them are discussed next.

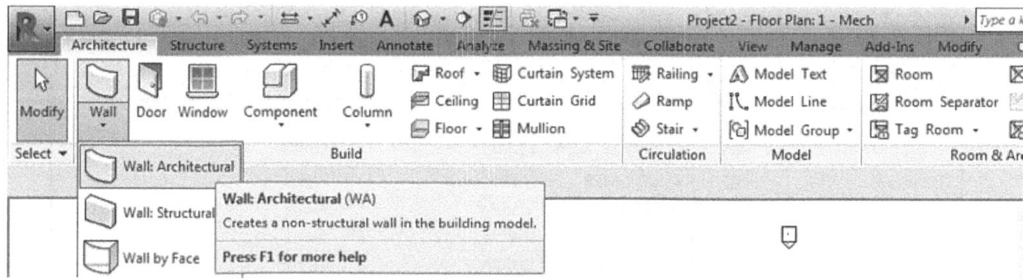

*Figure 3-25 Invoking the **Wall: Architectural** tool from the **Wall** drop-down*

Specifying Architectural Wall Properties

In Autodesk Revit, walls like other elements, has two sets of properties, type and instance. These set of properties control the appearance and the behavior of the concerned element.

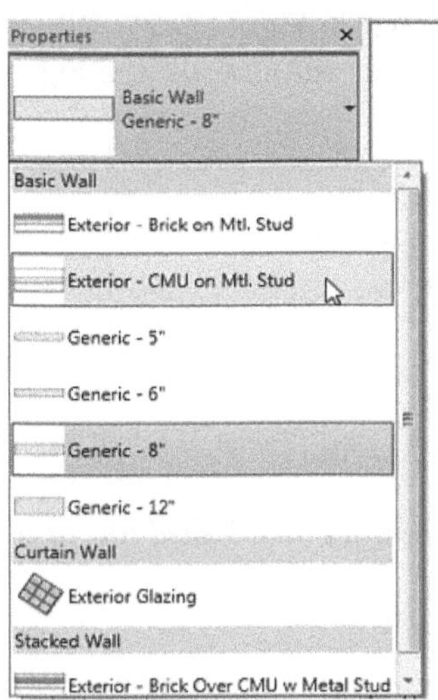

***Figure 3-26** Selecting an exterior wall type from the **Type Selector** drop-down list*

Specifying Instance Properties

After invoking the **Wall: Architectural** tool, the instance properties of the wall will be displayed in the **Properties** palette. The **Properties** palette also contains the **Type Selector** drop-down list. You can select the family and the type of the proposed wall from this drop-down list. This palette shows various instance properties and their corresponding values for the specified instance of the element. The options in this palette depend on the type and instance of the selected element or the element to be created as well as on the options selected in the **Type Selector** drop-down list. The properties of exterior walls are displayed in different categories such as **Constraints**, **Structural**, **Dimensions**, and **Identity Data**, each representing a set of properties corresponding to the title. You can use the twin arrows on the extreme right of the title to collapse the properties for each title. Some of the important parameters are discussed next.

In the **Properties** palette, the **Location Line** parameter indicates the reference line used for creating a wall. In 3D environment, the location line in a wall refers to a plane that does not get modified, even if the wall parameters are changed. To assign a value to the **Location Line** parameter, click in the value field corresponding to this parameter; a drop-down list will be displayed. Click on the drop-down list to view the available options. The options in the drop-down list are given next.

Wall Centerline	-	Center line of the entire composite wall
Core Centerline	-	Center line of the structural core of the wall
Finish Face: Exterior	-	Exterior face of the wall as the location line
Finish Face: Interior	-	Interior face of the wall as the location line
Core Face: Exterior	-	Exterior face of the core
Core Face: Interior	-	Interior face of the core

The location line is indicated by a dashed line, which appears while sketching a wall segment. For example, on selecting **Wall Centerline** as the location line parameter, you will notice a dashed line in the middle of the wall, as shown in Figure 3-27. When you select **Finish Face: Interior**, dashed line appears on the interior face of the wall, see Figure 3-28.

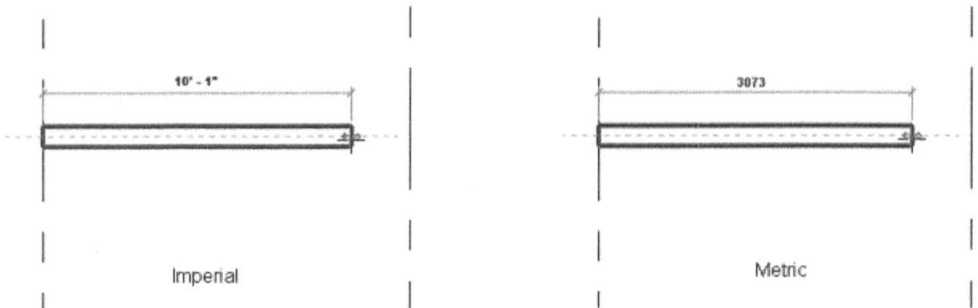

Figure 3-27 *The appearance of a dashed line at the center of the wall*

Note

While developing a design, you may need to modify certain parameters of the exterior wall such as its thickness and composition, based on the final selection of materials and their specifications. Considering this flexibility, the location line parameter enables you to create the walls.

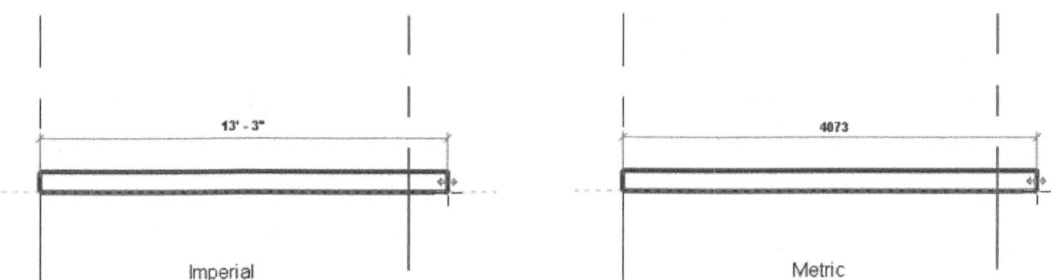

Figure 3-28 *The appearance of a dashed line at the interior face of the wall*

In Autodesk Revit, you can specify the height of walls by applying the base and top constraints with respect to the levels defined in the project. This means, if you set the base and the height parameter of a top story and apply these constraints, all walls will be sketched with the same base and the top. To create a wall segment that is not related to these components and levels, you can type the desired height in the column of the **Unconnected Height** instance parameter. The default value for the unconnected height in Imperial is 20' 0" or in Metric is 8000 mm. The various instance parameters for walls and their usage are given next. The values of some of the instance parameters will be available only after an instance is created. The instance parameters of the wall are given in the table below.

Instance Parameter	Description
Location Line	Line or reference plane for sketching the wall
Base Constraint	Level or reference plane of the base of a wall
Base is Attached	Check box showing whether or not the base of the wall is attached to any other element
Base Offset	Height of the wall from its base constraint

Base Extension Distance	Distance of the base of the layers in a wall
Top Constraint	Whether the wall height is defined by specified levels or is unconnected
Unconnected Height	Explicit height of the wall
Top Offset	Distance of the top of the wall from the top constraint
Top Extension Distance	Distance of the top of a layer on a wall
Room Bounding	Whether the wall constitutes the boundary of a room
Related to Mass	Whether the wall relates to a massing geometry
Structural Usage	Defines the specific structural usage of a wall
Length	Indicates the value of the length of a wall
Area	Indicates the value of the surface area of a wall
Volume	Indicates the value of the volume of a wall
Comments	Specific comments that give description of a wall
Mark	To add a unique value or label to each wall
Phase Created	Phase in which a wall is created
Phase Demolished	Phase in which a wall was demolished
Image	Specifies the name of the image of the wall. To specify an image name, click on the Value field; a Browse button will be displayed. Choose the Browse button; the **Manage Images** dialog box will be displayed. Use this dialog box to specify the image for the wall. The specified image will be displayed in the Schedule.

Specifying Type Properties

The type properties of a wall specify the common parameters shared by certain elements in a family. Any changes made in the type properties of a wall element will affect all individual elements of that family in the project. To specify the type properties of an element, invoke the **Wall: Architectural** tool; the **Modify | Place Wall** tab will be displayed. In this tab, choose the **Type Properties** tool from the **Properties** panel; the **Type Properties** dialog box will be displayed. Using this dialog box, you can modify the type properties of the selected wall type such as **Structure, Function, Coarse Scale Fill Pattern,** and so on.

In Autodesk Revit 2017, in the **Type Properties** dialog box, you can view the analytical properties of the wall such as the **Thermal Mass, Thermal Resistance,** and **Heat Transfer Coefficient**. The analytical properties that you can edit are: **Absorptance** and **Roughness**. You can also define the composition of the wall type. To do so, choose the **Edit** button in the **Value** column of the **Structure** parameter; the **Edit Assembly** dialog box will be displayed, as shown in Figure 3-29. In the **Edit Assembly** dialog box, choose the **Preview** button; a preview box will be displayed. The preview box will display sectional detail of the selected wall type.

In Autodesk Revit, a wall is a composite building element and can consist of several layers. The **Layers** area in the **Edit Assembly** dialog box displays multiple layers of the selected wall, each with a specific function, material, and thickness. The layer on the top of the table represents the exterior side of a wall and the last layer represents the interior face. The **Layers** area, displays the selected wall type, refer to Figure 3-29. In this case, it is **Exterior- Brick on Mtl. Stud**. This wall type has ten layers. Each layer of the composite wall is assigned a specific function and priority based on its usage. The layers available in Autodesk Revit can be broadly classified into the categories given next.

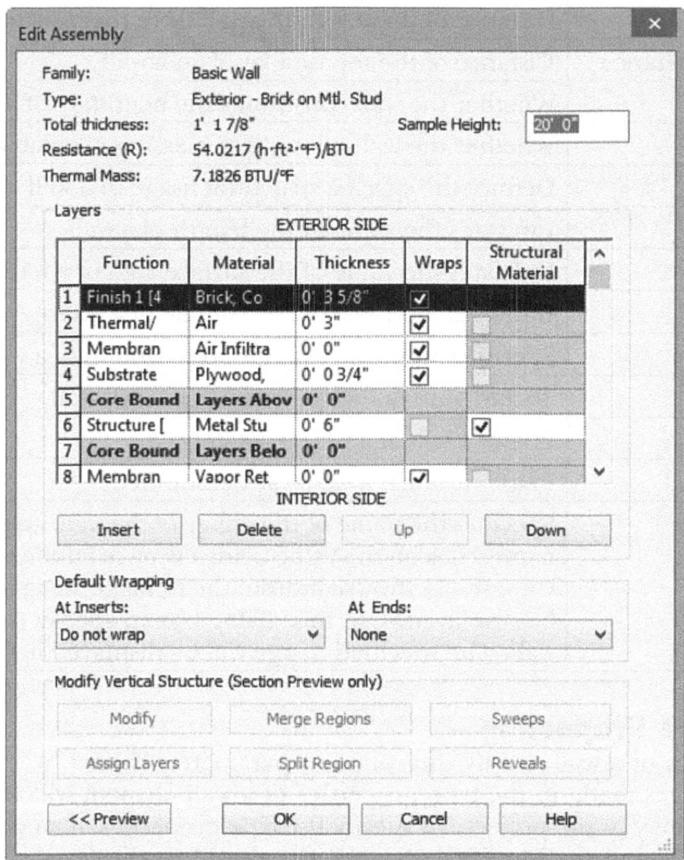

***Figure 3-29** The **Edit Assembly** dialog box for a wall type*

Structure [1]- Consists of main supporting element of the structure such as concrete, brick, wood, metal stud, and so on.

Substrate [2] - Consists of material that functions as substructure, such as foundation and plywood.

Thermal/Air Layer - Indicates the air cavity or the thermal insulation layer.

Membrane Layer - A zero thickness layer primarily used for the prevention against water vapor penetration.

Finish 1 [4] - Exterior finish such as metal, brick, and stone.

Finish 2 [5] - Interior finish such as paint, gypsum wall board, and so on.

Note

The numbers placed next to certain layers show the priority set of the layer and enables Autodesk Revit to work out the joinery detail of wall segments at corners and intersections according to the priority. When joined, a higher priority layer takes precedence over a lower priority layer.

In the **Edit Assembly** dialog box, the **Material** column displays the material specification, whereas the **Thickness** column displays the thickness of each layer. The total thickness of this composite wall is the sum of thickness of all layers. In the present case, the total thickness of wall is **1'1 7/8"** in Imperial or **350 mm** in Metric which is given beside the **Total thickness** parameter on the top of the dialog box. You can click on the **View** drop-down list and select **Section: Modify type attributes** to view the section of the wall.

Note

*The **View** drop-down list will only be visible if you choose the **Preview** button in the **Edit Assembly** dialog box.*

Autodesk Revit enables you to add and remove layers by using the **Insert** and **Delete** buttons, respectively provided in the **Layers** area in the **Edit Assembly** dialog box. To shift the layers, choose the **Up** and **Down** buttons. You can also create your own layers. You will learn more about materials, layers, and composite walls in the later chapters. The **Default Wrapping** area in the **Edit Assembly** dialog box has two drop-down lists namely, **At Inserts** and **At Ends**. The options in these drop-down lists allow wrapping of a compound wall at the end and at the inserts (for doors and windows). From the **At Inserts** drop-down list, you can select any of the following options: **Exterior, Interior, Both**, and **Do not wrap**. Similarly, from the **At Ends** drop-down list, you can select any of the following options: **Exterior, Interior**, or **None**. The wrapping in the walls can be viewed in a plan view. After, specifying various options in the **Edit Assembly** dialog box, choose the **OK** button; the dialog box will close. Also, choose the **OK** button again to close the **Type Properties** dialog box.

Sketching Walls

The next step after selecting the wall type from the **Properties** palette is to select the sketching tool. Autodesk Revit provides several sketching tools, such as **Line, Rectangle**, and so on to sketch the walls of different shapes. These tools, along with the **Options Bar**, can be invoked from the **Draw** panel in the **Modify | Place Wall** tab, as shown in Figure 3-30.

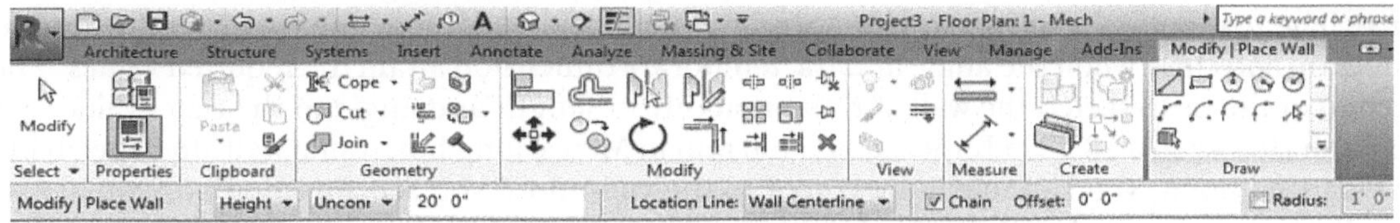

Figure 3-30 The ***Modify / Place Wall*** *tab*

In the **Modify | Place Wall** tab, you can access different sketching tools from the **Draw** panel and the **Options Bar** in the **Modify | Place Wall** tab. On invoking these tools, you can sketch different wall profiles. The procedures for sketching the straight and circular wall profiles are discussed next.

Sketching Straight Wall Profiles

You can sketch straight walls using the **Line** tool by specifying the start point and the endpoint of the wall segment. To specify the location of the start point, click in the drawing area and move the cursor, you will notice that a wall segment starts from the specified point and the changing dimension dynamically appears on it. This dimension is called the temporary dimension or listening dimension, and it shows the length and angle of the wall segment at any given location of the cursor, as shown in Figure 3-31.

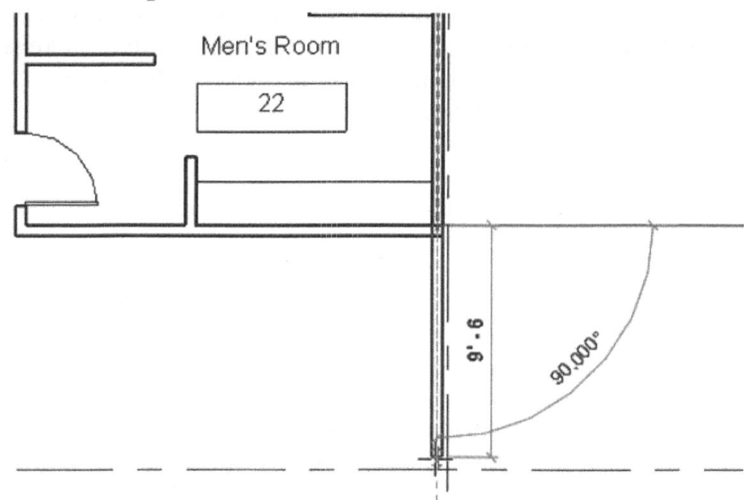

Figure 3-31 *The temporary dimensions displayed while sketching a wall*

Also, notice that the cursor moves in increments by the value set in the **Dimension Snaps** area of the **Snaps** dialog box (See Chapter 2, Setting Snaps). The angle subtended by the wall on the horizontal axis is also displayed and it keeps changing dynamically as you move the cursor to modify the inclination of the wall. Also notice that, on bringing the cursor near the horizontal or the vertical axis, a dashed line will appear on the wall segment. This is called the alignment line and it helps you sketch the components with respect to the already created components. You will also notice that a tooltip is displayed indicating that the wall segment being sketched is horizontal or vertical.

Autodesk Revit provides you with the flexibility of specifying the length of the walls in different ways. The first option is to specify the starting point of the wall, move the cursor in the desired direction and click, when the angle and the temporary dimension attain the required values. The second option is to sketch the wall and then modify its length and angle to the exact value. For example, to sketch a 18'0" in Imperial or 5400 mm in Metric long horizontal wall after specifying the starting point, you can move the cursor to the right until you see a dashed horizontal line parallel to the sketched wall. Click when the temporary dimension shows 20'0" in Imperial or 6000mm in Metric approximately. Note that the length of the wall may not be exactly 18'0" in Imperial or 5400mm in Metric. You can now use the wall controls to modify the dimensions of the wall to its exact value.

To modify the wall, select the wall segment and view its control and properties. As you select the wall segment, it gets highlighted in blue and the symbols appear above the wall segment. The exact dimension of the sketched wall is visible in the dimension text of the temporary dimension. The conversion control symbol, which appears below the dimension value, is used to convert the temporary dimension into a permanent dimension. The two blue arrows, that also appear on the upper face of the wall, indicate the flip control symbol for the sketched walls. They appear on the side interpreted as the exterior face of the wall. By default, the walls drawn from the left to right have the external face on the upper side and the walls drawn from the top to bottom have it on the right side. You can flip the orientation of the wall by clicking on the arrows symbol. Alternatively, you can place the cursor over the flip control symbol and notice the change in its color. After the color of the flip control changes, press SPACEBAR to flip the wall. The two blue dots that appear at the two ends of the wall segments are the drag control symbols. You can use them to stretch and resize the walls. To set the wall to the exact length, click on the temporary dimension; an edit box will appear showing the current dimension of the wall segment. Now, you can replace it by typing the exact length. For example, you can enter **9' 3"** in Imperial or **2775 mm** in Metric in the edit box, as shown in Figure 3-32. Next, press ENTER; the length of the wall will be modified to 9' 3" in Imperial or 2775 mm in Metric.

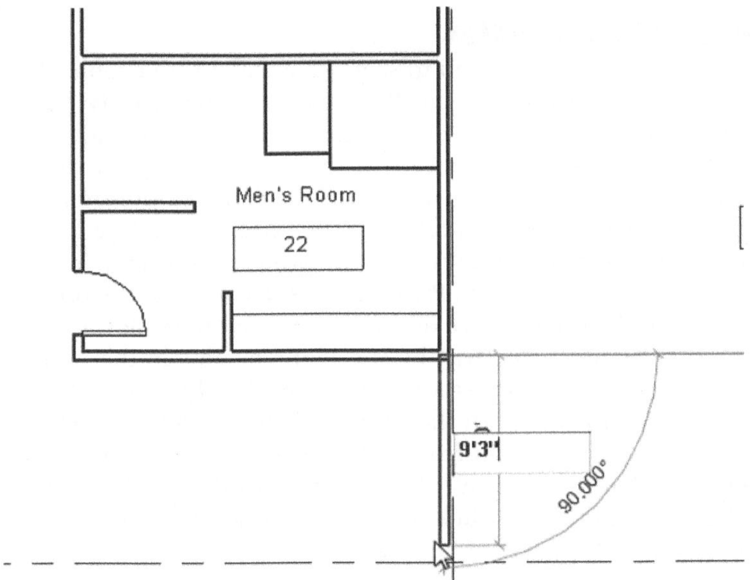

Figure 3-32 *Entering the value of the length in the edit box*

Alternatively, you can create a straight wall by typing the dimension for the length before choosing the endpoint. As soon as you start typing the length, an edit box appears above the dimension line. Enter the value of the length and press ENTER to create a wall segment of the specified length. To sketch a wall at a given angle, sketch it at any angle and then click on the angular dimension symbol; an edit box will appear. In the edit box, you can enter the exact angular dimension from the horizontal axis to which the wall will be inclined.

Note

*The **Project Browser** shows **Level 1** in bold letters. This indicates that the wall has been sketched in that level.*

On invoking the **Wall: Architectural** tool, you can set various options in the **Options Bar** before you start to sketch the wall. The options that you can specify in the **Options Bar** are related to the following options: level to which the wall height or depth will be constrained, the location line of the wall, the offset distance of the wall if offsetted from the specified location line, and the creation method of the wall. In the **Options Bar**, you can specify the offset distance in the **Offset** edit box. By specifying a value in this edit box, you can create a wall that starts at a specified offset distance from a point defined in an existing element. After entering the offset value and selecting the sketching option, click near the element to define the offset distance. When you move the cursor, the wall will start at the specified distance from the selected point. For example, this option can be used for creating boundary walls that are placed at a specific distance from the building profile.

Also, in the **Options Bar**, you can select the **Chain** check box to ensure that you can create a continuous wall profile with a number of wall segments. It enables you to create a continuous wall with wall segments connected end to end. The end point of the previous wall becomes the start point to the next wall.

Sketching Circular Wall Profiles

The **Circle** tool in the list box can be used to sketch a circular wall profile. To sketch a circular wall profile, invoke the **Circle** tool from the **Draw** panel of the **Modify | Place Wall** tab and click in the drawing area to specify the center point of the circular wall. You will notice that a circular wall profile is extending dynamically with the specified point as the center and the other end attached to the cursor, as shown in Figure 3-33. The temporary radial dimension will also be displayed. Click when the desired value for the radius is displayed. Alternatively, before clicking on the second point, type the value for the radius of the circular profile. As you type, the value will be displayed in the edit box. Press ENTER to complete the profile. Notice that the dimension that you entered is the distance of the center point to the location line of the profile. Alternatively, you can create a circular wall by specifying a value in the Radius edit box in the **Options Bar**. To do so, invoke the **Circle** tool from the **Modify | Place Wall** tab; various options will be displayed in the **Options Bar**. In the **Options Bar**, select the check box preceding the **Radius** edit box to activate it. In the **Radius** edit box, specify a value for the radius of the circle. Now, in the drawing window as you move the cursor, you will find the preview of the circular wall profile with the specified radius. Click on a specified point in the drawing area; a circular wall profile with the specified radius will be created.

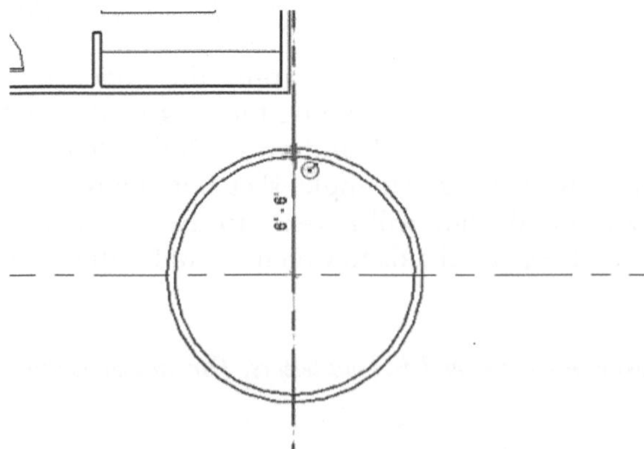

Figure 3-33 *Circular wall profile being created*

USING DOORS IN A BUILDING MODEL

A door is one of the most frequently used components in a building model. It helps in accessing various exterior and interior spaces in a project. Autodesk Revit provides a variety of predefined door types. You can access these door types by using the options from the **Type Selector** drop-down list of the **Properties** palette. You can also load other door types from the **US Imperial** folder. A wall acts as a host element for doors. This means that a door can be placed only if there exists a wall. When you add a door to a wall, Autodesk Revit intuitively creates an opening in it.

In Autodesk Revit, the doors are not loaded in any of the default templates. To add doors, you need to add the door types to the current file. To do so, choose the **Load Family** tool from the **Load from Library** panel of the **Insert** tab; the **Load Family** dialog box will be displayed. In this dialog box, you can browse to **US Imperial > Doors** folder for Imperial or **US Metric > Doors** folder for Metric and select the desired door type(s) from the displayed list of families. After selecting the door types, choose the **Open** button; the **Load Family** dialog box will close and the desired door types will be added in the current project. Now, you can add the doors to the building model as required. The procedure for adding doors to a building model is described next.

Adding Doors

You can add doors to a building model by using the **Door** tool. You can invoke this tool from the **Build** panel. Alternatively, you can type **DR** to invoke this tool. Note that in Revit, the door types are not loaded in the default templates. Therefore, if you are using any of the templates for the project and invoking the door for the first time, the **Revit** window displays the message that no doors family is loaded and prompts to load one. To load a door family, choose the **Yes** button from the **Revit** window; the **Load Family** dialog box will be displayed. Select the desired family(ies) for Imperial from the **US Imperial > Doors** folder or for Metric from the **US Metric > Doors** folder and choose the **Open** button the **Load Family** dialog box will close and the **Specify Types** dialog box will be displayed. Select the desired type(s) from the **Type** area of the dialog box. Note that you can use the CTRL key to select multiple types from the **Type** area. After selecting the desired type, choose the **OK** button in the **Specify Types** dialog box. The selected types of door will be loaded in the project.

Now, to add a door, invoke the **Door** tool from the **Build** panel of the **Architecture** tab; the **Modify | Place Door** tab will be displayed in the ribbon. In this tab, select the desired door type from the **Type Selector** drop-down list in the **Properties** palette. This drop-down list displays the door types loaded in the current project. After selecting a door type, click on the desired location of a wall to add the door. After adding the door to the building model, you can view and modify its properties. To do so, select the door; the instance properties of the door will be displayed in the **Properties** palette, as shown in Figure 3-34.

Now, to modify the type properties of the selected door type, choose the **Edit Type** button from the **Properties** palette; the **Type Properties** dialog box for the selected door type will be displayed, as shown in Figure 3-35. In this dialog box, change the parameters as required and then choose the **Preview** button to view the graphical image of the selected door type.

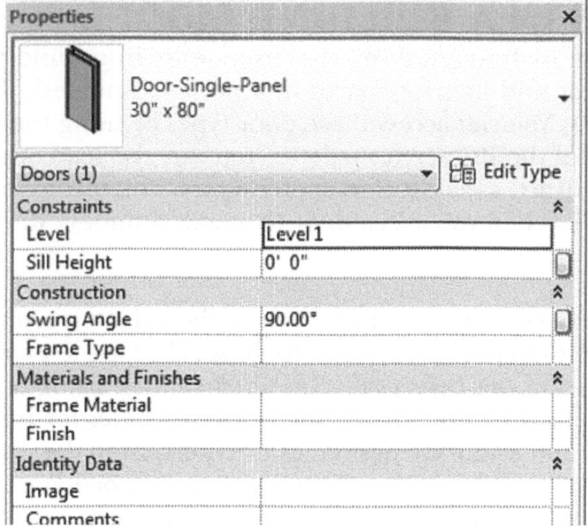

Figure 3-34 *Instance properties of a door*

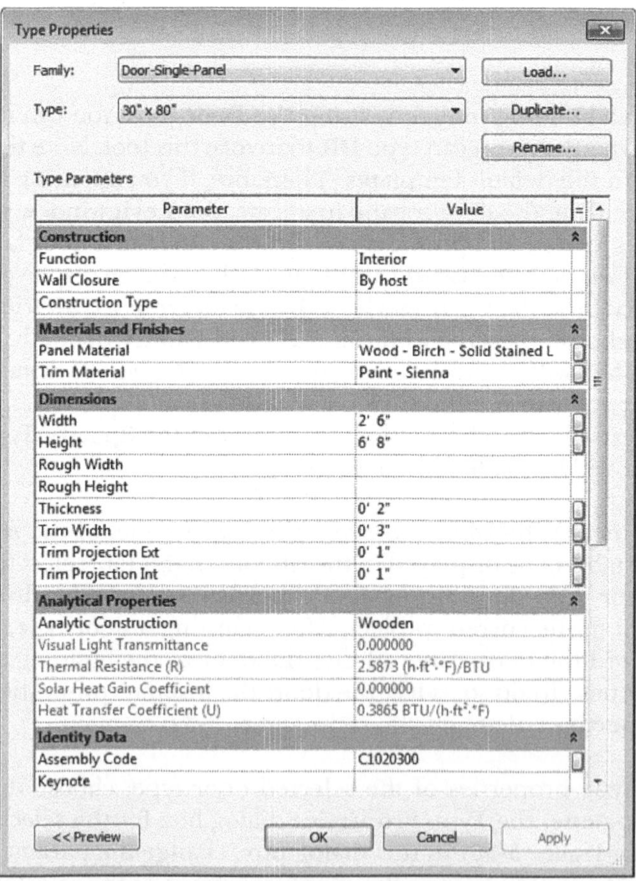

Figure 3-35 *The **Type properties** dialog box displaying the properties of a door*

Understanding Door Properties

The **Type Properties** dialog box displays the values of different parameters of a door. The type parameters are arranged under different heads based on their properties such as **Construction**, **Materials and Finishes**, **Dimensions**, **Identity Data**, and **IFC Parameters**. The parameters associated with each property are listed under each head. For example, the **Dimensions** head includes the dimensional type parameters associated with the door type such as, **Height**, **Width**, **Trim Width**, and so on. You have the option of either using the default values for these parameters or modifying them to the desired values. However, before modifying the type properties of a predefined door type, it is recommended to create a copy of the original door type and modify the desired properties of the new door type. The **Duplicate** button available on the top right corner in this dialog box can be used to create a copy of a door type. When you choose this button, the **Name** edit box will be displayed, prompting you to assign a name to the new door type. Enter a name in this edit box and choose the **OK** button; a new door type is created, which inherits the properties of the parent door type. Now, its parameters can be modified, as desired. Use the **Rename** button to give a new name to the selected door type. You can use the **Load** button, provided on the top right corner of the dialog box to load a door type of the required family from the additional libraries.

Note

Renaming a door type does not alter its properties. For example, in Imperial if you rename ***36"x 84"*** *to* ***34"x 84"****, its width will still remain 36", irrespective of its name. In Metric, if you rename* ***0915 x 2134mm*** *to* ***0860 x 2134mm****, its width will still remain* ***0915mm****.*

Door Type Properties

If you change the type properties of a door, the properties of all instances of that door type in the project will also change. The door type properties are described in the table given next.

Parameter Name	Description
Function	Sets the door function value to Interior or Exterior. This value will be used at the time of scheduling.
Wall Closure	Sets the layer wrapping for the door type.
Construction Type	Describes the composition of the door.
Door Material	Refers to the finish material of the door panel which can be selected from the available materials list.
Frame Material	Refers to the finish material of the door frame and can be selected from the available materials list.
Height	Sets the height of the door.
Trim Projection Ext	Thickness of the trim projection at the exterior side.
Trim Projection Int	Thickness of the trim projection at the interior side.
Trim Width	Width of the trim at both the sides.

Width	Width of the door can be set in this column.
Rough Width	Used for scheduling or exporting.
Rough Height	Used for scheduling or exporting.
Assembly Code	Refers to the assembly code for the door type that can be selected from the hierarchical list.
Keynote	This is a new parameter available for all model elements, detail components, and materials under identity data.
Model	Name to be given to the model door type.
Manufacturer	Name of the manufacturer of the door type.
Type Comments	Additional information or comments to be added to the door type, primarily for including in schedules.
URL	Web link of the door type manufacturer.
Description	Text describing the door type.
Assembly Description	Text describing the assembly of the door type.
Type Mark	Each door can be assigned a unique value that may be generated in a sequence of creation of the door type.
Fire Rating	Fire rating of the door.
Cost	Cost of the door, primarily for costing purpose.

Door Instance Properties

The door instance properties, available in the **Properties** palette, refer to the instance properties of a particular door. On changing these properties, the properties of only that particular instance in the project is changed. The description of various instance parameters is given in the table next.

Parameter Name	**Description**
Level	Shows the layer to which the door belongs and can be used to move it to a different level.
Sill Height	Refers to the distance or height of the sill of the door from the specified level.
Frame Type	Refers to the type of frame used for the door instance.
Swing Angle	Refers to the swing angle of the door.
Frame Material	Specifies the material used for the frame of the instance.
Finish	Refers to the finish applied to the door and frame.
Image	Specifies the name of the image for the door instance.

Comments	Describes the door instance.
Mark	Specifies the mark of the selected door.
Phase Created	Specifies whether the door is a part of the new construction or an existing construction.
Phase Demolished	Specifies whether the door is a part of the existing building or a new structure, or none.
Head Height	Refers to the height of the top of the door from the specified level.

Adding a Door to a Wall

Doors can be added to a building model in the plan, section, elevation or a 3D view, by clicking at the desired location in a wall. After invoking the **Door** tool and selecting the door type, move the cursor over the wall on which it is to be added. The '+' symbol over the cursor indicates that an element is being added. You will notice that the door symbol appears, when the cursor is moved over the wall. When the cursor comes close to the upper or lower face of the wall, the door symbol appears on it, as shown in Figure 3-36. The door symbol appears on the lower face when the cursor comes near to that face. Also, a temporary dimension appears indicating the distance of the center of the door opening from adjacent walls or wall edges.

Using the temporary dimensions displayed, you can add the door at the desired location. Alternatively, you can first add the door at an approximate location on the wall and then modify its location to the exact dimension. When a door is added, an opening is automatically created in the wall and the edges are also completed. After selecting the door, you will notice that the horizontal and vertical twin arrow symbols appear in the door along with a tag number. To flip the swing-side of the door, click on the twin arrow key that appears parallel to the wall edge. To shift the door to the other side of the wall, click on the twin arrow key that appears perpendicular to the wall edge (vertical, in this case). To move the added door to the exact dimension, click on the particular temporary dimension text and enter the exact value, as shown in Figure 3-37. The door shifts to the desired location.

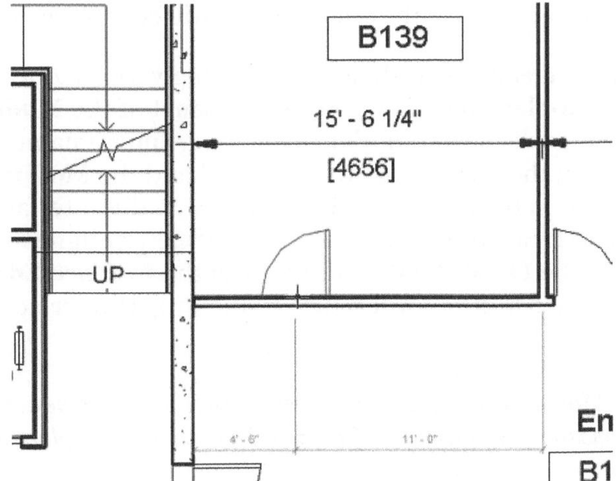

***Figure 3-36** The appearance of the door symbol on the wall*

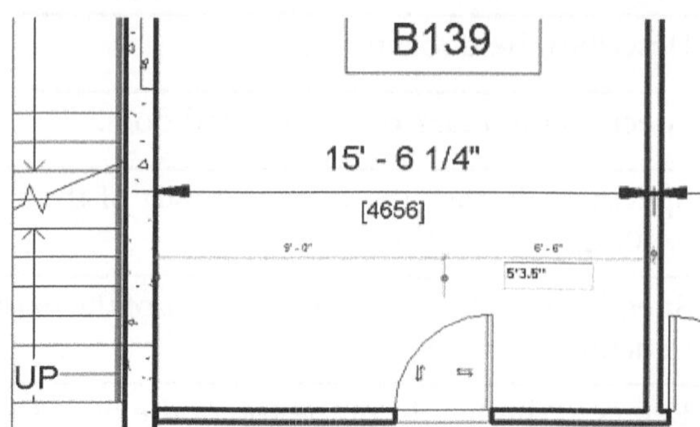

Figure 3-37 *Entering the value in the edit box to position the door*

Note

A door can be placed in any type of wall, regardless of the height of the door. Autodesk Revit displays alert messages if the door is not placed appropriately.

In Autodesk Revit, when doors are inserted, door tags are generated automatically. They assist in marking the doors and later arranging them in the form of a schedule. The door type tag number increments sequentially, when you place a door by using the **Door** tool or when you copy and paste it into the building model. You can, however, give a specific mark or tag to doors individually. To add a tag to the door, ensure that the **Tag on Placement** button is chosen from the **Tag** panel of the **Modify | Place Door** contextual tab. The visibility of door tags can be controlled by using the **Visibility/Graphics Overrides for Floor Plan** dialog box. This dialog box can be invoked by typing **VG**, or by selecting the desired door from the drawing and choosing the **Visibility/ Graphics** tool in the **Graphics** panel in the **View** tab. Next, if you want to hide the door tags, choose the **Annotation Categories** tab from the **Visibility/Graphics Overrides for Floor Plan** dialog box and clear the **Door Tags** check box. When you invoke the **Door** tool, the option for adding a horizontal or vertical door tag becomes available in the **Options Bar**. You can set the orientation of the door tags to horizontal or vertical by selecting the **Horizontal** or **Vertical** option from the drop-down list displayed in the **Options Bar**.

To change a door type, select the particular instance; the properties and the type of the selected door will be displayed in the **Properties** palette. In the **Properties** palette, select a new door type from the **Type Selector** drop-down list; the selected door will be replaced with the new door type.

In Autodesk Revit, you can create a new door type by using various tools. To create a new door type, choose the **Model In-place** tool from the **Mode** panel of the **Modify | Place Door** tab; the **Name** dialog box will be displayed. In this dialog box, enter a name in the **Name** edit box and choose the **OK** button; the dialog box will be closed and the **Modify** tab will be displayed along with the various tools in the Family Editor interface. In this interface, you can use various tools from different tabs to create the doors that are specifically designed for that instance. After creating the door choose the **Finish Model** button from the **In-Place Editor** panel; the Family Editor interface will be closed and you will return to the Project interface.

Note

On invoking the ***Model In-place*** *tool, the Family Editor mode will be activated. In this mode, you can use various massing tools from the* ***Create*** *tab to create an in-place door assembly.*

Apart from the door types available in the **Type Selector** drop-down list, you can use other door types from additional libraries. To access them, choose the **Load Family** tool in the **Mode** panel of the **Modify | Place Door**; the **Load Family** dialog box will be displayed. Additional door types are available in the **Doors** sub folder of the **US Imperial** folder. Select a door type to view its image in the **Preview** area. After selecting the door type, choose the **Open** button. The selected family of doors will be added to the **Type Selector** drop-down list in the **Properties** palette for that project.

ADDING WINDOWS IN A BUILDING MODEL

Windows form an integral part of any building project. Autodesk Revit provides several in-built window types that can be easily used and added to the building model. Like doors, windows are also dependent on the walls that act as their host element. In Autodesk Revit, the windows are not loaded in any of the default templates. To add the windows, you need to add the window families to the current file. To do so, choose the **Load Family** tool from the **Load from Library** panel of the **Insert** tab; the **Load Family** dialog box will be displayed. In this dialog box, you can browse to **US Imperial > Windows** folder for Imperial or **US Metric > Windows** folder for Metric and select the desired window type(s) from the displayed list of families. After selecting the window families, choose the **Open** button; the **Load Family** dialog box will close and the **Specify Types** dialog box will be displayed. Select the desired type(s) from the **Type** area of the dialog box. Note that you can use the CTRL key to select multiple types from the **Type** area. After selecting the desired type choose the **OK** button in the **Specify Types** dialog box and the desired window types will be added in the current project. Now, you can add the window to the building model as required. The procedure for adding windows to a building model is described next.

Adding Windows

In Autodesk Revit, you can add windows to a building model by using the **Window** tool. To do so, invoke the **Window** tool from the **Build** panel of the **Architecture** tab; the **Modify | Place Window** tab will be displayed. In this tab, select the window type from the **Type Selector** drop-down list in the **Properties** palette. To add a window to a building model, move the cursor over the wall and click to place it either in the upper face or in the lower face. After adding the window, you can view and also change its instance parameters. To do so, select the window from the drawing; the **Properties** palette will be displayed. You can use this palette to view and modify various instance parameters of the selected window such as its Level, Head Height, Sill Height and others. To modify and view the type parameters of the window, choose the **Edit Type** button in the **Properties** palette; the **Type Properties** dialog box will be displayed. In this dialog box, choose the **Preview** button to view the graphical image of the selected window type.

Understanding Window Properties

The **Type Properties** dialog box displays the type parameters for different components of a window such as **Glass Pane Material**, **Sash Material**, **Default Sill Height**, **Width**, **Height**, and so on. You can click in the value column of each parameter and select the required options or use the **Load** button provided on the top right corner of the dialog box to load a window family type from the additional libraries. The **Duplicate** button can be used to create a copy of the window type with a different name. The new window inherits the properties of the parent window type and its parameters can be modified as desired. By using the **Rename** button, you can give a new name to the selected window type.

Window Type Properties

When you change the type properties of a window type, the properties of all instances of that window type in the project will also change. Various type parameters and their corresponding descriptions are given in the following table:

Parameter Name	Description
Wall Closure	Sets layer wrapping for the window type
Construction Type	Describes the composition of the window
Glass Pane Material	Refers to the finish and material of the glass pane and can be selected from the available materials list
Sash Material	Refers to the material assigned to the sash of the window
Trim Exterior Material	Sets the exterior trim material
Trim Interior Material	Sets the interior trim material
Height	The value used to set the height of the window
Default Sill Height	Distance of the window from the bottom of the wall, the default value is 3'0" in Imperial or 915.0 mm for Metric
Trim Projection - Ext.	The value used to set the exterior projection
Trim Projection - Int.	The value used to set the interior projection
Trim Width - Exterior	The value used to set the width of exterior projection
Trim Width - Interior	The value used to set the width of interior projection
Width	Refers to the width of the window
Window Inset	Refers to the inset of the window from the wall face
Rough Width	The value used for scheduling or exporting
Rough Height	Used for scheduling or exporting
Keynote	This is a new parameter available for all model elements, detail components, and materials under identity data
Model	Name to be given to the window type
Manufacturer	Name of the manufacturer of the window type
Type Comments	Additional information or comments to be added to the window type, primarily for creating schedules
URL	Weblink of the manufacturer
Description	Text describing the window type
Assembly Description	Text describing the assembly
Type Mark	Unique value assigned to each window
Cost	Cost of the window, primarily for costing purpose

Window Instance Properties

Changing the instance properties of a window, changes the properties of only that instance of the window in the project. The instance properties of a window are given in the table given next.

Parameter Name	**Description**
Level	Shows the layer to which the window belongs and can be used to move the window to a different level
Sill Height	Refers to the distance or height of the sill of the window from the specified level
Image	Specifies the name of the image of the window type. The specified image will be displayed in the Schedule.
Comments	Description of the window instance not covered in the type properties
Mark	Can be used to specify or modify the mark of the selected window
Phase Created	Specifies whether the window is part of a new construction or an existing construction
Phase Demolished	Specifies whether the window is a part of an existing building or new structure
Head Height	Refers to the height of the top of the window from the specified level

Note that the properties available in the **Type Properties** dialog box may vary depending on the type of window you will select from the **Type Selector** drop-down list in the **Properties** palette.

Adding a Window to a Wall

To add a window to a wall, invoke the **Window** tool from the **Architecture** tab of the ribbon and select the window type from the **Type Selector** drop-down list in the **Properties** palette. Next, move the cursor close to the wall on which it needs to be added. The window symbol appears when the cursor is moved over the wall. When the cursor comes close to the lower face of the wall, the window appears on that face. The window appears on the upper face when the cursor comes near to it, as shown in Figure 3-38. Also, notice a temporary dimension, which indicates the distance of the center of the window opening from the adjacent walls or wall edges. You can also use the temporary dimensions to add the window by clicking at the appropriate location on the wall. Autodesk Revit automatically creates an opening in the wall and the edges are also completed.

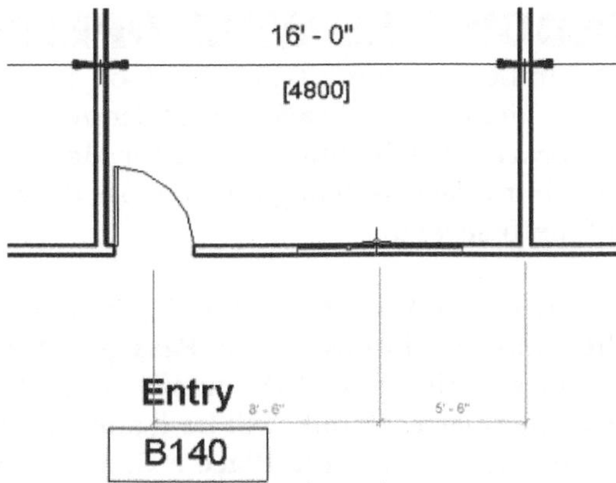

Figure 3-38 *The appearance of the window symbol on the wall*

You will also notice a twin arrow symbol on the window, along with a tag number. Click on the symbol to flip the orientation of the window. The flip arrow symbol will appear on the side that is interpreted as the inner side of the window. You can specify the exact position of the window with respect to the adjacent walls or edges after placing it at the approximate location. To specify the dimensional location of a window, click on the particular temporary dimension text and type the exact dimension. The window will shift to the desired location. Window tags are automatically generated in Autodesk Revit. Unlike doors, however, each window of the same type bears the same tag. Different window types have preassigned marks, which can be changed using the **Type Properties** dialog box. Window tags are used for creating the window schedule.

Note

The window tag numbers increases as you place or copy them in the project. You can also give them a specific tag number individually.

Similar to the door tags, the visibility of the window tags can also be controlled in the drawing. To hide the window tags, invoke the **Visibility/Graphics for Floor Plan** dialog box and choose the **Annotation Categories** tab from it. Next, clear the **Window Tags** check box.

Note

*On clearing the **Window Tags** check box in the **Annotation Categories** area of the **Visibility/Graphics for Floor Plan** dialog box, the tags become hidden, but still remain a part of the project.*

In Autodesk Revit, you can create the windows that are specifically designed for a location or an instance. To do so, choose the **Model In-place** tool from the **Mode** panel of the **Modify |Place Window** tab; the **Name** dialog box will be displayed. In this dialog box, enter the name of the window type in the **Name** edit box and choose the **OK** button; the dialog box will be closed and the **Modify** tab will be displayed. Now, the Family Editor mode will be activated, and in this mode, you can use various tools to create the in-place window. Apart from the window types displayed in the **Type Selector** drop-down list, you can access other window types as well. To add other window types in the **Type Selector** drop-down list, choose the **Load Family** tool from the **Mode** panel of the **Modify | Place Window** tab; the **Load Family** dialog box will be displayed. In this dialog box, add additional window types from the **Library > US Imperial > Windows** folder for Imperial or **Library > US Metric > Windows** folder for Metric.

DOORS AND WINDOWS AS WALL OPENINGS

Autodesk Revit also provides in-built opening types for door and windows. These types are available in the **Openings** subfolder of the **Libraries > US Imperial** folder for Imperial or the **Openings** subfolder of the **Libraries > US Metric** folder for Metric that can be accessed from the **Load Family** dialog box. To invoke this dialog box, choose the **Load Family** tool from the **Load from Library** panel of the **Insert** tab.

To add an opening for door, invoke the **Load Family** dialog box and then from the **Openings** subfolder select any of the following family types: **Passage Opening-Cased** or **Passage Opening-Elliptical Arch**. After selecting any of the family type, choose the **Open** button in the **Load Family** dialog box; the selected family will be loaded in the project. Now, to place the selected opening type in the wall, choose the **Place a Component** tool from **Architecture > Build > Component** drop-down; the **Modify | Place Component** tab will be displayed. In the **Properties** palette, ensure that the desired opening type is selected in the **Type Selector** drop-down list. Next, click in a desired location in the wall to insert the door opening. In the **Properties** palette, you can also edit the width and height of the door opening.

Similar to adding a door opening, you can insert a window opening. To do so, invoke the **Load Family** dialog box and then select any of the two family types from the **Openings** subfolder: **Opening with Trim** or **Opening**. To place the window opening in the wall you will follow the same method as used for inserting the door opening.

OPENINGS IN THE WALL

You can create rectangular openings in a curved or straight wall. To cut an opening in a wall, you can use a plan, elevation, or sectional view. Generally, the sectional or elevation view is preferred as locating and placing such views is easy. To cut a rectangular opening in a wall, open a preferred elevation or a section view in which the host wall of the opening is visible. Next, choose the **Wall: Architectural** tool from the **Opening** panel of the **Architecture** tab and then select the wall that will host the opening. Click in the desired area in the wall to mark the start point or the first corner point of the rectangular opening. As you move the cursor, a rectangle with its temporary dimensions appears. Click at the desired point in the wall to mark the other corner point of the rectangular opening. Now, you can use the temporary dimensions displayed on the opening to modify the placement of the opening. Next, choose the **Modify** button from the **Select** panel to exit the tool. After exiting the tool, you can select the created opening to modify its properties such as its height, top offset, base offset, and so on from the **Properties** palette.

CREATING ARCHITECTURAL FLOORS

You can add a floor to the current level of a building model using the **Floor: Architectural** tool. You can invoke this tool from the **Build** panel of the **Architecture** tab. On invoking this tool, the **Modify | Create Floor Boundary** tab will be displayed. You can use this tab to draw, annotate, and edit a floor boundary for your building model as well as to assign properties to them. The **Draw** panel of the **Modify | Create Floor Boundary** tab consists of various tools that are used to draw the floor sketches. These sketches define the boundary of the floor. To define the boundary of the floor, you can either pick the existing walls or sketch the boundary in the plan view by using lines. You can also sketch the boundary in the 3D view, provided that the work plane is set to the plan view.

Similar to other model components, the floor tool has associated type and instance properties. Once you sketch the floor, the **Properties** palette will display the instance parameters of floor. The **Type Selector** drop-down list in this palette displays the floors available in Autodesk Revit's library. This palette can be used to modify the instance properties of the floor such as the level at which the floor is to be created, the height offset of the floor from the specified level, and so on. To modify the type properties of a floor, choose the **Edit Type** button from the **Properties** palette; the **Type Properties** dialog box will be displayed, as shown in Figure 3-39.

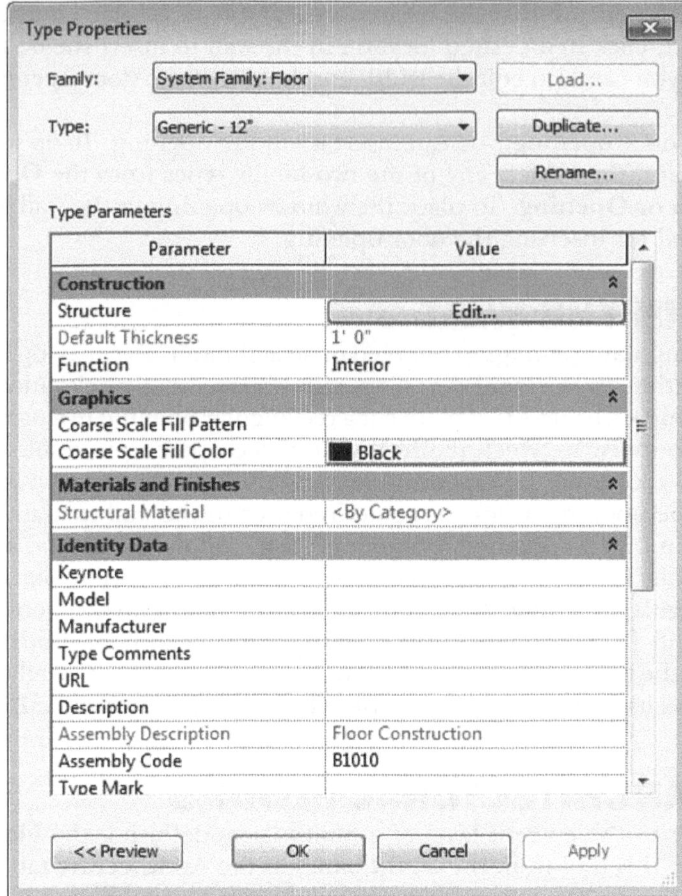

***Figure 3-39** The **Type Properties** dialog box*

You can set the type parameters for the floor in it. You can also create a new floor type by using the **Duplicate** button. To edit the structural elements of the floor, choose the **Edit** button in the **Value** column for the **Structure** type parameter; the **Edit Assembly** dialog box will be displayed, showing the structure of the floor type with its different layers. In the **Edit Assembly** dialog box, the **Insert** or **Delete** button can be used to customize the new floor type based on the specific project requirement.

Note

The type and instance properties may vary depending on the floor type selected. Autodesk Revit Help provides a detailed explanation of all properties associated with floor types.

Sketching the Floor Boundary

To create a floor, you need to sketch its boundary. There are two methods to sketch a boundary. The first method is to pick the already created walls using the **Pick Walls** tool to define the floor boundary. The other method is to draw the floor profile using the draw tools such as line, rectangle, polygon, arc, and others from the **Draw** panel of the **Modify | Create Floor Boundary** tab.

By default, the **Pick Walls** tool is chosen in the **Draw** panel of the **Modify | Create Floor Boundary** tab. This tool can be used to sketch the floor for the spaces bound by the connected walls. The **Option Bar** displays the **Offset** edit box, which can be used to specify the offset distance of the floor sketch line from an existing wall. The **Extend into wall (to core)** check box is used to extend the floor to the wall core and assists in creating a joint between the floor and the wall core. If the **Pick Walls** tool is not chosen by default, then invoke this tool and move the cursor near to the wall. You will notice that as the cursor is brought near to the face of the wall, a dashed line appears along with its inner or outer face. You can choose either of the faces of the wall to sketch the floor. Click when the dashed line appears at the appropriate location; a magenta line with flip and drag controls as well as two parallel lines will be displayed on the wall, as shown in Figure 3-40. The flip control can be used to flip the line between the two faces of the wall.

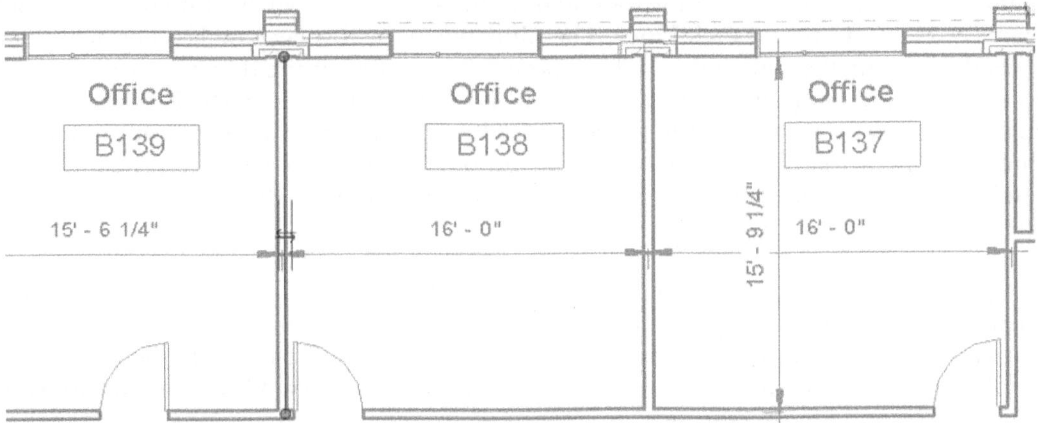

Figure 3-40 *The line with flip and drag control representing an edge of the floor is displayed*

Similarly, you can select other walls to define the floor boundary. The sketched boundary must form a closed profile with all edges connected to each other. After completing the floor boundary, you can edit it by using the drag controls and various tools in the **Modify** panel of the **Modify | Create Floor Boundary** tab. After the floor profile has been sketched, choose the **Finish Edit Mode** button from the **Mode** panel; the floor will be created, as shown in Figure 3-41. As the floor created will not be visible in the plan view, you can use the **Default 3D View** tool from the **View** tab to view it.

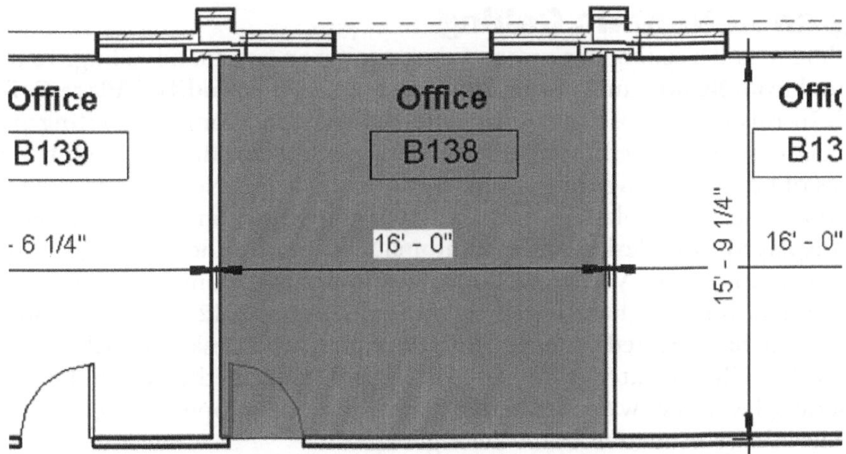

Figure 3-41 *The created floor boundary*

The other option to sketch the floor profile is to draw it using the sketching tools from the **Draw** panel. You can choose the appropriate sketching tool to sketch the floor boundary based on its shape. The functions of the sketching tools are the same as those used for creating a wall. While using the **Line** tool, you can select the **Chain** check box in the **Options Bar** to sketch the lines that are connected end-to-end. Also, you can specify the value in the **Offset** edit box in the **Options Bar** to sketch lines at a specified offset distance from a point on an existing element. Using the editing tools in the **Modify** panel of the **Modify | Create Floor Boundary** tab, you can edit the sketched profile.

In the sketched floor boundary, you can provide slope. To do so, invoke the **Slope Arrow** tool from the **Draw** panel; a list box containing tools to draw the slope arrow will be displayed. The list box contains two tools: **Line** and **Pick Lines**. The **Line** tool in the display panel is chosen by default. You need to specify the start point and endpoint of the arrow in the drawing. After specifying the start point and endpoint, you can modify its instance properties in the **Properties** palette. Using this palette, you can modify the associated properties such as specification method to define the slope arrow, the level at which the tail of the slope arrow will rest, height offset at the tail of the arrow, and more. You can attain the desired slope in the floor using the instance properties in the **Properties** palette.

After you complete the profile and add specifications for the floor, choose the **Finish Edit Mode** button from the **Mode** panel; the floor will be created and the **Modify | Floors** tab will be displayed. In this tab, you can use various modification tools to modify the floor created. This tab consists of nine panels: **Properties**, **Clipboard**, **Geometry**, **View**, **Dimension**, **Create**, **Modify**, **Mode**, and **Shape Editing**.

PLACING CEILINGS

You can add a ceiling to a building model by using the **Ceiling** tool. To do so, invoke this tool from the **Build** panel in the **Architecture** tab; the **Modify | Place Ceiling** tab with various tools for creating the ceiling will be displayed. Since the ceilings are not visible in the floor plan, they are created in the ceiling plan head of each discipline. You can add a ceiling to a project using three different methods, by adding automatic ceiling, by sketching the ceiling, and by using the pick walls method.

Creating an Automatic Ceiling

The first method to add a ceiling to a project is by creating an automatic ceiling. To do so, choose the **Ceiling** tool from **Build** panel in the **Architecture** tab; the **Modify | Place Ceiling** tab will be displayed. In this tab, choose the **Automatic Ceiling** tool from the **Ceiling** panel. In the **Properties** palette, select the ceiling type from the **Type Selector** drop-down list. You can select different types of built-in ceiling that can be used from this list. Now, to add the ceiling to the entire room, open the ceiling plan, move the cursor inside the room, and click when the ceiling boundary is displayed. Autodesk Revit will automatically create the ceiling from the center of the room. For example, when you move the cursor inside the room for creating an automatic ceiling, its boundary is highlighted in red, as shown in Figure 3-42. Click to create the ceiling, automatically. If you have created the ceiling in a floor plan, Autodesk Revit will display a warning indicating that the ceiling created will not be visible in it. You can then open the ceiling plan of the corresponding level to view the created ceiling. You can also open the section view through the room to view the cross-section of the ceiling.

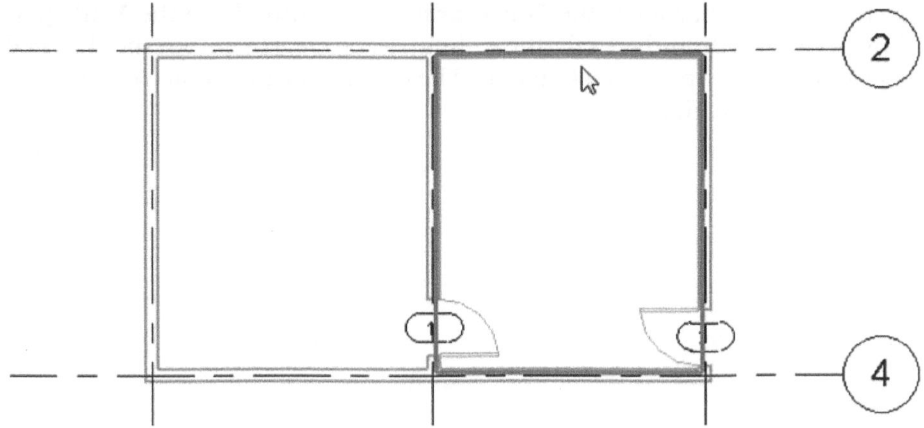

Figure 3-42 The highlighted ceiling boundary

Sketching a Ceiling

You can sketch a ceiling boundary to create it. To do so, choose the **Ceiling** tool from the **Build** panel; the **Modify | Place Ceiling** tab will be displayed. In this tab, choose the **Sketch Ceiling** tool from the **Ceiling** panel; the **Modify | Create Ceiling Boundary** tab will be displayed. This tab contains various tools for sketching and modifying the ceiling boundary. To start the sketch of the ceiling boundary, choose the **Boundary Line** tool from the **Draw** panel; a list box containing various drawing tools will be displayed on the right of this panel, as shown in Figure 3-43.

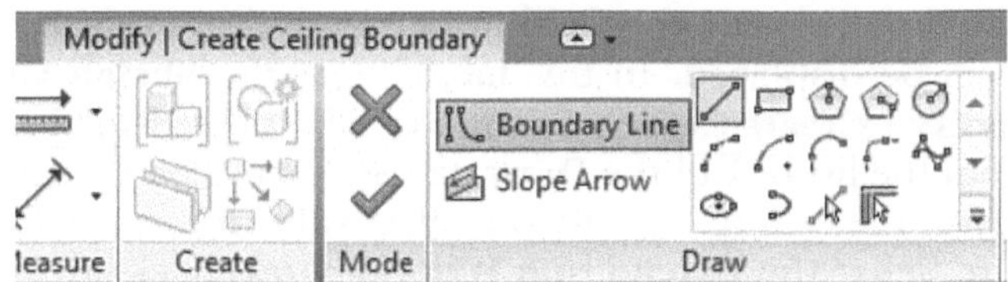

Figure 3-43 Different sketching tools for ceiling

The **Line** tool is chosen by default in the **Draw** panel. You can use this tool and the other drawing and modification tools displayed in the **Modify | Create Ceiling Boundary** tab to complete the sketch. Figure 3-44 shows a ceiling boundary that is sketched using various tools displayed in the **Modify | Create Ceiling Boundary** tab.

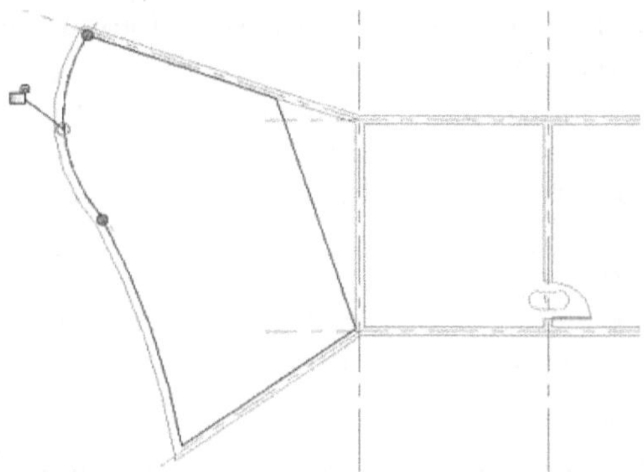

Figure 3-44 The sketched ceiling boundary

After completing the sketch, choose the **Finish Edit Mode** button from the **Mode** panel of the **Modify | Create Ceiling Boundary** tab; the ceiling will be created within the sketched profile. Display the section view to view the ceiling in it. The ceiling will appear at a certain height from the floor level, as shown in Figure 3-45.

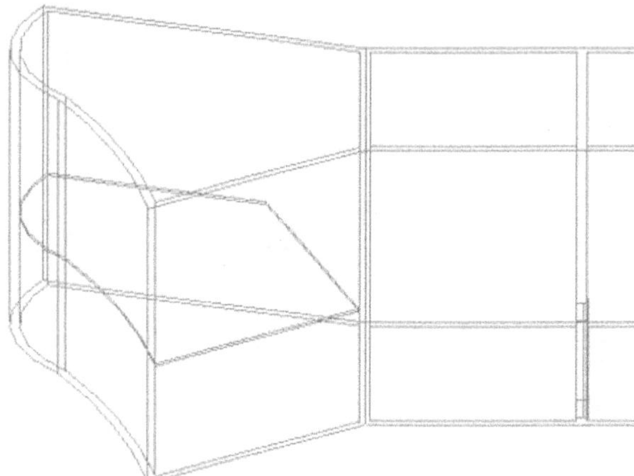

Figure 3-45 *The three dimensional view displaying the ceiling at a height*

Using the Pick Walls Method

The third method to create the ceiling is by picking the wall faces. This is a common method for creating ceilings. To do so, choose the **Ceiling** tool from the **Architecture** tab; the **Modify | Place Ceiling** tab will be displayed. In this tab, choose the **Sketch Ceiling** tool from the **Ceiling** panel; the **Modify | Create Ceiling Boundary** tab will be displayed. In this tab, choose the **Pick Walls** tool from the list box of the **Draw** panel; you will be prompted to pick the walls to define the boundary of the ceiling. Specify the offset value for the ceiling in the **Offset** edit box in the **Options Bar**. Select the **Extend into Wall (to core)** check box, if you want the offset to be measured from the core layer of the walls. Next, pick the walls to create the sketch for the ceiling. In the **Properties** palette, select the ceiling type from the **Type Selector** drop-down list. Next, choose the **Finish Edit Mode** button from the **Mode** panel of the **Modify | Create Ceiling Boundary** tab; the ceiling will be created.

Modifying a Ceiling

You can modify a ceiling after it has been created. To modify the ceiling, select it; the **Modify | Ceiling** tab will be displayed. From this tab, you can use various modification and editing tools to make changes on the selected ceiling. To edit the selected ceiling, you can use the editing tools such as **Copy**, **Rotate**, **Move**, and **Mirror**. You can also modify the properties of the selected ceiling based on its sketch. To do so, choose the **Edit Boundary** tool from the **Mode** panel; the **Modify | Ceiling > Edit Boundary** tab will be displayed and the sketch mode will be activated for the selected ceiling in the drawing. Now, you can modify the sketch profile by using the drag controls and other editing tools. Select the edge(s) of the ceiling boundary; the instance properties for the selected edges(s) of the ceiling profile will be displayed in the **Properties** palette. In this palette, you can enter the required values of various instance parameters for the selected edge(s) of the ceiling boundary.

You can view and edit the instance properties of a ceiling. To do so, select the ceiling from the drawing; the instance properties of the ceiling will be displayed in the **Properties** palette. This palette displays the instance parameters of the selected ceiling such as the level, height offset from level, and so on.

Being a level-based element, ceilings are created at a specified distance from the base level. This distance is specified in the **Height Offset From Level** instance parameter in the **Properties** palette. For example, to create a ceiling of 10' height for Imperial or 3000mm for Metric from Level 2, you can select it as the value for the **Level** instance parameter and enter the value **10'** for Imperial or **3000mm** for Metric in the **Height Offset From Level** instance parameter.

The **Edit Type** button in the **Properties** palette is used to invoke the **Type Properties** dialog box. Choose the **Edit Type** button; the **Type Properties** dialog box for the selected ceiling type will be displayed. In the **Type Properties** dialog box, you can create a duplicate type to create a new ceiling type. To do so, choose the **Duplicate** button; the **Name** dialog box will be displayed. In this dialog box, enter a name for the new ceiling type in the **Name** edit box and choose **OK**; the **Name** dialog box will close and new type of ceiling will be created. In the **Type Properties** dialog box, choose the **Edit** button in the **Value** column for the **Structure** type parameter to display the **Edit Assembly** dialog box. This dialog box displays the structure of the ceiling type with its various layers. The **Insert** or **Delete** button can be used to customize the new ceiling type, based on the specific project requirement.

Note

*When you select the created ceiling in the section view and choose the **Edit** button, Autodesk Revit displays the **Go To View** dialog box. You can select the view that you want to open for editing the ceiling boundary sketch.*

CREATING ROOMS

Room is a part of Revit building elements. Revit provides you the flexibility of creating rooms independent of room tags. Rooms can be created only in the plan view. You can also add rooms from the room schedules. Rooms and areas have the same graphical representation. Also, Revit forms the basis for creating spaces.

Adding Rooms

You can add rooms in the plan view of a specified discipline by using the **Room** tool. To do so, invoke this tool from the **Room & Area** panel, as shown in Figure 3-46; the **Modify | Place Room** tab will be displayed. Now, move the cursor inside the closed boundary that you need to define as room in the drawing; a symbol with a cross hair graphics attached to the cursor will appear. Notice that the size of this cross hair graphics will change according to the area of the room space of the closed boundary. Before you insert the room, you can select the type of room from the **Type Selector** drop-down list in the **Properties** palette. You can select any of the three options: **Room Tag**, **Room Tag With Area**, and **Room Tag With Volume** from the **Type-Selector** drop-down list. You can select the **Room Tag** option to display the inserted room with the tag only. Similarly, you can select the **Room Tag With Area** or **Room Tag With Volume** option from the **Type Selector** drop-down list to attach the room tag to the room to display the information regarding the area or volume of the room. After selecting the required option from the **Type Selector** drop-down list, choose the **Highlight Boundaries** tool from the **Room** panel of the **Modify | Place Room** tab; the **Autodesk Revit 2017** message box will be displayed, informing that the room bounding elements are highlighted in the drawing. Choose the **Close** button to close the message box.

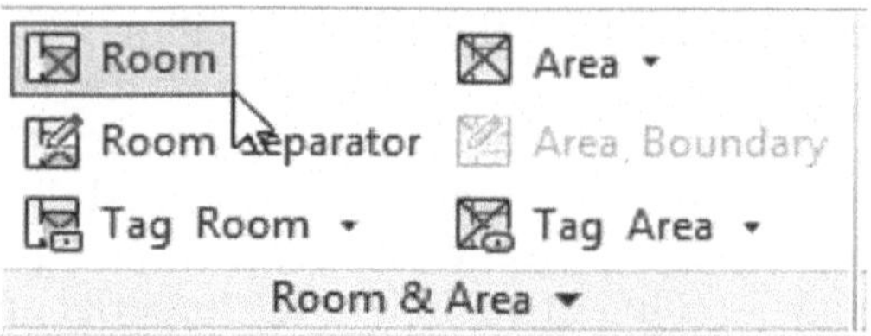

*Figure 3-46 Invoking the **Room** tool*

To add a room with a room tag, choose the **Tag on Placement** tool from the **Tag** panel. You can specify the level up to which the boundary of a room will extend vertically or in upward direction. To do so, select an option from the **Upper Limit** drop-down list in the **Options Bar**. For example, if you have added a room to the floor plan of **Level 1** and you desire to extend the room to **Level 2**, select the **Level 2** option from the **Upper Limit** drop-down list. You can extend the room boundary above the level specified in the **Upper Limit** drop-down list. To do so, click in the **Offset** edit box in the **Options Bar**. The default value displayed in this edit box is **10'** for Imperial or **3000mm** for Metric. You can enter a positive value to extend the room boundary above the level that you have selected from the **Upper Limit** drop-down list. Similarly, you can enter a negative value to extend the room boundary below the selected level. You can orient the room tag horizontally or vertically with reference to the current view, or align it with the walls and boundary lines present in the building model. To specify the orientation of the room tag, select an option from the drop-down list displayed next to the **Offset** edit box in the **Options Bar**. You can select the **Leader** check box to place the room tag with a leader.

To add a room, click in an area enclosed by the room bounding elements such as walls, as shown in Figure 3-47. The room will be added and the area of the room will be equal to the area enclosed by the walls.

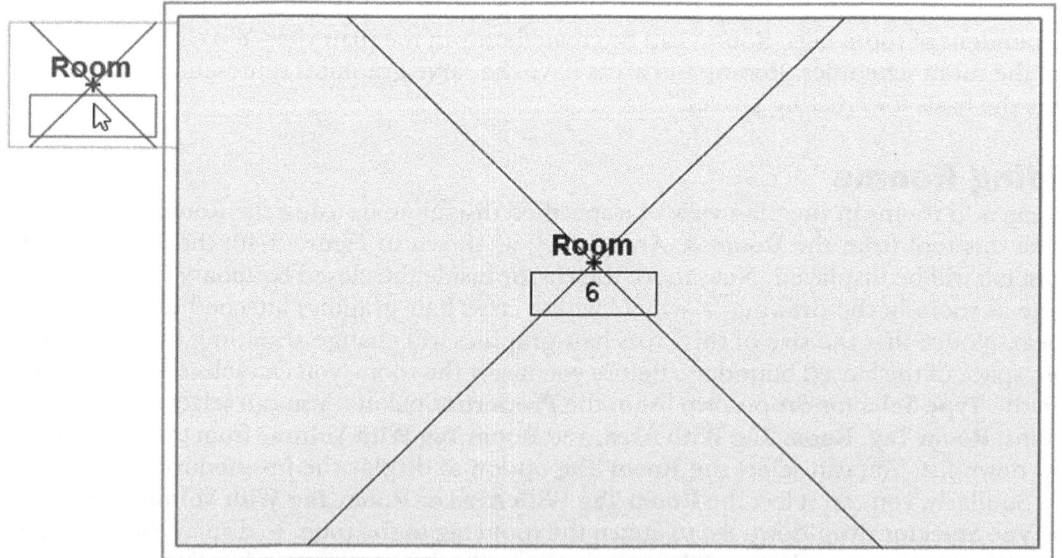

Figure 3-47 The graphical representation of the room

You can also add a room in a free space or in an area that is not enclosed completely, and then add walls or other room bounding elements to the room. In such an instance, the room will be created and the area of the room will be equal to the area enclosed by the walls added later. Figure 3-48 shows a room added to the area that is not enclosed and Figure 3-49 shows the room added after enclosing the area by adding a wall segment. On placing a room in a free space or in an area that is not enclosed, Revit will display a warning message that the room is not in a properly enclosed region.

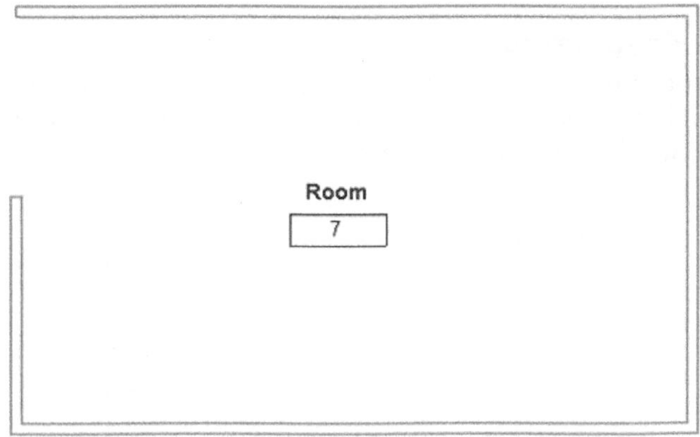

Figure 3-48 *Room added in an open boundary*

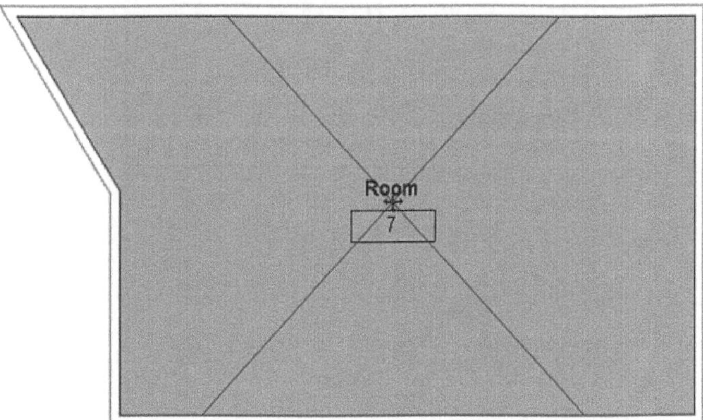

Figure 3-49 *Room created after adding the wall*

Creating Rooms from Room Schedules

Revit provides you with the flexibility to add rooms from the room schedules. You can add a new room in a room schedule and place the same room in the plan view. To do so, invoke the **Room** tool and select the room type from the **Room** drop-down list in the **Options Bar**. Next, select the room tag from the **Type Selector** drop-down list. The room types will be available in the **Room** drop-down list only when you have added rooms in a room schedule. After selecting the room type from the drop-down list, click in the drawing to place the room; the room will be added with a room tag in the drawing.

Note

If you do not select the room type from the ***Room*** *drop-down list in the* ***Options Bar****, a new room will be created and numbered after the last number of the room in the schedule.*

Room Bounding Elements

You can use different elements as room bounding elements. These elements define the boundary of the room and help in calculating the area and volume of the room. Walls, roofs, ceilings, curtain systems, floors, columns, and room separation lines can be used as room bounding elements. Revit calculates the area based on the area enclosed by room bounding elements and the room height.

Modifying Room Properties

You can modify the room properties by changing the values of the room parameters in the **Properties** palette. To do so, select the room and click when the crosshair graphics is displayed; the **Properties** palette will be displayed, as shown in Figure 3-50.

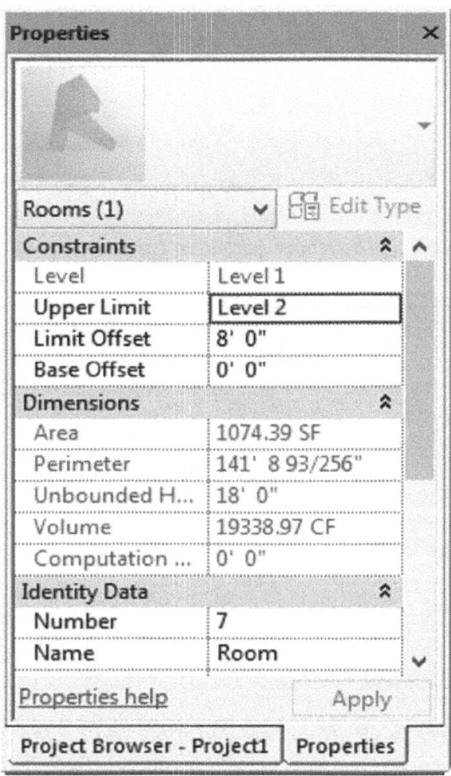

*Figure 3-50 The **Properties** palette displaying the properties of room*

Understanding Room Instance Parameters

The different instance parameters of a room are described in the table given next.

Instance Parameter	Value and Description
Level	Refers to the base level of the room. Level 1 is the default value.

Upper Limit	Refers to the upper boundary of the room. The specified level + the value defines the upper limit of the room. You can select the level from the **Level** drop-down list.
Limit Offset	Refers to the value specified to be added in the level to set the total height of the room. This parameter can also have negative value.
Area	Refers to the total area calculated using the room bounding elements.
Perimeter	Refers to the perimeter of the room.
Unbounded Height	Total height defined by the sum of the room base level, upper limit and the limit offset.
Volume	Refers to the total volume of the room. The volume is computed only when you select the **Areas and Volumes** radio button in the **Area and Volume Computations** dialog box.
Number	Refers to the room number assigned according to the number of rooms added.
Name	Refers to the room name. The default name is **Room**. You can assign any name to the room.
Comments	You can enter some specific comments or description about the room.
Occupancy	Refers to the type of occupancy for structure. You can specify occupancy as per the requirement. You can define any name for this parameter.
Base/Ceiling Finish	It is a user-defined parameter. In this parameter, you can define any type of finish for the base and the ceiling such as GWB.
Wall/Floor Finish	Refers to the finish for the walls of the room such as metal paints and coatings of the walls and tiles for the floor.
Occupant	Refers to the name of the occupant.
Phase	Refers to the name of the phase in which the room is created.

Calculating Room Volumes

To enable the room volume computations, choose the **Area and Volume Computations** tool from the **Room & Area** panel; the **Area and Volume Computations** dialog box will be displayed. In the **Volume Computations** area of the **Computations** tab, select the **Areas and Volumes** radio button. By default, the **Areas only** radio button is selected in the **Volume Computations** area. Next, choose the **OK** button; the volume computation of the room will be enabled and displayed in its instance properties. To view the computed volume of a room, select it from the drawing; the **Properties** palette will be displayed. In the **Properties** palette, the value in the value column of the **Volume** parameter shows the computed volume of the room.

Note

In Revit, the volume calculations of the room are done considering the finish face of the room-bounding element. When you select a room, the outline and the color fill display the exact periphery and the enclosed area used for calculating the volume of the room.

While computing the room volume, the room volume calculation engine of Autodesk Revit looks up and down from the measurement height to access the vertical limit of the room-bounding element. You can set the lower and upper limits of the room bounding elements using the **Properties** palette. The **Base Offset** parameter in the value column in this palette defines the limit of the lower boundary. It is used to limit the extent of the room with no floors or prevent floors to leak from floor openings while computing the volume of the room. The volume is also displayed in the drawing view if the rooms are added in the drawing view with the **Room Tag With Volume** option selected from the **Type Selector** drop-down list.

CUTTING OPENINGS IN A WALL, FLOOR, AND CEILING

In Autodesk Revit, you can create an opening in the wall, floor, structural floor, ceiling, and structural elements such as beams and braces. To do so, invoke any of the tools from the **Opening** panel of the **Architecture** tab, as shown in Figure 3-51. From this panel, you can choose any of these five options, **By Face**, **Wall**, **Vertical**, **Shaft**, or **Dormer** to create an opening. In Revit, to create openings, you need to change the **Discipline** parameter of view to **Architecture**.

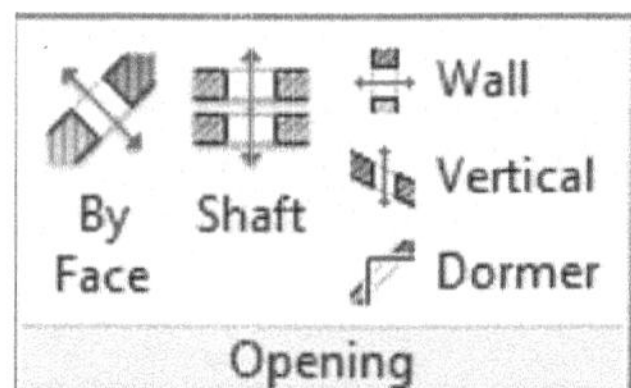

Figure 3-51 *The tools in the **Opening** panel*

Creating Openings Using the By Face Tool

You can use the **By Face** tool to create openings on the faces of floors, or ceilings in the building model. This tool is useful in a project when you need to cut an opening in a floor for stairway and in the ceiling for a chimney. To do so, invoke this tool from the **Opening** panel; you will be prompted to select a planar face of required floor, ceiling, beam, or column. Select the face on which you want to create the opening; the **Modify | Create Opening Boundary** tab will be displayed. In this tab, you can use various tools to sketch the opening in desired view. Now, open the required view and sketch the opening using the reference planes, as shown in Figure 3-52. After sketching the opening boundary on the selected face, choose the **Finish Edit Mode** button from the **Mode** panel to finish the sketch of the opening and then exit the **Modify | Create Opening Boundary** tab. Figure 3-53 shows the opening created perpendicular to the selected face.

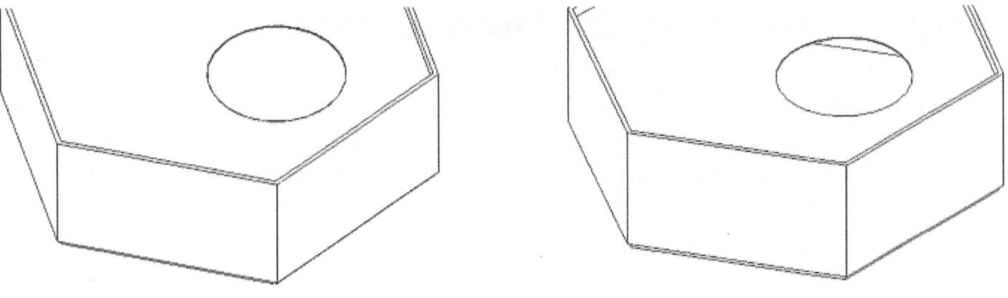

Figure 3-52 Sketching the opening in the ceiling plan using the reference planes

Figure 3-53 Opening created perpendicular to the selected face

Creating Openings Using the Vertical Tool

To cut a vertical opening, choose the **Vertical** tool from the **Opening** panel and select the required ceiling, or floor; the **Modify | Create Opening Boundary** tab will be displayed. You can use various tools from this tab to sketch the boundary of the opening. Sketch the opening in the appropriate view using the sketching tools. After sketching the opening boundary, choose the **Finish Edit Mode** button from the **Mode** panel; a vertical opening will be created in the selected element. You can use the sketching tools to draw a sketch of appropriate size, as shown in Figure 3-54. The opening can also be viewed in the 3D view, as shown in Figure 3-55.

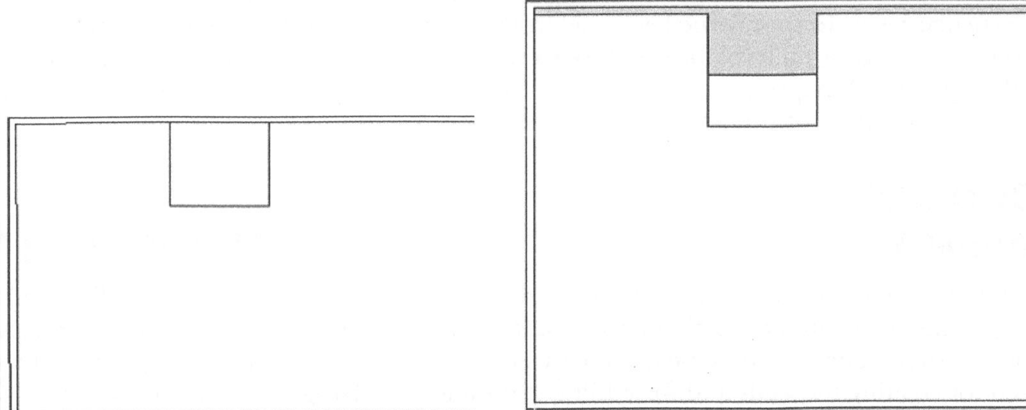

Figure 3-54 Sketching the opening in the ceiling plan view

Figure 3-55 3D view of the opening in ceiling

Creating Openings Using the Wall Tool

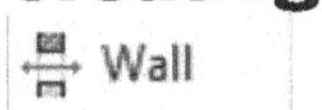

To create a rectangular opening in a wall, choose the **Wall** tool from the **Opening** panel in the **MEP** tab; you will be prompted to select a wall. Select the wall in which you want to cut an opening and then sketch a rectangular opening of the required size by clicking and dragging the cursor.

Creating Openings Using the Dormer Tool

To create a dormer opening in the dormer roof, choose the **Dormer** tool from the **Opening** panel; you will be prompted to select the roof in which you want to create a dormer opening. Select the roof; the screen will enter the sketch mode. Choose the **Pick Roof/ Wall Edges** tool from the **Pick** panel of the **Modify | Edit Sketch** tab and pick the boundary of the dormer to create the dormer opening. Next, choose the **Finish Edit Mode** button from the **Mode** panel; a dormer opening will be created.

Note

The boundary that you will pick for the dormer opening in a roof should be an edge of the selected roof, wall, or both, and should form a closed loop.

Creating Openings Using the Shaft Tool

To cut an opening up to the entire height of a building, choose the **Shaft** tool from the **Opening** panel; the **Modify | Create Shaft Opening Sketch** tab will be displayed. Choose a suitable sketching tool from this tab to create an opening of the required shape. Next, choose the **Finish Edit Mode** button from the **Mode** panel; the opening will be created passing through the entire height of the building. Make sure that before sketching the opening, you select the required work plane and the view to sketch the opening.

You can also specify the levels that will be cut by the opening. It will help you to restrict the opening to a particular level. To specify the levels, select the opening; the **Modify | Shaft Openings** tab will be displayed. Select a level for the **Base Constraint** parameter in the **Properties** palette to start the opening. Next, select a level for the **Top Constraint** parameter to end the opening. The opening will be cut through the selected levels.

TUTORIALS

Tutorial 1 — Office Building I

In this tutorial, you will create the exterior and interior walls, add grids, and modify levels in office building based on the sketch plan shown in Figure 3-56. The dimensions have been given only for reference and are not to be used in this tutorial. The project file and the parameters to be used for creating the walls and for adding grids and modifying levels are given next.

(Expected time: 30 min)

1. Project file-
   For Imperial *Systems Default*
   For Metric *Systems-Default_Metric*
2. Exterior Wall type-
   For Imperial **Generic- 9".**
   For Metric **Generic- 230mm.**
3. Interior Wall type-
   For Imperial **Generic - 5".**
   For Metric **Generic - 90mm.**
4. Location line parameter- **Wall Centerline**; Top Constraint- **Up to Level 2**.
5. Rename Level 1 as the Ground Floor
6. Grids to be created in the plan view.

7. File name to be assigned:

   For Imperial *c03_Office_BuildingI_tut1.rvt*
   For Metric *M_c03_Office_BuildingI_tut1.rvt*

   The following steps are required to complete this tutorial:

a. Open the required template file.
   For Imperial *Systems Default*
   For Metric *Systems-Default_Metric*
b. Invoke the **Wall: Architectural** tool from the ribbon.
c. Select the required exterior wall type from the **Properties** palette.
   For Imperial **Generic- 9"**
   For Metric **Generic- 230mm**
d. Select the required interior wall type from the **Properties** palette.
   For Imperial **Generic- 5"**
   For Metric **Generic- 90mm**
e. Modify Top Constraint- **Up to Level: Level 2** and Location Line - **Wall Centerline** as wall properties using the **Properties** palette, refer to Figure 3-57.
f. Invoke the **Rectangle** tool and then sketch the exterior walls based on the given parameters, refer to Figures 3-58 through 3-62.
g. Sketch the interior walls based on the given parameters, refer to Figures 3-63 through 3-69.
h. Modify levels by renaming them, refer to Figure 3-70.
i. Add grids using the **Grid** tool, refer to Figures 3-71 through 3-73.
j. Save and close the project.

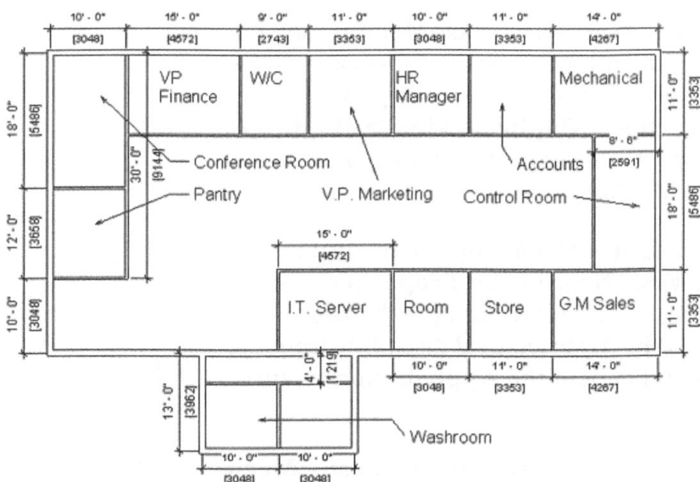

Figure 3-56 Sketch plan for creating exterior walls for the Office Building

Opening a New Project and Using the Template File

1. Choose **New > Project** from the **Application Menu**; the **New Project** dialog box is displayed.

2. In the **New Project** dialog box, choose the **Browse** button and then select the following template:

   For Imperial **Systems-Default**
   For Metric **Systems-Default_Metric**

Next, choose the **Open** button and then the **OK** button; the desired template file is loaded. Notice that the **Project Browser** now shows several views that are preloaded in the template file.

3. In the **Project Browser**, select **1-Mech** under the **Mechanical** head, if it is not selected by default and right-click to display a flyout. From this flyout, choose **Duplicate View > Duplicate; 1 - Mech Copy 1** is displayed under the **Mechanical** head.

4. Double click on **1 - Mech Copy 1** to display the corresponding view. Now, in the **Properties** palette, click on the value field corresponding to the **Discipline** parameter. Select the **Architectural** discipline from the drop-down list and choose the **Apply** button to apply the changes.

5. Now, the **Architectural** head is added under the **Views (Discipline)** in the **Project Browser** and under that head, **1 - Mech Copy 1** is displayed.

6. Select the **1 - Mech Copy 1** under the **Architectural Plan** head and right-click to display a flyout. From the flyout, choose the **Rename** option; the **Rename View** dialog box is displayed. Enter **Level 1** in the **Name** edit box and choose the **OK** button; the dialog box is closed and the view is renamed to **Level 1**.

7. Repeat the procedure followed in steps 3 through 6 to duplicate another level as **Level 2** from **Mechanical** head into **Architectural** head, as shown in Figure 3-57.

8. In the **Project Browser**, select **East-Mech** under the **Mechanical** head and **Elevations** sub-head of the **Mechanical** head and right-click to display a flyout. From this flyout, choose **Duplicate View > Duplicate; East - Mech Copy 1** is displayed under the **Elevations** sub-head in the **Mechanical** head.

9. Double-click on **East - Mech Copy 1** to display the corresponding view. Now, in the **Properties** palette, click on the value field corresponding to the **Discipline** parameter. Select the **Architectural** discipline from the drop-down list and choose the **Apply** button to apply the change.

10. Now, in the **Project Browser** window, **East - Mech Copy 1** is displayed under the **Views (Discipline) > Architectural > Elevations (Building Elevation)**.

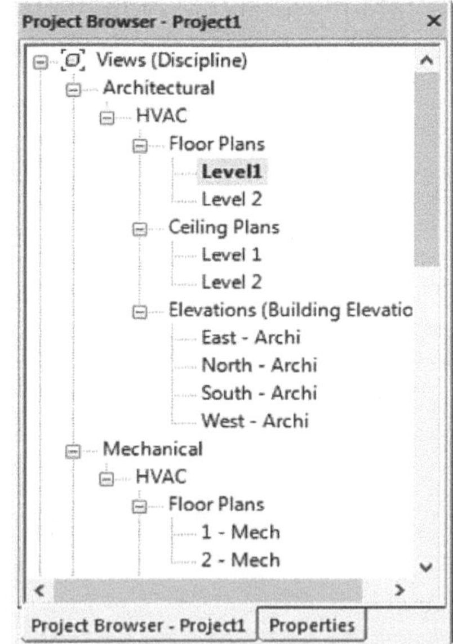

***Figure 3-57** The **Properties** Palette displaying other views under the **Elevations** sub-head*

11. Select **East - Mech Copy 1** under the **Architectural Plan** head and right-click to display a flyout. From the flyout, choose the **Rename** option; the **Rename View** dialog box is displayed. Enter **East - Archi** in the **Name** edit box and choose the **OK** button; the dialog box is closed and the view is renamed to **East - Archi**.

12. Repeat the procedure followed in steps 8 through 10 to add other views under the **Elevations** sub-head, refer to Figure 3-57.

Invoking the Wall: Architectural Tool and Selecting the Wall Type

In this section, you will sketch an architectural wall using the **Wall** tool.

1. Double-click on the **Level 1** view under the **Views (Discipline) > Architectural > HVAC > Floor Plans**; the corresponding view is displayed.

2. Invoke the **Wall: Architectural** tool from the **Architecture > Build > Wall** drop-down; the **Modify | Place Wall** tab is displayed.

3. In the **Type Selector** drop-down list of the **Properties** palette, select the **Generic - 8"** wall type for Imperial or **Generic - 200mm** wall type for Metric unit system.

4. In the **Properties** palette, choose the **Edit Type** button; the **Type Properties** dialog box is displayed.

5. Choose the **Duplicate** button from the upper right corner of this dialog box; the **Name** dialog box is displayed. Enter **Generic- 9"** for Imperial (**Generic- 230mm** for Metric system) in the **Name** edit box and then choose the **OK** button; the dialog box is closed and the **Generic - 9"** for Imperial system (**Generic - 230mm** for Metric system) is selected in the **Type** drop-down list.

6. Now, choose the **Edit** button from the value field corresponding to the **Structure** parameter; the **Edit Assembly** dialog box is displayed.

7. In the **Edit Assembly** dialog box, click on the value field of **Thickness** column corresponding to the **Structure[1]** function parameter. Enter **9"** for Imperial or enter **230mm** for Metric and then choose the **OK** button; the **Edit Assembly** dialog box is closed.

8. Now, choose **OK** button; the **Type Properties** dialog box is closed and the **Generic - 9"** wall type is selected in Imperial system or **Generic - 230mm** is selected in the **Type Selector** drop-down list.

Modifying the Properties of the Exterior Wall

After sketching the wall type, you need to modify the instance properties of the wall type using the **Properties** palette.

1. In the **Properties** palette, ensure that the **Location Line** parameter has **Wall Centerline** as the default value. Click in the value field of the **Top Constraint** instance parameter; a drop-down list is displayed. Select **Up to Level: Level 2** from the drop-down list displayed, as shown in Figure 3-58 and choose the **Apply** button.

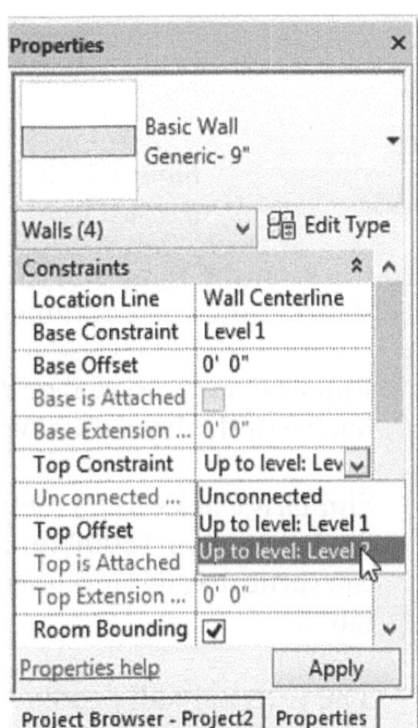

***Figure 3-58** Setting the **Top Constraint** parameter using the **Properties** palette*

Sketching the Exterior Wall Segment

In this section, you will sketch the exterior wall segment.

1. Invoke the **Rectangle** tool from the **Draw** panel of the **Modify | Place Wall** tab.
2. To specify the first point, click between the four elevation symbols in the drawing area. Next, move the cursor toward right to draw a rectangle. On doing so, a rectangle starts creating from a specified point. Now, click to specify the endpoint, as shown in Figure 3-59.

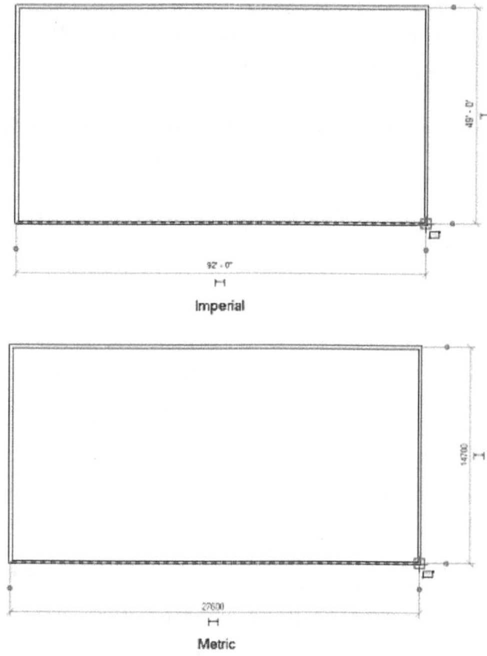

***Figure 3-59** The temporary dimensions being displayed on the sketched wall*

3. Click on the temporary dimension of the horizontal wall displayed; an edit box appears showing the current dimension of the wall segment.
4. Enter **80'** for Imperial or **24000 mm** for Metric in the edit box and then press ENTER; the length of the horizontal wall is modified to the entered value.
5. Similarly, click on the temporary dimension of vertical wall; an edit box appears. Enter **40'** for Imperial or **12000 mm** for Metric in the edit box and then press ENTER; the length of the vertical wall is modified to the entered value. Press ESC twice to exit the **Modify | Walls** tab.

The external wall profile is drawn with the specified dimensions, as shown in Figure 3-60.

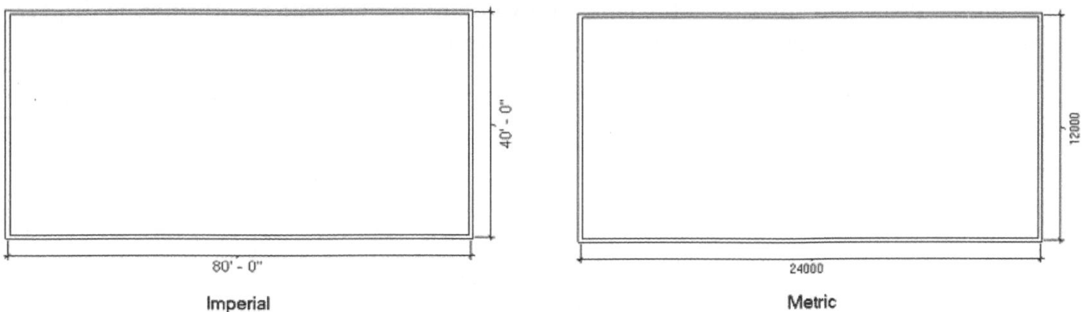

Figure 3-60 The completed exterior wall segment of Office Building

Sketching Other Exterior Wall Segments

In this section, you need to create other exterior wall segments.

1. Choose the **Wall: Architectural** tool from the **Architecture > Build > Wall** drop-down; the **Modify | Place Wall** tab is displayed.

2. Choose the **Line** tool from the **Draw** panel of the **Modify | Place Wall** tab. Ensure that the **Chain** check box is selected in the **Options Bar**. Now, place the cursor to the lower left corner of the wall and move toward right. When temporary dimension appears, enter **20'** for Imperial or enter **6000 mm** for Metric and then press ENTER.

3. Draw **13'0"** line in Imperial system or **3900 mm** line in Metric system from that point in downward direction, as shown in Figure 3-61.

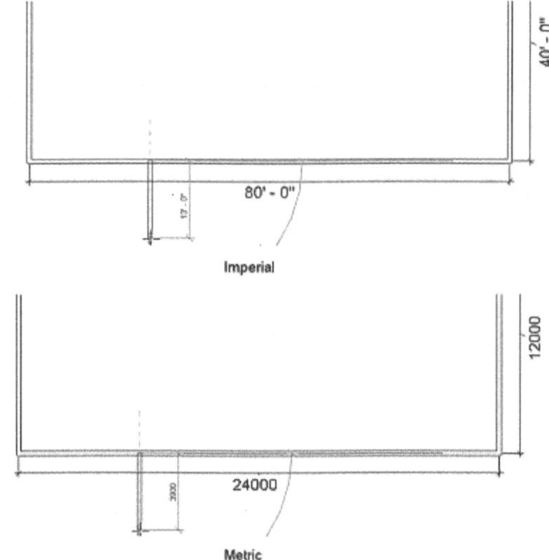

Figure 3-61 The other exterior wall segment created outside the Office Building

4. After drawing the line, the wall starts creating dynamically with one end attached to the specified point and the other end attached to the cursor. Move the cursor horizontally toward the right so that you see a dashed horizontal line inside the wall segment. Now, enter **20'0"**

for Imperial or **6000 mm** for Metric, as the value of the length; an edit box is displayed with the dimension you have entered, as shown in Figure 3-62.

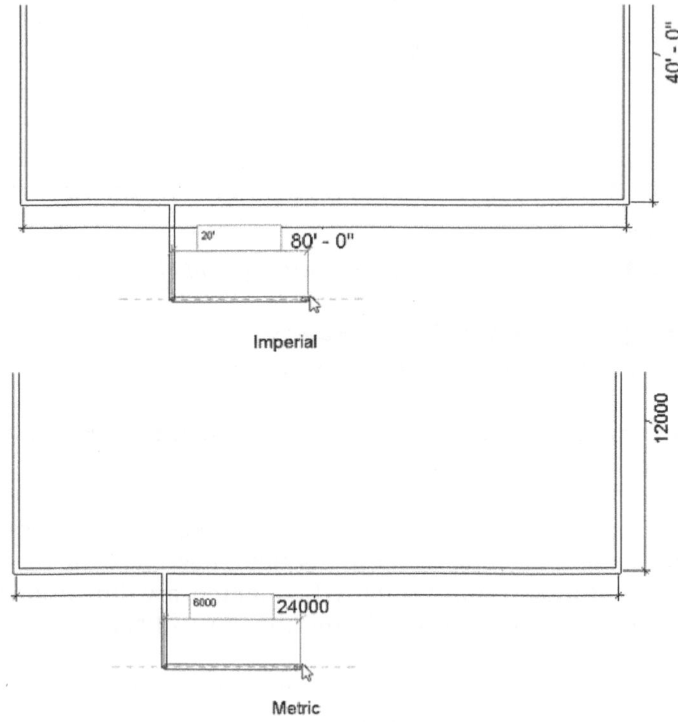

Figure 3-62 *Creating the second exterior wall segment*

5. To draw the third wall segment, move the cursor upward and enter **13'** for Imperial or enter **3900 mm** for Metric as the value of the length and press ENTER. The other exterior wall segments are created, as shown in Figure 3-63.

6. Now, press ESC or choose the **Modify** button to clear the selection.

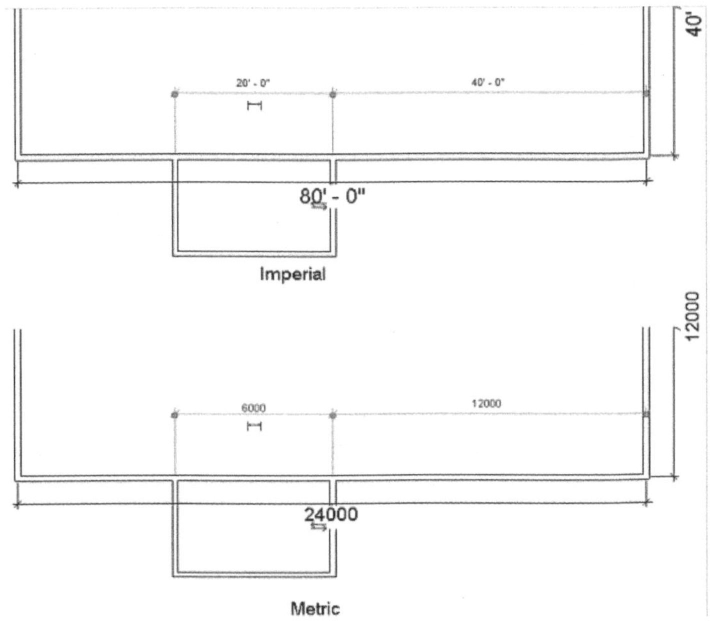

Figure 3-63 The completed exterior profile of Office Building

Selecting the Interior Wall Type

In this section, you will select the interior wall type.

1. Invoke the **Wall: Architectural** tool; the wall instance parameters are displayed in the **Properties** palette. In this palette, select the required wall type from the **Type Selector** drop-down list, as shown in Figure 3-64.

   For Imperial **BasicWall Generic - 5"**
   For Metric **BasicWall Generic - 90mm**

2. In the **Options Bar**, select the **Wall Centerline** option from the **Location Line** drop-down list, if it is not selected by default.

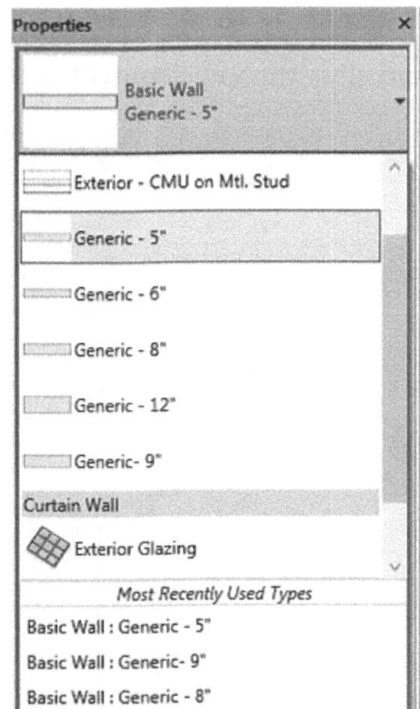

*Figure 3-64 Selecting the interior wall type from the **Type Selector** drop-down list*

Sketching Other Interior Walls

Next, you will sketch the other horizontal or vertical interior walls by specifying their start point and end point using different object snap options.

1. Move the cursor near the top left end of the wall and then start moving the cursor horizontally toward the right. Enter **10'0"** for Imperial or **3000 mm** for Metric when the temporary dimensions and the intersection object snap appear, as shown in Figure 3-65. Now, press ENTER; the starting point of the first interior wall is specified.

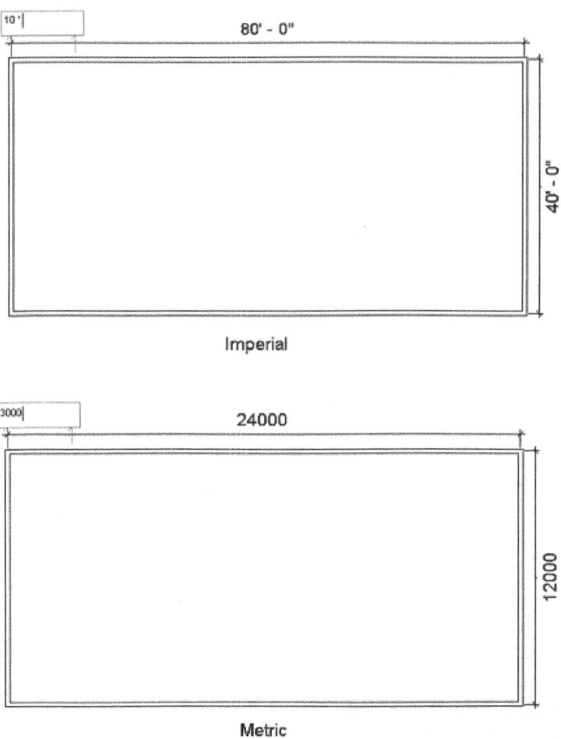

Figure 3-65 *Specifying the distance for starting the first interior wall segment*

2. Next, move the cursor vertically downward and enter **30'** for Imperial (**9000 mm** for Metric) and close the wall segment, as shown in Figure 3-66; the interior wall segment is sketched.

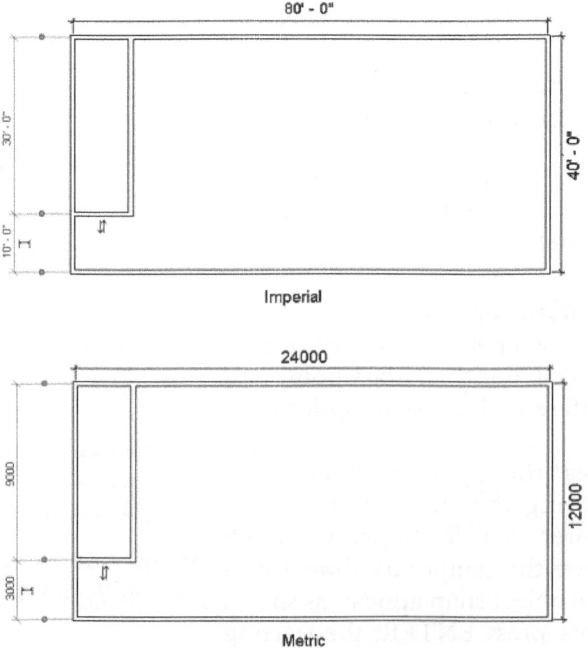

Figure 3-66 *Specifying the first interior wall segment*

3. To sketch the second interior wall, move the cursor to the upper endpoint of the interior wall you just created and then move the cursor vertically downward. Enter 11'0" for Imperial or 3300 mm for Metric when the temporary dimension and the intersection object snap appears as shown in Figure 3-67.

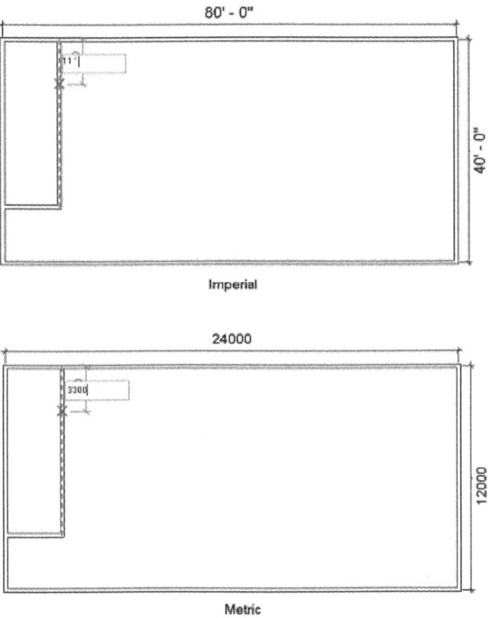

Figure 3-67 *Specifying the starting point of second interior wall segment*

4. Press SHIFT and move the cursor toward the right near the right exterior wall segment. Now, click to specify the location of the endpoint of the wall segment; the second interior wall segment is sketched, as shown in Figure 3-68.

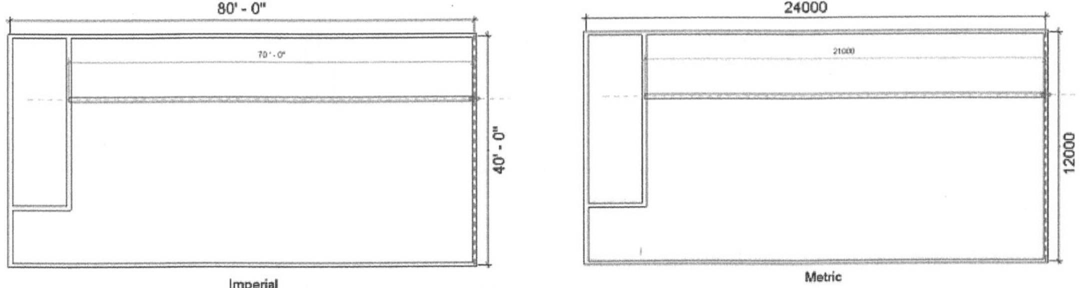

Figure 3-68 *Sketching the second interior wall*

5. To sketch the third interior wall, place the cursor toward the lower right corner of the wall segment and move the cursor upward. Enter **11'0"** for Imperial or **3300** mm for Metric and then press ENTER, as shown in Figure 3-69; the starting point of the interior wall is specified.

6. Next, move the cursor in the horizontal direction toward the left. Enter **50'0"** for Imperial and **15000** for Metric and then press ENTER, as shown in Figure 3-70. Ensure that the

Chain option is selected. Now, move the cursor vertically downward near the lower exterior wall segment; the interior wall segment is sketched, as shown in Figure 3-71.

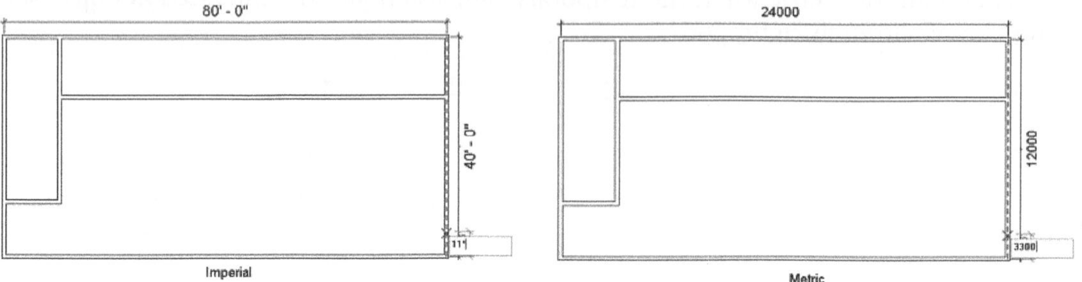

Figure 3-69 *Specifying the distance for starting the first interior wall segment*

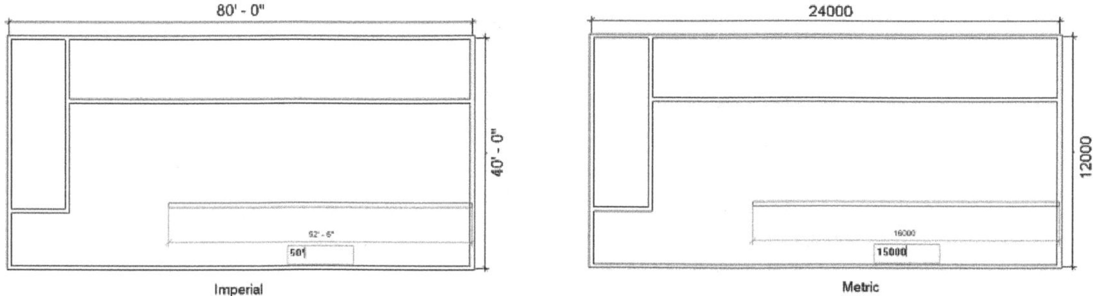

Figure 3-70 *Specifying the distance for starting the interior wall segment*

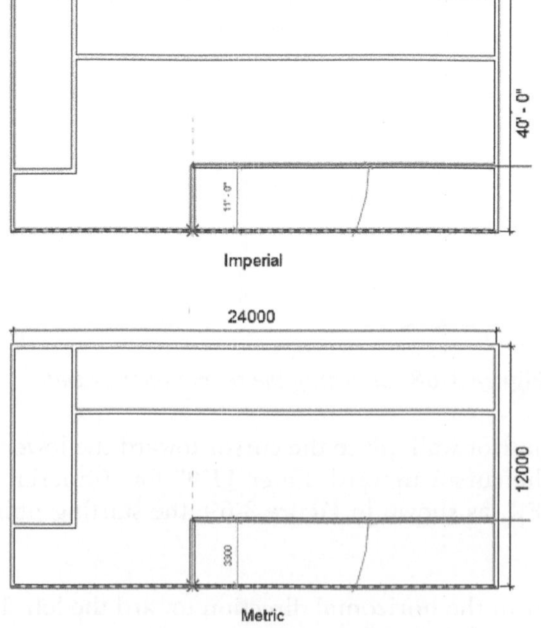

Figure 3-71 *Sketched wall segment*

7. Similarly, you can draw other interior walls by using the **Line** tool, refer to Figure 3-72.

8. Choose the **Modify** button to exit the tool.

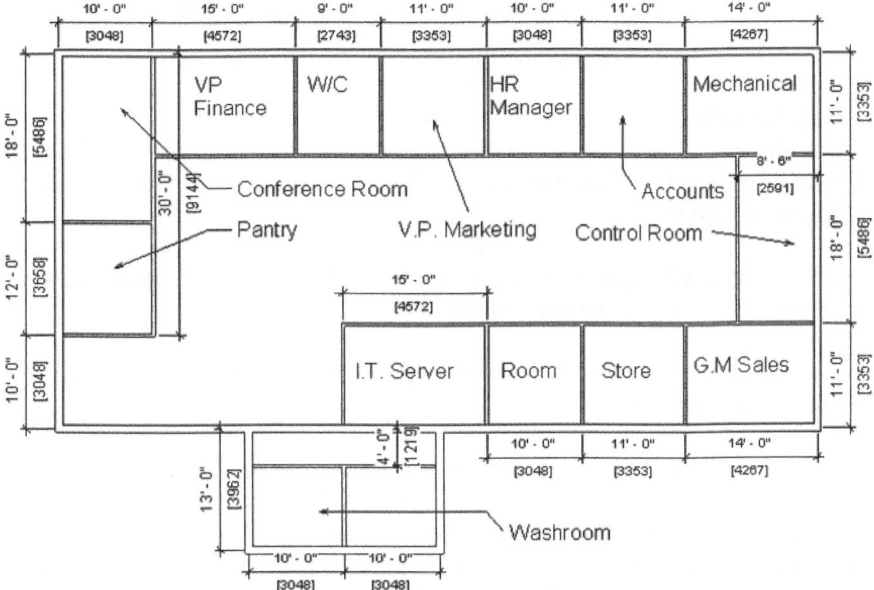

Figure 3-72 Layout of internal walls for Office Building

Modifying Levels

In this section, you will invoke the **Level** tool in the elevation view.

1. In the **Project Browser**, double-click on the **North - Archi** under the **Elevations (Building Elevation)** head; the north elevation is displayed within the existing levels in the drawing window.

2. Choose the **Zoom in Region** tool from the Navigation Bar to enlarge the right portion of the elevation showing the levels, refer to Figure 3-73.

3. To rename the levels, move the cursor over **Level 1** in the **Project Browser** and right-click; a shortcut menu is displayed.

4. Choose the **Rename** option from the shortcut menu; the **Rename View** dialog box is displayed.

5. In this dialog box, enter **Ground Floor** in the **Name** edit box and choose the **OK** button; you are prompted to verify whether you want to rename the corresponding levels and views.

6. Choose the **Yes** button to rename the level and views. The level is immediately renamed in the elevation view.

7. Similarly, rename the **Level 2** as **Roof** , as shown in Figure 3-73.

Figure 3-73 Renamed levels and views for the Office Building

Creating Grid Lines

You can use the plan view to add grids to the project using the **Grid** tool. Grids are automatically numbered as they are created. Now, you will create Grids in the sequence as shown in the sketch plan.

1. Double-click on **Ground Floor** from the **Floor Plans** head in the **Project Browser** to display the ground floor plan in the drawing window.

2. Next, choose the **Grid** tool from the **Datum** panel of the **Architecture** tab; the **Modify | Place Grid** tab is displayed.

3. Now, ensure that the **Line** tool is chosen in the **Draw** panel.

4. Move the cursor near the top left corner of the exterior wall profile and keep it moving till a vertical extension line is displayed. Click to specify the start point of the grid line when the temporary dimension of **3'0"** for Imperial or **900 mm** for metric is displayed from the centerline of the exterior wall, as shown in Figure 3-74.

5. Move the cursor vertically downward and click outside the south wall to specify the endpoint of the grid line, as shown in Figure 3-75.

Note

*If grid lines are not visible in the drawing, choose the **Visibility/Graphics** tool from the **Graphics** panel of the **View** tab to display the **Visibility/Graphic Overrides for Floor Plan** dialog box. In the **Annotation Categories** tab of this dialog box, select the **Grids** check box; the grid lines will become visible.*

The same procedure can be followed to draw grid lines for the interior walls. As the thickness of the interior wall is 5" or 90 mm, you can specify 2 1/2" or 64 mm as the offset distance to draw grid lines for the interior walls.

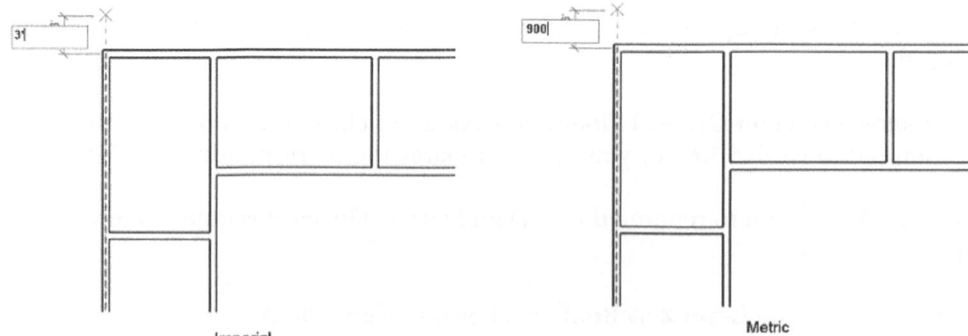

Figure 3-74 Specifying the start point of the grid line

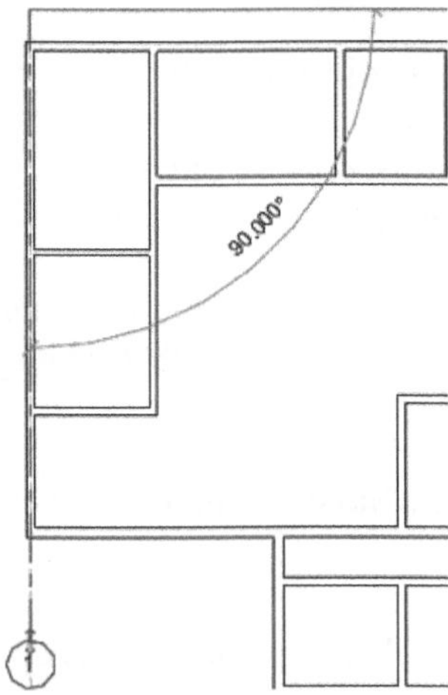

Figure 3-75 *Specifying the grid line drawn at first point*

6. Repeat steps 3, 4, and 5 to create other vertical and horizontal grid lines in the sequence of their numbers using the alignment line feature. After adding grid lines, press ESC twice to exit. Figure 3-76 shows the floor plan after adding grid lines.

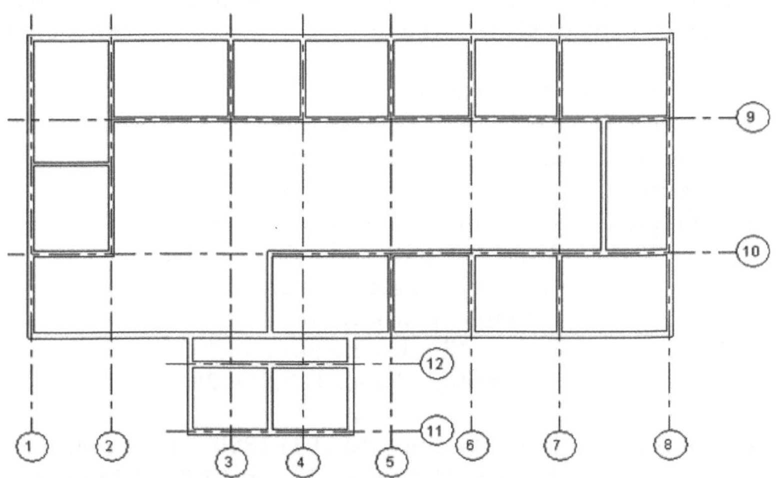

Figure 3-76 *The horizontal and vertical grid lines created for wall centerline*

Note

You can rename a grid by selecting it from the drawing and then entering a value corresponding to the value column for the ***Name*** *parameter in the* ***Properties*** *palette. The entered value will be the new name of the grid.*

This completes the tutorial for creating walls, adding grids, and modifying levels of the building envelope project.

Saving the Project

In this section, you need to save the project and the settings using the **Save As** tool.

1. To save the project with the settings, choose **Save As > Project** from the **Application Menu**; the **Save As** dialog box is displayed.

2. In this dialog box, browse to *C:\rmp_2017\c03_rmp_2017_tut* and then enter **c03_Office_BuildingI_tut1** for Imperial or **M_c03_Office_BuildingI_tut1** for Metric in the **File Name** edit box.

3. Now, choose the **Save** button; the **Save As** dialog box closes and the project file is saved.

Closing the Project

1. To close the project, choose the **Close** option from **Application Menu.**

Tutorial 2 Office Building II

In this tutorial, you will add doors and windows and also add a floor and a ceiling to the *c03_Office_BuildingI_tut1.rvt* project file for Imperial or *M_c03_Office_BuildingI_tut1.rvt* project file for Metric created in Tutorial 1 of Chapter 3. Refer to Figure 3-77 for adding these elements. The dimensions and the text have been given for reference and are not to be added. The project file name and parameters to be used are given next. **(Expected time: 30 min)**

1. Project File created in Tutorial 1 of Chapter 3.
   For Imperial *c03_Office_BuildingI_tut1.rvt*
   For Metric *M_c03_Office_BuildingI_tut1.rvt*
2. Door types to be used
   For Imperial
   1- **Double - Panel 1: 72" x 78"**
   2 and 3- **Single - Flush: 30" x 84"**
   4,5 and 6 **Single - Flush Vision: 36" x 84"**
   7- **Single- Glass 1: 36" x 84"**
   8 to 16- **Single - Decorative 2: 36" x 84"**
   17- **Double - Panel 1: 72" x 78"**

   For Metric
   1- **M_Double - Panel 1: 1830 x 1981 mm**
   2 and 3- **M_Single - Flush: 0762 x 2134 mm**
   4,5 and 6 **M_Single - Flush Vision: 0915 x 2134 mm**
   7- **M_Single- Glass 1: 0915 x 2134 mm**
   8 to 16- **M_Single - Decorative 2: 0915 x 2134 mm**
   17- **M_Double - Panel 1: 1830 x 1981 mm**
3. Window types to be used
   For Imperial
   Fixed- **24" x 48"**
   Fixed- **60" x 48"** (with modified width)

   For Metric
   M_Fixed- **0610 x 1220 mm**
   M_Fixed- **1524 x 1220 mm** (with modified width)

4. Floor type:
   For Imperial **Generic 12"**, Extents- to wall core.
   For Metric **Generic 300 mm**, Extents- to wall core.
5. Ceiling type:
   For Imperial **Generic**, Level- 8'6" from the floor level.
   For Metric **Generic**, Level- 2590 mm from the floor level.
6. File name to be assigned:
   For Imperial *c03_Office_BuildingII_tut2.rvt*
   For Metric *M_c03_Office_BuildingII_tut2.rvt*

The following steps are required to complete this tutorial:

a. Open the required file and hide the annotation tag such as grids.
   For Imperial *c03_Building-EnvelopeI_tut1.rvt file*
   For Metric *M_c03_Building-EnvelopeI_tut1.rvt file*
b. Add doors by invoking the **Door** tool and selecting the type of door from the **Type Selector** drop-down list, refer to Figures 3-78 through 3-81.
c. Invoke the **Window** tool. Select the window type by using the **Type Selector** drop-down list.
d. Place the windows, as shown in Figure 3-77.
e. Place the windows at the exact location as per the given dimensions, refer to Figures 3-82 through 3-86.
f. Create the floor using the **Floor** tool, refer to Figures 3-88 through 3-90.
g. Create the ceiling using the **Ceiling** tool.

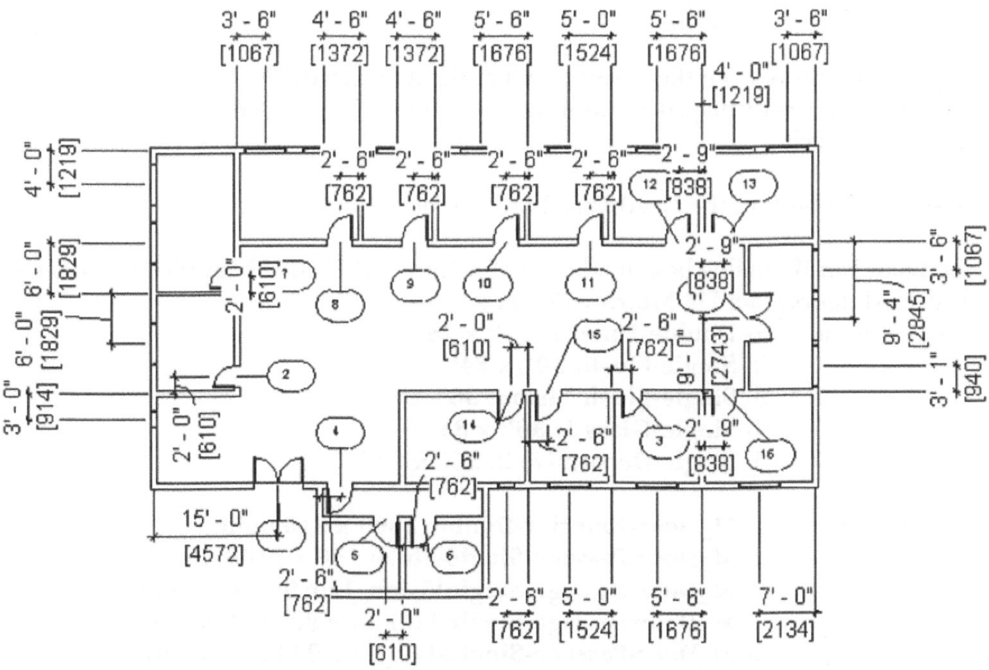

Figure 3-77 *Sketch for adding doors and windows to the Office Building project*

Opening the Existing Project and Hiding Annotation Tags

In this section, you will open the specified project and then hide the annotation symbols and tags such as grids using the **Visibility/Graphics** tool.

1. Choose **Open > Project** from **Application Menu** and open the *c03_Office_BuildingI_tut1.rvt* project file for Imperial or *M_c03_Office_BuildingI_tut1.rvt* for Metric created in Tutorial 1 of Chapter 3. You can also download this file from *http://www.cadcim.com*. The path of the file is as follows: *Textbooks > Civil/GIS > Revit MEP > Exploring Autodesk Revit 2017 for MEP*.

2. Now, to hide the annotation symbols and tags such as grids, choose the **Visibility/Graphics** tool from the **Graphics** panel of the **View** tab; the **Visibility/Graphics Overrides for Floor Plan: Ground Floor** dialog box is displayed.

3. Choose the **Annotation Categories** tab from this dialog box, and clear the check box corresponding to the **Grids** under the **Visibility** column.

4. Now, choose the **Apply** button and then the **OK** button; the **Visibility/Graphics Overrides for Floor Plan: Ground Floor** dialog box is closed and the specified settings are applied to the plan view of the Ground Floor.

Adding Doors

In this section, you need to add doors at an approximate location and then modify their location by specifying the exact dimension. You will use the **Load Family** tool to load the desired door type in the project.

1. Invoke the **Door** tool from the **Build** panel of the **Architecture** tab. Alternatively, type **DR**; the **Revit** window is displayed prompting you to load the door family, as no door family is loaded in the Revit.

2. Choose the **Yes** button; the **Load Family** dialog box is displayed.

3. In the **Load Family** dialog box, load doors for Imperial from **US Imperial>Doors** and for Metric, load doors from **US Metric>Doors :**

   For Imperial
   1- **Double-Panel 1: 72" x 78"**
   2- **Single-Flush: 30" x 84"**
   3- **Single-Flush Vision: 36" x 84"**
   4- **Single-Glass 1: 36" x 84"**
   5- **Single-Decorative 2: 36" x 84"**

   For Metric
   1- **M_Door-Exterior-Double 1800 x 2100mm**
   2- **M_Door-Passage-Single-Flush 750 x 2100mm**
   3- **M_Door-Passage-SingleVision_Lite 900 x 2100mm**
   4- **M_Door-Passage-Single-Full_Lite 900 x 2100mm**
   5- **M_Door-Passage-Single-Two_Lite 900 x 2100mm**

4. On invoking the **Door** tool, the properties of the door to be added are displayed in the **Properties** palette. In the palette, select the desired type of door from the **Type Selector** drop-down list.
   For Imperial **Single-Flush: 30" x 84"**
   For Metric **M_Door-Passage-Single-Flush 750 x 2100mm**

5. Before placing the door, ensure that the **Tag on Placement** tool is not selected in the **Tag** panel of the **Modify | Place Door** tab.

6. Move the cursor close to the interior wall of the pantry area to display the door symbol, as shown in Figure 3-78. Notice that as you move the cursor, the side of the door is changed. Click on the interior wall; the door is created at the specified location along with a tag on it.

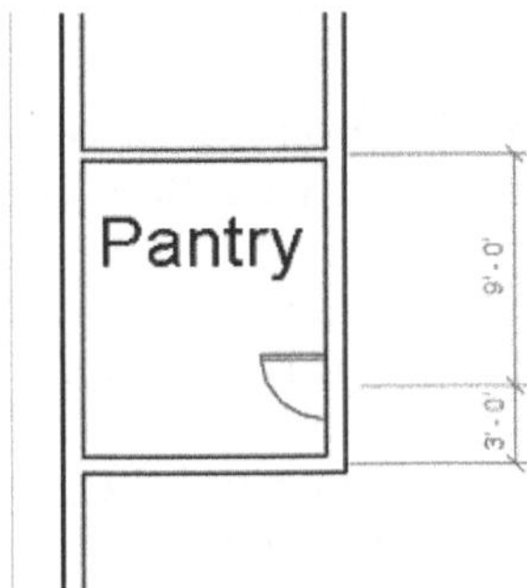

Figure 3-78 *Specifying the location of the pantry door*

7. To move the door to the exact location, choose the **Modify** button in the **Select** panel of the **Modify | Place Door** tab and select the door added in the drawing; the selected door gets highlighted in blue and the controls and the related temporary dimensions are displayed in it.

8. Since the location of the door is given with reference to the side interior wall, click on the lower temporary dimension, and then enter **2'0"** for Imperial or **600 mm** for Metric, as shown in Figure 3-79. Next, press ENTER; the door moves to the specified location.

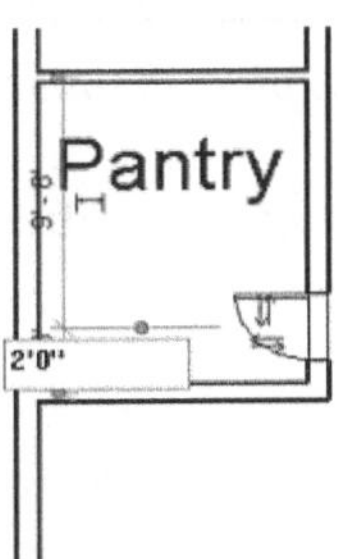

Figure 3-79 *Moving the door to the exact location*

9. Choose the **Modify** button from the **Select** panel and then select the door inserted in the drawing; the door gets highlighted and its controls are displayed. Next, flip the door swing, as shown in Figure 3-80.

Figure 3-80 *Flipping the door*

10. To place the door type at the entrance, invoke the **Door** tool from the **Build** panel; the **Modify | Place Door** tab is displayed.

11. In the **Type Selector** drop-down list, select the desired door type, as specified in the project parameters.

For Imperial	**Double - Panel 1: 72" x 78"**
For Metric	**Double - Panel 1 : 1830 x 1981 mm**

12. Move the cursor near the exterior wall side near to the washroom, as shown in Figure 3-81, and click to add the entrance door close to this location.

13. Choose the **Modify** button and select the door and then click on the right side dimension to set it to **5'0"** for Imperial or **1500 mm** for Metric, as specified in Figure 3-81.

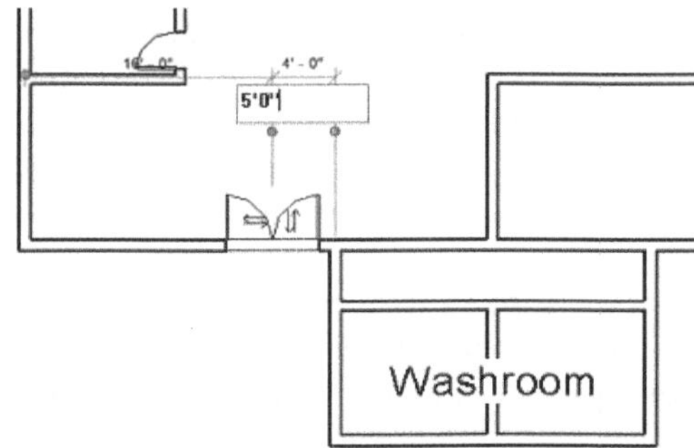

Figure 3-81 *Using the dimension to place the door at the exact location*

14. Add the other types of door in other areas at a specified distance from the internal wall, refer to Figure 3-77.

Tip

Doors and door openings can also be added in 3D view, sections, and elevations. However, you need to choose the appropriate view to place the door. You can use the temporary dimensions to place the door at the exact location. In case, if the door is not placed correctly, Autodesk Revit displays a message to alert you about the conflict and prompts you to take an appropriate action.

Adding Windows

In this section, you will add windows to the building envelope project.

1. Invoke the **Window** tool from the **Build** panel of the **Architecture** tab; Revit window is displayed prompting you to load a family as no window family is loaded. Choose the **Yes** button; the **Load Family** dialog box is displayed.

2. In the **Load Family** dialog box, select the **Fixed** family type from the **Windows** folder of the **US Imperial** folder or **M_Fixed** for Metric from the **US Metric** folder. Next, choose the **Open** button; the dialog box is closed.

3. Click on the **Type Selector** drop-down list to view the in-built window types. To create the window number 1, select the desired window type from the drop-down list.
   For Imperial **Fixed 24" x 48"**
   For Metric **Fixed 0610 x 1220 mm**

4. Move the cursor close to the exterior wall of the reception to display the window symbol, as shown in Figure 3-82. Add the window by clicking on the inner face of the exterior wall; the window is created at the specified location.

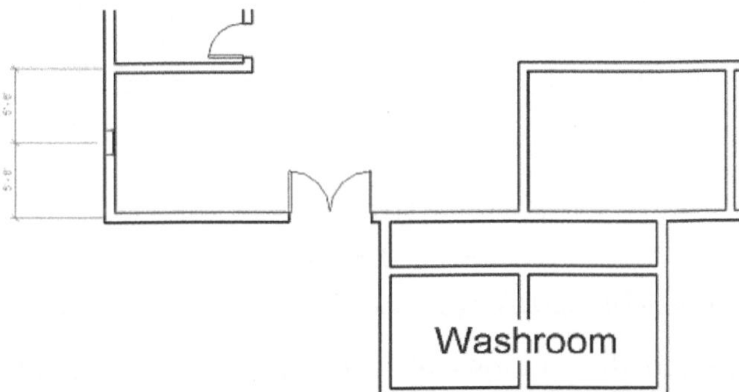

Figure 3-82 *Adding the window at the Reception area*

5. To move the window to the exact location, choose the **Modify** button from the **Select** panel and then select the window from the drawing; it gets highlighted in blue and its controls are displayed.

6. Click on the upper temporary dimension and enter **3'0"** for Imperial or **900 mm** for Metric, as shown in Figure 3-83. Press ENTER; the window is moved to the specified location. Similarly, add other windows of the same type near the internal wall of the I.T. Server room (mentioned in Tutorial 1) by invoking the **Window** tool from the **Build** panel, refer to Figure 3-77.

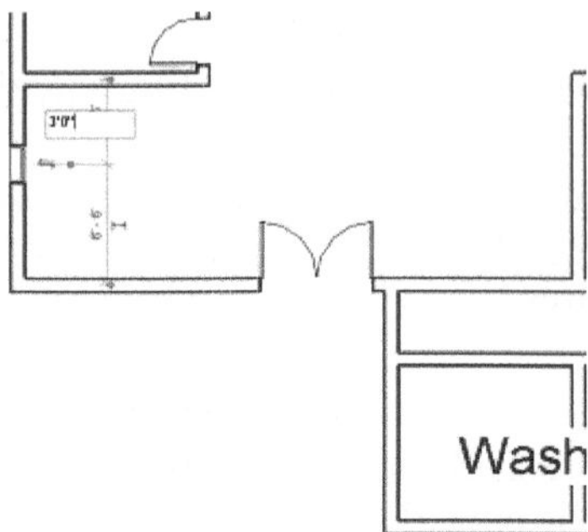

Figure 3-83 Specifying the exact location of the window

7. After adding the window in internal wall of the IT Server room, you need to move it to the exact location. To do so, select the window; it is highlighted in blue. Click on the left temporary dimension; an edit box is displayed. Enter **2'0"** for Imperial or **600 mm** for Metric in the edit box, as shown in Figure 3-84, and then press ENTER; the window is moved to the desired location. Press ESC and exit.

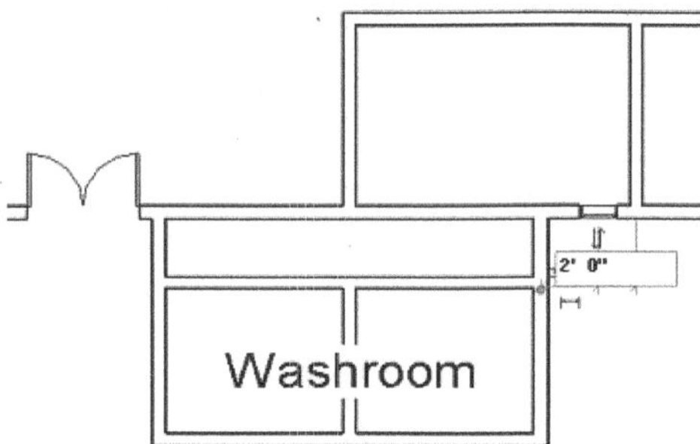

Figure 3-84 Specifying the location of the IT Server window

Now, you need to add the windows of type 2 in the drawing. These windows have a modified width of 5'0" in Imperial or 1500 mm for Metric. To add these windows, select the **Fixed: 24" x 48"** window type in Imperial system, **Fixed: 0610 x 1220 mm** window type in Metric system and then create its duplicate. Modify its width to 5'0" for Imperial or 1500 mm for Metric by using the **Type Properties** dialog box and add the window at the desired location.

8. Invoke the **Window** tool from the **Build** panel of the **Architecture** tab; the **Modify | Place Window** tab is displayed.

9. In the **Type Selector** drop-down list, select the **Fixed: 24" x 48"** window type for Imperial or **Fixed: 0610 x 1220 mm** window type for Metric. Next, choose the **Edit Type** button in the **Properties** palette; the **Type Properties** dialog box is displayed.

10. In this dialog box, choose the **Duplicate** button; the **Name** dialog box is displayed. In the **Name** edit box, enter **60" x 48"** for Imperial or enter **1524 x 1220 mm** for Metric and then choose the **OK** button.

11. In the **Value** field for the **Width** type parameter, enter **5'0"** for Imperial or **1524mm** for Metric and then choose the **Apply** and **OK** buttons to close the **Type Properties** dialog box and return to the drawing window.

    Notice that the **Fixed: 60" x 48"** window type in Imperial or **Fixed: 1524 x 1220 mm** window type in Metric is added in the **Type Selector** drop-down list.

12. Move the cursor near the exterior wall of the pantry and click to place the window, as shown in Figure 3-85. Press ESC twice to exit.

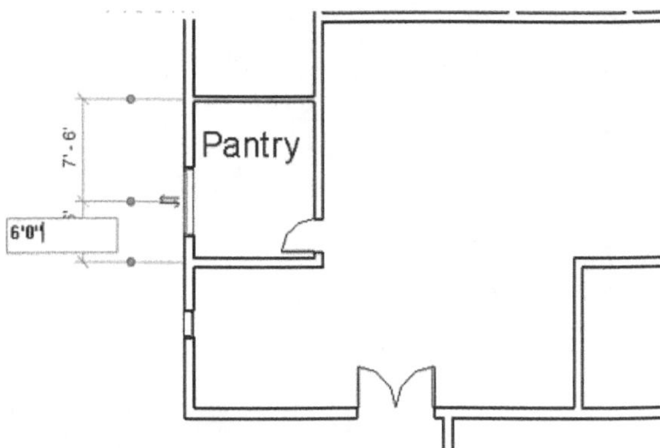

Figure 3-85 *Specifying the location of the bedroom window*

13. Now, select the added pantry window; the window gets highlighted in blue color and its controls are displayed. Click on the temporary dimension displayed at the bottom and enter **6'0"** for Imperial or **1800 mm** for Metric to specify the location of the pantry window, refer to Figure 3-85; the window is moved to the desired location. Similarly, add the windows of the same type to the walls of the other rooms and specify their respective locations based on the given sketch plan, refer to Figures 3-86.

    This completes the tutorial of adding doors and windows to the *Building Envelope II* project. The Level 1 plan should look similar to the plan shown in Figure 3-86.

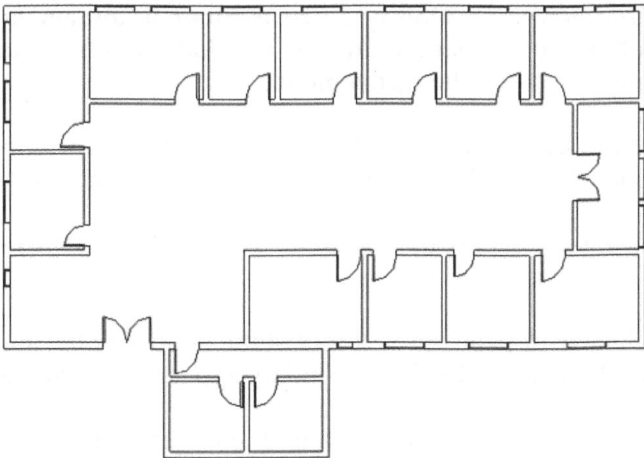

Figure 3-86 *Complete project plan with doors and windows*

Note

You can place doors and windows at nearby position, refer to Figure 3-86.

14. To view the plan in 3D, choose the **Default 3D View** tool from **View > Create > 3D View** drop-down; the 3D view of the project is displayed, as shown in Figure 3-87.

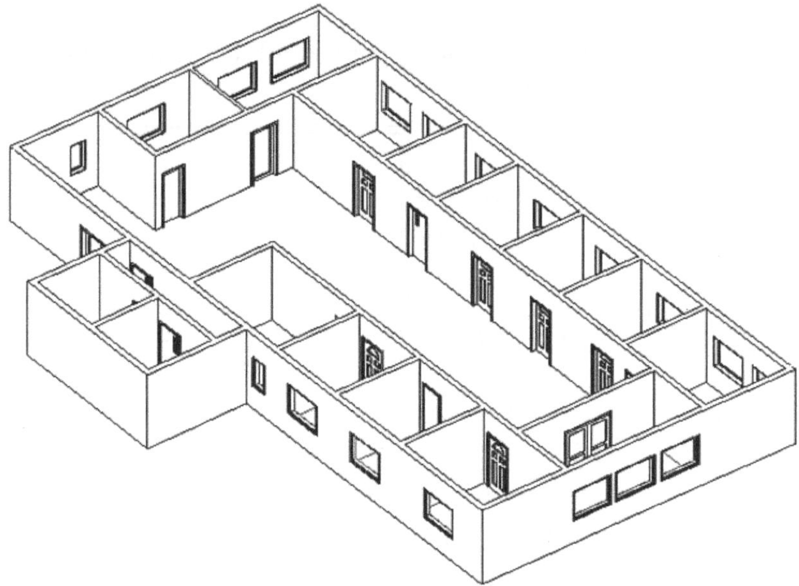

Figure 3-87 *3D view of the project*

Creating the Floor

In this section, you will add floor to the building using the **Floor** tool.

1. Double-click on the **Ground Floor** under the **Floor Plans** head; the corresponding view is displayed.

2. To add a floor to the building, choose the **Floor: Architectural** tool from **Architecture > Build > Floor** drop-down; the **Modify | Create Floor Boundary** tab is displayed along with the **Options Bar**. Notice that the drawing area fades when you invoke the **Floor** tool, which indicates that you are in the sketch mode.

3. In the **Options Bar**, select the **Extend into wall (to core)** check box, if it is not selected. Also, notice that the **Pick Walls** tool is chosen by default in the **Draw** panel.

4. Move the cursor near the center of the north wall of the building plan; the wall is highlighted. Now, click to draw the line.

5. Similarly, move the cursor near the west wall of the building plan and click when the wall is highlighted. On doing so, a sketched boundary appears in magenta color.

6. Repeat the procedure followed in steps 3 and 4 and sketch the boundary of the floor on other walls, as shown in Figure 3-88.

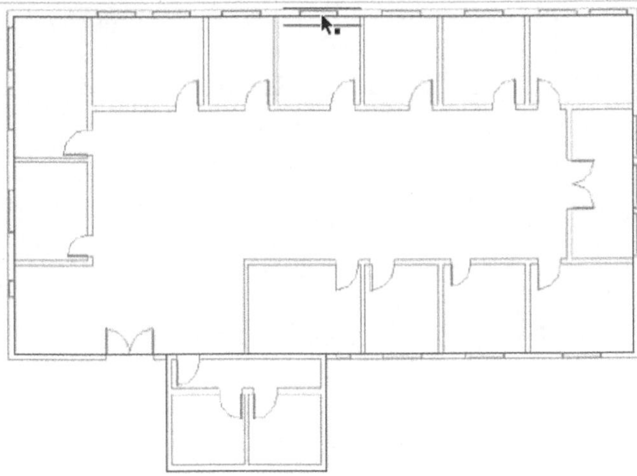

Figure 3-88 The floor boundary sketched using the ***Pick Walls*** *tool*

7. After sketching, you will notice that the floor boundary intersects at the interior wall of washroom. To separate the floor boundary, choose the **Split Element** tool from the **Modify** panel of the **Modify | Create Floor Boundary** tab.

8. Now, split the boundary at the corners where line intersects and then select the split element and press DELETE.

9. Next, choose the **Finish Edit Mode** button from the **Mode** panel to complete the sketching of the floor.

10. By default, **Floor : Generic 12”** option for Imperial (**Floor : Generic 300mm** for Metric) from the **Type Selector** drop-down list in the **Properties** palette is selected, as shown in Figure 3-89.

11. Choose the **Modify** button from the **Select** panel of the **Modify | Floor** tab to exit the **Floor: Architectural** tool. The floor is created for the project, as shown in Figure 3-90.

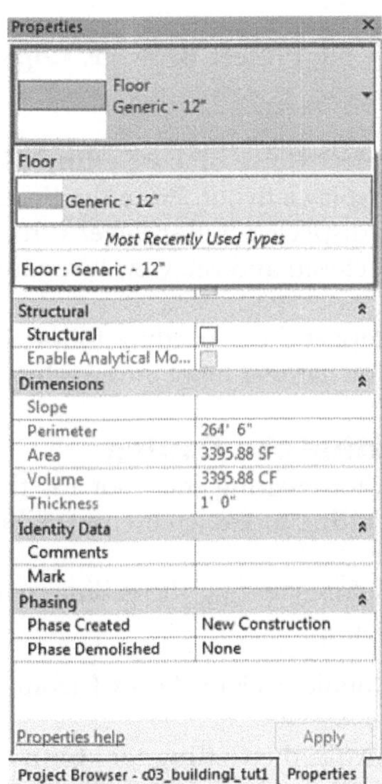

Figure 3-89 Selecting the ***Generic 12”*** *floor type*

Creating the Ceiling Head under Architectural Head

1. In the **Project Browser**, select **1-Ceiling Mech** under the **Mechanical** head and right-click to display a flyout. From this flyout, choose **Duplicate Views > Duplicate**; the **Copy of 1 - Ceiling Mech** option is displayed under the **Mechanical** head.

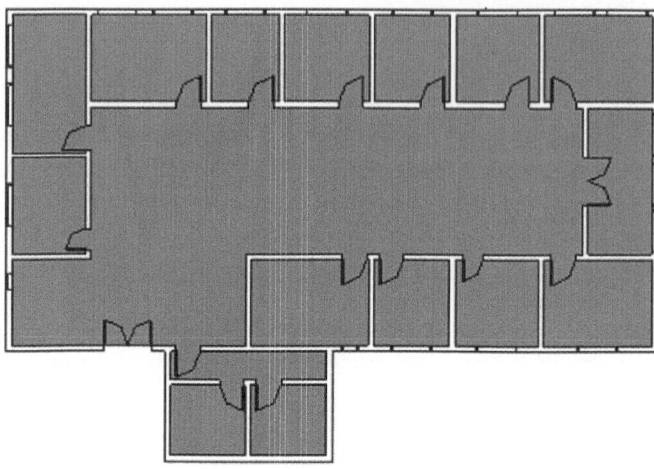

Figure 3-90 *The* ***Generic 12"*** *type of the floor created*

2. Double click on **Copy of 1 - Ceiling Mech** to display the corresponding view. Now, in the **Properties** palette, click on the value field corresponding to the **Discipline** parameter. Select the **Architectural** discipline from the drop-down list and choose the **Apply** button to apply the changes.

3. In the **Project Browser, Copy of 1 - Ceiling Mech** is displayed under the **Architectural** head.

4. Select **Copy of 1 - Ceiling Mech** under the **Architectural Plan** head and right-click to display a flyout. From the flyout, choose the **Rename** option; the **Rename View** dialog box is displayed. Enter **Level 1** in the **Name** edit box and choose the **OK** button; the dialog box is closed and the view is renamed to **Level 1**.

5. Repeat the procedure followed in steps 1 through 5 to add another level as **Level 2** from **Mechanical** head into **Architectural** head.

Creating the Ceiling

After creating the floor for the project, you need to add a ceiling to it. You will use the **Ceiling** tool to create the ceiling.

Before creating the ceiling, transform the current view to the ceiling plan view of the first floor.

1. Double-click on **Level 1** from the **Ceiling Plans** head in the **Project Browser**.

2. Invoke the **Ceiling** tool from the **Build** panel of the **Architecture** tab; the **Modify | Place Ceiling** tab is displayed.

3. To assign a type to the ceiling, click on the **Type Selector** drop-down list in the **Properties** palette and then select the **Generic** option from it.

Next, you need to define the exact height of the ceiling.

4. In the **Properties** palette, click on the value field of the **Height Offset From Level** instance parameter and enter **8'6"** for Imperial or **2590 mm** for Metric. Next, choose the **Apply** button; the new height is assigned to the ceiling.

5. Next, move the cursor on any of the enclosed space and click to create a ceiling. Note that the created ceiling is not distinctly visible in the ceiling plan because the ceiling type selected has a plain board finish.

6. Repeat step 5 to create individual ceilings for every enclosed space in the *Office Building II* project. After creating all the ceilings, press ESC twice.

7. Choose the **Default 3D View** tool from the **3D View** drop-down of the **Create** panel in the **View** tab; the 3D view of the project with the ceiling created is displayed. You can move the cursor over the ceiling of the room to highlight and display it, as shown in Figure 3-91.

Note
*If the 3D view is in halftone grey, you need to change the discipline of the 3D view to **Architecture** or **Coordination** from the instance properties displayed in the **Properties** palette.*

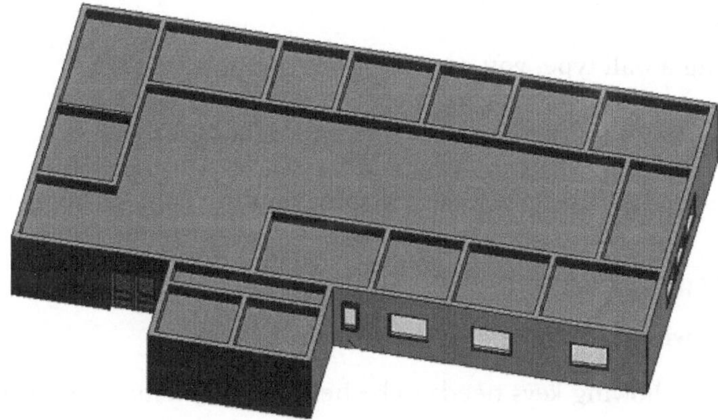

Figure 3-91 *Displaying the ceiling of the Office Building II project*

Saving the Project

In this section, you need to save the project and the settings using the **Save As** tool.

1. To save the project with the settings, choose **Save As > Project** from the **Application Menu**; the **Save As** dialog box is displayed.

2. In this dialog box, browse to *C:\rmp_2017\c03_rmp_2017_tut* and then enter **c03_Office_BuildingII_tut2** for Imperial or **M_c03_Office_BuildingII_tut2** for Metric in the **File Name** edit box.

3. Now, choose the **Save** button; the **Save As** dialog box closes and the project file is saved.

Closing the Project

1. To close the project, choose the **Close** option from **Application Menu**.

Self-Evaluation Test

Answer the following questions and then compare them to those given at the end of this chapter:

1. Using the __________ button in the **Properties** palette, a copy of an existing door type can be created.

2. You can select a wall type from the __________ drop-down list.

3. The __________ tool can be used to attach walls to the floor.

4. Using the __________ tool, you can create grids by picking elements.

5. The __________ type parameter indicates the height of a door.

6. You can control the visibility of a level head. (T/F)

7. You cannot copy or array grids. (T/F)

8. After creating a wall type, you can modify its properties. (T/F)

9. You can add doors and windows in plan view only. (T/F)

10. You can use the **By Face** tool to cut openings on the faces of floors and ceilings. (T/F)

Review Questions

Answer the following questions:

1. Which of the following keys needs to be held to add elements to a selection?

   a) TAB b) CTRL
   c) SHIFT d) ESC

2. Which of the following parameters of a door is an instance property?

   a) **Level** b) **Thickness**
   c) **Door Material** d) **Fire Rating**

3. Which of the following sketching tools can be used to create a curved wall?

   a) **Rectangle** b) **Fillet Arc**
   c) **Line** d) **Polygon**

4. You can create a radial grid pattern using the **Grid** tool. (T/F)

5. Levels, once created, cannot be modified. (T/F)

6. You can create an opening in the ceiling using the **Cut** tool. (T/F)

7. The **Chain** option can be enabled or disabled without exiting the **Wall: Architectural** tool. (T/F)

8. The location line parameter is an instance property of a wall. (T/F)

9. Walls can be attached to the floors using the **Join Geometry** tool. (T/F)

10. Door tags increase automatically as you add doors to a project. (T/F)

EXERCISE

Exercise 1 Residential Building

Create the exterior and interior walls of a residential building and then add doors and windows to them. Create floor and ceiling and then add grids to the walls of the Residential building, refer to Figure 3-92. Do not add dimensions or texts as they are given only for reference. Figure 3-93 shows the three dimensional view of the residential building with the added floors and ceilings. The project parameters for this exercise are given next. **(Expected time: 1 Hour)**

1. Project File -
   For Imperial **Systems-Default.**
   For Metric **Systems-Default_Metric.**
2. Discipline - **Architectural.**
3. Rename Level 1 - First Floor, Level 2 - Second Floor.
4. Exterior wall type -
   For Imperial **Basic Wall - Exterior Brick on Mtl. Stud.**
   For Metric **Basic Wall - Exterior Brick on Mtl. Stud.**
5. Interior wall type -
   For Imperial **Basic Wall: Generic- 5".**
   For Metric **Basic Wall: Generic- 90 mm.**
6. Height of wall - **Top Constraint** - **Upto Level 2.**
7. Door type to be used:
   For Imperial Main door - **Double - Glass 2 - 36" x 84"**
   Bedroom doors - **Single - Flush 30" x 84"**
   Washroom door - **Single Flush Vision - 36" x 84"**
   For Metric Main door - **Double - Glass 2 - 1830 x 1981mm**
   Bedroom doors - **Single - Flush 0762 x 2134mm**
   Washroom door - **Single Flush Vision - 0915 x 2134 mm**
8. Window type to be used:
   For Imperial **Fixed with Trim - 36" x 24"**
   For Metric **Fixed with Trim - 0915 x 0610 mm**
9. Floor type -
   For Imperial **Floor: Generic- 12".**
   For Metric **Floor: Generic- 300mm**

10. Ceiling type - **Generic.**
11. File name to be assigned:
    For Imperial *c03_Residential-Building_exer1.rvt*
    For Metric *M_c03_Residential-Building_exer1.rvt*

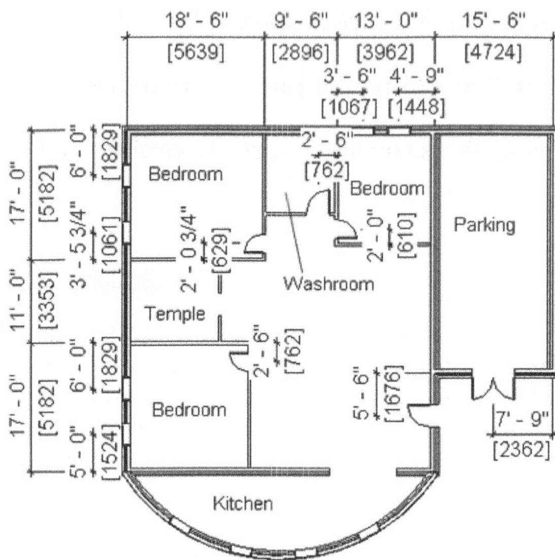

Figure 3-92 *Sketch plan of walls with doors and windows, and floor and ceiling added to the building*

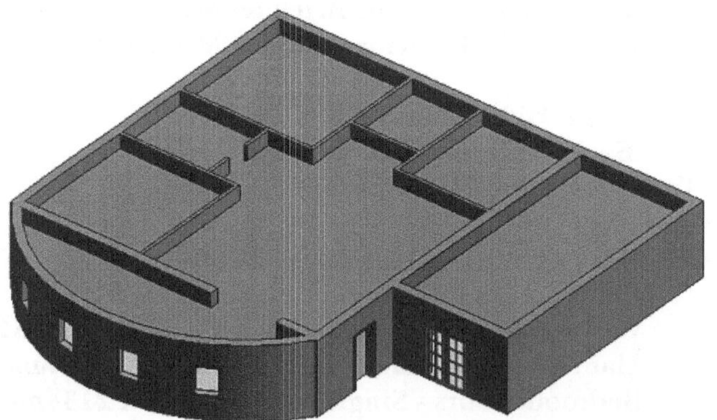

Figure 3-93 *Three dimensional view of residential building with added floors and ceilings*

Answers to Self-Evaluation Test

1. Duplicate 2. Type-Selector, 3. Attach Top/Base, 4. Pick Line, 5. Height, 6. T, **7.** F, **8.** T, **9.** F, **10.** T

Chapter 4

Creating Spaces and Zones and Performing Load Analysis

Learning Objectives

After completing this chapter, you will be able to:

- *Create Spaces*
- *Modify Spaces*
- *Create Zones*
- *Modify Zones*
- *Perform Heating and Cooling Load Analysis*

INTRODUCTION

In Autodesk Revit, you can model the spaces and create zones to efficiently track the building design and construction changes within a project file. In Revit, you can assign the HVAC load to the spaces in the model and export the space load data via a gbXML file to an external simulation software program.

While designing HVAC systems, modeling the building space accurately is one of the key criteria for correct designing. During the mechanical designing of a project, most of the time is spent on modeling the building correctly in a load-simulating program, such as Trane TRACE 700 or Carriers Hourly Analysis Program (HAP). Although these programs are essential for mechanical designer, setting up the building accurately using these programs can be a tedious task.

In an MEP model, each space is set up individually and the physical construction and the usage of each space is also different. Alterations to the building design or space usage by the architect during this phase will require returning to previously modeled spaces and modifying them. This is time-consuming and can often be a point of conflict, when changes occur later in the design phase.

In this chapter, you will learn the process of preparing the space model and create zones for analysis. Also, you will learn how to perform the heating and cooling analysis in Revit 2017. Further, you will learn how to export the gbXML data to a load-simulating software.

SPACE MODELING FOR BUILDING ANALYSIS

Modeling spaces accurately and efficiently in a building model is necessary for successful load analysis. In Revit, various components of a building have to be modeled for each space, as each component plays a vital role in building load analysis. The components that are to be modeled include building construction component, internal load component, and external load factors. These components should be considered for each space that is being created. Note that each of these components has several significant inputs that can affect the loads within the space.

Creating Spaces

Creation of spaces in a building model is necessary before performing a load analysis. In Revit, the spaces are created from room bounding elements such as walls, floors, ceilings, roofs, and room separation lines. After creating the initial set-up for the MEP project and linking the desired architectural model in the project or creating the building envelope, the architectural elements that make up a room define your space accurately.

Figure 4-1 shows a linked architectural model. Select the linked model from the drawing area; the properties of the linked model will be displayed in the **Properties** palette. In the palette, choose the **Edit Type** button; the **Type Properties** dialog box will be displayed. In this dialog box, select the check box corresponding to the **Room Bounding** parameter; the spaces in the linked model will be bounded by room. Now, choose **OK** and **Apply** to close the **Type Properties** dialog box.

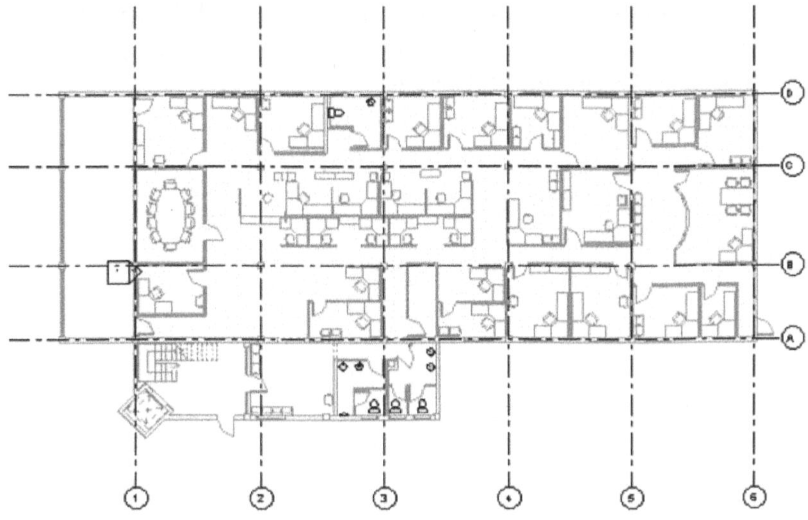

Figure 4-1 *The linked architectural model*

Note

*In the **Type Properties** dialog box for the linked model, if you clear the check box and place a space in the model, the **Warning** message box will be displayed informing you that the created space will not be in an enclosed region, and subsequently, Revit will not be able to calculate load data for that space if HVAC analysis is attempted on the model.*

Placing Spaces

In Autodesk Revit 2017, you can place spaces in a model manually or automatically. To create a space automatically, open a floor plan that contains the area where you want to place a space from the **Project Browser**. Now, choose the **Space** tool from the **Space & Zones** panel of the **Analyze** tab; the **Modify | Place Space** contextual tab and the **Options Bar** with various options will be displayed, as shown in Figure 4-2.

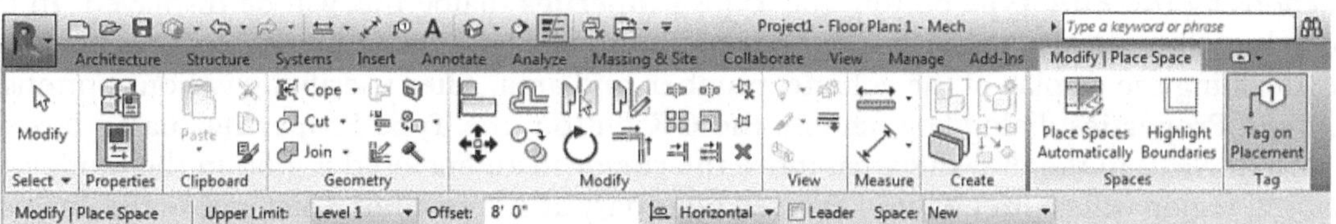

Figure 4-2 *The options in the **Modify / Place Space** contextual tab*

In the **Modify | Place Space** contextual tab, the **Tag on Placement** button is chosen by default. As a result, the tag will be attached to the space in the model. You can choose the button again to detach the tag from the space when you place the space in the model. In the **Modify | Place Space** contextual tab, you can choose the **Highlight Boundaries** button in the **Spaces** panel to highlight all the bounding elements in the current view. This will help you to know which elements are bounded by the building elements before you place the space in the model. On choosing the **Highlight Boundaries** button from the **Spaces** panel, the bounding elements will be highlighted, as shown in Figure 4-3. Also, the **Autodesk Revit 2017** message box will be displayed. This message box will inform you that the space bounding elements are highlighted and it displays all the warnings related to the space. You can choose the **Expand** button to view the warnings in detail. Choose the **Close** button in the **Autodesk Revit 2017** message box to close it. On closing the message box, you will notice that the space highlights will disappear and now you can continue to add space in the model.

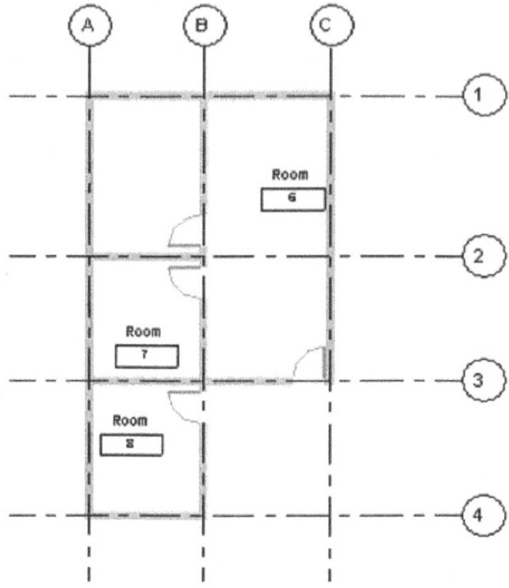

Figure 4-3 *The highlighted bounding elements*

In the **Options Bar**, you can select an option from the **Upper Limit** drop-down list to specify the level upto which the created space will be extended in the elevation. After specifying the upper limit of the space, you can specify the offset value beyond which the space will be extended by entering a value in the **Offset** edit box in the **Options Bar**. Now, in the **Properties** palette, select an option from the **Type Selector** drop-down list to specify the type of space tag. Also, in the **Properties** palette, you can specify various instance properties of the space such as its dimensions, level constraints, electrical loads, mechanical flow, and so on. In the **Properties** palette, you can choose the **Edit Type** button to modify the type properties of the space tag. On choosing the **Edit Type** button, the **Type Properties** dialog box will be displayed. In this dialog box, you can specify various options to modify the type properties of the space tag such as controlling the display of the volume, number, and area. After specifying various options in the **Type Properties** dialog box, choose the **OK** button; the **Type Properties** dialog box will be closed. Next, in the drawing area, move the cursor to an enclosed region in the model; the enclosed region will be highlighted by a red boundary and cross lines. Click inside the enclosed region; the space will be created in the enclosed region. By default, the space will not be visible in the project view. To display the spaces in the current view, you need to change the visibility settings of spaces using the **Visibility/Graphics Overrides** dialog box. The various options to display the space categories in the **Visibility/Graphics Overrides** dialog box are discussed in the next section.

Displaying Spaces in the Project View

As discussed earlier, to display the spaces in the Project view, you need to invoke the **Visibility Graphics** dialog box. To do so, choose the **Visibility Graphics** tool from the **Graphics** panel of the **View** tab; the **Visibility/Graphics Override** dialog box will be displayed. In this dialog box, ensure that the **Model Categories** tab is chosen by default. Additionally, in the **Visibility** column of the displayed tab, ensure that the **Spaces** check box is selected. Now, click on the "**+**" icon corresponding to the **Spaces** category to expand it. In the expanded **Spaces** category, select the **Interior** check box. To apply the settings to the current view, choose the **Apply** button in the **Visibility/Graphic Overrides** dialog box. Next, choose the **OK** button to close the displayed dialog box. The created spaces are now visible in the project. You can select the displayed spaces and modify their instance and type properties and the space tag by using the **Properties** palette and the **Type Properties** dialog box, respectively.

Modifying Instance Properties of a Space

After inserting a space in the project, you can modify its instance properties. To do so, select the desired space from the drawing; various properties corresponding to the selected space will be displayed in the **Properties** palette. These properties are discussed in the table given next.

Properties	Description
Constraints	
Level	Specifies the level at which the space is placed.
Upper Limit	Specifies the level upto which the space will be extended in height.
Limit Offset	Specifies the distance by which the space will increase its height above the level specified in the **Upper Limit** parameter.
Base Offset	Specifies the distance by which the space will increase its depth below the level specified in the **Level** parameter.
Electrical-Lighting	
Average Estimated Illumination	Specifies the mean illumination of the space. This value is calculated by dividing the summation of the illumination contributed by each lighting fixture at the lighting calculation work plane divided by the area of space. The value displayed in its value field will be read only and will be dependent on the properties of the light fixtures inside it.
Room Cavity Ratio	Specifies the Room Cavity Ratio of the space. The Room Cavity Ratio (RCR) is expressed in the form of equation: RCR= (2.5*RCH*P)/A, where P= Perimeter of the Space, A= Area of the Space, RCH=Room Cavity Height (Height of the Lighting Fixture-Height of the Lighting Workplane).
Lighting Calculation Workplane	Specifies the height of the workplane at which the illumination calculation is performed. By default, the value displayed in its value field is **2'6"(762mm)**.
Lighting Calculation Luminaire Plane	Specifies the height of the lighting fixture(s) placed. The value displayed in its value field is read-only and is derived from the properties of the lighting fixtures placed inside the space.
Ceiling Reflectance	Specifies the reflectance of the space based on the surface and color properties of the ceiling placed inside it. The value is specified in percent. By default, **75%** is displayed in its value field.

Wall Reflectance	Specifies the reflectance of the space based on the surface and color properties of the walls enclosing it. The value is specified in percent. By default, **50%** is displayed in its value field.
Floor Reflectance	Specifies the reflectance of the space based on the surface and color properties of the floor placed inside it. The value is specified in percent. By default, **20%** is displayed in its value field.
Electrical Loads	
Design HVAC Load per area	Specifies the total HVAC load for the space. You can specify a value in its value field. Alternatively, you can specify the value by performing the heating and cooling load analysis or retrieve it from a gbXML file.
Design Other Load per area	Specifies the total load for the space. You can specify a value in its value field. Alternatively, you can specify the value by performing the heating and cooling load analysis or retrieve it from a gbXML file.
Mechanical-Flow	
Specified Supply Airflow	Specifies the airflow supplied inside the space. The supply airflow refers to the volume of air supplied to circulate inside the space in unit time. You can specify a value in its value field. Alternatively, you can specify the value by performing the heating and cooling load analysis or retrieve it from a gbXML file.
Calculated Supply Airflow	Specifies the total airflow required inside the space to heat and cool it. You can specify a value in its value field. Alternatively, you can specify the value by performing the heating and cooling load analysis or retrieve it from a gbXML file.
Actual Supply Airflow	Specifies the total airflow supplied in the space. This value is the sum of the airflow that is supplied from all the air terminals inside the space. The value specified in its value field is read-only.
Specified Exhaust Airflow	Specifies the airflow that leaves from the space.
Return Airflow	Specifies the method to calculate the return airflow inside the space. To specify a value, click in its value field and select any of the following options from the drop-down list displayed: **Specified**, **Specified Supply Airflow**, **Calculated Supply Airflow**, and **Actual Supply Airflow**.
Specified Return Airflow	Specifies the total return airflow in the space. You can specify a value in its value field if the **Specified** option is assigned to the **Return Airflow** parameter.
Actual Return Airflow	Specifies the sum of the airflows for all return air terminals inside the space.
Dimensions	
Area	Specifies area of the room associated with space. The area of the space is calculated by using all the room-bounding elements enclosing the space.
Perimeter	Specifies the perimeter of the space.

Unbounded Height	Specifies the unbounded height of the room associated with the space. The unbounded height of the room depends on the following room height parameters: **Level**, **Upper Limit**, **Limit Offset**, and **Base Offset.**
Volume	Specifies the computed volume of the room associated with the space. The value of the computed volume will be displayed only when the **Areas and Volumes** radio button is selected from the **Volume Computations** area of the **Area and Volume Computations** dialog box. You can invoke the **Area and Volume Computations** dialog box by choosing the **Area and Volume Computations** tool from the **Room & Area** panel in the **Architecture** tab.
Identity Data	
Number	Specifies the unique number given to the space. If you assign a duplicate number, a warning message will be displayed while placing the space.
Name	Specifies the name of the space.
Room Number	Specifies the number of the room associated with the space.
Room Name	Specifies the name of the room associated with the space.
Comments	Specifies the comment assigned to the space.
Occupant	Specifies the name of the occupant, who will utilize this space. The occupant can be a person, a department, an organization, or others relevant to the occupancy.
Energy Analysis	
Occupiable	Specifies whether the space is occupied by the occupant or not. If the space is occupied, select the check box displayed in its value field. If the space is unoccupied, as in case of plenums, shafts, chases, and so on, clear the check box displayed in its value field.
Plenum	Specifies whether the space is a plenum space or not. To specify the space as plenum, select the check box corresponding to it in its value field. To make it a regular space, clear the check box displayed in its value field.
Zone	Indicates the name of the zone to which the space is assigned to.
Condition Type	Specifies how the heating and cooling loads are calculated for the space. To specify a type for this parameter, click in its value field and select any of the following options: **Heated**, **Cooled**, **Heated and cooled**, **Unconditioned**, **Naturally vented**, and **Vented**.
Space Type	Specifies the type of space. The type of space is defined by its utility. As such each space type will have different utilization in terms of human load factor and energy consumption. To specify a type for space, click in the value field corresponding to the parameter; a browse button will be displayed. Choose the browse button; the **Space Type Settings** dialog box will be displayed. In this dialog box, you can select a type from the list box and choose the **OK** button; the selected type will be assigned to the parameter.

Construction Type	Specifies the type of construction assigned to the space. To assign a construction type to the space, click in the value field corresponding to the parameter; a browse button will be displayed. Choose the browse button; the **Construction Type** dialog box will be displayed. You can use this dialog box to select an existing construction type or create a new construction type and assign it to the space.
People	This parameter will be displayed in the **Properties** palette only when you select an existing space. It specifies the heat load generated by people inhabitating the space. To do so, choose the **Edit** button corresponding to the **People** parameter; the **People** dialog box will be displayed. You can use various options in this dialog box to specify the occupancy and the heat gain in the space.
Electrical Loads	This parameter will be displayed in the **Properties** palette only when you select an existing space. It specifies the electric load required for the space. To specify the electric load of the space, choose the **Edit** button corresponding to the **Electric Loads** parameter; the **Electrical Loads** dialog box will be displayed. You can use various options in this dialog box to specify the lighting values and the power required in the space.
Calculated Heating Load	Specifies the total heating load of the space. The value for this parameter will be displayed after performing heating and cooling load analysis. If the heating and cooling load analysis is not performed, the **Not Computed** text will be displayed in its value field.
Design Heating Load	Specifies the total heating load for the space. Alternatively, you can specify the value by performing the heating and cooling load analysis or retrieve it from a gbXML file.
Calculated Cooling Load	Specifies the total cooling load for the space. Alternatively, you can specify the value by performing the heating and cooling load analysis or retrieve it from a gbXML file.
Design Cooling Load	Specifies the total cooling load for the space.

Modifying Spaces

After adding spaces to the model, you may need to modify the design specification or adjust the spaces depending on the result of the heating and cooling load analysis. In some cases, you may need to increase or decrease the vertical extents of the space. You may also need to split, combine, delete, or move a space. These modifications are discussed next.

Splitting the Space

In a project, you may need to split an existing space or a given area into two or multiple spaces or areas to accommodate the changes made in the design. To do so, you can use the **Space Separator** tool from the **Spaces & Zones** panel in the **Analyze** tab. On invoking this tool, the **Modify | Place Space Separation** contextual tab will be displayed. In this tab, you can use various sketching tools from the **Draw** panel to sketch separation lines. You can use separation lines to divide spaces. You can also use separation lines to create multiple areas from one large area.

Note

While drawing the separation lines, you need to ensure that the area you define should be closed.

In a model, you can sketch the separation line(s) in a closed area (with no spaces) or in an existing space. To sketch the separation line(s) in a closed area, invoke the **Line** tool (for illustration), if it is not chosen by default from the **Draw** panel. Next, in the **Options Bar**, ensure that the **Chain** check box is selected by default. The selection of the **Chain** check box in the **Options Bar** will help you to create multiple line segments connected to each other. Now, in the drawing area, move the mouse on the desired point to specify the start point of the separation line, refer to Figure 4-4.

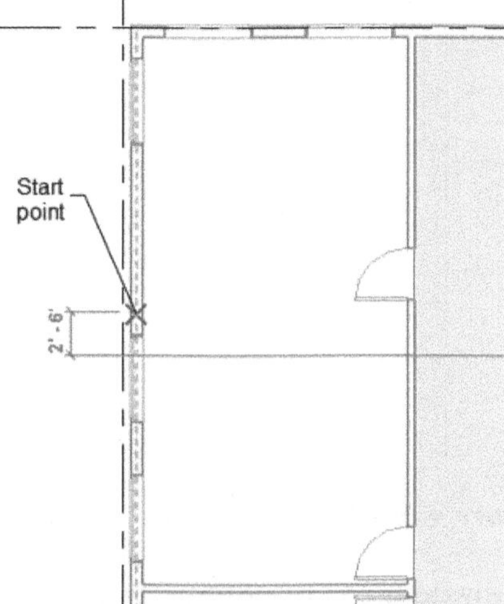

Figure 4-4 *Specifying the start point of the separation line*

Next, draw more lines to define the periphery of the desired areas, refer to Figure 4-5.

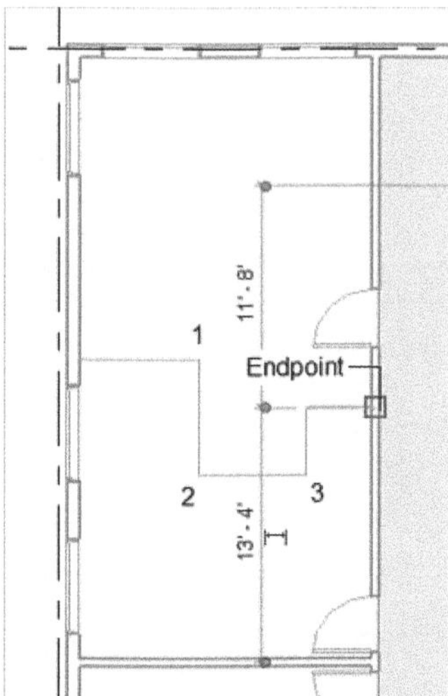

Figure 4-5 *Specifying other points in the specified area*

After sketching the separation lines, choose the **Modify** button from the **Select** panel to exit the sketching mode. Now, choose the **Space** tool from the **Spaces & Zones** panel of the **Analyze** tab and then move the cursor on either side of the separation line; the space with a tag will be displayed along with the cursor, refer to Figure 4-6.

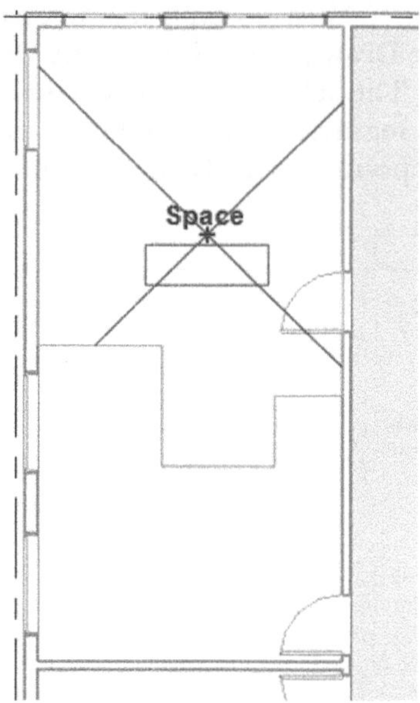

Figure 4-6 *Clicking inside the created area*

Click to add the space in the newly defined area. Similarly, you can add a space to the other areas. In a project, you may require to add a separation line to redefine an existing space. To do so, choose the **Space Separator** tool, as discussed, and then invoke the sketching tool from the **Draw** panel to enable the sketching mode. Now, click on any desired point inside the space to specify the start point, refer to Figure 4-7.

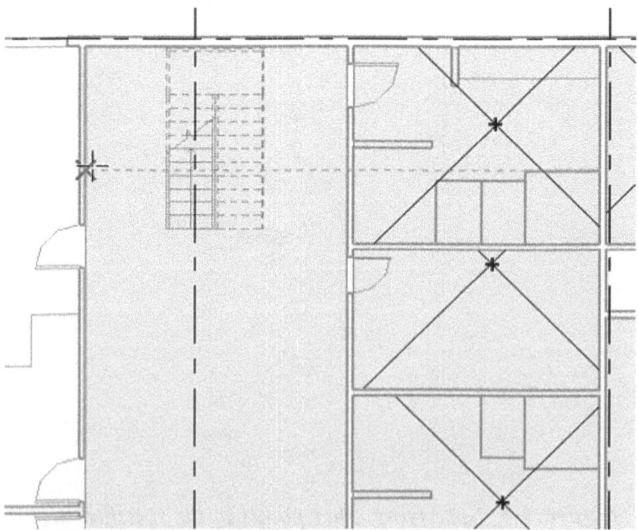

Figure 4-7 *Specifying the start point of the separation line*

Next, sketch the other lines as required. On sketching the lines, the boundaries of the existing space will be adjusted according to the separation lines specified, refer to Figure 4-8.

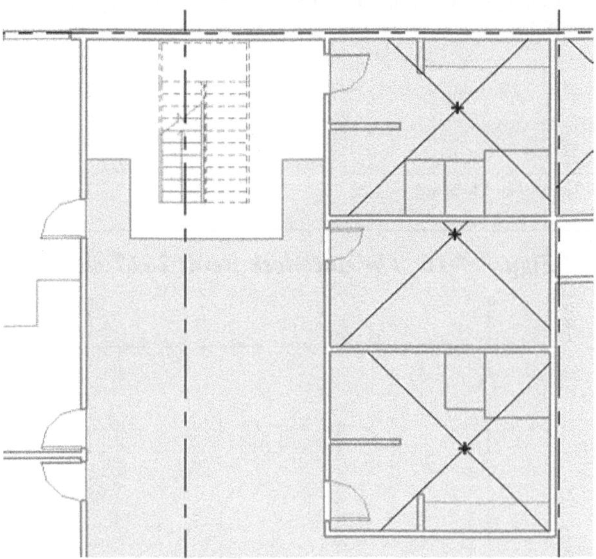

Figure 4-8 *Space adjusted according to the specified separation line*

Moving the Space

In a project, you may need to move a space from one location and place it in the other. To move a space, place the cursor on it; the space will be highlighted, refer to Figure 4-9.

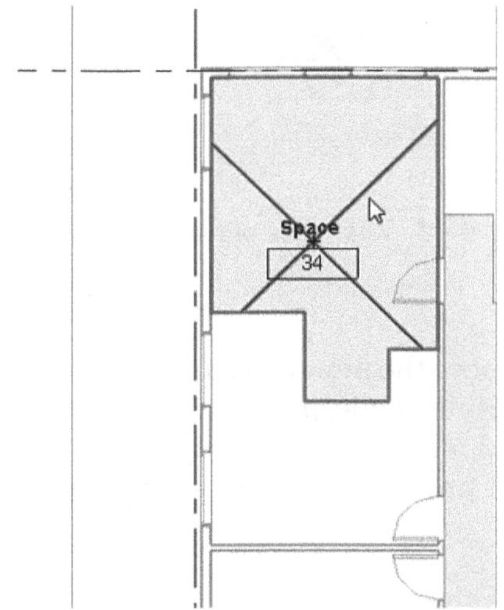

Figure 4-9 *The space to be relocated is highlighted*

Press and hold the cursor and drag it to a location where you desire to move the space. When the space is moved to a new location, release the mouse; the **Autodesk Revit 2017** message box will be displayed, as shown in Figure 4-10. Choose the **Move to Space** button in the message box; the message box will be closed and the space is moved to a new location, refer to Figure 4-11.

*Figure 4-10 The **Autodesk Revit 2017** message box*

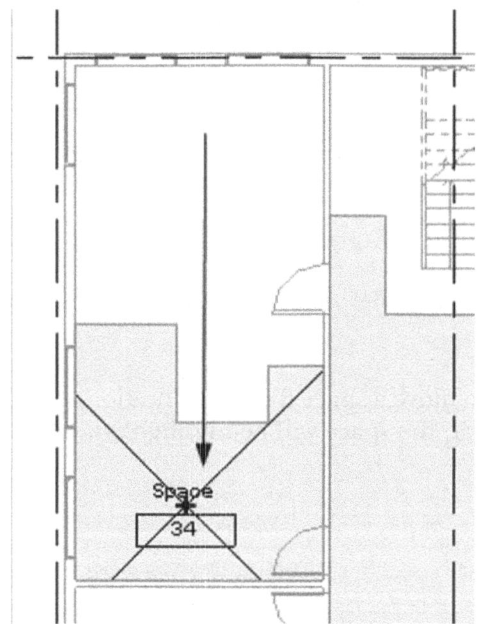

Figure 4-11 The space moved to a new location

Removing the Spaces

In a project, you may need to remove the unwanted space(s) from the model to avoid discrepancies in schedules and inaccurate results while performing heating and cooling load analysis. To remove a space from the model, either you can unplace it or permanently delete it from the project. The method to unplace and delete spaces are discussed next.

Unplacing a Space

Unplacing a space in a project refers to removing the space from the current location and keeping it reserved, so that you can place it at another location later during the project redesign. This reduces the hassle of adding the space information again. To unplace a space, open the floor plan view that displays the space and then select space from it; the **Modify | Spaces** contextual tab will be displayed. In this contextual tab, choose the **Delete** tool from the **Modify** panel; the space will be removed from the model and a **Warning** message box will be displayed, as shown in Figure 4-12. This message box will inform you that although the space was deleted from all the model views, its information will still remain in the project. The unplaced space is displayed in the schedule and the text **Not Placed** is displayed for the space that has been removed, as shown in Figure 4-13.

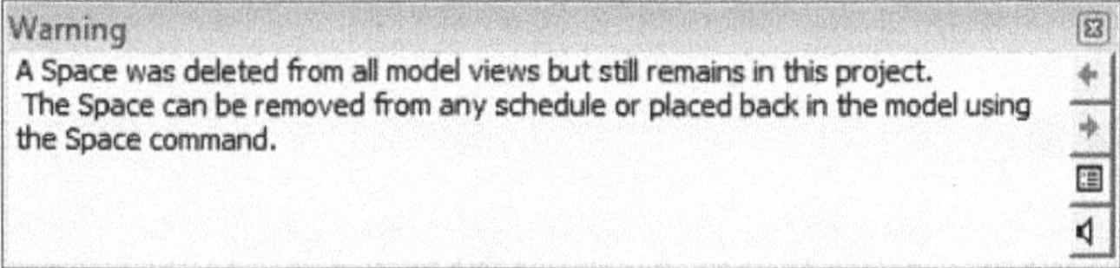

***Figure 4-12** The **Warning** message box displayed for the unplaced space*

<Space Schedule>

A	B	C
Name	Number of People	Area
Open	12.240352	3764 SF
Office	0.758216	Not Placed
Office	0.904483	Not Placed
Office	0.616304	190 SF
Office	0.761483	234 SF
Office	0.794336	244 SF
Office	0.843442	259 SF
Stairwell	0.823797	253 SF
Office	0.751872	231 SF
Office	0.757952	233 SF
Office	0.751872	231 SF

***Figure 4-13** The space schedule displaying the unplaced space*

Alternatively, you can remove the space from the model by selecting it and then pressing the DELETE key. Also, you can remove the space by pressing the CTRL+X keys.

Deleting a Space

You can also remove a space and its information completely from a model. To do so, you need to open the schedule of the spaces in the project view and then in the opened schedule, refer to Figure 4-13, select the row or rows corresponding to the desired space(s) and then right-click; a shortcut menu will be displayed. Choose the **Delete Row** option from the shortcut menu; the row will be deleted and also a **Revit** message box is displayed informing you that the selected spaces and its associated tags will also be deleted.

Computing the Volume of the Spaces

To compute the volume of the added spaces, choose the **Area and Volume Computations** tool from the **Space & Zones** panel in the **Analyze** tab. On doing so, the **Area and Volume Computations** dialog box will be displayed, as shown in Figure 4-14. In the **Volume Computations** area of the **Computations** tab, select the **Areas and Volumes** radio button. Next, choose the **OK** button; the volume computation of the space will be enabled and will be displayed in the instance properties for the selected space. To view the calculated volume of a space, select it from the drawing; the **Properties** palette will be displayed. In the **Properties** palette, the value in the value column of the **Volume** parameter indicates the computed volume of the space, as shown in Figure 4-15.

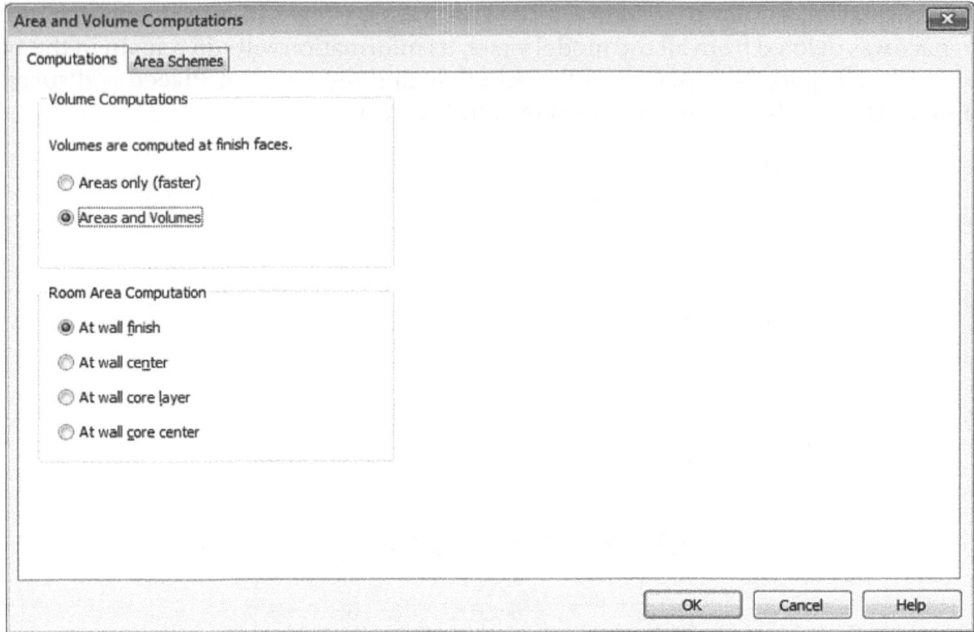

Figure 4-14 *The* ***Area and Volume Computations*** *dialog box*

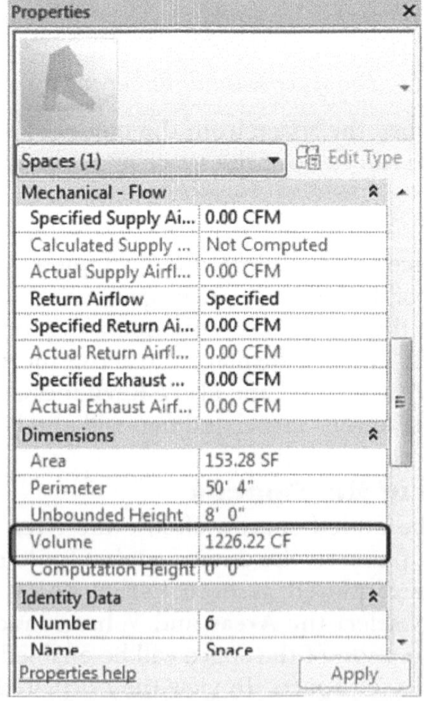

Figure 4-15 *The* ***Properties*** *palette displaying the computed volume of a selected space*

Note

In Revit, the volume calculations of the spaces and rooms are done considering the finish face of the room bounding element. When you select a space, the outline and the color fill display the exact periphery and the enclosed area which are used for calculating the volume of the room.

While computing the space volume, the room volume calculation engine of Autodesk Revit looks up and down from the measurement height to access the vertical limit of the room-bounding element. You can set the lower and upper limits of the room-bounding elements using the **Properties** palette. The **Base Offset** parameter in the value column in this palette defines the limit of the lower boundary. It is used to limit the extent of the spaces that have no floor.

The volume is also displayed in the drawing view if the spaces are added to it with the **Space Tag With Volume** option selected from the **Type Selector** drop-down list. Figure 4-16 shows a space along with its computed volume.

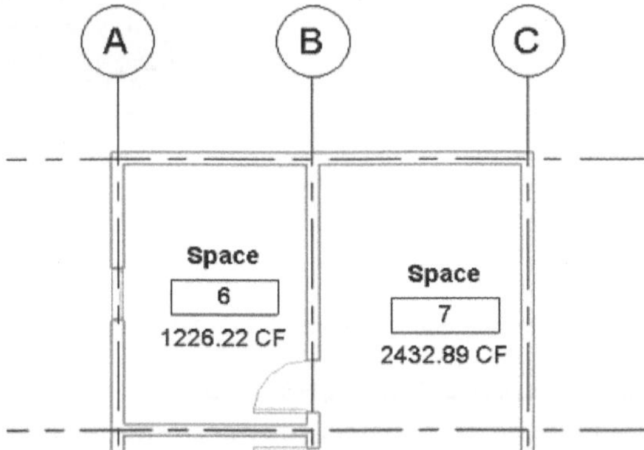

Figure 4-16 *The space tags displaying the volume of the spaces*

COLOR SCHEMES

Color schemes, as shown in Figure 4-17 are used to represent and categorize different spaces in the project graphically by using color codes. In other words, color schemes are used to color the spaces, rooms, and areas in a view. You can create color schemes and then apply them to different plan views. You can create different color schemes for the first and second floors of a building. A color scheme can be created based on specific categories such as gross area, rentable area, or an instance property of the space such as room cavity ratio, calculated cooling load, space type, area per person, perimeter, number, name, and more. You can also create a color scheme depending on the utilization of different spaces in a building. For example, you can assign different colors to represent areas such as office, storage, or accounts. Then, you can add a color scheme legend to help you identify different areas by the colors assigned to them. To create a color scheme for spaces, first you need to create and edit different color schemes using the **Edit Color Scheme** dialog box and then apply a scheme to the project view. The various options for creating, editing, and applying a color scheme to the spaces in a project view are discussed next.

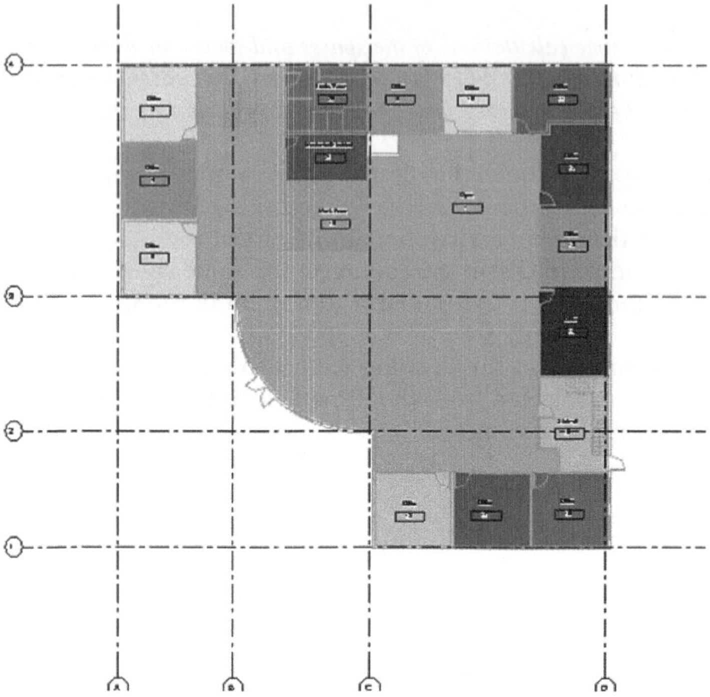

Figure 4-17 The color scheme of spaces categorized by its assigned number

Creating and Editing Color Schemes

Before creating a color scheme, the areas and the spaces should be defined in the plan view. You can create a color scheme based on any parameter of the space. For example, if you want to create a color scheme for spaces on the basis of space number, area, or names, make sure that the spaces are numbered and named in the plan view. To create a color scheme, you need to invoke the **Edit Color Scheme** dialog box. To do so, choose the **Color Schemes** tool from the **Spaces & Zones** panel in the **Analyze** tab; the **Edit Color Scheme** dialog box will be displayed, as shown in Figure 4-18. Alternatively, you can display the **Edit Color Scheme** dialog box by choosing the **<none>** button displayed in the value column corresponding to the **Color Scheme** parameter in the **Properties** palette for the current view. Now, in the **Schemes** area of the **Edit Color Scheme** dialog box, select the category for the color scheme from the **Category** drop-down list. Next, choose the **Duplicate** button in the **Schemes** area; the **New color scheme** dialog box will be displayed. Specify the name for the color scheme in the dialog box and choose the **OK** button; the name will be added in the **Schemes** area. Enter a title for the color scheme legend in the **Title** edit box in the **Scheme Definition** area. Next, select the parameter for the color scheme from the **Color** drop-down list; a message prompting you to make a new color scheme will be displayed. Choose the **OK** button to continue. Note that the options in the **Color** drop-down list will vary depending on the category selected.

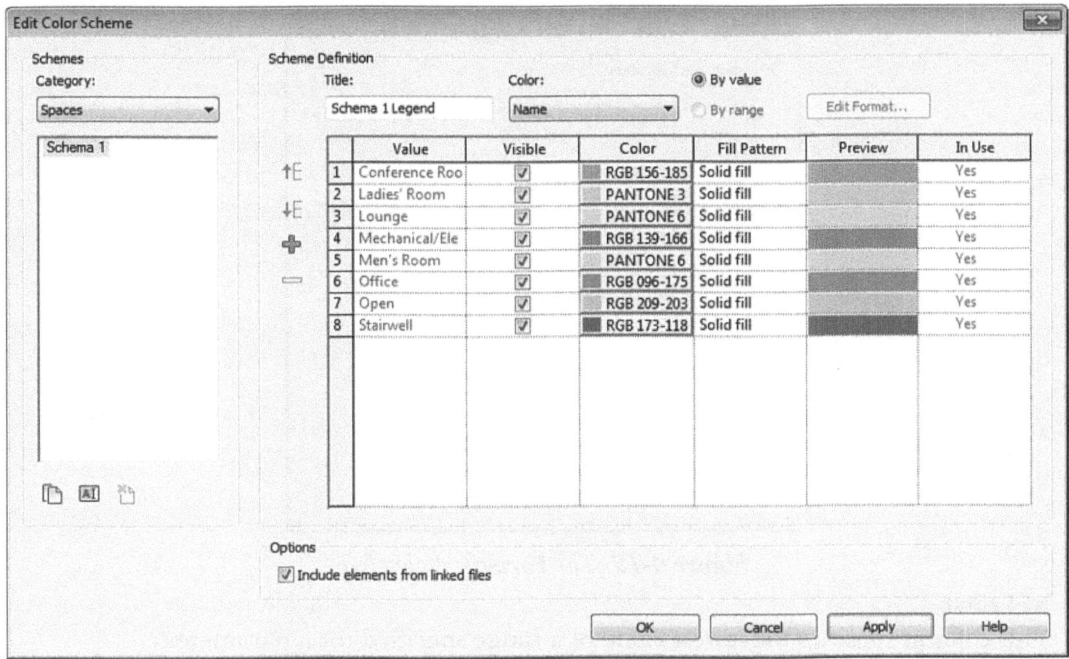

***Figure 4-18** The **Edit Color Scheme** dialog box*

Note

*Make sure you select the correct parameter from the **Color** drop-down list to create a color scheme. The values for the parameters should be predefined. For example, if you select the **Number of People** parameter to create a color scheme for the plan view, then the **People** parameter in the **Properties** palette for the spaces must be predefined.*

In the **Edit Color Scheme** dialog box, the **By value** radio button is selected by default. As a result, the color schemes are created based on the values of the selected parameter. Select the **By range** radio button to create a color scheme based on certain ranges of parameter values. The **By range** radio button will be available only when you select a parameter from the **Color** drop-down list in the **Scheme Definition** area that has a numeric value assigned to it. On selecting the **By range** radio button, the **Edit Format** button will be enabled and the unit format used for the parameter will be displayed on the right. Choose the **Edit Format** button; the **Format** dialog box will be displayed, as shown in Figure 4-19. Clear the **Use project settings** check box in the **Format** dialog box; the options in the dialog box will be enabled. Select the required values for the **Units** and **Rounding** options to set the format of the specified units. Choose the **OK** button; the scheme definition values will be added in the columns. You can modify the values in the columns as required. The columns displayed in the **Scheme Definition** area are discussed next.

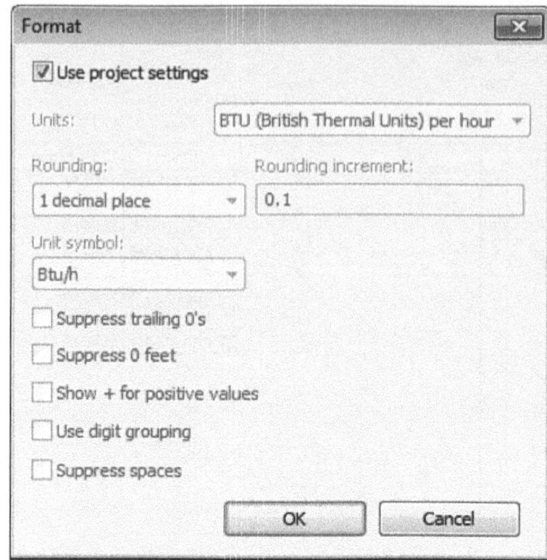

*Figure 4-19 The **Format** dialog box*

At Least

This column specifies the lowest value of a range specified for a parameter.

Less Than

This column specifies the lowest value of a range specified for a parameter and cannot be modified.

Caption

This column specifies the legend text for the range specified for a parameter. Click in the column to edit the text.

Visible

This column indicates the visibility of the value in the color scheme legend. By default, the **Visible** check box is selected indicating that the values are visible in the legend. Clear the check box in the column to make the value invisible in the color scheme legend.

Color

This column specifies the color assigned to the range/ class interval. Click on the default color value in the **Color** column; the **Color** dialog box will be displayed. Select the required color and choose the **OK** button; the selected color will be applied to the range/ class interval and is displayed in the column.

Fill Pattern

This column specifies the fill pattern assigned to a value by default. Click on the default value in the column and then click on the down arrow displayed on the right. Select the suitable fill pattern from the drop-down list displayed.

Preview

This column displays the preview of the color and pattern used for a particular range.

In Use

This column indicates that if a particular value from a range of values is in use in a project, you cannot modify the values in this column.

You can move a row up or down in the **Scheme Definition** area by using the **Move Rows Up/Down** buttons on the left. These buttons will be available only after selecting the **By Value** radio button. To add a new value to the color scheme, choose the **Add Value** button on the left. You can clear the check box, if you do not want to apply color schemes to rooms and areas from the linked files. Choose the **Apply** and then the **OK** button after creating the color scheme.

Applying a Color Scheme to the Spaces

To apply a color scheme in the required plan view, you can use the **Properties** palette of the current view. In the **Properties** palette of the current view, choose the **<none >** button in the **Value** column of the **Color Scheme** parameter; the **Edit Color Scheme** dialog box will be displayed. Select the required color scheme and choose the **OK** button; colors will be applied to the areas or rooms based on the color scheme selected.

Now, to apply the color scheme in the project view, click on the value field corresponding to the **Color Scheme Location** parameter in the **Properties** palette; a drop-down list will be displayed. You can either select **Background** or **Foreground** from the list. On selecting the **Foreground** option, all the elements in the area or room such as furniture or walls, except the columns, will be colored. On selecting the **Background** option only the background or the floor will be colored.

Adding Color Scheme Legends

The color scheme legends help you identify different rooms and areas through different colors assigned to them. The color scheme legends are included in the **Annotation Tag** category. You can place multiple color scheme legends anywhere in the plan view. The color scheme legend belongs to the annotation category and is affected by the Annotation crop region. If you do not want to place the color scheme legend on the view, you can exclude it by adjusting the Annotation crop region of that view.

To add a color fill legend, choose the **Color Fill Legend** tool from the **Color Fill** panel of the **Annotate** tab; the **Modify|Place Color Fill Legend** tab will be displayed. In the **Properties** palette, select the color scheme from the **Type Selector** drop-down list and then click in the drawing area to place the legend; the color scheme legend will be placed in the drawing view. Figure 4-20 shows a floor plan view with a color scheme and the color scheme legend for the rooms. The color scheme is created based on the area occupied by each room.

You can drag and stretch the color scheme legend by using the drag symbol displayed after selecting the color scheme legend.

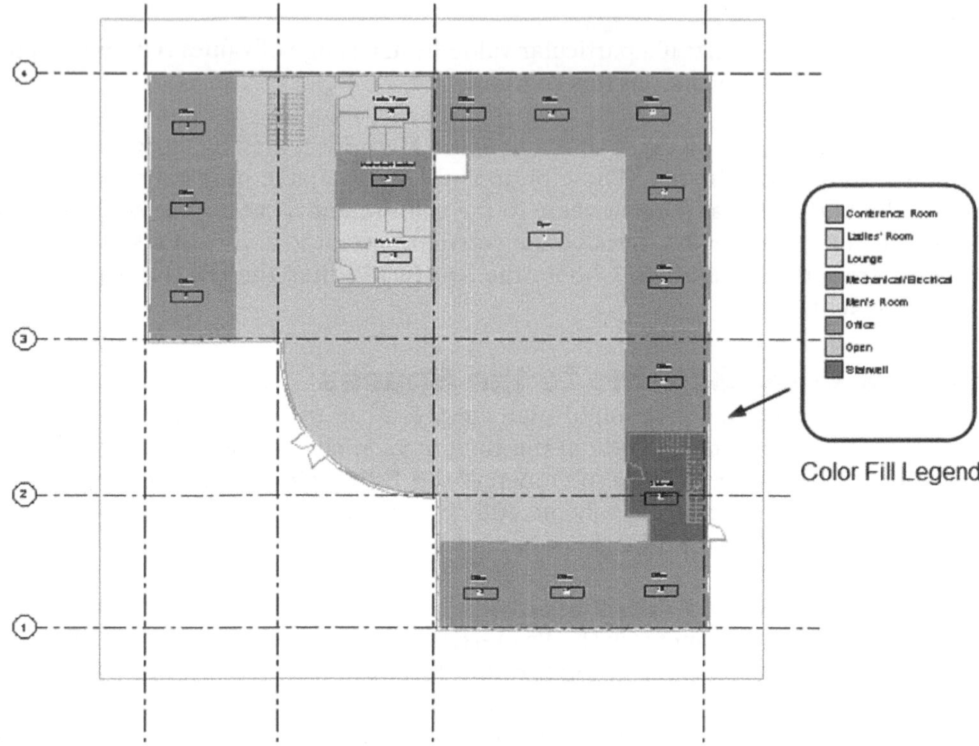

Figure 4-20 The floor plan displaying the color scheme

Modifying a Color Scheme

To modify a color scheme, select the existing color scheme legend from the drawing area and choose **Scheme > Edit Scheme** from the **Modify Color Fill Legends** tab; the **Edit Color Scheme** dialog box will be displayed. In this dialog box, modify the colors, fill patterns, title, parameter, and other values as required and choose the **Apply** button to view the changes. Choose the **OK** button to retain the changes.

Modifying a Color Scheme Legend

To modify a color scheme legend, select the existing color scheme legend and drag the blue circular drag control to move the color swatches into new columns. Also, drag the cursor down to move the color swatches into one column. Next, choose the **Edit Type** button in the **Properties** palette; the **Type Properties** dialog box will be displayed. In this dialog box, you can modify various parameters related to text, swatches, and other elements in the **Color Fill** legend. After modifying the parameters, choose the **OK** button to close the dialog box. You can also display the title of the color scheme legend by selecting the **Show Title** check box.

CREATING ZONES FROM SPACES

In an MEP project, spaces that have common environmental and design requirements are grouped to form zones. Zones are formed in order to provide control on the quality or condition of similar spaces. These conditions refer to the temperature, humidity, and other information factors. By creating zones in a building, you can control the airflow to a given group of spaces, depending on the changes in the design specifications. For example, you can shut off the airflow to an area that is not occupied or increase the airflow to spaces when the changes in the space load increases.

In a zone, you can add both occupied and unoccupied areas. You can also add spaces to different levels of the same zone. You can create a zone schedule and use it to modify the zones. Every zone contains zone information, such as heating and cooling temperatures and outdoor air information. Revit uses both zone and space information during heating and cooling loads analysis to determine the energy demands of the building.

The zone properties of a zone collects information from various spaces in it. The information can be the heating and cooling temperature set points alongwith other space properties. It is used with a heating and cooling loads analysis to determine the energy demands of the building.

In Revit, all projects have one zone namely **Default** zone. All spaces in Revit are initially placed in this zone. You can also create an unbounded zone in the **Default** zone. These zones have no spaces assigned to them. You can create zones in order to satisfy the environmental requirements for areas in a project, and add spaces later. Unbounded zones can be created for design purposes, fire protection zones, and retaining information. Unbounded zones retain zone properties that you specify, and you can move (drag) them within a view for design purposes. Only unbounded zones can be moved. After a space is assigned (added) to a zone, the zone is bounded by the space(s) assigned to it, and the zone cannot be moved. Unlike a space, an unbounded zone will not snap to a bounded area. In the next sections, you will learn how to create and modify a HVAC zone in a Revit project.

Adding and Modifying HVAC Zones

Before you add a new zone, open the project view and then invoke the **System Browser** window by selecting the **System Browser** check box from **View > Windows > User Interface** drop-down. In the **System Browser** window, select the **Zones** option from the **View** drop-down list; the **Zones** list box with a **Default** node will be displayed. On expanding the **Default** node, you will notice that all the spaces in the project are displayed under it by default.

Now, to add a new zone to the project, choose the **Zone** tool from the **Spaces & Zones** panel of the **Analyze** tab; the **Edit Zone** contextual tab will be displayed, as shown in Figure 4-21. Also, you will notice that the current view gets faded and a zone icon with a "+" symbol will appear along with the cursor. In the **Edit Zone** tab, ensure that the **Add Space Zone** tool is chosen by default in the **Mode** panel and then move the cursor over a space and click when the specified space is highlighted. On clicking the specified space, its color fades and it is added to the new zone. Similarly, you can click on other spaces in the project view to add to it to the same zone. Now, at this stage, you can choose the **Remove Space** tool from the **Mode** panel, to remove an unwanted space that you have added in the zone. On doing so, a "-" symbol along with the zone icon and the cursor is displayed. Place the cursor on the space to be removed from the zone and click when it is highlighted; the specified space will be removed from the zone and the color of the space fades.

***Figure 4-21** The **Edit Zone** contextual tab*

After adding and removing a space from the zone, you can view the properties of the zone in the **Properties** palette. If the **Properties** palettes is not displayed, choose the **Properties** button from the **Properties** panel of the **Edit Zone** tab; various properties of the zones are displayed in the **Properties** palette. These properties are discussed in the table given next.

Properties	Description
Constraints	
Level	Specifies the level at which the zone is placed.
Mechanical Flow	
Calculated Supply Airflow	This is a read-only parameter. The value field of this parameter shows the total supply airflow to the zone that is calculated by performing the heating and cooling load analysis or can be read from a gbXML file.
Calculated Supply Airflow per area	This is read-only parameter. The value for this parameter will be generated by dividing the value of the **Calculated Supply Airflow** of the zone parameter by the total area of the zone. This value will only be displayed after performing the heating and cooling load analysis.
Dimensions	
Occupied Area	This is a read-only parameter. The value in the value field of this parameter shows the sum of the areas for all of the occupied spaces in the zone.
Gross Area	This is a read-only parameter. The value field of this parameter shows the sum of the areas for all the occupied and unoccupied spaces in the zone.
Occupied Volume	This is a read-only parameter. The value field of this parameter shows the sum of the volume for all occupied spaces in the zone.
Gross Volume	This is a read-only parameter. The value field of this parameter shows the sum of volumes for all the occupied and unoccupied spaces in the zone.
Perimeter	This is a read-only parameter, and is disabled for the **Default** zone. The value field of this parameter shows the sum of the perimeter for all the spaces in the zone. Note that the common edges of the adjacent spaces are taken as single edge while calculating the perimeter.
Identity	
Comments	Specifies the comments for the zone.
Name	Specifies the name of the zone.
Phasing	
Phase	Specifies the project phase to which the zone belongs.
Energy Analysis	
Service Type	Specifies the heating and cooling service type for the zone. Click on the value field corresponding to this parameter and select a specific service type from the drop-down list displayed.

Coil Bypass	Specifies the manufacturer's coil bypass factor. This factor is a measure of the efficiency of the HVAC system of the zone that indicates the volume of air passing through the coil which is unaffected by the coil temperature.
Cooling Information	Specifies the cooling information of the zone. Choose the **Edit** button on the value field of this parameter; the **Cooling Information** dialog box will be displayed. In this dialog box, specify various information related to the cooling of the zone and choose **OK**; the values will be specified for this parameter.
Heating Information	Specifies the heating information for the zone. Choose the **Edit** button on the value field of this parameter; the **Heating Information** dialog box will be displayed. In this dialog box, specify various information related to the heating of the zone and choose **OK**; the values will be specified for this parameter.
Outdoor Air Information	Specifies the outdoor air information for the zone. Choose the **Edit** button on the value field of this parameter; the **Outdoor Air Information** dialog box will be displayed. You can specify information related to the outdoor air for the zone in this dialog box and choose **OK**; the values will be specified for this parameter.
Calculated Heating Load	Specifies the heating load calculated for the zone by heating and cooling loads analysis. The value is unavailable if no heating and cooling analysis is done.
Calculated Heating Load per area	Specifies the value of calculated heating load divided by the total area of the zone. The value is unavailable if no heating and cooling analysis is done.
Calculated Area per Heating Load	Specifies the value calculated by dividing the total area of the zone to the calculated heating load of the zone.
Calculated Cooling Load	Specifies the cooling load calculated for the zone by heating and cooling loads analysis. The value is unavailable if no heating and cooling analysis is done.
Calculated Cooling Load per area	Specifies the value of calculated cooling load divided by the total area of the zone. The value is unavailable if no heating and cooling analysis is done.
Calculated Area per Cooling Load	Specifies the value calculated by dividing the total area of the zone to the calculated cooling load of the zone.

After specifying various properties in the **Properties** palette and adding various spaces to the zone, choose the **Finish Editing Zone** button from the **Edit Zone** contextual tab to exit from the **Zone** tool. Now, you can choose the **Zone** tool again to create another zone in the project. To display various zones and related spaces, you can view the **System Browser** window, as shown in Figure 4-22.

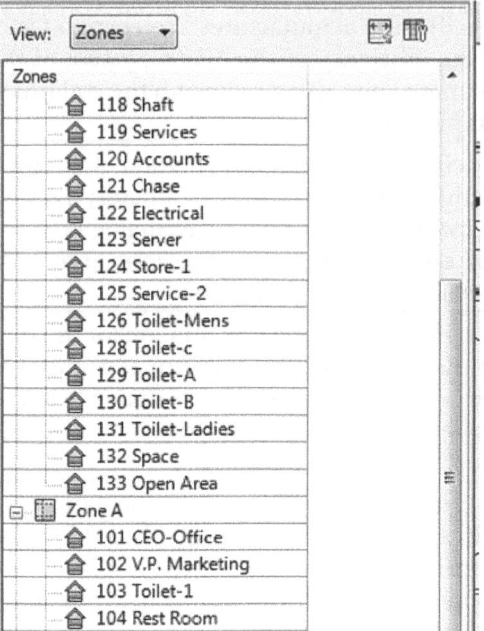

***Figure 4-22** The **System Browser** window displaying zones and spaces*

In the **System Browser**, you can select a zone and then edit it in the project view. On selecting a zone from the **System Browser** window, the spaces related to it will be highlighted in the project view and the **Modify | HVAC Zones** contextual tab will be displayed. In this tab, choose the **Edit Zone** tool from the **Zone** panel; the **Edit Zone** contextual tab will be displayed. The various tools in this tab have already been discussed in this section.

PERFORMING HEATING AND COOLING LOAD ANALYSIS

In a project, after defining the spaces and assigning them to zones, you may need to perform a detailed heating and cooling load analysis. The report generated from the analysis will help you to know how sustainable will be the building throughout the project. You can use the data from the report to design the HVAC system in the building for which the analysis has been made.

To perform the heating and cooling loads analysis, choose the **Heating and Cooling Loads** tool from the **Reports & Schedules** panel of the **Analyze** tab; the **Heating and Cooling Loads** dialog box will be displayed, as shown in Figure 4-23.

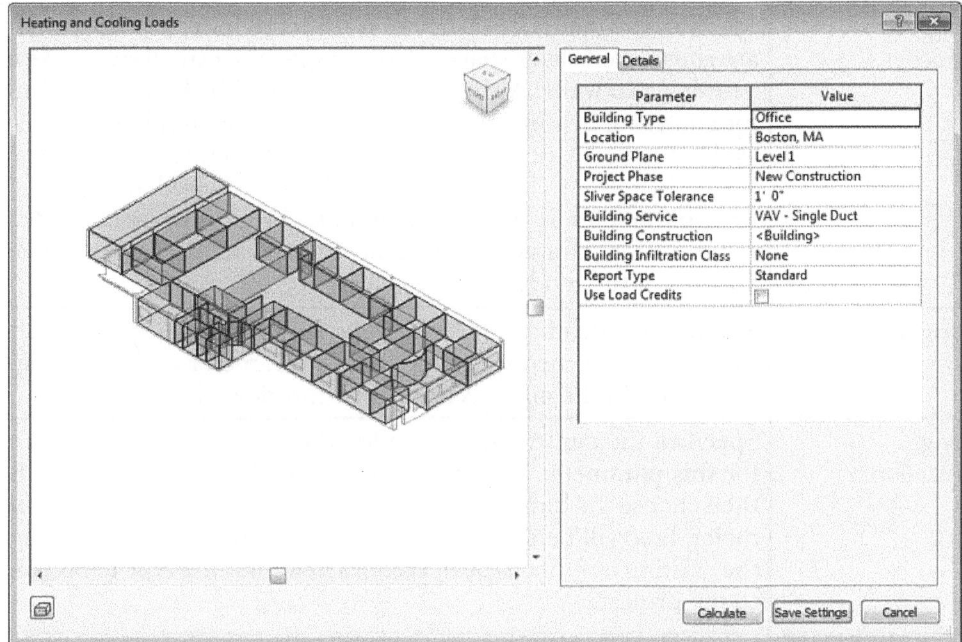

***Figure 4-23** The **Heating and Cooling Loads** dialog box displaying the options in the **General** tab*

In the left pane of this dialog box, the preview pane will be displayed. In this pane, a preview of the conceptual model along with the spaces will be displayed. In the right pane of this dialog box, various options related to the settings for the heating and cooling analysis will be displayed in two tabs: **General** and **Details**. The **General** tab is chosen by default. The options in this tab can be used to specify the information related to the project that will affect the heating and cooling loads analysis, only. The information in this tab can be modified before or after the loads analysis has been informed to make the report comply with the design specification. The various options in this tab are discussed in the table given next.

Parameter	**Description**
Building Type	Specifies the building type for the project. Click in the value field and select an option form the drop-down list displayed.
Location	Specifies the geographical location of the project. To modify it, choose the Browse button in the **Value** field and then specify the location and weather condition from the **Location Weather and Site** dialog box.
Ground Plane	Specifies the ground level for the building. Click in the **Value** field corresponding to this parameter and select a level from the drop-down list displayed.
Project Phase	Specifies the stage of construction of the project. Click in the **Value** field corresponding to this parameter and select any of the two options from the drop-down list displayed: **Existing** or **New Construction**.

Sliver Space Tolerance	Specifies the tolerance distances considered for computing areas that are considered sliver spaces. A sliver space is a small space like a gap between two walls. A sliver space is used with the analytical model for analyzing heating and cooling loads. For example, if there is new wall being constructed 1' (304mm) away from the existing wall for aesthetic reasons. This 1' gap is usually considered as a sliver space. This parameter is important because in an analytical model, the value in this parameter will remove the inaccuracies in the energy analysis of the model.
Building Service	Specifies the heating and cooling system used for the project. Click in the **Value** field corresponding to this parameter and select a system to be used in the analysis from the drop-down list displayed.
Building Construction	Specifies the construction type for the building. To specify a value for this parameter, click in the **Value** field corresponding to it and then choose the browse button displayed; the **Building Construction** dialog box will be displayed. You can use this dialog box to modify the existing building type or create a new building type to be assigned to the project.
Building Infiltration Class	The value specified for this parameter is an estimate of the outdoor air that will infiltrate the building envelope through leaks in it. Click on the **Value** field corresponding to this parameter and select any of the following options from the drop-down list displayed: **Loose**, **Medium**, **Tight**, and **None**. In Revit, the value specified for each of these options is given below: Loose: 0.076 cfm/sqft (0.396 L/s/m2) for tightly constructed walls Medium: 0.038 cfm/sqft (0.2 L/s/m2) for tightly constructed walls Tight: 0.019 cfm/sqft (0.09 L/s/m2) (for tightly constructed walls None: No infiltration
Report Type	Specifies the type of report that you need to generate from the analysis. Click on the **Value** field corresponding to this parameter and select any of the following options from the drop-down list displayed: **Simple**, **Standard**, or **Detailed**
Use Load Credits	Select the check box in the **Value** field corresponding to this parameter to register the information of the heating or cooling "credit" loads that take the form of negative loads in the analysis. For example, heat that leaves a zone through a partition or a glazing into another zone can be a negative load or credit.

After specifying various options in the **General** tab of the **Heating and Cooling Load** dialog box, choose the **Details** tab; various options in this tab will be displayed, as shown in Figure 4-24.

The **Details** tab displays all zones and spaces in the project as well as the corresponding zone and space information. In this tab, the **Spaces** radio button is selected by default. As a result, the preview pane in the left of this dialog box displays the spaces of the model. Alternatively, you can select the **Analytical Surface** radio button to display the analytical surface of the model in the preview pane.

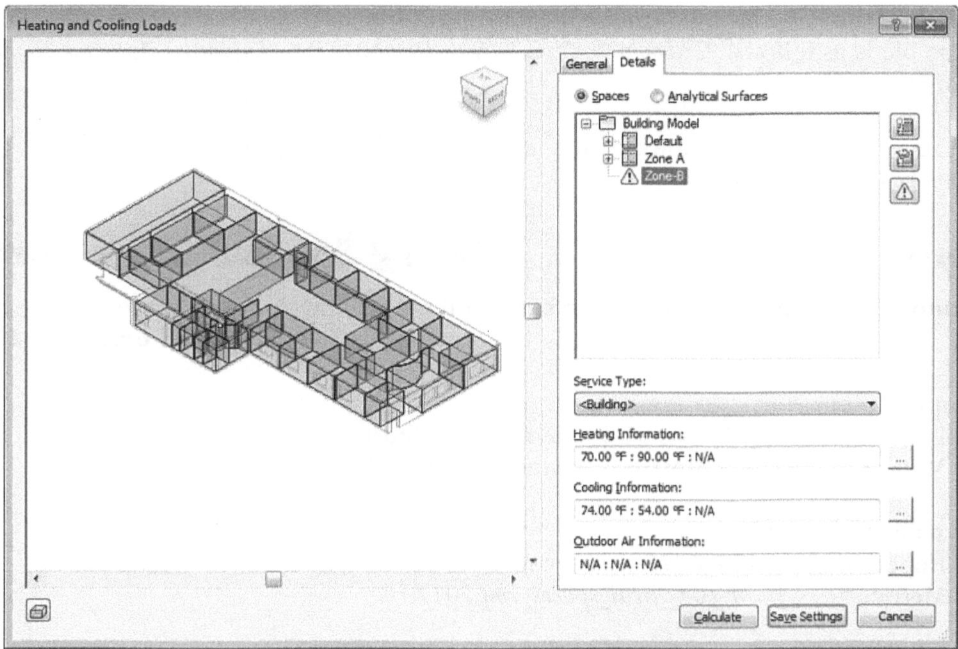

***Figure 4-24** The **Heating and Cooling Loads** dialog box displaying the options in the **Details** tab*

In the **Details** tab, the list box that is displayed below the **Spaces** and **Analytical Surfaces** radio buttons contains the hierarchical list of spaces and zones in the building model. You can use this list to view the space zone. Also, you can select any of the spaces or zones and modify various properties that are displayed below the list box. On selecting a space, the following properties are displayed below the list box: **Space Type**, **Construction Type**, **People**, and **Electrical Loads**. These properties have already been discussed in the earlier sections of this chapter. You can modify these properties for the selected space depending on your design requirement. On selecting a zone from the list box, the following properties are displayed below it: **Service Type**, **Heating Information**, **Cooling Information**, and **Outdoor Information**. You can modify these properties by using their respective dialog boxes which can be invoked by choosing the corresponding browse button. After specifying various properties of the spaces and zones, you can now view the model in the preview pane more closely. For example, if you want to highlight a particular space selected in the list box, choose the **Highlight** button displayed in the right of the list box. If you desire to view only the space selected in the list box, choose the **Isolate** button; the selected space will be displayed only in the preview pane. To get back the display of the entire model in the preview pane, choose the **Isolate** button again.

After viewing the spaces and the analytical surface and specifying various properties for the zones, choose the **Calculate** button; the report will be displayed in the drawing window along with the **Properties** palette displaying its properties. In the **Properties** palette, you can click on the value field corresponding to the **View Name** parameter and enter a new name. Choose the **Apply** button to apply the changed properties. In the **Project Browser**, the report will be added under the **Reports > Load Reports** node.

TUTORIALS

General instructions for downloading tutorial files:

1. Download the *c04_rmp_2017_tut.zip* file for this tutorial from *http://www.cadcim.com*. The path of the file is as follows: *Textbooks > Civil/GIS > Revit MEP > Exploring Autodesk Revit 2017 for MEP.*

2. Now, save and extract the downloaded folder at the following location: *C:\rmp_2017*

Tutorial 1 Placing Spaces- Office Space

In this tutorial, you will open a linked architectural model and then add spaces to it.

(Expected time: 1 hr 15 min)

1. Template file:
   For Imperial: **US Imperial > Systems-Default.**
   For Metric: **US Metric > Systems-Default_Metric**

2. File name to be used:
   For Imperial: *c04_archi_spaces_rmp2017.rvt*
   For Metric: *M_c04_archi_spaces_rmp2017.rvt*

3. File name to be assigned:
   For Imperial: *c04_Office-Space_tut1.rvt*
   For Metric: *M_c04_Office-Space_tut1.rvt*

The following steps are required to complete this tutorial:

a. Start a Revit 2017 session.
b. Open a new project and link an architectural model.
c. Add a Plenum level.
d. Rename and modify the Plenum level.
e. Place spaces in the 1-Mech view.
f. Rename and renumber the spaces.
g. Enable the space visibility.
h. Place space in the separated area.
i. Place space in the Chase area.
j. Save the project using the **Save As** tool.
k. Close the project using the **Close** tool.

Starting Autodesk Revit 2017

1. Start Autodesk Revit 2017 by choosing **Start > All Programs > Autodesk > Revit 2017 > Revit 2017**; the Revit interface window is displayed.

Opening a New Project and Linking the Architectural Model

In this section, you will open a new project and link the downloaded .rvt file to it.

1. Choose **New > Project** from the **Application Menu**; the **New Project** dialog box is displayed.

2. In the **New Project** dialog box, select the **Systems Template** (for Metric **Systems-Default_Metric**) from the **Template** file drop-down list and then choose the **OK** button; the **New Project** dialog box is closed and the new project is opened.

   In the new project file, you will download the architectural model in the current project view and then link the architectural model in the **1-Mech** view under the **Mechanical > HVAC > Floor Plans** view displayed in the **Project Browser**.

3. In the **Project Browser**, ensure that the **1-Mech** node is selected under **Mechanical > HVAC > Floor Plans** and then choose the **Link Revit** tool from the **Link** panel of the **Insert** tab; the **Import/Link RVT** dialog box is displayed. In this dialog box, browse to the *C:\rmp_2017\c04_rmp_2017_tut* folder and then select the *c04_archi_spaces_rmp2017.rvt* file. For Metric select the *M_c04_archi_spaces_rmp2017.rvt* file.

4. Now, choose the **Open** button; the selected file is linked to the current project and is displayed in the project view, as shown in Figure 4-25.

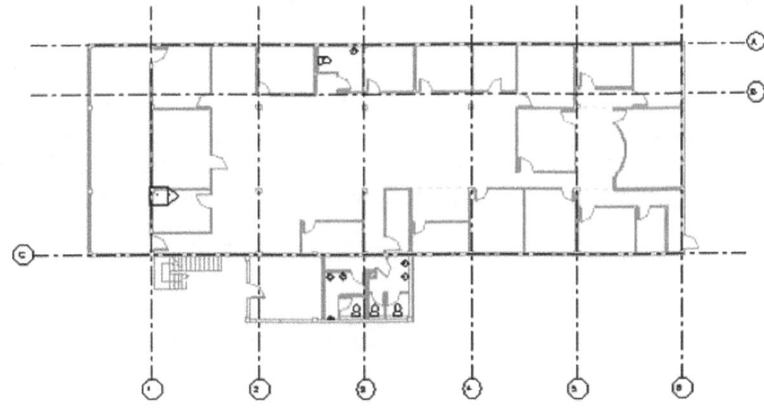

Figure 4-25 *The drawing view with the linked model*

5. Now, move the cursor over the linked model and click when a blue border is displayed around it; the **Modify | RVT Links** contextual tab is displayed.

6. In this tab, choose the **Type Properties** tool from the **Properties** panel; the **Type Properties** dialog box is displayed.

7. In this dialog box, select the check box displayed in the **Value** field corresponding to the **Room Bounding** parameter. The architectural components (such as walls and floors) are closed so that they are recognized as boundaries for spaces.

Note

While working with a linked file, make sure that the roof is defined as room bounding element and the ceiling is defined as a non-room bounding element. These components are defined in the architectural model file and not in the MEP model file.

8. In the **Type Properties** dialog box, choose the **OK** button to close it. Now, in the **Modify | RVT Links** contextual tab, choose the **Modify** button in the **Select** panel; the linking process of the architectural model is now complete.

Adding a Plenum Level

In this section, you will create a plenum level for the spaces. The plenum levels are created to place spaces in the plenum areas (between the ceiling and the floor) of the building. You must place spaces in all areas (occupied and unoccupied) of the building to achieve an accurate heating and cooling load analysis.

1. In the **Project Browser**, expand **Mechanical> HVAC> Elevations (Building Elevation)**, and double-click in the **East - Mech** node; the east elevation view is opened.

2. Choose the **Level** tool from the **Datum** panel of the **Architecture** tab; the **Modify | Place Level** tab is displayed along with various options in the **Options Bar**.

3. In the **Properties** palette, select the **Level Plenum** option from the **Type Selector** drop-down list.

4. In the **Options Bar**, ensure that the **Make Plan View** check box is selected and then choose the **Plan View Types** button; the **Plan View Types** dialog box is displayed, as shown in Figure 4-26. In this dialog box, you will notice that the **Ceiling Plan** and **Floor Plan** options are selected and highlighted in the **Select view types to create** list box.

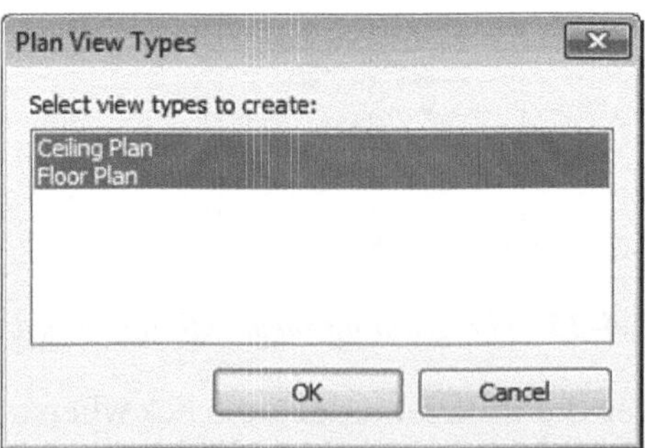

Figure 4-26 *The **Ceiling Plan** and the **Floor Plan** options selected in the **Plan View Types** dialog box*

5. In the list box, click on the **Ceiling Plan** option to clear the selection and then choose the **OK** button; the **Plan View Types** dialog box is closed.

6. Now, in the **Draw** panel of the **Modify | Place Level** contextual tab, ensure that the **Line** tool is chosen and then move and place the cursor near the endpoint of **Level 1** level. Move the cursor up. On doing so, you will notice a temporary dimension emerging from the left endpoint of the **Level 1**, as shown in Figure 4-27.

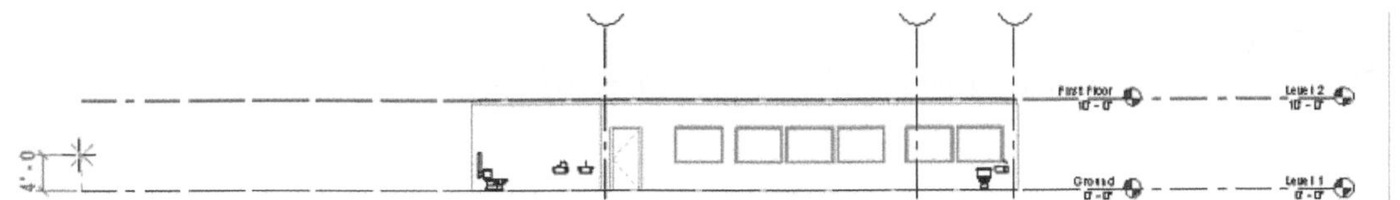

Figure 4-27 *The temporary dimension emerging from the **Level 1** line*

7. Now, type **8'6" (2591mm)** and press ENTER; the level starts at a distance of 8'6" (2591mm) from the **Level 1** level.

8. Now, move the cursor toward right and place it over the endpoint of **Level 1**. Click when the extension snap appears along with an alignment line emerging from **Level 1** line; the plenum level is created.

9. In the **Modify | Place Level** tab, choose the **Modify** button from the **Select** panel; you exit the **Level** tool.

10. In the **Project Browser**, double-click on the **Mechanical 3** (for Metric **Level 3**) node in **Mechanical > HVAC > Floor Plans** node; the floor plan view of the **Mechanical 3** level is displayed in the drawing window.

Renaming and Modifying the Plenum Level

1. In the **Properties** palette, click on the value field corresponding to the **View Name** parameter and enter **1-Mech-Plenum** in the edit box to replace the existing name. Press ENTER; the **Revit** message box is displayed. Choose the **Yes** button in the displayed message box; the level is renamed.

2. In the **Properties** palette, choose the **Mechanical Plan** button displayed in the value field corresponding to the **View Template** parameter; the **Apply View Template** dialog box is displayed.

3. In the dialog box, select the **<None>** option from the **Names** list box and then choose the **OK** button; the **Apply View Template** dialog box is closed.

4. In the **Properties** palette, choose the **Edit** button displayed in the value field corresponding to the **View Range** parameter; the **View Range** dialog box is displayed.

5. In the **Primary Range** area of the dialog box, select the **Level Above (Level 2)** option from the **Top** drop-down list. Also, select the **Associated Level (1-Mech-Plenum)** option from the **Bottom** drop-down list. Now, click in the **Offset** edit box displayed next to the **Cut plane** drop-down list and enter **1' (304mm)** to replace the existing value.

6. In the **View Depth** area of the **View Range** dialog box, select the **Associated Level (1-Mech-Plenum)** option from the **Level** drop-down list. Choose **Apply** and then **OK**; the **View Range** dialog box is closed.

7. In the **Project Browser**, under **HVAC > Floor Plans**, double-click on **1 - Mech** and maximize the window. Now, choose the **Close Hidden** button from the **Windows** panel of the **View** tab to close the displayed elevation view.

Note

*If none of the windows is maximized, then the **Close Hidden Windows** button is disabled.*

Placing Spaces in the 1-Mech View

In this section, you will place the spaces in the **1-Mech** floor plan view.

1. Choose the **Space** tool from the **Spaces & Zones** panel of the **Analyze** tab; the **Modify | Place Space** tab is displayed.

2. In the **Tag** panel of this tab, make sure that the **Tag on Placement** button is chosen by default. In the **Options Bar**, select the **1-Mech-Plenum** option from the **Upper Limit** drop-down list.

   In the **Options Bar**, ensure that the **0'0"** (**0.0**) value is specified in the **Offset** edit box, the **Horizontal** option is selected in the drop-down list displayed next to the **Offset** edit box, the **Leade**r check box is cleared and the **New** option is selected in the **Space** drop-down list.

3. In the drawing area, zoom into the office area located in the upper-left corner of the building. Now, place the cursor in it, until the space snaps to the room-bounding elements, as shown in Figure 4-28. Click when the room bounding is highlighted; the new space is placed with the default name **Space** and number **1**.

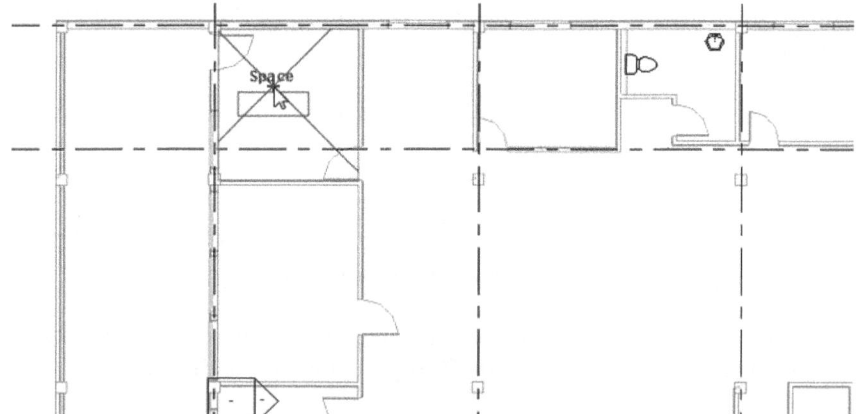

Figure 4-28 *Placing the space inside the room-bounding area*

4. Ensure that the **Space** tool is invoked. Then, press ZF; the project view is zoomed to fit the drawing area. This displays the entire floor plan placed at the center of the drawing area.

Tip

*You can right-click in the drawing window and select the **Zoom to Fit** option from the shortcut menu displayed*

5. Now, move the cursor to the large open area at the center of the floor plan, and after the space snaps to the room bounding elements, click to place a space, as shown in Figure 4-29.

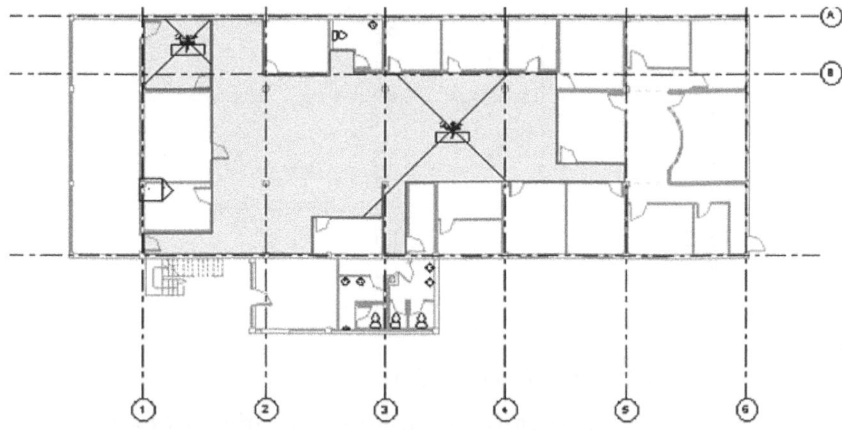

Figure 4-29 *The space added to the large open area*

Make sure that you have placed the space tag toward right in the open space. Later in the tutorial, you will separate the open space near the entrance and place a space there.

6. In the **Modify | Place Space** contextual tab, choose the **Modify** button from the **Select** panel; the **Space** tool is exited.

Renaming and Renumbering the Spaces

In this section, you will rename and renumber the spaces added.

1. Zoom in the space tag in the office area in the upper-left corner and then click on the **Space** text; an edit box is displayed. Enter **CEO-Office** in the edit box and press ENTER; the space name is changed.

2. Now, in the same space, double- click on the text **1**; an edit box is displayed. Enter **101** to replace the previous number and press ENTER; the space number is changed.

3. Repeat steps 1 and 2 and rename and renumber the space at the central area as **Central Area** and **110**, respectively, refer to Figure 4-30.

Enabling the Space Visibility

In this section, you will enable the visibility of the space interior fills and markers.

1. Ensure that the **1-Mech** floor plan view is active and then choose the **Visibility/Graphics** tool from the **Graphics** panel of the **View** tab; the **Visibility/Graphics Override for Floor Plan: 1-Mech** dialog box is displayed.

2. In the dialog box, ensure that the **Model Categories** tab is chosen by default, and then in the **Visibility** column, expand the **Spaces** node. Ensure that the check box corresponding to the **Spaces** node is selected.

3. Now, under the **Spaces** node, ensure that the **Color Fill** check box is selected and then select the **Interior** and **Reference** check boxes.

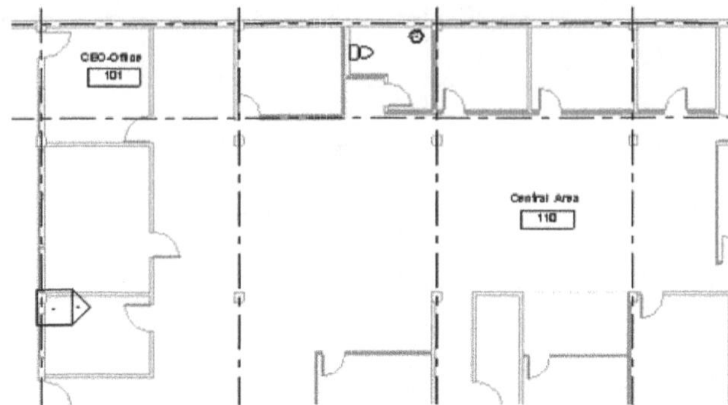

Figure 4-30 The central area space renamed and renumbered

4. Choose the **OK** button; the the **Visibility/Graphics Override for Floor Plan1-Mech** dialog box is closed and the added spaces will be displayed with the specified settings, as shown in Figure 4-31.

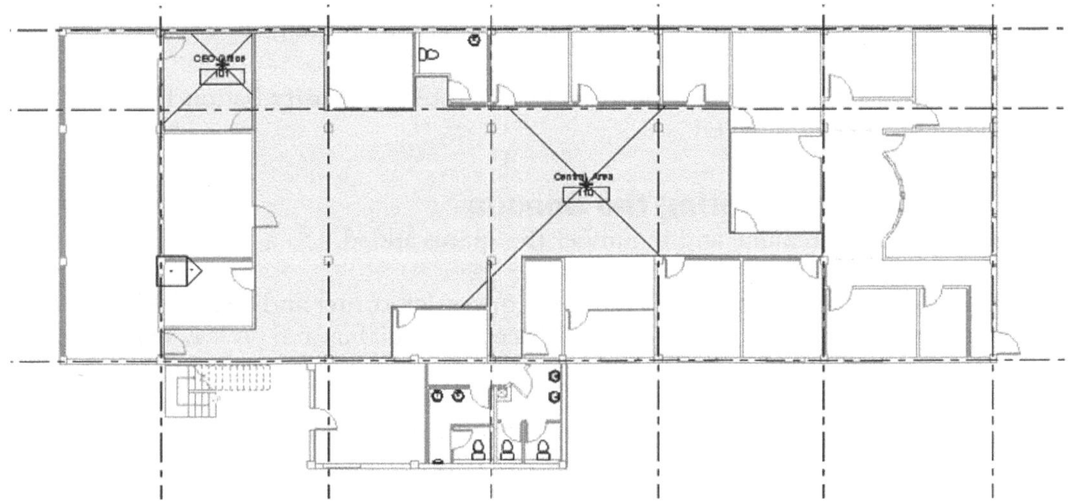

Figure 4-31 The markers and the interior fills displayed in the added spaces

Splitting the Space

You need to place a space in the area next to the building entrance because this area will be heated and cooled more often than the rest of the open spaces. The entrance area is considered semi-bounded. To place a space in this area, you need to make it fully-bounded by drawing space separation lines. In this section, you will split the **Central Area** space.

1. Ensure that the **1 - Mech** view is active and enter ZR; the cursor changes into a zoom region icon. Click at the point above the **CEO-Office** space area and drag the mouse downward right below the **Central Area** space, refer to Figure 4-32. and click; the central region of the office area is zoomed.

2. Choose the **Space Separator** tool from the **Spaces & Zones** panel of the **Analyze** tab; the **Modify | Place Space Separation** contextual tab is displayed. In the **Draw** panel of the tab, ensure that the **Line** tool is chosen by default. Also, in the **Options Bar**, ensure that the **Chain** check box is selected and the value specified in the **Offset** edit box is **0'0" (0.0)**.

3. Now, place the cursor at the endpoint of the space boundary of the **Central Area** near the **Toilet** area, as shown in Figure 4-33. Click when the **Endpoint** snap marker appears; the start point of the separation line is specified.

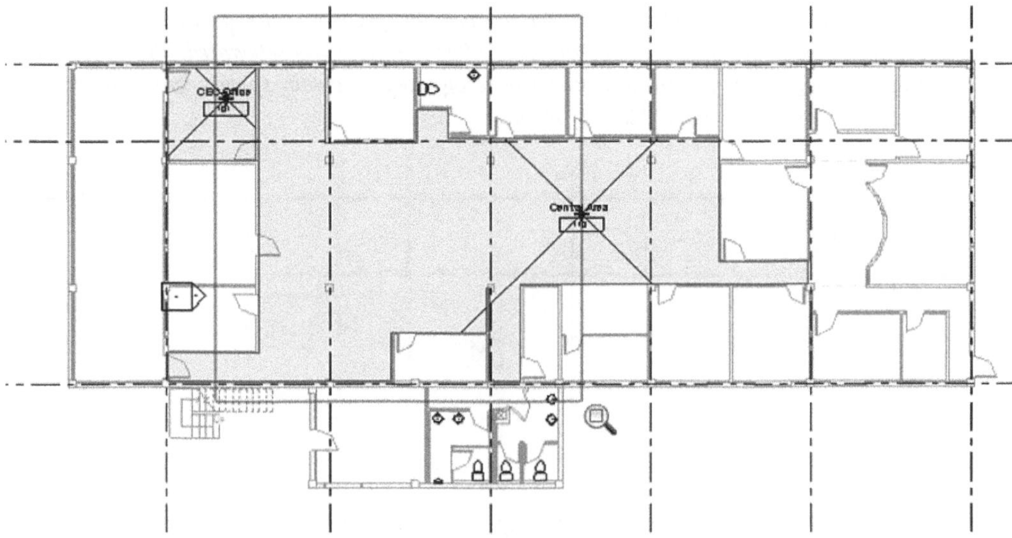

Figure 4-32 *Specifying the zoom area*

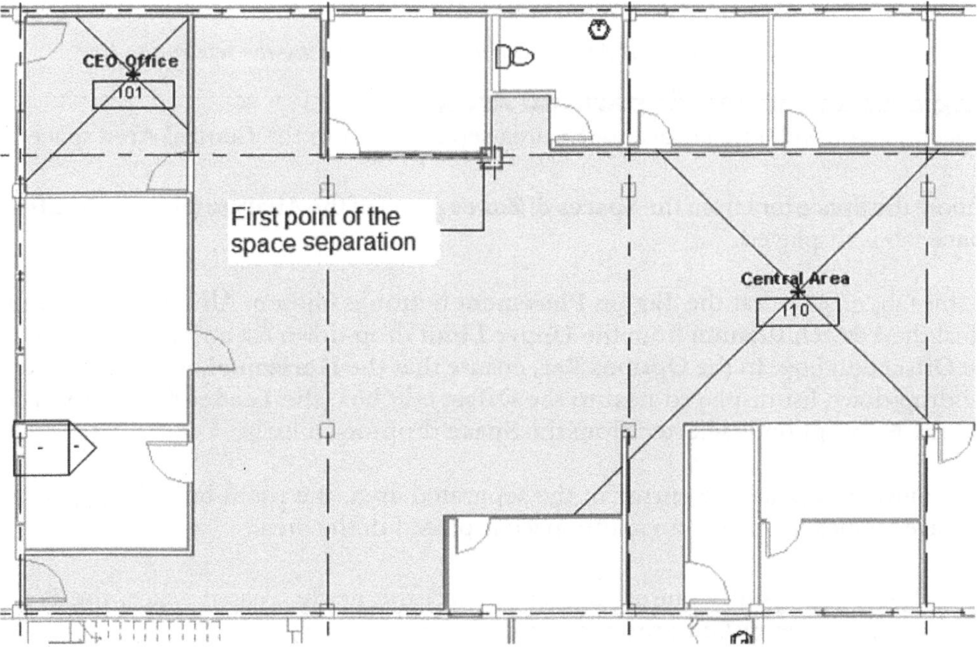

Figure 4-33 *Specifying the start point of the separator line*

4. Now, move the cursor vertically downward; a dashed line along with temporary dimension appears. Enter **26'5" (8052mm)** and press ENTER; the separation line is created and the **Central Area** is adjusted to the new separation line, as shown in Figure 4-34. Now, choose

the **Modify** button in the **Select** panel of the **Modify | Place Space Separation** contextual tab to exit the **Space Separator** tool.

Note

Space separation lines are MEP-specific room bounding lines that separate areas where a wall is not required or is not possible to create one. After the areas are separated, spaces can be placed in them. Although room separation lines are recognized in Revit, space separation lines are not recognized in Architecture discipline of Revit.

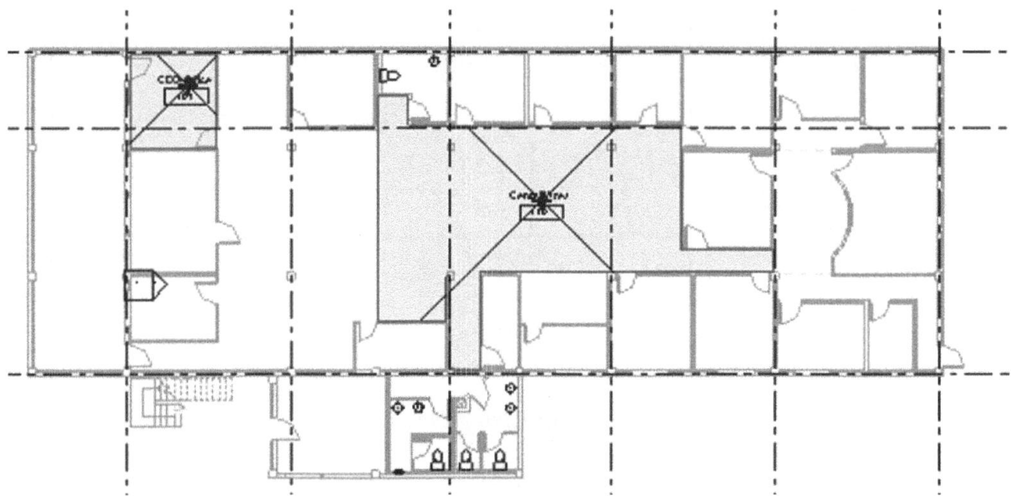

Figure 4-34 *The **Central Area** space adjusted on adding the separation line*

Placing a Space in the Separated Area

In this section, you will add a space to the area separated from the **Central Area** space.

1. Choose the **Space** tool from the **Spaces & Zones** panel of the **Analyze** tab; the **Modify | Place Space** tab is displayed.

2. In this tab, ensure that the **Tag on Placement** button is chosen. Also, in the **Options Bar**, select the **1-Mech Plenum** from the **Upper Limit** drop-down list and then enter **0"(0.0)** in the **Offset** edit box. In the **Options Bar**, ensure that the **Horizontal** option is selected from the drop-down list displayed next to the **Offset** edit box, the **Leader** check box is cleared, and the **New** option is selected from the **Space** drop-down list.

3. Now, move and place the cursor in the separated area; the room bounding space snap is displayed. Click inside the area, the space is placed in the area.

4. Now, choose the **Modify** button and then select the newly created space; the **Properties** palette displays the instance property of the selected space.

5. In the **Properties** palette, click in the value field corresponding to the **Number** parameter. Next, type **115** and press ENTER.

6. Now, click in the value field of the **Name** parameter. Then, type **Lounge** and press ENTER. Choose the **Modify** button from the **Select** panel of the **Modify | Spaces** tab to exit the modification of the space.

The space number and the name is changed, as shown in Figure 4-35.

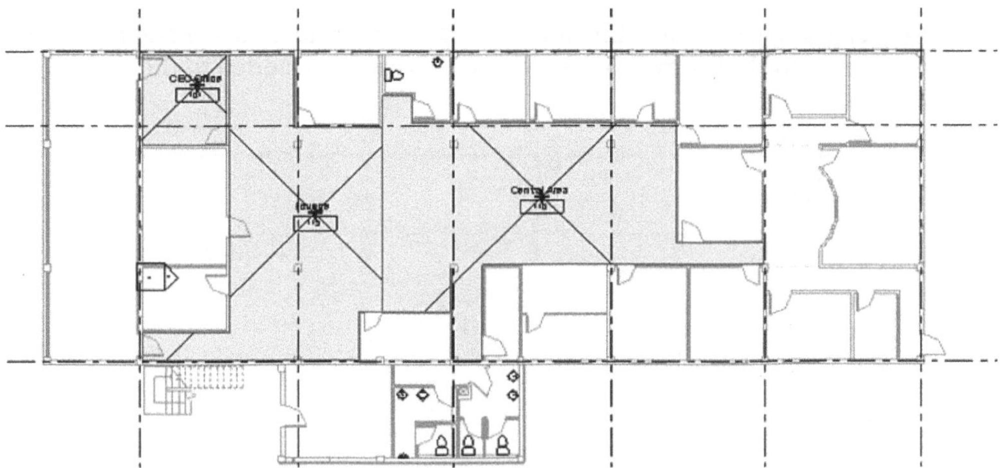

Figure 4-35 The added space renamed and renumbered

Placing a Space in the Chases Area

In this section, you will add a space to the chases area. Note that the space components are placed in chases to permit a reliable heating and cooling load analysis.

1. Zoom in the chases area that is located below the central area, as shown in Figure 4-36.

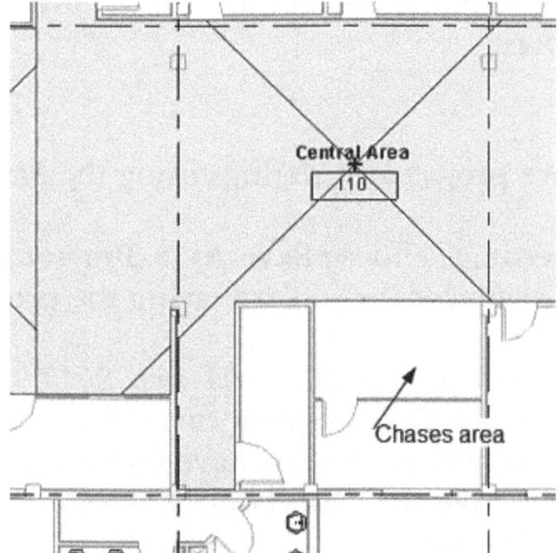

Figure 4-36 Zooming in the chases area

2. Invoke the **Space** tool from the **Spaces & Zones** panel of the **Analyze** tab and then in the **Options Bar**, select **Level 2** from the **Upper Limit** drop-down list.

3. Click in the **Offset** edit box, enter **1'6" (457mm)**, and press ENTER.

4. Next, click in the chases area, refer to Figure 4-37, and click when the space snap is highlighted.

5. Now, choose the **Modify** button from the **Select** panel of the **Modify | Place Space** contextual tab and then select the added space.

6. In the **Properties** palette, enter **Chases** and **121** in the value fields of **Name** and **Number** edit boxes, respectively. Figure 4-37 shows the **Chases** space added to the model.

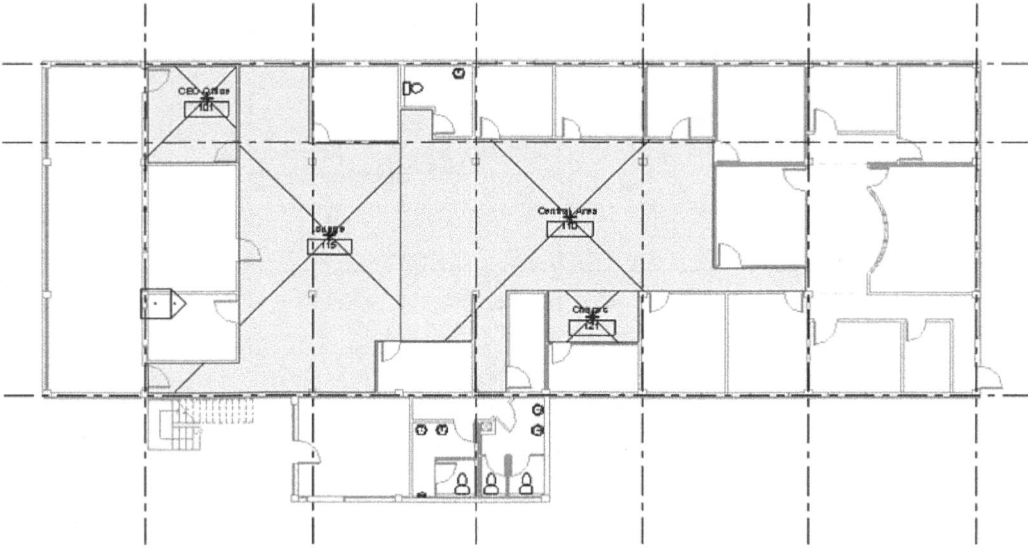

Figure 4-37 *Chases space added to the model*

7. Choose the **Modify** button from the **Select** panel of the **Modify | Space** contextual tab to exit the selection of the space.

Saving the Project

In this section, you need to save project and settings using the **Save As** tool.

1. To save the project with settings, choose **Save As > Project** from the **Application Menu**; the **Save As** dialog box is displayed, as you are saving the project for the first time.

2. In this dialog box, browse to the *c:\rmp_2017\c04_rmp_2017_tut* folder and then in the **File name** edit box, enter the text **c04_Office-Space_tut1** (for Metric **M_c04_Office-Space_tut1**) and then choose the **Options** button; the **File Save Options** dialog box is displayed. In this dialog box, ensure that the **Active view/sheet** option is selected from the **Source** drop-down list in the **Thumbnail Preview** area.

3. Now, choose the **OK** button; the **File Save Options** dialog box is closed and the **Save As** dialog box is displayed.

4. In this dialog box, choose the **Save** button to save the current project file with the specified name and close the **Save As** dialog box.

Closing the Project

1. To close the project, choose the **Close** option from **Application Menu**; the file is closed.

   This completes Tutorial 1 of Chapter 4.

Tutorial 2 Creating Zones- Office Space

In this tutorial, you will assign spaces to the zones in the building, and verify the zones in the **System Browser** window. Zones allow you to control the spacial environment and to perform an accurate heating and cooling load analysis. **(Expected time: 30 min)**

File to be used:
For Imperial: *c04_tut2_zones_rmp2017*
For Metric: *M_c04_tut2_zones_rmp2017*

File name to be assigned:
For Imperial: *c04_Office-Space_tut2.rvt*
For Metric: *M_c04_Office-Space_tut2.rvt*

The following steps are required to complete this tutorial:

a. Open the project file
b. Modify the visibility of spaces.
c. Display spaces in the **System Browser**.
d. Assign spaces to zones.
e. Setting the visibility of zones.
f. Rename the zones.
g. Save the project by using the **Save As** tool.
h. Close the project by using the **Close** tool.

Opening the Project

In this section, you will open the downloaded project.

1. Choose **Open > Project** from **Application Menu**; the **Open** dialog box is displayed.

2. In the **Open** dialog box, browse to *C:\rmp_2017\c04_rmp_2017_tut* and select the *c04_tut2_zones_rmp2017.rvt* file. Now, choose **Open**; the selected file opens in the Revit interface.

Note

The architectural model named c04_archi_spaces_rmp_2017.rvt linked in this tutorial file is located in the c04_rmp_2017_tut folder. It is recommended to maintain the relative path to the architectural model. However, if the link is lost, you need to reload the file using the ***Manage Links*** *dialog box which has already been discussed in the previous chapters.*

Modifying the Visibility Settings of the Spaces

In this section, you will clear the markers in the spaces.

1. Ensure that the **1-Mech** floor plan view is active. Next, type VG; the **Visibility/Graphic Overrides For Floor Plan: 1-Mech** dialog box is displayed.

2. In the dialog box, ensure that the **Model Categories** tab is chosen. Also, in this tab ensure that the **Mechanical** check box is selected in the **Filter list** drop-down list. Now, expand the **Spaces** nodes in the **Visibility** column.

3. In the expanded **Spaces** node, clear the **Reference** check box.

4. Choose **Apply** and **OK**; the **Visibility/Graphic Overrides For Floor Plan: 1-Mech** dialog box is closed and the reference lines are removed from the spaces, as shown in Figure 4-38.

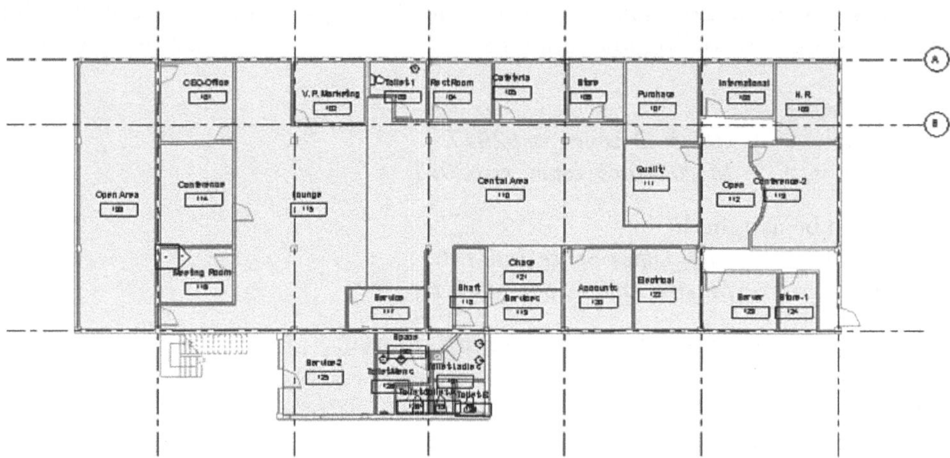

***Figure 4-38** Reference lines removed from spaces*

Note that all the space reference lines have been hidden to provide a clear view of the floor plan.

Displaying Spaces in the System Browser

In this section, you will invoke the **System Browser** window to view spaces in the model.

1. Ensure that the **1-Mech** floor plan view is active and then select the **System Browser** check box from **View > Windows > User Interface** drop-down; the **System Browser** window is displayed.

Note

*You can also press F9 (with the drawing area active) to invoke the **System Browser** window.*

2. In the **System Browser** window, select the **Zones** option from the **View** drop-down list; a list of zones in the drawing is displayed in the **Zones** list box.

3. In the list box, expand the **Default** node; all the spaces in the model are displayed under it, as shown in Figure 4-39.

This is a hierarchical list of spaces and zones to which spaces have been assigned. Notice that **Default** is the current zone.

Note

*A space cannot be placed in an area without being added to a zone. After a space is placed in an area, it is automatically added to the **Default** zone. It is recommended to add each space to a zone created to remove it from the **Default** zone.*

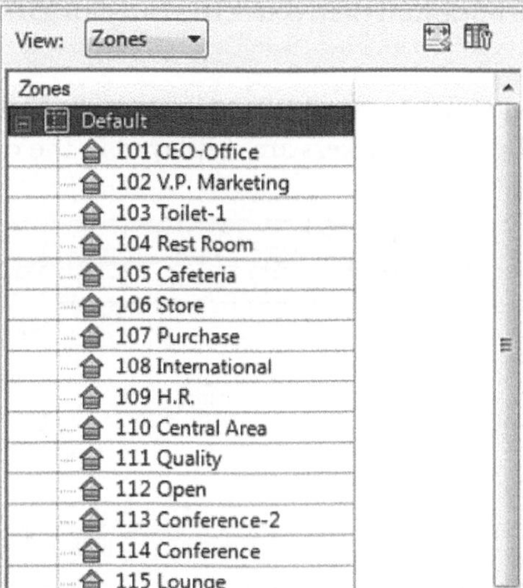

***Figure 4-39 The System Browser** window displaying the spaces under the **Default** node*

Assigning Spaces to Zones

You will assign spaces to a zone and then using the **System Browser** window confirm that the spaces are in the new zone. You also need to assign a zone to spaces on the same level.

1. Choose the **Zone** tool from the **Spaces and Zones** panel in the **Analyze** tab; the **Edit Zone** contextual tab is displayed and the drawing becomes faded.

2. In the **Mode** panel of the **Edit Zone** contextual tab, ensure that the **Add Space** tool is chosen and then in the drawing area, place the cursor on **V.P. Marketing** space located in the upper-left corner of the building; the space is highlighted. Now, click on the highlighted space; the space is added to a new zone **1**.

3. Similarly, click on the following spaces: Toilet-1(103), Rest Room(104), Cafeteria(105), Store(106) Purchase(107), International(108), and HR(109).

4. Now, choose the **Finish Editing Zone** button from the **Edit Zone** panel of the **Edit Zone** tab.

   Notice that the added spaces are now displayed under the **1** node in the **Zones** list box of the **System Browser**.

Setting the Visibility of the Zones

In this section, you will specify the visibility settings of the zones.

1. Type VG; the **Visibility/Graphics Override for Floor Plan1-Mech** dialog box is displayed.

2. Expand the **HVAC Zones** node and then select the **Interior Fill** and **Reference Lines** check boxes.

3. Choose **Apply** and **OK** to close the **Visibility/Graphics Override for Floor Plan: 1-Mech** dialog box. Notice that the zone markers are displayed in the drawing window, as shown in Figure 4-40.

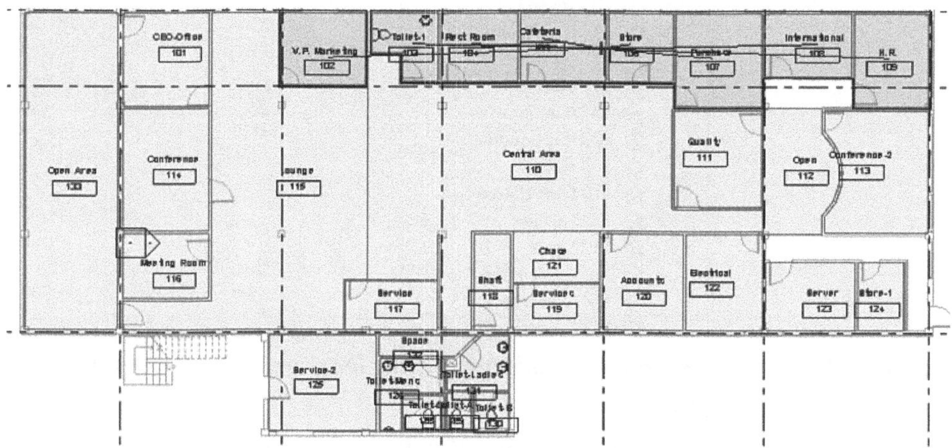

Figure 4-40 *Zone markers displayed in the added zone*

Renaming the Zone

1. In the **System Browser**, click on the **1** node in the **Zones** list box; the **Modify | HVAC Zones** contextual tab is displayed.

2. In this tab, choose the **Edit Zone** tool from the **Zone** panel; the **Edit Zone** contextual tab is displayed.

3. In the contextual tab, double-click in the **Properties** button; the **Properties** palette of the selected zone is displayed.

4. Click in the value field corresponding to the **Name** edit box and enter **Office-North-Zone** and press ENTER.

5. Now, choose the **Finish Editing Zone** button from the **Edit Zone** panel; the zone is renamed.

   In the **System Browser**, the **Office-North-Zone** node is displayed with the spaces assigned to it.

Saving the Project

In this section, you need to save the project and the settings using the **Save As** tool.

1. To save the project with the settings, choose **Save As > Project** from the **Application Menu**; the **Save As** dialog box is displayed as you are saving the file for the first time.

2. In this dialog box, browse to the *C:|rmp_2017|c04_rmp_2017_tut* folder and then in the **File name** edit box, enter **c04_Office-Space_tut2** (For Metric enter **M_c04_Office-Space_tut2**) and choose the **Options** button; the **File Save Options** dialog box is displayed.

3. In this dialog box, enter **5** in the **Maximum backups** edit box and then choose **OK**; the **File Save Options** dialog box is closed and the **Save As** dialog box is displayed.

4. In this dialog box, choose the **Save** button to save the current project file with the specified name and to close the **Save As** dialog box.

Closing the Project

1. To close the project, choose the **Close** option from the **Application Menu**.

   The file is closed and this completes Tutorial 2 of Chapter 4.

Tutorial 3 Heating and Cooling Load Analysis

In this tutorial, you will perform the Heating and Cooling load analysis of the space model. Also, you will export the model to gbXML file format. **(Expected time: 45 min)**

File name to be used:
For Imperial: *c04_tut3_analysis_rmp2017*
For Metric: *M_c04_tut3_analysis_rmp2017*

File name to be assigned for export:
For Imperial: *c04_Office-Space_tut3-gb.xml*
For Metric: *M_c04_Office-Space_tut3-gb.xml*

File to be assigned:
For Imperial: *c04_Office-Space_tut3.rvt*
For Metric: *M_c04_Office-Space_tut3.rvt*

The following steps are required to complete this tutorial:

a. Open the project file.
b. Specify the project information.
c. Verify the area and volume settings
d. Verify the building information.
e. Verify the space information.
f. Perform the Heating and Cooling Loads analysis.
g. Export the model information to *.gbXML* file format.
h. Save the project using the **Save As** tool.
i. Close the project by using the **Close** tool.

Opening the Project File

1. Choose **Open > Project** from the **Application Menu**; the **Open** dialog box is displayed.

2. In the dialog box, select the *c04_tut3_analysis_rmp2017.rvt* (for Metric *M_c04_tut3_analysis_rmp2017.rvt*) file and then choose the **Open** button; the project file is opened.

Note

The architectural model named c04_archi_spaces_rmp_2017.rvt linked in this tutorial file is located in the c04_rmp_2017_tut folder. In the ***Manage Links*** *dialog box, it is recommended to assign the* ***Path Type*** *of the linked architectural model to* ***Relative****. However, if the link is lost, you need to reload the file using the* ***Manage Links*** *dialog box which has already been discussed in the previous chapters.*

Specifying the Project Information

In this section, you will set the project information for the project.

1. Choose the **Project Information** tool from the **Settings** panel of the **Manage** tab; the **Project Properties** dialog box is displayed.

2. In this dialog box, choose the **Edit** button corresponding to the **Energy Settings** parameter; the **Energy Settings** dialog box is displayed.

3. In this dialog box, ensure that the **Office** option is selected in the **Value** field corresponding to the **Building Type** parameter.

4. Next, click in the **Value** field corresponding to the **Location** parameter; a browse button is displayed. Choose the button; the **Location Weather and Site** dialog box is displayed. In this dialog box, ensure that the **Location** tab is chosen by default and then select **Default City List** from the **Define Location by** drop-down list, if it is not selected by default.

5. Now, select the **Indianapolis, IN** option from the **City** drop-down list.

6. In the **Location Weather and Site** dialog box, choose the **Weather** tab and then select the **Use closest weather station(INDIANAPOLIS)** check box, if it is not selected by default.

7. In the **Weather** tab, ensure that **-2 °F** (**-19 °C**) and **1.0** values are specified in the **Heating Design Temperatures** and **Clearness Number** edit boxes, respectively.

8. Now, choose **OK**; the **Location Weather and Site** dialog box is closed and the selected option is displayed in the **Value** field corresponding to the **Location** parameter.

9. In the **Energy Settings** dialog box, retain the default settings for the remaining parameters, refer to Figure 4-41, and then choose the **OK** button; the **Energy Settings** dialog box is closed. Again, choose the **OK** button to close the **Project Properties** dialog box.

Verifying the Area and Volume Settings

1. Choose the **Area and Volume Computations** tool from the **Spaces & Zones** panel of the **Analyze** tab; the **Area and Volume Computations** dialog box is displayed.

2. In this dialog box, ensure that the **Computations** tab is chosen by default and then in the **Volume Computations** area, select the **Area and Volumes** radio button, if it is not selected by default.

3. In the **Room Area Computation** area, select the **At wall finish** radio button, if it is not selected by default.

4. Now, choose the **OK** button; the **Area and Volume Computations** dialog box is closed.

Note

*The **Areas and Volumes** option must be selected for a space to perform an accurate heating and cooling loads analysis.*

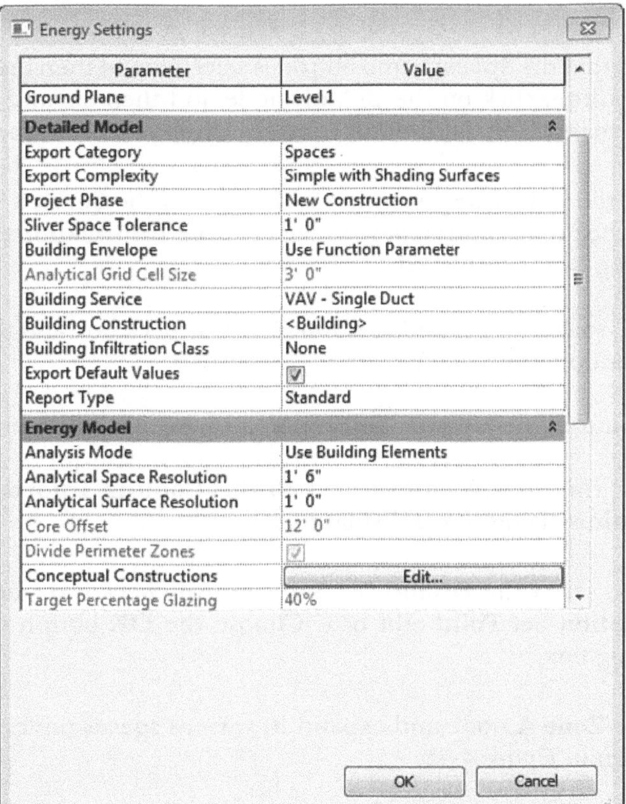

Figure 4-41 *The default values in the **Energy Settings** dialog box*

Verifying the Building Information

1. Choose the **Heating and Cooling Loads** tool from the **Reports & Schedules** panel of the **Analyze** tab; the **Heating and Cooling Loads** dialog box is displayed.

2. In this dialog box, ensure that the **General** tab is chosen by default and then click on the **Value** field corresponding to the **Building Infiltration Class** parameter; a drop-down list is displayed.

3. Select the **Tight** option from the displayed drop-down list.

4. Click on the **Value** field corresponding to the **Report Type** parameter and then select the **Detailed** option from the drop-down list displayed.

5. Select the check box displayed in the **Value** field corresponding to the **Use Load Credits** parameter.

   After verifying and setting the building information, you will verify and specify the space information of the building.

Verifying the Space Information

1. In the **Heating and Cooling Loads** dialog box, choose the **Details** tab; various options in this tab are displayed.

2. In this tab, ensure that the **Spaces** radio button is selected and then in the list box displayed below the radio button, click on the **Default** node and then expand it. Note that various settings and information for the **Default** zone are displayed below the list box.

3. Now, ensure that the **<Building>** option is selected in the **Service Type** drop-down list, and then choose the browse button next to the **Heating Information** edit box; the **Heating Information** dialog box is displayed.

4. In this dialog box, select the **Humidification Control** check box and then enter **15%** in the **Humidification Set** point edit box.

5. Choose the **OK** button; the **Heating Information** dialog box is closed.

6. Similarly, choose the browse button next to the **Cooling Information** edit box; the **Cooling Information** dialog box is displayed.

7. In the dialog box, select the **Humidification Control** check box and then enter **85%** in the **Dehumidification Set Point** edit box. Choose the **OK** button to close the **Cooling Information** dialog box.

8 Next, click on the **Zone A** node and expand it; various spaces under it are displayed in a hierarchy, as shown in Figure 4-42.

9. To view the spaces in **Zone A**, choose the **Highlight** button displayed on the right of the dialog box, refer to Figure 4-43; various spaces are highlighted in the preview pane displayed in the left pane.

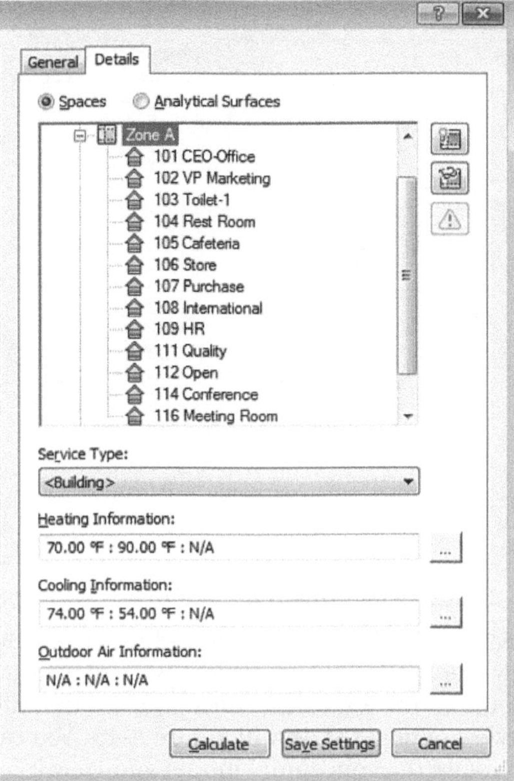

***Figure 4-42** The **Zone A** node expanded with various nodes*

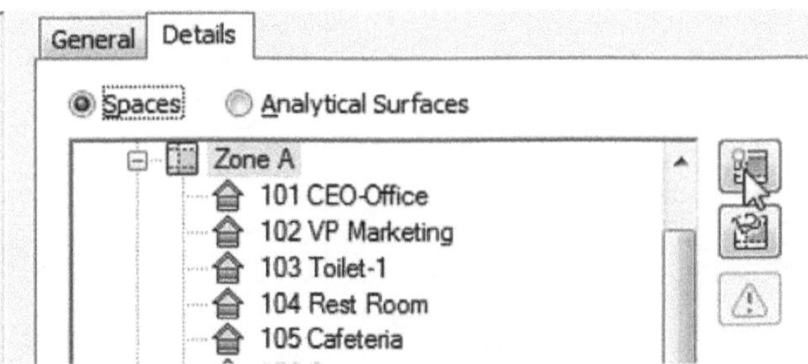

***Figure 4-43** Choosing the **Highlight** button*

10. Similarly, select the **Zone B** node; the spaces in the **Zone B** are highlighted in the conceptual model displayed in the preview pane. Now, choose the **Isolate** button displayed below the **Highlight** button in the **Heating and Cooling Loads** dialog box; the spaces in **Zone B** are displayed in isolation from the main conceptual model in the preview pane, as shown in Figure 4-44.

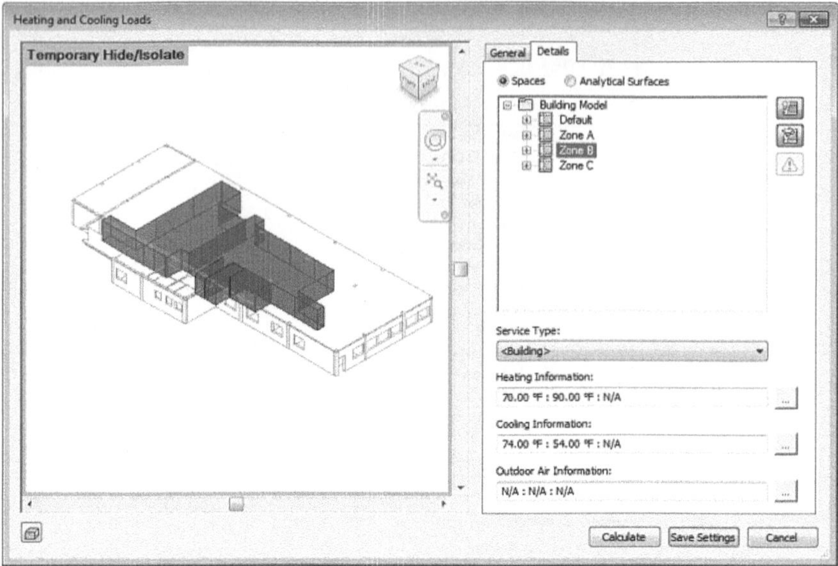

*Figure 4-44 Spaces in the **Zone B** are highlighted in the preview pane*

11. In the **Details** tab, select the **Analytical Surface** radio button and then choose the **Isolate** button again; the analytical model of the project is displayed in the preview pane. Now, choose the **Highlight** button; the analytical conceptual model without the space highlights is displayed in the preview pane, as shown in Figure 4-45. You can use the **ViewCube** tool in the preview pane to rotate the conceptual model and view it from all sides.

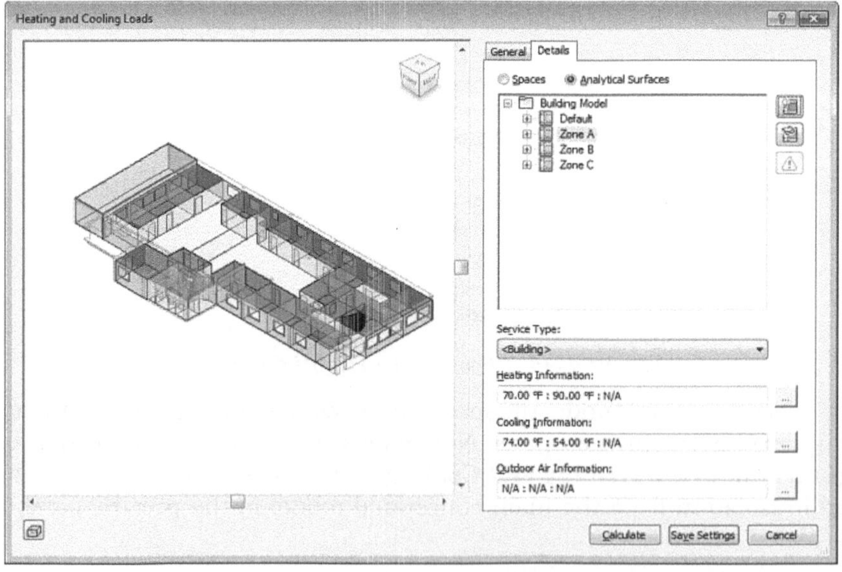

Figure 4-45 The analytical surfaces of the model with space highlights displayed in the preview pane

Tip

*You can use the **View Cube** tool to spin, pan, and zoom the model to have a better view of the space.*

Performing the Heating and Cooling Loads Analysis

1. In the **Heating and Cooling Loads** dialog box, choose the **Calculate** button; the heating and load analysis is performed and the report is displayed in the drawing window, as shown in Figure 4-46.

Project Summary

Location and Weather	
Project	Project Name
Address	
Calculation Time	Thursday, May 07, 2015 2:43 PM
Report Type	Standard
Latitude	39.78°
Longitude	-86.15°
Summer Dry Bulb	94 °F
Summer Wet Bulb	80 °F
Winter Dry Bulb	-2 °F
Mean Daily Range	19 °F

Building Summary

Inputs	
Building Type	Office
Area (SF)	5,447
Volume (CF)	45,636.58
Calculated Results	
Psychrometric Message	One or more zones have psychrometric errors
Peak Cooling Total Load	-
Peak Cooling Month and Hour	-
Peak Cooling Sensible Load	-
Peak Cooling Latent Load	-
Maximum Cooling Capacity	-
Peak Cooling Airflow	-

Figure 4-46 *The Heating and Cooling load report*

You can scroll down and view the entire report. Also, notice that in the **Project Browser**, the load report is added as the **Loads Report(1)** node under **Reports > Load Reports**, refer to Figure 4-47. You can click on the **Loads Report(1)** node to view the report whenever required.

Revit performs a heating and cooling loads analysis using the integrated heating and cooling loads analysis engine. In this analysis, various factors are analyzed including analytical and inner volumes of the spaces.

2. Review the loads report to analyze the project, weather, space, and zone information of the building model.

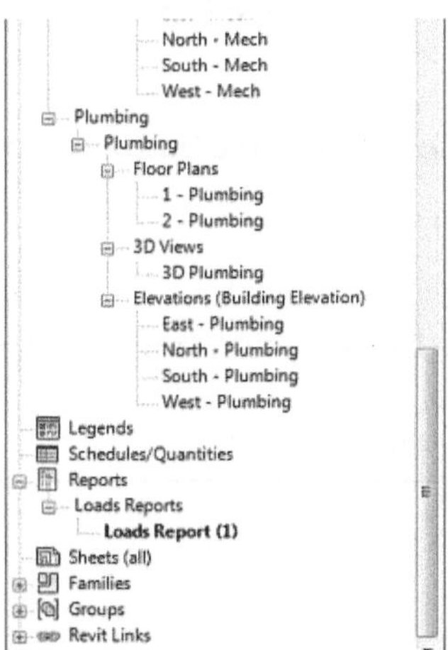

Figure 4-47 *The **Project Browser** displaying the **Loads Report(1)** node*

Note

You must perform a new heating and cooling loads analysis each time you modify building, space, or zone information, or make any changes to the model, otherwise the loads report or schedules will not reflect your changes.

After you have performed the load analysis of the model using the IES engine, you can export the model information to a third party software and compare the results. To export the model information to a third party software, you need to create a gbXML file.

Exporting the Model Information to gbXML File

In this section, you will export the model information into gbXML file format.

1. Choose **Export > gbXML** from the **Application Menu**; the **Export gbXML Settings** dialog box is displayed.

2. Retain all the default settings in the dialog box and then choose the **Next** button; the **Export to gbXML -Save to Target Folder** dialog box is displayed.

3. Browse to the *C:\rmp_2017\c04_rmp_2017_tut* folder and type **c04_office-space-tut3-gb** (for Metric, **M_c04_office-space-tut3-gb**)in the **File name** edit box. Choose **Save**; the file is saved in the *.xml* file format.

Saving the Project

In this section, you need to save the project and settings using the **Save As** tool.

1. To save the project with the settings, choose **Save As > Project** from the **Application Menu**; the **Save As** dialog box is displayed as you are saving the project for the first time,.

2. In this dialog box, browse to the *C:\rmp_2017\c04_rmp_2017_tut* folder and then in the **File name** edit box, enter **c04_Office-Space_tut3** (for Metric, **M_c04_Office-Space_tut3**)and then choose the **Options** button; the **File Save Options** dialog box is displayed.

3. Now, choose the **OK** button; the **File Save Options** dialog box is closed and the **Save As** dialog box is displayed.

4. In the displayed dialog box, choose the **Save** button to save the current project file with the specified name.

Closing the Project

1. To close the project, choose the **Close** option from the **Application Menu**; the file is closed.

   This completes Tutorial 3 of Chapter 4.

Self-Evaluation Test

Answer the following questions and then compare them to those given at the end of this chapter:

1. The__________tool is used to split a space into two or multiple spaces.

2. The **Zone** tool is available in the _________ panel of the **Analyze** tab.

3. Before performing load analysis, you need to create spaces in a building model. (T/F)

4. Color schemes are used to categorize different spaces in a project by using color codes. (T/F)

5. You cannot place multiple color scheme legends in the plan view. (T/F)

Review Questions

Answer the following questions:

1. Which of the following tools is used to invoke the **Edit Color Scheme** dialog box?

   a) **Endpoints** b) **Zone**
   c) **Color Schemes** d) **Space**

2. In a Zone, you can add only occupied areas. (T/F)

3. The **Heating and Cooling Loads** tool is used to perform the heating and cooling load analysis in a project. (T/F)

4. In Revit, the volume calculations of the spaces and rooms are done considering the finish face of the room bounding element. (T/F)

5. You cannot remove the space and its information from a model. (T/F)

EXERCISE

Exercise 1 Creating Spaces

Download the *c04_Conference-Center_exer1.rvt* (for Metric *M_c04_Conference-Center_exer1.rvt*)file from *http://www.cadcim.com*. The path of the file is as follows: *Textbooks > Civil/GIS > Revit > Exploring Autodesk Revit 2017 for MEP*.

In this exercise, you will open an architectural model and then add spaces to it. Name and number the spaces, as shown in Figure 4-48.

Note
You can add properties to the spaces as per your design requirement.

1. Project view to be used :
   Views > Floor Plans > Mechanical > 1ST FLOOR- HVAC Space

2. File name to be assigned: *c04_Conference-Center_exer1a.rvt* (For Metric *M_c04_Conference-Center_exer1a.rvt*).

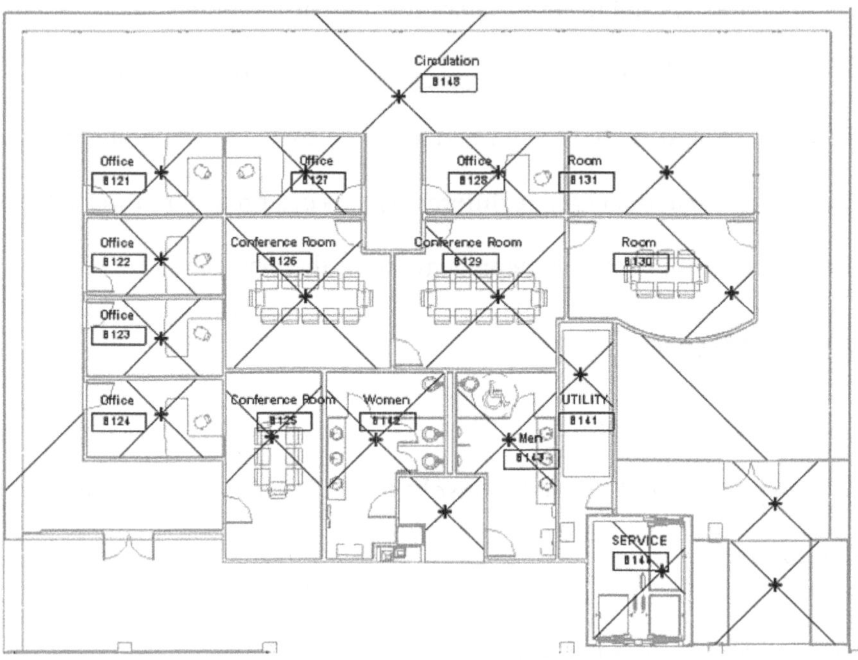

Figure 4-48 *Spaces created for the Conference-Center project*

Answers to Self-Evaluation Test

1. Space Separator, 2. Spaces & Zones, 3. T, **4.** T, **5.** F

Chapter 5

Creating an HVAC System

Learning Objectives

After completing this chapter, you will be able to:

- *Create an HVAC system*
- *Generate an HVAC system layout*
- *Create ducts and duct fittings*

INTRODUCTION

In this chapter, you will learn about various tools and options to create HVAC systems for a project. In Revit, you can use different tools to create, modify, and inspect HVAC systems in a project. These tools allow you to model and analyze systems and check whether your project design values meet the engineering standards fixed by the organization you are working with.

CREATING AN HVAC SYSTEM

In an MEP project, the HVAC system is designed for three important functions, namely heating, ventilating, and air conditioning of a building. These three functions are closely interrelated and the design, installation, and control systems of these functions are integrated into one or more HVAC systems in a project.

While working in an HVAC system for an MEP project, you will place air terminals and mechanical equipment. Next, you will create supply, return, and exhaust systems to connect the components of the HVAC system and create system groups.

In Revit, you create the HVAC systems using different tools available in the **HVAC**, **Fabrication**, and **Mechanical** panels of the **Systems** tab, as shown in Figure 5-1. Apart from these tools, you can use automatic system creation tools to create duct routing layouts to connect the supply and return system components to the HVAC system.

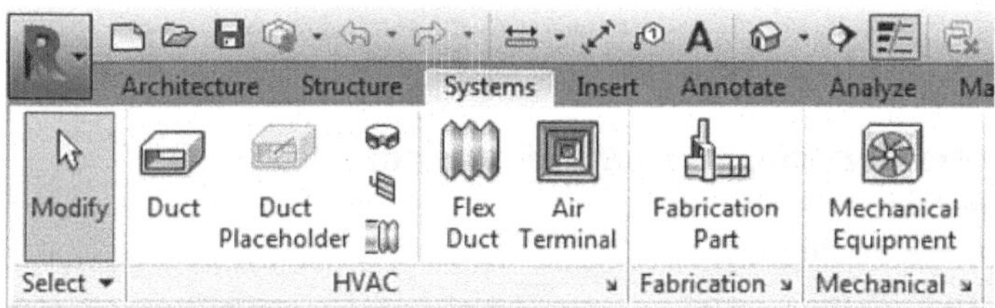

***Figure 5-1** Different tools displayed in the **HVAC, Fabrication,** and **Mechanical** panels to create an HVAC system*

While working in an HVAC system, you will perform various tasks, which are described next.

Adding Supply Air Terminals

While working in an HVAC system, it is important that you add sufficient air terminals to the spaces to fulfil its air flow requirement. In Revit, adding air terminals involves loading the appropriate type of air terminal from the library, specifying the appropriate offset value (for non-hosted air terminals), and setting the designed air flow for the air terminal.

To load the air terminals into a project, choose the **Load Family** tool from the **Load from Library** panel of the **Insert** tab; the **Load Family** dialog box will be displayed. In this dialog box, browse to **US Imperial > Mechanical > MEP > Air Side Components > Air Terminals** folder (for Metric browse to **US Metric > Mechanical > MEP > Air Side Components > Air Terminals** folder). In the **Air Terminals** folder, as shown in Figure 5-2, select the desired family(ies) of air supply terminal and choose **Open**; the **Load Family** dialog box will be closed and the selected family(ies) will be loaded in the project and can be used to create the HVAC System. Next, to add the air terminals, you can use the **Air Terminal** tool in the **HVAC** panel of the **Systems** tab. The process of adding air terminals has been described later in this chapter.

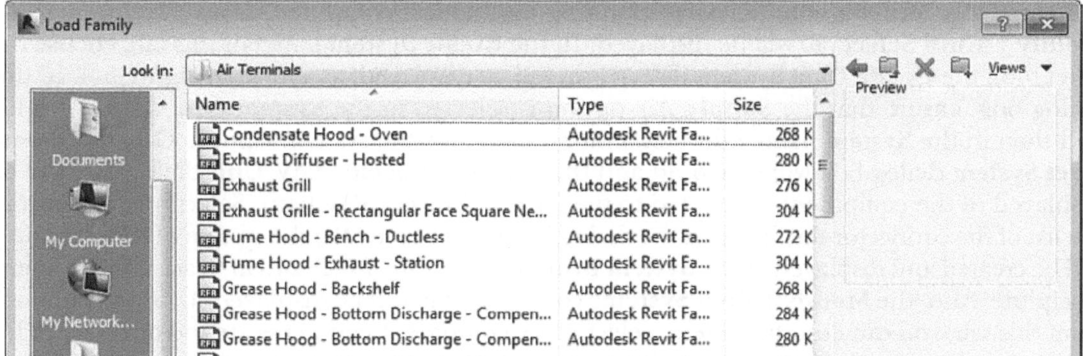

***Figure 5-2** Partial view of the **Load Family** dialog box displaying various families of air terminals*

Adding Air Equipment

While designing an HVAC system, you need to add sufficient and specified air equipment to control the flow of air from the duct to the air terminals. In Revit, adding air equipment involves loading the appropriate type of air equipment family(ies), placing the offset, and rotating the equipment in the proper direction to connect it to the ducts in the HVAC system. To load the air equipment into your project, invoke the **Load Family** dialog box and then browse to **US Imperial > Mechanical > MEP > Air Side Components > Air Terminals** folder (for Metric browse to **US Metric > Mechanical > MEP > Air Side Components** folder). In the **Air Side Components** folder, as shown in Figure 5-3, you can use the **Air Handling Units** and **Terminal Units** sub-folders to load various families of air equipment required for the HVAC system.

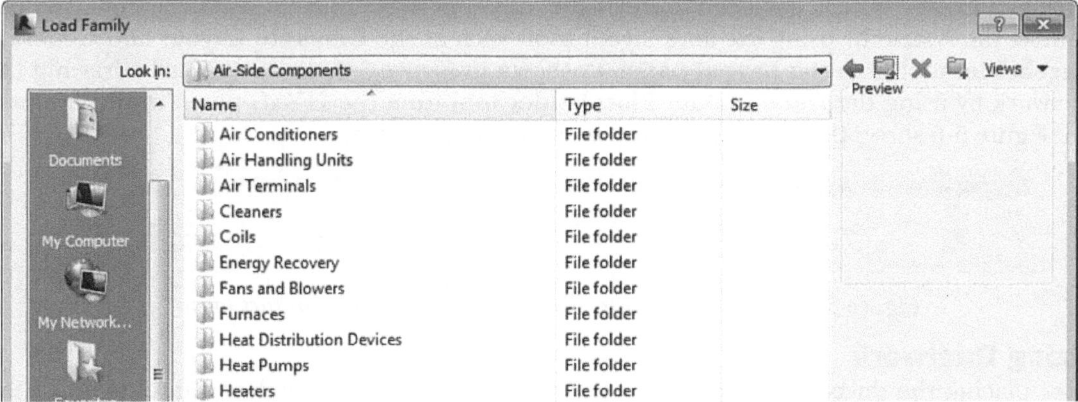

***Figure 5-3** Partial view of the **Load Family** dialog box displaying various sub-folders for air equipment*

To add different air equipment in the HVAC system, you can use the **Mechanical Equipment** tool from the **Mechanical** panel of the **Systems** tab. The process of adding different air equipment has been discussed later in this chapter.

Creating Air Supply System

After adding the air terminals and the air equipment, you need to connect the supply air terminals and equipment together to create an air supply system. To create an air supply system, select the air supply terminals and its corresponding mechanical equipment from the drawing; the **Modify | Multi Select** tab will be displayed. In the **Create System** panel of this tab, choose the **Duct** tool; the **Create Duct System** dialog box will be displayed, as shown in Figure 5-4. In this dialog box, ensure that the **Supply Air** option is selected in the **System type** drop-down list and then in the **System name** edit box, enter a name for the system. Choose **OK**; the **Create Duct System** dialog box will be closed and the **Select Connector VAV Unit** dialog box will be displayed (if the equipment connected to the air terminal is a VAV box). Select an option from the list of the connector displayed in the dialog box and choose **OK**; the system of the air supply will be created and displayed in the **System Browser** under the **Mechanical** head of the **Systems** discipline. Also, the **Modify | Duct Systems** contextual tab will be displayed. Using the options from this tab, you can edit the system, select more equipment and generate the duct layout for the air supply system.

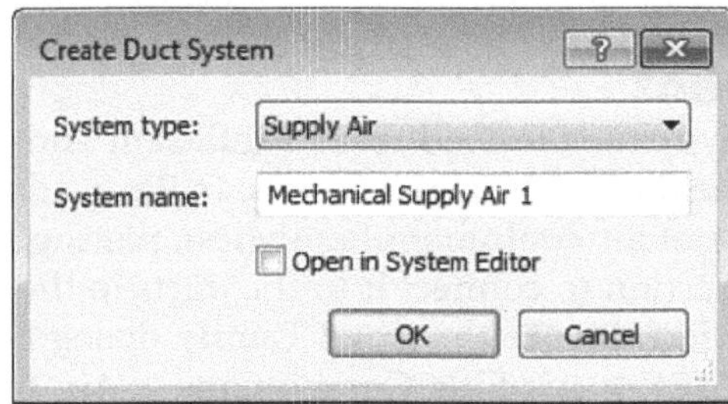

*Figure 5-4 The **Create Duct System** dialog box*

Creating Ductwork

After creating the system, you need to create the ductwork to connect the airflow system. You can connect the system by using the auto layout tools such as the **Generate Layout** and **Generate Placeholder** tool from the **Layout** panel, as shown in Figure 5-5, or by manually drawing the ductwork by using the **Duct** or **Duct Placeholder** tool from the **HVAC** panel in the **Systems** tab. Figure 5-6 shows the ducts connected in an air supply system.

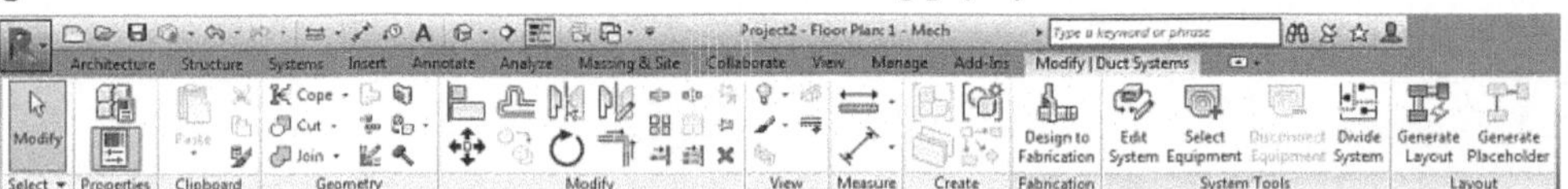

*Figure 5-5 The **Layout** panel displaying various tools for duct layout*

Sizing Ductwork

After placing the ducts, it is required to size the duct as per the air flow requirement of the space. It helps in controlling the discharge of air in the air ducts. The sizing of ducts will be based on the static or friction method, or both, depending on the design requirement. To size the duct, select the duct in the HVAC system from the drawing and then choose the **Duct/ Pipe Sizing** tool from the **Analysis** panel of the **Modify | Ducts** tab; the **Duct Sizing** dialog box will be displayed, as shown in Figure 5-7. You can use the options in this dialog box to specify the method by which the ducts will be sized in a system. Choose **OK**; the dialog box will be closed and the selected duct will be sized as per the specified method. Figure 5-8 shows a sized duct in an air flow system.

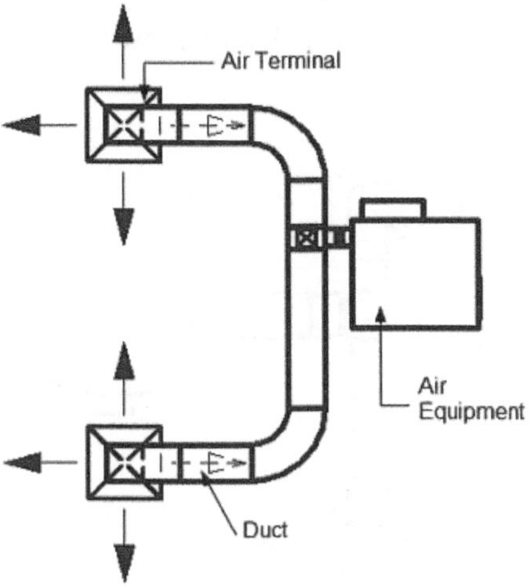

Figure 5-6 The air supply system

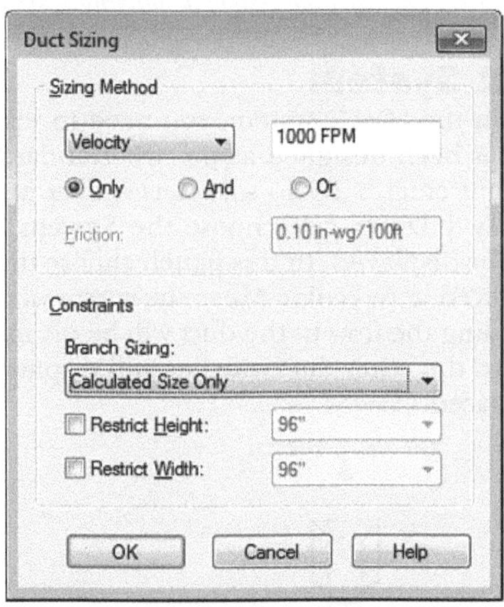

*Figure 5-7 The **Duct Sizing** dialog box displaying various options for sizing ducts*

Creating Return Air Terminals, Air System, and Air Ductwork

After creating the air supply system, you need to add air terminals for return air to the HVAC system. To add the return air terminal, first you will load the required return air terminal families from the **Load Family** dialog box. The families of the return air terminals are available in the **Air Terminals** folder. You can browse this folder and select the desired family for return air terminals and load it to the project file. Next, choose the **Air Terminal** tool from the **HVAC** panel of the **Systems** tab. Now, specify the offset value, and settings for the CFM flow. After inserting the air return terminals, you will create a system for return air as created for supply air. The return air system will connect the return air terminals and equipment together.

In this system, you will also create a duct work for return air. You can create the ductwork either by using the auto layout tools or by manually drawing ductwork.

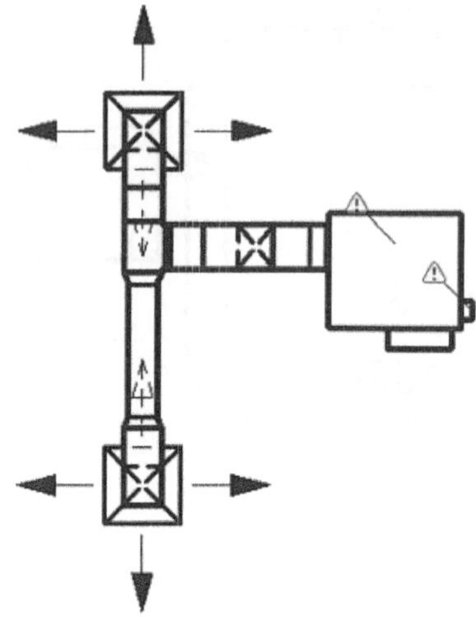

Figure 5-8 *The air flow system displaying a sized duct*

Inspecting the Duct System

After creating the ductwork in the HVAC system, you need to inspect the airflow in the duct to make sure that the duct has been designed as per the standards and the air in the duct is flowing as per the design requirement. To do so, select a duct in the system and then in the **Analysis** panel of the **Modify | Ducts** tab, choose the **System Inspector** tool; the **System Inspector** floating panel will be displayed. In this panel, choose the **Inspect** tool; arrows inside the duct sections will be displayed in red color. Move the cursor in the section of the duct; a flag displaying information regarding the flow in the duct will be displayed, as shown in Figure 5-9. As you move the cursor toward the other duct, the flag will display the information of the duct on which the cursor will be placed.

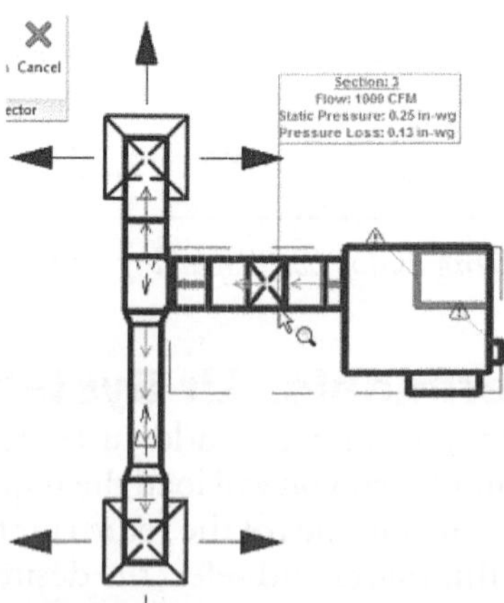

Figure 5-9 *The flag displaying the information of a duct in the system*

Checking the Duct System

After inspecting the air flow in the system, you need to check the connectivity of the ductwork in the system. To do so, choose the **Check Duct Systems** tool from the **Check Systems** panel in the **Analyze** tab; the various disconnects in the ducts, if any, will be shown as warning in the drawing.

Creating Duct Legend

After creating the ducts, you will create duct legend to indicate color fills associated with the ductworks in the HVAC system. The duct legend will help you to visualize the air flow requirement in different ducts with the help of color fills. To create a duct legend, choose the **Duct Legend** tool from the **Color Fill** panel in the **Analyze** tab and click in the drawing view; the **Choose Color Scheme** dialog box will be displayed. In the dialog box, select any of the options from the **Color Scheme** drop-down list and choose **OK**; the color fills will be displayed in the ducts and legend will be displayed at the location where you have clicked. Figure 5-10 shows a color fill legend and color fills in ducts in an HVAC layout.

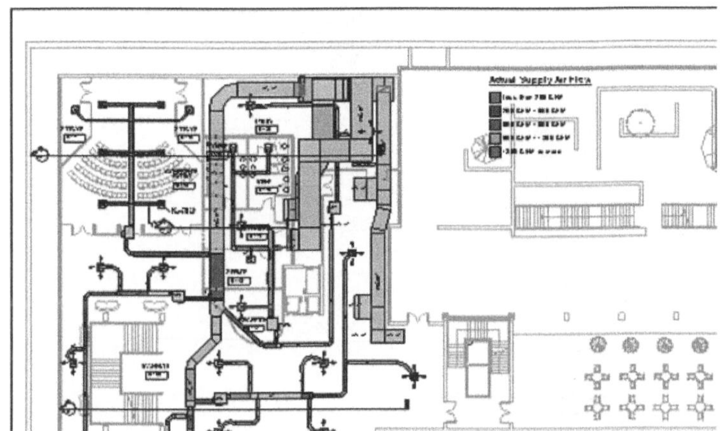

Figure 5-10 *The duct legend and color fills displayed in an HVAC layout*

Different Components of an HVAC System

The components of an HVAC system include various types of mechanical equipment and air terminals that you will add to the project. In an MEP project, you will add these components in the floor plan view or in the ceiling plan view.

The air terminals can be a hosted or non-hosted to a ceiling. To place the hosted air terminals, you need to activate the desired ceiling plan view from **Views > Mechanical > HVAC > Ceiling Plans** node in the **Project Browser**. The equipment are generally non-hosted families. To place the equipment, activate the desired floor plan view from **Views > Mechanical > HVAC > Floor Plans** node of the **Project Browser**.

The various options to add different air terminals and mechanical equipment to an HVAC system are discussed next.

Placing Air Terminals

The air terminals in an HVAC system are responsible to discharge air in the spaces of the project. In MEP, you will use the information associated with air terminals to calculate loads for the spaces in an HVAC system. While adding the air terminals in the spaces, you will size them as per the design requirement.

To add an air terminal to the project, activate the desired plan view from the **Project Browser** and then choose the **Air Terminal** tool from the **HVAC** panel of the **Systems** tab; the **Modify | Place Air Terminal** contextual tab will be displayed and various instance properties of the air terminal to be placed will be displayed in the **Properties** palette, as shown in Figure 5-11.

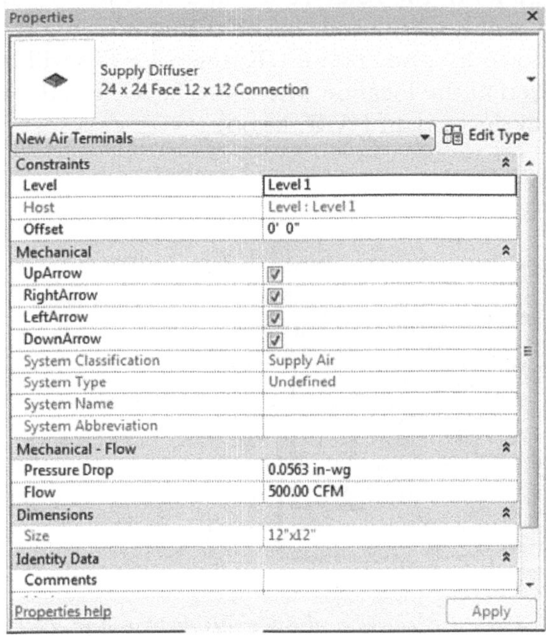

*Figure 5-11 The **Properties** palette displaying the instance properties of an air terminal*

In the **Properties** palette, by default, the **Supply Diffuser: 24 x 24 Face 12x12 Connection** (for Metric **Supply Diffuser: 600 x 600 Face 300 x 300 Connection**) will be selected in the **Type Selector** drop-down list. You can select other diffuser types as per the requirement of the system from the **Type Selector** drop-down list. Under the **Constraints** head, you can click in the value field corresponding to the **Level** parameter and select an option to specify the level to which the air terminal can be constrained. Also, click in the **Offset** parameter and enter a suitable value to specify the vertical offset distance of the air terminal from the level it will be constrained to. Under the **Mechanical** head, you can select or clear the check boxes corresponding to the **UpArrow**, **RightArrow**, **LeftArrow**, and **DownArrow** parameters to control the visibility of the arrows in the air terminal. Under the **Mechanical-Flow** head in the **Properties** palette, click in the value fields corresponding to the **Pressure Drop** and **Flow** parameters to specify the drop in pressure and the flow rate, respectively, in the air terminal.

Next, click in the drawing area to place the air terminal. Note that if you select a hosted type air terminal, the level and the offset distance of the air terminal will be determined by the host such as ceiling.

To place a hosted type air terminal, ensure that the desired ceiling plan view is activated from the **Project Browser**. Next, invoke the **Air Terminal** tool from the **HVAC** panel of the **Systems** tab and select a hosted air terminal type from the **Type Selector** drop-down list in the **Properties** palette. Now, specify the various properties in the **Properties** palette and choose the **Place on Face** button from the **Placement** panel of the **Modify | Place Air Terminal** contextual tab. Move the cursor in the ceiling grid; a preview of the air terminal will be displayed. Click to place the air terminal at a desired location, as shown in Figure 5-12. After placing the air terminal, you can modify its properties by selecting it and changing the desired parameters from the **Properties** palette. Also, you can change the flow parameter of the selected air terminal from the **Options Bar** by specifying a desired value in the **Flow** edit box.

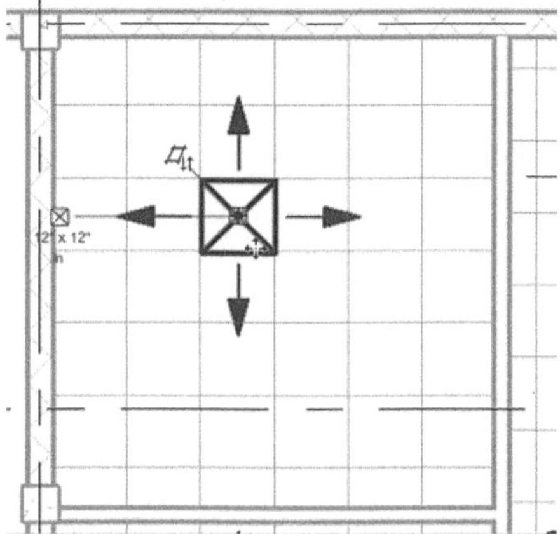

***Figure 5-12** The air terminal placed in a ceiling*

Tip

*In Revit MEP, you can add an air terminal directly to a duct by using the **Air Terminal on Duct** tool from the **Layout** panel of the **Modify | Place Air Terminal** contextual tab.*

Placing Mechanical Equipment

In an HVAC system, the mechanical equipment such as a Variable Air Volume (VAV) unit, FCU, and AHU are used to supply air to the air terminals in a project. To add a mechanical equipment to a project, activate the desired floor plan view from **Views > Mechanical > HVAC > Floor Plans** node in the **Project Browser**. Next, choose the **Mechanical Equipment** tool from the **Mechanical** panel of the **Systems** tab; the **Modify | Place Mechanical Equipment** contextual tab will be displayed. In this tab, you can choose the **Load Family** tool to invoke the **Load Family** dialog box. You can use the **Load Family** dialog box to load the desired families of the mechanical equipment into the project. In the **Properties** palette, you can select the type of equipment from the **Type Selector** drop-down list to place it in a project. If the particular type is not listed, you can load additional families from the library by using the **Load Family** dialog box. The families of a mechanical equipment have multiple connectors depending on the type of family selected. For example, a VAV unit has a supply connector and a return connector that are defined in the family.

After selecting an equipment type from the drop-down list, you can modify various instance properties of the mechanical equipment in the **Properties** palette, as shown in Figure 5-13.

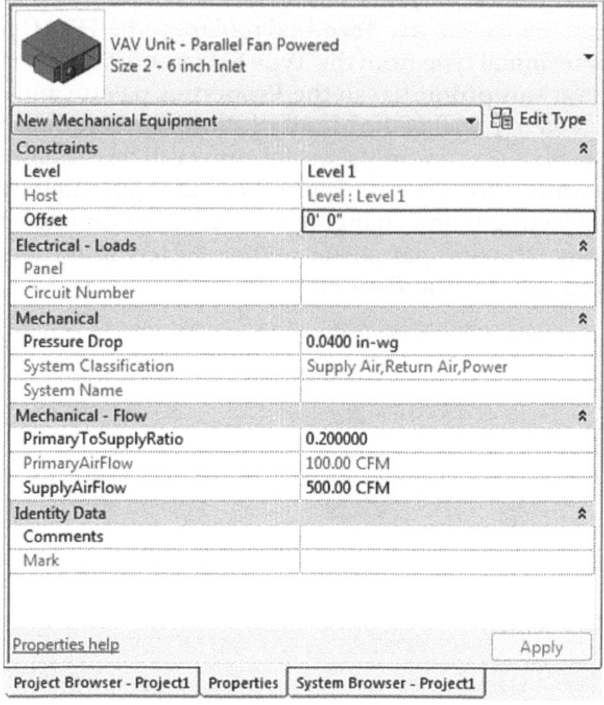

Figure 5-13 *The* ***Properties*** *palette displaying various instance properties of a VAV mechanical equipment*

Note

The properties in the ***Properties*** *palette will vary depending upon the type of equipment selected in the* ***Type Selector*** *drop-down list.*

Under the **Constraints** head, you can click in the value field corresponding to the **Level** parameter and select a level from the drop-down list displayed. The selected level will be used as a reference level to define the vertical offset of the equipment. To define the vertical offset, click in the value field corresponding to the **Offset** parameter and specify a value in it. Under the **Mechanical** head, click in the value field corresponding to the **Pressure Drop** parameter and enter a value to specify the pressure drop in the VAV mechanical equipment. By default, a value of **0.0400 in-wg** (**10 Pa**) will be specified in this parameter. Under the **Mechanical-Flow** heading in the **Properties** palette, you can click in the value field corresponding to the **Supply Air Flow** parameter and enter a value to specify the total airflow supply for all the terminals connected to the equipment. By default, a value of **500 CFM** (**236 L/S**) will be specified to this parameter. After specifying the properties in the **Properties** palette, click in the drawing area at a desired location to place the mechanical equipment. Figure 5-14 shows a placed VAV unit of the **VAV Unit - Parallel Fan Powered Size 2-6 inch Inlet** (for Metric **VAV Unit - Parallel Fan Powered Size 2-150mm Inlet**) type.

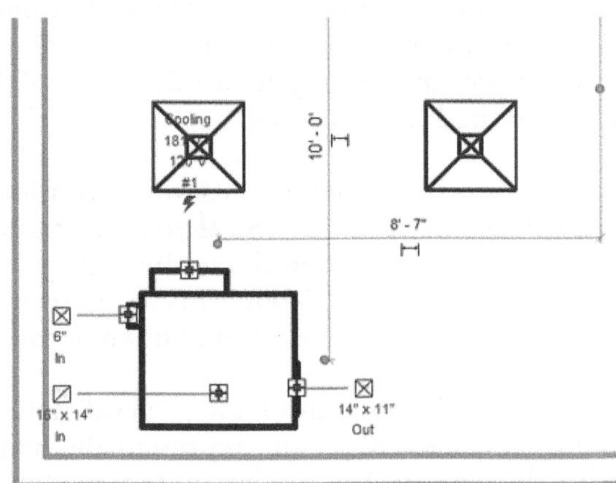

Figure 5-14 *The mechanical equipment (VAV unit) placed*

Note

*A mechanical equipment will be added by default at the finished floor elevation. While placing the equipment, you can select the **Rotate after Placement** check box on the **Options Bar** or press SPACEBAR to rotate the equipment.*

Recommended Practices for Creating HVAC Systems

While working in an HVAC system, there are certain recommended practices that help you to create HVAC systems effectively. These practices are as follows:

1. While placing air terminals and equipment, it is recommended to copy the existing air terminals and equipment to the desired locations. This will help the copied elements in inheriting the properties such as elevation and type from the parent element. This practice will save time because you do not have to specify similar information for multiple components.

2. It is always recommended to schedule information related to spaces in the project, which will be useful during the design process of the HVAC system, irrespective of whether the information will become part of the design documentation or not.

3. While scheduling information for the spaces in the project, it is always recommended to use conditional formatting in the schedules that you create to identify design problems.

4. It is recommended to use the schedule views to update the properties of different equipment. This practice will quickly update multiple components without selecting and editing the components in the drawing.

GENERATING HVAC SYSTEM LAYOUTS

After you create an HVAC system, you will add different components to it and use automatic layout tools to review possible routing solutions. The automatic layout tools will provide you with multiple layout solutions that you can explore to suit your design requirement. If you do not find the required set of connections, you can manually modify the layout path solutions.

An HVAC system layout is a representation of the physical connection between different components in an HVAC system. For example, you can create duct layouts to connect air system components. Revit will provide you with tools to generate the layout of the ductwork automatically when components are added to the HVAC systems.

While creating a system layout, only those components will be considered that are connected to the same system and are displayed in the plan view. If you select a component in 3D, section, or elevation view, all components that are connected to the same system, even if they reside on the multiple levels, will be considered for the layout. This is important when you create a layout for components that are connected to the same system but are located on different levels.

While generating layouts using the automatic layout tool, you will notice that each layout solution consists of blue and green layout lines. Blue lines represent the main duct layout, and green lines represent the branches duct layout. You can generate three types of routing solutions for a layout: Network, Perimeter, and Intersection. The table below describes the solution types.

Solution Type	**Description**
Network	Provides up to six solutions, each consisting of a main segment with branches at 90 degrees from the main segment.
Perimeter	Provides five solutions that wrap the main segment around the perimeter of the components.
Intersection	Provides up to eight solutions, each consisting of a main segment routed over the connectors of the components. Each solution consists of branches extending perpendicular from the main segment down to the components.

To create an auto layout for the HVAC system, select the mechanical equipment and the air terminals that you want to connect; the **Modify | Multi-Select** contextual tab will be displayed, as shown in Figure 5-15.

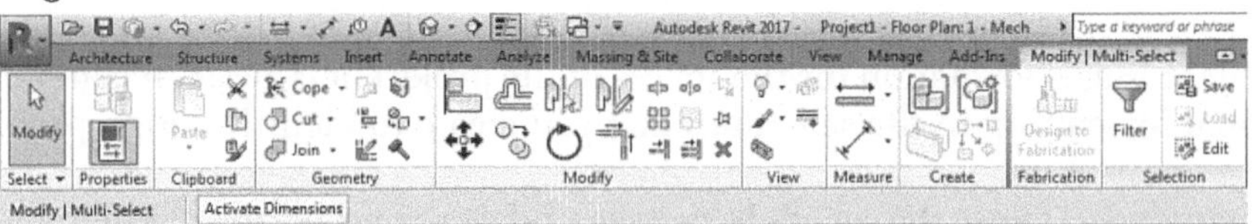

***Figure 5-15** The options in the **Modify / Multi-Select** contextual tab*

In this tab, choose the **Duct** tool from the **Create Systems** panel; the **Create Duct System** dialog box will be displayed. In this dialog box, ensure that the **Supply Air** option is selected in the **System type** drop-down list and then enter the text **Supply System-01** in the **System name** edit box. Choose **OK**; the dialog box will be closed and the **Select Connector** dialog box will be displayed. Keep the default option in the dialog box and choose **OK**; a blue dotted rectangle will be displayed around the system in the drawing and the **Modify | Duct Systems** contextual tab will be displayed. In this tab, choose the **Edit System** tool from the **System Tools** panel in the **Modify | Duct Systems** tab; the **Edit Duct System** tab will be displayed. You can use the options in this tab to edit the system such as adding or removing any component. Next, choose the **Finish Editing System** tool from the **Mode** panel in the **Edit Duct System** tab; the HVAC system will be created.

Next, to generate the layout, select any of the air terminal components in the system that you have created; the **Modify | Air Terminals** tab will be displayed. In this tab, choose the **Generate Layout** tool from the **Layout** panel; the **Generate Layout** tab will be displayed, as shown in Figure 5-16.

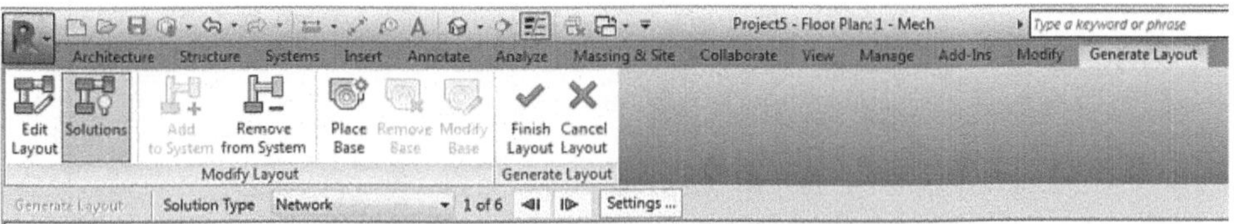

Figure 5-16 *The options in the **Generate Layout** tab*

In the **Options Bar** of this tab, choose the **Settings** button; the **Duct Conversion Settings** dialog box will be displayed, as shown in 5-17.

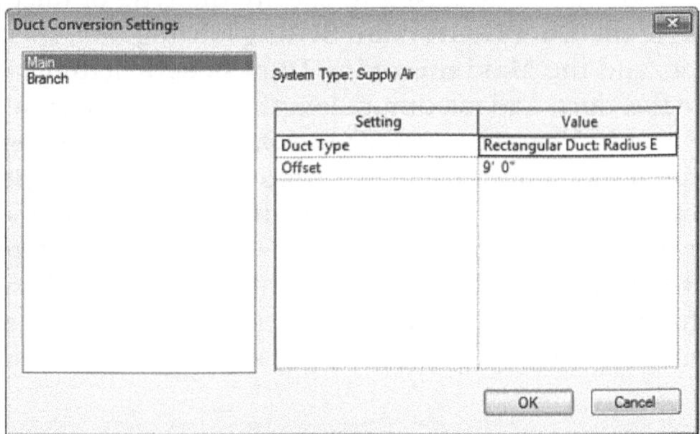

Figure 5-17 *The **Duct Conversion Settings** dialog box*

In the left pane of the dialog box, ensure that the **Main** option is selected. As a result, the right pane of the dialog box will display various options related to the **Main** option. In the right pane, click in the **Value** field corresponding to the **Duct Type** settings and select an option for the duct type of the main duct from the drop-down list displayed.

Next, click in the **Value** field corresponding to the **Offset** settings and enter a value to specify the vertical offset for the main duct. Next, in the left pane of the **Duct Conversion Settings** dialog box, select the **Branch** option; the various options related to the **Branch** option will be displayed in the right pane, as shown in Figure 5-18.

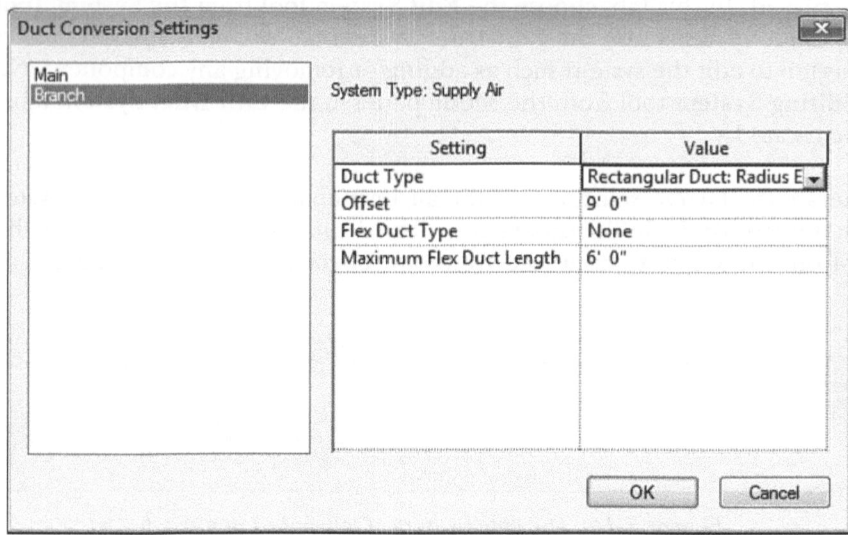

Figure 5-18 *The options for branch ducts in the* ***Duct Conversion Settings*** *dialog box*

In the right pane, click in the **Value** field corresponding to the **Duct Type** setting and select an option from the drop-down list displayed to specify the type of duct for the branch duct. Next, in the right pane of the **Duct Conversion Settings** dialog box, specify the values for the **Offset**, **Flex Duct Type**, and the **Maximum Flex Duct Length** settings to specify the vertical offset value, type of the flex duct, and maximum length of the flex duct, respectively, to be used for branch duct in the layout. Next, choose **OK**; the **Duct Conversion Settings** dialog box will be closed. In the **Options Bar**, select an option from the **Solution Type** drop-down list. For example, you can select the **Network** option from the drop-down list. On selecting this option, a default solution for network will be displayed in the drawing view. In the **Options Bar**, choose the **Next Solution** button to preview the next solution of the layout in the drawing view. Figure 5-19 displays a network solution for an air supply system. In the **Generate Layout** tab, choose the **Finish Layout** tool; the layout will be generated. Figure 5-20 shows a three dimensional view of an HVAC system.

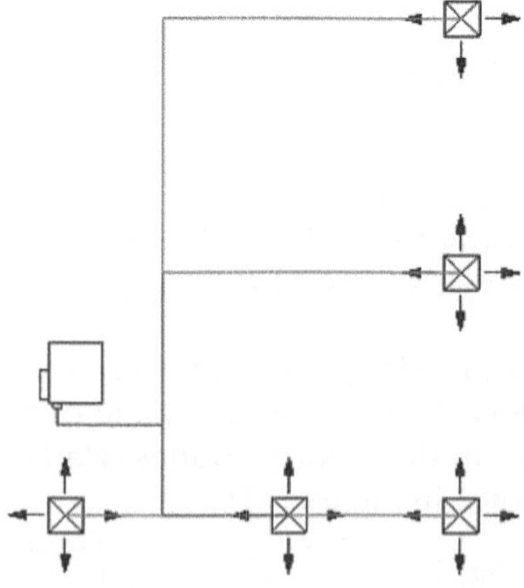

Figure 5-19 *Floor plan displaying a network solution of the HVAC system layout*

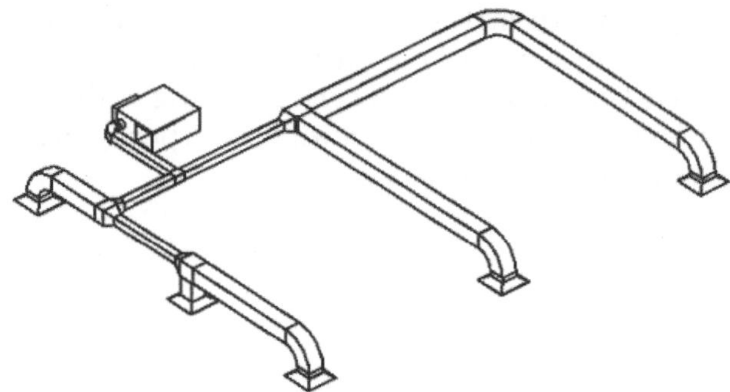

Figure 5-20 Three-dimensional view of an HVAC system layout

CREATING DUCTS AND DUCT FITTINGS

In an HVAC system, the ducts are used to supply and remove air from a space. The airflow inside the ducts includes supply air, return air, and exhaust air.

In Revit, the ducts are created using the automatic connection snaps. When you place the duct segments in a project, Revit automatically connects two segments of the ducts with appropriate duct fittings. This method saves your time as there will be no need to join or trim elements.

Creating Ducts

To create a duct segment in a drawing, open the desired view from the **Project Browser** and then choose the **Duct** tool from the **HVAC** panel in the **Systems** tab; the **Modify | Place Duct** contextual tab will be displayed, as shown in Figure 5-21.

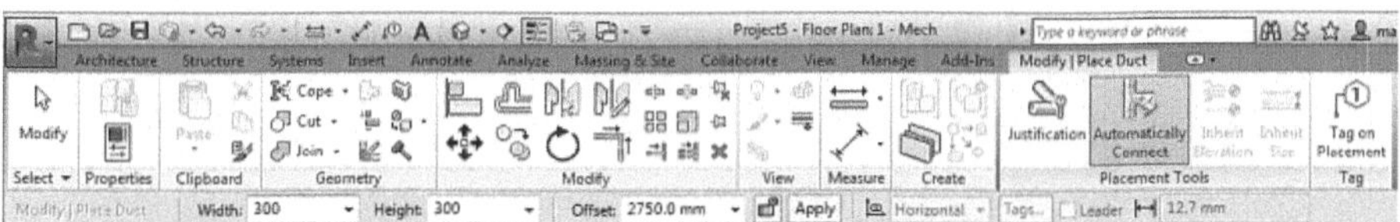

***Figure 5-21** Different options in the **Modify / Place Duct** contextual tab*

In the **Placement Tools** panel of this tab, the **Automatically Connect** button is chosen by default. As a result, the startpoint and the endpoint of the duct will snap the connector of the equipment or component and connect automatically to it. In case you want the duct to inherit the elevation of the component to which it will be snapped, you can choose the **Inherit Elevation** button in this panel. Similarly, you can choose the **Inherit Elevation** button to enable the duct to inherit the size of the equipment to which it will be snapped. In the **Tag** panel of the **Modify | Place Duct** tab, choose the **Tag on Placement** button to place the tag on the duct.

In the **Options Bar**, you can enter a value in the **Width** and **Height** edit boxes to specify the width and depth of the duct, respectively. By default, the value is set to **12"(300)** in both the edit boxes. Next, in the **Offset** edit box, enter a vertical offset distance of the duct. By default, **9' (2750.0 mm)** offset distance is specified in this edit box. You can choose the **Lock/unlock Specified Elevation** button displayed next to the **Offset** edit box to lock the offset value. Next, choose the **Apply** button to apply the settings specified in the **Options Bar** to the drawing.

In the **Properties** palette, as shown in Figure 5-22, you can select an option from the **Type Selector** drop-down list to specify a type of the duct to be placed. Under the **Constraints** head in the **Properties** palette, click in the value field corresponding to the **Horizontal Justification** parameter and select an option from the drop-down list to specify the horizontal justification of the duct, when you place it in the plan view.

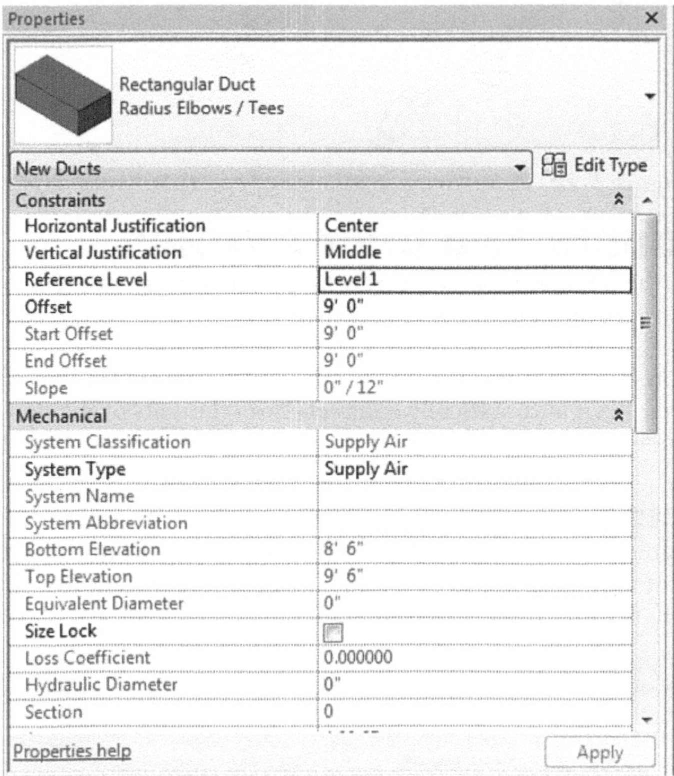

***Figure 5-22** Different instance properties of the duct*

By default, the **Center** option will be selected. The other options that you can select from the drop-down list are: **Left** and **Right**. You can click in the value field corresponding to the **Vertical Justification** parameter and select an option from the drop-down list displayed to specify the vertical justification of the duct. The vertical justification will be used in measuring the vertical offset distance of the duct. Under the **Constraints** head, click in the value field corresponding to the **Reference Level** parameter and select a level to specify the reference level of the duct. This parameter will be used as a reference of the vertical offset distance. Next, you can click in the value field of the **Offset** parameter and enter a value in it to specify the offset distance of the duct with reference to the level specified for the **Reference Level** parameter.

Under the **Mechanical** head of the **Properties** palette, click in the value field corresponding to the **System Type** parameter and select an option from the drop-down list to specify the type of system specified for the duct. By default, the **Supply Air** option is selected. In the drop-down list, you can also select the **Exhaust Air** or **Return Air** option. Under the **Mechanical** head, you can select the check box corresponding to the **Size Lock** parameter to lock the size of the duct for editing.

After specifying various options in the **Properties** palette, click in the drawing area to specify the start point of the duct. You can also snap to the connector point of an existing equipment to automatically connect to it. To do so, place the cursor at the connector point of the equipment; a snap will appear, as shown in Figure 5-23. Now, click at the snapped point and drag the cursor toward the desired direction; a preview of the duct with specified cross-section and justification will appear along with the cursor, as shown in Figure 5-24. Now, click on the desired location to specify the end point of the duct segment. On clicking at the desired location, a duct segment will be created. You can now click on more locations to define other duct segments. After defining the duct segments, choose the **Modify** button from the **Select** panel to exit the tool. Figures 5-25 and 5-26 show the elevation and three dimensional views, respectively, of a ductwork in an HVAC system.

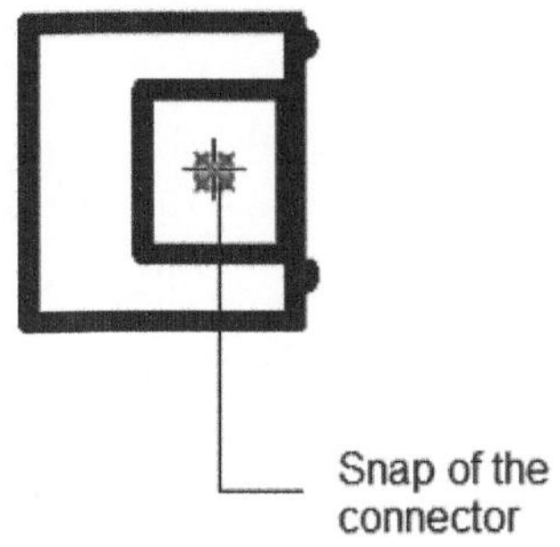

Figure 5-23 *The appearence of the snap point at the connector*

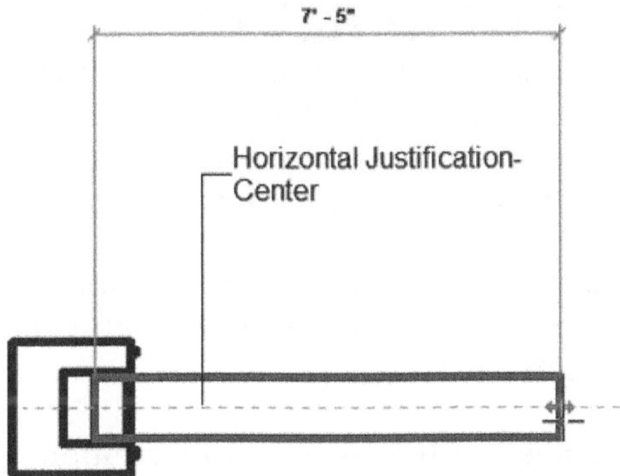

Figure 5-24 *The appearance of a duct segment along with the cursor*

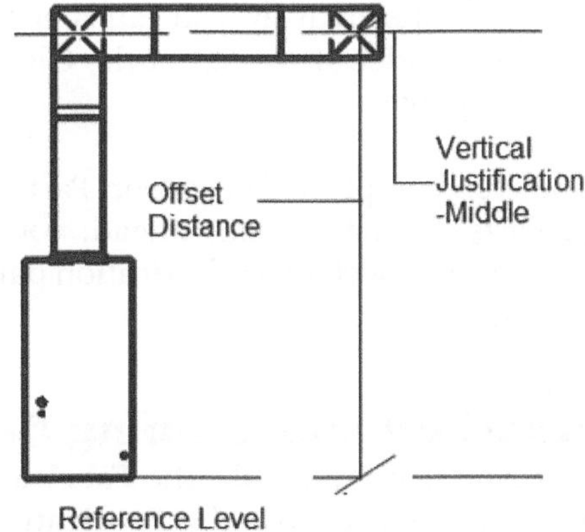

Figure 5-25 *The elevation view of a duct system*

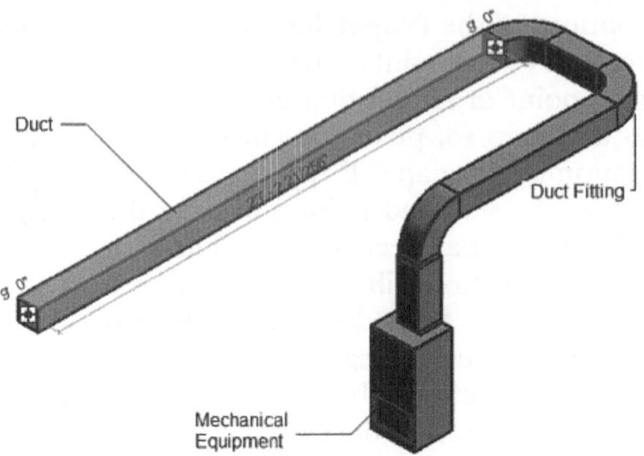

Figure 5-26 Three dimensional view of a duct system

FABRICATION DETAILS IN REVIT

In Autodesk Revit, you can create a model with fabrication parts reflecting the fabrication intent of the model. This will enable you to share a more detailed model with the contractors and thereby produce more accurate estimates and bids. In addition, you can quickly generate fabrication-level models, and move directly to fabrication retaining all the information in the model required in BIM.

The creation of fabrication parts can have different workflows. You can place a fabrication part and then detail it or you can convert a Revit model with generic duct, pipe, or electrical containment parts into fabrication parts.

For any of the workflows, you need to first specify a fabrication configuration. A fabrication configuration consists of fabrication content and associated data of the products to support coordinated modeling and detailing for fabrication and construction. The configuration specified must be saved in a specified network or on a local drive. Every Revit model will have a unique configuration of fabrication. Alternatively, you can specify a fabrication profile which is a collection of services specific to a model. If you select the Global profile, all services in the specified configuration are made available

After configuring the fabrication, you can place Fabrication Parts in a Revit model or convert Generic Parts into Fabrication Parts. In the sections ahead, you will learn to configure the fabrication and add load services in the project, place fabrication parts in the model, and convert generic parts into fabrication parts.

Configuring the Fabrication and Loading Services

To configure fabrication in Revit, you need to invoke the **Fabrication Settings** dialog box. To open the **Fabrication Settings** dialog box, choose the **Fabrication Settings** button from the **Fabrication** panel of the **Systems** tab, refer to Figure 5-27. Alternatively, you can press FS to display the **Fabrication Settings** dialog box shown in Figure 5-28. In this dialog box, the following tabs are displayed: **Fabrication configuration** and **Connection Indicators**. The **Fabrication configuration** tab is chosen by default. The options in the **Fabrication configuration** tab help in specifying a fabrication configuration and profile, and load fabrication services into the model. The options in the **Connection Indicators** tab help to specify connection indicators for the **Route and Fill** tool.

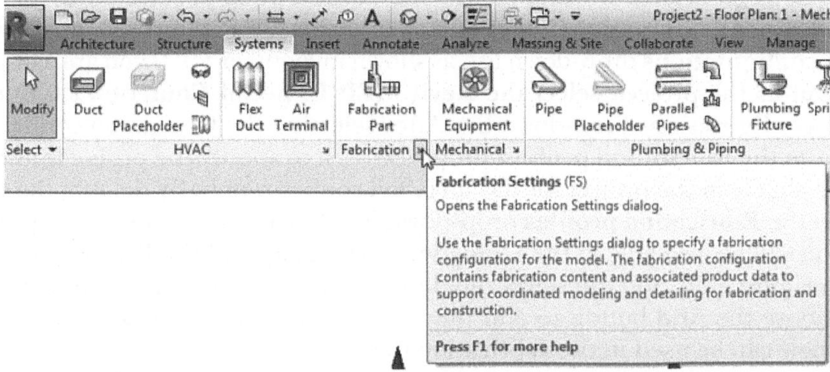

*Figure 5-27 Choosing the **Fabrication Settings** button from the **Fabrication** panel*

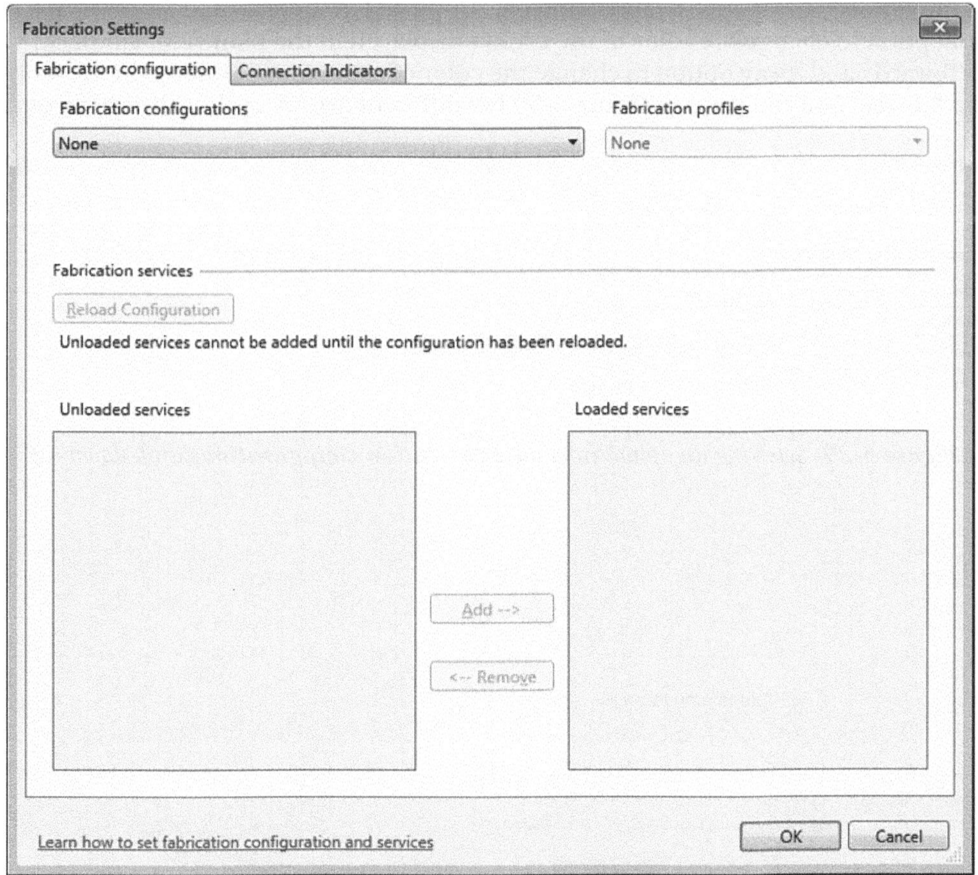

*Figure 5-28 The **Fabrication Settings** dialog box*

Fabrication configurations Tab

In the **Fabrication configurations** tab of the **Fabrication Settings** dialog box, you can select a fabrication configuration from the **Fabrication configurations** drop-down list. In the **Fabrication configurations** drop-down list, the **None** option is selected by default. You can also select **Revit MEP Imperial Content V2.0** or **Revit MEP Metric Content V2.0** from the **Fabrication configurations** drop-down list, as shown in Figure 5-29. If you are using the Imperial system of unit in the project, select the **Revit MEP Imperial Content V2.0** option from the **Fabrication configurations** drop-down list. After selecting the fabrication configuration, select an option from the **Fabrication profiles** drop-down list to specify the profile for filtering the list of services avaliable in the project for the specified configuration. By default, the **Global** option is selected in the **Fabrication profiles** drop-down list. As a result, all the services of the specified configuration will be available in the **Unloaded services** area of the **Fabrication configuration** tab, refer to Figure 5-30. You can select the desired service(s) from the **Unloaded services** area and then choose the **Add** button to add them to the **Loaded services** area. The services that are loaded now can be used in the Fabrication detailing.

Connection Indicators Tab

In the **Colors** area of the **Connection Indicators** tab, various options are available to change the color of the connection arrow in a fabrication part displayed in the plan and 3d views. You can use the **Plan** option to change the color of the arrows displayed in the plan view. Similarly, you can use the **Towards** and **Away** option to change the color of the arrows displayed in the fabrication part in a 3d view. You can refer to Figure 5-30 for different arrows in the fabrication parts.

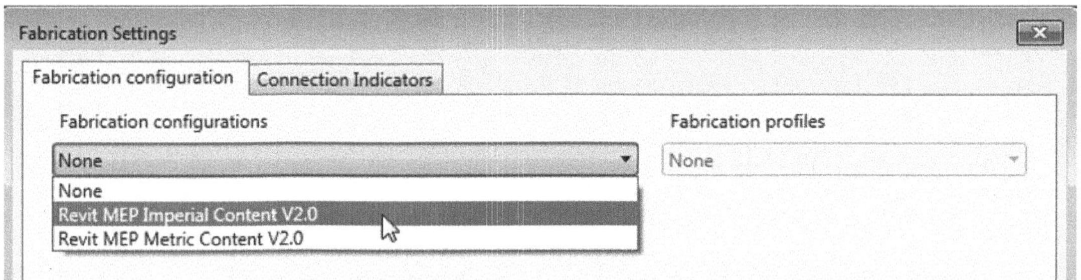

***Figure 5-29** Selecting an option from the **Fabrication configurations** drop-down list*

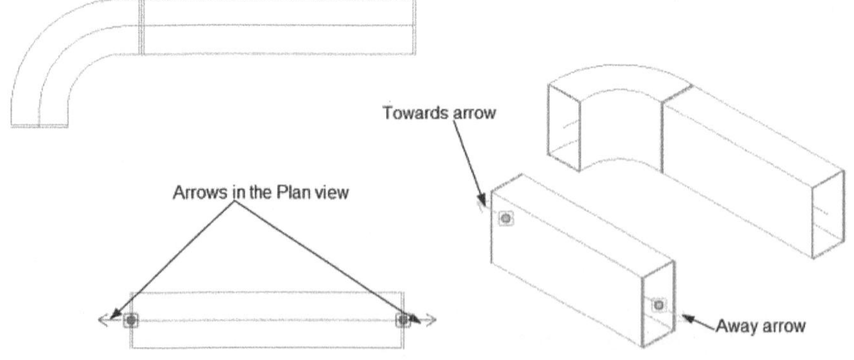

***Figure 5-30** Display of different arrows in the fabrication parts*

Placing the Fabrication Parts

After configuring the Fabrication and loading the services, you can place the fabrication parts in the model. To place the fabrication parts in a model, choose the **Fabrication Part** tool from the **Fabrication** panel of the **Systems** tab. On doing so, the **MEP Fabrication Parts** palette will be displayed in the screen, as shown in Figure 5-31. Alternatively, you can invoke the **Fabrication Part** tool by pressing PB. In the **Fabrication Parts** palette, select the desired service from the **Service** drop-down list. Note that the services that are loaded in the **Fabrication Settings** dialog box will only be displayed in the **Service** drop-down list. After selecting the desired option from the **Service** drop-down list, select the group to which the part will belong from the **Group** drop-down list. On doing so, the list of parts belonging to the specified group will be displayed in the display area of the palette. Now, choose a particular part from the display area and add it in the project to place the fabrication.

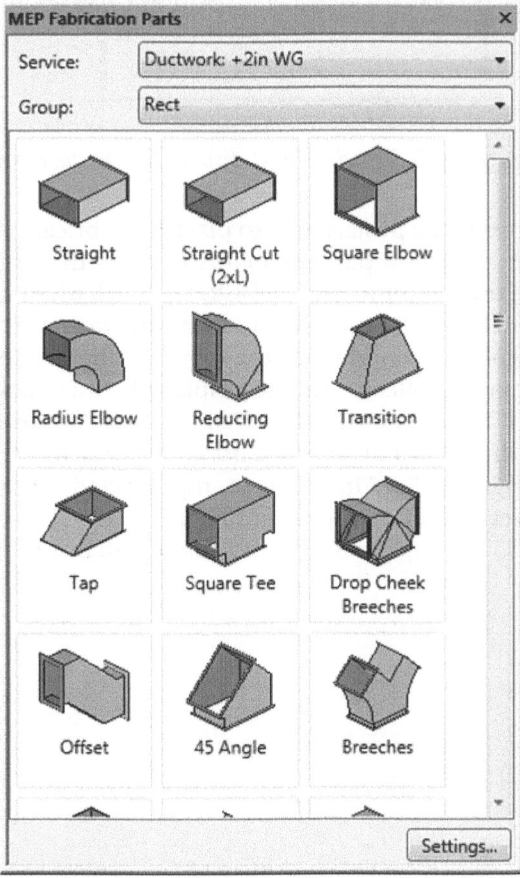

Figure 5-31 The ***MEP Fabrication Parts*** *palette*

Placing a Fabricated Rectangular Ductwork

You can place the fabrication of a ductwork in a specified Mechanical view. The placing of a fabricated ductwork is illustrated with an example given next. In this example, you will add fabrication of a rectangular ductowork with radius elbows and half strap hangers in a Mechanical plan view of an MEP project. To place the fabrication ductwork, choose the **Fabrication Settings** button from the **Fabrication** panel of the **Systems** tab; the **Fabrication Settings** dialog box will be displayed. In this dialog box, select the **Revit MEP Imperial Content V2.0** option from the **Fabrication configuraitons** drop-down list. Ensure that the **Global** option is selected in the **Fabrication profiles** drop-down list. In the **Fabrication services** area of the dialog box, select the **Ductwork+2in WG** option from the **Unloaded services** list box. Now, choose the **Add** button; the selected option will be added to the **Loaded services** area. Choose the **OK** button; the **Fabrication Settings** dialog box will be closed. Next, choose the **Fabrication Part** tool from the **Fabrication** panel of the **Systems** tab; the **MEP Fabrication Parts** palette will be displayed. In this palette, select the **Rect** option from the **Group** drop-down list. Now, select the **Straight** option from the display area; the duct part will appear with the cursor in the drawing area, as shown in Figure 5-32.

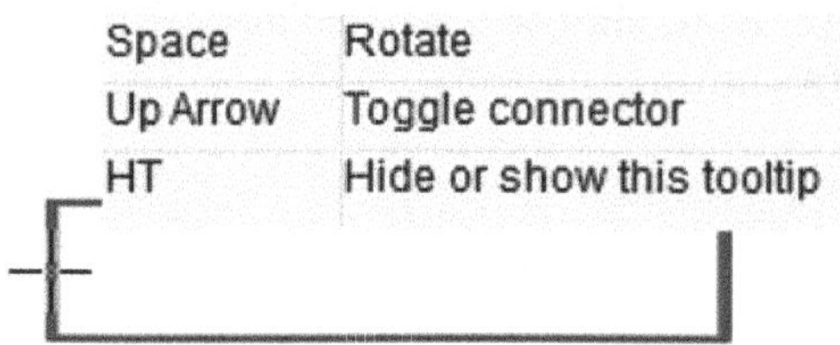

Figure 5-32 *The duct part displayed with the cursor*

Click in the desired space inside the project area to place the fabrication part. Now, select **Radius elbow** from the display are; the elbow part will be displayed with the cursor. Place the cursor at the right end of the placed duct, refer to Figure 5-32, and click when a magenta colored control appears. On doing so, the elbow will get connected with the ductwork. Now, select the **Straight Cut(2xL)** part from the display area and place the cursor at the unconnected end of the placed elbow; a magenta colored point collector will be displayed. Now, click to add the **Straight Cut** part to the fabrication part. Next, you will add a hanger to the fabrication part. To do so, select the **Hangers** option from the **Group** drop-down list and then select the **Full Strap** option from the part list, as shown in Figure 5-33. On doing so, the selected part will be displayed with the cursor. Place the cursor over the duct as shown in Figure 5-34. Click on the desired location to add the hanger. Figure 5-35 display the 3d view of the duct fabrication.

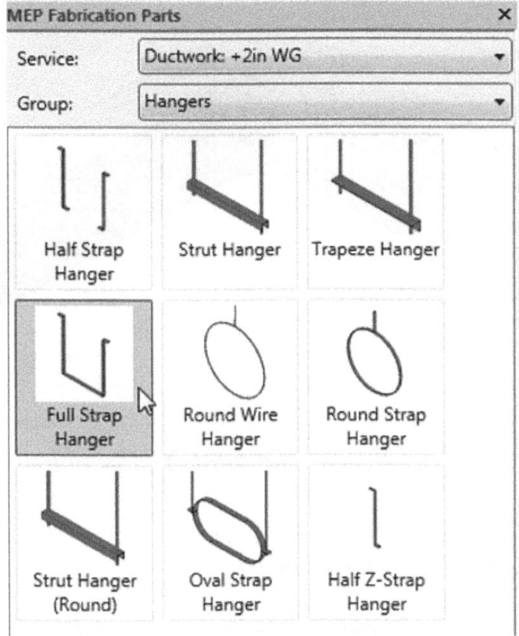

Figure 5-33 *Selecting* ***Full Strap Hanger*** *from the list*

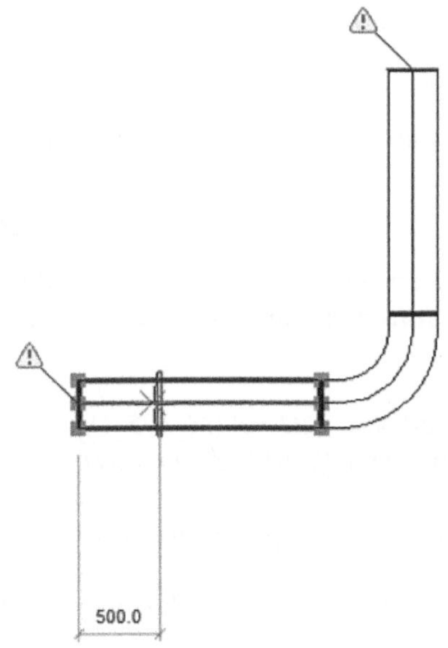

Figure 5-34 *Placing* ***Full Strap Hanger***

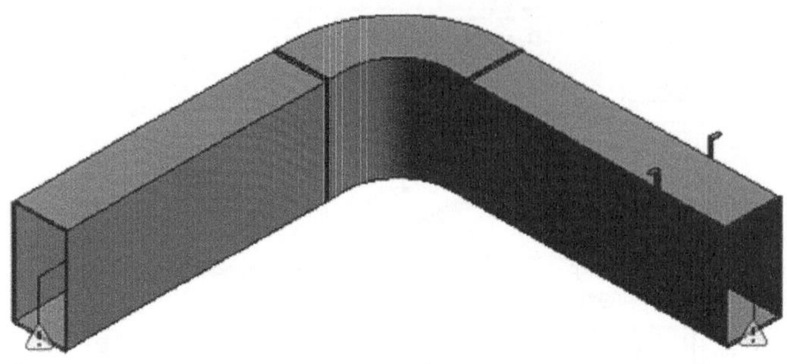

Figure 5-35 *3D view of the placed fabricated part*

TUTORIALS

General instructions for downloading tutorial files:

1. Download the *c05_rmp_2017_tut.zip* file for this tutorial from *http://www.cadcim.com*. The path of the file is as follows: *Textbooks > Civil/GIS > Revit MEP > Exploring Autodesk Revit 2017 for MEP*.

2. Now, save and extract the downloaded zip file at the following location: *C:\rmp_2017\c05_rmp_2017_tut*

Note
The default unit system used in the tutorials is Imperial.

Tutorial 1 Placing Air Terminals

In this tutorial, you will place air terminals in the ceiling of the rooms. Also, you will create new views, modify air terminal parameters, and place air terminals in the ceiling plan.

(Expected time: 45 min)

1. File to be used: *c05_Office-Space_tut1.rvt (M_c05_Office-Space_tut1.rvt)*
2. File name to be assigned: *c05_Office-Space_tut1a.rvt (M_c05_Office-Space_tut1a.rvt)*

The following steps are required to complete this tutorial:

a. Open the *05_Office-Space_tut1.rvt (M_05_Office-Space_tut1.rvt)* file.
b. Modify the ceiling plan.
c. Add the supply air terminal.
d. Add the return and exhaust air terminal.
e. Save the project by using the **Save As** tool.

Opening a Project

In this section, you will open the *c05_Office-Space_tut1.rvt (M_ c05_Office-Space_tut1.rvt)* file.

1. Choose **Open > Project** from the **Application Menu**. On doing so, the **Open** dialog box is displayed.

2. In the **Open** dialog box, browse to *C:\rmp_2017\c05_rmp_2017_tut* and select the *c05_Office-Space_tut1.rvt.* (*M_c05_Office-Space_tut1.rvt*) file. Now, choose the **Open** button; the selected file opens in the Revit interface.

Note

The architectural model named c04_archi_spaces_rmp_2017.rvt (for Metric M_c04_archi_spaces_rmp_2017.rvt) linked in this tutorial file is located in the c04_rmp_2017_tut folder. It is recommended to maintain the relative path to the architectural model. However, if the link is lost, you need to reload the file using the ***Manage Links*** *dialog box which has already been discussed in the previous chapters.*

Modifying the Ceiling Plan View

In this section, you will modify the ceiling plan view using the **View Range** dialog box.

1 In the **Project Browser**, expand **Views (Discipline) > Mechanical > HVAC > Ceiling Plans**, and double-click on **1 - Ceiling Mech** to make it an active view.

2. In the **Properties** palette, choose the **Edit** button corresponding to the **View Range** parameter under the **Extents** head; the **View Range** dialog box is displayed.

3. In the **Primary Range** area of this dialog box, select the **Associated Level (Level1)** option from the **Top** drop-down list and then enter **8' 4"** (**2540mm**) in the **Offset** edit box.

4. Enter **0** in the **Offset** edit box corresponding to the **Cut plane** drop-down list.

5. In the **View Depth** area of the **View Range** dialog box, select the **Associated Level (Level 1)** option from the **Level** drop-down list and enter **8' 4"** (**2540mm**) in the **Offset** edit box corresponding to the **Level** drop-down list.

6. Choose **Apply** and then **OK**; the specified settings are applied to the current view and the **View Range** dialog box is closed.

Note

On modifying the ranges of the ceiling plan view, the various fixtures and fittings in the model will be visible.

Adding the Supply Air Terminal

In this section, you will place the supply air terminals in the ceiling of the rooms.

1. Choose the **Air Terminal** tool from the **HVAC** panel of the **Systems** tab; the **Modify | Place Air Terminal** contextual tab is displayed.

2. Choose the **Load Family** tool from the **Mode** panel of the contextual tab; the **Load Family** dialog box is displayed.

3. In the dialog box, browse to **US Imperial > Mechanical > MEP > Air Side Components > Air Terminals** folder (for Metric, browse to **US Metric > Mechanical > MEP > Air Side Components > Air Terminals** folder) and then select the **Supply Diffuser - Hosted (M_Supply Diffuser-Hosted)** family from the list displayed.

4. Next, choose **Open**; the **Load Family** dialog box is closed and the selected family is loaded in the project file.

5. In the **Properties** palette, select the **Supply Diffuser - Hosted: Workplane-based Supply Diffuser** option (for Metric **M_SupplyDiffuser - Hosted: Workplane-based Supply Diffuser**) from the **Type Selector** drop-down list.

6. In the **Placement** panel of the **Modify | Place Air Terminal** contextual tab, choose the **Place on Face** button.

7. In the drawing area, move the cursor toward the upper left corner of the plan into the **CEO-Office** area and click to place at the location shown in Figure 5-36.

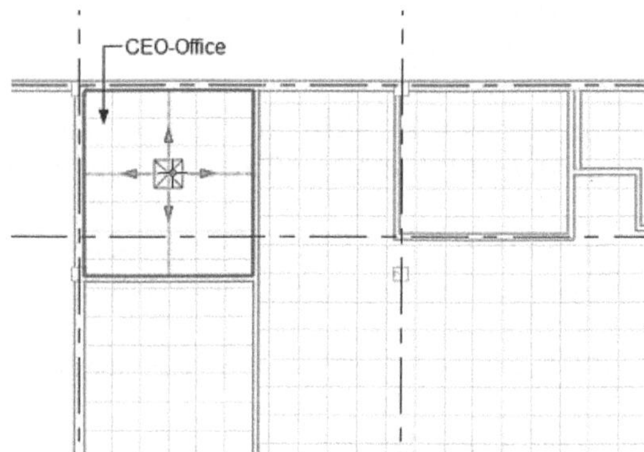

***Figure 5-36** The supply air terminal placed in the CEO-Office area*

Note
The air terminal will be placed on the ceiling.

8. In the **Properties** palette, enter **300 CFM (150 L/S)** in the edit box corresponding to the **Flow** parameter under the **Mechanical - Flow** head.

9. Now, choose the **Modify** button from the **Select** panel to exit the **Air Terminal** tool.

10. Select the added air terminal and place the cursor at the center grip of the air terminal; the center grip turns red and the **Drag** tooltip appears. Press the left mouse button and drag the air terminal to fit it inside the ceiling tile, as shown in Figure 5-37.

11. After placing the air terminal, release the left mouse button.

12. Next, ensure that the air terminal is selected and then choose the **Copy** tool from the **Modify** panel; a dashed box is displayed around the selected air terminal.

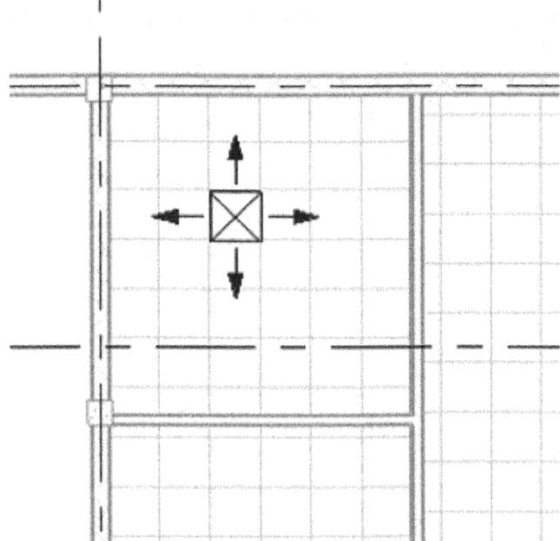

Figure 5-37 Placing the supply air terminal inside the ceiling tile

13. In the **Options** Bar, select the **Multiple** check box.

14. In the drawing area, place the cursor at the center of the air terminal and click when the **Midpoint** snap is displayed, as shown in Figure 5-38.

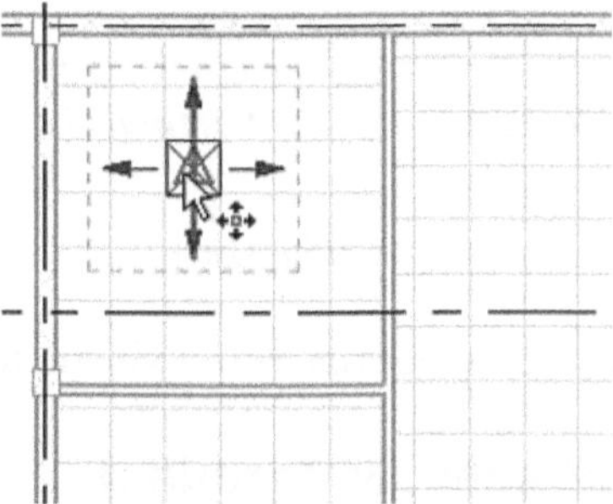

Figure 5-38 Placing the cursor at the center of the air terminal

15. Move the cursor vertically down and click when the vertical dimension appears as **12' (3658mm)**, as shown in Figure 5-39.

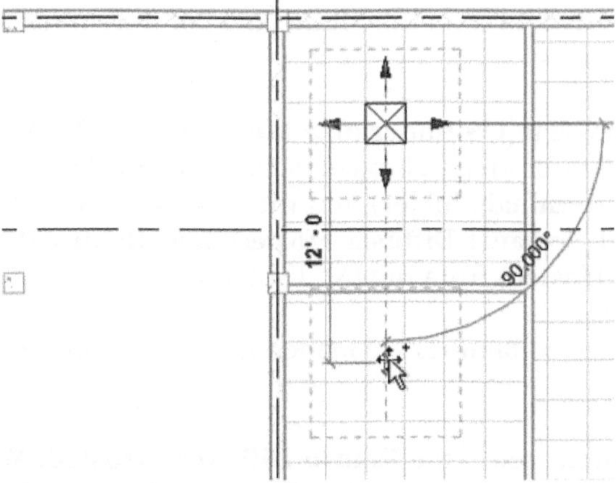

Figure 5-39 Copying the air terminal to the other area

16. Similarly, copy and place the other air terminals at required locations, as shown in Figure 5-40.

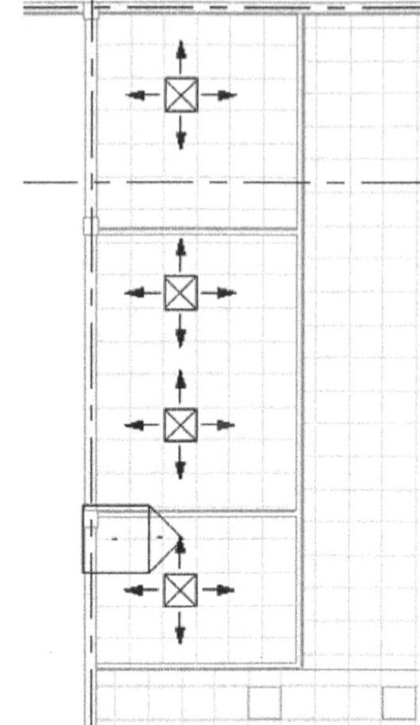

Figure 5-40 *Placing the air terminals in other areas*

Note

The placement of the air terminals may not be exact.

17. Choose the **Modify** tool from the **Select** panel to exit the tool.

Adding the Return and Exhaust Air Terminal

In this section, you will add the return and exhaust air terminal to the plan.

1. Choose the **Air Terminal** tool from the **HVAC** panel of the **Systems** tab; the **Modify | Place Air Terminal** contextual tab is displayed.

2. Choose the **Load Family** tool from the **Mode** panel of the contextual tab; the **Load Family** dialog box is displayed.

3. In the dialog box, browse to **US Imperial > Mechanical > MEP > Air Side Components > Air Terminals** folder (for Metric, browse to **US Metric > Mechanical > MEP > Air Side Components > Air Terminals** folder) and then using the CTRL key, select the **Exhaust Diffuser - Hosted (M_Exhaust Diffuser-Hosted)** and **Return Diffuser - Hosted** families **(M_Return Diffuser-Hosted)** from the list displayed.

4. Choose **Open**; the selected families are loaded in the file and the **Load Family** dialog box is closed.

5. In the **Properties** palette, select the **Return Diffuser - Hosted: Workplane-based Return Diffuser** option (for Metric, select the **M_ Return Diffuser - Hosted: Workplane-based Return Diffuser** option) from the **Type Selector** drop-down list.

6. In the **Properties** palette, click in the value field corresponding to the **Flow** parameter and enter **300 CFM** (for Metric, **150 L/S**).

7. Choose the **Place on Face** button from the **Placement** panel in the **Modify|Place Air Terminal** contextual tab.

8. Next, in the drawing area, move the cursor in the Lounge area next to the CEO-Office room and then click inside the ceiling tile, as shown in Figure 5-41.

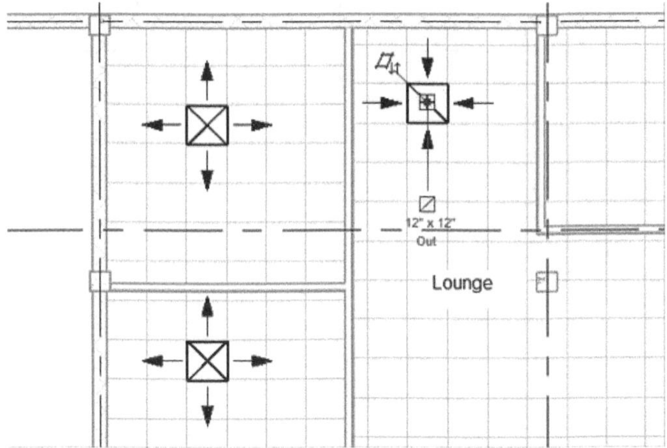

Figure 5-41 *Placing the return air terminal in the Lounge area*

9. Now, click inside the ceiling tile in the Lounge area to place the other return air terminals, as shown in Figure 5-42.

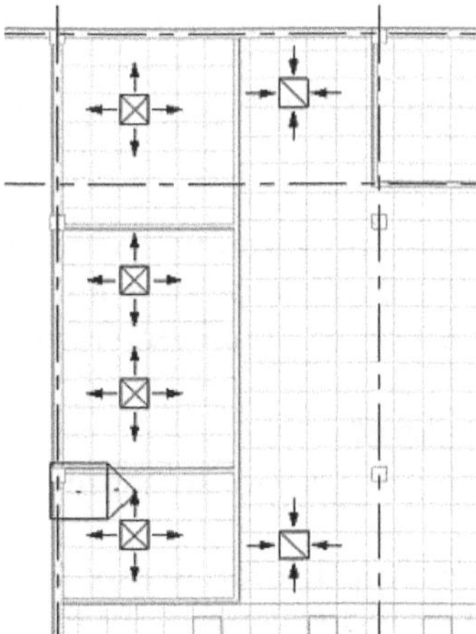

Figure 5-42 *Placing the other return air terminal in the Lounge area*

10. Next, in the **Properties** palette, select the **Exhaust Diffuser - Hosted: Workplane-based Exhaust Diffuser** type (for Metric, select the **M_Exhaust Diffuser - Hosted: Workplane-based Exhaust Diffuser**) from the **Type Selector** drop-down list.

11. In the **Properties** palette, click in the value field corresponding to the **Flow** parameter and enter **250 CFM** (for Metric, **120 L/S**).

12. In the drawing area, move the cursor to the Toilet 1 area, and click inside the ceiling tile at the location, as shown in Figure 5-43, to place the exhaust air terminal.

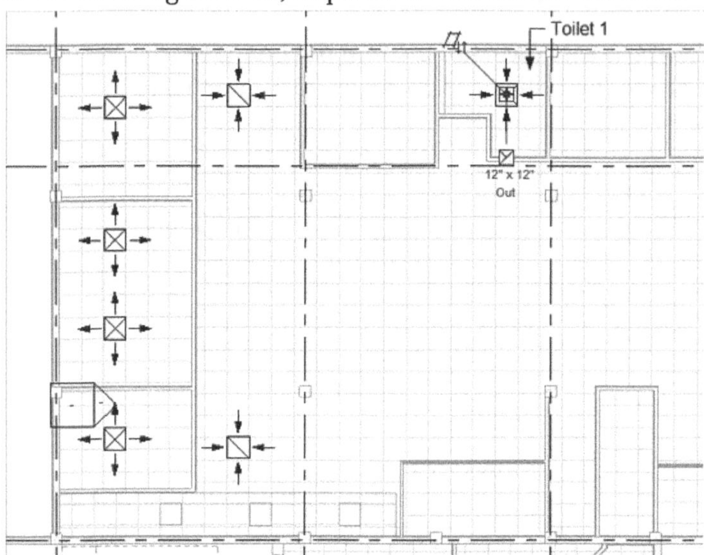

***Figure 5-43** Placing the exhaust air terminal in the Toilet 1 area*

13. Choose the **Modify** button from the **Select** panel to exit the tool.

Note

You can add more air terminals to complete the requirement of the HVAC system in the Office-Space area.

After you place the return and exhaust air terminals, remember to modify the airflow display arrows for air terminals that requires 2-way and 3-way blow patterns by setting the **UpArrow**, **RightArrow**, **LeftArrow**, and **DownArrow** parameters from the **Properties** palette

Saving and Closing the Project

In this section, you need to save the project and the settings using the **Save As** tool.

1. Choose **Save As > Project** from **Application Menu**. As you are saving the project for the first time, the **Save As** dialog box is displayed.

2. In this dialog box, browse to *C:|rmp_2017|c05_rmp_2017_tut* and in the **File name** edit box, enter **c05_Office-Space_tut1a (M_c05_Office-Space_tut1a)** and then choose the **Save** button to save the current project file with the specified name and to close the **Save As** dialog box.

3. Choose the **Close** option from the **Application Menu**.

   The file is closed and this completes the tutorial.

Tutorial 2 Creating Schedules-Air Terminals

In this tutorial, you will create a schedule for the supply air system for the *Office-Space* project. Instead of placing this schedule on sheets as a construction document, you will use it as a design tool to determine whether the correct amount of airflow is being supplied to each of the rooms in the model. You can then use the schedule to adjust the air terminal airflow properties to precisely meet the design requirements. **(Expected time: 45 min)**

1. File to be used: *c05_Office-Space_tut2.rvt (M_c05_Office-Space_tut2.rvt)*
2. File name to be assigned: *c05_Office-Space_tut2a.rvt (M_c05_Office-Space_tut2.rvt)*

The following steps are required to complete this tutorial:

a. Open the file.
b. Create the schedule.
c. Add the **Calculated Value** parameter.
d. Format the **Calculated Value** parameter.
e. Use the schedule to modify air terminals.
f. Save the project as *c05_Office-Space_tut2a.rvt (c05_Office-Space_tut2a.rvt)* by using the **Save As** tool.
g. Close the project by using the **Close** tool.

Opening a Project

In this section, you will download the *c05_Office-Space_tut2.rvt* file from *www.cadcim.com* and then open the file.

1. Choose **Open > Project** from **Application Menu**. On doing so, the **Open** dialog box is displayed.

2. In the **Open** dialog box, browse to *C:\rmp_2017\c05_rmp_2017_tut* and select the *c05_Office-Space_tut2.rvt. (M_c05_Office-Space_tut2.rvt)* file. Now, choose the **Open** button; the selected file opens in the Revit interface.

Note

The architectural model named c04_archi_spaces_rmp_2017.rvt (for Metric M_c04_archi_spaces_rmp_2017.rvt) linked in this tutorial file is located in the c04_rmp_2017_tut folder. It is recommended to maintain the relative path to the architectural model. However, if the link is lost, you need to reload the file using the ***Manage Links*** *dialog box which has already been discussed in the previous chapters.*

Creating the Schedule

1. Choose the **Schedule/Quantities** tool from **View > Create > Schedules** drop-down; the **New Schedule** dialog box is displayed.

2. In this dialog box, click on the **Filter list** drop-down list and then select the **Mechanical** check box from the list displayed. Now, select the **Air Terminals** option from the **Category** list.

3. In the **New Schedule** dialog box, enter **Air-Terminals-Office** in the **Name** edit box. Also, ensure that the **Schedule building components** radio button is selected and then choose **OK**; the **Schedule Properties** dialog box is displayed.

4. Ensure that the **Fields** tab is chosen and then in the **Available fields** area, select the **Flow** option.

5. Choose the **Add parameter(s)** button; the **Flow** option is added to the **Scheduled fields (in order)** area.

6. Next, in the **Available fields** area, press the CTRL key and select the **Mark** and **System Type** options. Choose the **Add parameter(s)** button; the selected options are added to the **Scheduled fields (in order)** area.

7. Select the **Space** option from the **Select available fields from** drop-down list.

8. In the **Available fields** area, press the CTRL key and select the following options: **Space: Actual Supply Airflow**, **Space: Calculated Supply Airflow**, **Space: Name**, and **Space: Number**. Choose the **Add parameter(s)** button; the selected options are added to the **Scheduled fields (in order)** area.

9. In the **Scheduled fields (in order)** area, select the **Space: Number** option and then click the **Move parameter up** button six times to place the **Space Number** at the top of the list. Similarly, select the other options also appearing in the sequence and place them in the order, as shown in Figure 5-44.

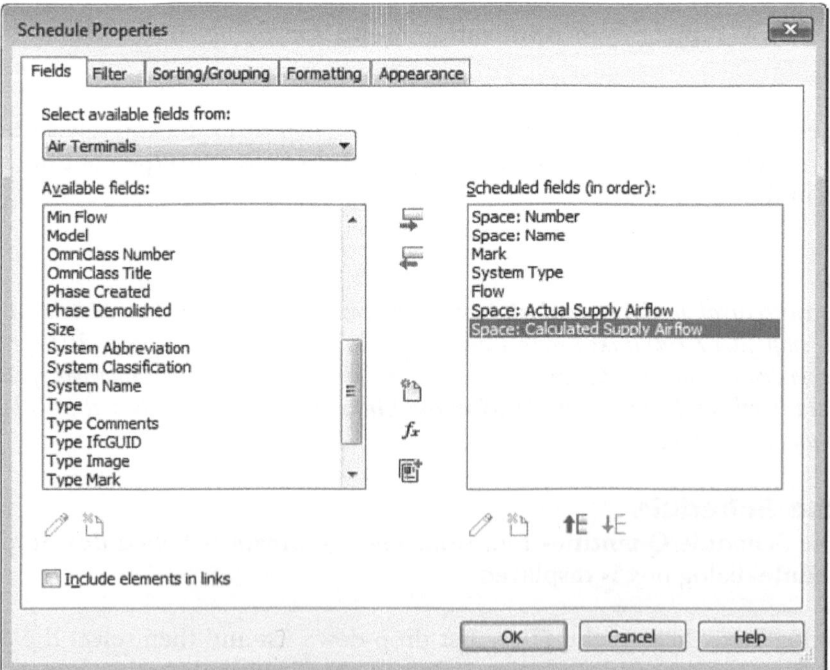

***Figure 5-44** The **Schedule Properties** dialog box displaying the order of the fields*

Creating the Calculated Value Parameter

1. In the **Schedule Properties** dialog box, choose the **Add calculated parameter** button; the **Calculated Value** dialog box is displayed.

2. In this dialog box, enter **Difference in Airflow** in the **Name** edit box. Ensure that the **Formula** radio button is selected.

3. Select the **HVAC** option from the **Discipline** drop-down list.

4. Select the **Air Flow** option from the **Type** drop-down list.

5. Choose the button displayed next to the **Formula** edit box; the **Fields** dialog box is displayed.

6. In this dialog box, select the **Space: Actual Supply Airflow** option from the **Select the field to be added to the formula** area and choose **OK**; the selected option is displayed in the **Formula** edit box.

7. In the **Formula** edit box, enter **"-"** symbol next to the **Space: Actual Supply Airflow** text and then choose the button displayed next to it; the **Fields** dialog box is displayed again.

8. In this dialog box, select the **Space: Calculated Supply Airflow** option from the **Select the field to be added to the formula** area and choose **OK**; the selected option is displayed in the **Formula** edit box next to the "-" symbol.

9. In the **Calculated Value** dialog box, choose the **OK** button; the **Difference in Airflow** option is added to the **Scheduled fields (in order)** area, as shown in Figure 5-45.

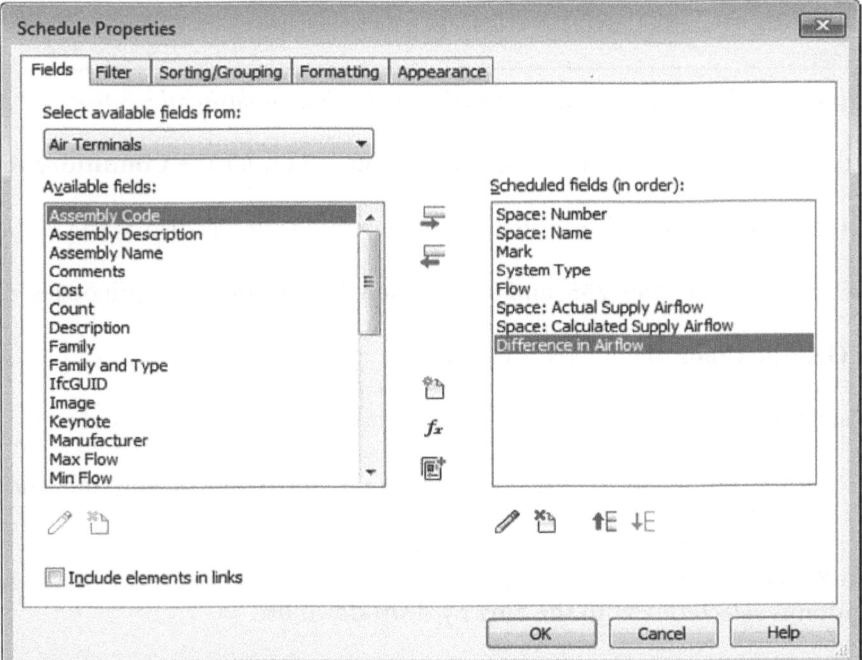

***Figure 5-45** The **Schedule Properties** dialog box displaying added parameter*

Formatting the Calculated Value Parameter

1. In the **Schedule Properties** dialog box, choose the **Formatting** tab; various options in this tab are displayed.

2. In the **Fields** area, select the **Difference in Airflow** option and then choose the **Conditional Format** button; the **Conditional Formatting** dialog box is displayed.

3. In the **Condition** area of the displayed dialog box, ensure that the **Difference in Airflow** option is selected in the **Field** drop-down list.

4. Select the **Not Between** option from the **Test** drop-down list.

5. Enter **-20 CFM (-9.5 L/s)** and **20 CFM (9.5 L/s)** in the edit boxes available in the **Value** area, as shown in Figure 5-46.

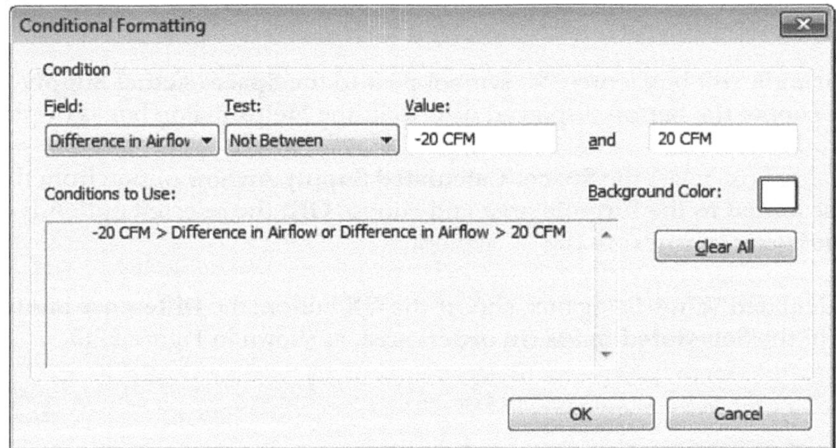

***Figure 5-46** The **Conditional Formatting** dialog box displaying the entered values*

Notice that the conditions that you specified are displayed under the **Conditions to Use** area.

6. Choose the **Background Color** swatch; the **Color** dialog box is displayed.

7. In this dialog box, enter **255, 255,** and **0** in the **Red, Green,** and **Blue** edit boxes, respectively.

8. Choose **OK**; the **Color** dialog box is closed.

9. In the **Conditional Formatting** dialog box, choose **OK**; the dialog box closes.

10. In the **Schedule Properties** dialog box, choose the **Sorting/Grouping** tab; the options in this tab are displayed.

11. Select the **Space: Number** option from the **Sort by** drop-down list. Ensure that the **Ascending** radio button is selected next to the **Sort by** drop-down list.

12. Select the **Header** and **Footer** check boxes and then select the **Count and totals** option from the drop-down list displayed next to it.

13. Select the **Blank line** check box. Ensure that the **Grand totals** check box is cleared and the **Itemize every instance** check box is selected.

14. Choose the **Filter** tab. Next, ensure that the **(none)** option is selected in the **Filter by** drop-down list.

15. Choose **OK** from the **Schedule Properties** dialog box; the new schedule named **Air-Terminals-Office** opens and is located under **Schedules/Quantities** in the **Project Browser**. Notice that the data is sorted according to the space number. The values in yellow color in the **Difference in Airflow** column indicate that the actual amount of air being supplied to the room does not meet the design airflow requirements within the range of plus or minus **20 CFM (9.5 L/S)**.

Using the Schedule to Modify Air Terminals

1. In the **Project Browser**, double-click on the **1 - Mech** node under **Views > Mechanical > HVAC > Floor Plans**.

2. Enter ZR from the keyboard, and draw a zoom region around **CEO-Office** area located on the left of the floor plan.

3. Enter WT from the keyboard; the floor plan and the schedule displays simultaneously in the drawing area.

4. Click in the schedule view and select the **500 CFM (236 L/S) Flow** parameter (in the **Flow** column) for the air terminal in the **CEO-Office** area.

5. Delete the value and enter **200 CFM (95 L/S)** in the **Flow** parameter. Next, press ENTER; the value field background of the **Difference in Airflow** parameter changes to white, indicating that it now complies with the CEO-Office airflow design requirements.

6. Click in the drawing area of the **Floor Plan: 1 - Mech** view and then choose the **Tag All** tool from the **Annotate** tab; the **Tag All Not Tagged** dialog box is displayed.

7. In this dialog box, select the **All objects in current view** radio button and then ensure that the **Air Terminal Tags** option is selected in the **Category** column. Now, choose **Apply** and **OK**; the dialog box closes and the tags for the air terminals are displayed in the drawing view. The tags display the **Flow** parameter of the air terminals in the view, as shown in Figure 5-47.

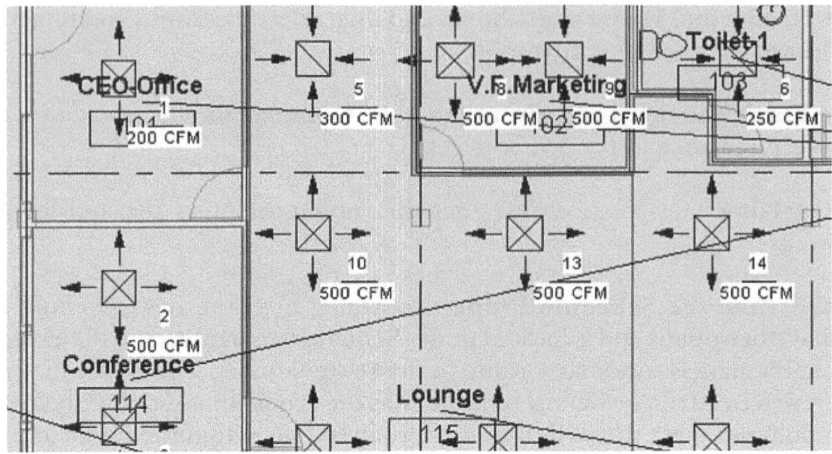

Figure 5-47 *Floor plan showing the modified parameters of the air terminals*

Saving and Closing the Project

In this section, you need to save the project and the settings using the **Save As** tool.

1. Choose **Save As > Project** from **Application Menu**. As you are saving the project for the first time, the **Save As** dialog box is displayed.

2. In this dialog box, browse to *C:\rmp_2017\c05_rmp_2017_tut* and then in the **File name** edit box, enter **c05_Office-Space_tut2a** and then choose the **Save** button to save the current project file with the specified name and to close the **Save As** dialog box.

3. To close the project, choose the **Close** option from **Application Menu**.

   The file is closed and this completes the tutorial.

Self-Evaluation Test

Answer the following questions and then compare them to those given at the end of this chapter:

1. The **Air Terminal** tool is available in the ________ panel of the _________ tab.

2. The main functions of an HVAC system are Heating, ________, and _________ in a building project.

3. In an HVAC system, air equipment are added to control the flow of air from duct to the air terminals. (T/F)

4. To create an air supply system, you need to connect the air terminals and air equipment together. (T/F)

5. You can use the **Mechanical Equipment** tool to add different air equipment in an HVAC system. (T/F)

Review Questions

Answer the following questions:

1. Which of the following tools is used to configure the size of the duct?

   a) **Duct** b) **Air Terminal**
   c) **Duct/Pipe Sizing** d) None of these

2. Which of the following tools is used to inspect the airflow in the duct?

   a) **Load Family** b) **System Inspector**
   c) **Pipes** d) **Sprinklers**

3. Which of the following tools is used to check the connectivity of the ductwork in the system?

   a) **System Inspector** b) **Generate Layout**
   c) **Check Duct Systems** d) None of these

4. Creating duct legend helps you to visualize the air flow requirement in different ducts. (T/F)

5. In an HVAC system, ducts are used to supply and remove air from space. (T/F)

EXERCISE

Exercise 1 HVAC System

Download the *c05_Conference-Center_exer1.rvt* (for Metric *M_c05_Conference-Center_exer1.rvt)* file from *http://www.cadcim.com*. The path of the file is as follows: *Textbooks > Civil/GIS > Revit MEP > Exploring Autodesk Revit 2017 for MEP*.

Open the *c05_Conference-Center_exer1.rvt* file and create an HVAC system in the conference room for the *Conference-Center* project. While creating the HVAC system, you will add air terminals to the spaces, as shown in Figure 5-48. You will also create the duct system for the air terminals, as shown in Figure 5-49.

(Note : 1 CFM = 0.47 L/s)

1. Project view to be used :
   Floor Plans > Mechanical > 1ST FLOOR- HVAC DUCT
2. Family type to be used:
   Air Terminals
   For Imperial Rectangular Diffuser- Round Connection : 24*24 -10 Neck
   For Metric M_Supply Diffuser - Rectangular Face Round Neck : 600*600 - 250 Neck
   Duct System
   For Imperial Rectangular Duct : Galvanized
   For Metric Rectangular Duct : Galvanized

3. File name to be assigned: *c05_Conference-Center_exer1a.rvt*

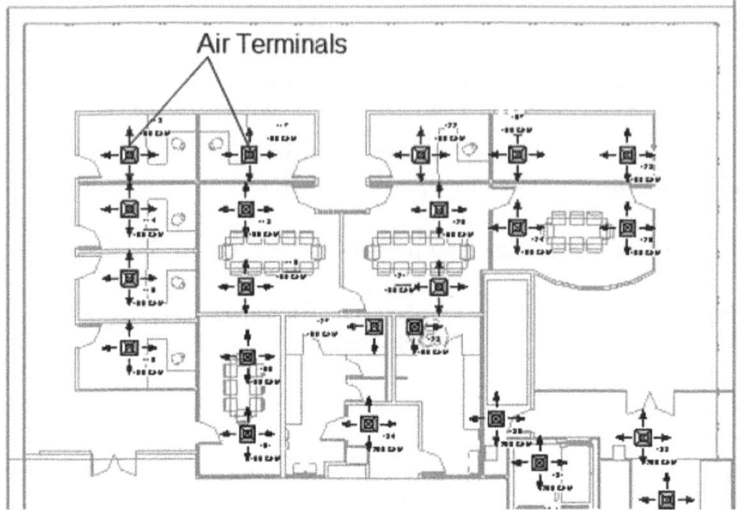

Figure 5-48 *Air Terminals added in the space*

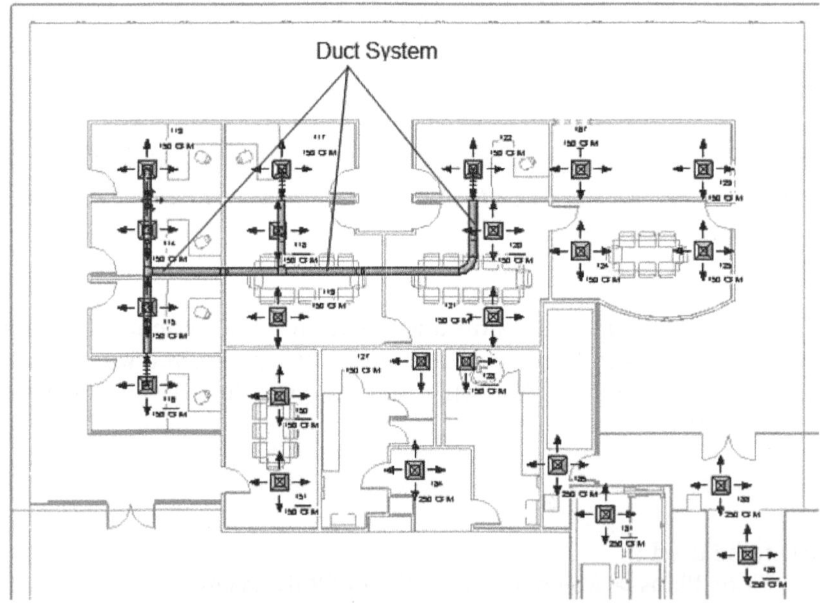

Figure 5-49 *Duct system created for the air terminals*

Answers to Self-Evaluation Test

1. HVAC, Systems, 2. Ventilating, Air Conditioning, **3.** T, **4.** T, **5.** T

Chapter 6

Creating an Electrical System

Learning Objectives

After completing this chapter, you will be able to:

- *Add electrical equipments*
- *Add power and system devices*
- *Add lighting fixtures*
- *Specify electrical settings*
- *Create power distribution systems*
- *Perform lighting analysis*
- *Add electrical circuits and wires*

INTRODUCTION

In this chapter, you will learn various procedures and tools available in Revit MEP to create an electrical system in a project. You will learn to add various power and system devices and lighting fixtures. You will also learn to modify various electrical settings, add conduits, cable trays, and specify the Power Distribution System for a project.

ADDING ELECTRICAL EQUIPMENT

In an MEP project, the electrical equipment consists of panels and transformers. This equipment plays an important role in the functioning of the building. The process of adding electrical equipment in a building is discussed next.

Adding Transformers

A transformer is an electrical equipment that is used to transform power from one circuit to another without changing the frequency of the input current. The primary use of transformer in a building is to transform the electricity from one voltage to another (generally from higher to lower) and distribute the electricity in the circuits of the building. In general, transformers are essential for the transmission, distribution, and utilization of electrical energy in a building project.

In Revit MEP, you can model and add transformers of various sizes with different ratings and voltage requirement. In a project, you can represent a transformer as a symbol or as a physical model. The transformer that you will add can be added in a floor or can be mounted in the wall. In Revit, you can add both wet and dry transformers. Figure 6-1 shows a general purpose dry type transformer of the following specification: construction encapsulated, primary voltage 240 x 480 V, and NEMA 3R.

Figure 6-1 *A dry type transformer of 240 x 480 V, NEMA 3R*

Before you add a transformer in a project, you need to load the desired family type. To do so, choose the **Load Family** tool from the **Load from Library** panel in the **Insert** tab; the **Load Family** dialog box will be displayed. In this dialog box, browse to **US Imperial > Electrical > MEP > Electric Power > Generation and Transformation** folder (for Metric browse to **US Metric > Electrical > MEP > Electric Power > Generation and Transformation** folder). In this folder, you can select the following transformer families based on your requirement: **Dry Type Transformer - 480-208Y120 - NEMA Type 2** (for Metric **M_Dry Type Transformer - 480-208Y120 - NEMA Type 2**), **Dry Type Transformer - 480-208Y120 - NEMA Type 3R**, (for Metric **M_ Dry Type Transformer - 480-208Y120 - NEMA Type 3R**), and **Wet Type Transformer - 12000-480Y277**(for Metric, **M_Wet Type Transformer - 12000-480Y277**). Note that the **Dry**

Type Transformer - 480-208Y120 - NEMA Type 3R (for Metric **M_Dry Type Transformer - 480-208Y120 - NEMA Type 3R**) family is a hosted family. After selecting the desired families of the transformer, choose the **Open** button; the selected families are loaded in the project. To place the transformer in the project, invoke the desired power floor plan of the model. Next, choose the **Electrical Equipment** tool from the **Electrical** panel of the **Systems** tab; the **Modify | Place Equipment** contextual tab will be displayed along with the **Properties** palette displaying the various properties of the selected type. In the **Properties** palette, you can select the type of transformer from the **Type Selector** drop-down list. After selecting the type of the transformer, you can now modify its instance and type properties. The various instance and type properties are discussed next.

Instance Properties of the Transformer

The instance properties of the transformer are displayed in the **Properties** palette. These properties will be displayed in the palette on placing a transformer or selecting a transformer from the model. Some of the important instance properties of a transformer that you can modify are discussed in the table next.

Properties	**Description**
Level	Specifies the level at which the transformer will be constrained.
Offset	Specifies the vertical offset value with reference to the specified level at which the transformer will be placed.
Secondary Distribution	Specifies the secondary distribution for the selected transformer type.
Mounting	Specifies the type of mounting in which the transformer will be installed.
Panel Name	Specifies the name of the panel in which it will be circuited.
Max#1 Pole Breakers	Specifies the maximum number of breakers for single phase circuit.
Feed	Specifies the name of the feeder to which the transformer will be connected. A feeder is a circuit conductor between the power supply source and a final branch circuit over current device.
Short Circuit Rating	Specifies the short circuit rating for the transformer.
Distribution System	Specifies the name of the distribution system of the transformer. A distribution system is a circuit of users linked to a generating station and substations that is typically arranged in either a radial or in an interconnected manner. Local distribution systems transport power within a building.

Type Properties of the Transformer

The type properties of a transformer refer to the properties of the transformer type selected from the **Type Selector** drop-down list in the **Properties** palette. To view and edit the type properties of a transformer, select its type from the **Type Selector** drop-down list and then choose the **Edit Type** button in the **Properties** palette; the **Type Properties** dialog box will be displayed. Some of the important type properties of the transformer type are discussed in the table given next.

Properties	**Description**
Primary Voltage	Specifies the voltage of the transformer at primary end.
Primary Number of Poles	Specifies the number of poles at the primary end.
Load Classifications	Specifies the classifications of the load for the transformer.
Voltage	Specifies the output voltage of the transformer.
Wattage	Specifies the output power of the transformer.
Transformer Length	Specifies the length of the transformer.
Transformer Height	Specifies the height of the transformer.
Transformer Width	Specifies the width of the transformer.

Next, after specifying various type properties in the **Type Properties** dialog box, choose **OK**; the **Type Properties** dialog box will be closed. Now, zoom into the drawing area and place the cursor at the desired location. Next, in the **Tag** panel of the **Modify | Place Equipment** tab, choose the **Tag on placement** button to display the tag along with the transformer that you will add.

Note

*On choosing the **Tag on placement** button, the **No Tag Loaded** window will be displayed, if no tag is loaded in the project. In this window, choose the **Yes** button to load the tag; the **Load Family** dialog box will be displayed. In this dialog box, browse to **US Imperial > Annotations > Electrical folder** (for Metric browse to **US Metric > Annotations > Electrical** folder) and then select any of the following: **Electrical Equipment Tag (M_Electrical Equipment Tag)** or **Electrical Equipment Type Mark Tag (M_Electrical Equipment Tag)**. After selecting the desired family, choose **Open**; the **Load Family** dialog box will be closed.*

Now, in the **Options Bar**, you can select the **Rotate after placement** check box to rotate the transformer while you place it in the drawing area. Also, in the **Options Bar,** click on the drop-down list displayed next to the **Rotate after placement** check box and select the **Horizontal** or **Vertical** option from it to specify the alignment of the tag. In the **Options Bar**, you can also select the **Leader** check box to display a leader line with the tag. On selecting the **Leader** check box, the edit box next to it will be enabled. Enter a value in this edit box to specify the length of the leader line that will be displayed with the tag. Next, click at the desired place in the drawing area; the transformer will be displayed with various connectors, as shown in Figure 6-2.

After placing the transformer, choose **Modify** from the **Select** panel to exit the **Electrical Equipment** tool. Next, you can modify the instance properties of the transformer. To do so, select the transformer from the drawing area and then in the **Properties** palette, edit its properties.

Also, you can edit the type properties of the selected transformer. To do so, choose the **Edit Type** button from the **Properties** palette; the **Type Properties** dialog box will be displayed. Use the options in this dialog box to edit the properties. After editing the desired properties, choose **OK**; the **Type Properties** dialog box will be closed and the modified properties are assigned to the selected transformer.

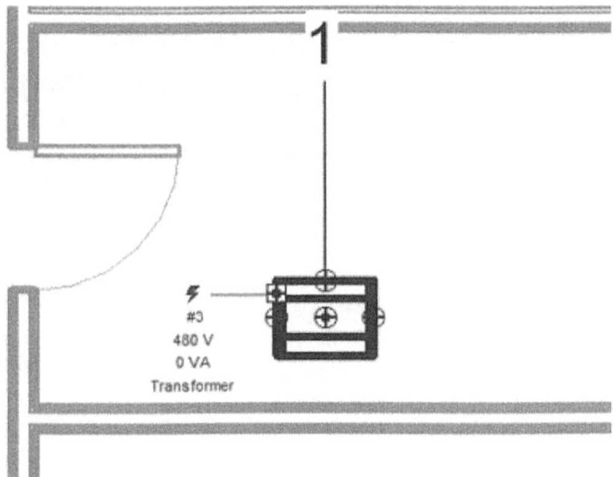

Figure 6-2 A transformer placed

Placing Switchboard Components

In an MEP project, a switchboard is an assembly of the following components: Circuit Breaker, Utility, Metering, and Transformer switchboards. Figure 6-3 shows an electrical switchboard with circuit breakers and safety switches.

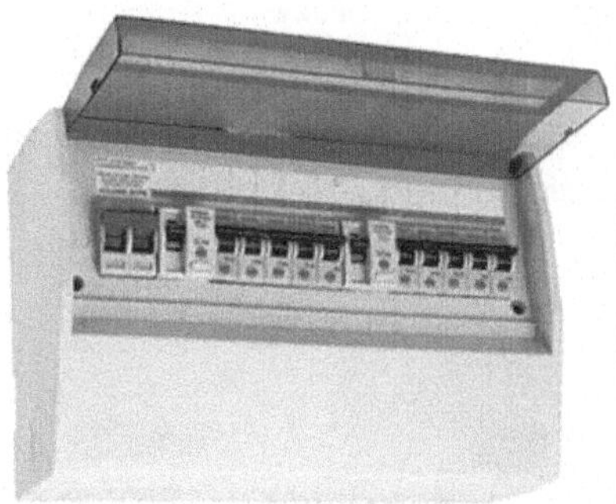

Figure 6-3 An electrical switchboard with circuit breakers and safety switches

Before adding the components to the project, you need to load their families to it. To do so, choose the **Load Family** tool from the **Load from Library** panel in the **Insert** tab; the **Load Family** dialog box will be displayed. In this dialog box, browse to **US Imperial > Electrical > MEP > Electric Power > Distribution** (for Metric browse to **US Metric > Electrical > MEP > Electric Power > Distribution** folder) and then select the following families based on the design requirement: **Circuit Breaker Switchboard (M_Circuit Breaker Switchboard), Metering Switchboard (M_Metering Switchboard), Utility Switchboard (M_Utility Switchboard)**, and **Transformer Switchboard (M_Transformer Switchboard)**. After selecting the desired family(ies) of the switchboard, choose **Open**; the **Load Family** dialog box will be closed and the selected family(ies) will be loaded in the project. Next, to insert the various components of the switchboard, choose the **Electrical Equipment** tool from the **Electrical** panel of the **Systems** tab; the **Modify | Place Equipment** contextual tab will be displayed. In this tab, ensure that the **Tag on Placement** button is chosen by default. As a result, a tag will be attached to the switchboard component when it is added. In the **Options Bar**, you can select the **Rotate after placement** check box if you want to rotate the component when you place it in the drawing area. You can use other options from the **Options Bar** to specify the alignment of tag and the display of the leader with the tag. After specifying the options in the **Options Bar**, select the type of the switchboard from the **Type Selector** drop-down list in the **Properties** palette. After selecting the type, you can modify the instance properties of the switchboard from the various properties displayed in the **Properties** palette. The properties that you can modify in the **Properties** palette are same as discussed for the transformers. After modifying the properties in the **Properties** palette, you can edit the type properties of it. To modify the type properties of the switchboard type, choose the **Edit** button; the **Type Properties** dialog box will be displayed, as shown in Figure 6-4.

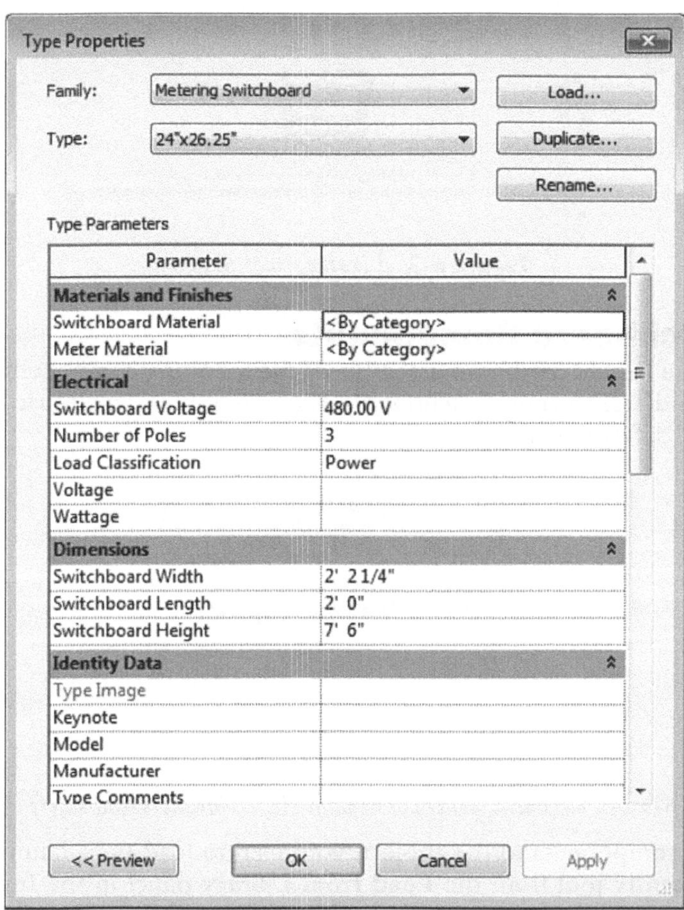

***Figure 6-4** The **Type Properties** dialog box of a Metering Switchboard*

In this dialog box, you can edit various properties of the switchboard such as the material of the switch, voltage of the switchboard, dimensions of the switchboards, and so on. After modifying the properties, move the cursor to the desired area where you want to place the switchboard. Notice that the preview of the selected type is attached to the cursor when you move it in the drawing area. You can use the SPACEBAR to rotate the switchboard prior to placement. Next, click in the desired place to add the switchboard component. Next, without exiting the command, select another switchboard component type from the **Type Selector** drop-down list and then click at the place next to the added switchboard component to add it. Repeat this procedure to add other components to complete the switchboard assembly. Refer to Figure 6-5 for the complete assembly of the switchboard in a 3D view.

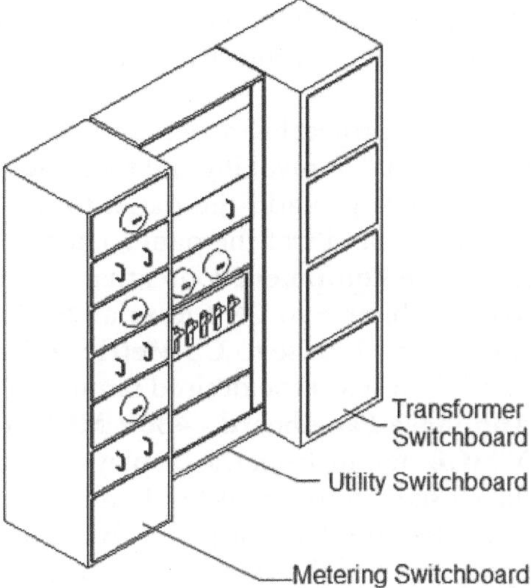

Figure 6-5 *The complete assembly of a switchboard*

After adding the switchboard components to the drawing, you can select them individually. Next, in the **Properties** palette, specify an option for the **Distribution System** parameter to assign a distribution system connected to it.

Placing the Panel Board or Distribution Board

The panel board, also referred as distribution board, is an important element of an electrical system. The function of the panel board in an electrical system is to protect the distribution system and the electrical connection in a building from various problems such as overloading, short-circuiting, and so on. Figure 6-6 shows electrical panel board for an office building.

Figure 6-6 *The electrical panel board for an office building*

There are different names referred to panel board, depending on the users such as breaker panel, circuit breaker panel, consumer unit or CU, electrical panel, fuseboard, fusebox, breaker box, load centre/center, power breaker, service panel, and DB board (South Africa). In this textbook, the panel board or the distribution board will be referred to as panels. Panels are made up of fuse links, bus bars, switches, and automated protective equipment.

In Revit MEP, you can add a panel to a project by invoking the **Electrical Equipment** tool from the **Electrical** panel of the **Systems** tab. On invoking the tool, the **Modify | Place Equipment** contextual tab will be displayed. Before you add the panel to the project, load the family of the panel into the project. To load the family of the panel, choose the **Load Family** tool from the **Mode** panel of the **Modify | Place Equipment** contextual tab; the **Load Family** dialog box will be displayed. In this dialog box, browse to **US Imperial > Electrical > MEP > Electric Power > Distribution** folder (for Metric browse to **US Metric > Electrical > MEP > Electric Power > Distribution** folder) and then select the desired family of the panel. For example, you can select the **Lighting and Appliance Panelboard - 480V MCB** (for Metric **M_Lighting and Appliance Panelboard - 480V MCB**) family from the displayed folder. Now, choose **Open**; the **Load Family** dialog box will be closed and the selected family will be loaded into the project. Now, in the **Properties** palette, select the type of panel from the **Type Selector** drop-down list. You can modify the type properties of the selected panel type. To do so, choose the **Edit Type** button from the **Properties** palette; the **Type Properties** dialog box will be displayed. In this dialog box, click in the value field of the **Default Elevation** parameter and enter a value to specify the elevation height of the panel from the level at which it will be placed. Next, in the **Type Properties** dialog box, you can specify the classification of the load in the panel by assigning a value to the **Load Classification** parameter. To assign a value to this parameter, click in the value field corresponding to it and then choose the browse button displayed in it; the **Load Classifications** dialog box will be displayed. In this dialog box, use various options to specify the load class to the panel. After specifying various options, choose **OK**; the **Load Classifications** dialog box will be closed and the desired load classification will be assigned to the **Load Classification** parameter.

In the **Type Properties** dialog box, you can specify the values for other parameters such as **Voltage, Wattage, Width, Height**, and so on. After specifying the values for the parameters, choose **Apply** and **OK**; the **Type Properties** dialog box will be closed and the specified parameters will be assigned to the selected type. Next, in the **Properties** palette, you can specify various instance parameters such as **Offset, Schedule Header Notes, Schedule Footer Notes, Mounting, Mains, Circuit Naming, Distribution System**, and more. After specifying the parameters in the palette, choose **Apply** to apply the instance properties to the panel.

Next, in the **Modify | Place Equipment** contextual tab, the **Place on Vertical Face** tool will be chosen by default. As a result, you can place the panel at the vertical face of the desired wall in the project. Alternatively, you can choose the **Place on Face** or the **Place on Workplane** tool from the **Placement** panel to place the panel on the face of an element (for example, a floor) or at a point in the current workplane, respectively. You can choose the **Place on Vertical Face** tool, if it is not chosen by default from the **Placement** panel and then place the cursor at the face of the desired wall; the preview of the panel will be displayed along with the cursor at the face of the wall, as shown in Figure 6-7. You can use the SPACEBAR to flip the side of placement of the panel. Now, click to place the panel at the desired location. After placing the panel, you can load more panels as per your design requirement and add them in the project. Now, choose the **Modify** button from the **Select** panel of the **Modify | Place Equipment** tab to exit the tool.

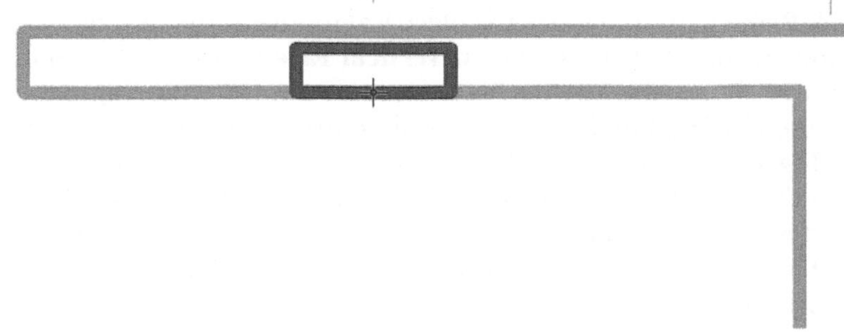

Figure 6-7 *The panel placed at the face of the wall*

ADDING POWER AND SYSTEM DEVICES

Devices consist of receptacles, switches, junction boxes, telephones, communications, and data terminal devices, nurse call devices, wall speakers, starters, smoke detectors, and fire alarm manual pull stations. Electrical devices are often hosted components (receptacles that must be placed on a wall or work plane). Figure 6-8 shows various electrical devices that can be used in an electrical system of a project. The procedure of adding various electrical fixtures to a project is discussed next.

Figure 6-8 *Various electrical devices*

Adding Electrical Fixtures

In an MEP project, while designing the electrical system, you need to add various electrical fixtures for power distribution. To do so, double-click on the desired power floor plan in the **Project Browser** to make it active and then invoke the **Electrical Fixture** tool from **Systems > Electrical > Device** drop-down; the **Modify | Place Devices** contextual tab will be displayed.

In this tab, the **Place on Vertical Face** button is chosen in the **Placement** panel of the **Modify | Place Devices** tab by default. As a result, you can place the electrical fixture at the face of a host element such as wall, at the desired elevation. Alternatively, you can choose the **Place on Face** or **Place on Work Plane** button to place the electrical fixture at the face of an element or at the desired workplane. Ensure that the **Place on Vertical Face** button is chosen in the **Placement** panel. Next, you can choose the **Tag on Placement** button from the **Tag** panel to attach a tag with the fixture; the **No Tag Loaded** window will be displayed. To load a tag, choose the **Yes** button; the **No Tag Loaded** window will be closed and the **Load Family** dialog box will be displayed. In this dialog box, browse to **US Imperial > Annotations > Electrical** (for Metric **US Metric > Annotations > Electrical**) and then select the **Electrical Fixture Tag** family and choose **OK**; the **Load Family** dialog box will be closed and the selected family of the tag will be loaded in the project.

Next, in the **Options Bar**, you can click on the drop-down list and select the **Horizontal** or **Vertical** option to specify the alignment of the tag when it is placed with the fixtures. Next, in the **Options Bar**, choose the **Tags** button; the **Loaded Tags** dialog box will be displayed. In this dialog box, click on the **Loaded Tags** field corresponding to the **Electrical Fixture** category and select an option from the drop-down list displayed to specify the type of tag that you want to display with the fixture.

After selecting an option from the drop-down list, choose **OK**; the **Loaded Tags** dialog box will be closed. Next, in the **Properties** palette, select the type of electrical fixture from the **Type Selector** drop-down list. In the drop-down list, the **Duplex Receptacle: Standard** option is selected by default (for Metric **M_Duplex Receptacle: Standard**). To add other types of power receptacle and electrical fixtures in the drop-down list, choose the **Load Family** tool from the **Mode** panel of the **Modify | Place Devices** contextual tab; the **Load Family** dialog box will be displayed. In this dialog box, browse to **US Imperial > Electrical > MEP > Electric Power** folder (for Metric, browse to **US Metric > Electrical > MEP > Electric Power** folder) and to select various families of receptacle, choose the **Terminals** folder. In this folder, select various families of power receptacle such as **Simplex Receptacle** (**M_Simplex Receptacle**), **Special Purpose Receptacle** (**M_Special Purpose Receptacle**), **Quadruplex Receptacle** (**M_Quadruplex Receptacle**), and so on from the list displayed in it. After selecting the families, choose **Open**; the **Load Family** dialog box will be closed and the selected families will be loaded in the project. You can now select various types of the loaded families from the **Type Selector** drop-down list in the **Properties** palette. After selecting the desired type from the **Type Selector** drop-down list, you can edit and verify various instance parameters of the fixture that you will add to the project. These parameters are displayed in the **Properties** palette, refer to Figure 6-9.

In the **Properties** palette, the value field corresponding to the **Host** parameter displays the host of the fixture. This parameter is read-only. The host of a fixture can be a level, wall, face of an equipment, or others. By default, the **<not associated value>** will be displayed corresponding to this parameter because the fixture is not added to the view. In the **Properties** palette, you can click in the value field corresponding to the **Elevation** parameter and enter a value to specify the height of the fixture from the hosted level. Also, you can assign a horizontal offset distance of the fixture by specifying a value corresponding to the **Offset** parameter. In the **Properties** palette, you can select an option from the value field corresponding to the **Schedule Level** parameter to specify the level in which the fixture will be hosted. By default, the current level will be specified in the value field of this parameter. Next, after verifying and editing the instance properties of the fixture, move the cursor and place it on the face of the wall at which you want to place the fixture. On placing the cursor on the face of the wall, the preview of the fixture will be displayed. You can use the SPACEBAR to flip the preview and align the placement of the fixture.

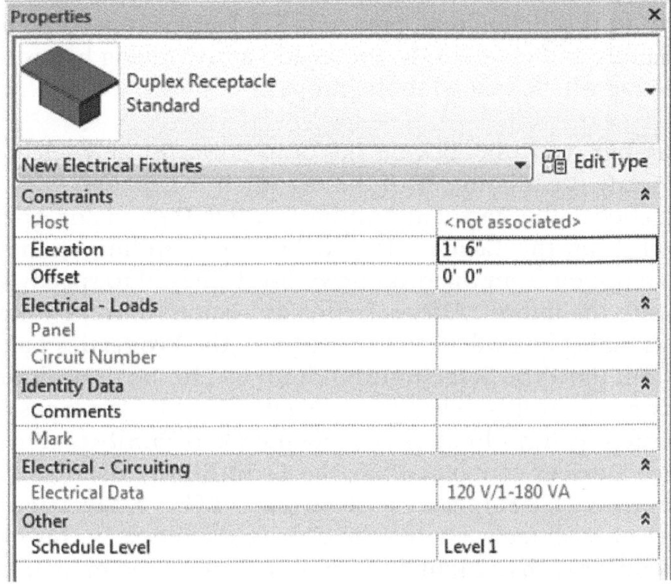

Figure 6-9 *The various instance parameters for the electrical fixture*

Now, click at the desired location; the selected fixture will be placed in the project view. Choose the **Modify** button from the **Select** panel to exit the **Electrical Fixture** tool.

You can change the type properties of the selected fixture type. To do so, you can select an existing fixture or at the time of placing a fixture, choose the **Edit** button in the **Properties** palette; the **Type Properties** dialog box will be displayed. You can use, verify, and modify various parameters such as **Default Elevation, Switch Voltage, Load,** and more. The parameters displayed in the **Type Properties** dialog box will vary depending upon the type of fixture you select. After specifying various type properties of the fixture, choose **OK**; the **Type Properties** dialog box will be closed. After adding the electrical fixture, you can select it and modify its various instance and type properties.

Adding Lighting Devices

In an MEP project, while designing the electrical system you need to add various lighting devices such as switches, daylight sensors, and more. To add the lighting devices, you can use the **Lighting** tool.

Before invoking this tool, double-click on the desired power floor plan in the **Project Browser** to make it active and then invoke the **Lighting** tool from **Systems > Electrical > Device** drop-down; the **Modify | Place Lighting Device** contextual tab will be displayed. In this tab, the **Place on Vertical Face** button is chosen in the **Placement** panel of the **Modify | Place Devices** tab by default. As a result, you can place the electrical fixture at the face of a host element such as wall, at the desired elevation. Alternatively, you can choose the **Place on Face** or **Place on Work Plane** button to place the electrical fixture at a face of an element or at a desired workplane. Ensure that the **Place on Vertical Face** button is chosen from the **Placement** panel. Next, you can choose the **Tag on Placement** button from the **Tag** panel to attach a tag with the fixture. On choosing the **Tag on Placement** button, the **No Tag Loaded** window will be displayed. To load a tag, choose the **Yes** button; the **No Tag Loaded** window will be closed and the **Load Family** dialog box will be displayed. In this dialog box, browse to **US Imperial > Annotations > Electrical** and then select the family and choose **OK**; the **Load Family** dialog box will be closed and the selected family of the tag will be loaded in the project.

Next, in the **Options Bar**, you can click on the drop-down list and select the **Horizontal** or **Vertical** option to specify the alignment of the tag when it is placed with the fixtures. Next, in the **Options Bar**, choose the **Tags** button; the **Loaded Tags** dialog box will be displayed. In this dialog box, click on the **Loaded Tags** field corresponding to the **Lighting Devices** category and select an option from the drop-down list displayed to specify the type of tag that you want to display with the fixture. After selecting an option from the drop-down list, choose **OK**; the **Loaded Tags** dialog box will be closed. Next, in the **Properties** palette, select the type of electrical fixture from the **Type Selector** drop-down list. In the drop-down list, the **Lighting Switches: Three Way** option will be selected by default. To add other types of power receptacle and electrical fixtures to the drop-down list, choose the **Load Family** tool from the **Mode** panel of the **Modify | Place Devices** contextual tab; the **Load Family** dialog box will be displayed. In this dialog box, browse to **US Imperial > Electrical > MEP > Electric Power** folder and to select various families of receptacle, choose the **Terminals** folder. In this folder, select various families of power receptacle such as **Lighting Switches**, **Switch**, and more from the list displayed in it. After selecting the families, choose **Open**; the **Load Family** dialog box will be closed and the selected families will be loaded in the project. You can now select the various types of the loaded families from the **Type Selector** drop-down list in the **Properties** palette. After selecting the desired type from the **Type Selector** drop-down list, you can edit and verify various instance parameters of the fixture that you will add in the project. These parameters are displayed in the **Properties** palette, refer to Figure 6-10.

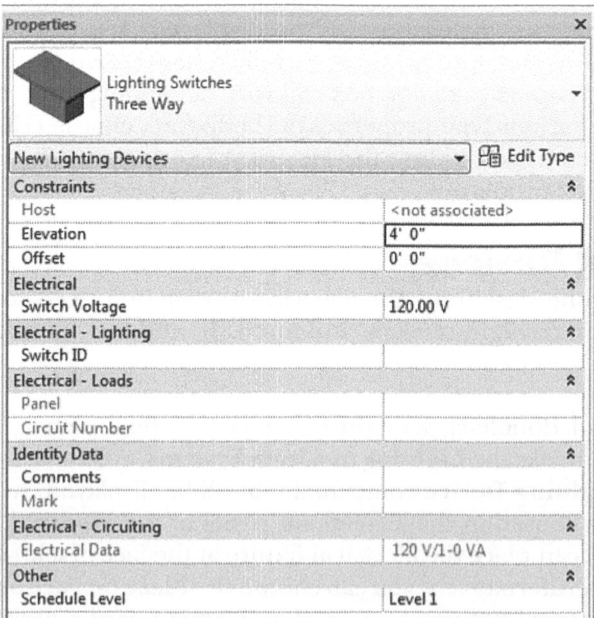

Figure 6-10 *The instance parameters for the lighting device*

In the **Properties** palette, the value field corresponding to the **Host** parameter displays the host of the fixture. This parameter is read-only. The host of a device can be a level, wall, face of an equipment, or others. By default, the **<not associated value>** will be displayed corresponding to this parameter because the device is not added to the view. In the **Properties** palette, you can click in the value field corresponding to the **Elevation** parameter and enter a value to specify the height of the device from the hosted level. Also, you can specify a value corresponding to the **Switch Voltage** parameter to assign a switch voltage to the device. In the **Properties** palette, you can select an option from the value field corresponding to the **Switch ID** parameter to specify identification to the switch. After verifying and editing the instance properties of the fixture, move the cursor and place it on the face of the wall at which you want to place the fixture. On placing the cursor on the face of the wall, the preview of the fixture will be displayed. You can use the SPACEBAR to flip the preview and align the placement of the fixture. Now, click at the desired location; the selected fixture will be placed in the project view. Choose the **Modify** button from the **Select** panel to exit the **Lighting** tool.

You can change the type properties of the selected device type. To do so, you can select a device or at the time of placing a lighting device, choose the **Edit** button in the **Properties** palette; the **Type Properties** dialog box will be displayed. You can use, verify, and modify various parameters in this dialog box such as **Default Elevation**, **Load Classification**, **Apparent Load**, and so on. The parameters displayed in the **Type Properties** dialog box will vary depending upon the type of fixture you select. After specifying the various type properties of the fixture, choose **OK**; the **Type Properties** dialog box will be closed. After adding the lighting device, you can select it and modify its various instance and type properties.

Adding Communication Devices

In an MEP project, while designing the electrical system, you need to add various communication devices such as Intercom, Intercom Substation, Speaker, and more. To add various communication devices to the project, you can use the **Communication** tool.

Before invoking this tool, double-click on the desired power floor plan in the **Project Browser** to make it active and then invoke the **Communication** tool from **Systems > Electrical > Device** drop-down; the **Modify | Place Communication Device** contextual tab will be displayed. In this tab, the **Place on Vertical Face** button is chosen in the **Placement** panel of the **Modify | Place Devices** tab by default. As a result, you can place the communication device at the face of a host element such as wall, at the desired elevation. Alternatively, you can choose the **Place on Face** or **Place on Work Plane** button to place the electrical fixture at a face of an element or at a desired workplane. Ensure that the **Place on Vertical Face** button is chosen from the **Placement** panel. Next, you can choose the **Tag on Placement** button from the **Tag** panel to attach a tag with the fixture. On choosing the **Tag on Placement** button; the **No Tag Loaded** window will be displayed, if there is no tag loaded in the project. To load a tag, choose the **Yes** button; the **No Tag Loaded** window will be closed and the **Load Family** dialog box will be displayed. In this dialog box, browse to **US Imperial > Annotations > Electrical** and then select the family and choose **OK**; the **Load Family** dialog box will be closed and the selected family of the tag will be loaded in the project.

Next, in the **Options Bar**, you can click on the drop-down list and select the **Horizontal** or **Vertical** option to specify the alignment of the tag when it is placed with the fixtures. Next, in the **Options Bar**, choose the **Tags** button; the **Loaded Tags** dialog box will be displayed. In this dialog box, click on the **Loaded Tags** field corresponding to the **Communication Devices** category and select an option from the drop-down list displayed to specify the type of tag that you want to display with the fixture. After selecting an option from the drop-down list, choose **OK**; the **Loaded Tags** dialog box will be closed. Next, in the **Properties** palette, select the type of electrical fixture from the **Type Selector** drop-down list. To add other types of communication devices to the drop-down list, choose the **Load Family** tool from the **Mode** panel of the **Modify | Place Devices** contextual tab; the **Load Family** dialog box will be displayed. In this dialog box, browse to **US Imperial > Electrical > MEP > Information and Communication > Communication** folder and select various families of communication device such as **Speaker - Round, Speaker - Clock, TV - Square** and more from the list displayed in it. After selecting the families, choose **Open**; the **Load Family** dialog box will be closed and the selected families will be loaded in the project. You can now select the various types of the loaded families from the **Type Selector** drop-down list in the **Properties** palette. After selecting the desired type from the **Type Selector** drop-down list, you can edit and verify various instance parameters in the **Properties** palette.

Next, after verifying and editing the instance properties of the fixture, move the cursor and place it on the face of the wall on which you want to place the fixture. On placing the cursor on the face of the wall, the preview of the fixture will be displayed. You can use the SPACEBAR to flip the preview and align the placement of the fixture. Now, click at the desired location; the selected fixture will be placed in the project view. Choose the **Modify** button from the **Select** panel to exit the **Communication** tool.

ADDING LIGHTING FIXTURES

In a project, a light fixture (US English), or light fitting (UK English), or luminaire (IEC, International Electrotechnical Commission) is an electrical device which will be used to create artificial light by using various types of electric lamps. A light fixture comprises of a fixture body and a light socket that will hold the lamp and allow its replacement on requirement.

A light fixture will also require a switch to control the light and an electrical connection to a power source. In a project, light fixture can be moveable or fixed at a point. A light fixture can also have other features, such as reflectors for directing the light, an aperture (with or without a lens), an outer shell or housing for lamp alignment and protection, and an electrical ballast or power supply. The classification of light fixture is based on the fixture installation, the function of the light, and the type of lamp. Figure 6-11 shows various types of ceiling lighting fixtures that can be used in a project.

In Revit MEP, most of the lighting fixtures are hosted components that are placed on a host component (a ceiling or wall). To place a lighting fixture in a view, invoke the view in which you want to add the fixtures. Note that the lighting fixtures will be added either in a floor plan or in a ceiling plan depending on its type. For example, if you desire to place a ceiling hosted lighting fixture, double-click on the desired view under **Electrical > Lighting > Ceiling Plans** node in the **Project Browser**. Next, choose the **Lighting Fixture** tool from the **Electrical** panel of the **Systems** tab; the **Modify | Place Fixture** contextual tab will be displayed. Now, before you insert a lighting fixture in the project, you need to load the families of the lighting fixtures. To do so, choose the **Load Family** tool from the **Mode** panel; the **Load Family** dialog box will be displayed.

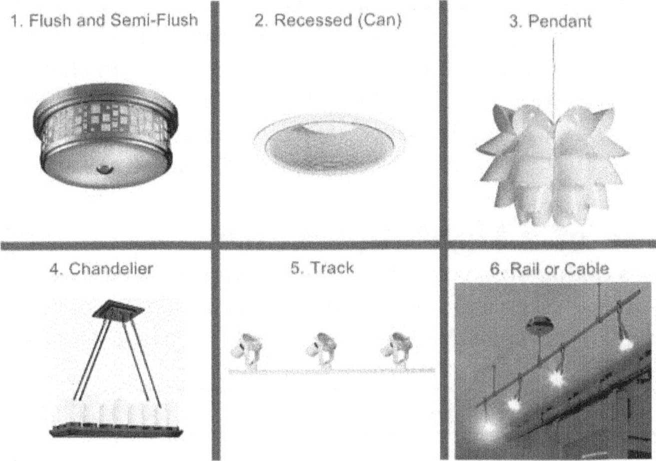

***Figure 6-11** The various types of ceiling lighting fixtures*

In this dialog box, browse to **US Imperial > Lighting > MEP** folder (for Metric, browse to **US Metric > Lighting > MEP** folder) and then choose the **External** or **Internal** folder to view different families of the lighting fixtures. You can choose the **External** folder if you desire to view and load the family files for external lighting in the project. Alternatively, choose the **Internal** folder to load families of the lighting fixtures for internal lighting; the families related to internal lighting fixture will be displayed in a list, as shown in Figure 6-12.

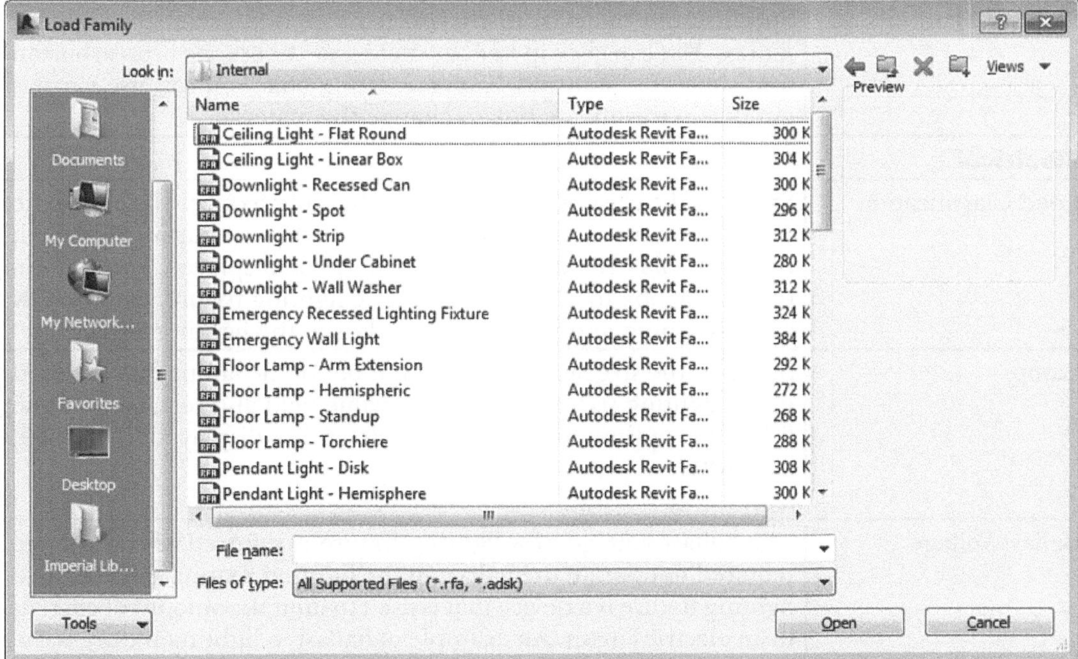

***Figure 6-12** The Load Family dialog box displaying the families for internal lighting fixtures*

In the dialog box, you can select the **Ceiling Light - Flat Round** family (for Metric **M_ Ceiling Light - Flat Round)** (ceiling -host) and then choose **Open**; the **Load Family** dialog box will be closed and the selected family will be loaded in the project. In the **Properties** palette, select the type of light fixture from the **Type Selector** drop-down list. For the loaded **Ceiling Light - Flat Round** family, you can select the **Ceiling -Flat Round : 60 W-277V (M_Ceiling -Flat Round : 60 W-277V)** option from the **Type Selector** drop-down list. You can change the type properties of the selected type. To do so, choose the **Edit Type** button from the **Properties** palette; the **Type Properties** dialog box will be displayed. In this dialog box, you can specify various type properties of the selected lighting fixture type that are discussed next.

Type Properties of a Lighting Fixture

In the **Type Properties** dialog box, you can specify various properties to specify the constraint, material, electrical settings, electrical loads, and identification data of the lighting fixture type. The various parameters in the **Type Properties** dialog box are discussed in the table given next.

Properties	**Description**
Constraint	
Default Elevation	Specifies the default elevation of the light fixture.
Material and Finishes	
Light Box Material	Specifies the material for the body of the lighting fixture. To change the material, click in its corresponding value field and choose the browse button displayed in it to display the **Material Browser** dialog box. You can use various options in this dialog box to edit material of the light box and choose **OK** to close it.
Diffuser Material	Specifies the material of the reflector or diffuser of the lighting fixture. You can click in its value field and choose the browse button to display the **Material Browser** dialog box. You can use various options in this dialog box to change the material.
Electrical	
Load Classification	Specifies the class of the load for the lighting fixture. To change the class, click in its value field and choose the browse button displayed; the **Load Classifications** dialog box will be displayed. You can use this dialog box to assign a class to the lighting fixture. Choose **OK** after assigning and specifying the class to the lighting fixture.
Lamp	Specifies the size factor and the number of the lamps that are used in the lighting fixture. Click in its value field and select any of the following options from the drop-down list displayed: **T8**, **A-19**, and **A-21**.
Ballast Voltage	The ballast voltage of a lighting fixture is referred as the voltage required to operate the ballast in the lighting fixture. A ballast in a lighting fixture is a device that is used to limit the amount of current in an electric circuit. An example of ballast in lighting fixture is the inductive ballast used in fluorescent lamps.
Ballast Number of Poles	Specifies the number of poles or leads in the lighting circuit. You can change the value of this parameter by using the spinner displayed in its value field.

Electrical Loads	
Apparent Load	Specifies the apparent load in the lighting fixture. This value will be used by Revit MEP to define the real and reactive power used by a fixture. To determine the apparent load, you need to multiply the apparent current by the voltage. This parameter is measured in volt ampere (VA).
Photometric (The following parameters will not affect rendering)	
Tilt Angle	Specifies the angle of tilt of the light source to direct its light.
Light Loss Factor	Specifies a value that will be used to calculate the amount of light lost (or gained) due to environmental factors such as dust and ambient temperature. Choose the button in its value field; the **Light Loss Factor** dialog box will be displayed. You can use this dialog box to change various options affecting the light loss factor.
Initial Intensity	Specifies the amount of brightness of the light. To change the value, choose the button in the value field corresponding to its parameter; the **Initial Intensity** dialog box will be displayed. You can use various options in this dialog box to change the intensity of the light that is emitted from the lighting fixture.
Photometric Web File	Specifies the name of the IES file that will define the light emitted from the light source. This parameter is available when the **Light Distribution** parameter is set to **Photometric Web**.
Color Filter	Specifies the color of the light that will be emitted from the light source. Choose the button in the value field corresponding to this parameter; the **Color** dialog box will be displayed. You can select the required color from this dialog box.

After assigning the type properties in the **Type Properties** dialog box, choose **OK** to close it. Now, you can modify various instance properties of the lighting fixture in the **Properties** palette. After specifying various options in the **Properties** palette, choose the **Place on Face** tool from the **Placement** panel in the **Modify | Place Fixture** tab and then place the cursor over the ceiling grid; the preview of the lighting fixture will be displayed. Click at the desired location in the ceiling grid to place the lighting fixture, as shown in Figure 6-13.

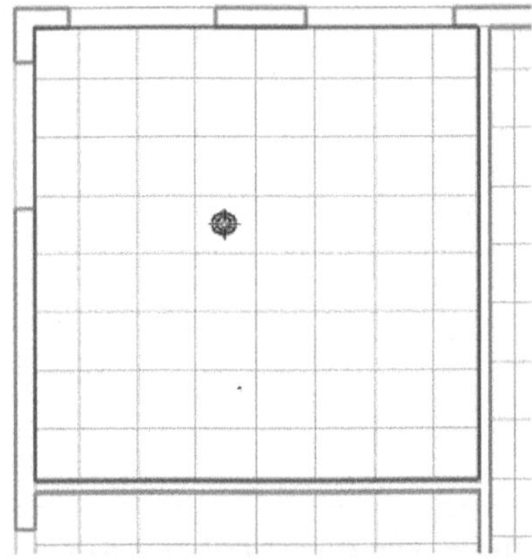

Figure 6-13 *The lighting fixtures placed in the ceiling plan*

After placing the lighting fixture, you can add more lighting fixtures by clicking on the desired locations in the ceiling grid. Now, choose **Modify** from the **Select** panel to exit the **Lighting Fixture** tool.

After adding the lighting fixtures, you can select them and modify their instance as well as type properties.

SPECIFYING THE ELECTRICAL SETTINGS

After placing the fixtures, devices, and equipment in the electrical system, you need to specify various settings that will enable you to connect these equipment and fixtures and also define how wiring and electrical information is displayed.

While specifying the electrical settings for the electrical system, you can define the types of voltages available for distribution and the characteristics of the distribution system. By specifying these settings, you can properly connect devices with the equipment and prevent connecting wiring objects to wrong panels. While specifying the electrical settings for the electrical system, you can also set the visibility behavior of tick marks. The tick marks will be used to display wire counts and the way wire tags. All the settings that you will specify are specific to the project you are working. You can specify these settings and save them as template so that it can be used for other projects in future.

To specify the electrical settings for the project, choose the **Electrical Settings** button from the **Electrical** panel of the **Systems** tab; the **Electrical Settings** dialog box will be displayed, as shown in Figure 6-14. In this dialog box, you can specify wiring, cable tray, and conduit settings. In the dialog box, you can also specify settings for voltage definitions, distribution systems, load calculations, and panel schedules. The procedure and options to set various elements and definitions using the **Electrical Settings** dialog box are discussed next.

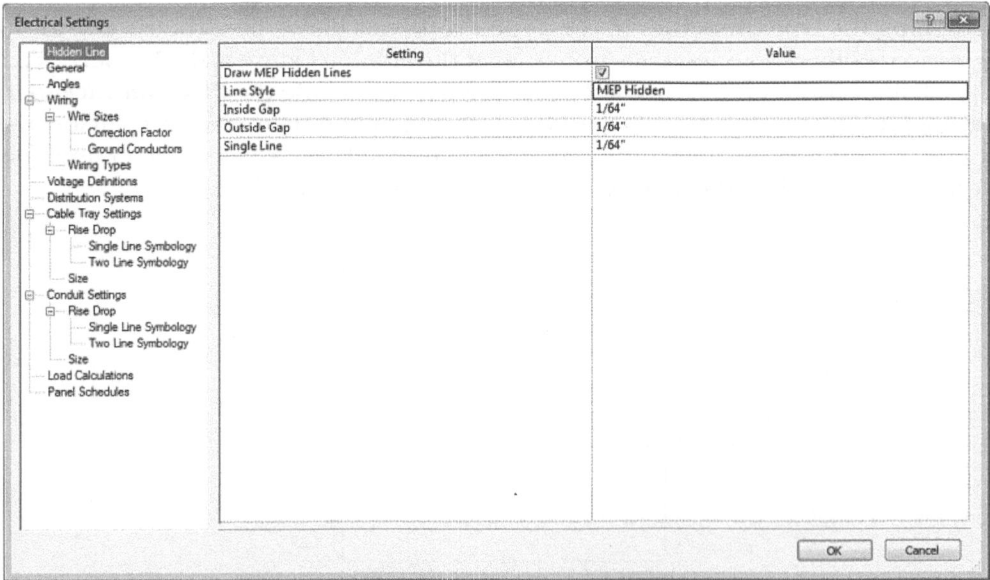

***Figure 6-14** The **Electrical Settings** dialog box*

Setting the Wires

In the **Electrical Settings** dialog box, you can specify various settings of the wire such as its display in the plan view, size in the circuit, and various settings for its correction factor and specifications for its ground conductors. To specify the settings of the wires in the **Electrical Settings** dialog box, click on the **Wiring** option displayed in the left pane of the dialog box; various options for setting the specification of the wiring are displayed in a table in the right pane of the dialog box, as shown in Figure 6-15. The various settings for the **Wiring** option are discussed in the table given next.

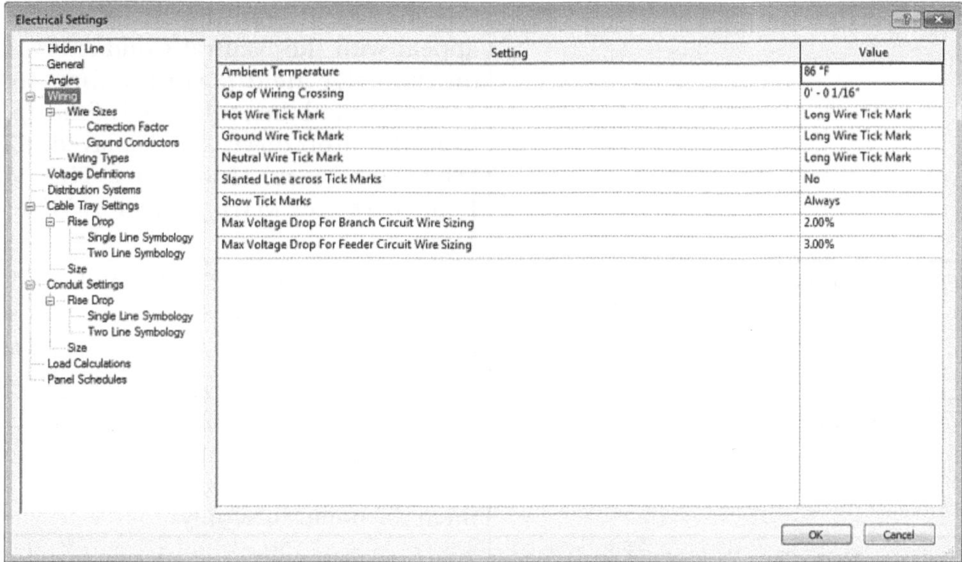

Figure 6-15 *The various options for **Wiring** in the **Electrical Settings** dialog box*

Settings	**Description**
Ambient Temperature	Specifies the ambient temperature to be used for applying a correction factor to the load of a circuit. By default, the value for this setting will be assigned as **86°F** (30°C). For this temperature, a correction factor of 1 for any of the three wire temperature ratings will be applicable.
Gap of Wiring Crossing	Specifies the size of the gap that Revit MEP displays when wires cross each other. Refer to Figure 6-16.
Hot Wire Tick Mark	Specifies the style of the tick mark that will appear with the Hot Conductors. Click on the value field corresponding to this parameter and then select any of the four options: **Circle Wire Tick Mark**, **Hook Wire Tick Mark**, **Long Wire Tick Mark**, and **Short Wire Tick Mark**.

Ground Wire Tick Mark	Specifies the style of the tick mark that will appear with the Ground Conductors. Click on the value field corresponding to this parameter and then select any of the four options from the drop-down list displayed: **Circle Wire Tick Mark**, **Hook Wire Tick Mark**, **Long Wire Tick Mark**, and **Short Wire Tick Mark**.
Neutral Wire Tick Mark	Specifies the style of the tick mark that will appear with the Neutral Conductors. Click on the value field corresponding to this parameter and then select any of the options from the drop-down list displayed: **Circle Wire Tick Mark**, **Hook Wire Tick Mark**, **Long Wire Tick Mark**, and **Short Wire Tick Mark**.
Slanted Line across Tick Marks	Specifies whether to display a slanted line across the tick mark or not. Click in the value field corresponding to the setting and select **Yes** or **No** from the drop-down list displayed.
Show Tick Marks	Specifies the condition for the display of the tick marks. You can specify an option to always hide tick marks, show them, or show them for home runs only.
Max Voltage Drop For Branch Circuit Wire Sizing	Specifies the maximum voltage drop for the wires in the branches.
Max Voltage Drop For Feeder Circuit Wire Sizing	Specifies the maximum voltage drop for the wires in the feeders.

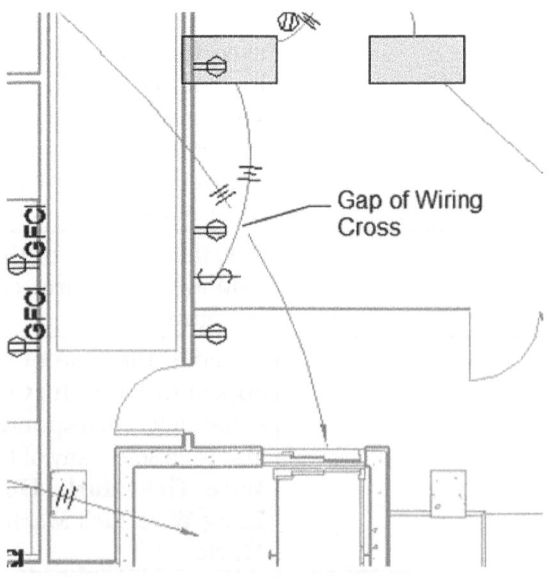

***Figure 6-16** The gap created in wiring cross*

Next, after setting the options for the wirings, you can set the correction factor for the wiring sizes. The correction factor is a factor based on temperature to be used in load calculations. You can set correction factors for the three wire temperature ratings for both aluminum and copper wires. To specify the correction factors for the wires, click **Wiring > Wiring Sizes > Correction Factor** node from the left pane of the **Electrical Settings** dialog box; various options to set the correction factors for the wiring of different sizes are displayed in the right pane, as shown in Figure 6-17.

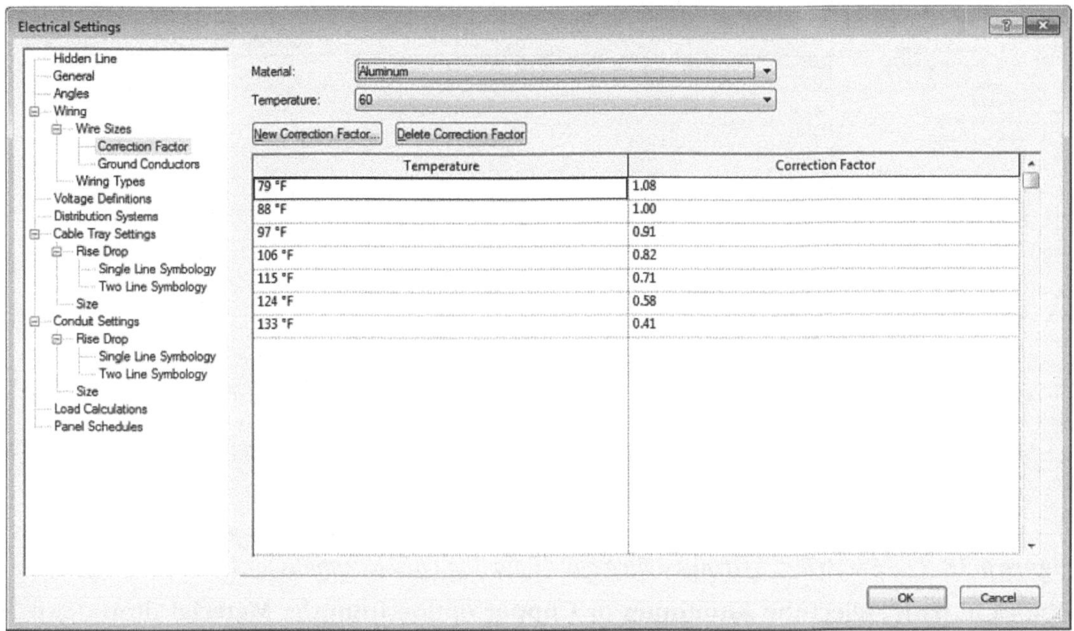

Figure 6-17** The **Electrical Settings** dialog box displaying various options for **Correction Factor

In the right pane of the **Electrical Settings** dialog box, you can select an option from the **Material** drop-down list to specify the material of the wiring for which you will set the correction factor. By default, the **Aluminum** option will be selected from the **Material** drop-down list. As a result, you can set the correction factors for **Aluminum** wires at different temperatures. Alternatively, you can select the **Copper** option from the **Material** drop-down list. Next, to set the temperature to assign the correction factors for the wires, select an option from the **Temperature** drop-down list; the table displaying correction factors for various temperatures will be displayed below the **Temperature** drop-down list. To add a new entry to the table, choose the **New Correction Factor** button which is located below the **Temperature** drop-down list; the **New Correction Factor** dialog box will be displayed. In the **Temperature** edit box of this dialog box, enter a value to specify the temperature for the correction factor. In the **Correction Factor** edit box, specify a value for the correction factor that you desire to specify. Choose **OK**; the **New Correction Factor** dialog box will be closed and the specified values in the **New Correction** dialog box will be added to the table. You can also delete any of the correction factor entries from the table. To do so, select the desired correction factor from the table, the value in the **Correction Factor** column in the table will be highlighted. Choose the **Delete Correction Factor** button; the **Delete Setting** dialog box will be displayed. Choose **Yes**; the dialog box will be closed and the selected settings will be deleted from the table.

After setting the options for **Correction Factor**, click on **Wiring > Wire Sizes > Ground Conductors** node in the left pane of the **Electrical Settings** dialog box; the various options for specifying the settings for ground conductors are displayed in the right pane of the dialog box, as shown in Figure 6-18.

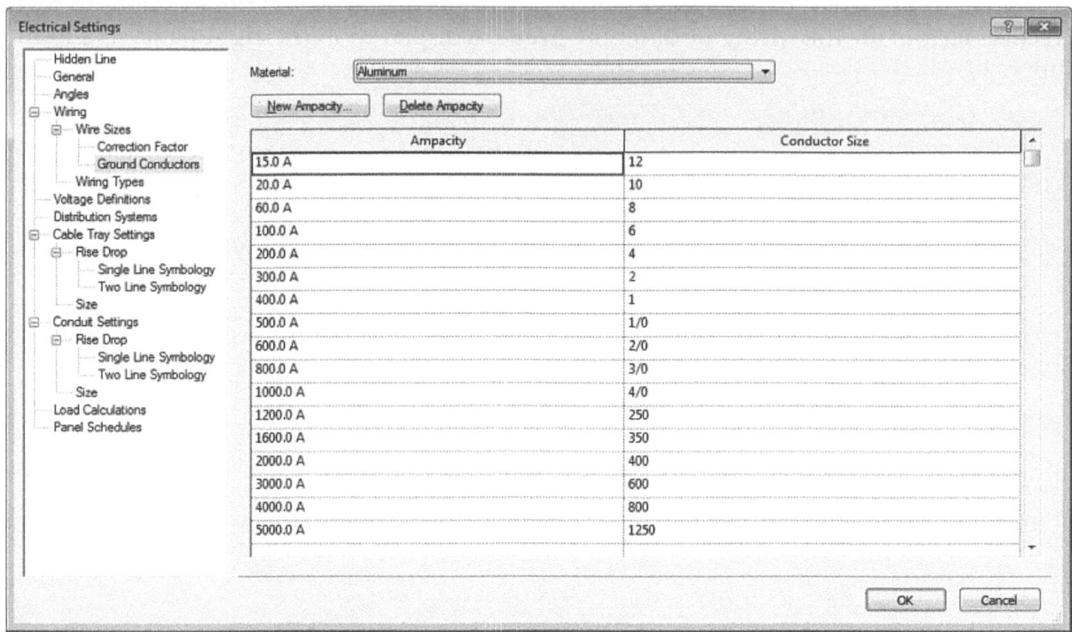

Figure 6-18** The **Electrical Settings** dialog box displaying various options for **Ground Conductors

In the right pane, select the **Aluminum** or **Copper** option from the **Material** drop-down list to select the material for the ground conductor; the table containing the different sizes of the ground conductor with their ampacity will be displayed below the drop-down list. To add a new row in the table, choose the **New Ampacity** button; the **New Ampacity** dialog box will be displayed. In this dialog box, enter a value in the **Ampacity** edit box to specify the value of the current of the wire in amperes. Next, in the **Wire Size** edit box, enter a value to specify the wire size for the conductor for which the ampacity will be set. The value that you will enter will be in multiples of 1/8"(#) (for Metric it will be in mm). For example, if you enter **12** in the **Wire Size** edit box, the size of the wire will be 12/8" or #12 (for Metric, it will be in mm). After specifying the size of the wire in the **Wire Size** edit box, choose **OK**; the **New Ampacity** dialog box will be closed and the desired values will be added to a new row in the table. To delete an entry (row) from the table, select it and choose the **Delete Ampacity** button; the **Delete Setting** dialog box will be displayed. Choose **Yes**; the dialog box will be closed and the selected rows will be deleted from the table.

After specifying the settings for the ground conductor, click on **Wiring > Wiring Types** node in the left pane of the **Electrical Settings** dialog box; the various options related to the settings of the wire types will be displayed in the right pane, as shown in Figure 6-19. The right pane for the **Wiring Types** displays a table showing various wire types with specifications for material, temperature, rating, insulation, neutral size, max size, neutral multiplier, and neutral requirement.

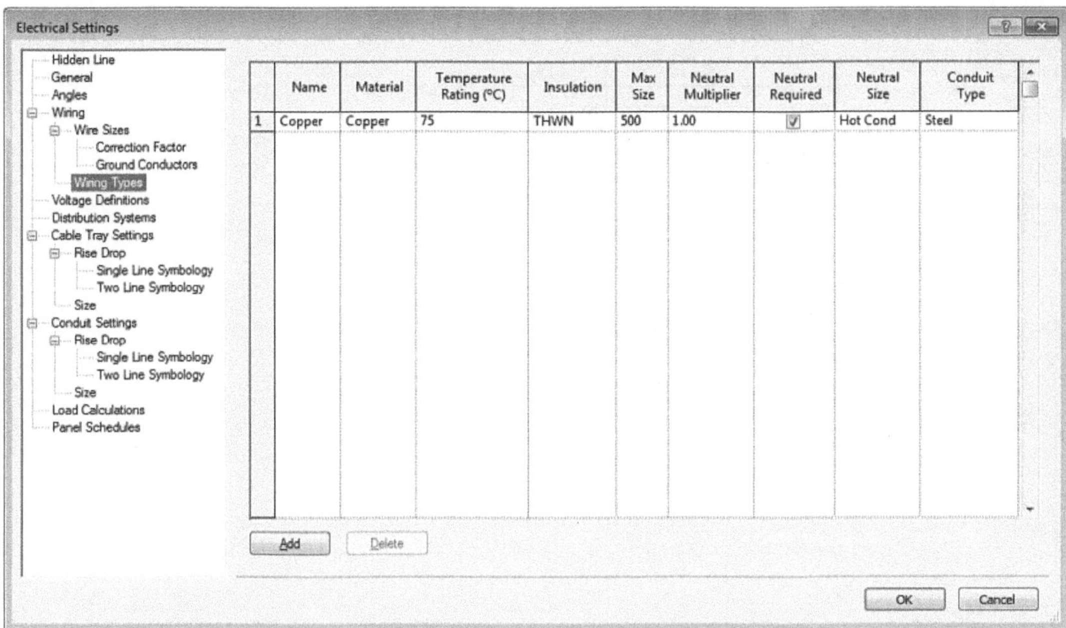

Figure 6-19** The **Electrical Settings** dialog box displaying various options for **Wiring Types

To change the specification of any type, click the column corresponding to the wire type and modify it. For example, click in the cell of the **Temperature Rating** column corresponding to any of the type and select an option from the drop-down list displayed; the temperature rating for the specified wire type will change. Similarly, you can click in the cell of other columns corresponding to the wire type and specify the settings as required. You can add a wire type to the table. To do so, choose the **Add** button displayed at the bottom of the right pane; a row with default values for all columns will be added below the last row in the table. You can change the values in the desired columns for the newly added wire type. You can delete a wire type from the table. To do so, select a row corresponding to the desired wire type and then choose the **Delete** button; the wire type will be deleted from the table.

Now, after setting the wiring specifications, correction factor, ground conductor specifications, and wire types, you can now click on the **Voltage Definition** node in the left pane of the **Electrical Settings** dialog box to set the voltage definition of the electrical system. The various options for setting the voltage definition of an electrical system are discussed next.

Setting the Voltage Definition

The voltage definition in an electrical system refers to the specification that will be laid to define the minimum and maximum values for the voltages used in a project. This definition will allow you to specify different voltage ratings on devices or equipment that are placed in the project. The voltages defined will be used to establish different distribution system definitions. On clicking the **Voltage Definitions** node in the **Electrical Settings** dialog box, various options to define the voltages will be displayed in a table in the right pane, as shown in Figure 6-20. The table displays various voltage definitions with specifications such as **Name**, **Value**, **Minimum**, and **Maximum** arranged in various columns. You can add a voltage definition to the table. To do so, choose the **Add** button; a row will be added in the table.

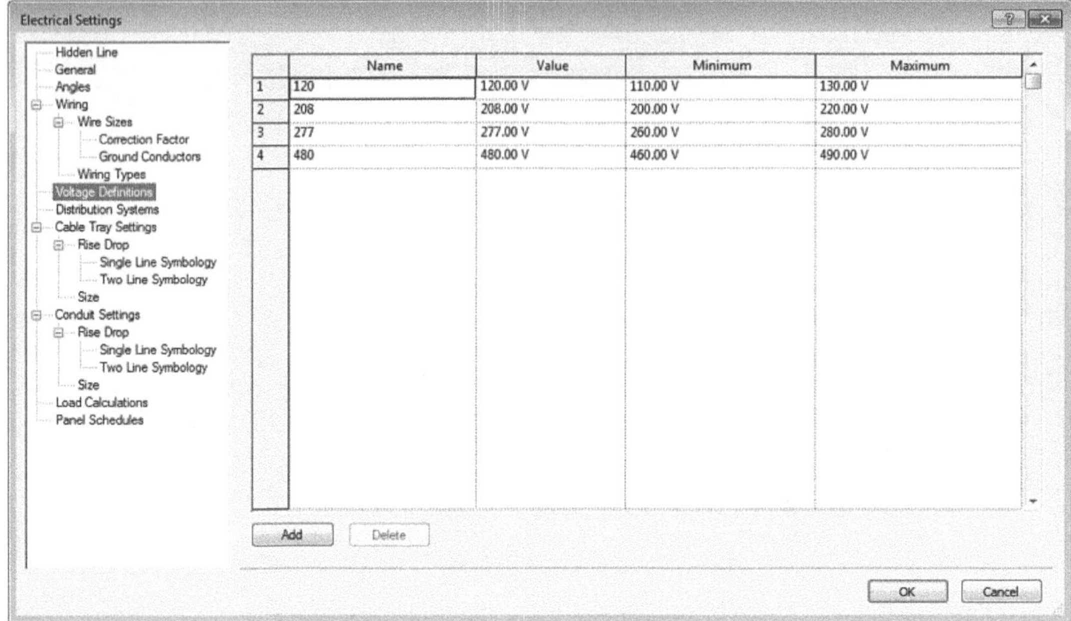

Figure 6-20** The **Electrical Settings** dialog box displaying various options for **Voltage Definitions

You can click in any of the cell of the column in the table and enter the desired value for the specification defining the voltage. For example, you can click in any of the cell in **Maximum** column and enter a value to specify the maximum voltage for a specified voltage definition.

You can delete a voltage definition from the table. To do so, select the row for the desired voltage definition and then choose the **Delete** button; the selected row for the voltage definition will be deleted from the table. Next, after setting the voltage definitions for the electrical system, you can set the specification for the distribution system in the project. The various options that can be used to set the distribution system of the project will be discussed next.

Setting the Distribution System

You can define the distribution systems to be used in your project. To do so, click in the **Distribution Systems** node in the **Electrical Settings** dialog box; the various options to specify the distribution system will be displayed in the right pane of the dialog box in a table. The table displays various specifications for the distribution system such as the Name, Phase, Configuration, Wires, L-L Voltage (Line to Line Voltage), and L-G Voltage (Line to Ground Voltage) in columns. You can click in the cell under any column for the corresponding distribution system and then assign a value to it. For example, you can click in the cell of the **L-L Voltage** column corresponding to a distribution system and select an option from the drop-down list displayed. You can create a new distribution system and add it to the table. To do so, choose the **Add** button in the **Electrical Settings** dialog box; a new row will be added to the table. You can click in the cell of the **Name** column of the newly added row and enter a name for the distribution. Similarly, click on the cells of the other columns of the newly added row and specify the desired parameters for the distribution system you have added. After setting the distribution system, you can specify the settings for cable tray, conduit, load calculations, and panel schedules. Various options to set the load calculations for the electrical system are discussed.

Setting the Load Calculations

You can specify the settings of the load classification and demand factor applied to circuits in the electrical system. To do so, click in the **Load Calculations** node in the left pane of the **Electrical Settings** dialog box; various options for **Load Calculations** will be displayed in the right pane. In the right pane, choose the **Load Classifications** button; the **Load Classifications** dialog box will be displayed, as shown in Figure 6-21.

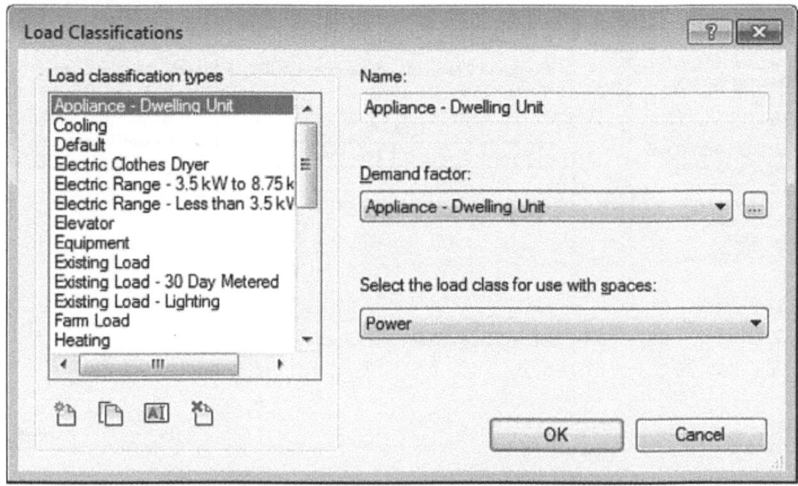

***Figure 6-21** The **Load Classifications** dialog box*

In this dialog box, select a type from the **Load classification types** area; the various specifications related to the selected type will be displayed in the right of the area. For example, if you select the **Power** option in the **Load classification types** area; the specifications for the selected option will be displayed in its right. You can also create new classification types. To do so, select any type from the **Load classification types** area and then choose the **New** button displayed below it; the **Name** dialog box will be displayed. In this dialog box, enter a name in the **Name** edit box and then choose **OK**; the **Name** dialog box will be closed and the new type will be added and displayed in the **Load classification types** area of the **Load Classifications** dialog box. Ensure that the new classification type is selected in the **Load classification types** area, select an option from the **Demand factor** drop-down list to specify the demand factor for the new type of load classification. Alternatively, choose the browse button next to the **Demand factor** drop-down list; the **Demand Factors** dialog box will be displayed, as shown in Figure 6-22.

In this dialog box, select a type from the **Demand factor types** area; the specifications for the selected type will be displayed in the right of the area. You can select an option from the **Calculation method** drop-down list to specify the calculation method for calculating the demand factor for the load in the load classification. On selecting the calculation method from the **Calculation method** drop-down list, the options related to the selected method will be displayed below the drop-down list. After specifying various options in the **Demand Factors** dialog box, choose **OK**; the dialog box will be closed and the **Load Classifications** dialog box will be displayed. In the dialog box, select an option from the **Select the load class for use with spaces** drop-down list to specify the load class for the system that will be used with spaces.

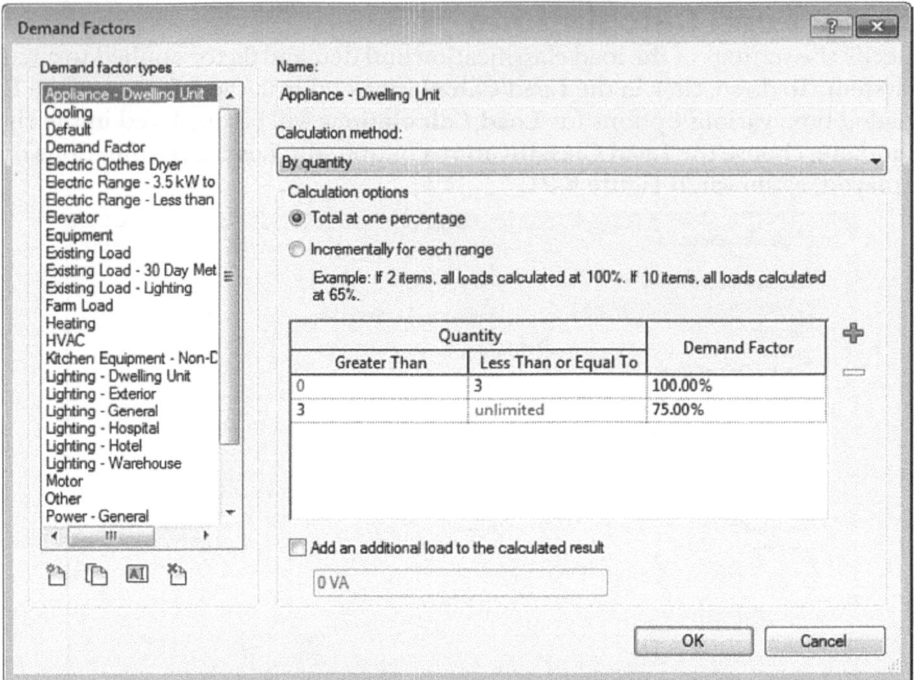

***Figure 6-22** The **Demand Factors** dialog box*

In the **Load Classifications** dialog box, you can also create a new load classification type by using the **New** button. Also, you can delete an existing classification type by choosing the **Delete** button. You can rename an existing load classification type by choosing the **Rename** button.

In the **Electrical Settings** dialog box, you can choose the **Demand Factors** button to display the **Demand Factors** dialog box. The use of various options in the **Demand Factors** dialog box has already been discussed. After specifying various options in this dialog box, choose **OK** to close it.

In the **Electrical Settings** dialog box, select the **Run calculations for loads in space** check box to enable load calculations for loads in spaces. After specifying various options in the **Electrical Settings** dialog box for **Load Calculation**, click on the **Panel Schedules** node to modify the settings for panel schedules in the project. The options to modify the settings for panel schedules are discussed next.

Setting the Panel Schedules

To specify the settings for the panel schedules, click on the **Panel Schedules** node in the left pane of the **Electrical Settings** dialog box; various options to set the panel schedule will be displayed, as shown in Figure 6-23.

In the value field of the **Spare Label** parameter, you can specify the default label text to be applied to the **Load Name** parameter for any spares in the panel schedule. In the value field of the **Include Spares in Panel Totals** parameter, you can select the check box to include spares in the panel totals when you add load values to spares in a panel schedule. Also, in the value field of the **Merge multi-poled circuits into a single cell** parameter, you can select the check box to merge 2 or 3 pole circuits into a single cell in a panel schedule.

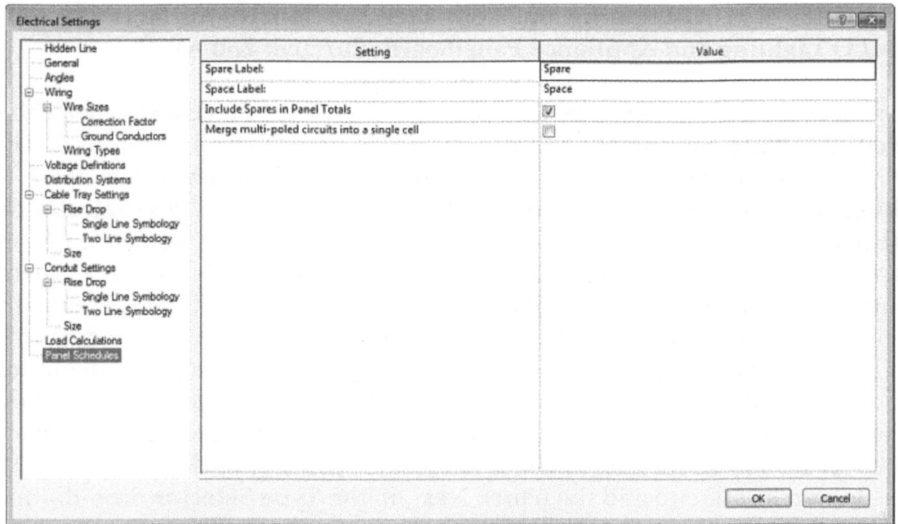

Figure 6-23 *The options for* ***Panel Schedules***

After specifying the various parameters in the **Electrical Settings** dialog box, choose **OK** to apply the settings to the project and close the dialog box.

CREATING POWER DISTRIBUTION SYSTEM

After you place all the electrical components and equipment in a project, the next step will be to create a system to set a path for the flow of electricity through them. The system that you will create between various electrical panels and the transformer will be called as Power Distribution System.

To create a power distribution system, you need to create a distributive relationship between the transformer and the panels. This relationship will enable you to track loads from the branch circuit panels to the main electrical equipment. You will learn the creation of distribution system from the example given next.

In this example, you will create a power distribution system between a transformer and two panels. To do so, you need to first place the transformer and the panels in the project view.

To place the transformer, choose the **Electrical Equipment** tool from the **Electrical** panel of the **System** tab and then in the **Properties** palette, select the **Dry Type Transformer-408 -208Y-NEMA Type 2: 75 KVA** (**M_Dry Type Transformer-408 -208Y-NEMA Type 2: 75 KVA**) option from the **Type Selector** drop-down list. In the **Options Bar**, select the **480/277** option from the **Distribution System** drop-down list. Next, in the palette, select the **120/208 Wye** from the drop-down list displayed corresponding to the **Secondary Distribution** parameter. In the **Properties** palette, click on the value field corresponding to the **Panel Name** parameter and then type **T1**. Now, move the cursor and place it at a location in the floor plan where you want to place the transformer. Now, click to add the transformer. Choose **Modify** from the **Select** panel. After adding the transformer, you will add the panels. For this example you will add the panels of the following types: **208V MCB Lighting and Appliance Panelboard - Surface: 225 A (Breaker)** (for Metric **M_208V MCB Lighting and Appliance Panelboard - Surface: 225 A**

(Breaker)) and **480 V MLO Lighting and Appliance Panelboard -Surface: 250 A** (for Metric **M_480 V MLO Lighting and Appliance Panelboard -Surface: 250 A**).

To add the panels, choose the **Electrical Equipment** tool from the **Electrical** panel of the **Systems** tab; the **Modify | Place Equipment** contextual tab will be displayed. Next, in the **Properties** palette, select the **480 V MLO Lighting and Appliance Panelboard-Surface: 250 A** (**M_480 V MLO Lighting and Appliance Panelboard-Surface: 250 A**) from the **Type Selector** drop-down list. Note that if the type is not available, then you can load the family type from **US Imperial > Electrical > Electric Power > Distribution** folder (**US Metric > Electrical > Electric Power > Distribution**) by using the **Load Family** tool in the **Mode** panel of the contextual tab. After selecting the type in the **Properties** palette, click in the value field corresponding to the **Panel Name** edit box and type **H1**. Click in the value field corresponding to the **Distribution System** parameter and select the **480/277 Wye** option from the drop-down list displayed. Next, choose the **Place on Face** tool from the **Placement** panel in the **Modify|Place Equipment** contextual tab and then place and move the cursor to a location where you desire to place the panel. Click at the desired location to add the panel. Next, in the **Type Selector** drop-down list, select the **208V MCB Lighting and Appliance Panelboard - Surface**: **225 A (Breaker)** (for Metric **M_208V MCB Lighting and Appliance Panelboard - Surface**: **225 A (Breaker)**) type and then in the **Properties** palette, click in the value field corresponding to the **Panel Name** parameter and type **L1**. Click in the value field corresponding to the **Distribution System** parameter and then select the **120/208 Wye** option from the displayed drop-down list. Next, in the floor plan view, move and place the cursor at the desired location and then click to add the panel. Choose **Modify** from the **Select** panel to exit the tool.

Now, select the added panel marked **L1** and then in the **Create Systems** panel, choose **Power**; the **Modify | Electrical Circuits** contextual tab will be displayed. In this tab, choose the **Select Panel** tool from the **System Tools** panel and then in the **Options Bar**, select the **T1** option from the **Panel** drop-down list. On doing so, a dotted rectangular box will be displayed around the selected panel and the transformer.

Next, select the transformer, place the cursor over the cursor symbol to highlight it and then right-click on the connector symbol; a shortcut menu will be displayed. Choose the **Create Power Circuit** option from the shortcut menu and then choose the **Select Panel** tool from the **System Tools** panel in the **Electrical Circuit** contextual tab; a symbol will appear along with the cursor. Now, select the panel **H1** from the drawing view; the selected panel will be added to the distribution system.

PERFORMING LIGHTING ANALYSIS

Lighting analysis is used to help you plan the type of light fixtures that will be added to the project. You can create a schedule of the spaces in the project that will display the light fixtures and the lighting criteria for the project. Further, you can review this schedule while placing light fixtures. This will enable you to analyze the difference between the planned and actual requirement of illumination of the spaces due to the light fixtures. Figure 6-24 shows a simple version of this type of schedule. The last column is a calculated value that shows the difference between the required lighting level and the actual level. A difference greater than 6 footcandles causes the cell to turn brown. Since there are no lights in the model yet, none of the spaces have the required lighting level. Hence every cell in the column appears brown. The objective of a lighting designer will be to achieve a schedule with no brown cells in the final stage. The procedure of performing the lighting analysis has been discussed in the Tutorial 1 of this Chapter.

<Lighting Analysis>								
A	B	C	D	E	F	G	H	I
Required Illuminati	Average Estimated Illumination	Ceiling Reflectanc	Floor Reflectance	Lighting Calculatio	Name	Number	Wall Reflectance	Delta
30 fc	15 fc	0.75	20.00%	2' - 6"	CEO-Office	101	0.50	-15.07 fc
30 fc	0 fc	0.75	20.00%	2' - 6"	V.P. Marketing	102	0.50	-30.00 fc
30 fc	0 fc	0.75	20.00%	2' - 6"	Toilet-1	103	0.50	-30.00 fc
30 fc	0 fc	0.75	20.00%	2' - 6"	Rest Room	104	0.50	-30.00 fc
30 fc	0 fc	0.75	20.00%	2' - 6"	Cafeteria	105	0.50	-30.00 fc
20 fc	0 fc	0.75	20.00%	2' - 6"	Store	106	0.50	-20.00 fc
30 fc	0 fc	0.75	20.00%	2' - 6"	Purchase	107	0.50	-30.00 fc
30 fc	0 fc	0.75	20.00%	2' - 6"	International	108	0.50	-30.00 fc
30 fc	0 fc	0.75	20.00%	2' - 6"	H.R.	109	0.50	-30.00 fc
45 fc	0 fc	0.75	20.00%	2' - 6"	Central Area	110	0.50	-45.00 fc
30 fc	0 fc	0.75	20.00%	2' - 6"	Quality	111	0.50	-30.00 fc
20 fc	0 fc	0.75	20.00%	2' - 6"	Open	112	0.50	-20.00 fc
35 fc	0 fc	0.75	20.00%	2' - 6"	Conference-2	113	0.50	-35.00 fc
35 fc	0 fc	0.75	20.00%	2' - 6"	Conference	114	0.50	-35.00 fc
25 fc	0 fc	0.75	20.00%	2' - 6"	Lounge	115	0.50	-25.00 fc
35 fc	0 fc	0.75	20.00%	2' - 6"	Meeting Room	116	0.50	-35.00 fc
30 fc	0 fc	0.75	20.00%	2' - 6"	Service-1	117	0.50	-30.00 fc
20 fc	0 fc	0.75	20.00%	2' - 6"	Shaft	118	0.50	-20.00 fc
20 fc	0 fc	0.75	20.00%	2' - 6"	Service-2	119	0.50	-20.00 fc
30 fc	0 fc	0.75	20.00%	2' - 6"	Accounts	120	0.50	-30.00 fc

***Figure 6-24** A typical lighting schedule*

CREATING CIRCUITS

In the electrical system for a project, circuits are the sub-systems that Revit will use for electrical design. In a project, the circuit can be created for devices or fixtures without selecting a panel. While working in a project, it is important to demarcate the difference between wires and circuits. Circuits are the actual connection between devices or fixtures whereas the wires are representation of these connections, symbolically.

In a project, when you place devices or fixtures, you can assign them to a system by creating a circuit for them. The type of circuit that will be created for the devices or fixtures is dependent on the connectors in their families. The available circuits are: **Power-Balance**, **Power-Unbalanced**, **Communication**, **Controls**, **Fire Alarm**, **Telephone**, and **Security**. For example, to create a **Power** circuit for a power device, select the power device (receptacle) in the drawing; the **Modify | Electrical Fixtures** tab will be displayed. In this tab, choose the **Power** button from the **Create Systems** tool; the **Modify | Electrical Circuits** contextual tab will be displayed. In the **System Tools** panel of the contextual tab, choose the **Edit Circuit** tool; the **Edit Circuit** contextual tab will be displayed. In the **Edit Circuit** panel of the tab, ensure that the **Add to Circuit** tool is chosen by default. Now, in the drawing area, select the devices that you want to add to the circuit and then choose the **Finish Editing Circuit** button in the **Mode** panel; the circuit will be created between the devices. Next, to view the circuit, select any of the device that you have added to the circuit and then choose the **Electrical Circuits** contextual tab; the circuit between the fixtures will be displayed in a dotted line. In the **Systems Tool** panel of the **Electrical Circuits** contextual tab, the name of the circuit will be displayed as **<unnamed>** in the **System Selector** drop-down list. This is because the panel is not selected for this circuit. To select a panel for the circuit, choose the **Select Panel** tool in the **System Tools** panel; the **Options Bar** will display the **Panel** drop-down list. From the **Panel** drop-down list, select a panel; the circuit will be complete and also notice that the **<unnamed>** option in the **System Selector** drop-down list in the **Electrical Circuits** tab will be replaced by a new option **1**. Choose the **Modify** button in the **Select** panel to exit the tool.

Note that when you select a panel from the **Panel** drop-down list in the **Options Bar**, only those panels will be available for selection whose distribution system matches the connector properties of the device selected in the circuit.

ADDING WIRES TO THE CIRCUIT

In a project, you can draw the wires for the circuit manually. To add the wires in the project, you can choose any of the following tools: Arc Wire, Spline Wire, and Chamfered Wire. You can choose any of these tools from **Systems > Electrical > Wire** drop-down. To draw an arc shaped wire, choose the **Arc Wire** tool; the **Modify | Place Wire** tool will be displayed. In the **Tag** panel of this tab, choose the **Tag on Placement** button to display the tag with the wires. In the **Properties** palette, you can select the type of the wire from the **Type Selector** drop-down list. Next, in the drawing view, click at a desired point to specify the start point of the wire. Now, click at a point to define the second point of the arc. To complete the sketch of the arc wire, click at a desired point in the drawing area to specify the end point of the wire; the wire will be created. You can modify the instance properties of the wire by using the various parameters displayed in the **Properties** palette. After modifying the instance properties of the wire, choose **Modify** from the **Select** panel to exit the tool. Similarly, you can create a spline or chamfered wire by using the **Spline Wire** and **Chamfered Wire** tools from **Systems > Electrical > Wire** drop-down, respectively.

TUTORIALS

General instructions for downloading tutorial files:

1. Download the *c06_rmp_2017_tut.zip* file for this tutorial from *http://www.cadcim.com*. The path of the file is as follows: *Textbooks > Civil/GIS > Revit MEP > Exploring Revit 2017 for MEP*.

2. Now, save and extract the downloaded folder at the following location:
   C:\rmp_2017\c06_rmp_2017_tut

Tutorial 1 — Planning the Electrical Systems

In this tutorial, you will specify the settings for the electrical system and also load the family components required for the project. **(Expected time: 45 min)**

1. File to be used:
   For Imperial: *c06_archi_elec_tut1.rvt*
   For Metric: *M_c06_archi-elec_tut1.rvt*

2. File name to be assigned:
   For Imperial *c06_Office-Space_tut1a.rvt*
   For Metric *M_c06_Office-Space_tut1a.rvt*

The following steps are required to complete this tutorial:

a. Open the *c06_archi_elec_tut1.rvt* (For Metric *M_c06_archi_elec_tut1.rvt*) project file.
b. Specify the electrical settings.
c. Load family components.
d. Save the project.
e. Close the project.

Opening the Project File

1. Choose **Open > Project** from the **Application Menu**; the **Open** dialog box is displayed.

2. In the dialog box, browse to *c:\rmp_2017\c06_rmp_2017_tut* folder and then select the *c06_archi_elec_tut1.rvt* (*M_ c06_archi_elec_tut1.rvt*) file. Next, choose the **Open** button; the project file is opened.

Note

*The architectural model named c04_archi_spaces_rmp_2017.rvt (for Metric M_c04_archi_spaces_rmp_2017.rvt) linked in this tutorial file is located in the c04_rmp_2017_tut folder. It is recommended to maintain the relative path to the architectural model. However, if the link is lost, you need to reload the file using the **Manage Links** dialog box which has already been discussed in the previous chapters.*

Specifying Electrical Settings

1. Choose the **Electrical Settings** button from the **Electrical** panel of the **Systems** tab; the **Electrical Settings** dialog box is displayed.

2. In the left pane of this dialog box, click on **Wiring > Wiring Types** node; a table is displayed.

3. Choose the **Add** button in the dialog box; a new row is displayed in the table.

4. In this row, specify the settings as follows:

   Name: **AL-THHN** Material: **Aluminium** Temperature Rating: **75**
   Insulation: **THHN** Max Size: **500**
   Neutral Required: Select the check box Conduit Type: **Steel**
   Neutral Size: **Hot Conductor Size**

5. Next, in the left pane of the dialog box, select the **Voltage Definitions** node; a table is displayed.

6. In the table, retain the default settings for all the parameters, refer to Figure 6-25.

	Name	Value	Minimum	Maximum
1	120	120.00 V	110.00 V	130.00 V
2	208	208.00 V	200.00 V	220.00 V
3	240	240.00 V	220.00 V	250.00 V
4	277	277.00 V	260.00 V	280.00 V
5	480	480.00 V	460.00 V	490.00 V

***Figure 6-25** The table displaying the specified parameter for the **Voltage Definitions** node*

7. In the left pane of the dialog box, select the **Distribution Systems** node; a table is displayed in the right pane.

8. Retain the default settings in this table, as shown in Figure 6-26.

	Name	Phase	Configuration	Wires	L-L Voltage	L-G Voltage
1	120/208 Wye	Three	Wye	4	208	120
2	120/240 Single	Single	None	3	240	120
3	480/277 Wye	Three	Wye	4	480	277

***Figure 6-26** The table displaying the specified parameter for the **Distribution Systems** node*

9. In the left pane of the dialog box, click on the **Load Calculations** node; various options related to the calculations of the electrical load are displayed in the right pane.

10. In the right pane, choose the **Load Classifications** button; the **Load Classifications** dialog box is displayed, as shown in Figure 6-27.

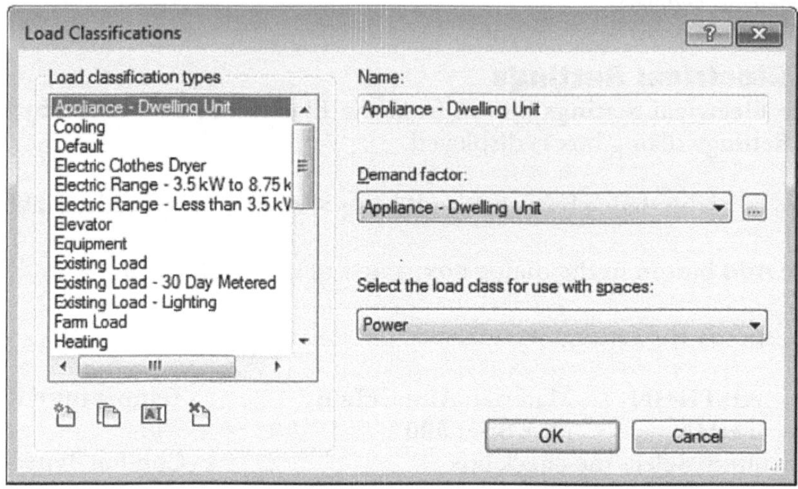

***Figure 6-27** The **Load Classifications** dialog box*

11. In the **Load classification types** area of this dialog box, select the **Other** option and then in the right side of the dialog box, ensure that the **Other** option is selected in the **Demand Factor** drop-down list.

12. Choose the browse button displayed next to the **Demand Factor** drop-down list; the **Demand Factors** dialog box is displayed, as shown in Figure 6-28.

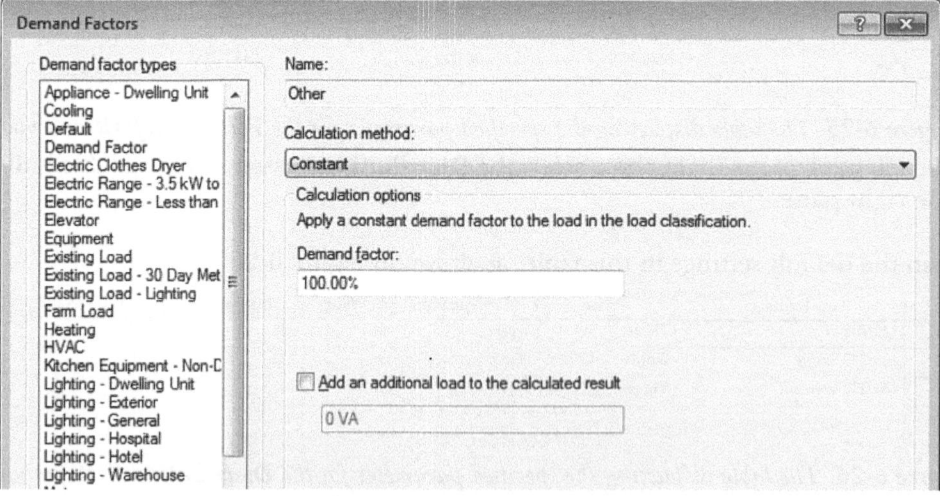

***Figure 6-28** Partial view of the **Demand Factors** dialog box*

13. In this dialog box, ensure that the **Other** option is selected in the **Demand factor types** area and then select the **By load** option from the **Calculation method** drop-down list; a table is displayed below it.

14. In the **Calculation options** area, select the **Incrementally for each range** radio button and then choose the **Split the selected row** button (icon displayed in '+' symbol) twice. On doing so, two rows are added to the table, refer to Figure 6-29.

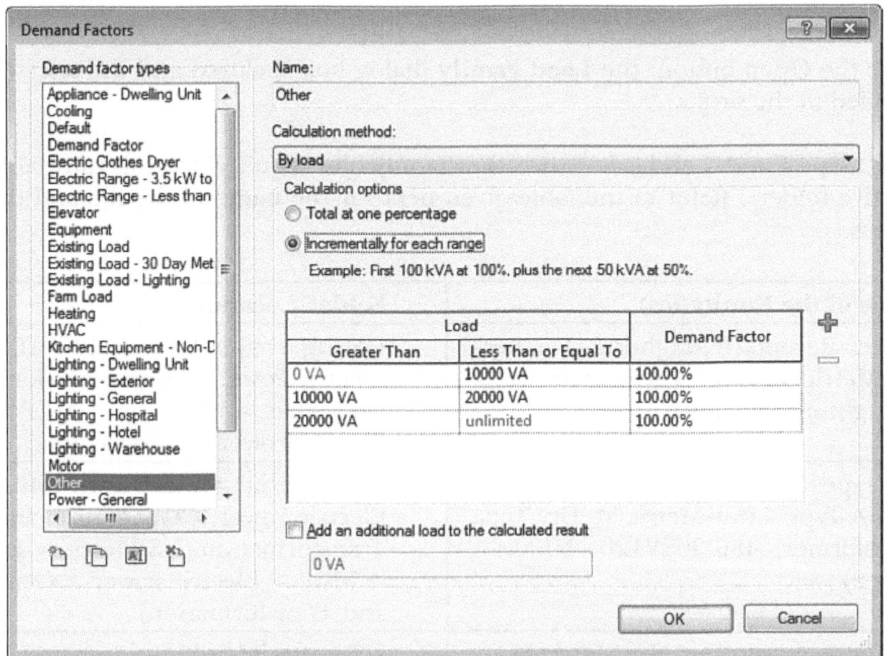

Figure 6-29 The rows added in the table

15. Now, assign the settings in this table, as given in Figure 6-30.

Load		Demand Factor
Greater Than	Less Than or Equal To	
0 VA	2000 VA	100.00%
2000 VA	70000 VA	50.00%
70000 VA	unlimited	30.00%

Figure 6-30 The settings specified in the rows added

16. Choose **OK**; the **Demand Factors** dialog box is closed. Next, choose **OK** twice in the **Load Classifications** and **Electrical Settings** dialog boxes to close them.

Loading the Electrical Components

1. Choose the **Load Family** tool from the **Load from Library** panel of the **Insert** tab; the **Load Family** dialog box is displayed.

2. In the dialog box, browse to **US Imperial > Electrical > MEP > Electric Power > Distribution** folder (for Metric, browse to **US Metric > Electrical > MEP > Electric Power > Distribution)** and then select the *Lighting and Appliance Panelboard - 208V MLO - Surface.rfa* (for Metric, *M_ Lighting and Appliance Panelboard - 208V MLO - Surface.rfa*) file from it.

3. Press and hold the CTRL key, and then select the *Lighting and Appliance Panelboard - 480V MCB - Surface.rfa* (for Metric, *M_Lighting and Appliance Panelboard - 480V MCB - Surface.rfa*) file.

4. Choose the **Open** button; the **Load Family** dialog box is closed and the selected families are loaded in the project.

5. Repeat Steps 1 and 2 and select the other family files required for this tutorial from their respective folders. Refer to the table given next for the name of the file and their folder locations.

Name of the Family(ies)	Folder Location
Duplex Receptacle, Lighting Switches (for Metric M_Duplex Receptacle, M_Lighting Switches)	US Imperial > Electrical > MEP > Electric Power > Terminals (for Metric US Metric > Electrical > MEP > Electric Power > Terminals)
Dry Type Transformer - 480-208Y120 - NEMA Type 2 (for Metric M_Dry Type Transformer - 480-208Y120 - NEMA Type 2)	US Imperial > Electrical > MEP > Electric Power > Generation and Transformation (US Metric > Electrical > MEP > Electric Power > Generation and Transformation)
Troffer Corner Insert (for Metric M_ Troffer Corner Insert)	US Imperial > Lighting > MEP > Internal (US Metric > Lighting > MEP > Internal)

Saving and Closing the Project

In this section, you need to save the project and the settings.

1. Choose **Save As > Project** from **Application Menu**; the **Save As** dialog box is displayed.

2. In this dialog box, browse to the *C:\rmp_2017\c06_rmp_2017_tut* folder and then in the **File name** edit box, enter the text **c06_Office-Space_tut1a** (for Metric, **M_c06_Office-Space_ tut1a**) and then choose the **Save** button to save the current project file with the specified name and to close the **Save As** dialog box.

3. Choose the **Close** option from **Application Menu**; the file is closed.

Tutorial 2 Analyzing the Illumination Requirement

In this tutorial, you will analyze the illumination level required for the different spaces in the office-space building. This analysis will then be used for designing the electrical system for the office-space building. **(Expected time: 1hr 15 min)**

1. File to be used:
   For Imperial: *c06_Office-Space_tut1a.rvt*
   For Metric: *M_06_Office-Space_tut1a .rvt*

2. File name to be assigned:
   For Imperial: *c06_Office-Space_tut2.rvt*
   For Metric: *M_c06_Office-Space_tut2.rvt*

The following steps are required to complete this tutorial:

a. Open the *c06_Office-Space_tut1a .rvt* (*M_c06_Office-Space_tut1a.rvt*) project file.
b. Define the required illumination parameter.
c. Create a key schedule for the required illumination level.
d. Enter the required illumination level.
e. Assign the space keys to the spaces.
f. Assign space color fills.
g. Compare the illumination level.
h. Save and Close the project.

Opening the Project File

1. Choose **Open > Project** from the **Application Menu**; the **Open** dialog box is displayed.

2. In the dialog box, browse to the *c:\rmp_2017\c06_rmp_2017_tut* folder and then select the *c06_Office-Space_tut1a.rvt* (*M_06_Office-Space_tut1a.rvt*) file and then choose the **Open** button; the project file is opened.

Defining the Required Illumination Level Parameter

1. Choose the **Project Parameters** tool from the **Settings** panel of the **Manage** tab; the **Project Parameters** dialog box is displayed.

2. In the **Project Parameters** dialog box, choose the **Add** button; the **Parameter Properties** dialog box is displayed.

3. In the **Parameter Type** area of this dialog box, ensure that the **Project Parameter** radio button is selected.

4. Next, in the **Categories** area click on the **Filter list** drop-down list and select the **Mechanical** check box from the options displayed, if it is not selected by default. Now, select the **Spaces** check box from the list box displayed below the **Filter list** drop-down list.

5. In the **Parameter Data** area of the dialog box, click in the **Name** edit box and enter the text **Required Illumination Level**. Next, select the **Electrical** option from the **Discipline** drop-down list.

6. Now, select the **Illuminance** and **Electrical-Lighting** options from the **Type of Parameter** and **Group parameter under** drop-down lists, respectively.

7. Next, in the **Parameters Properties** dialog box, ensure that the **Instance** and the **Values are aligned per group type** radio buttons are selected.

8. Choose the **OK** button; the **Parameter Properties** dialog box is closed and the **Project Parameters** dialog box is displayed.

9. In the **Parameters available to elements in this project** area of this dialog box, ensure that the **Required Illumination Level** option is selected and then choose the **OK** button; the **Project Parameters** dialog box is closed.

10. The new parameter you created applies to all spaces in the project. To verify this, you can look at the properties of one of the spaces. To do so, select a space in the project view; the new parameter is displayed under the **Electrical-Lighting** head in the **Properties** palette, as shown in Figure 6-31.

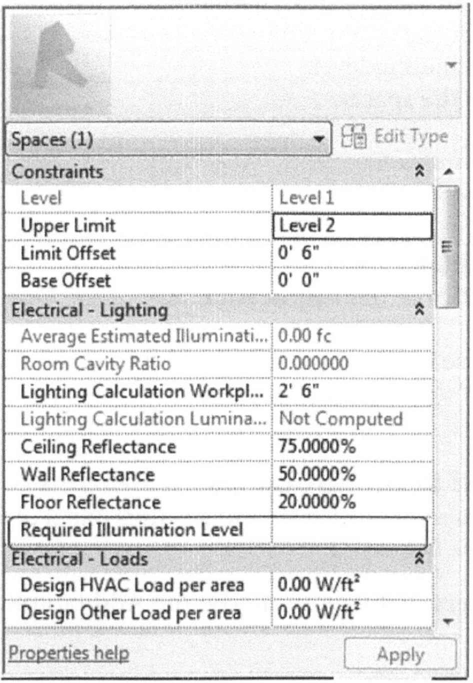

***Figure 6-31** The new parameter added in the **Properties** palette*

Creating a Key Schedule for the Required Illuminance Level

You can use the new parameter to enter a value for the illuminance required for each space. However, there are many spaces in this project that have similar lighting requirements, and it is more efficient to create a key schedule and use it to assign the required illuminance values based on the space type. In this section, you will create a key schedule to define the illumination level of each of the space type in the project.

1. Invoke the **Schedule/Quantities** tool from the **Reports & Schedule** panel of the **Analyze** tab; the **New Schedule** dialog box is displayed.

2. In this dialog box, select the **Spaces** option from the **Category** list box and then click in the **Name** edit box and type **Required Illumination-Spaces.**

3. Select the **Schedule keys** radio button and then in the **Key name** edit box, type **Illumination Levels (fc).**

4. Choose **OK**; the **New Schedule** dialog box is closed and the **Schedule Properties** dialog box is displayed.

5. In the dialog box, ensure that the **Key Name** option is added in the **Scheduled fields (in order)** list box.

Note

*In a BIM project, you can use a schedule either as a design interface (Key schedule) or as a documentation tool (Schedule building components). To create a key schedule, select the **Schedule keys** radio button in the **New Schedule** dialog box. Alternatively, in the **New Schedule** dialog box, select the **Schedule building components** radio button to create the schedule of building components.*

6. In the **Schedule Properties** dialog box, ensure that the **Fields** tab is chosen by default. Now, select the **Required Illumination Level** option from the **Available fields** list box and choose the **Add parameter(s)** button; the **Required Illumination Level** field is added in the **Scheduled fields (in order)** area of the **Schedule Properties** dialog box.

7. Choose **OK**; the dialog box is closed and the **Modify Schedule/Quantities** contextual tab is displayed. Also, the schedule is displayed in the drawing area.

8. Now, drag the borders of the columns in the schedule horizontally to get the desired column width so that the text in the schedules is fully visible.

Note

You can double-click on column dividers to auto-fit column width to its content.

Entering the Required Illumination Level Requirements in the Key Schedule

1. Choose the **Insert Data Row** tool from **Modify Schedule/Quantities > Rows** panel; a row is added in the schedule, as shown in Figure 6-32. Similarly, add seven more rows. Refer to Figure 6-33 for the schedule displaying eight rows.

<Required Illumination-Spaces>	
A	B
Key Name	Required Illumination Leve
1	

__Figure 6-32__ A row added in the schedule

<Required Illumination-Spaces>	
A	B
Key Name	Required Illumination Level
1	
2	
3	
4	
5	
6	
7	
8	

__Figure 6-33__ All rows added in the schedule

2. In the schedule displayed in the drawing area, enter the values under the **Key Name** and the **Required Illumination Level** columns, as per the table given next. Refer to Figure 6-34 for viewing the values entered.

Key Name	**Required Illumination Level** -(fc)
Office-Private	30
Open Office	45
Main Entrance	45
Conference	35
Lounge	25
Restroom	30
Services-Electrical/Mech	20
Circulation	20

<Required Illumination-Spaces>	
A	B
Key Name	Required Illumination Level
Circulation	20 fc
Conference	35 fc
Lounge	25 fc
Main Entrance	45 fc
Office-Private	30 fc
Open Office	45 fc
Restroom	30 fc
Services-Electrical/Mech	20 fc

__Figure 6-34__ The schedule displaying all the values specified under the __Key Name__ Column

Tip

The entries in the key schedules are automatically sorted alphabetically by the __Key Name__. However, you can change the sort keys for the added schedule. To do so, select the __Required Illumination-Spaces__ schedule from the __Project Browser__ and then in the __Properties__ palette, edit the __Sorting/Grouping__ parameter.

Assigning the Space Keys to the Spaces

1. In the **Project Browser**, double-click on the **1-Lighting** node under **Electrical > Lighting > Floor Plans.**

2. Next, choose the **Tag All** tool from the **Tag** panel of the **Annotate** tab; the **Tag All Not Tagged** dialog box is displayed.

3. In this dialog box, ensure that the **All objects in current view** radio button is selected. Next, select the **Space Tags** option displayed in the **Category** column and choose **Apply** and then **OK**; the **Tag All Not Tagged** dialog box is closed and the space tags are displayed in the drawing.

4. In the upper left corner of the floor plan, select the space with the name and number displayed as **CEO-Office** and **101**.

5. On selecting the space, the properties related to it are displayed in the **Properties** palette.

6. In the **Properties** palette, click in Value field corresponding to the **Illumination Levels (fc)** parameter and select the **Office-Private** option from the drop-down list displayed, as shown in Figure 6-35, and choose **Apply**.

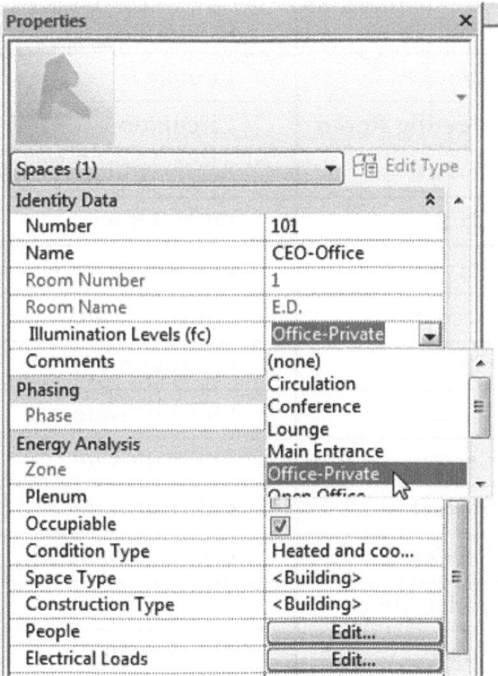

***Figure 6-35** Selecting the **Office-Private** option from the drop-down list*

7. Now, repeat the procedure followed in step 6 to assign the specified key name for the remaining spaces as per the table given next.

Office Number	Name	Illumination Levels (fc)-Key Name
101	CEO-Office	Office-Private
102	V.P. Marketing	Office-Private
103	Toilet-1	Restroom
104	Rest Room	Restroom
105	Cafeteria	Restroom
106	Store	Services-Electrical/Mech
107	Purchase	Office-Private
108	International	Office-Private
109	H.R.	Office-Private
110	Central Area	Open Office
111	Quality	Office-Private
112	Open	Circulation
113	Conference-2	Conference
114	Conference	Conference
115	Lounge	Lounge
116	Meeting Room	Circulation
117	Service	Services-Electrical/Mech
118	Shaft	Open Office
119	Service-2	Services-Electrical/Mech
120	Accounts	Office-Private
121	Chase	Circulation
122	Electrical	Office-Private
123	Server	Office-Private
124	Store-1	Office-Private
125	Services	Office-Private
126	Toilet-Mens	Restroom
127	Space	Circulation
128	Toilet-C	Restroom
129	Toilet-A	Restroom
130	Toilet-B	Restroom
131	Toilet-Ladies	Restroom

8. Choose the **Modify** button from the **Select** panel to exit the selection.

Assigning Space Color Fills

1. In the **Properties** palette, choose the **<none>** option corresponding to the **Color Scheme** parameter; the **Edit Color Scheme** dialog box is displayed.

2. In the **Schemes** area of the displayed dialog box, ensure that the **Spaces** option is selected from the **Category** drop-down list. Next, in the list box displayed in the **Schemes** area, select the **Schema 1** option; various options for editing the schema are displayed in the **Scheme Definition** area.

3. In the **Scheme Definition** area, enter **Lighting Analysis** in the **Title** edit box. In this area, select the **Required Illumination Level** option from the **Color** drop-down list; the **Colors Not Preserved** window is displayed, as shown in Figure 6-36.

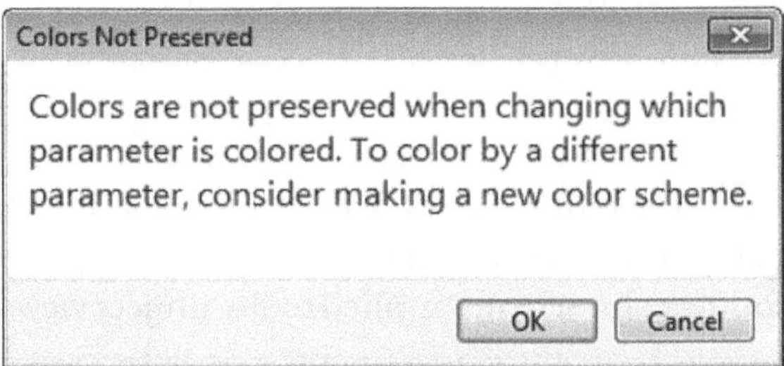

***Figure 6-36** The **Colors Not Preserved** window*

4. In this window, choose **OK**; the window is closed and the default color scheme is displayed in a table in the **Edit Color Scheme** dialog box.

5. In the **Scheme Definition** area, select the **By range** radio button and then select the first cell in the second row; the **Add Value** button (+ icon) is displayed on the left of the table. Choose the **Add Value** button twice; two rows will be added below the selected cell, as shown in Figure 6-37.

6. Choose **Apply** and then **OK**; the **Edit Color Scheme** dialog box is closed and the color scheme is applied in the drawing.

7. Next, choose the **Color Fill Legend** tool from the **Color Fill** panel in the **Annotate** tab; the legend is displayed along with the cursor.

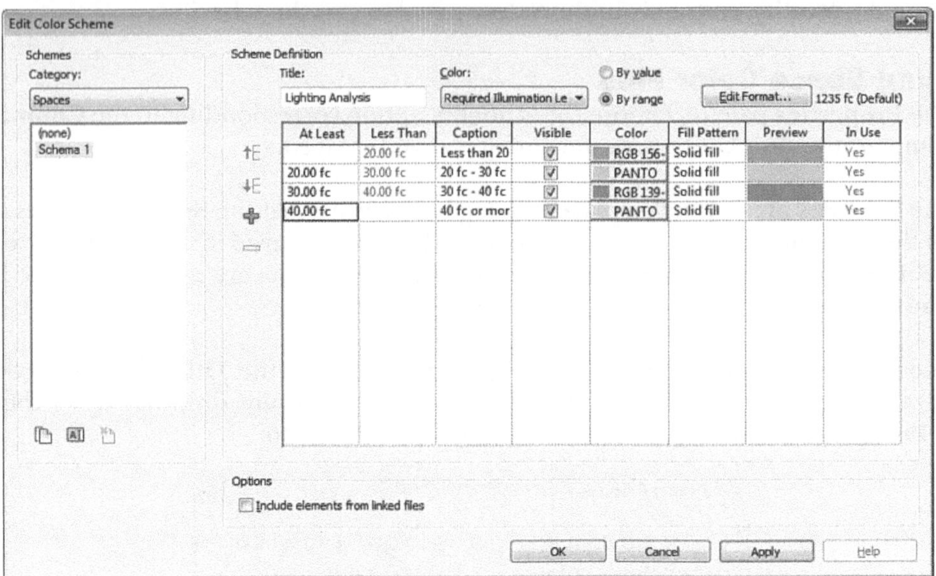

Figure 6-37 *The* ***Edit Color Scheme*** *dialog box with added rows*

8. In the drawing area, click at a suitable point near the floor plan; the legend is displayed. Refer to Figure 6-38 for the color scheme applied to the project view and the inserted legend.

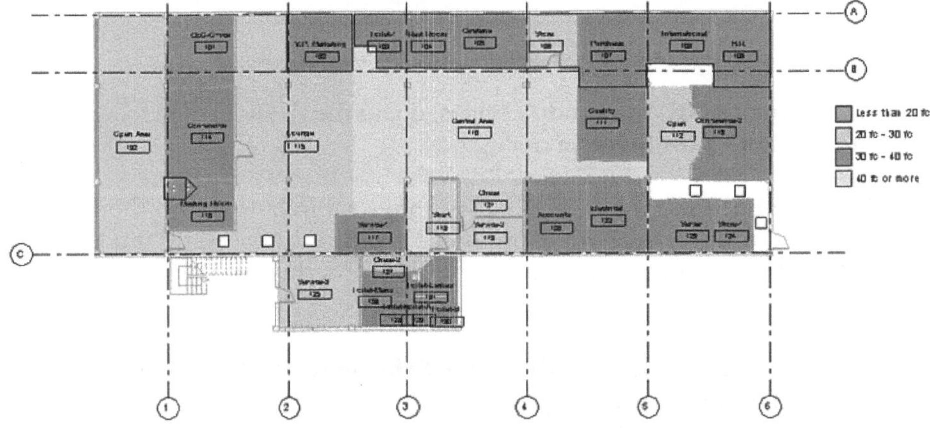

Figure 6-38 *The applied color scheme with the legend*

Comparing the Illumination Level

1. Choose the **Schedule/Quantities** tool from the **Reports & Schedules** panel of the **Analyze** tab; the **New Schedule** dialog box is displayed.

2. In this dialog box, select the **Spaces** option from the **Category** list box and then in the **Name** edit box, enter **Lighting Analysis**.

3. Ensure that the **Schedule building components** radio button is selected and then choose **OK**; the **Schedule Properties** dialog box is displayed.

4. In this dialog box, ensure that the **Fields** tab is chosen by default and then in the **Available fields** area, click on the **Name** option. Now, press and hold the CTRL key and select the following fields: **Number, Required Illumination Level, Average Estimated Illumination, Ceiling Reflectance, Wall Reflectance, Floor Reflectance**, and **Lighting Calculation Workplane.**

5. Choose the **Add parameter(s)** button; the selected fields are added in the **Schedule fields (in order)** area, as shown in Figure 6-39.

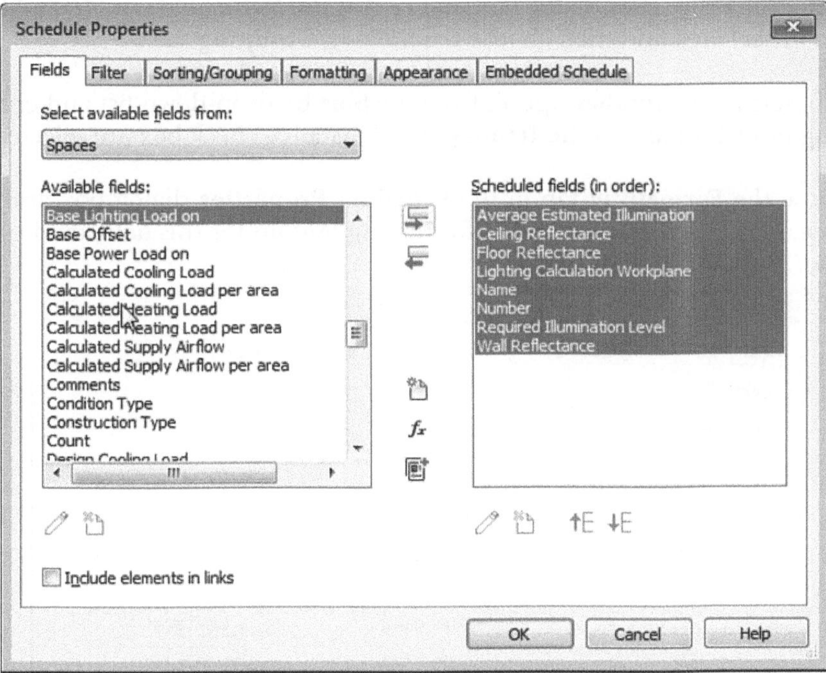

*Figure 6-39 The added fields in the **Fields** tab*

6. Next, choose the **Add calculated parameter** button; the **Calculated Value** dialog box isdisplayed. In this dialog box, enter **Delta** in the **Name** edit box and then select the **Formula** radio button if it is not selected by default.

7. In the **Calculated Value** dialog box, select the **Electrical** and the **Illuminance** options from the **Discipline** and **Type** drop-down lists, respectively.

8. Now, choose the browse button next to the **Formula** edit box; the **Fields** dialog box is displayed. In the displayed dialog box, select the **Average Estimated Illumination** option from the **Select the field to be added to the formula** list box and then choose **OK**; the **Fields** dialog box is closed and the selected field is displayed in the **Formula** edit box.

9. Now, in the **Formula** edit box, add the "-" symbol after the text **Average Estimated Illumination** and then again choose the browse button next to the edit box; the **Fields** dialog box is displayed.

10. In the **Select the field to be added to the formula** list box of the dialog box, select the **Required Illumination Level** option and choose **OK**; the **Fields** dialog box is closed and the formula **Average Estimated Illumination-Required Illumination Level** is displayed in the **Formula** edit box.

11. Choose **OK**; the **Calculated Value** dialog box is closed and the **Schedule Properties** dialog box is displayed.

12. In the **Schedule Properties** dialog box, notice that the **Delta** field is added in the **Schedule Fields (in order)** area and then choose the **Sorting/Grouping** tab.

13. In this tab, select the **Number** option from the **Sort by** drop-down list and ensure that the **Ascending** radio button and the **Itemize every instance** check box are selected by default.

14. Now, choose the **Formatting** tab in the **Schedule Properties** dialog box and then in the **Fields** area, select the **Delta** value; the formatting options for this field are displayed in the right pane; as shown in Figure 6-40.

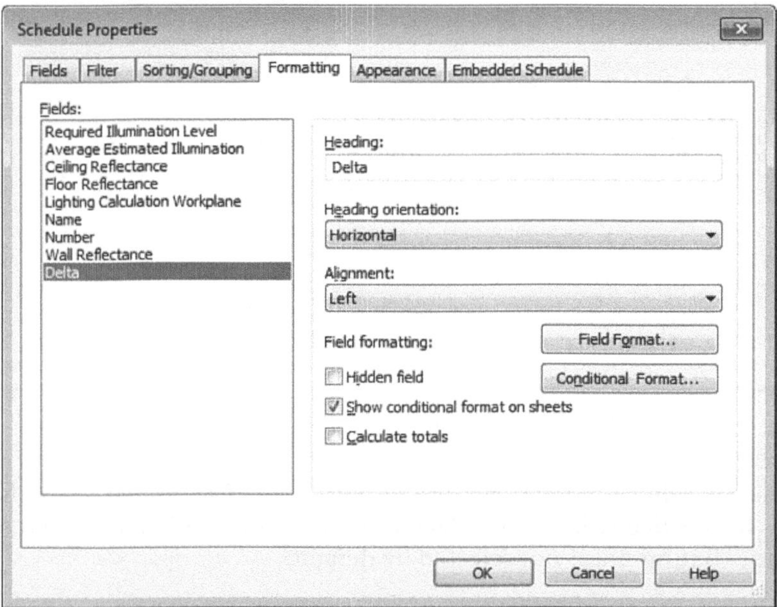

***Figure 6-40** The formatting options for the **Delta** field*

15 Next, choose the **Conditional Format** button; the **Conditional Formatting** dialog box for the selected field is displayed.

16. In this dialog box, select the **Not Between** option from the **Test** drop-down list and then in the **Value** area, enter **-10 fc** and **10 fc** in the left and right edit boxes displayed. On entering the values, the text -**10.00 fc > Delta or Delta > 10.00 fc** is displayed in the **Conditions to Use** text box, refer to Figure 6-41.

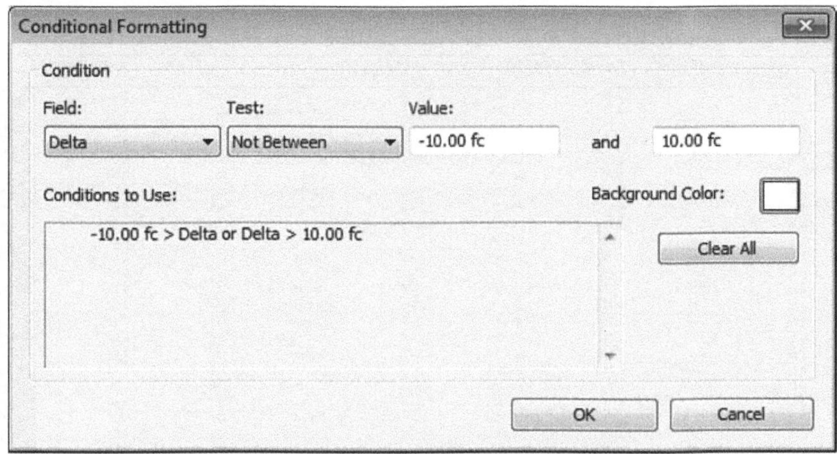

***Figure 6-41** The **Conditional Formatting** dialog box*

17. In the **Conditional Formatting** dialog box, choose the **Background Color** swatch; the **Color** dialog box is displayed.

18. In the **Color** dialog box, enter the values in the specified edit boxes as given next.

    Red: **128** Green: **64** Blue: **64**

19. Next, choose **OK** twice; the **Color** and the **Conditional Formatting** dialog boxes are closed. And, the **Schedule Properties** dialog box with the **Formatting** tab chosen is displayed.

20. Next, in the **Schedule Properties** dialog box, select the **Ceiling Reflectance** option from the **Fields** list box and then choose the **Field Format** button; the **Format** dialog box is displayed.

21. In this dialog box, clear the **Use project settings** check box and then select the **Fixed** option from the **Units** drop-down list.

22. Next, ensure that the **2 decimals places** option is selected in the **Rounding** drop-down list and then choose **OK**; the **Format** dialog box is closed.

23. Next, repeat the procedure as explained in steps 21 and 22 for the **Wall Reflectance** and **Floor Reflectance** options.

24. After assigning the field formatting values for the specified fields, choose **OK**; the **Schedule Properties** dialog box is closed and the **<Lighting Analysis>** schedule is displayed in the drawing window, as shown in Figure 6-42.

<Lighting Analysis>

A	B	C	D	E	F	G	H	I
Required Illuminati	Average Estimated Illumination	Ceiling Reflectanc	Floor Reflectance	Lighting Calculatio	Name	Number	Wall Reflectance	Delta
30 fc	15 fc	0.75	20.00%	2' - 6"	CEO-Office	101	0.50	-15.07 fc
30 fc	0 fc	0.75	20.00%	2' - 6"	V.P. Marketing	102	0.50	-30.00 fc
30 fc	0 fc	0.75	20.00%	2' - 6"	Toilet-1	103	0.50	-30.00 fc
30 fc	0 fc	0.75	20.00%	2' - 6"	Rest Room	104	0.50	-30.00 fc
30 fc	0 fc	0.75	20.00%	2' - 6"	Cafeteria	105	0.50	-30.00 fc
20 fc	0 fc	0.75	20.00%	2' - 6"	Store	106	0.50	-20.00 fc
30 fc	0 fc	0.75	20.00%	2' - 6"	Purchase	107	0.50	-30.00 fc
30 fc	0 fc	0.75	20.00%	2' - 6"	International	108	0.50	-30.00 fc
30 fc	0 fc	0.75	20.00%	2' - 6"	H.R.	109	0.50	-30.00 fc
45 fc	0 fc	0.75	20.00%	2' - 6"	Central Area	110	0.50	-45.00 fc
30 fc	0 fc	0.75	20.00%	2' - 6"	Quality	111	0.50	-30.00 fc
20 fc	0 fc	0.75	20.00%	2' - 6"	Open	112	0.50	-20.00 fc
35 fc	0 fc	0.75	20.00%	2' - 6"	Conference-2	113	0.50	-35.00 fc
35 fc	0 fc	0.75	20.00%	2' - 6"	Conference	114	0.50	-35.00 fc
25 fc	0 fc	0.75	20.00%	2' - 6"	Lounge	115	0.50	-25.00 fc
35 fc	0 fc	0.75	20.00%	2' - 6"	Meeting Room	116	0.50	-35.00 fc
30 fc	0 fc	0.75	20.00%	2' - 6"	Service-1	117	0.50	-30.00 fc
20 fc	0 fc	0.75	20.00%	2' - 6"	Shaft	118	0.50	-20.00 fc
20 fc	0 fc	0.75	20.00%	2' - 6"	Service-2	119	0.50	-20.00 fc
30 fc	0 fc	0.75	20.00%	2' - 6"	Accounts	120	0.50	-30.00 fc
20 fc	0 fc	0.75	20.00%	2' - 6"	Chase	121	0.50	-20.00 fc
30 fc	0 fc	0.75	20.00%	2' - 6"	Electrical	122	0.50	-30.00 fc
30 fc	0 fc	0.75	20.00%	2' - 6"	Server	123	0.50	-30.00 fc
30 fc	0 fc	0.75	20.00%	2' - 6"	Store-1	124	0.50	-30.00 fc

***Figure 6-42** The **Lighting Analysis** schedule displaying different illumination levels*

Note

*The created schedule displays the value of **Average Estimated Illumination Level** for all the spaces as **0**. This is because you have not yet added lighting fixtures to any of the spaces. Also, notice that the **Delta** has been calculated for each of the occupied spaces, and in every case, the value in the **Delta** column is highlighted. This is because the value is not within the +/-10 fc range that you specified in the **Conditional Formatting** dialog box.*

Saving and Closing the Project

In this section, you need to save the project and the settings using the **Save As** tool.

1. Choose **Save As > Project** from **Application Menu**. As you are saving the project for the first time, the **Save As** dialog box is displayed.

2. In this dialog box, browse to the *C:\rmp_2017\c06_rmp_2017_tut* folder and then in the **File name** edit box, enter the text **c06_Office-Space_tut2** (for Metric **M_c06_Office-Space_tut2**) and then choose the **Save** button to save the current project file with the specified name and to close the **Save As** dialog box.

3. To close the project, choose the **Close** option from **Application Menu**. This completes Tutorial 2 of Chapter 6.

Tutorial 3 Adding the Lighting Fixtures and Switches

In this tutorial, you will use the views and schedules that you created in Tutorial 2 to place electrical devices and lighting fixtures in the North zone of the office-space project. Once the fixtures and devices are added, you will create the power and lighting consumption schedule.

(Expected time: 45 min)

1. File to be used:
   For Imperial: *c06_Office-Space_tut2.rvt*
   For Metric: *M_c06_Office-Space_tut2.rvt*

2. File name to be assigned:
   For Imperial: *c06_Office-Space_tut3.rvt*
   For Metric: *M_c06_Office-Space_tut3.rvt*

The following steps are required to complete this tutorial:

a. Open the *c06_Office-Space_tut2.rvt (M_c06_Office-Space_tut2.rvt)* project file.
b. Modify the display of the Lighting Analysis Schedule.
c. Create a key schedule for the required illumination level.
d. Add switches in the spaces.
e. Add power receptacles in the spaces.
f. Create power and lighting consumption schedule.
g. Save and close the project.

Opening the Project File

1. Choose **Open > Project** from the **Application Menu**; the **Open** dialog box is displayed.

2. In the dialog box, browse to *c:\rmp_2017\c06_rmp_2017_tut* folder and then select the *c06_Office-Space_tut2.rvt* file (*M_c06_Office-Space_tut2.rvt*). Then, choose the **Open** button; the project file is opened with the Lighting Analysis Schedule displayed.

Modifying the Display of the Lighting Analysis Schedule

1. In the displayed schedule, click on the header text of the **Required Illumination** column and then right-click when the entire column is highlighted; a shortcut menu is displayed. Select the **Hide Columns** option from the shortcut menu; the **Required Illumination** column is hidden.

2. Repeat the procedure explained in step 1 to hide the following columns: **Ceiling Reflectance, Floor Reflectance**, **Lighting Calculation Workplane**, and **Wall Reflectance**. On specifying the settings, the schedule is displayed, as shown in Figure 6-43.

<Lighting Analysis>			
A	B	C	D
Average Estimated Illumin	Name	Number	Delta
0 fc	CEO-Office	101	-30.00 fc
0 fc	V.P. Marketing	102	-30.00 fc
0 fc	Toilet-1	103	-30.00 fc
0 fc	Rest Room	104	-30.00 fc
0 fc	Cafeteria	105	-30.00 fc
0 fc	Store	106	-20.00 fc
0 fc	Purchase	107	-30.00 fc
0 fc	International	108	-30.00 fc
0 fc	H.R.	109	-30.00 fc
0 fc	Central Area	110	-45.00 fc
0 fc	Quality	111	-30.00 fc
0 fc	Open	112	-20.00 fc
0 fc	Conference-2	113	-35.00 fc
0 fc	Conference	114	-35.00 fc
0 fc	Lounge	115	-25.00 fc
0 fc	Meeting Room	116	-35.00 fc
0 fc	Service-1	117	-30.00 fc

***Figure 6-43** The **Lighting Analysis** schedule displaying the modified schedule*

3. Next, in the **Project Browser**, double click on the **1-Ceiling Elec** sub-node under **Electrical > Lighting > Ceiling Plans** node.

4. Type **WT**; the ceiling plan and the schedule are displayed side by side in the interface. Next, resize the view containing the schedule to show all the columns, refer to Figure 6-44.

5. Next, zoom in to the upper left corner of the plan and then choose the **Lighting Fixture** tool from the **Electrical** panel of the **Systems** tab; the **Modify | Place Fixture** contextual tab is displayed and a symbol of fixture appears with the cursor.

6. In the **Properties** palette, select the **Troffer Corner Insert: 2x4 3Lamp** (for Metric, **M_Troffer Corner Insert: 600x1200 3 Lamp**) option from the **Type Selector** drop-down list.

7. Now, move the cursor into the **CEO-Office** area (**101**) space, and click at the location, as shown in Figure 6-45.

8. Next, zoom out and move the cursor into the **V.P. Marketing** (**102**) space and click at the location, as shown in Figure 6-46.

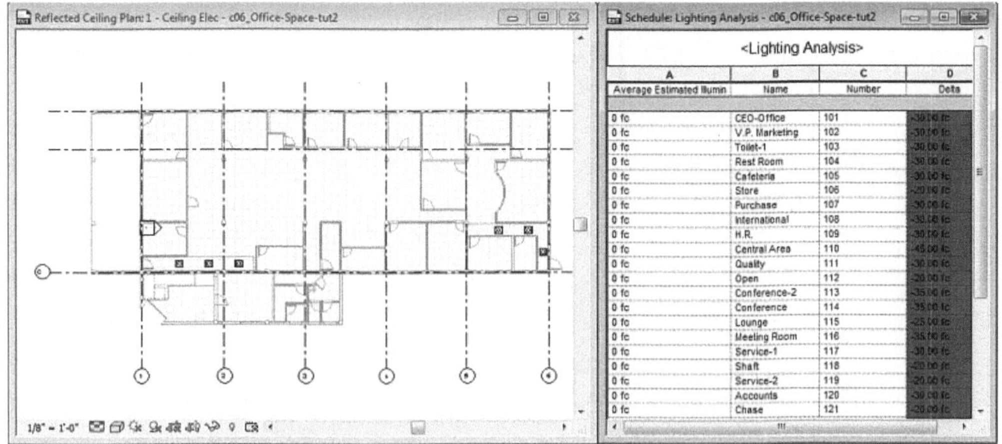

***Figure 6-44** The **Lighting Analysis** schedule and ceiling plan views displayed side by side*

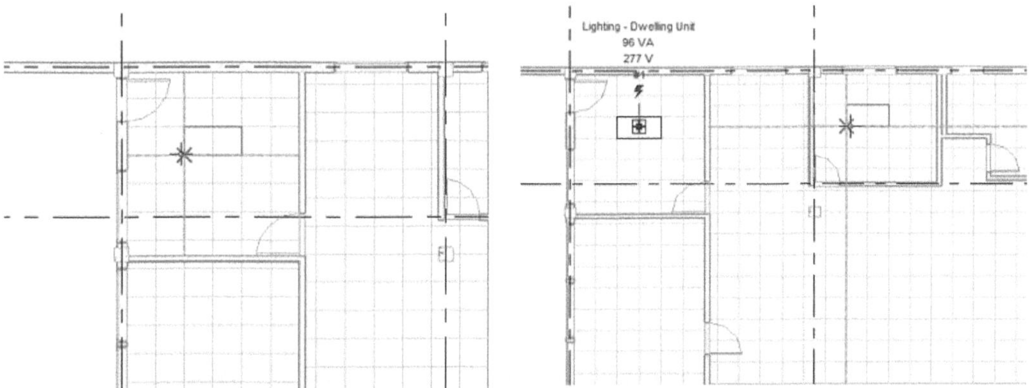

***Figure 6-45** Placing the light fixture in the **CEO-Office** area*

***Figure 6-46** Placing the light fixture in the **V.P. Marketing** area*

Notice that in the **Lighting Analysis** schedule view, the **Delta** value for both the spaces is not highlighted as the lighting requirement of these spaces has been fulfilled.

9. Now, repeat the procedure given in step 8 and place the lighting fixtures in all the areas of the North Zone of the office, as shown in Figure 6-47. After adding all the fixtures, choose **Modify** from the **Select** panel of the **Modify | Place Fixture** contextual tab.

   After adding the light fixtures in all the specified areas, you will notice that in the schedule view, the **Delta** values for **Toilet 1** and **Store** areas are still highlighted. This is because the illumination in these spaces does not fulfill the design requirement. As such, you will change the type of lighting fixtures in these areas.

10. Zoom into the **Toilet 1** space and select the added lighting fixture, refer to Figure 6-48. Now, in the **Properties** palette, select the **Troffer Corner Insert: 2x4 2 Lamp** (for Metric, **M_Troffer Corner Insert: 600x1200 2 Lamp**) from the **Type Selector** drop-down list.

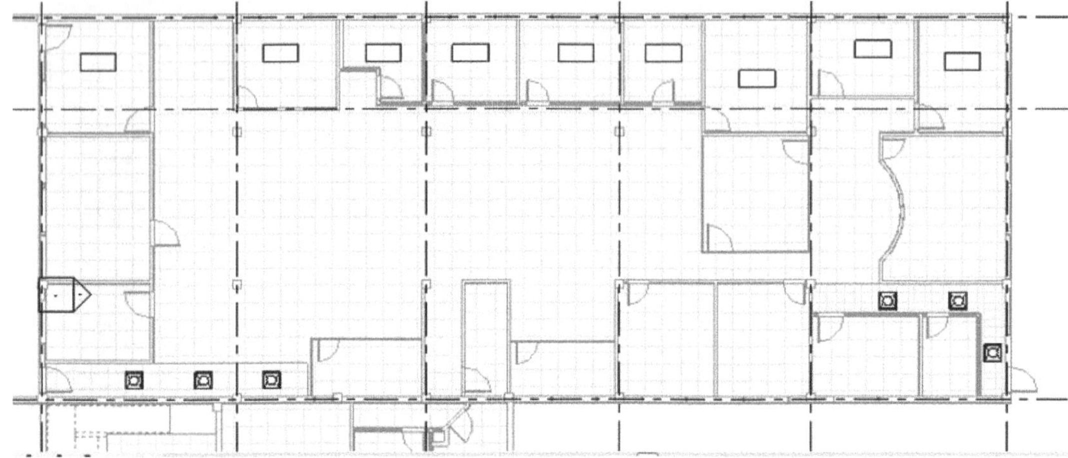

Figure 6-47 *The lighting fixtures placed in all the areas of North zone*

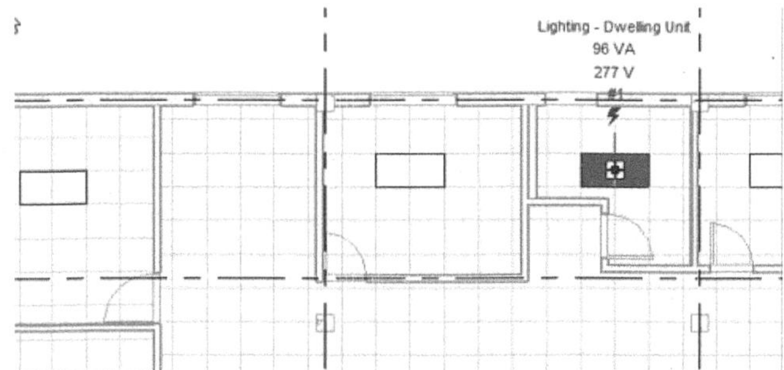

Figure 6-48 *Selecting the lighting fixture in the* ***Toilet 1*** *space*

11. Repeat the procedure in step 10 and change the type of lighting fixture in the **Store 1** area to **Troffer Corner Insert: 2x4 2Lamp** (for Metric, **M_Troffer Corner Insert: 600x1200 2 Lamp**) type. Now, choose **Modify** from the **Select** panel of the **Modify | Place Fixture** contextual tab.

    Notice that the **Toilet 1** and the **Store** areas are not highlighted. This is because the design requirement for both the areas has been fulfilled.

Tip

You can add more lighting fixtures to complete the lighting requirement of the Office-Space area.

Adding Switches in the Spaces

1. Choose the **Lighting** tool from the **Systems > Electrical > Device** drop-down; the **Modify | Place Lighting Device** contextual tab is displayed.

2. In the tab, ensure that the **Place on Vertical Face** button is chosen by default and then in the **Properties** palette, select the **Lighting Switches: Single Pole** (for Metric, **M_Lighting Switches: Single Pole**) option from the **Type Selector** drop-down list.

3. Zoom into the **CEO-Office** space area in the upper left corner of the plan and move the cursor into it. Place the cursor on the inner face of the right wall; a **$** symbol appears with the cursor on the face of the wall. Position the cursor at the desired location, as shown in Figure 6-49 and click; the switch is placed.

Figure 6-49 *Switch added at the inner face of the right wall*

4. Next, continue adding switches to all the areas of the office in which the lighting fixtures are placed. For location of the switches, refer to Figure 6-50.

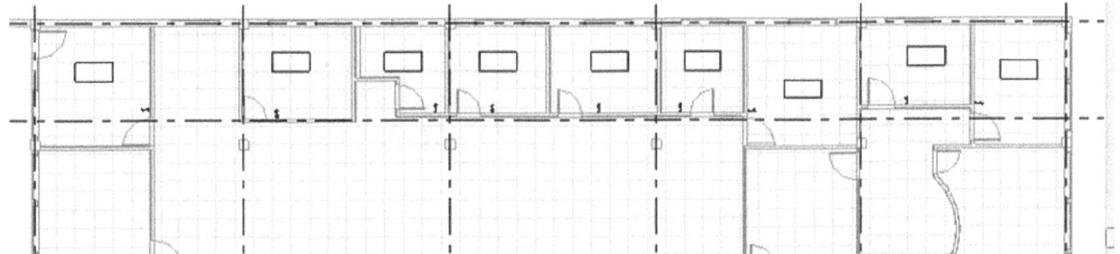

Figure 6-50 *The switch added in all the spaces of North zone*

After adding the switches, choose **Modify** from the **Select** panel of the **Modify | Place Lighting Device** tab.

Note

You can add more switches to complete the requirement of switches in the Office-Space project.

Adding Power Receptacles in the Spaces

1. In the **Project Browser**, double-click on the **1-Power** sub-node under **Electrical > Power > Floor Plans** node; the project view is changed to the power plan of level 1. Maximize the window of the project view, if needed.

2. Now, choose the **Electrical Fixture** tool from **Systems > Electrical > Device** drop-down; the **Modify | Place Devices** contextual tab is displayed.

3. In the tab, ensure that the **Place on Vertical Face** button is chosen by default and then select **Duplex Receptacle: Standard** (for Metric, **M_Duplex Receptacle: Standard**) from the **Type Selector** drop-down list.

4. Now, zoom into the **CEO-Office** space area and then move the cursor and place it on the inner face of the left wall; a symbol appears. Position the cursor on the inner face of the left wall, as shown in Figure 6-51, and click; the receptacle is added. Similarly, add three more receptacles at the inner face of the wall of the **CEO-Office** space area, as shown in Figure 6-52.

5. Repeat the procedure in step 4 and add more power receptacles on the areas having the lighting fixtures. For the placement of the power receptacles, refer to Figure 6-53.

   You can add more switches to complete the requirement of switches in the Office-Space area.

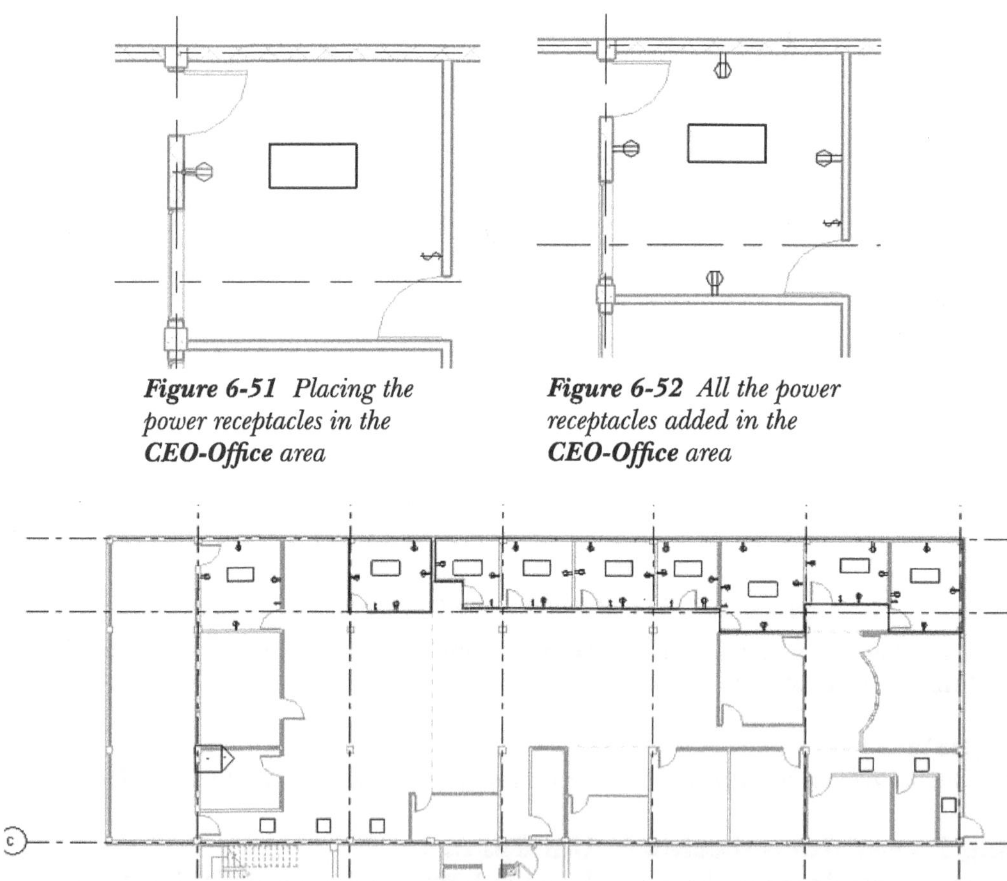

__Figure 6-51__ Placing the power receptacles in the __CEO-Office__ area

__Figure 6-52__ All the power receptacles added in the __CEO-Office__ area

__Figure 6-53__ The power receptacles added in all the spaces of North zone

Creating Power and Lighting Consumption Reports

In this section, you will create a consumption usage report for power and lighting in this project. With the introduction of local energy codes, the amount of electricity consumed by different systems within the building is becoming increasingly important to the design. You can refer to this report at the time of HVAC designing to determine spaces and count fixtures.

1. Choose the **Electrical Settings** button from the **Electrical** panel of the **Systems** tab; the **Electrical Settings** dialog box is displayed.

2. In the displayed dialog box, select the **Load Calculations** option from the list box in the left pane and then in the right pane, select the **Run calculations for loads in spaces** check box.

3. Choose **OK**; the **Electrical Settings** dialog box is closed.

4. Choose the **Schedule/Quantities** tool from the **Report & Schedules** panel of the **Analyze** tab; the **New Schedule** dialog box is displayed.

5. In the dialog box, select the **Spaces** option from the **Category** list box and then in the **Name** edit box, enter **Power and Lighting Consumption**. Ensure that the **Schedule building components** radio button is selected by default and then choose **OK**; the **Schedule Properties** dialog box is displayed.

6. In the **Available fields** list box, select the **Number** option and then press and hold the CTRL key and select the following options: **Name, Area, Actual Lighting Load, Actual Power Load, Actual Lighting Load per area**, and **Actual Power Load per area**.

7. After selecting the specified options, choose **Add parameter(s)**; the selected fields are displayed in the **Schedule fields (in order)** list box.

8. Next, choose the **Sorting/Grouping** tab in the **Schedule Properties** dialog box and then select the **Number** option from the **Sort by** drop-down list and then ensure that the **Ascending** radio button is selected. Also, ensure that the **Itemize every instance** check box is selected by default.

9. Choose **OK**; the **Schedule Properties** dialog box is closed and the **Power and Lighting Consumption** schedule is displayed in the drawing area, as shown in Figure 6-54.

<Power and Lighting Consumption>

A	B	C	D	E	F
Name	Number	Actual Lighting Lo	Actual Lighting Load per area	Actual Power Lo	Actual Power Loa
CEO-Office	101	96 W	0.62 W/ft²	720 W	4.63 W/ft²
V.P. Marketing	102	96 W	0.82 W/ft²	720 W	6.17 W/ft²
Toilet-1	103	80 W	1.15 W/ft²	360 W	5.16 W/ft²
Rest Room	104	96 W	0.99 W/ft²	540 W	5.55 W/ft²
Cafeteria	105	96 W	0.88 W/ft²	720 W	6.59 W/ft²
Store	106	80 W	0.95 W/ft²	720 W	8.59 W/ft²
Purchase	107	96 W	0.63 W/ft²	720 W	4.71 W/ft²
International	108	96 W	0.92 W/ft²	720 W	6.93 W/ft²
H.R.	109	96 W	0.74 W/ft²	720 W	5.54 W/ft²
Central Area	110	0 W	0.00 W/ft²	0 W	0.00 W/ft²
Quality	111	0 W	0.00 W/ft²	0 W	0.00 W/ft²
Open	112	0 W	0.00 W/ft²	0 W	0.00 W/ft²

Figure 6-54 *The light and power consumption schedule*

Note

The schedule that you have created displays the values of ***Actual Lighting Load, Actual Lighting Load per area, Actual Power Load,*** *and* ***Actual Power Load per area*** *for some spaces as* ***0.*** *This is because you have not yet added lighting fixtures and power receptacles to any of these spaces.*

Saving and Closing the Project

In this section, you need to save the project and the settings using the **Save As** tool.

1. Choose **Save As > Project** from **Application Menu**. As you are saving the project for the first time, the **Save As** dialog box is displayed.

2. In this dialog box, browse to the *C:|rmp_2017|c06_rmp_2017_tut* folder and then in the **File name** edit box, enter **c06_Office-Space_tut3**. Choose the **Save** button to save the current project file with the specified name and to close the **Save As** dialog box.

3. To close the project, choose the **Close** option from **Application Menu**. This completes Tutorial 3 of Chapter 6.

Self-Evaluation Test

Answer the following questions and then compare them to those given at the end of this chapter:

1. The electrical equipment used to transform power from one circuit to another is called __________.

2. The __________ tool is used to place the electrical equipment.

3. You can choose the **Electrical Equipment** tool from the __________ panel of the **Systems** tab.

4. The __________ tool is used to place a tag for the element that you place.

5. You can place the element on a selected workplane by choosing the __________ button.

6. The **Place on Vertical Face** button is used to place the element on the selected face of the host element. (T/F)

7. You can add lighting fixtures either in the floor plan view or in the ceiling plan. (T/F)

Review Questions

Answer the following questions:

1. Which of the following is an electrical fixture device?

   a) Pipe b) Receptacles
   c) Ducts d) None of these

2. Which of the following options is used to invoke the **Electrical Settings** dialog box?

   a) **Electrical Settings** b) **Mechanical Settings**
   c) **Component** d) **Set**

3. Which of the following tools is used to draw an arc shaped wire?

   a) **Spline Wire** b) **Chamfered Wire**
   c) **Arc Wire** d) None of these

4. In Revit MEP, to add a transformer in a project, you need to load the desired family type. (T/F)

5. Electrical devices are hosted components that can be placed on a wall or a workplane. (T/F)

6. The ballast voltage is the voltage required to operate the ballast in the lighting fixture. (T/F)

7. You can use the **Communication** tool to add light fixtures in a project. (T/F)

EXERCISE

Exercise 1 Placing Lighting Fixtures and Switches

Download the *c06_Conference-Center_exer1.rvt* file (for Metric *M_c06_Conference-Center_exer1.rvt*) from *http://www.cadcim.com*. The path of the file is as follows: *Textbooks > Civil/GIS > Revit MEP > Exploring Autodesk Revit MEP 2017*.

In this exercise, you will add the lighting fixtures, switches, and junction boxes for spaces in the 1ST Floor-ELEC LIGHT'G view. Refer to Figure 6-55 for the placement of various components.

1. Project view to be used:
   Floor Plans > Electrical > 1ST Floor-ELEC LIGHT'G

2. Family type to be used:
   Lighting Fixtures
   For Imperial Duplex Receptacle: Standard and M_Duplex Receptacle: GFCI
   For Metric M_Duplex Receptacle: Standard and M_Duplex Receptacle: GFCI
   Switches
   For Imperial Lighting Switches: Single Pole
   For Metric M_ Lighting Switches: Single Pole
   Junction Boxes
   For Imperial Junction Boxes-Load: 4" Square 120-1
   For Metric M_Junction Boxes-Load: 4" Square 120-1
3. Elevation
   Switches: 3' 9" (1145mm)
   Receptacles: 1'3" (381mm)
   Junction Boxes: 8' (2438mm)

4. File name to be assigned: *c06_Conference-Center_exer1a.rvt* (for Metric *M_ c06_ Conference-Center_exer1a.rvt*)

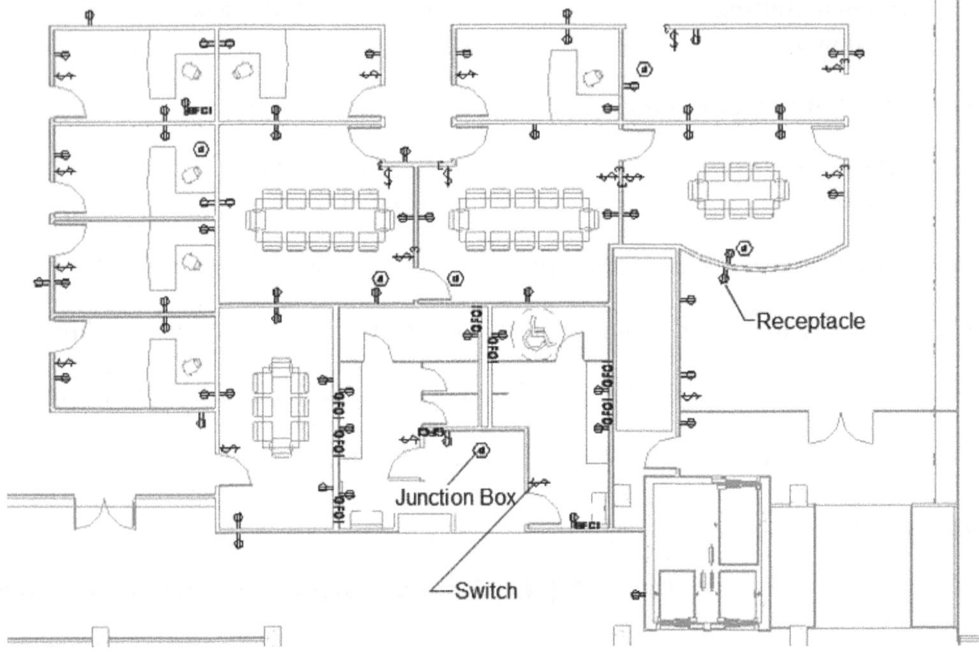

Figure 6-55 *The placement of various electrical components in the project*

Answers to Self-Evaluation Test

1. transformer, **2**. **Electrical Equipment**, **3**. **Electrical**, **4**. **Tag on Placement**, **5**. **Place on Work Plane**, **6**. F, **7**. T

Chapter 7

Creating Plumbing Systems

Learning Objectives

After completing this chapter, you will be able to:

- *Add plumbing fixtures*
- *Create pipe settings*
- *Auto route the pipe*
- *Manually route the pipe*

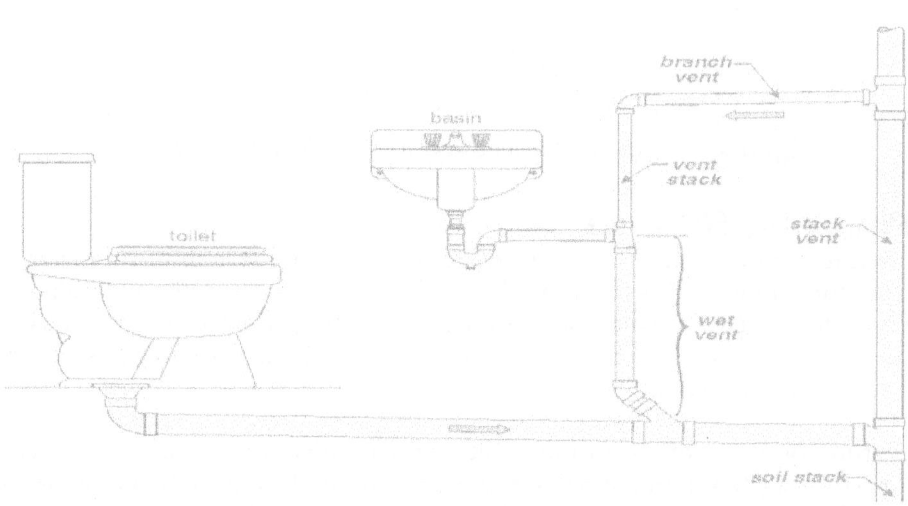

INTRODUCTION

A plumbing system is a network of pipes, drain fittings, valves, valve assemblies, and devices that are installed in a building to distribute water for drinking, washing, and heating, and also to drain the waste out of the building. In this chapter, you will learn various steps involved in creating a plumbing system in a building.

CREATING A PLUMBING SYSTEM

To create a plumbing system in Revit, you will need to add plumbing fixtures, define various pipe settings, and then route the pipe to connect the fixtures to supply water or drain the waste out of it. Figure 7-1 shows a typical plumbing system in a building. In Revit, you can create the plumbing system under the **Plumbing** discipline. To start working in a plumbing system, expand **Plumbing > Floor Plans** node in the **Project Browser** and then click on the desired level. In the **Project Browser**, the following floor plans are available under the **Floor Plans** node: **1-Plumbing** and **2-Plumbing**. You can select any of these floor plans and start creating the plumbing system. The steps involved in creating a plumbing system are discussed next.

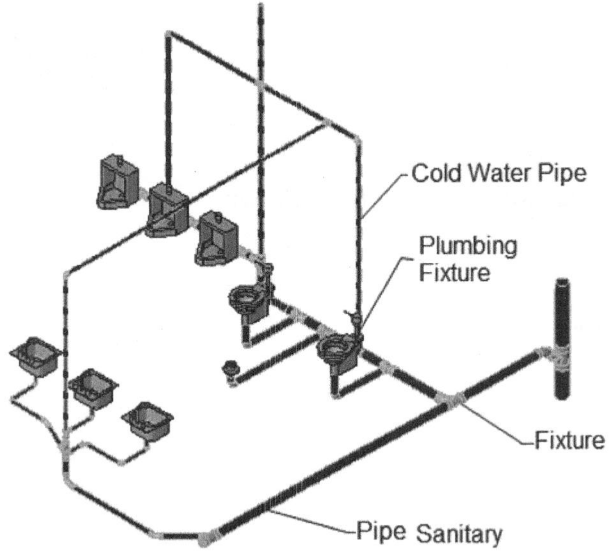

***Figure 7-1** A typical plumbing system in a building project*

Adding Plumbing Fixtures

A plumbing fixture is a device that is connected to the plumbing system to supply and drain water away from the building. It is configured according to its usage in the plumbing system. The plumbing fixtures that are commonly used in a building project are: bathtubs, bidets, kitchen sinks, channel drains, trench drains, showers, lavatories bathroom sinks, urinals, tap valves, water closets, and so on.

A plumbing fixture comprises of one or more water outlets and a drain. It also contains a flood rim which allows the supply water to overflow when the water in the fixture is full. In the fixtures, both hot and cold water can be supplied. All plumbing fixtures in a building have traps in their drains. These traps are used to trap small amount of water to create a water seal between the ambient air space and the inner space of the drain system. This will prevent the foul gases to enter into the building through drains.

To add a plumbing fixture, choose the **Plumbing Fixture** tool from the **Plumbing & Piping** panel of the **Systems** tab; the **Modify | Place Plumbing Fixture** contextual tab will be displayed. In this tab, choose the **Load Family** tool from the **Mode** panel; the **Load Family** dialog box will be displayed. In this dialog box, browse to **US Imperial > Plumbing > MEP > Fixtures** folder; various folders for fixture families will be displayed, as shown in Figure 7-2. For the Metric system, you can browse to **US Metric > Plumbing > MEP > Fixtures** folder. Select the desired folder and then select the family(ies) you want to use in the project. After selecting the desired family(ies) from the specified folder, choose **Open**; the **Load Family** dialog box will be closed and the selected family(ies) will be loaded in the drawing. Next, in the **Properties** palette, select the type of fixture from the **Type Selector** drop-down list. The plumbing fixture can be a wall hosted type in case of the **Urinal -Wall Hung : 3/4" Flush Valve** type (For Metric system, the plumbing fixture can be of the **M_Urinal -Wall Hung : 20mm Flush Valve** type) or can be a face hosted in case of the **Single - Island - Single 18" x18"- Private** type or for Metric system the **M_Single - Island - Single 455 mm x 455 mm Private** type.

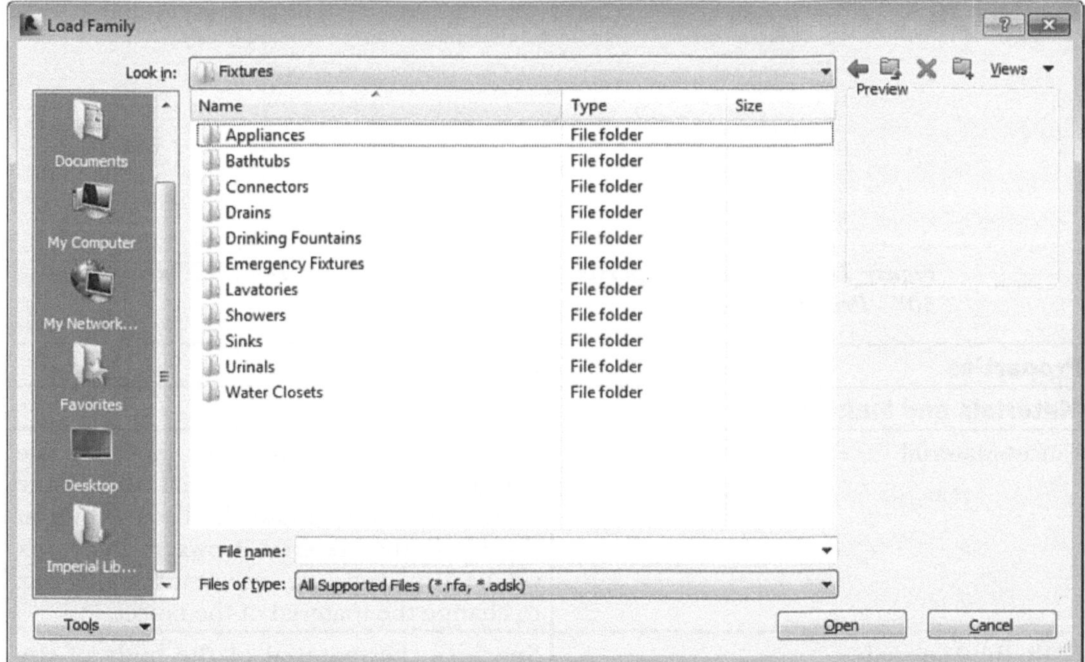

***Figure 7-2** The **Load Family** dialog box displaying different folders for the fixtures*

For example, to add a plumbing fixture, you can select the **Bath Tub : 42" x 30" - Private** type from the **Type Selector** drop-down list. For Metric system, select the **M_Bath Tub : 1065 mm x 760 mm - Private** type. Next, in the **Properties** palette, you can modify various instance properties of the fixture. To modify the type properties of the selected plumbing fixture, choose the **Edit Type** button in the **Properties** palette; the **Type Properties** dialog box will be displayed, as shown in Figure 7-3. You can use this dialog box to edit type properties of the selected fixture type. In this case, it is **Bath Tub : 42" x 30" - Private** type (or for Metric **M_Bath Tub : 1065 mm x 760 mm - Private** type).

The various type properties of the selected type are discussed in the table given next.

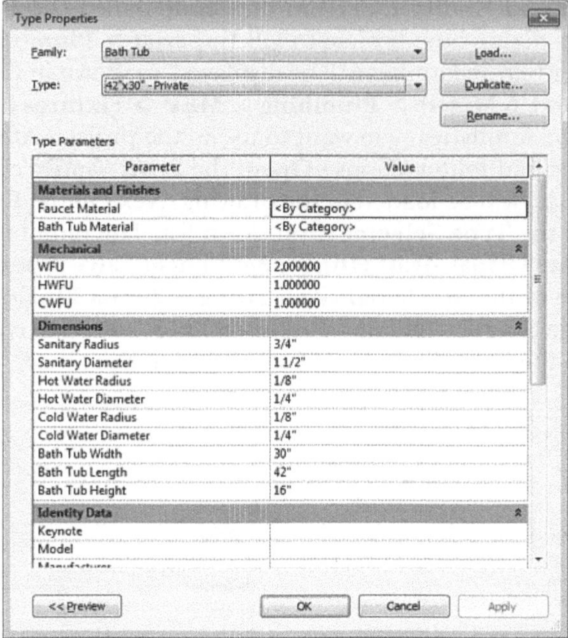

*Figure 7-3 The **Type Properties** dialog box for the **Bath Tub : 42" x 30" - Private** type*

Properties	**Description**
Materials and Finishes	
Faucet Material	Specifies the material of the faucet in the bathtub. To change the material, click in the **Value** field and choose the browse button displayed; the **Material Browser** dialog box will be displayed. You can use this dialog box to change the material of the faucet.
Bath Tub Material	Specifies the material of the body of the bathtub. To change the material, click in the **Value** field and choose the browse button displayed; the **Material Browser** dialog box will be displayed. You can use this dialog box to change the material of the bathtub.
Mechanical	
WFU	Specifies the water fixture units (Load value) for the domestic water supply in the bathtub.

HWFU	Specifies the water fixture unit for the hot water in the bathtub.
CWFU	Specifies the water fixture unit for the cold water in the bathtub.
Dimensions	
Sanitary Radius	Specifies the radius of the sanitary outlet of the bathtub.
Hot Water Radius	Specifies the radius of the connector for the hot water in the bathtub.
Cold Water Radius	Specifies the radius of the connector for the cold water in the bathtub.
Bath Tub Width	Specifies the width of the bathtub.
Bath Tub Length	Specifies the length of the bathtub.
Identity Data	
Keynote	Specifies the keynote value for the bathtub.
Model	Specifies the model of the bathtub.
Cost	Specifies the cost of the project.

After assigning the type properties for the selected type, choose the **OK** button in the **Type Properties** dialog box to close it. Next, in the **Properties** palette, you can modify the instance properties of the plumbing fixture.

The various instance properties that you can modify in the plumbing fixture are briefly explained in the table given next.

Properties	**Description**
Constraints	
Level	Specifies the level of the bathtub.
Host	Specifies the host for the bathtub.
Offset	Specifies the offset value of the bathtub from the host level.
Plumbing	
Flow Pressure	Specifies the flow pressure of the outlet pipes in the bathtub.
Mechanical	
System Classification	This is a read-only parameter. It specifies the system classification of the bathtub.
System Type	Specifies the system type to which the bathtub belongs.
System Name	Specifies the name of the system to which the bathtub belongs.
System Abbreviation	Specifies the abbreviation for the system to which the bathtub belongs.

Identity Data	
Comments	Specifies the comment for the bathtub.
Phasing	
Phase Created	Specifies the phase in which the component was added.
Phase Demolished	Specifies the phase in which the component is demolished.

After assigning the instance properties, you can place the bathtub at the desired location. To do so, move the cursor in the drawing area. You will notice that the preview of the bathtub will be displayed along with the cursor. Click at the desired location; the bathtub will be placed. Figure 7-4 shows a three-dimensional view of the bathtub with various connectors.

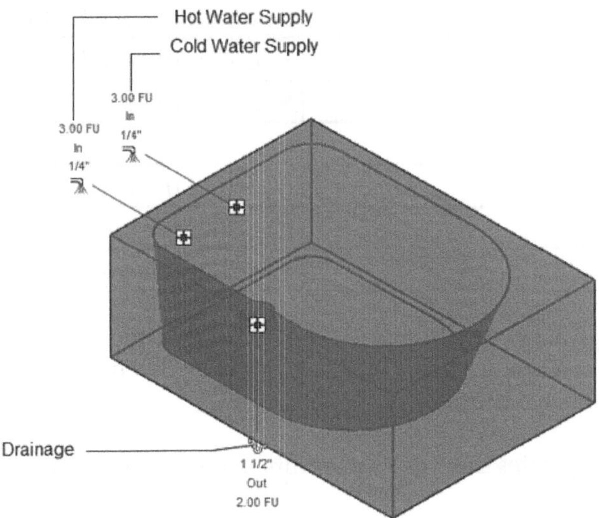

***Figure 7-4** The **Bath Tub : 42" x 30" - Private** type plumbing fixture with various connectors*

Specifying the Pipe Settings

After placing the fixtures at their required location in the drawing, you now need to create a pipe system that will connect the fixtures with the pipes. The pipe system consists of a network of pipes and fixtures to supply water to the building and also to drain the waste out of the building. Before you create the network for these utilities, you need to set the specification of the pipe and pipe fixtures to be used in the pipe system. In Revit, you can specify the type of pipe, different sizes of pipe, and the material of the pipe before creating network of the pipe system. The various procedures to set the pipe system are discussed next.

Creating the Pipe Type

Before you create a pipe system (network), it is important to create various types of pipes to be used in the pipe system. To create a new type of pipe, expand **Families > Pipes > Pipe Types** in the **Project Browser**. Under the **Pipe Types** node, right-click on the **Standard** sub-node; a shortcut menu will be displayed. From the shortcut menu, choose the **Duplicate** option; another sub-node with the name **Standard 2** will be added under the **Pipe Types** node. Now, select the **Standard 2** node and right-click; a shortcut menu will be displayed. From the shortcut menu, choose the **Type Properties** option; the **Type Properties** dialog box will be displayed, as shown in Figure 7-5.

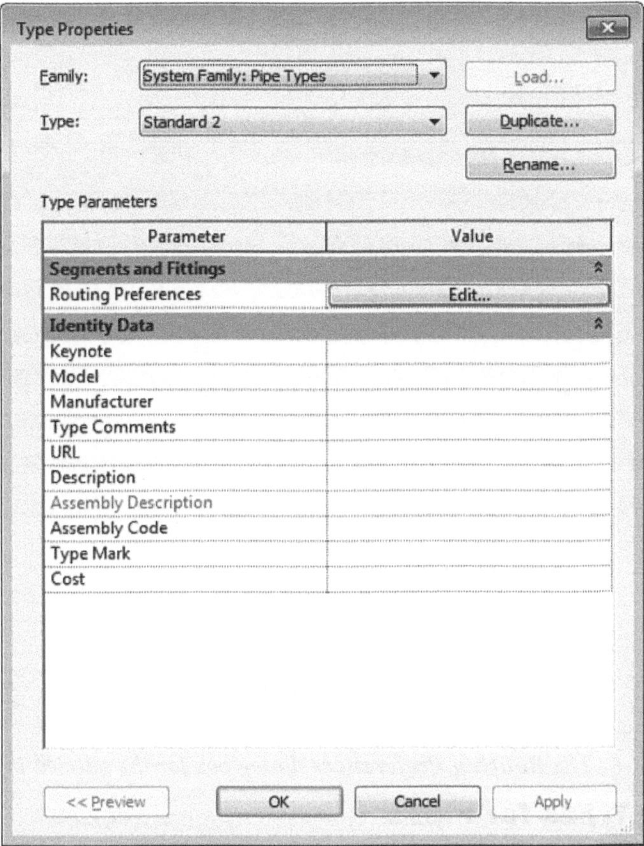

***Figure 7-5** The **Type Properties** dialog box for the pipe types*

In the **Type Properties** dialog box, choose the **Edit** button displayed in the **Value** field corresponding to the **Routing Preferences** parameter; the **Routing Preferences** dialog box will be displayed, as shown in Figure 7-6.

Using the option in this dialog box, you can set the specifications for various entities in the pipe system such as the pipe segments, pipe fittings, pipe junctions, and so on. Also, in this dialog box, you can use the options to specify the size ranges of the pipe to be used in the pipe system. After specifying the options in the **Routing Preferences** dialog box, choose the **OK** button to close it. Now, in the **Type Properties** dialog box, you can specify the parameters such as **Keynote**, **Model**, **Cost**, and so on that are specific to the type of pipe you have created.

Also, in the **Type Properties** dialog box, you can choose the **Rename** button to rename the type you have created. On choosing the **Rename** button, the **Rename** dialog box will be displayed. In the **New** edit box of this dialog box, enter text to specify the new name of the pipe type and then choose **OK**; the **Rename** dialog box will be closed. For example, you can enter **PVC-Sanitary** in the **New** edit box of the **Rename** dialog box. When the **Rename** dialog box will be closed, the new name will appear in the **Type** drop-down list in the **Type Properties** dialog box. After specifying various options in the **Type Properties** dialog box, choose **OK** to close it. You have now created a new pipe type for the pipe system. Now, you will create fittings for the pipe system. The process of creating fittings for the pipe system is discussed next.

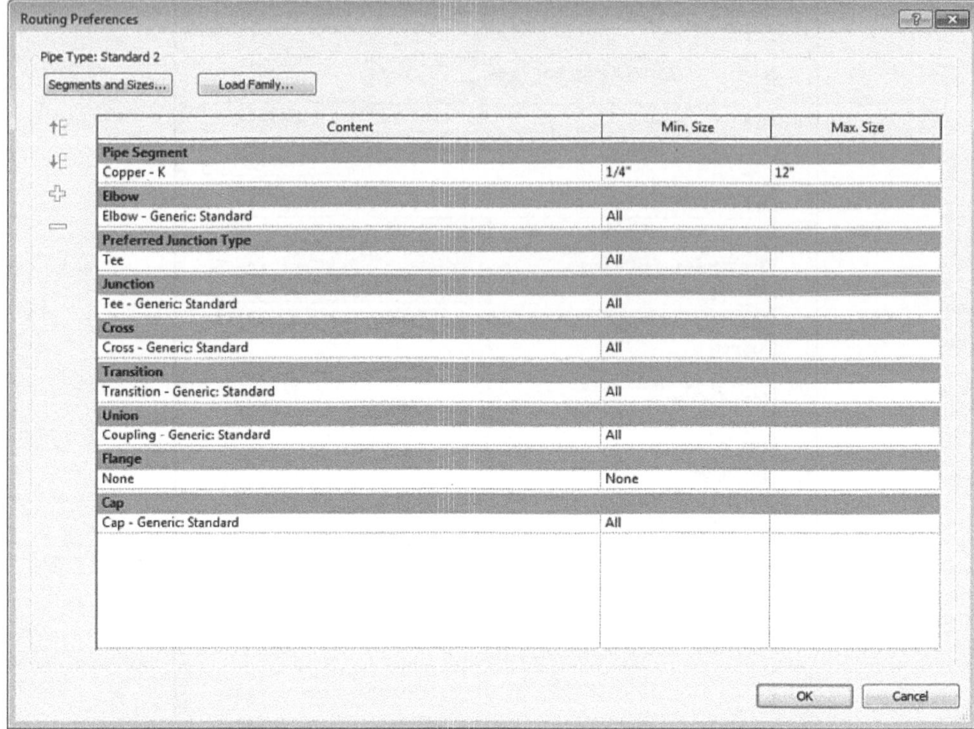

*Figure 7-6 The **Routing Preferences** dialog box for the selected pipe type*

Creating Fitting Types for Pipes

The pipe fittings in a pipe system include bends, elbow, cap, cross, coupling, tee, transition, reducer, plug, and so on. Before you create a pipe system, you can specify various types for each of these fittings. To view the existing fittings available in MEP, expand **Families > Pipe Fittings** in the **Project Browser**; various available fittings for the pipe system are displayed in the **Pipe Fittings** node, as shown in Figure 7-7.

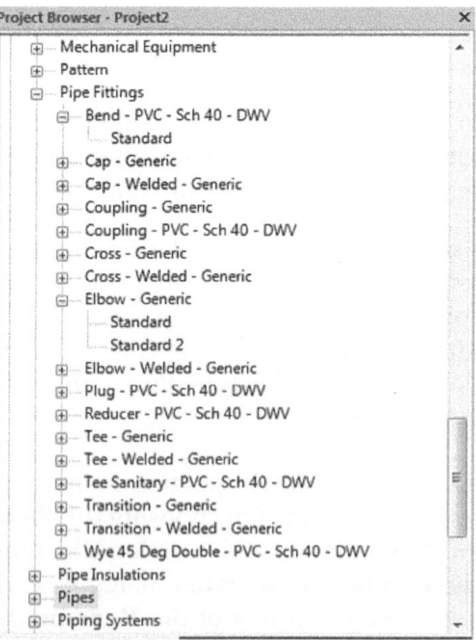

*Figure 7-7 The **Project Browser** displaying various pipe fittings*

You can expand the nodes corresponding to these fittings and create a new type for them. For example, to create a new type for the elbow, expand the **Elbow Generic** node and then right-click on the **Standard** sub-node; a shortcut menu will be displayed. Choose the **Duplicate** option from the shortcut menu; the **Standard 2** sub-node will be created under the **Elbow-Generic** node. Now, select the **Standard 2** sub-node and click; the **Type Properties** dialog box will be displayed for the elbow type. In this dialog box, click in the **Value** field corresponding to the

Loss Method parameter and select an option from the drop-down list displayed in it. From the drop-down list, you can select any of the following options: **None**, **K Coefficient**, and **K Coefficient from Table**.

These options are used to specify the resistance coefficient K for the pipe fitting. If you select the **K Coefficient** option, the **K Coefficient** parameter will become active. You can enter a suitable value in the **Value** field corresponding to this parameter to specify the friction loss coefficient of the pipe. If you select the **K Coefficient from Table** option, the **K Coefficient Table** parameter will become active. Click in the **Value** field corresponding to this parameter and select the desired table to specify the loss coefficient for the pipe fitting. Alternatively, you can specify the **Not Defined** option for the **Loss Method** parameter to ignore the loss coefficient for the pipe fitting. In the **Type Properties** dialog box for the new pipe type, you can specify other parameters such as **Keynote**, **Model**, **Manufacture**, **Cost**, **Lookup Table Name**, and more. After specifying various parameters in the **Type Properties** dialog box, choose **OK**; the dialog box will close and a new type will be added under the **Elbow-Generic** node. You can rename the created type. To do so, select the created type and right-click; a shortcut menu will be displayed. Choose the **Rename** option from the shortcut menu and type a new name in the edit box displayed.

Similarly, you can create new types for other pipe fittings listed in the **Pipe Fittings** node. After creating different types of fittings for the Pipe system, now you will set various materials for the pipe in the pipe system.

Setting the Pipe Material and Pipe Size

To set the material for the pipe system, choose the **Mechanical Settings** button in the **Plumbing & Piping** panel of the **Systems** tab; the **Mechanical Settings** dialog box will be displayed. In this dialog box, choose **Pipe Settings > Segments and Sizes** option from the left panel; various options related to the pipe segments and its sizes are displayed in the right pane, as shown in Figure 7-8.

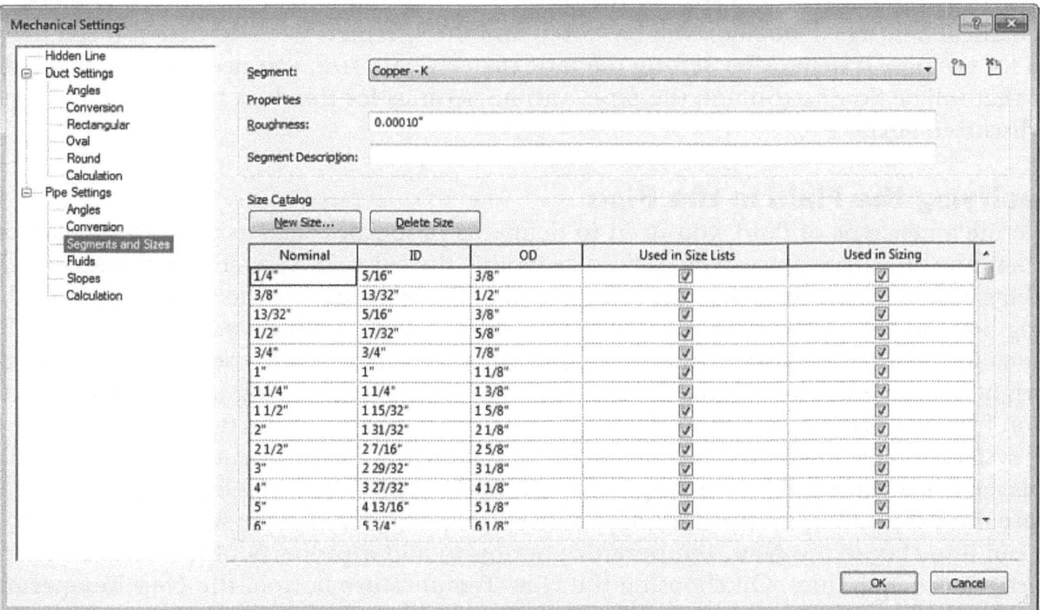

Figure 7-8** The **Mechanical Settings** dialog box displaying various options for **Segments and Sizes

Click on the **Segment** drop-down list and select an option to define the material for the pipe segment; various sizes of the pipe related to the selected material will be displayed in the **Size Catalog** area.

On selecting a particular material, a table will be displayed in the **Size Catalog** area. In this table, you can click in the value field corresponding to the required columns to modify the existing sizes such as outer diameter, inner diameter, nominal diameter, and so on. In the displayed table, you can add more sizes. To do so, choose the **New Size** button in the **Size Catalog** area; the **Add Pipe Size** dialog box will be displayed, as shown in Figure 7-9.

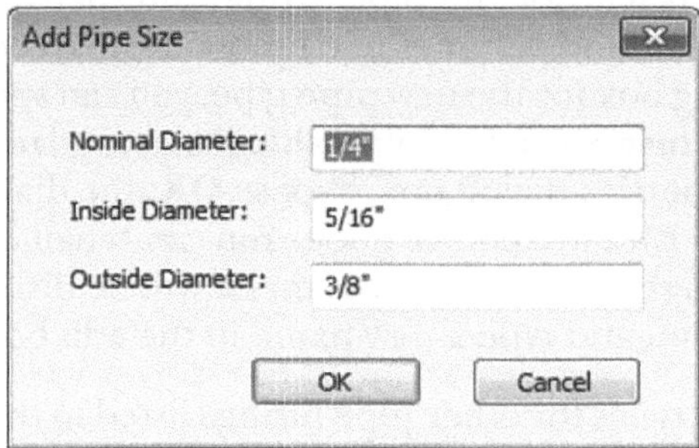

*Figure 7-9 The **Add Pipe Size** dialog box*

In the dialog box, you can specify the sizing values of the pipe such as its inner diameter, nominal diameter, and outer diameter in the **Inside Diameter**, **Nominal Diameter**, and **Outside Diameter** edit boxes, respectively. After specifying these values, choose **OK**; the **Add Pipe Size** dialog box will be closed and a new size will be added to the table in the **Size Catalog** area. You can also delete a size from the table. To do so, select the required size from the table and then choose the **Delete Size** button from the **Size Catalog** area; the selected size will be deleted from the table.

After setting the material and size for the pipe to be used in the pipe system, choose **OK**; the **Mechanical Settings** dialog box will be closed and the specified size and material can now be used for the pipe system. After setting the pipe material and size, you need to specify the fluid type that will be flowing through the pipe. Various settings for the fluid to be used in the pipe are discussed next.

Specifying the Fluid in the Pipe

To define a new type of fluid, you need to define its properties such as viscosity, density, and temperature. To create a new type of fluid or modify the existing type, choose the **Mechanical Settings** button in the **Plumbing & Piping** panel of the **Systems** tab; the **Mechanical Settings** dialog box will be displayed. In the dialog box, expand **Pipe Settings > Fluids** node; various options to modify the existing fluid type and to create a new fluid type will be displayed in the right pane, as shown in Figure 7-10. In the right pane of the dialog box, you can select an option from the **Fluid Name** drop-down list to specify the name of the fluid to be used for the pipe system; a table displaying various properties of the fluid at different temperatures will be displayed below the **Fluid Name** drop-down list. In this table, you can select a temperature and choose the **Delete Temperature** button to delete the entire entry for the specified temperature. You can also choose the **New Temperature** button to add a property of the selected fluid at a particular temperature. On choosing the **New Temperature** button, the **New Temperature** dialog box will be displayed. In this dialog box, you can click on the **Temperature** edit box and enter a value in it to specify the temperature for which you want to define the property of the fluid. In the **New Temperature** dialog box, you can also click on the **Viscosity** and **Density** edit boxes to specify the viscous and weight properties of the fluid.

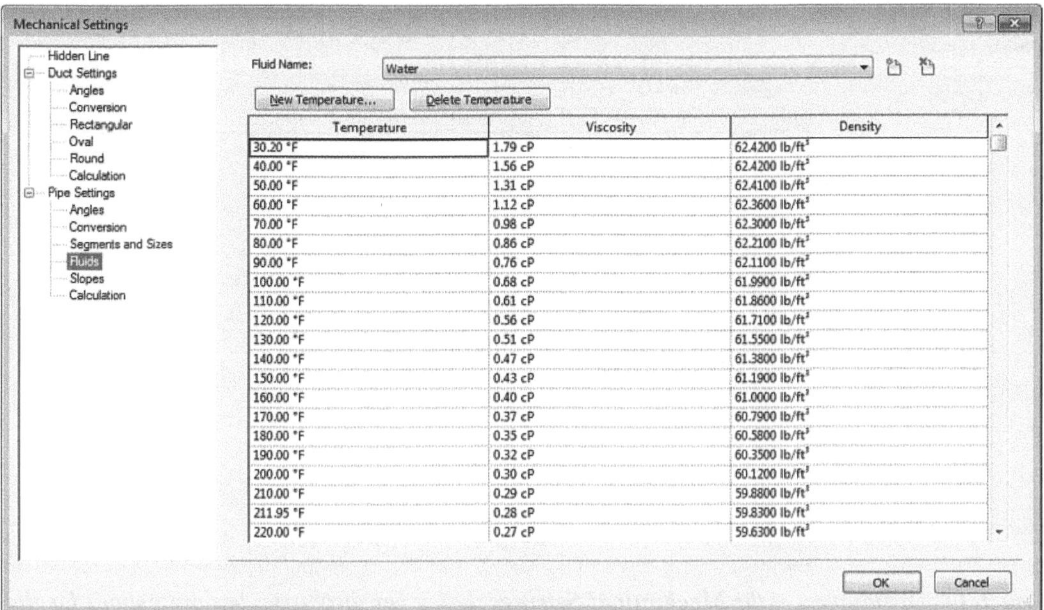

__Figure 7-10__ The __Mechanical Settings__ dialog box displaying various options for fluids

After specifying various properties in the **New Temperature** dialog box, choose **OK**; the dialog box will be closed and an entry for the new temperature and its properties will be displayed in the table. Next, in the right pane for the **Fluids** option, choose the **Add Fluid** button displayed next to the **Fluid Name** drop-down list in the **Mechanical Settings** drop-down list; the **New Fluid** dialog box will be displayed. In this dialog box, enter a name in the **New Fluid Name** edit box to specify a name of the fluid you want to add. Next, select an option from the **New Fluid Based on** drop-down list to specify the fluid type whose property the new fluid will inherit. Now, choose the **OK** button; the dialog box will be closed and the new fluid will be added as an option in the **Fluid Name** drop-down list. Now, choose the **OK** button in the **Mechanical Settings** dialog box to close it.

Setting the Slope of the Pipe

After specifying the type of fluid in the pipe, you can specify a new slope parameter or delete the existing slope parameter for the pipe to be used in the pipe system. To specify the slope of the pipe, choose the **Mechanical Settings** button from the **Plumbing & Piping** panel in the **Systems** tab; the **Mechanical Settings** dialog box will be displayed. In the left pane of this dialog box, expand **Pipe Settings > Slopes**; various options for setting the slope of the pipe will be displayed in the right pane, as shown in Figure 7-11. In the right pane of the dialog box, a table displaying the existing slope values is displayed. In the table, you can select a slope value from the **Slope Values** column and choose the **Delete Slope** button; the selected value will be deleted from the table. You can also add a new value in the table. To do so, choose the

New Slope button; the **New Slope** dialog box will be displayed. In the **Slope Value** edit box of the dialog box, enter a value to specify the new slope and choose **OK**; the **New Slope** dialog box will be closed and the new value specified will be added to the table. Now, choose **OK**; the **Mechanical Settings** dialog box will be closed.

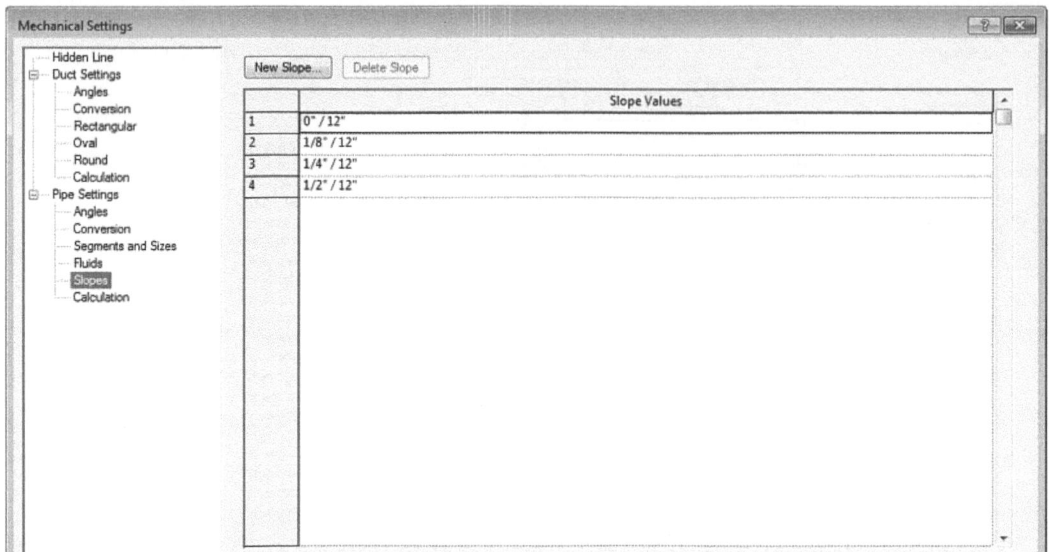

***Figure 7-11** Partial view of the **Mechanical Settings** dialog box displaying various options for slopes*

Specifying the Calculation Method for the Pressure of the Pipe

After specifying various settings for the slope, you can now specify and view the methods to calculate the pressure drop and the flow conversion in the pipe system. To specify and view the calculation methods, invoke the **Mechanical Settings** dialog box and then select **Pipe Settings > Calculations** from the left pane; various options related to the calculation methods are displayed in the right pane, as shown in Figure 7-12.

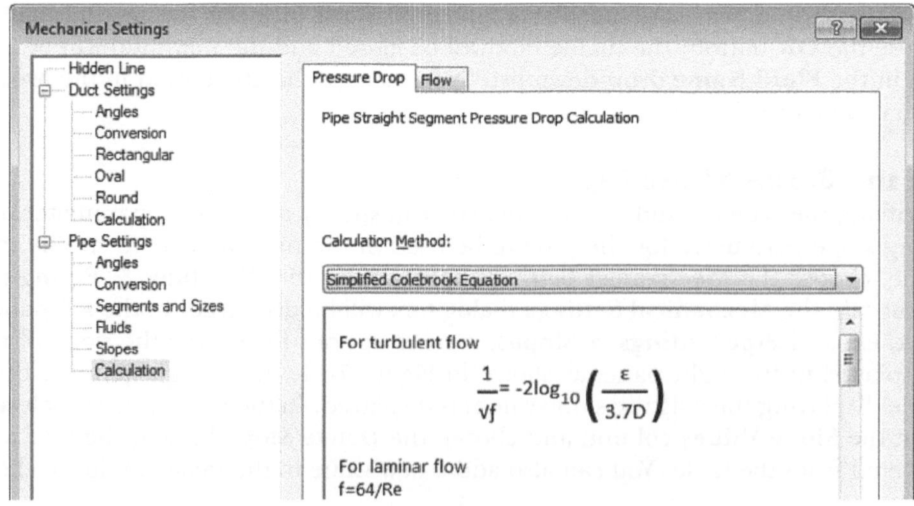

***Figure 7-12** Partial view of the **Mechanical Settings** dialog box displaying various options for calculating pressure*

In this pane, the **Pressure Drop** tab is chosen by default. In this tab, the **Simplified Colebrook Equation** option is selected by default in the **Calculation Method** drop-down list. To select a different method for the calculation of pressure drop in the pipe click on the **Calculation Method** drop-down list and then select **Colebrook Equation**, **Haaland Equation**, or **Simplified Colebrook Equation** from the drop-down list displayed.

Tip

The selection of the calculation method depends on the design intent and the type of flow. The decision of selecting the method is solely to be taken by the piping engineer or the design team.

In the right pane of the **Mechanical Settings** dialog box, choose the **Flow** tab to specify and view the method to convert the fixture units into volumetric flow. In the **Flow** tab, the **Plumbing Fixture Flow** option is selected by default in the **Calculation Method** drop-down list. In the list box below the drop-down list, the description of the method will be displayed. After specifying various calculation methods, choose **OK**; the **Mechanical Settings** dialog box will be closed.

Tip

*The **Plumbing Fixture Flow** method converts the **Fixture Units** specified in the plumbing fixture into volumetric flow using values found in International Plumbing Code(IPC)-Table E103.3(3), 2012. The flow units of the fixtures are displayed in their type properties.*

Routing Pipes in the Pipe System

Enhanced

While creating a pipe system, routing of the pipe is the most important task. Routing of a pipe involves connecting the fixtures with it such that the waste from the building system is easily drained to the sewer and the water is supplied to the building as per the requirement. In the **Plumbing** discipline of an MEP project, the pipes are routed above ceilings, in walls, in chases, and under floor slabs. The routing of the pipes should be correctly designed in coordination with the structural and architectural model of the building.

In Revit, you can route a pipe using three methods: Auto Routing, Manual Routing, and Slope. The process of routing pipes using all the three methods is discussed next.

Auto Routing Pipes

In this method, you can generate the layout of the pipe network automatically based on certain calculation algorithms. Before you route the pipe automatically, ensure that the pipe settings are specified and the plumbing fixtures are placed at their desired location. To begin the process of Auto routing, you need to select the desired plumbing fixtures from the model. For example, if you select a water closet, as shown in Figure 7-13, the **Modify | Plumbing Fixtures** contextual tab will be displayed. In this tab, choose the **Piping** tool from the **Create Systems** panel; the **Create Piping System** dialog box will be displayed, as shown in Figure 7-14. You can select the desired sanitary system and the system required for the distribution of water from the **System type** drop-down list. Next, enter the name of the system in the **System name** edit box.

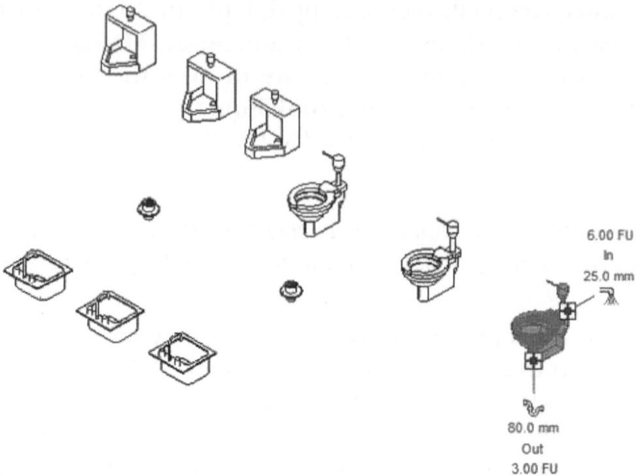

***Figure 7-13** The water closet selected for pipe system*

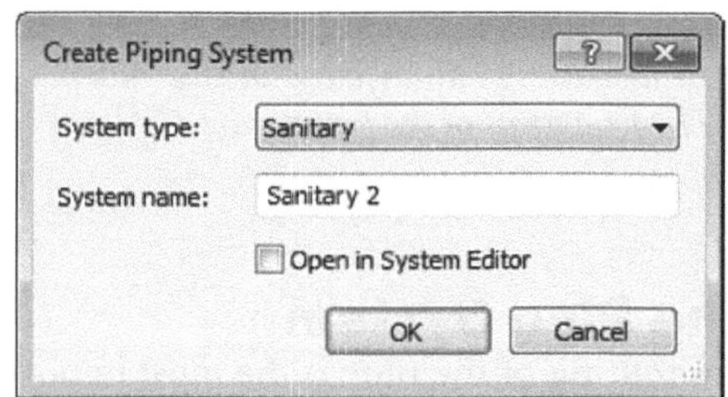

***Figure 7-14** The **Create Piping System** dialog box*

After specifying parameters in the **Create Piping System** dialog box, choose **OK**; the dialog box will be closed and the selected plumbing fixture will be displayed inside a dotted box, as shown in Figure 7-15. Also, the **Modify | Piping Systems** contextual tab will be displayed. In this tab, you can use the options to modify the piping system that you have created. Now, you will learn to add more fixtures to the system.

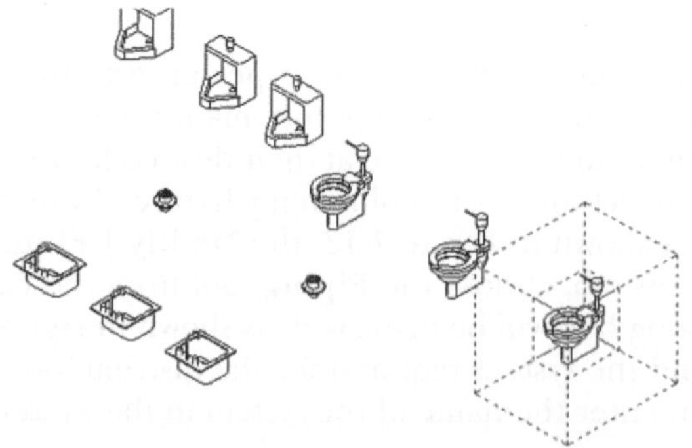

***Figure 7-15** The dotted box around the selected fixture*

Adding more Fixtures

To add more fixtures to the system, choose the **Edit System** tool from the **System Tools** panel. Next, choose the **Add to System** tool, if it is not chosen by default, from the **Editing Piping System** panel; all fixtures, except the selected fixture, will appear faded and a "+" symbol will appear with the cursor. Click on the fixtures that you want to add to the system. Now, choose the **Finish Editing System** button from the **Edit Piping System** panel of the **Edit Piping System** contextual tab.

Creating Layout

Now, to generate the routing automatically, select any of the fixtures added in the system; the **Modify | Plumbing Fixtures** tab will be displayed. In this tab, you can choose the **Generate Layout** or **Generate Placeholder** tool from the **Layout** panel to create the routing. If you choose the **Generate Placeholder** tool from the **Layout** panel, the **Generate Layout** tab will be displayed and also a preview of the layout with default solution will be displayed in the drawing area, as shown in Figure 7-16.

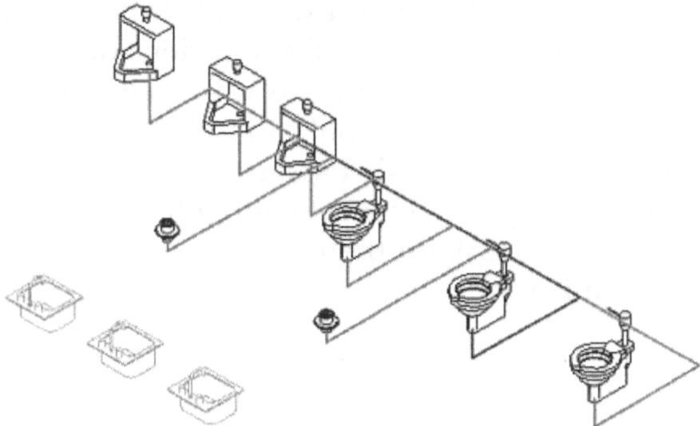

Figure 7-16 *Default solution 1 of the pipe system*

In the **Generate Layout** tab, choose the **Place Base** tool to add a base in the system to provide an outlet for the flow in the pipe. On choosing the **Place Base** tool, the preview of the base will be displayed with the cursor. After selecting the option from the **Options Bar**, move the cursor and place the outlet in a desired area as per the design. You can place the base at chase or at an open space. To place the outlet, click on the desired point; the outlet will be placed and the **Options Bar** displays the default values of the **Offset** and **Diameter** parameters of the outlet.

Tip

If you want to create a piping system with physical pipes and fittings, choose the ***Generate Layout*** *tool in the* ***Piping Systems*** *tab as a substitute for the* ***Generate Placeholder*** *tool. The* ***Generate Placeholder*** *tool can be used when you need to create the pipe system only to view the pipe arrangement and to analyze the flow in the pipe.*

Also, in the **Modify Layout** panel of the **Generate Layout** tab, the **Modify Base** tool is chosen by default. As a result, you can choose the **Remove Base** tool from this panel to remove the added outlet from the system.

Generating Solution of the Layout

Now, in the **Generate Layout** contextual tab, you can choose the **Solutions** tool from the **Modify Layout** panel to list the options for the solution of the system. On choosing this tool, the **Solution Type** drop-down list will be displayed in the **Options Bar.** In this drop-down list, you can select the options to derive a solution for the pipe system. The various options that you can select from the **Solution Type** drop-down list are: **Network, Perimeter, Intersections,** and **Custom**. If you select the **Network** option, you will have five solutions for the pipe system. The numbers of solutions are based upon the complexity of the network. To get the preview of the solutions available for the **Network** option, select the arrows displayed next to the **Solution Type** drop-down list. As you select an arrow, the text displayed next to it shows the solution number. Also, on selecting the arrow, the solution number will change and the preview corresponding to the solution will be displayed in the drawing area. Figures 7-17 to 7-20 display various solutions for the **Network** option in the pipe system. After selecting the solution for the pipe system, choose the **Settings** button from the **Options Bar**; the **Pipe Conversion Settings** dialog box will be displayed. In this dialog box, you can specify the type and offset value of the branch and the main pipe that will be used in the pipe system. After specifying various options in the **Pipe Conversion Settings** dialog box, choose **OK**; the dialog box will be closed. Now, in the **Modify Layout** panel, you can choose the **Edit Layout** tool to modify the layout generated by the Auto routing method. After choosing the **Edit Layout** tool, move the cursor to any of the pipe segments and click; the pipe segment will be highlighted in blue color and a move icon will be displayed on the segment. Click on the move icon and drag the cursor to relocate the pipe segment, as shown in Figure 7-21.

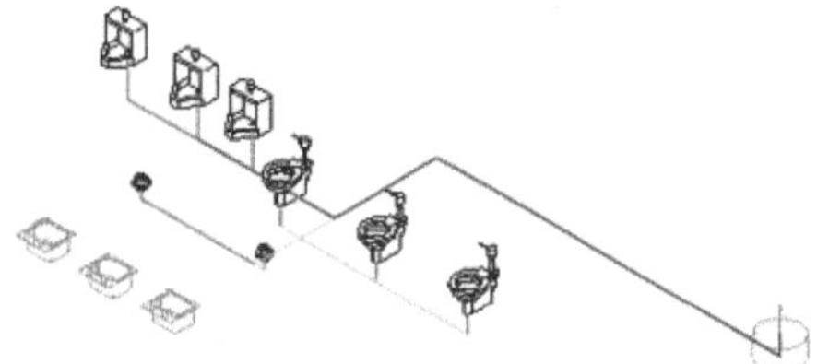

Figure 7-17 *The solution 2 of the pipe system*

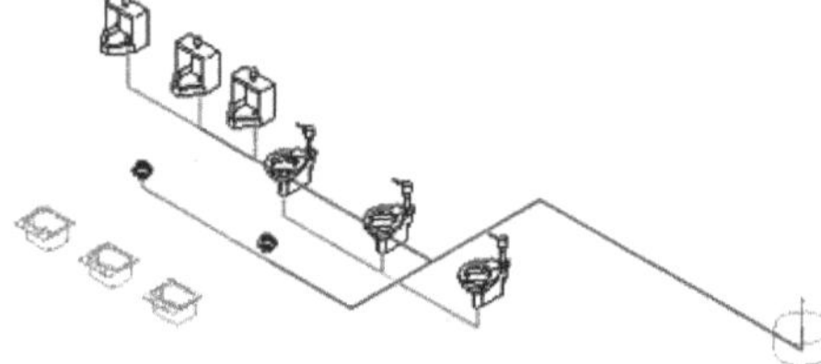

Figure 7-18 *The solution 3 of the pipe system*

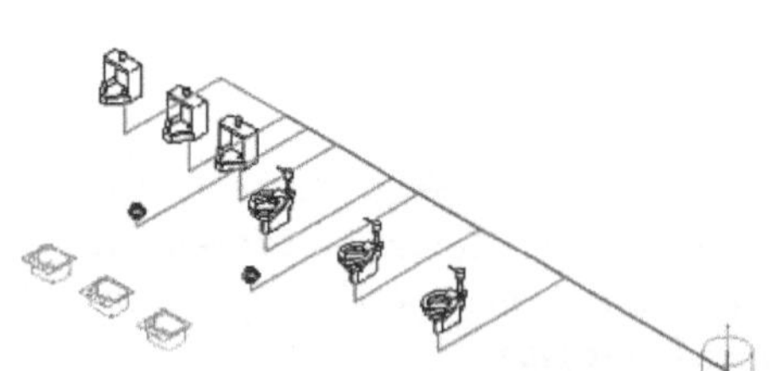

Figure 7-19 *The solution 4 of the pipe system*

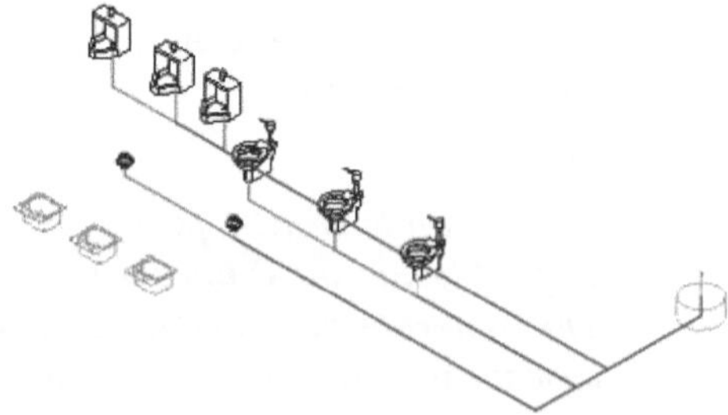

Figure 7-20 *The solution 5 of the pipe system*

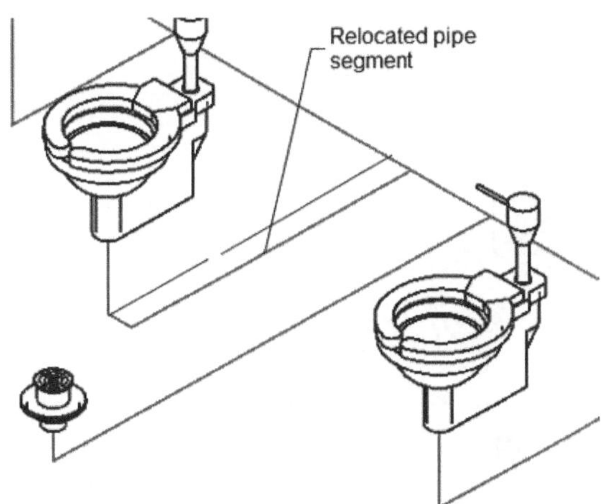

Figure 7-21 *The relocated pipe segment*

When you select a pipe segment, the offset value of the pipe will be displayed next to it. Click on the offset value and enter a new offset value in the edit box displayed. After entering a value in the edit box, press ENTER; the selected pipe segment will be adjusted to the new offset value specified. Now, choose the **Finish Layout** button from the **Generate Layout** panel of the **Generate Layout** tab; the layout of the sanitary system as placeholders will be generated, refer to Figure 7-22. Next, you can inspect the pipe system to check the flow of fluids in the pipe system. To do so, select the required placeholder segment and then choose the **System Inspector** tool from the **Analysis** panel of the **Modify | Pipe Placeholders** contextual tab; the **System Inspector** floating panel will be displayed. In this panel, choose the **Inspect** tool; arrows in the placeholder segments showing the direction of the flow or slope will be displayed, as shown in Figure 7-23.

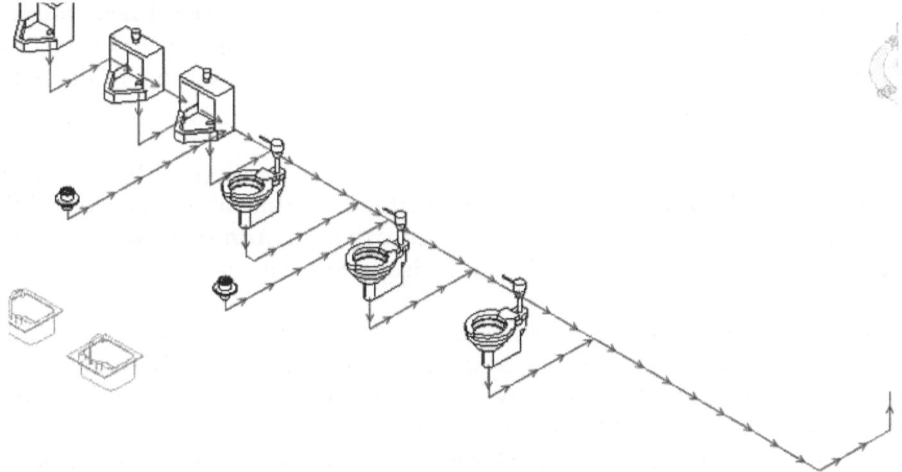

Figure 7-22 *The sanitary system with arrows displayed*

Now, place the cursor over the desired placeholder segment; a tag will be displayed, as shown in Figure 7-23.

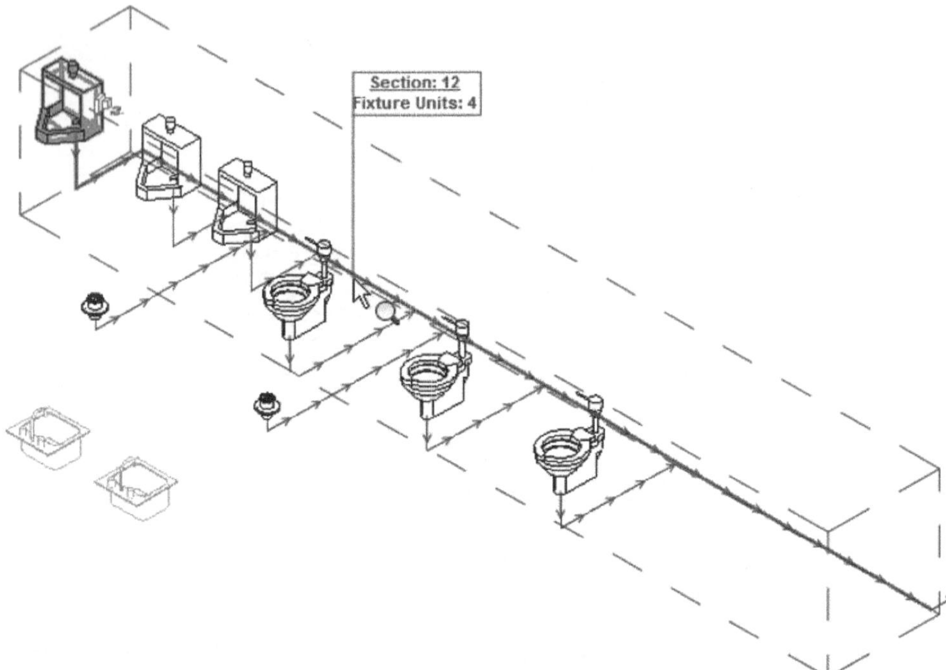

Figure 7-23 *The tag showing the information of the placeholder segment*

The tag will display the section number and the number of fixture units. Similarly, move the cursor over the other placeholder segments and view the tag related to them. Choose the **Finish** button in the **System Inspector** panel to finish the system inspection. Now, you can convert the placeholder segment(s) into pipe. To do so, select the placeholder segment(s); the **Modify | Pipe Placeholders** tab will be displayed. In the **Options Bar**, specify the diameter of the pipe in the **Diameter** edit box and then choose the **Convert Placeholder** tool; the pipe will be created in the selected segment. Similarly, select the placeholder segments that you want to convert into pipes and choose the **Convert Placeholder** tool from the **Edit** panel to create the pipe in those segments.

Next, to add more fixtures to the sanitary system, select the desired fixture in the system and then choose the **Piping Systems** contextual tab. In this tab, choose the **Edit System** tool from the **System Tools** panel and then ensure that the **Add to System** button is chosen in the **Edit Piping System** panel of the **Edit Piping System** contextual tab.

Now, select the other fixture(s) that you want to add to the system. After selecting the desired fixture(s), choose the **Finish Editing System** button from the **Mode** panel; the selected fixture(s) will be added to the system. Next, you will modify the layout of the piping system to accommodate the newly added fixture to the system. To do so, select the added fixture in the system from the drawing; the **Modify | Plumbing Fixtures** tab will be displayed. In this tab, choose the **Generate Layout** tool from the **Layou**t panel; the pipe(s) will be connected to added fixtures to accommodate them in the system. In the **Options Bar**, you select an option from the **Solution Type** drop-down list and set the desirable solution for the layout of the pipe system. Next, after selecting the option for the layout, choose the **Finish Layout** button from the **Generate Layou**t panel to complete the piping system using the auto routing process.

Tip

*In Autodesk Revit, you can use the **Fabrication Parts** tool to place the fabrication parts of the pipe. You can also convert an existing pipe to a fabrication part. To do so, choose a pipe segment from the existing pipe layout and then choose the **Design to Fabrication** tool from the **Fabrication** panel of the **Modify / Place Pipe** contextual tab.*

Manually Routing Pipes

The auto route method of routing pipes may not be economical or feasible in some conditions. As such, you can use various tools to manually add the pipe segments to the network. To manually add pipes, you can work in a floor plan view for the **Plumbing** discipline or in a section view. Invoke the desired view and then choose the **Pipe** tool from the **Plumbing & Piping** panel of the **Systems** tab; the **Modify| Place Pipe** contextual tab will be displayed, as shown in Figure 7-24.

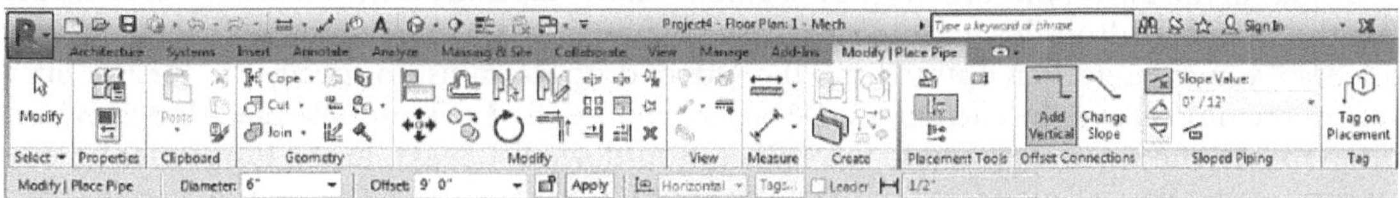

***Figure 7-24** The **Modify / Place Pipe** contextual tab*

In the **Placement Tools** panel of this tab, the **Automatically Connect** tool is chosen by default. As a result, you can snap cursor to the required component segment. The feature of snapping the component is called the auto connecting feature of a pipe in Revit. The selection of this tool is useful when you connect the pipe segments at different elevations. You can disable the auto connecting feature by choosing the **Automatically Connect** tool. In the **Placement Tools** panel of the **Modify| Place Pipe** contextual tab, you can choose the **Inherit Elevation** button to enable the start point or the endpoint of the pipe segment to inherit its elevation from the component it is snapped to. Similarly, you can choose the **Inherit Size** button to enable the pipe segment to inherit its cross-sectional size from the component it is snapped to. In the **Placement Tools** panel, you can choose the **Justification** button to specify the vertical and horizontal justification of the pipe segment. On choosing the **Justification** button, the **Justification Setting** dialog box will be displayed. In this dialog box, you can specify values for the **Horizontal Justification**, **Horizontal Offset**, and **Vertical Justification** parameters. After specifying the various options, choose **OK**; the **Justification Setting** dialog box will be closed.

After specifying various options in the **Placement Tools** panel in the **Modify | Place Pipe** tab, you can use various options in the **Sloped Piping** panel to specify the slope of the pipe segment. In the **Sloped Piping** panel, choose the **Slope: Off** button to draw the pipe segment without a slope definition. To assign an upward or downward slope to the pipe segment, choose the **Slope: Up** or **Slope: Down** button, respectively. Next, you can select an option from the **Slope Value** drop-down list in the **Sloped Piping** panel to define the slope value of the pipe segment. You can choose the **Show Slope Tooltip** to enable the display of a tooltip while you draw the pipe. The tooltip will display the offset value of the start point of the pipe segment and also the slope information of the pipe segment. Figure 7-25 shows a tooltip with information about the pipe segment being sketched. In the **Sloped Piping** panel of the **Modify |Place Pipe** tab, choose the **Ignore Slope Connect** tool to ignore the current slope of the pipe segment when it will be connected to a component.

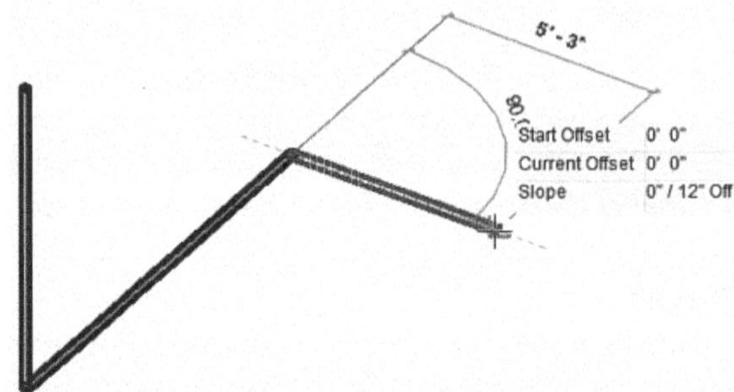

Figure 7-25 The tooltip displayed on sketching the pipe segment

In the **Tag** panel of the **Modify | Place Pipe** tab, choose the **Tag on Placement** button to enable the display of the tag on placing the pipe segment. In the **Options Bar**, you can select an option from the **Diameter** drop-down list to specify the diameter of the pipe segment that you want to add. Also, you can select an option from the **Offset** drop-down list to specify the vertical offset value of the pipe above the current level. You can choose the **Lock/unlock Specified Elevation** button to lock the value specified in the **Offset** drop-down list. Next, in the **Properties** palette, you can select a type of pipe from the **Type Selector** drop-down list. Next in the drawing area, click at the desired point to specify the start point of the pipe; a pipe segment will emerge from the specified point. Next, click at the desired point to specify the pipe segment. You can create multiple segments of the pipe using the assigned offset, slope, and cross-section values to complete the pipe layout. After completing the layout, choose **Modify** from the **Select** panel of the **Modify | Place Pipes** contextual tab to exit the sketching of the pipe.

Modifying a Pipe Segment

To modify a pipe segment, select it from the drawing; the **Modify | Pipes** contextual tab and the **Properties** palette will be displayed with the values of the instance parameters of the pipe segment selected. Also, you will notice that the selected pipe is highlighted in blue color and the connectors are displayed at its two endpoints along with the value of offset of the endpoints. In the **Edit** panel of the **Modify|Pipes** contextual tab, choose options to modify the justification, slope constraints, and capping at the open end of the pipe segment. Using the tool from the **Pipe Insulation** panel, you can add insulation cover to a pipe segment. To do so, choose the **Add Insulation** tool; the **Add Pipe Insulation** dialog box will be displayed. In this dialog box, select the type of insulation from the **Insulation Type** drop-down list and then specify a thickness value in the **Thickness** edit box. Next, choose the **Edit Type** button next to the **Insulation Type** drop-down list; the **Type Properties** dialog box will be displayed. You can use this dialog box to edit the type of insulation applied to the pipe. In the **Type Properties** dialog box, click in the **Value** field corresponding to the **Material** parameter and then choose the browse button; the **Material Browser** dialog box will be displayed. In this dialog box, specify the material to be used for insulation and then choose the **OK** button; the **Material Browser** dialog box will be closed.

In the **Type Properties** dialog box, you can also edit other type properties of the insulation such as its keynote, model, manufacturer, cost, and so on. After modifying the parameters, choose **OK** to close the **Type Properties** dialog box. Similarly, choose the **OK** button to close the **Add Pipe Insulation** dialog box; the insulation cover will be added to the pipe segment. Next, you can choose the **Edit Insulation** tool from the **Pipe Insulation** panel to modify the insulation added. Also, you can choose the **Remove Insulation** tool from the **Pipe Insulation** panel to remove the pipe insulation from the pipe segment. Next, you can modify the instance properties of the selected pipe segment from the **Properties** palette. For example, you can modify various parameters such as **Horizontal Justification, Vertical Justification, Reference Level, Offset, System Type, Diameter, Pipe Segment,** and so on in this palette. After specifying various instance parameters, choose **Modify** from the **Select** panel to exit the modification process.

Placing Fittings

After placing the pipe, you can add various fittings to it. The fittings that you can add to a pipe include elbows, tees, wyes, crosses, unions and other types of fittings. Some of the fittings can be placed at endpoints of the pipe segment or directly at a point along the length of the pipe segment. To add a pipe fitting to the pipe segment, choose the **Pipe Fittings** tool from the **Plumbing & Piping** panel of the **Systems** tab; the **Modify | Place Pipe Fittings** contextual tab will be displayed. In the **Level** drop-down list of the **Options Bar**, select the level to which the pipe fitting will be associated. Also, you can select the **Rotate after placement** check box if you want the pipe fitting be rotated at the time of its placement.

Next, in the **Properties** palette, select a type for the fittings from the **Type Selector** drop-down list. Also, in the **Properties** palette, you can specify various instance properties of the pipe fitting such as **Offset, Insulation Thickness, Nominal Radius,** and more. After specifying the instance properties of the fitting, place the cursor at the end of the pipe fitting or at the desired location along the pipe. Notice that the preview of the fitting will be displayed with the cursor. For example, if you select the **M_Pipe Elbow : Standard** type from the **Type Selector** drop-down list, the preview of the selected type will be displayed with the cursor in the drawing area.

As you move the cursor and place it at the endpoint of the pipe, the elbow will snap to the end of the pipe and will resize according to the diameter of the pipe. Click when the elbow snaps to the endpoint; the elbow will be placed and connected to the pipe segment, as shown in Figure 7-26.

Now, choose **Modify** from the **Select** panel of the **Modify | Place Pipe Fittings** contextual tab to exit the **Pipe Fittings** tool. You can now modify the properties and connection of the pipe fitting. To do so, select the added fitting in the drawing; the **Modify | Pipe Fittings** tab will be displayed and also instance properties related to the fittings will be displayed in the **Properties** palette. In the **Modify | Pipe Fittings** tab, you can choose the tools from the **Layout** panel to connect the pipe fittings with other pipe segments. In the **Edit** panel, you can use various tools to modify the slope, justification, and end cap of the pipe fitting. And, in the **Pipe Insulation** panel, you can use various tools to add an insulation to the pipe fitting.

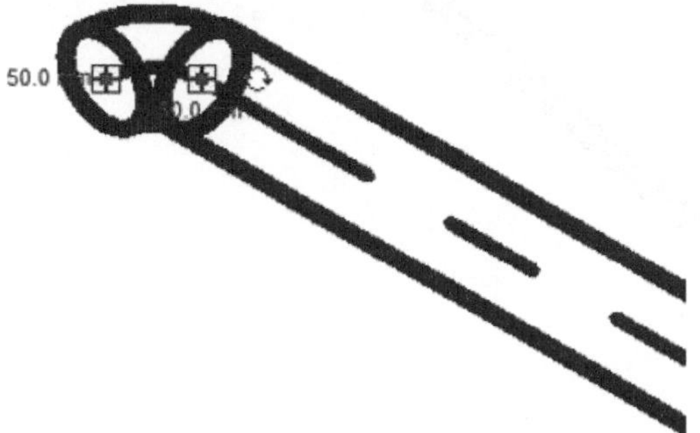

Figure 7-26 *The elbow placed at the end of the pipe segment*

Next, in the **Option Bar**, you can select an option from the **Diameter** drop-down list to modify the diameter of the pipe fixture. Also, you can select or specify an option in the **Offset** edit box to modify the existing offset value of the pipe fixture. In the **Properties** palette, you can modify various instance properties of the selected pipe fitting. Next, choose **Modify** from the **Select** panel to exit the modification.

Placing Pipe Accessories

Similar to placing pipe fittings, you can add pipe accessories to the pipe segment. The pipe accessories include valves, connectors, venturi flow meter, pressure gauge, temperature gauge, air separator, and so on. The families of pipe accessories can be loaded from the **Accessories** and the **Valves** folders which are located at **US Imperial > Pipe** folder location (for Metric **US Metric > Pipe** folder location) by using the **Load Family** tool from the **Load from Library** panel in the **Insert** tab. After loading the required families, choose the **Pipe Accessories** tool from the **Plumbing & Piping** panel of the **Systems** tab. On doing so, the **Modify | Place Pipe Accessory** tab will be displayed. In the **Options Bar**, select the desired level from the **Level** drop-down list and then in the **Properties** palette, select a type of accessory from the **Type Selector** drop-down list. For example, you can select the **Double Check Valve - 2.5-10 Inch** type (for Metric **Double Check Valve - 65-250mm)** from the **Type Selector** drop-down list and then in the **Properties** palette, specify the instance properties of the accessory such as **Pressure Drop, Flow, Loss Method**, and more. After specifying the instance properties, move the cursor in the drawing area and place it over the pipe at a location where you want to add the accessory. As you move the cursor, you will notice that the preview of the selected type of accessory will be displayed with it. Place the cursor and click when it snaps to the pipe at the desired location; the pipe accessory will be placed, as shown in Figure 7-27. Choose **Modify** from the **Select** panel of the **Modify | Place Pipe Accessory** tab to exit the tool.

After placing the accessory, you can select it and modify its properties and connections to the pipe. On selecting the pipe accessory, its various controls will be displayed, as shown in Figure 7-28. You can use these controls to rotate and flip the accessory to the desired direction. Also, you can use the controls to add pipe segments to the inlet and outlet connectors of the accessory, if required.

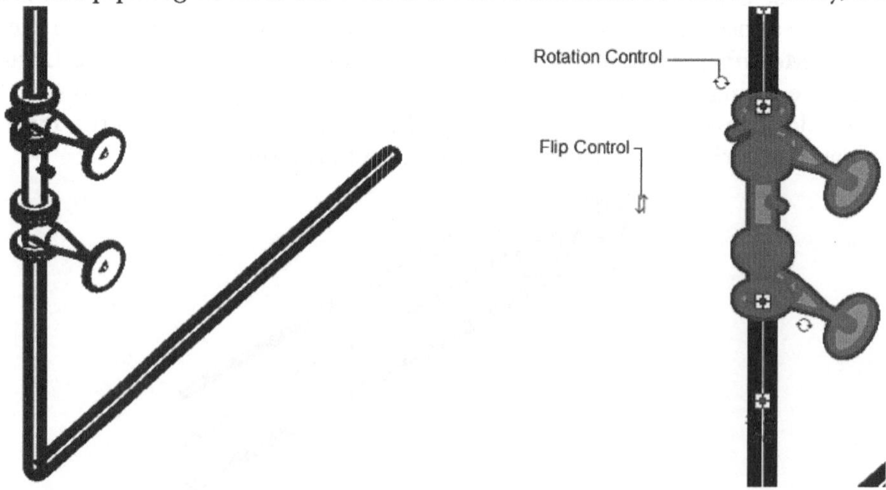

Figure 7-27 *The* ***Double Check Valve - 2.5-10 Inch*** *type pipe accessory placed at the pipe*

Figure 7-28 *The various controls of the selected pipe accessory*

TUTORIAL

General instructions for downloading tutorial files:

1. Download the *c07_rmp_2017_tut.zip* file for this tutorial from http://www.cadcim.com. The path of the file is as follows: *Textbooks > Civil/GIS > Revit MEP > Exploring Autodesk Revit 2017 for MEP.*

2. Now, save and extract the downloaded folder at the following location: *C:\rmp_2017*

Note

The default unit system used in the tutorials is Imperial.

Tutorial 1 Office-Space

In this tutorial, you will create a plumbing system for the *Office-Space* project with the following parameters and project specifications: **(Expected time: 45 min)**

1. File name to be used:
   For Imperial *c07_Office-Space_tut1.rvt*
   For Metric *M_c07_Office-Space_tut1.rvt*
2. File name to be assigned:
   For Imperial *c07_Office-Space_tut1a.rvt*
   For Metric *M_c07_Office-Space_tut1a.rvt*

The following steps are required to complete this tutorial:

a. Open the project file
b. Load the plumbing component families.
c. Configure the piping systems.
d. Adding the plumbing fixtures.
e. Set the view range.
f. Place the floor drain.
g. Create the sanitary system.
h. View the plumbing system in 3D.
i. Save the project by using the **Save As** tool.
   For Imperial *c07_Office-Space_tut1a.rvt*
   For Metric *M_c07_Office-Space_tut1a.rvt*
j. Close the project by using the **Close** tool.

Opening a Project

1. Choose **Open > Project** from **Application Menu**; the **Open** dialog box is displayed.

2. In the **Open** dialog box, browse to *C:\rmp_2017\c07_rmp_2017_tut* and select the desired file.
   For Imperial *c07_Office-Space_tut1*
   For Metric *M_c07_Office-Space_tut1*

3. Now, choose **Open**; the selected file opens in the Revit interface.

Loading the Plumbing Component Families

1. Choose the **Load Family** tool from the **Load from Library** panel of the **Insert** tab; the **Load Family** dialog box is displayed.

2. In this dialog box, browse to **US Imperial > Plumbing > MEP > Fixtures > Urinals** folder and then select the **Urinal - Wall Hung.rfa** file and choose **Open**; the selected family is loaded in the current project. For the Metric system, browse to **US Metric > Plumbing > MEP > Fixtures > Urinals** folder and then select the **M_Urinal - Wall Hung.rfa** file.

3. Repeat the procedure followed in steps 1 and 2 and select the other family files required for this tutorial from their respective folders. Refer to the table given next for the name of the files and their folder location.

Name of the Family Catagory(ies)	Folder Location (Imperial)	Folder Location (Metric)
Water Closet - Flush Valve - Floor Mounted (Imperial) M_Water Closet - Flush Valve - Floor Mounted (Metric)	US Imperial > Plumbing > MEP > Fixtures > Water Closets	US Metric > Plumbing > MEP > Fixtures > Water Closets
Tee - PVC - Sch 40 (Imperial) M_Tee - PVC - Sch 40 (Metric)	US Imperial > Pipe > Fittings > PVC > Sch 40 > Socket-Type	US Metric > Pipe > Fittings > PVC > Sch 40 > Socket-Type
Bend - PVC - Sch 40 - DWV (Imperial) M_Bend - PVC - Sch 40 - DWV (Metric)	US Imperial > Pipe > Fittings > PVC > Sch 40 > Socket-Type > DWV	US Metric > Pipe > Fittings > PVC > Sch 40 > Socket-Type > DWV

Note

*In case, the families are already present in the project, the **Family Already Exists** dialog box is displayed. Choose the **Overwrite the existing version and its parameter values** option; the family is loaded.*

Configuring the Piping Systems

1. In the **Project Browser**, double-click on the **PVC-DWV** sub-node from **Families > Pipes > Pipe Types** node; the **Type Properties** dialog box is displayed.

2. In this dialog box, choose the **Duplicate** button; the **Name** dialog box is displayed.

3. In this dialog box, type the **Sanitary-PVC** text in the **Name** edit box.

4. Choose **OK**; the **Name** dialog box is closed and the **Type Properties** dialog box appears.

5. In the **Type Properties** dialog box, ensure that the **Sanitary-PVC** option is selected in the **Type** drop-down list and then choose the **Edit** button displayed in the **Value** field corresponding to the **Routing Preferences** parameter; the **Routing Preferences** dialog box is displayed.

6. In this dialog box, click in the desired field and select the required options from the drop-down list displayed. The options to be selected are given in Figure 7-29.

7. After assigning the specified values in the **Routing Preferences** dialog box, choose **OK** to close it.

8. In the **Type Properties** dialog box, again choose the **Duplicate** button; the **Name** dialog box is displayed. In this dialog box, type **Sanitary Vent- PVC** in the **Name** edit box and choose **OK**; the **Name** dialog box is closed.

9. In the **Type Properties** dialog box, ensure that the **Sanitary Vent-PVC** option is selected by default and then choose the **Edit** button corresponding to the **Routing Preference** parameter; the **Routing Preferences** dialog box is displayed.

10. In this dialog box, choose the **Load Family** button; the **Load Family** dialog box is displayed.

11. In the **Load Family** dialog box, browse to **US Imperial > Pipe > Fittings > PVC > Sch 40 > Socket-Type > DWV** folder and then select the **Tee Vent - PVC - Sch 40 - DWV** family from the list. For Metric system, browse to **US Metric > Pipe > Fittings > PVC > Sch 40 > Socket-Type > DWV** folder and then select the **M_Tee Vent - PVC - Sch 40 - DWV** family from the list. Choose **Open**; the **Load Family** dialog box is closed. In the **Routing Preferences** dialog box, click in the **Content** field for **Junction** and select the **Tee-Vent PVC - Sch 40 - DWV: Standard** option for Imperial and **M_Tee Vent - PVC - Sch 40 - DWV : Standard** for Metric from the drop-down list displayed.

12. Next, in the **Routing Preferences** dialog box, keep the settings for the other values unchanged, refer to Figure 7-29 and then choose the **OK** button; the **Routing Preferences** dialog box is closed.

13. In **Type Properties** dialog box, choose **OK** to close it.

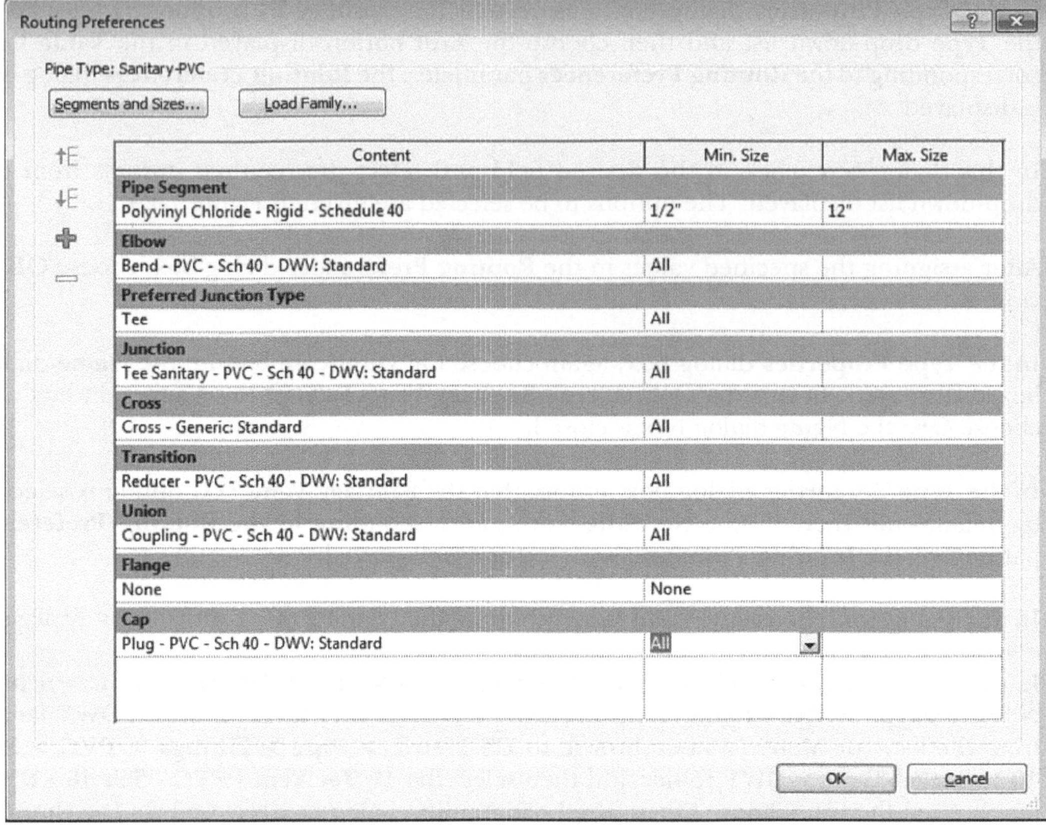

*Figure 7-29 The **Routing Preferences** dialog box*

Adding the Plumbing Fixtures

In this section, you need to add 1 toilet, 2 urinals, 2 sinks, and a floor drain to the floor plan of the Office-Space project.

1. Choose the **Plumbing Fixture** tool from the **Plumbing & Piping** panel of the **Systems** tab; the **Modify | Place Plumbing Fixture** contextual tab is displayed. In this tab, choose the **Tag on Placement** button from the **Tag** panel, if it is not chosen by default. This enables the placing of the tag along with the fixture.

2. In the **Properties** palette, select the **Water Closet-Flush Valve -Floor Mounted Private-1.6 gpf** option from the **Type Selector** drop-down list. For Metric system, select **M_Water Closet-Flush Valve -Floor Mounted Private-6.1 Lpf**.

3. In the **Options Bar**, select the **Rotate after placement** check box.

4. Next, zoom in the toilet area in the south. Now, move the cursor inside the toilet area and click at the location shown in Figure 7-30.

5. Next, in the **Options Bar**, enter **-90** in the **Angle** edit box and press ENTER; the fixture is placed at the specified location, as shown in Figure 7-31.

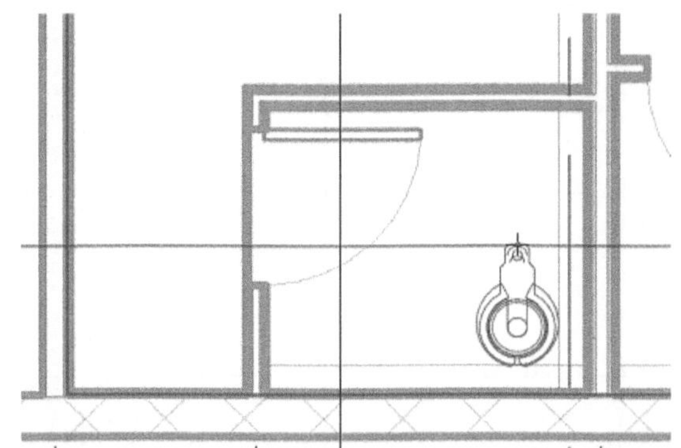

Figure 7-30 *The fixture placed at the specified location*

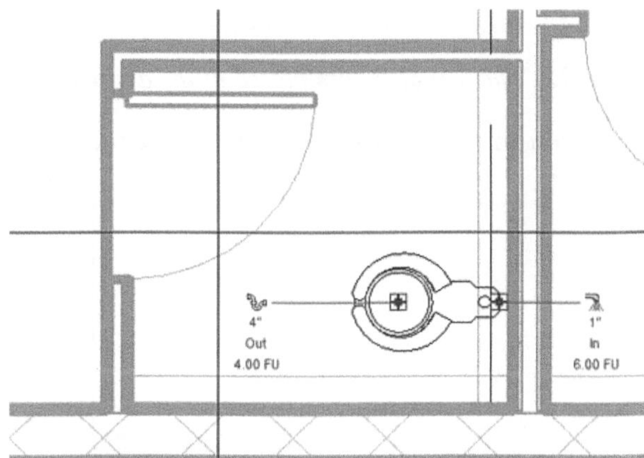

Figure 7-31 *The fixture placed after rotation*

6. Choose **Modify** from the **Select** panel to exit the **Plumbing Fixture** tool.

7. Next, choose the **Plumbing Fixture** tool from the **Plumbing & Piping** panel of the **Systems** tab; the **Modify | Place Plumbing Fixture** contextual tab is displayed.

8. In the **Properties** palette, select the **Urinal Wall Hung 3/4" Flush Valve** from the **Type Selector** drop-down list. Also, click in the value field of the **Elevation** parameter and type **1'6"**. For Metric system, select the **Urinal Wall Hung 20 mm Flush Valve** from the **Type Selector** drop-down list. Then, in the **Properties** palette, click in the value field of the **Elevation** parameter and type **450**.

9. In the **Properties** palette, ensure that the **Level 1** option is specified corresponding to the **Schedule Level** parameter.

10. Now, in the **Placement** panel of the **Modify | Place Plumbing Fixture** contextual tab, ensure that the **Place on Vertical Face** button is chosen. Next, place the cursor at a location in the toilet area, as shown in Figure 7-32. Click to place the fixture at the specified location.

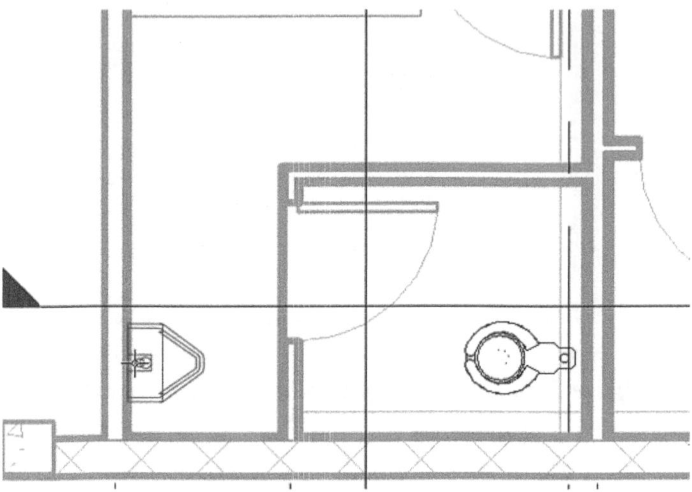

***Figure 7-32** The urinal fixture placed at the desired location*

11. Repeat the procedure given in step 10 to place another urinal of the same type, as shown in Figure 7-33.

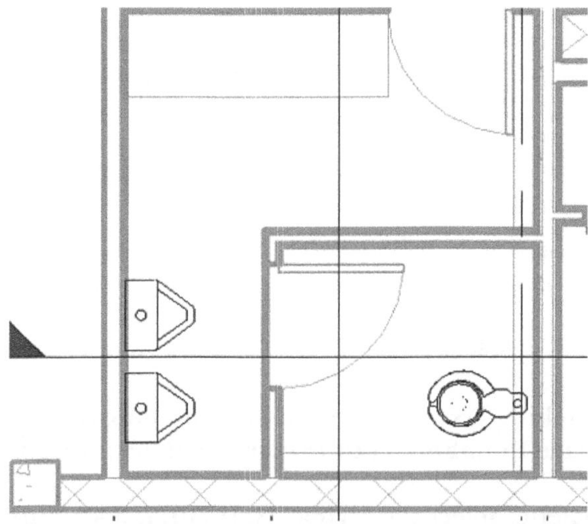

***Figure 7-33** The second urinal fixture placed at the specified location*

12. After placing the urinals, choose the **Modify** tool to exit the selection.

13. Choose the **Plumbing Fixture** tool from the **Plumbing & Piping** panel of the **Systems** tab; the **Modify | Place Plumbing Fixture** contextual tab is displayed.

14. In the **Properties** palette, select the **Sink-Island-Single 18"x18"-Private** type from the **Type Selector** drop-down list. For Metric system, select the **M_Sink-Island-Single 455 x455mm-Private** type.

15. Now, choose the **Place on Face** tool from the **Placement** panel of the **Modify | Place Plumbing Fixture** contextual tab.

16. Move the cursor at the face of the slab and click, refer to Figure 7-34; the sink is placed.

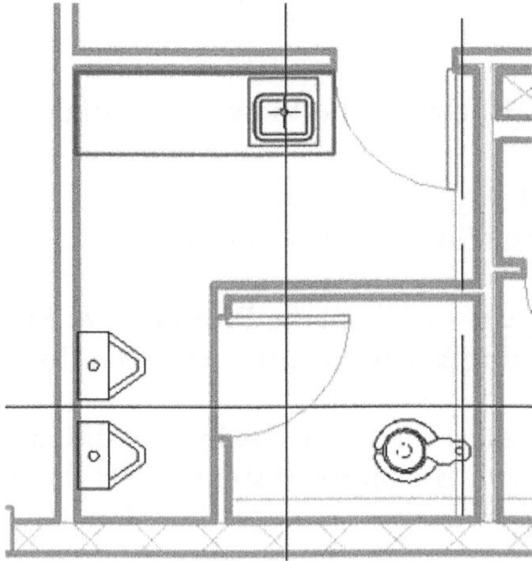

Figure 7-34 *The preview of the sink fixture displayed*

17. Add one more sink as done in previous steps. For placing the sink, refer to Figure 7-35.

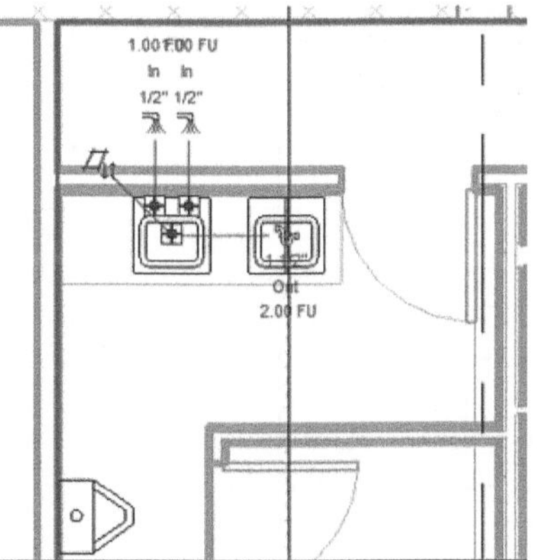

Figure 7-35 *The second sink fixture placed*

18. Choose **Modify** from the **Select** panel of the **Modify | Place Plumbing Fixture** contextual tab.

Setting the View Range

In this section, you will set the view range of the floor plan view.

1. In the **Properties** palette, choose the **Edit** button corresponding to the **View Range** parameter; the **View Range** dialog box is displayed.

2. In the **Primary Range** area of this dialog box, ensure that the **Associated Level (Level1)** option is selected in the **Bottom** drop-down list and enter **-5' (-1500 mm)** in the **Offset** edit box displayed next to it.

3. In the **View Depth** area of this dialog box, ensure that the **Associated Level (Level1)** option is selected in the **Level** drop-down list and then enter **-5' (-1500 mm)** in the **Offset** edit box displayed next to it.

4. Choose **Apply** and then **OK** to close the **View Range** dialog box.

Placing the Floor Drain

In this section, you will place the floor drain in the view.

1. Choose the **Plumbing Fixture** tool from the **Plumbing & Piping** panel of the **Systems** tab; the **Modify | Place Plumbing Fixture** contextual tab is displayed.

2. In the **Properties** palette, select the **Floor Drain - Round: 5" Strainer - 2" Drain** from the **Type Selector** drop-down list. For Metric system, select the **Floor Drain - Round: 125mm Strainer - 50mm Drain** option.

3. Choose the **Place on Face** tool from the **Placement** panel and then move the cursor to the location shown in Figure 7-36, and click; the floor drain is placed.

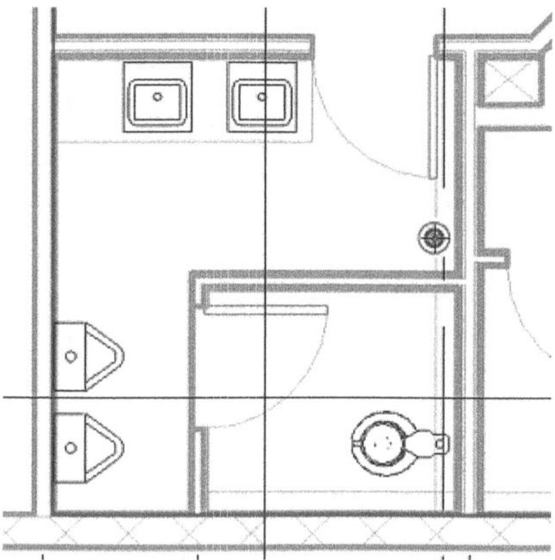

Figure 7-36 *The location of the floor drain*

4. Now, choose the **Modify** button from the **Select** panel to exit the **Plumbing Fixture** tool.

Creating the Sanitary System

1. Choose the **Analyze** tab and then choose the **Show Disconnects** button from the **Check Systems** panel; the **Show Disconnects Options** dialog box is displayed.

2. In this dialog box, select the **Pipe** check box and choose the **OK** button; the **Show Disconnects Options** dialog box is closed and all the open connectors in the fixtures are displayed as warning symbols.

3. Choose the **Visual Style** button in the **View Control Bar** and then choose the **Wireframe** option from the flyout displayed.

4. Choose the **Mechanical Settings** button from the **Plumbing & Piping** panel of the **Systems** tab; the **Mechanical Settings** dialog box is displayed.

5. In the left-pane of this dialog box, choose **Pipe Settings > Conversions**; the right-pane displays various properties related to the pipe settings, refer to Figure 7-37.

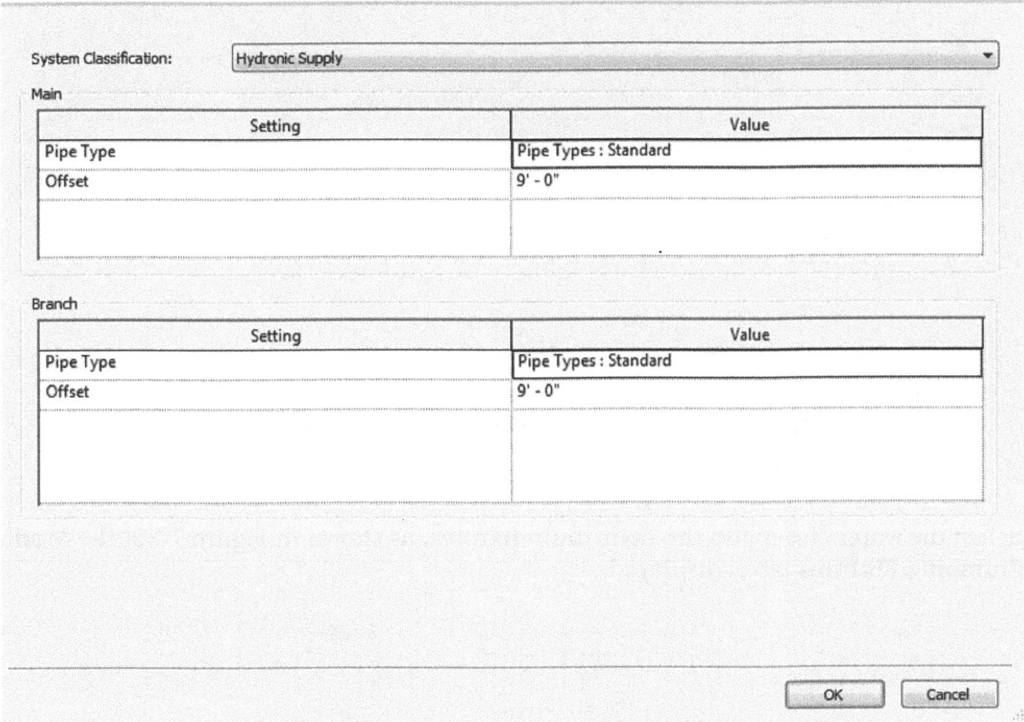

Figure 7-37 *Various properties displayed related to pipe settings*

6. In the right panel, select the **Sanitary** option from the **System Classification** drop-down list.

7. In the **Main** area, click in the **Value** field corresponding to the **Pipe Type** parameter and select the **Pipe Types : PVC - DWV** option from the drop-down list displayed.

8. Specify the other settings in the **Main** and **Branch** areas, as shown in Figure 7-38. For Metric system, specify **-305** for the **Offset** parameters.

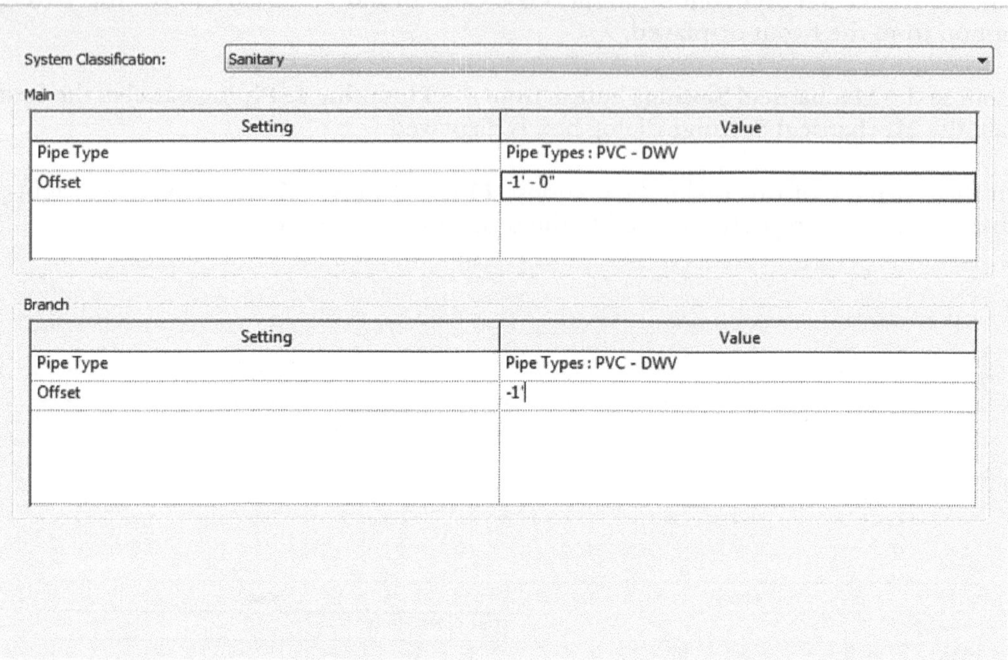

***Figure 7-38** The pipe settings for the **Sanitary** system*

9. Choose **OK**; the **Mechanical Settings** dialog box is closed.

10. Select the water closet and the floor drain fixtures, as shown in Figure 7-39; the **Modify | Plumbing Fixtures** tab is displayed.

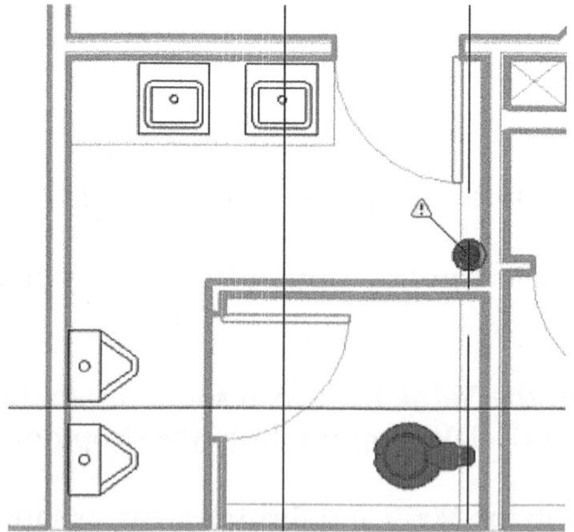

***Figure 7-39** The floor drain and the water closet fixtures selected*

11. In the **Create Systems** panel, choose the **Piping** tool; the **Create Piping System** dialog box is displayed.

12. In this dialog box, ensure that the **Sanitary** option is selected in the **System** type drop-down list.

13. In the **System name** edit box, type **Drainage System -Toilet 1** and choose **OK**; the fixtures in the system are bounded in a rectangular box, as shown in Figure 7-40.

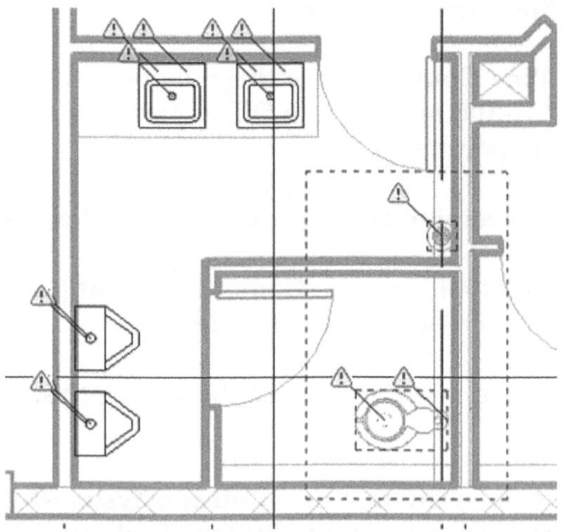

Figure 7-40 *The fixtures in the system bounded in a rectangular box*

14. Choose the **Generate Layout** tool from the **Layout** panel; the **Generate Layout** contextual tab is displayed.

15. In the **Options Bar**, ensure that the **Network** option is selected in the **Solution Type** drop-down list and then choose the **Next Solution** button, "**>**"; the text **2 of 5** is displayed before it and a solution is displayed in the drawing, as shown in Figure 7-41.

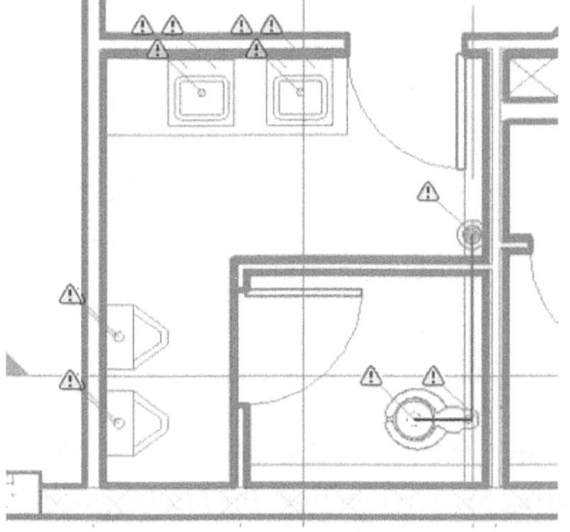

Figure 7-41 *The layout solution for the system*

16. In the **Options Bar**, choose the **Settings** button; the **Pipe Conversion Settings** dialog box is displayed.

17. In the left pane of this dialog box, ensure that the **Main** option is selected and then in the right pane, enter **-1'** (**-305 mm**) in the **Offset** parameter. Next, select the **Pipe Types: PVC - DWV** option in the **Pipe Type** parameter.

18. In the left pane of the **Pipe Conversion Settings** dialog box, select the **Branch** option. In the right pane, enter **-1'** (**-305 mm**) for the **Offset** parameter and select **Pipe Types: PVC - DWV** for the **Pipe Type** parameter.

19. Choose **OK**; the **Pipe Conversion Settings** dialog box is closed.

20. Choose the **Finish Layout** tool from the **Generate Layout** panel of the **Generate Layout** tab; the pipe system is created between the fixtures.

21. Select the floor drain fixture and then choose the **Piping Systems** tab; the options in this tab are displayed.

22. In the **Piping Systems** tab, ensure that the **Drainage System-Toilet 1** option is selected in the **System Selector** drop-down list in the **System Tools** panel and then choose the **Edit System** tool; the **Edit Piping System** contextual tab is displayed.

23. In this tab, ensure that the **Add to System** button is chosen in the **Edit Piping System** panel and then select the two urinals and sinks, refer to Figure 7-42.

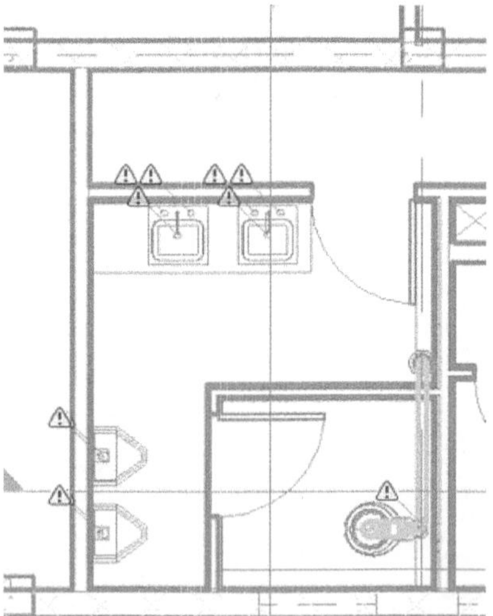

Figure 7-42 *The two urnials and sinks selected*

24. Choose the **Finish Editing System** tool from the **Mode** panel; the urinals and the sinks are added to the system.

25. Next, select any of the two urinals added to the system and then choose the **Generate Layout** tool from the **Layout** panel of the **Modify | Plumbing Fixture** tab; the default layout is displayed in the drawing area.

26. In the **Options Bar**, ensure that the **Network** option is selected in the **Solution Type** drop-down list and the choose the **Next Solution** button four times; the text **5 of 5** is displayed before the button and the solution layout is displayed in the drawing area, as shown in Figure 7-43.

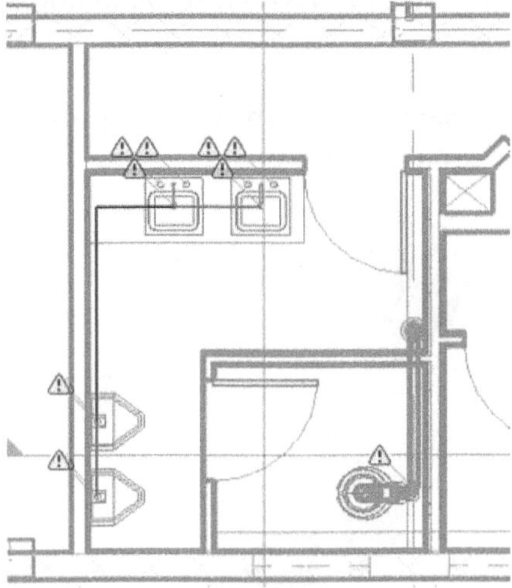

Figure 7-43 *The solution layout of the added fixture*

27. Choose the **Finish Layout** tool from the **Generate Layout** panel of the **Generate Layout** tab; the layout is generated.

Viewing the Plumbing System in 3D

In this section, you will display the 3D view of the plumbing system.

1. Choose the **Manage Links** tool from the **Manage Project** panel of the **Manage** tab; the **Manage Links** dialog box is displayed.

2. In this dialog box, select the **c07_ archi_ plumbing_tut1** option for Imperial (**M_c07_ archi_ plumbing_tut1** option for Metric) in the **Linked File** column and then choose the **Unload** button; the **Unload Link** dialog box is displayed.

3. Choose the **Yes** button; the dialog box is closed.

4. Choose **OK** in the **Manage Links** dialog box to close it.

5. Choose the **Default 3D View** tool from **View > Create > 3D View** drop-down; the 3D view of the system is displayed, as shown in Figure 7-44.

Saving the Project

In this section, you need to save the project and the settings using the **Save As** tool.

1. Choose **Save As > Project** from the **Application Menu**; the **Save As** dialog box is displayed.

2. In this dialog box, browse to *C:\rmp_2017\ c07* folder. Next, in the **File name** edit box, enter the text **c07_Office-Space_tut1** for Imperial or **M_c07_Office-Space_tut1** for Metric and then choose the **Options** button; the **File Save Options** dialog box is displayed.

3. Now, choose the **OK** button; the **File Save Options** dialog box is closed and the **Save As** dialog box appears.

4. In the dialog box, choose the **Save** button; the current project file is saved with the specified name and the **Save As** dialog box is closed.

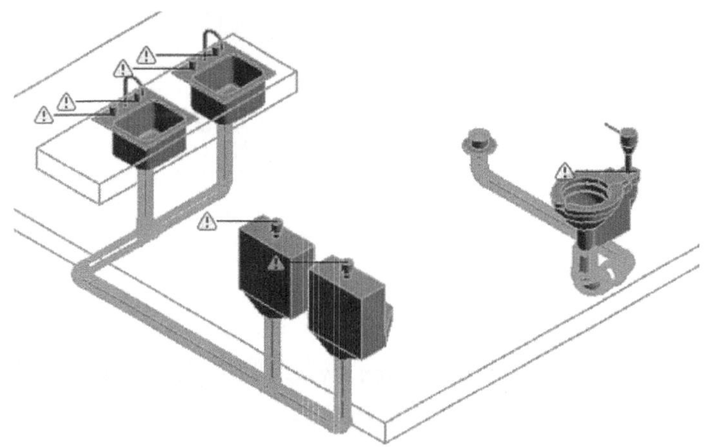

Figure 7-44 *The 3D view of the plumbing system*

Closing the Project

1. Choose the **Close** option from **Application Menu**; the file is closed and this completes the tutorial.

Self-Evaluation Test

Answer the following questions and then compare them to those given at the end of this chapter:

1. You can route the pipes in a plumbing system by using the__________ method.

2. The__________ parameter in the **Type Properties** dialog box specifies the material of faucet in the bathtub.
3. The __________ type parameter for a bathtub, specifies the water fixture unit for the cold water in it.

4. To create a new type of pipe, you need to expand **Families >__________> Pipe Types** node in the **Project Browser**.

5. You can load the family of pipe accessories from the __________ and the __________ folder located at **US Imperial (US Metric) > Pipe** folder.

6. A plumbing system is a network of pipes and drain fittings used to distribute water for drinking, washing, and heating, and to drain the waste out of the building. (T/F)
7. In Revit, you can create the plumbing system under any discipline. (T/F)
8. You can invoke the **Plumbing Fixture** tool from the **Architecture** tab. (T/F)
9. You cannot set the slope of the pipe in a plumbing system. (T/F)
10. All plumbing fixtures in a building have traps in their drains. (T/F)

Review Questions

Answer the following questions:

1. To view the existing fittings available in MEP, expand **Families >** __________node in the **Project Browser**.
2. The__________ parameter in the **Type Properties** dialog box for a bathtub specifies the water fixture unit for the hot water in it.
3. In the **New Temperature** dialog box, you can specify the viscous and weight properties of the fluid by using the **Viscosity** and __________edit boxes.
4. In the __________ dialog box, you can set the specifications for various entities in the pipe system such as the pipe segments, pipe fittings, and pipe junctions.
5. You can add insulation cover to a pipe segment using the __________ tool from the **Pipe Insulation** panel.
6. You cannot set the material of the pipes in the pipe system. (T/F)
7. A plumbing fixture comprises of one or more water outlets and a drain. (T/F)
8. In a plumbing system, it is not possible to supply both hot and cold water. (T/F)
9. You cannot convert a placeholder pipe into a solid pipe. (T/F)
10. You can inspect the flow of fluids in the pipe on creating a plumbing system. (T/F)

EXERCISE

Exercise 1 Community Center

Download the *c07_Community-Center_exer1.rvt* file for Imperial or *M_c07_Community-Center_exer1.rvt* file for Metric from *www.cadcim.com*. Create a sanitary system for the *Community-Center* project with the following parameters and project specifications. Figures 7-45 and 7-46 show sanitary system. **(Expected time: 1hr)**

1. Project View used for creating the plumbing system:
   Floor Plans > Mechanical > 1ST FLOOR- PLUMBING
2. Families to be used:
   For Imperial **Sink-Vanity Round 19"x19"**
   Toilet-Commercial-Wall-3D 15" Seat Height
   Urinal-Wall-3D
   For Metric **M_Sink-Vanity Round 482 x 482 mm**
   Toilet-Commercial-Wall-3D 380mm Seat Height
   Urinal-Wall-3D
3. Pipe Types: PVC
4. Offset Values:
   Main Pipe **-1'(-305mm)**
   Branch Pipe **-1'(-305mm)**
5. File name to be assigned:
   For Imperial *c07_Community-Center_exer1.rvt*
   For Metric *M_c07_Community-Center_exer1.rvt*

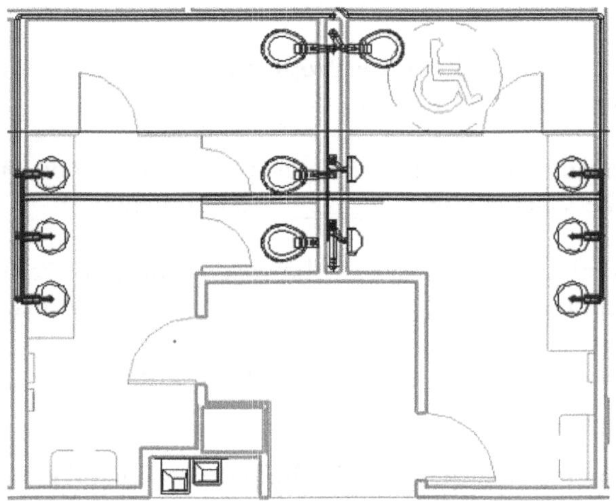

Figure 7-45 *Sanitary System*

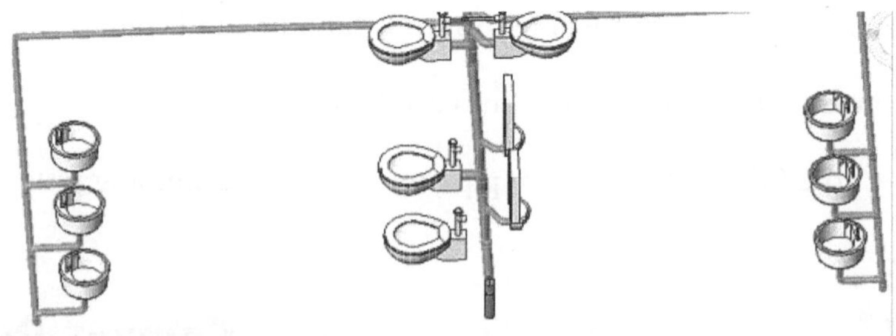

Figure 7-46 *The 3D view of a sanitary system*

Answers to Self-Evaluation Test

1. Auto Routing, **2. Faucet Material**, **3. WFU**, **4. Pipes**, **5. Accessories, Valves**, **6.** T, **7.** F, **8.** F, **9.** F, **10.** T

Chapter 8

Creating Fire Protection System

Learning Objectives

After completing this chapter, you will be able to:

- *Set up the fire protection system project*
- *Create space schedules*
- *Place sprinklers*

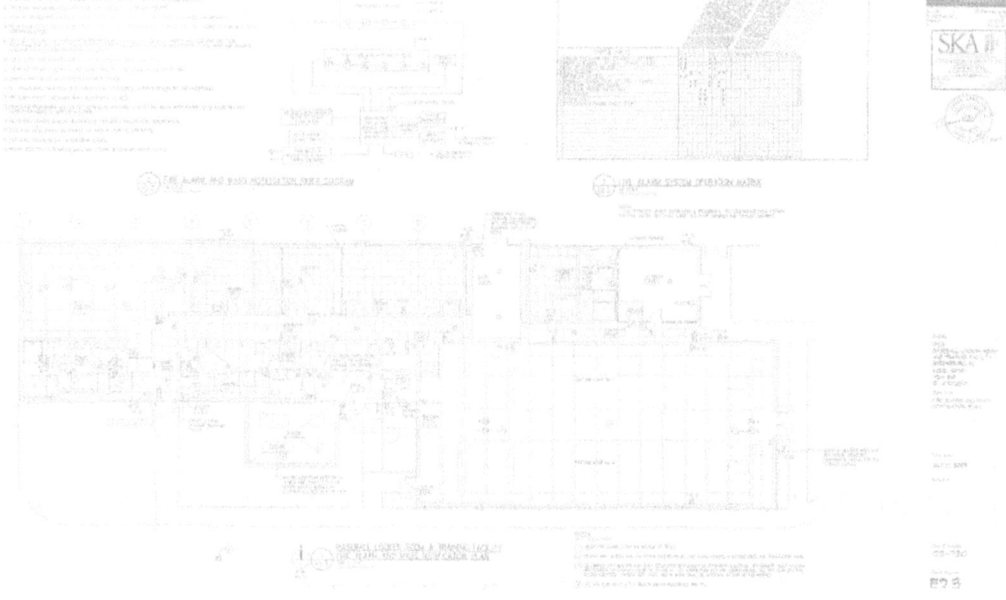

INTRODUCTION

Fire Protection or Fire Suppression is one of the major areas for a building design in a project. While designing a Fire Protection System for a project, the designer will use variety of methods and techniques. For example, for designing the schema of a fire protection plan, the designer should plan all the equipment required for the system. This will help in making the fire protection system more efficient and will also improve the coordination between other disciplines. A Fire Protection System consists of the following essential features: fire detection alarm, all types of fixed extinguishing systems, portable systems, private fire main and hydrants, pumping stations, smoke and heat evacuation system, centralized control system, auxiliary equipment, automotive and fire prevention system.

In this chapter, you will learn how to place fire protection equipment, create a wet fire protection system, create a dry protection system, and more.

FIRE PROTECTION SYSTEMS

A fire protection system comprises of sprinklers, pipes, and valves. In Revit, you can create a sprinkler system by placing sprinkler heads, such as upright and pendent as elements. These elements can be placed as hosted in the ceiling or as non-hosted elements. You can then connect the sprinklers with the pipes using the auto layout tools or by manually drawing the pipes. Further, you can check the fire protection system and its components for interferences with other components in a building. Figure 8-1 displays the 3d view of a fire protection system in an MEP project. The information stored within the system can be used for analysis or scheduling purposes. The various features and processes required for creating a fire protection system are discussed next.

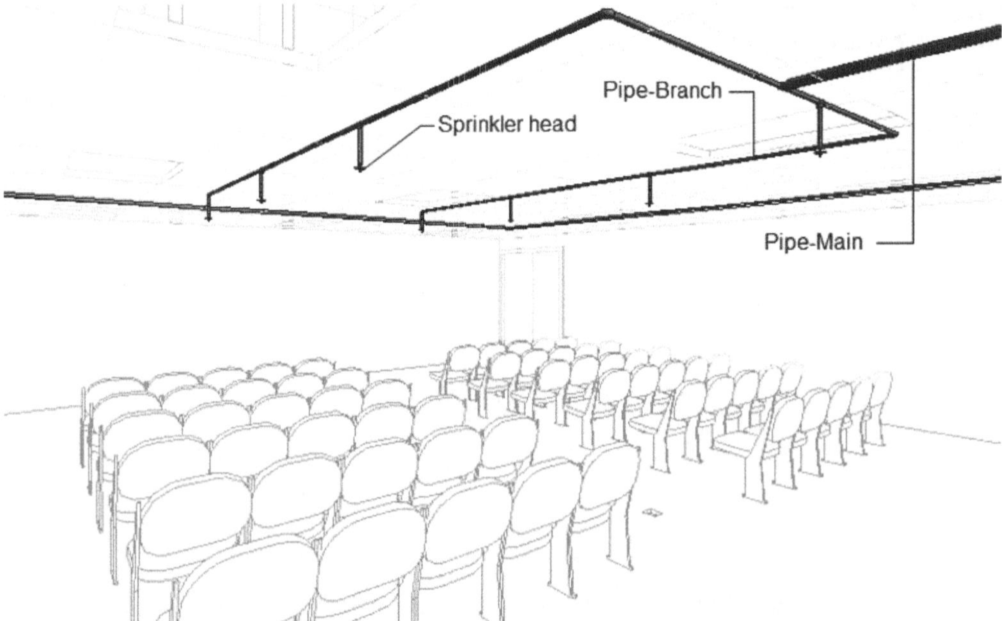

Figure 8-1 *Pictorial view of an auditorium with the Fire Protection System installed*

Sprinkler Libraries

A fire sprinkler, which is also called a sprinkler head, is an important component of a fire protection system. At the time of fire, the function of the sprinkler is to discharge water from its nozzle when a predetermined temperature has been exceeded. In an MEP project, you can use various sprinkler families for creating a fire protection system. To use the sprinkler families in a project, choose the **Load Family** tool from the **Load from Library** panel in the **Insert** tab; the **Load Family** dialog box will be displayed, as shown in Figure 8-2. In this dialog box, browse to **US Imperial > Fire Protection > Sprinklers** (for metric **US Metric > Fire Protection > Sprinklers)** folder and select any of the sprinkler families that you want to insert. Next, choose the **Open** button; the selected sprinkler will be loaded in the project view. You can use this sprinkler in the project.

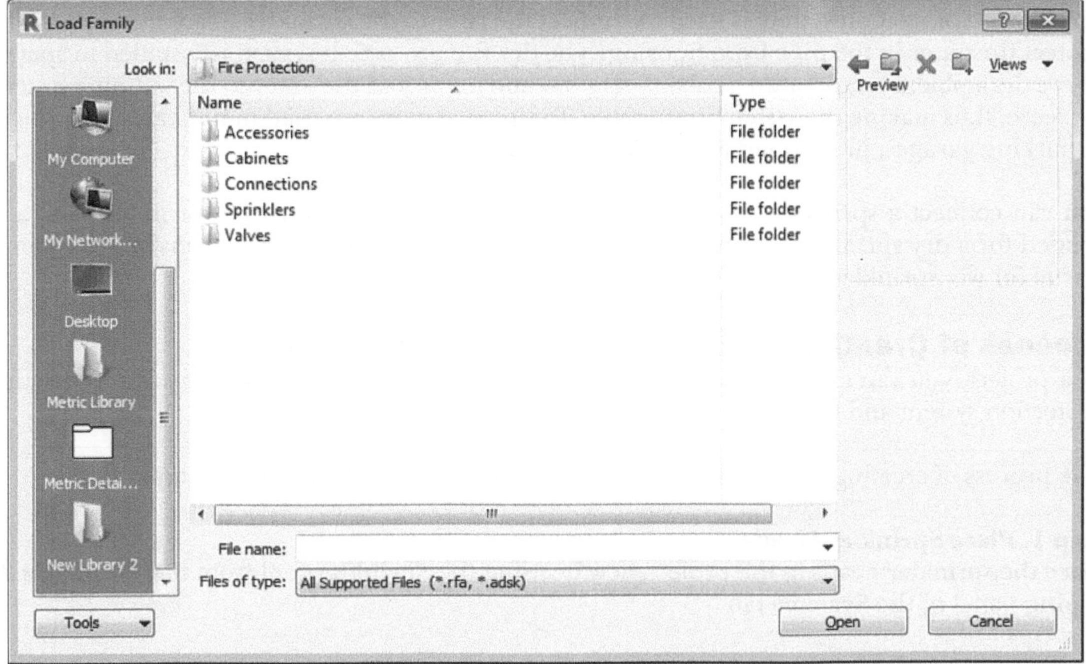

Figure 8-2 *The **Load Family** dialog box displaying various folders for fire protection equipments and accessories*

Piping Tools

In a fire protection system, the sprinklers are connected using pipes. You can connect the pipes manually to the sprinklers by using various tools in the **Plumbing &Piping** panel of the **Systems** tab, as shown in Figure 8-3. Alternatively, you can connect the sprinklers with the pipe by using the auto-routing feature of Revit 2017.

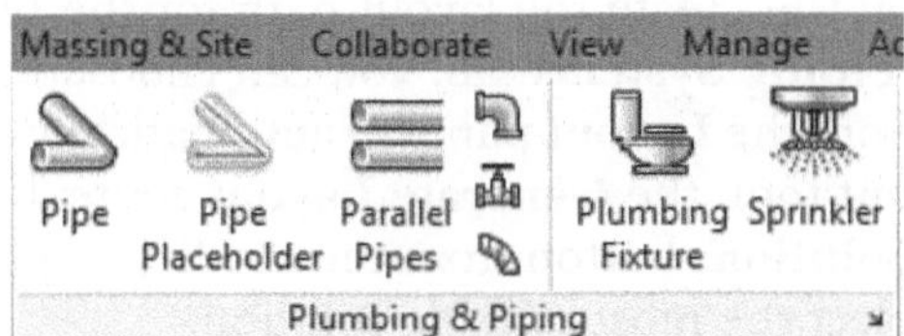

Figure 8-3 *The piping tools in the **Plumbing & Piping** panel*

Wet and Dry Fire Protection Systems

A wet pipe sprinkler system uses automatic sprinkler heads that discharge water immediately from sprinklers. At the time of fire the sprinklers get heated and opens to discharge water to mitigate the damage on the site. The wet fire protection system is used in a piping layout to connect fire risers with the sprinklers. A wet fire protection system comprises of automatic sprinklers and automatic alarm check valve. The automatic water sprinklers supply water under pressure through pipes when there is an alarm of fire. A dry pipe sprinkler system is sprinkler system employing automatic sprinklers that are attached to a piping system containing air or nitrogen under pressure, the release of which (as from the opening of a sprinkler) permits the water pressure to open a valve known as a dry pipe valve, and the water then flows into the piping system and out the opened sprinklers.

The dry fire protection system is used to connect the riser to the sprinkler head or standpipe to protect the water in the pipe from freezing. The dry fire protection system is installed in spaces where the ambient temperature remains very low and may cause the water in the wet pipe system to freeze, thus making the system inoperable. Dry pipe systems are used in unheated buildings, in parking garages, in canopies attached to heated buildings.

You can connect a sprinkler head to a wet or dry fire protection system. Sprinklers that are created for a dry sprinkler system can only be assigned to dry sprinkler systems and the same is true for wet sprinkler systems.

Process of Creating a Fire Protection System

In a project, you can create a fire protection system by associating sprinkler heads to the fire protection system and then inserting pipes which connect the system objects.

The process of creating a fire protection system is described in the following steps:

Step 1. Place Sprinkler Heads

Place the sprinkler heads in the project view by using the **Sprinkler** tool from the **Plumbing & Piping** panel of the **Systems** tab.

Step 2. Create the Sprinkler System

After placing sprinkler heads, you need to create the sprinkler system. To do so select the sprinklers that you have added and then invoke the **Piping** tool from the **Create Systems** panel of the **Modify | Sprinklers** tab. On choosing the **Piping** tool the **Create Piping System** dialog box will be displayed. In this dialog box, select the system type from the **System Type** drop-down list and then in the **System name** edit box enter the name of the system. Choose **OK**; the sprinkler system will be created and the **Modify| Piping System** contextual tab will be displayed.

Step 3. Create the Layout Path

After creating the system, you will create the layout path for the pipes to be connected to the sprinklers. In the **Modify | Piping Systems** tab, you can choose the **Generate Layout** tool or **Generate Placeholder** tool from the **Layout** panel to automatically route the piping system. On choosing the **Generate Layout** tool, the **Generate Layout** contextual tab will be displayed. In this tab, you can choose the **Solutions** button from the **Modify Layout** panel to browse through various solution types and select the most suitable solution.

Step 4. Save the Changes
After creating the layout path for pipes to be connected, choose the **Finish Layout** tool from the **Generate Layout** panel of the **Generate Layout** tab to save the changes and finalize the solution.

Guidelines for Creating a Fire Protection System
To create an efficient fire protection system, following are the recommended guidelines:

1. It is recommended to always place the sprinkler piping above the pendent type sprinkler heads and below the upright sprinkler heads. This is because a piping run in the opposite direction will not connect to the sprinkler as intended.

2. It is recommended to set an elevation for the piping head while using layout tools. This is because the layout tools will not find a solution for piping at an elevation above the upright heads or below the pendent sprinklers.

3. It is recommended not to define the size of sprinklers based on the flow information of individual sprinkler heads. This information is for scheduling, coordination, and analysis purposes only.

DESIGNING THE FIRE PROTECTION SYSTEM
In Revit, you can design both wet and dry fire protection systems. The designing of a fire protection system involves the following steps: setting up the fire protection system, creating the space schedule, placing sprinkler heads, and then connecting the sprinklers. To perform these steps, you need to create different views and pipe types, insert fittings, modify the pipes and fittings manually, create schedules, and size and tag the pipes. In the next sections, the procedure and the steps involved in designing a fire protection system are discussed next.

Setting Up a Fire Protection System Project
The setting up of a fire protection system, both wet and dry, involves various steps. First, you need to create a project view in which you can draw the layout of the fire protection system. Next, you need to create different pipe types and configure different conversion settings for the pipes that will be used to physically connect the sprinklers. Also, you need to sketch the supply pipe for the fire protection system. The steps involved in setting the fire protection system project are discussed next.

Creating the Project View
To create a project view, open the project file in which you want to create the fire protection system. Note that the project file will contain the architectural plan of the project. To create a project view for the fire protection system in the project file, expand **Views (Discipline) > Mechanical > HVAC > Floor Plans** node in the **Project Browser** and then right-click on the name of the plan view in which you want to create the fire protection system; a shortcut menu will be displayed. In the shortcut menu, choose **Duplicate View > Duplicate**; a copy of the view will be created and it will become the active view. The properties of the copied view will be based on the view selected. Next, to rename the created view, select it and then right-click; a shortcut menu will be displayed. In the shortcut menu, choose the **Rename** option; the **Rename View** dialog box will be displayed. In the **Name** edit box of the dialog box, enter the name of the view. For example, you can enter **1-Fire Protection** and choose **OK**; the **Rename View** dialog box will be closed and the selected view will be renamed.

Creating New Pipe Types

To create an efficient fire protection system, you need to create pipe types for both dry and wet fire protection systems. To create pipe types for the system, expand **Families > Pipes > Pipe Types** in the **Project Browser**, as shown in Figure 8-4.

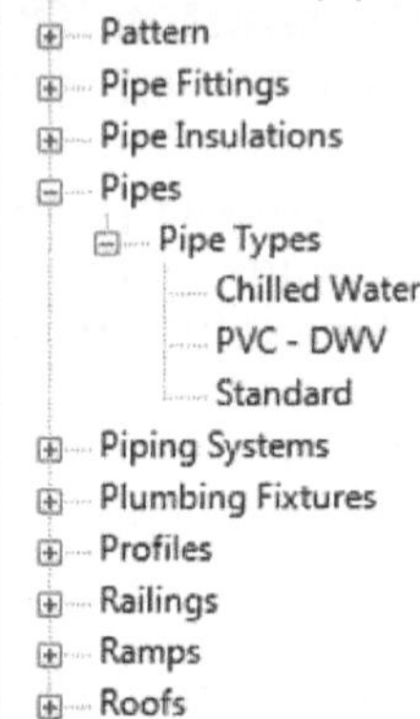

*Figure 8-4 The **Project Browser** displaying various pipe types*

Under the **Pipe Types** node, different pre-defined pipe types are displayed. To create new pipe types (dry and wet), select the **Standard** pipe type under the **Pipe Types** node and right-click; a shortcut menu will be displayed. In the shortcut menu, choose the **Duplicate** option; a copy of the **Standard** pipe type with the name **Standard 2** will be created below it. Double-click on **Standard 2**; the **Type Properties** dialog box will be displayed. In this dialog box, choose the **Duplicate** button; the **Name** dialog box will be displayed. In the **Name** edit box, enter **Fire Protection-Wet** and choose **OK**; the **Name** dialog box will be closed and the **Fire Protection-Wet** type will be created and displayed in the **Type** drop-down list in the **Type Properties** dialog box.

Next, to specify different specifications for the new pipe type, choose the **Edit** button displayed in the **Value** field corresponding to the **Routing Preferences** parameter; the **Routing Preferences** dialog box will be displayed. In the **Content** column of the dialog box, click on the drop-down list under the **Pipe Segment** head and select the material for the pipe segment of the new pipe type from the list displayed. For example, you can select the **Steel, Carbon - Schedule 40** option from the drop-down list for the **Fire Protection-Wet** pipe type, as shown in Figure 8-5. Now, choose the **OK** button; the **Routing Preference** dialog box will be closed and the desired specifications will be assigned to the new pipe type. Similarly, in the **Type Properties** dialog box, choose the **Duplicate** button to create the **Fire Protection-Dry** pipe type. Now, in the **Type Properties** dialog box, choose the **OK** button; the dialog box will be closed and the two pipe types namely **Fire Protection-Dry** and **Fire Protection-Wet** will be created and displayed under the **Pipe Types** node in the **Project Browser**.

Configuring the Pipe Conversion Settings

To configure the pipe, choose the **Mechanical Settings** button from the **Mechanical** panel in the **Systems** tab; the **Mechanical Settings** dialog box will be displayed. In this dialog box, ensure that the **Conversion** sub-node under the **Pipe Settings** node is selected in the left pane. The right pane of the dialog box will display various settings for the selected **Conversion** node. In the right pane, you can select an option from the **System Classification** drop-down list to specify the system for which the pipe will be configured. For example, you can select the **Fire Protection-Dry** or **Fire Protection-Wet** option for the dry or wet protection system, respectively. Next, to configure the main pipes for the selected system, you need to specify the **Pipe Type** and **Offset** settings in the **Main** area, as shown in Figure 8-6.

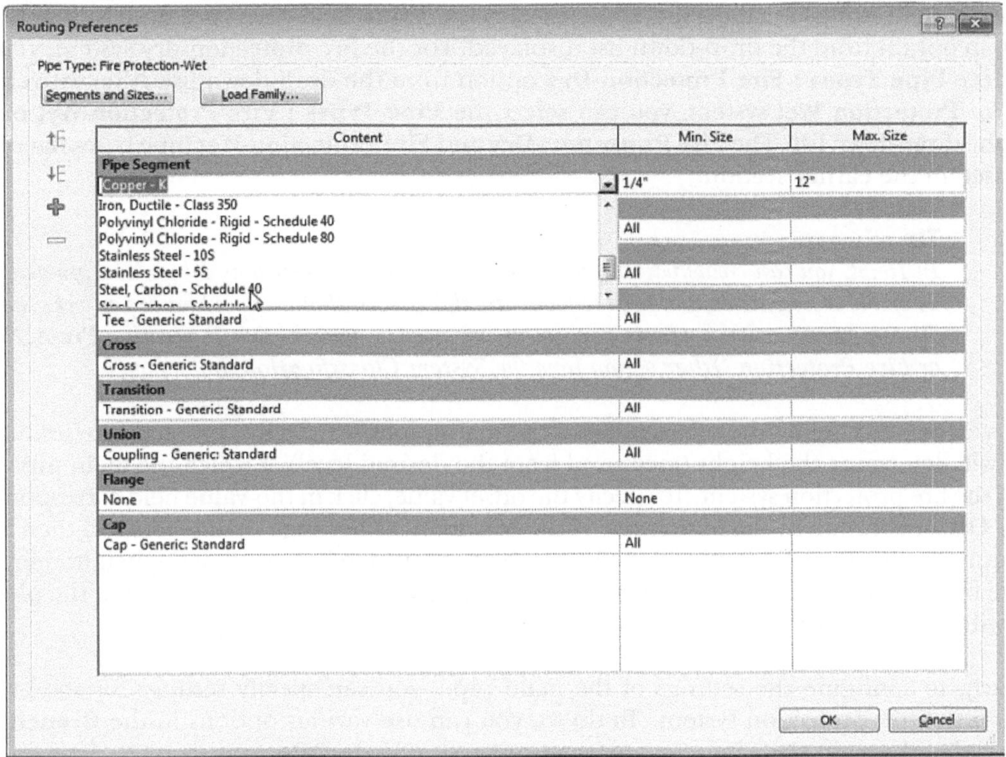

Figure 8-5 *Selecting the* ***Steel, Carbon - Schedule 40*** *option from the drop-down list in the* ***Routing Preferences*** *dialog box*

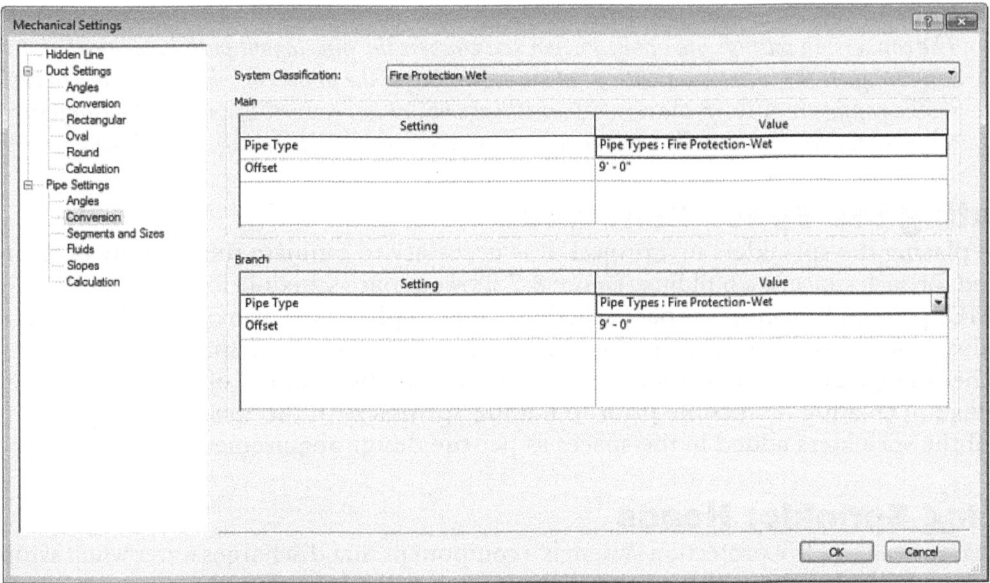

Figure 8-6 *The* ***Mechanical Settings*** *dialog box displaying various options for conversion settings of the pipe*

To specify the settings for the **Pipe Type**, click in the **Value** field corresponding to it and then select an option from the drop-down list displayed. For the fire protection-dry system, you can select the **Pipe Types : Fire Protection-Dry** option from the drop-down list. Alternatively, for the **Fire Protection Wet** system, you can select the **Pipe Types : Fire Protection-Wet** option from the drop-down list. The **Fire Protection-Dry** and **Fire Protection-Wet** pipe types have been discussed in the earlier section.

Tip

In Revit, you can create various other fire protection systems such as deluge and pre-action. To create these systems, you need to follow similar process that was used for dry or wet system. To create a pre-action fire protection system, you need to select the ***Fire Protection Pre-Action*** *or* ***Fire Protection Other*** *option from the* ***System Classification*** *drop-down list.*

Next, you need to define the offset value of the main pipes for the fire protection system. This value will determine the height (measured from the desired level) at which the main pipes will run in the fire protection system. To specify the offset value, click in the **Value** field corresponding to the **Offset** edit box in the **Main** area of the **Mechanical Settings** dialog box and then enter the desired value. By default, **9' - 0" (2750)** will be displayed in it. Note that the height reference for the fire protection system will run above the plenum level. As such the height of the plenum level will be the determining factor to specify the offset value for the pipes.

Similarly, to configure the settings of the main pipe, you can specify settings for the branch pipes of the fire protection system. To do so, you can use various options in the **Branch** area displayed in the right pane on selecting the **Conversion** node. After specifying various settings for the wet and dry pipe system, choose the **OK** button in the **Mechanical Settings** dialog box to apply the setting to the project and close the dialog box.

Note

The conversion settings are applied when you convert the pipe layout path to physical piping. You can configure the conversion settings at the beginning of the project or while doing it. However, you should configure or verify the conversion settings before you convert a layout path. Configuring the conversion settings is usually a one-time process unless you need to change them during your project.

Creating the Space Schedule

Before placing the sprinklers in a project, it is necessary to estimate the quantity of sprinklers required for each space in a building. Figure 8-7 shows a space schedule for fire protection system in an MEP project. By using the space schedule, you can place the sprinklers in the spaces as per the industry standards. To create a schedule for the estimation of the sprinkler, you can choose the **Schedule/Quantities** tool from the **Reports & Schedules** panel of the **Analyze** tab. The advantage of creating a schedule prior to adding sprinklers in the space is that you can keep track of the sprinklers added in the spaces as per the design requirement.

Placing Sprinkler Heads

A sprinkler head in a fire protection system is a component that discharges water when symptoms of fire have been detected, such as exceed in predetermined temperature. In an MEP project, sprinkler heads are available as hosted and non-hosted elements. The hosted sprinkler heads belong to face-based families. When you use these family types, you need to place them on a surface such as Wall, Ceiling, Slab, or a Soffit mounted. These surfaces can be a part of the linked architectural model or can be created as an envelope in the project file, whereas non-hosted sprinkler families are independent of surfaces and can be placed anywhere as per the project requirement. Note that the offset height parameter of the non-hosted sprinkler families must be set so that the heads can be located at proper elevation.

<Space Schedule-Fire Protection>

A	B	C	D	E
Number	Name	Level	Area	Sprinkler Quantity- Min. Required
101	CEO-Office	Level 1	156 SF	1.20
102	V.P. Marketing	Level 1	117 SF	0.90
103	Toilet-1	Level 1	70 SF	0.54
104	Rest Room	Level 1	97 SF	0.75
105	Cafeteria	Level 1	109 SF	0.84
106	Store	Level 1	84 SF	0.64
107	Purchase	Level 1	153 SF	1.18
108	International	Level 1	104 SF	0.80
109	H.R.	Level 1	130 SF	1.00
110	Central Area	Level 1	1015 SF	7.81
111	Quality	Level 1	160 SF	1.23
112	Open	Level 1	157 SF	1.21
113	Conference-2	Level 1	216 SF	1.66
114	Conference	Level 1	201 SF	1.55
115	Lounge	Level 1	844 SF	6.49
116	Meeting Room	Level 1	106 SF	0.81
117	Service	Level 1	84 SF	0.64
118	Shaft	Level 1	63 SF	0.49
119	Services	Level 1	75 SF	0.57
120	Accounts	Level 1	145 SF	1.11
121	Chase	Level 1	83 SF	0.64
122	Electrical	Level 1	139 SF	1.07

Figure 8-7 *The schedule displaying the quantity of sprinklers required for different spaces in a project*

Before placing sprinklers, you need to activate the desired floor plan or ceiling plan view of the fire protection system. To place the hosted sprinklers, it is recommended to open the ceiling plan view and then place them. You can place the non-hosted sprinklers in the floor plan view. Next, choose the **Sprinkler** tool from the **Plumbing & Piping** panel of the **Systems** tab; the **Modify | Place Sprinkler** contextual tab will be displayed. In this contextual tab, choose the **Load Family** tool from the **Mode** panel; the **Load Family** dialog box will be displayed. In this dialog box, to load the families of the sprinklers to be used in the fire protection system, browse to **US Imperial > Fire Protection > Sprinklers** (in Metric system, browse to **US Metric > Fire Protection > Sprinklers**) and select the desired family(ies) from the list displayed. From the list, you can select both hosted and non-hosted sprinklers as per the requirement of the system. After selecting the desired family(ies), choose **Open**; the **Load Family** dialog box will be closed and the selected family(ies) will be loaded in the current project.

Next, in the **Properties** palette, select the type of sprinkler from the **Type Selector** drop-down list. You can select either a hosted sprinkler type (such as **Sprinkler-Pendent-Hosted : 1/2"** (**M_Sprinkler-Pendent-Hosted : 15mm**)) or a non-hosted sprinkler type such as **Sprinkler-Dry-Upright : 1/2" Upright** (**M_Sprinkler-Dry-Upright : 15mm Upright**). Next, in the **Properties** palette, you can use various parameters to modify the instance properties of the sprinkler that you wish to add. The parameters in the **Properties** palette will differ for hosted and non-hosted sprinkler types.

After specifying various parameters in the **Properties** palette, you will now insert the sprinkler in the view. The method for placing a hosted and non-hosted sprinkler is different. Before placing the sprinkler, ensure that a hosted type is selected in the **Type Selector** drop-down list. You can place the sprinkler at the face of a surface such as wall or ceiling, at the vertical face of a wall, or in a workplane. The placement of the sprinklers depends on the type of hosted sprinkler selected in the **Type Selector** drop-down list. To place the sprinkler that will be hosted to a ceiling, choose the **Place on Face** button from the **Placement** panel in the **Modify | Place Sprinkler** contextual tab. Next, in the drawing area zoom to the ceiling and place the cursor in the ceiling tile; a preview of the sprinkler will be displayed. Click to place the sprinkler at the desired location, as shown in Figure 8-8. You can now click on other locations to place the sprinklers as per the design requirement. After placing the sprinklers, choose the **Modify** button from the **Select** panel to exit the tool.

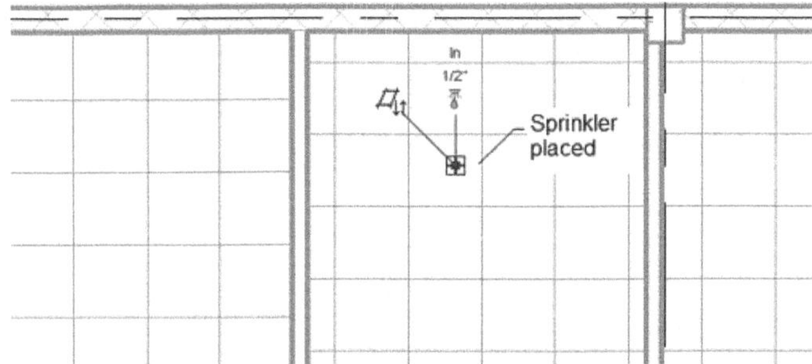

Figure 8-8 *The sprinkler placed in the project view*

Connecting the Sprinklers

After placing the sprinklers, now you need to connect them through a piping system. You can connect the pipes with sprinklers by either using the auto-routing method or by using the manual connection method.

To connect the sprinklers by using the auto-routing method, in the project view, select the sprinklers that you want connect with the pipes; the **Modify | Sprinklers** tab will be displayed. In this tab, choose the **Piping** tool from the **Create Systems** panel; the **Create Piping System** dialog box will be displayed, as shown in Figure 8-9.

Figure 8-9 *The* ***Create Piping System*** *dialog box*

In this dialog box, select the type of system from the **System type** drop-down list and then enter a name for the system in the **System name** edit box. Now, choose the **OK** button; the **Create Piping System** dialog box will be closed and the **Modify | Piping Systems** contextual tab will be displayed, as shown in Figure 8-10.

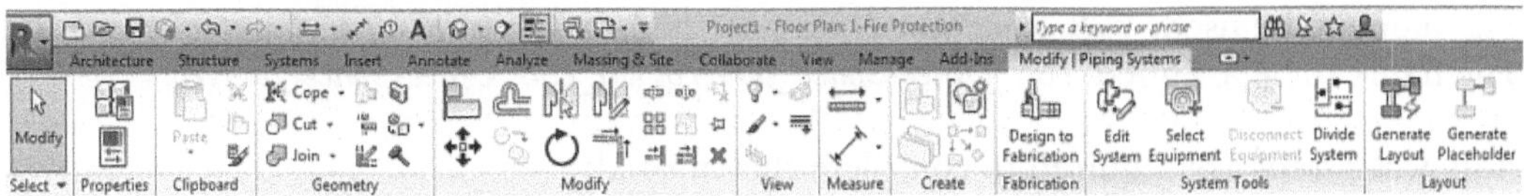

Figure 8-10 The Modify / Piping Systems contextual tab

From the **Layout** panel of this tab, choose the **Generate Layout** tool; the **Generate Layout** contextual tab will be displayed and also the sprinklers are connected with a default solution. In the **Options Bar**, select an option from the **Solution Type** drop-down list. You can select any of the three options from the drop-down list: **Network, Perimeter**, and **Intersections**. By default, the **Network** option will be selected in the drop-down list. Next to the **Solution Type** drop-down list, two buttons namely **Previous Solution** and **Next Solution,** are displayed. You can choose any of these buttons to display the solution of the pipe network in the drawing view. Next to the **Next Solution** button, choose the **Settings** button; the **Pipe Conversion Settings** dialog box will be displayed. You can use this dialog box to specify the pipe settings for the branch and main pipes in the pipe network. After specifying the options in the **Pipe Conversion Settings** dialog box, choose **OK**; the dialog box will be closed. In the **Generate Layout** tab, choose the **Finish Layout** button from the **Generate Layout** panel to complete the connection of the pipes with the sprinklers, as shown in Figure 8-11.

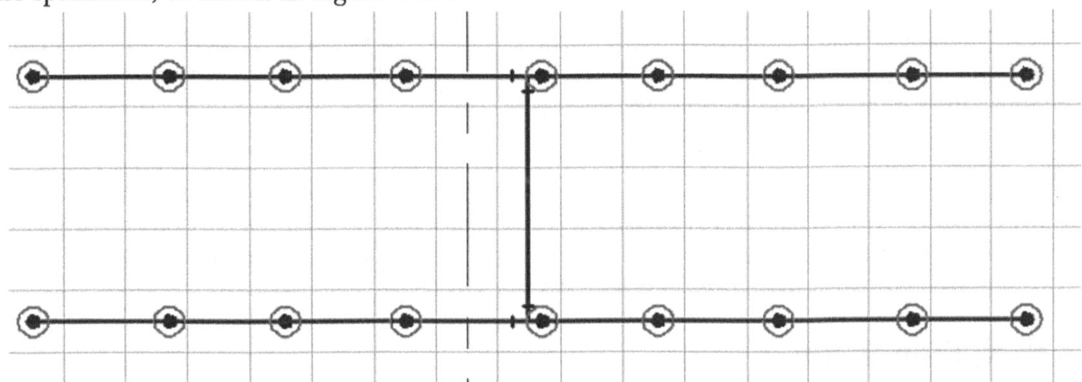

Figure 8-11 The sprinklers connected to the piping system

TUTORIAL

General instructions for downloading tutorial files:

1. Download the *c08_tutorial.zip* file for this tutorial from *http://www.cadcim.com*. The path of the folder is as follows: *Textbooks > Civil/GIS > Revit MEP > Exploring Autodesk Revit 2017 for MEP*.

2. Now, save and extract the downloaded zip file at the following location: *C:\rmp_2017\c08_rmp_2017_tut*

Tutorial 1 — Office Space- Fire Suppression

In this tutorial, you will create pipe types for dry and wet fire protection. Also, you will create a space schedule to estimate the quantity of sprinklers required for each space in the model.

(Expected time: 45 min)

1. File name to be used: *c08_office_fire_protections_tut1.rvt (M_ c08_office_fire_protections.rvt)*
2. File name to be assigned: *c08_Office-Space_tut1.rvt (M_c08_Office-Space_tut1.rvt)*

The following steps are required to complete this tutorial:

a. Open the *c08_office_fire_protections.rvt* (*M_ c08_office_fire_protections.rvt*) file.
b. Create pipe types.
c. Configure the pipe settings.
d. Create space schedule for estimating sprinklers.
e. Save the project using the **Save As** tool.
f. Close the project by using the **Close** tool.

Opening a Project

In this section, you will download the *c08_office_fire_protections.rvt (M_08_office_fire_protections.rvt)* file from *www.cadcim.com* and then open the file.

1. To open a file, choose **Open > Project** from **Application Menu**. On doing so, the **Open** dialog box is displayed.

2. In the **Open** dialog box, browse to *C:\rmp_2017\c08_rmp_2017_tut* and then select the *c08_office_fire_protections.rvt* file (for Metric, select the *M_c08_office_fire_protections.rvt*). Now, choose the **Open** button; the selected file opens.

Note

The architectural model named c04_archi_spaces_rmp_2017.rvt linked in this tutorial file is located in the c04_rmp_2017_tut folder. It is recommended to maintain the relative path to the architectural model. However, if the link is lost, you need to reload the file using the ***Manage Links*** *dialog box which has already been discussed in the previous chapters.*

Creating Pipe Types

In this section, you will create new pipe types for the fire suppression system.

1. In the **Project Browser**, click on the "**+**" symbol on the left of the **Families** node to expand it.

2. In the expanded **Families** node, click on **Pipes > Pipe Types > Standard**; the **Standard** node is highlighted.

3. Next, right-click; a shortcut menu is displayed. From the shortcut menu, select the **Duplicate** option; a duplicate node with the name **Standard 2** is created and is displayed under the **Standard** node.

4. Select the **Standard 2** node and then right-click; a shortcut menu is displayed. From the shortcut menu, choose the **Rename** option; the existing name is displayed in an edit box.

5. In the edit box, type **x** and press ENTER; the existing name is renamed, as shown in Figure 8-12.

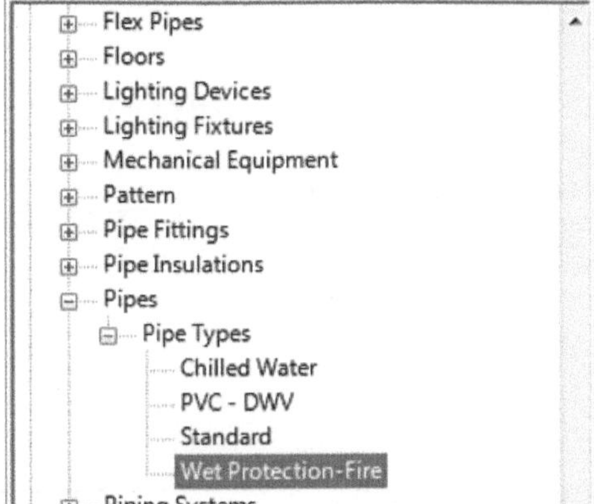

***Figure 8-12** The **Project Browser** displaying the **Wet Protection-Fire** type*

6. Next, ensure that the **Wet Protection-Fire** node is selected and then right-click; a shortcut menu is displayed. From the shortcut menu, choose the **Type Properties** option; the **Type Properties** dialog box is displayed.

7. In this dialog box, choose the **Duplicate** button; the **Name** dialog box is displayed.

8. In the **Name** edit box of the **Name** dialog box, type the **Dry Protection-Fire** text and then choose the **OK** button; the **Name** dialog box is closed and the **Dry Protection-Fire** type is displayed in the **Type** drop-down list in the **Type Properties** dialog box.

9. In the **Type Properties** dialog box, choose the **OK** button; the dialog box is closed. Notice that in the **Project Browser**, the **Dry-Protection-Fire** type is displayed under the **Pipe Types** head.

Configuring the Pipe Settings

In this section, you will configure the pipe types for the fire protection system.

1. Choose the **Mechanical Settings** button from the **Plumbing & Piping** panel of the **Systems** tab; the **Mechanical Settings** dialog box is displayed.

2. In the left pane of this dialog box, click on the **Conversion** node under the **Pipe Settings** node; various options related to the **Conversion** node are displayed in the right pane, as shown in Figure 8-13.

3. In the right pane, select the **Fire Protection Wet** option from the **System Classification** drop-down list.

4. In the **Main** area, click in the **Value** field corresponding to the **Pipe Type** parameter; a drop-down list is displayed.

5. From the drop-down list displayed, select the **Pipe Types: Wet Protection-Fire** option.

6. In the **Main** area, click in the **Value** field corresponding to the **Offset** parameter and replace the existing value of **9' - 0" (2750)** with **9' - 3" (2820)**.

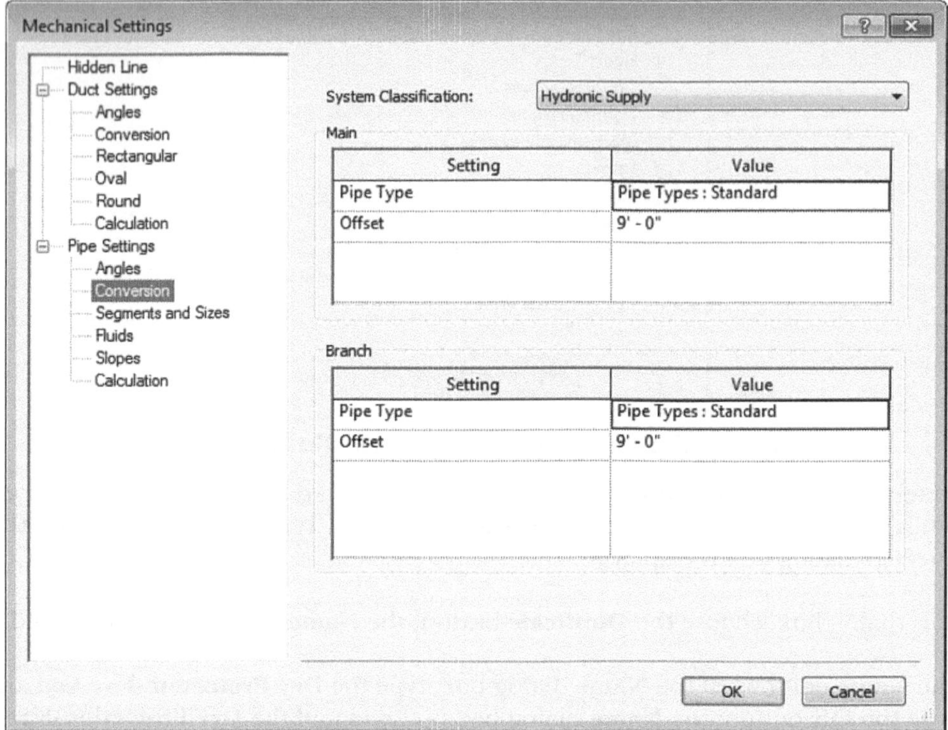

***Figure 8-13** Various options related to the **Conversion** node displayed in the **Mechanical Settings** dialog box*

7. In the **Branch** area, assign the same settings as specified in the **Main** area.

Note

The offset values specified for the main and branch pipes refers to the placement of the main and branch pipes with respect to the referenced level. Also, it is important to note that the branch offset allows you to automatically create branches that run above or below the main and other obstacles. This is useful for avoiding interference with pipes, duct, structural beams, or architectural components.

8. Now, repeat the procedure followed in steps 3 to 7 to assign the conversion settings for the **Dry Fire Protection** system. For creating the settings, use the following specifications:
   System Classification: **Fire Protection Dry**
   Pipe Type (Main and Branch areas): **Pipe Types : Dry Protection-Fire**
   Offset (Main and Branch area): **9'3"(2820 mm)**

9. After configuring the settings for the pipes, choose the **OK** button; the **Mechanical Settings** dialog box is closed.

Creating a Space Schedule for Estimating Sprinklers

In this section, you will create a space schedule and find out the quantity of the sprinklers in the spaces.

1. Choose the **Schedules/Quantities** tool from the **Reports & Schedules** panel of the **Analyze** tab; the **New Schedule** dialog box is displayed.

2. In the **Category** list box of the dialog box, click on the **Spaces** category. Now, in the **Name** edit box, enter a new name **Space Schedule-Fire Protection**. Also, ensure that in the **New Schedule** dialog box, the **Schedule building components** radio button is selected and the **New Construction** option is selected from the **Phase** drop-down list.

3. In the **New Schedule** dialog box, choose the **OK** button; the **Schedule Properties** dialog box is displayed with the **Fields** tab chosen, as shown in Figure 8-14.

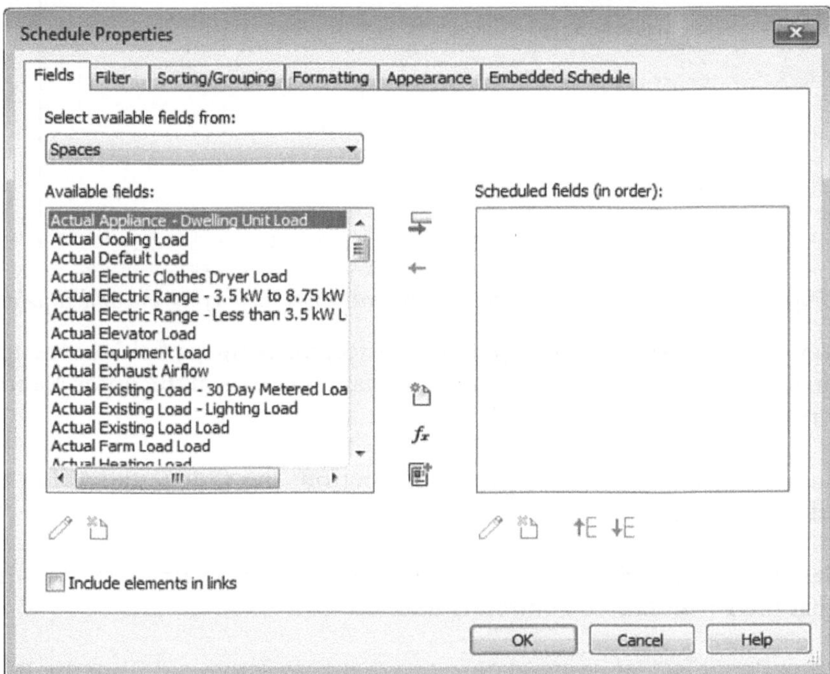

*Figure 8-14 The **Schedule Properties** dialog box with the **Fields** tab chosen*

4. In the **Available fields** area of the **Fields** tab, select the **Area** field. Now, press and hold the CTRL key and then select the following fields from the **Available fields** area: **Level**, **Name**, and **Number**.

5. Now, release the CTRL key and choose the **Add parameter(s)** button; the selected fields are added to the **Scheduled fields (in order)** area. Note that the added fields are selected and are highlighted in blue color, refer to Figure 8-15. Now, click on the **Number** field in the **Scheduled fields (in order)** area; other fields except the **Number** field get deselected.

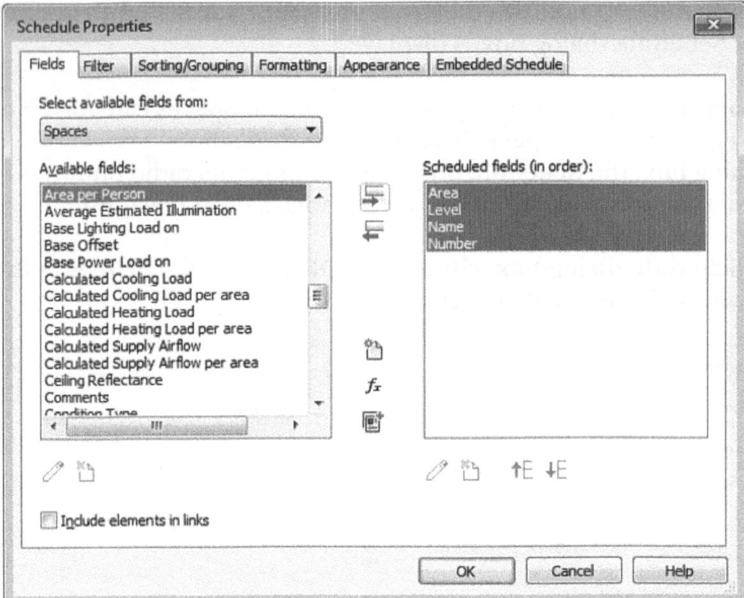

***Figure 8-15** The **Schedule Properties** dialog box displaying the added fields*

6. Now, choose the **Move parameter up** button thrice; the **Number** field moves up in the order above the **Area** field. Similarly, arrange the remaining fields in the order **Name, Level,** and **Area** (Top-Bottom), refer to Figure 8-16.

7. Now, choose the **Add calculated parameter** button; the **Calculated Value** dialog box is displayed.

8. In the **Name** text box of the dialog box, enter **Sprinkler Quantity- Min. Required** and then ensure that the **Formula** radio button is selected.

9. Also, ensure that the **Common** and **Number** options are selected from the **Discipline** and **Type** drop-down lists, respectively.

10. Now, in the **Calculated Value** dialog box, choose the browse button next to the **Formula** edit box; the **Fields** dialog box is displayed.

11. In the displayed dialog box, select the **Area** field and then choose the **OK** button; the dialog box is closed and the **Area** field is added to the **Formula** edit box.

12. In the **Formula** edit box, type **/130** (for Metric unit type **/12**) after the **Area** text to complete the formula as Area/130 (for Metric unit type Area/12).

    The fire protection code requires one sprinkler for every 130 square feet (sprinkler required for every 12 square meter).

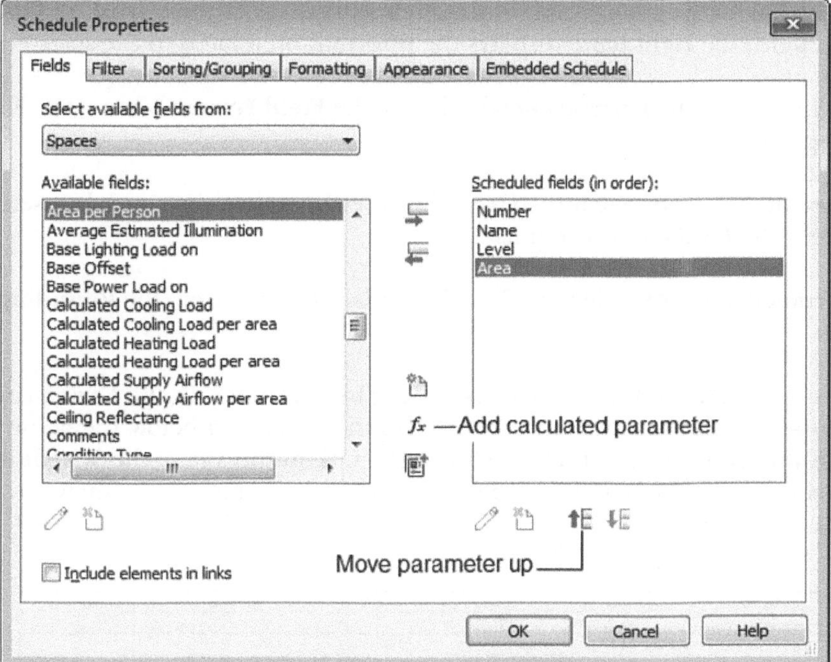

*Figure 8-16 The **Scheduled fields (in order)** area displaying the re-ordered fields*

Note

*The formula that you enter in the **Formula** edit box is case sensitive.*

13. Now, choose the **OK** button; the **Calculated Values** dialog box is closed and the **Sprinkler Quantity- Min. Required** parameter is added to the **Scheduled fields (in order)** area.

14. Choose the **Filter** tab from the **Schedule Properties** dialog box; the options in this tab are displayed.

15. Select the **Level** option from the **Filter by** drop-down list and also ensure that the **equals** option is selected in the drop-down list displayed next to it.

16. Next, select the **Level 1** option from the drop-down list located at the third position corresponding to the **Filter by** parameter, if it is not selected by default.

17. Now, ensure that the **(none)** option is selected in the **And** drop-down list.

18. In the **Schedule Properties** dialog box, choose the **Sorting/Grouping** tab and then select the **Number** option from the **Sort by** drop-down list. Also, ensure that the **Ascending** radio button located next to it is selected.

19. Now, ensure that the **(none)** option is selected in the **Then by** drop-down list and then select the **Grand totals** check box. Ensure that the **Title, count, and totals** option is selected in the drop-down list displayed next to it.

20. Choose the **Formatting** tab. Next, in the **Fields** area, select the **Sprinkler Quantity- Min. Required** field; the right pane displays the information related to the selected field.

21. In the right pane of the **Formatting** tab, choose the **Field Format** button; the **Format** dialog box is displayed.

22. In the **Format** dialog box, clear the **Use default settings** check box and then select the **Fixed** option from the **Units** drop-down list.

23. In the **Format** dialog box, select the **2 decimal places** option from the **Rounding** drop-down list.

24. Now, choose the **OK** button; the **Format** dialog box is closed. In the **Formatting** tab, select the **Calculate totals** option from the drop-down list located below the **show conditional format on sheets** check box and then choose the **OK** button again; the **Schedule Properties** dialog box is closed; the schedule is displayed in the drawing area, as shown in Figure 8-17.

<Space Schedule-Fire Protection>

A	B	C	D	E
Number	Name	Level	Area	Sprinkler Quantity- Min. Required
101	CEO-Office	Level 1	156 SF	1.20
102	V.P. Marketing	Level 1	117 SF	0.90
103	Toilet-1	Level 1	70 SF	0.54
104	Rest Room	Level 1	97 SF	0.75
105	Cafeteria	Level 1	109 SF	0.84
106	Store	Level 1	84 SF	0.64
107	Purchase	Level 1	153 SF	1.18
108	International	Level 1	104 SF	0.80
109	H.R.	Level 1	130 SF	1.00
110	Central Area	Level 1	1015 SF	7.81
111	Quality	Level 1	160 SF	1.23
112	Open	Level 1	157 SF	1.21
113	Conference-2	Level 1	216 SF	1.66
114	Conference	Level 1	201 SF	1.55
115	Lounge	Level 1	844 SF	6.49
116	Meeting Room	Level 1	106 SF	0.81
117	Service	Level 1	84 SF	0.64
118	Shaft	Level 1	63 SF	0.49
119	Services	Level 1	75 SF	0.57
120	Accounts	Level 1	145 SF	1.11

Figure 8-17 *The* ***Scheduled fields*** *area displaying the re-ordered fields*

You can refer to the minimum number of sprinklers per space data as you place sprinklers in order to satisfy the design and code requirements. Although, you rounded the data to 2 decimal places, you will want to round all the decimals up to the next whole number.

Note

A schedule in Revit is not only a construction document but also a design tool. When you change editable entries in the schedule to modify your system, you are actually editing information in a database of building information. As a result, each change is dynamic and is reflected throughout your project.

Saving the Project

In this section, you need to save the project and settings using the **Save As** tool.

1. To save the project with the specified settings, choose **Save As > Project** from **Application Menu**. As you are saving the project for the first time, the **Save As** dialog box is displayed.

2. In this dialog box, browse to *C:\rmp_2017\c08_rmp_2017_tut* and then in the **File name** edit box, enter **c08_Office-Space_tut1** (for Metric **M_c08_Office-Space_tut1**).

3. In the displayed dialog box, choose the **Save** button to save the current project file with the specified name and to close the **Save As** dialog box.

Closing the Project

1. To close the project, choose the **Close** option from **Application Menu**.

   The file is closed and this completes tutorial of Chapter 8.

Self-Evaluation Test

Answer the following questions and then compare them to those given at the end of this chapter:

1. The__________button is used to invoke the **Mechanical Settings** dialog box.

2. The **Sprinkler** tool is available in the _________ panel of the **Systems** tab.

3. In Revit, you can design only dry fire protection systems. (T/F)

4. You can place the sprinkler either in the floor plan view or in the ceiling plan view. (T/F)

5. It is recommended to set an elevation for the piping head while using the layout tools. (T/F)

Review Questions

Answer the following questions:

1. Which of the following tools is used to invoke the **Create Piping System** dialog box?

   a) **Sprinkler** b) **Plumbing Fixture**
   c) **Flex Duct** d) **Piping**

2. Which of the following tools is used to create a schedule for the estimation of the sprinkler?

   a) **Panel Schedules** b) **Sprinkler**
   c) **Schedule/Quantities** d) None of these

3. You can create a schedule for the estimation of the sprinkler by choosing the __________ tool.

4. In Revit, sprinkler heads are only available as hosted elements. (T/F)

5. A non-hosted sprinkler can be placed anywhere in a project. (T/F)

EXERCISE

Exercise 1 Fire Protection System

Download the *c08_Conference-Center_exer1.rvt* file from *http://www.cadcim.com*. The path of the file is as follows: *Textbooks > Civil/GIS > Revit MEP > Exploring Autodesk Revit 2017 for MEP*.

Open the *c08_Conference-Center_exer1.rvt* file and create a fire protection system in the conference room for the *Conference-Center* project. For location of the room, refer to Figure 8-18. While creating the fire protection system, you will add sprinklers and then create a wet pipe system, as shown in Figure 8-19.

1. Project view to be used :
   Ceiling Plans > Mechanical > 1 - Ceiling Mech

2. Family type to be used:
   Sprinklers
   For Imperial Sprinkler-Pendent_Semi-Recessed-Hosted : 1/2” Pendent
   For Metric M_Sprinkler - Pendent - Semi-Recessed - Hosted : 15mm Pendent

3. File name to be assigned: *c08_Conference-Center_exer1a.rvt*

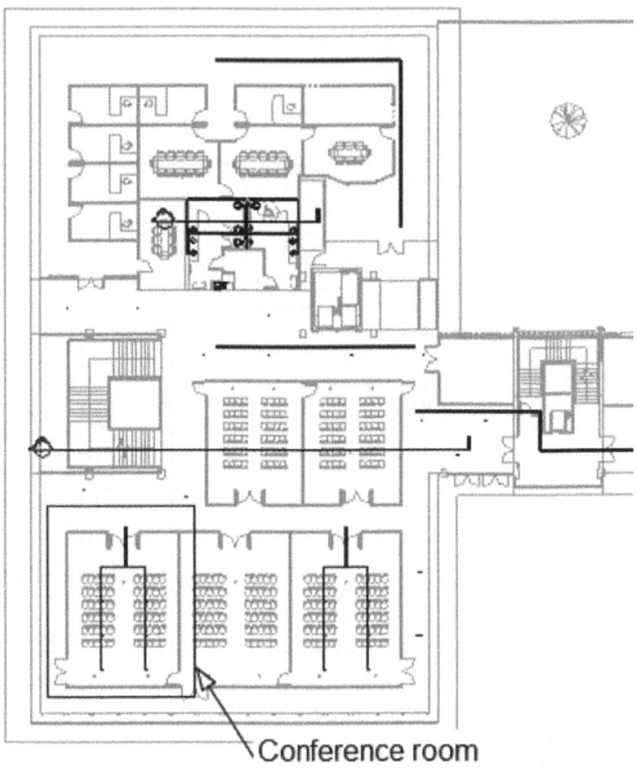

Figure 8-18 *The conference room for which fire protection system will be created*

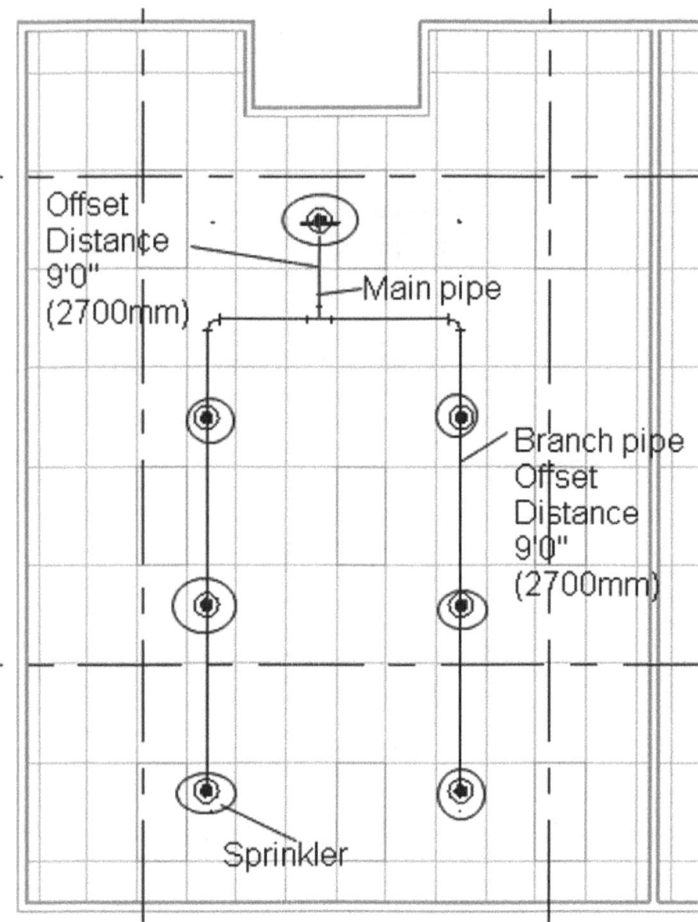

Figure 8-19 The fire protection system created for the conference room

Answers to Self-Evaluation Test

1. Mechanical Settings, 2. Plumbing & Piping, 3. F, **4.** T, **5.** T

Chapter 9

Creating Construction Documents

Learning Objectives

After completing this chapter, you will be able to:

- *Add dimensions*
- *Add text notes*
- *Add tags to elements*
- *Use callout views*
- *Create drafting views*
- *Duplicate views*
- *Add sheets to a projectx*

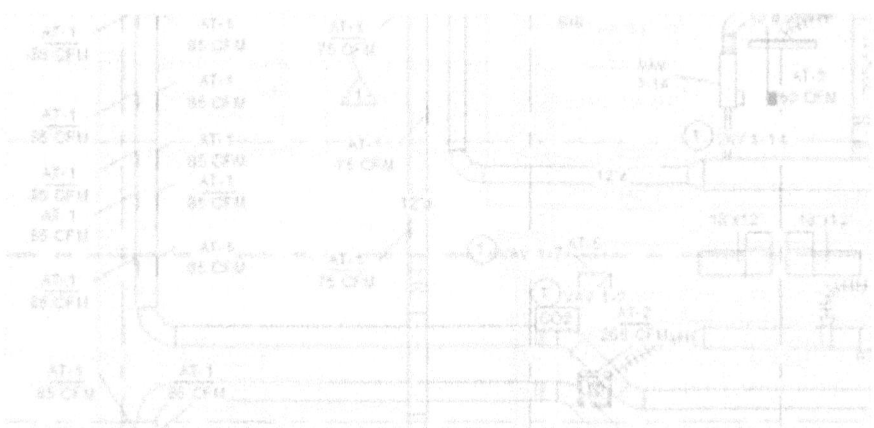

INTRODUCTION

In the previous chapters, you learned to create building envelopes, create different systems, analyze spaces, and more. In this chapter, you will learn to document a project and prepare it as a working drawing by using various tools and techniques in Revit. To document a system, you need to place dimensions in the plan view, add callout view, and place tags on ducts, equipment, machines, pipelines, and so on. In this chapter, you will learn various dimensioning terms and tools, tools for placing text notes, and the methods to place tags on elements in a project. You will also learn to add different views to the project, import and export views, and then add them to the sheets. Moreover, you will learn to prepare schedules and legends and to add them to the project sheets.

DIMENSIONING

Dimensions play a crucial role in the presentation of a project. Although the representation of MEP system in a project can convey how the appearance or design of the system would be, yet to materialize it at the site, there must be information and statistics regarding each element involved in the system. Since the design of a project is used for the actual assembly of the project, it is essential to describe each element of the project in terms of actual measurement parameters such as length, width, height, angle, radius, diameter, and so on. All these information can be added to a project by using dimensions. In most cases, information conveyed through dimensions is as important as the project view itself. The dimensions added to the project view ensure that the project drawings in the view are read and interpreted in an appropriate manner. Adding dimensions also helps in avoiding the discrepancies that may creep in between the elements used for generating the system drawings. In an MEP project, you can add dimensions based on the actual dimensions of the elements to be created. In other words, they are as real as the project elements themselves. The units used in the dimensions play an important role in describing the detailing that is required to complete a project. For example, the use of fractional inches in the dimensions indicates the amount of detailing required while generating a design. It also reflects the extent of detailing and the precision required to complete a project. Therefore, dimensions are used not only for specifying the sizes of elements, but also for guiding the people involved in the project, such as cost estimators, project managers, site engineers, contractors, supervisors, and so on.

Types of Dimensions

In Revit, you can create two types of dimensions for an element: temporary dimension and permanent dimension. Temporary dimensions appear while creating or selecting an element, but they do not appear in the project views. On the other hand, permanent dimensions appear in the views in which they are created and describe the size or distance of the elements. In Revit, you can add the dimensions denoting the length of elements such as ducts, pipes, cable trays, electrical conduits, and more. You can dimension the distance between them, arc length of a path made by them, angle between them, spot elevation of the level difference, and so on. While dimensioning a system, you can change various type parameters of the dimension such as its size, color, and so on by using the **Type Properties** dialog box. In the next section, you will learn about various entities in a dimension, various types of dimensions, adding dimensions to a project, and modifying the added dimensions.

In Revit, you can use two types of dimensions: temporary and permanent. By default, the units that are specified in the initial start-up of a project are used by both the dimensions. Unlike temporary dimensions, the permanent dimensions are view-specific. It means if you change the view of a project, the permanent dimensions will not be visible.

Using Temporary Dimensions

Revit displays temporary dimensions around the component or element when you place or sketch it in a view. The dimension that appears dynamically while drawing and placing an element is called temporary dimension. This type of dimension is not view-specific and may appear in any view while drawing or selecting an element. Temporary dimensions help you position elements at the desired location and references. While sketching the lines of desired length at the desired angle instantly, temporary dimensions can help you speed up your drafting work.

A temporary dimension appears only in three situations. First, when you draw an element; second, when you select an element; and third, when you select or place a component in a project.

When you place a component in a project, temporary dimensions turnout to be a useful tool to guide in exact placing of the component with respect to a fixed element or a component. While placing a component, the temporary dimensions are displayed at the nearest perpendicular element or component with a predefined snap increment setting. This helps in placing a component in a drawing properly. Figure 9-1 shows the temporary dimensions displayed while adding a return air diffuser to a project view.

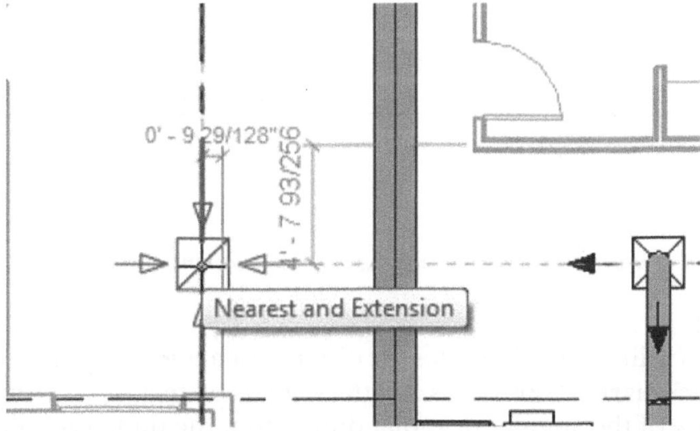

Figure 9-1 *Temporary dimensions displayed while placing a return air diffuser*

While using a temporary dimension, you can set the point of reference of the element being placed. To change the settings of the temporary dimension, invoke the **Temporary Dimensions** tool from **Manage > Settings > Additional Settings** drop-down; the **Temporary Dimension Properties** dialog box will be displayed, as shown in Figure 9-2. This dialog box contains two areas: **Walls** and **Doors and Windows**.

In the **Walls** area of the **Temporary Dimension Properties** dialog box, you can select any one of the four radio buttons, **Centerlines, Center of Core, Faces**, and **Faces of Core** to set the reference point for displaying temporary dimensions of walls. To change the point of reference for placing and referring doors and windows, you can select any of the two radio buttons, **Centerlines** and **Openings**, from the **Doors and Windows** area of the **Temporary Dimension Properties** dialog box. These settings help you to set the references of walls, doors, and windows for temporary dimensions while creating or placing elements or components in a system.

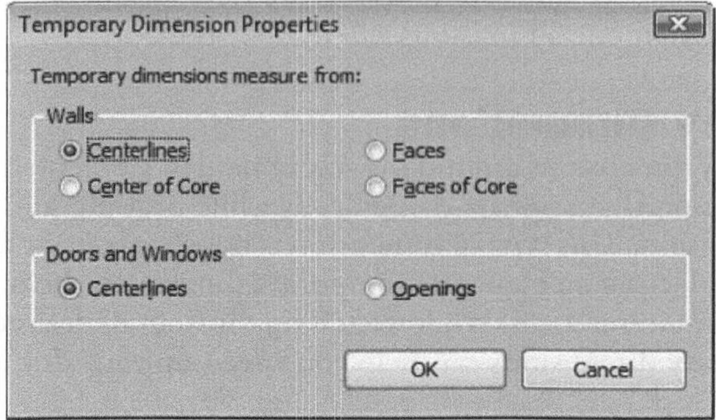

*Figure 9-2 The **Temporary Dimension Properties** dialog box*

Entities in a Dimension

Before using the dimensioning tools, it is important to understand various entities in a dimension. Figure 9-3 shows the terms used for various entities in a dimension. In the next section, these entities are discussed briefly.

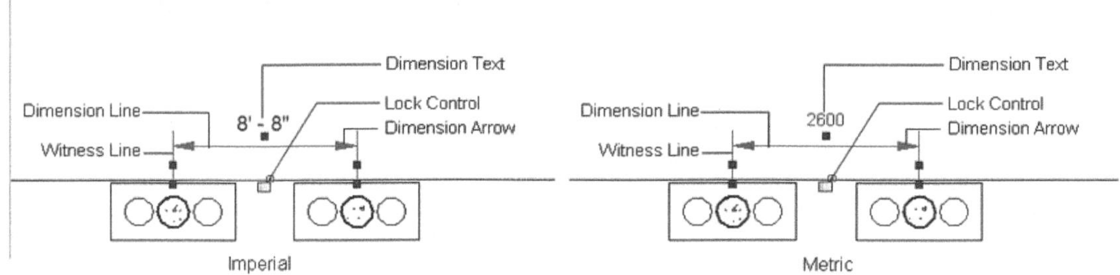

Figure 9-3 Various entities in a permanent dimension

Dimension Line

The dimension line in a dimension indicates the distance or angle being measured. By default, the dimension line has tick marks at both ends and the dimension text is placed along the dimension line. Note that in case of the angular or radial dimension, the dimension line will be an arc.

Dimension Text

The dimension text represents the actual measurement (dimension value) between the selected points. You cannot modify this value but can add prefixes or suffixes to it. Note that the dimension text value is automatically updated when the size of an element is modified.

Dimension Arrows

Dimension Arrows are added at the intersection of the dimension line and witness line. As drafting standards differ from company to company, Revit allows you to select tick marks from a range of in-built symbols.

Witness Lines

Witness lines are generated from a selected element and extend toward the dimension line. Generally, they are generated perpendicular to the dimension line. You can move the witness lines to a desired location by using the witness line drag controls. Alternatively, you can move the witness lines by first selecting the desired dimension and then moving the cursor and placing it above the witness line control; the color of the witness line control will change and at the same time, a tool tip with the text **Move Witness Line** will also be displayed. Next, right-click to display a shortcut menu. In the shortcut menu, choose the **Move Witness Line** option; an additional witness line will appear. Move this witness line and click at the desired reference point for the new location; the selected dimension will change to a new value and the desired witness line will move to a new location.

You can add an extra witness line to the existing dimension. To do so, select the desired dimension and then right-click; a shortcut menu will be displayed. In this shortcut menu, choose the **Edit Witness Line** option; an additional witness line with a dimension line will emerge from any of the witness lines of the selected dimension. Next, click on the desired reference; a dimension will be added in addition to the selected dimension. Figures 9-4 and 9-5 show the addition of a witness line to an existing dimension.

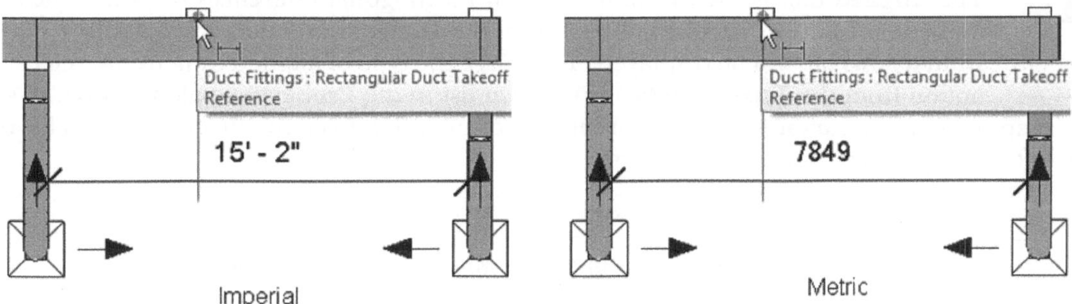

***Figure 9-4** Additional witness line emerging from the dimension*

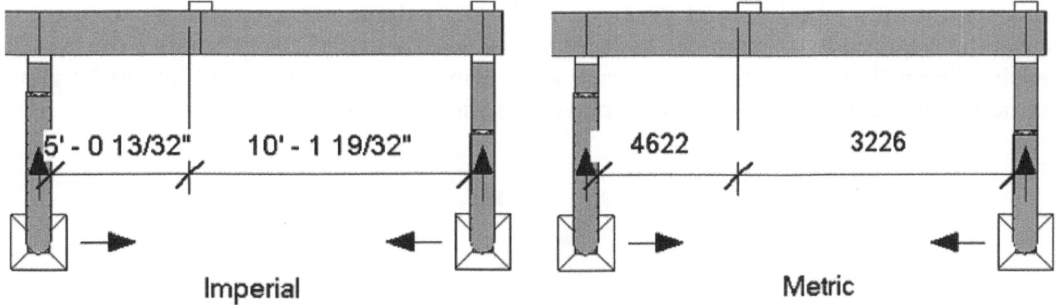

***Figure 9-5** Witness line added to the desired dimension*

Tip

*You can also edit witness lines by selecting the dimension and then choosing the **Edit Witness Lines** tool from the **Witness Lines** panel of the **Modify / Dimensions** contextual tab.*

Adding Permanent Dimensions

Permanent dimensions are added for a specific measurement. In Revit, you can access various dimension tools from the **Dimension** panel in the **Annotate** tab, as shown in Figure 9-6. You can choose appropriate dimension type and dimension tool to add dimensions to an element. The dimensioning tools are discussed next.

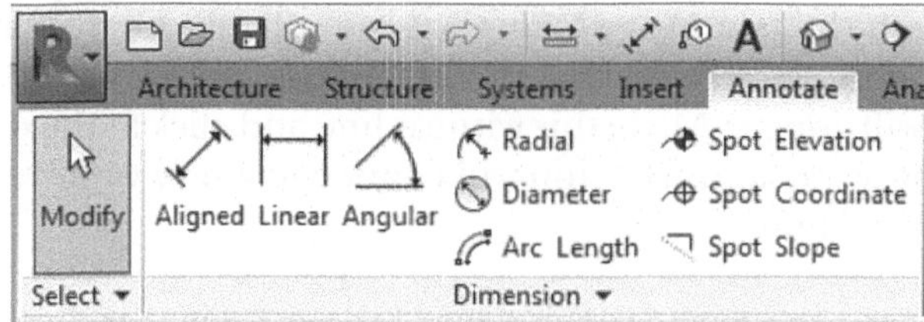

***Figure 9-6** Various dimensioning tools in the **Dimension** panel of the **Annotate** tab*

Aligned Tool

Ribbon: Annotate > Dimension > Aligned

The **Aligned** tool is used to dimension two orthogonal references or points such as wall-ends. To do so, invoke this tool from the **Dimension** panel; the **Modify | Place Dimensions** tab will be displayed. To change the type of aligned dimension, select an option from the **Type Selector** drop-down list in the **Properties** palette. Next, to set the snap point of the cursor for dimensioning, select an option from the first drop-down list on the left in the **Options Bar**, refer to Figure 9-7.

***Figure 9-7** Various options in the **Options Bar** for the **Aligned** tool*

For example, if you select the **Wall centerlines** option from the drop-down list, the cursor will snap to the centerline of the wall, if it is placed above the wall. Next, select the **Individual Reference** option from the **Pick** drop-down list. Place the cursor at a reference point on an element; the reference point will be highlighted. Next, click to specify the reference point. Then, place the cursor at the required location of the next reference point and click. As you move the cursor, a dimension line will appear. Move the cursor away from the component and left-click again; a permanent aligned dimension will be displayed, as shown in Figure 9-8.

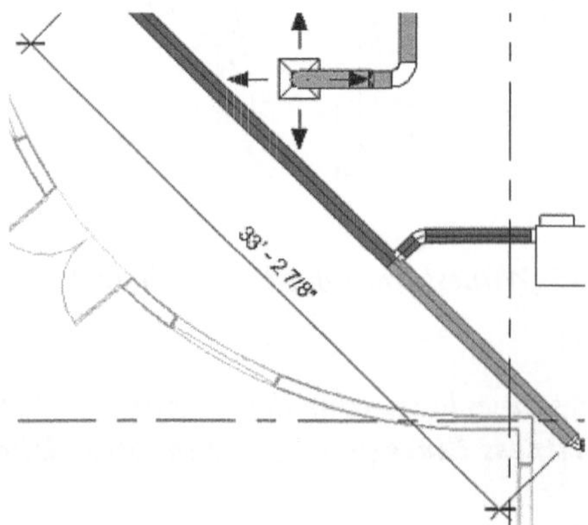

***Figure 9-8** Dimension created using the **Aligned** tool*

Linear Tool

Ribbon:	Annotate > Dimension > Linear

The **Linear** tool is used to dimension straight elements and distances. It measures the shortest distance between any two specified points. To measure the distance, invoke this tool from the **Dimension** panel in the **Annotate** tab. On doing so, the **Modify | Place Dimensions** tab will be displayed. From the **Properties** palette, click on the **Type Selector** drop-down list and select an option to assign a type to the linear dimension that you want to create. After selecting this option, select the first point by clicking at the appropriate location. After selecting the first point, select the second point of reference for the dimension; the dimension line will be displayed.

You can now move the cursor to the desired location and click to place the dimension. The dimension thus created will display various parameter controls. You can invoke any other tool or press ESC to exit the **Linear** tool. The linear dimension will be created, as shown in Figure 9-9.

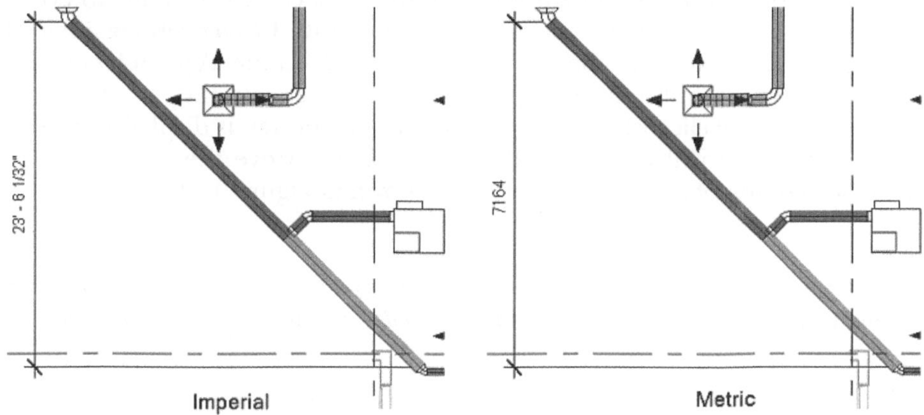

Figure 9-9 *Linear dimension created using the **Linear** tool*

Angular Tool

Ribbon:	Annotate > Dimension > Angular

The **Angular** tool is used to dimension an angle. It is also used to create a dimension arc (dimension line in the shape of an arc with arrows on both ends) to indicate the angle between two non-parallel elements, as shown in Figure 9-10. To dimension an angle, invoke the **Angular** tool from the **Dimension** panel; the **Modify | Place Dimensions** tab will be displayed. From the **Properties** palette, click on the **Type Selector** drop-down list and select an option. Now, move the cursor, click on the first reference, and then click on the other reference. On doing so, the angular dimension between the selected references will be displayed. Next, click at an appropriate place to locate the dimension displayed. Figure 9-10 shows an angular dimension between two round duct taps.

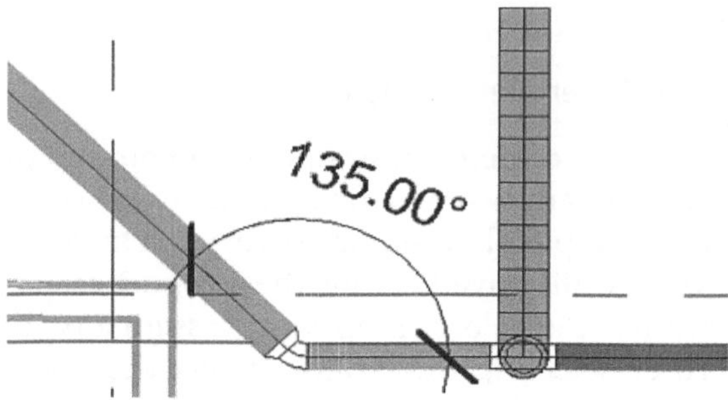

Figure 9-10 *Angular dimension created using the* ***Angular*** *tool*

Radial Tool

Ribbon: Annotate > Dimension > Radial

The **Radial** tool is used to dimension the radius of a circular profile. To do so, invoke the **Radial** tool from the **Dimension** panel; the **Modify | Place Dimensions** tab will be displayed. In the **Properties** palette of this tab, click on the **Type Selector** drop-down list and select an option from the list of types displayed. After selecting an option, move the cursor near the profile and click when the appropriate snap option is displayed; a center mark along with the dimension will automatically be generated. Move the cursor and place the dimension. Dimensioning of a round duct elbow is shown in Figure 9-11.

Note

In Revit, you can dimension the diameter of a circular profile. To do so, invoke the ***Diameter*** *tool from the* ***Dimension*** *panel of the* ***Annotate*** *tab and place the dimension as required.*

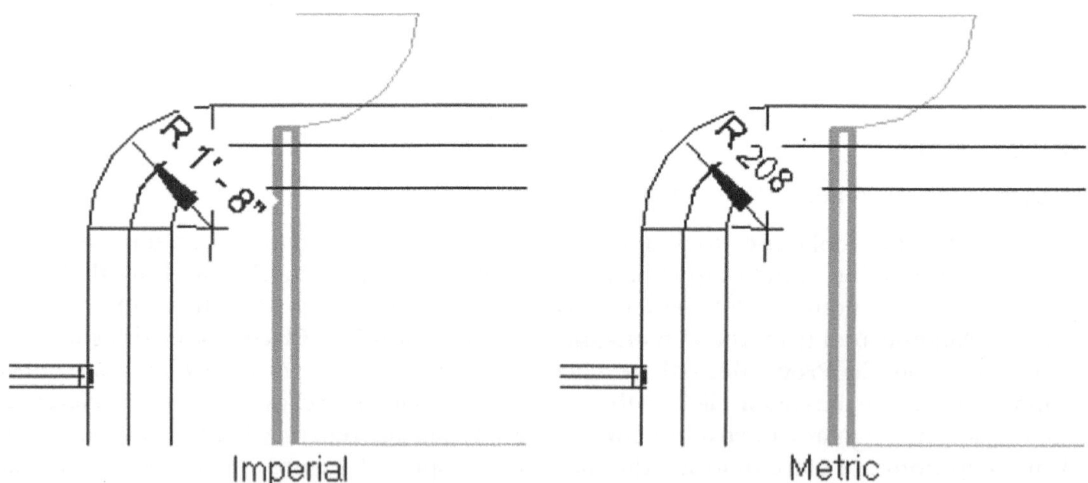

Figure 9-11 *Dimension created using the* ***Radial*** *tool*

Arc Length Tool

Ribbon: Annotate > Dimension > Arc Length

The **Arc Length** tool is used to dimension a curved duct or a curved cable tray based on its overall length. To dimension a curved duct, invoke this tool from the **Dimension** panel; the **Modify | Place Dimensions** tab will be displayed. In the **Properties** palette, select the dimension type from the **Type Selector** drop-down list. Next, move the cursor near the arc duct and click to specify the radial point. Select the start and end reference points between which the arc length is to be measured. Next, move the cursor away from the duct and click; the arc length dimension will be created, as shown in Figure 9-12.

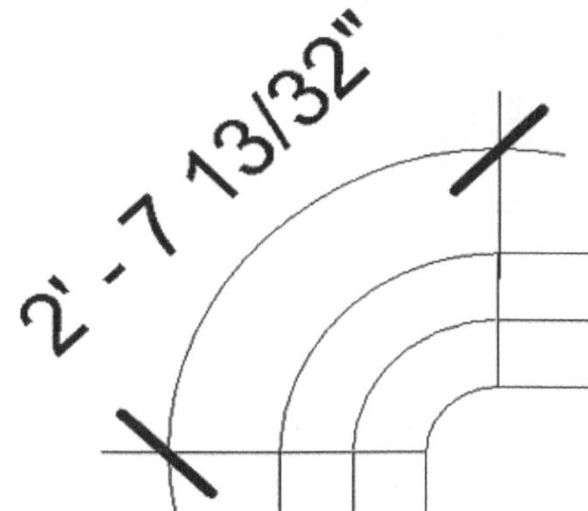

Figure 9-12 *Dimension created using the* ***Arc Length*** *tool*

Spot Elevation Tool

Ribbon: Annotate > Dimension > Spot Elevation

Spot Elevation The **Spot Elevation** tool is used to place a spot elevation at a point in the drawing area. Spot elevations display the elevation level of a point with respect to the base level. They can be placed in a plan, elevation, or 3D view. You can add spot dimensions on non-horizontal and non-planar surfaces. You can use the spot elevation to specify the elevation level of points on a floor, ramp, duct, machines, topographical surface, stairs, and other features. To place a spot elevation at a point, invoke the **Spot Elevation** tool from the **Dimension** panel; the **Modify | Place Dimensions** tab along with the **Options Bar** will be displayed. The **Leader** check box is selected by default in the **Options Bar**. As a result, a leader will be displayed along with the spot dimension placed in the drawing. You can clear this check box if you do not need the leader to be displayed along with the spot dimension in the drawing. In the **Options Bar**, the **Shoulder** check box is also selected by default. As a result, a shoulder line will be displayed along with a leader line in the spot dimension to be placed. You can clear the **Shoulder** check box to remove the shoulder line from the leader line.

Tip

In a BIM(Building Information Modeling) environment, the MEP engineers have to work in coordination with the other disciplines like Architecture and Structure. As a result, the ***Spot Elevation*** *tool will help the MEP engineers to locate the MEP elements in height of the 3d space. This will help to mitigate the coordination issues with the other disciplines can at an early stage of the project.*

You can also change the type of spot elevation by selecting an option from the **Type Selector** drop-down list. The options available in this drop-down list are: **Crosshair (Project)**, **Crosshair (Relative)**, **No Symbol (Project)**, **No Symbol (Relative)**, **Target (Project)**, and **Target (Relative)**. In Figure 9-13, you can see the spot elevation of a duct.

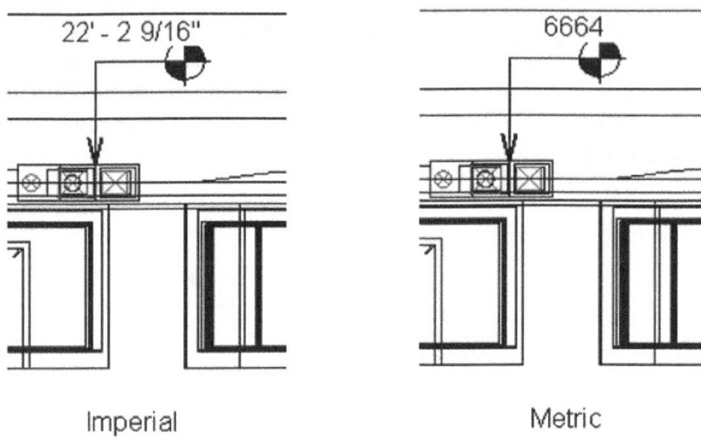

Figure 9-13 The spot elevation of the duct displayed

Note
*The placement of the shoulder line and the leader line in the spot elevation depends on the options that you select from the **Shoulder** and **Leader** drop-down lists in the **Options Bar**.*

Spot Coordinate Tool

Ribbon: Annotate > Dimension > Spot Coordinate

Spot Coordinate The **Spot Coordinate** tool is used to display spot coordinates (Northing and Easting) of a point in a project. You can place spot coordinates on floors, ducts, diffusers, machines, boundary lines, and other such elements in a project. Spot coordinates can also be placed on non-horizontal surfaces and non-planar edges.

To place spot coordinates, invoke the **Spot Coordinate** tool from the **Dimension** panel; the **Modify | Place Dimensions** contextual tab will be displayed. The options and the properties for the spot dimension will be displayed in the **Options Bar** and the **Properties** palette, respectively. In the **Options Bar**, you can select the **Leader** and **Shoulder** check boxes to control the display of shoulder and leader along with the spot coordinate dimension. By default, both the check boxes are selected. As a result, leader and shoulder will be displayed along with spot coordinate dimension. To turn off the display of the shoulder and leader, clear the **Shoulder** and **Leader** check boxes. After specifying options in the **Options Bar**, you can select the type of spot coordinate dimension from the **Type Selector** drop-down list in the **Properties** palette. Figure 9-14 shows a spot dimension placed on a rectangular diffuser with the **Horizontal** type.

Tip
*In an MEP project (Design-Build), finding the spot coordinates of MEP elements such as sprinklers, air terminals, sleeves, and others is a regular task. The **Spot Coordinate** tool helps the BIM team to compare the coordinates of these elements in Revit with those that are actually build in the site. This helps in the coordination of the model with the site.*

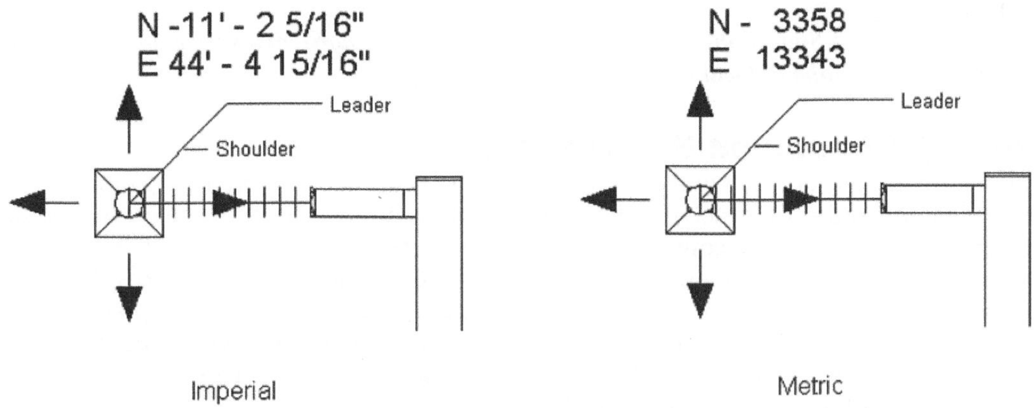

Figure 9-14 *Spot coordinate placed with the* ***Horizontal*** *type*

Spot Slope Tool

Ribbon:	Annotate > Dimension > Spot Slope

The **Spot Slope** tool is used to specify the slope of an edge or a face of an element at a point in a drawing. You can display the spot slope dimension in a plan, elevation, section, or 3D view. To add the spot slope at a point in the drawing, choose the **Spot Slope** tool from the **Dimension** panel; the **Modify | Place Dimensions** tab will be displayed. In the **Options Bar**, you can set the representation type for the spot slope dimension that you will place in the drawing. You can set an arrow or a triangle as the representation type for the spot slope dimension. Note that the **Arrow** option is selected by default in the **Slope Representation** drop-down list. You can select the **Triangle** option from the **Slope Representation** drop-down list to set the representation type of the spot slope dimension as a triangle. After setting the desired representation type, you can enter a value in the **Offset from Reference** edit box in the **Options Bar** to specify the offset distance of the slope symbol and the dimension text from the point referred for the dimension of the slope. In the Imperial system, by default, **1/16"** is displayed in this edit box. In Metric system by default, **1.5875 mm** is displayed in this edit box. After setting the parameters in the **Options Bar**, you can place the cursor on the sloping edge of a system element or a sloping face. As you place the cursor at a point, the slope dimension is displayed at the point. Click at the desired point to place the slope dimension and then click again to fix the vertical alignment of the slope dimension. Figure 9-15 shows the slope dimensions of an inclined beam and an inclined slab.

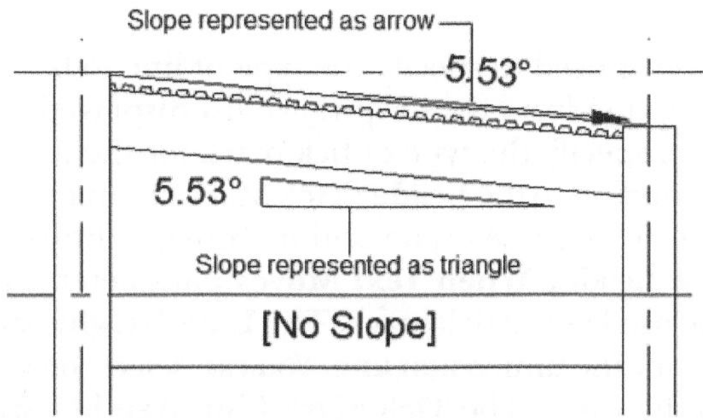

Figure 9-15 *Elevation of a structural model displaying the slope dimensions in different slope representation*

Note

*While using the **Spot Slope** tool, if you click on the face of a horizontal surface or on the straight edge, the **No Slope** text will be displayed.*

Modifying Dimension Parameters

You can modify the parameters of a dimension such as text font of a dimension, gap of witness line from element, and so on to achieve the desired dimension style. To do so, select the required dimension from the drawing; a contextual tab for the selected dimension type will be displayed. For example, for the linear dimension, the **Modify | Dimensions** tab will be displayed, and for the spot elevation dimension, the **Modify | Spot Elevations** tab will be displayed. In this tab, you can use various editing tools from their respective panels. When you select the desired dimension, its properties will be displayed in the **Properties** palette. Figure 9-16 shows the **Properties** palette of the selected linear dimension.

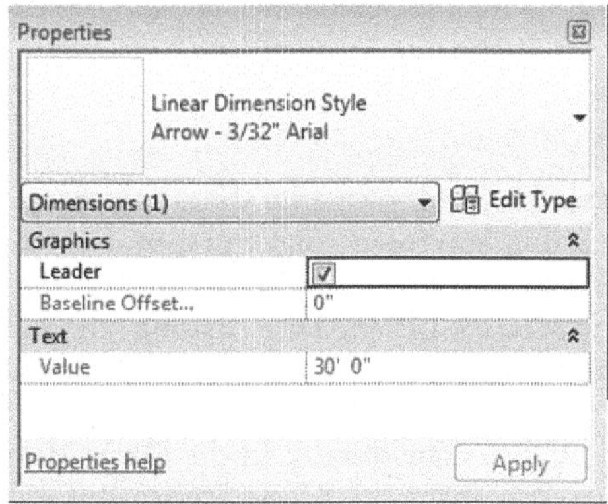

***Figure 9-16** The **Properties** palette displaying various properties of the linear dimension type*

In this palette, there are various instance parameters that can be modified from their respective heads. The appearance of these parameters depends upon the type of dimension selected in the drawing area. In the **Properties** palette, you can change the type properties of the selected dimension. To do so, choose the **Edit Type** button from the **Properties** palette; the **Type Properties** dialog box will be displayed, as shown in Figure 9-17. To create a new dimension style with the parameters most suitable to the project. Choose the **Duplicate** button from the **Type Properties**. Various type parameters available in this dialog box and their usage are discussed next.

The **Leader Type** parameter is used to specify the type of line to be drawn for the leader. You can select the **Arc** or **Line** option from the drop-down list displayed on clicking the **Value** field corresponding to it. You can specify the type of tick mark for the leader by selecting an option from the **Value** field corresponding to the **Leader Tick Mark** parameter. You can also set condition for the display of the leader. To do so, select an option from the drop-down list in the **Value** field corresponding to the **Show Leader When Text Moves** parameter. The **Tick Mark** parameter defines the mark type to be used as the tick mark. The **Line Weight** parameter is used to specify the line weight or thickness for the dimension line. You can select the value ranging from 1 to 16, depending on the desired thickness. The **Tick Mark Line Weight** parameter sets the thickness of the tick mark line. The **Dimension Line Extension** parameter is used to specify the distance upto which the dimension line can be extended beyond its intersection with the witness line.

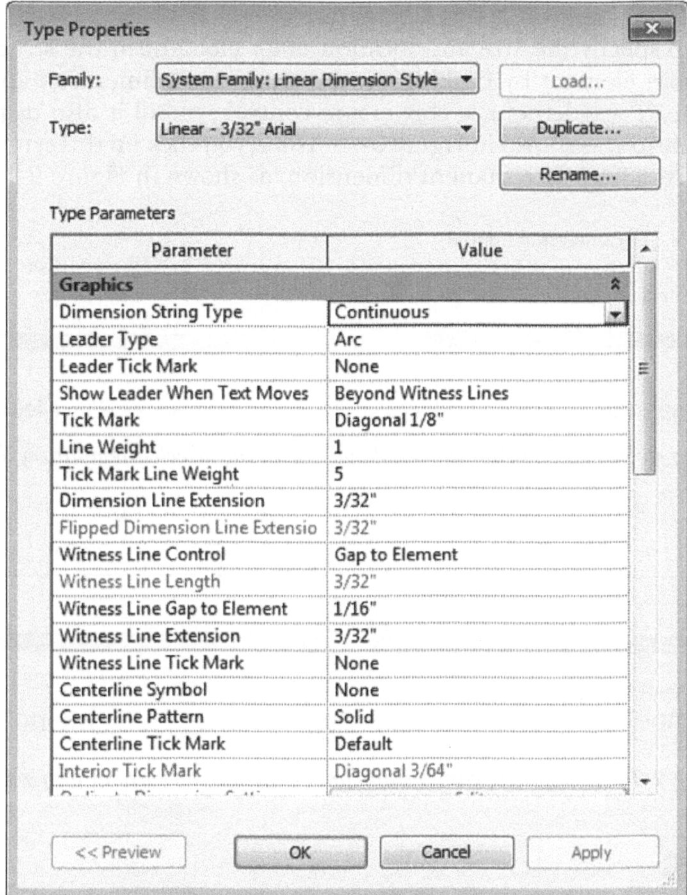

Figure 9-17 *The* ***Type Properties*** *dialog box*

To change the default label from **EQ** to a different text description for the dimension type. You can use the **Equality Text** parameter under the **Other** head. This custom label will be displayed for all equality texts created with this dimension type. Apart from various dimension settings, you can also set various parameters for the dimension text such as **Text Size**, **Text Offset**, and so on. After modifying the parameter(s), choose the **Apply** button to apply the changes.

Locking Permanent Dimensions

When you add a permanent dimension, a lock control symbol is displayed. It also gets displayed when you select a permanent dimension. This symbol can be used to lock or unlock the dimension of an element. When the symbol is unlocked, you can modify the dimension along with the element. When you lock a dimension, the element corresponding to it is also locked along with it. This means you cannot modify its dimension value. You can, however, move the element along with dimension. Once the dimension is locked, you must unlock it to change its value.

Converting Temporary Dimensions into Permanent Dimensions

As discussed, in the earlier sections of this chapter, temporary dimensions are displayed while creating various elements such as grids, ducts, panels, pipes, and other MEP system elements.

They can be used to specify the size and location of an element in the structural system. You can move or resize an element by clicking on the temporary dimension and entering a new value. When you create an element, a conversion control symbol is also displayed along with the temporary dimension, as shown in Figure 9-18. When you click on this symbol, the temporary dimension is converted into a permanent dimension, as shown in Figure 9-19.

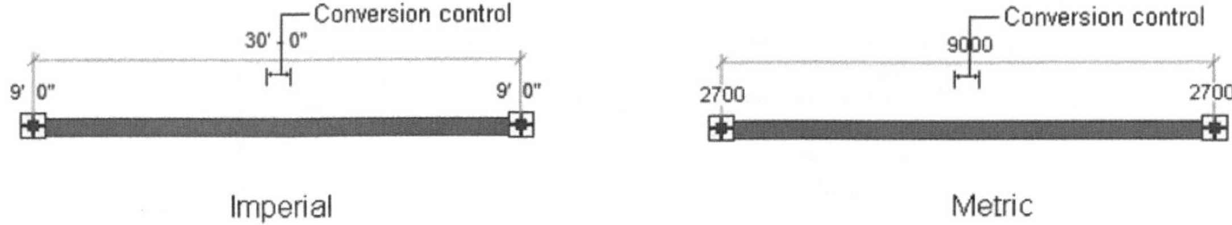

Figure 9-18 *The conversion control symbol displayed in the selected temporary dimension*

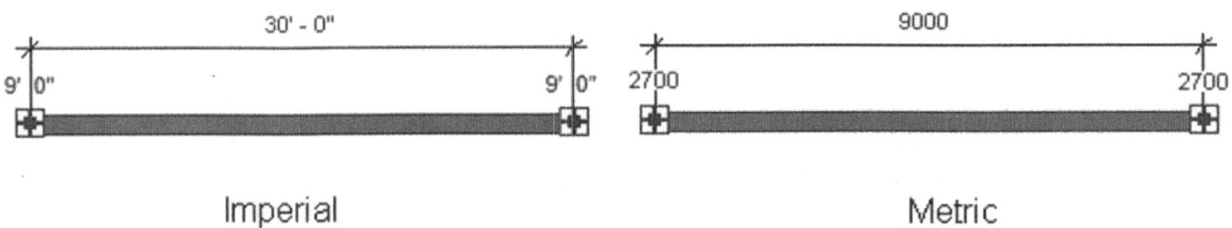

Figure 9-19 *Temporary dimension converted into permanent dimension*

TEXT NOTES

Enhanced

In Revit, text notes are important part of a project detail. They not only help in adding the specification of various elements but also in conveying the specific design intent. Revit provides a variety of options to add text notes to different system detail views by using the **Text** tool. Various options to add and modify a text in a model view are discussed next.

Adding Text Notes

Ribbon:	Annotate > Text > Text

In Revit 2017, text notes are view-specific entities. You can add different text notes to different views. Generally, text notes are added in the plan view, section view, callout view, or in drafting view. The selection of a view in which the text notes are added depends on the project requirement. To add a text note to a desired view, invoke the **Text** tool from the **Text** panel; the **Modify | Place Text** tab will be displayed, as shown in Figure 9-20.

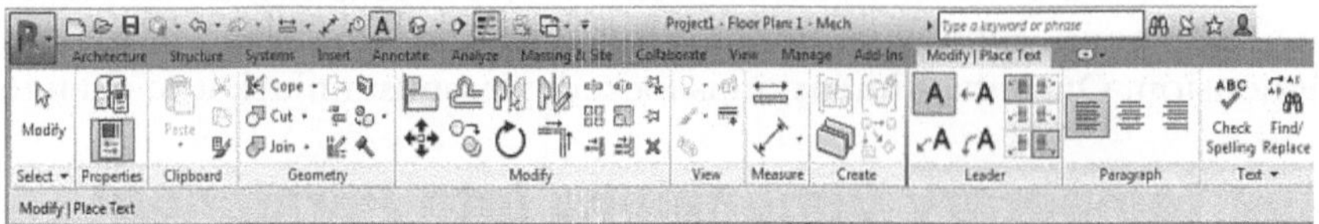

Figure 9-20 *Various options in the **Modify / Place Text** tab*

In this tab, you can use the tools in the **Leader** panel to add a leader with text. For instance, when using the text note, you can attach a straight leader line that has a single segment or double segments. Alternatively, you can also attach a curved leader line to a text note. The **No Leader** tool is chosen by default in the **Leader** panel. As a result, when a text note is inserted into the project view, no leader will get attached to the text note. To attach a straight leader line with one segment, choose the **One Segment** tool from the **Format** panel. You can choose the **Two Segments** tool or the **Curved** tool from the **Format** panel to attach a double segment straight leader line or a curved leader line to the text note. Figure 9-21 illustrates the usage of the leader options discussed earlier.

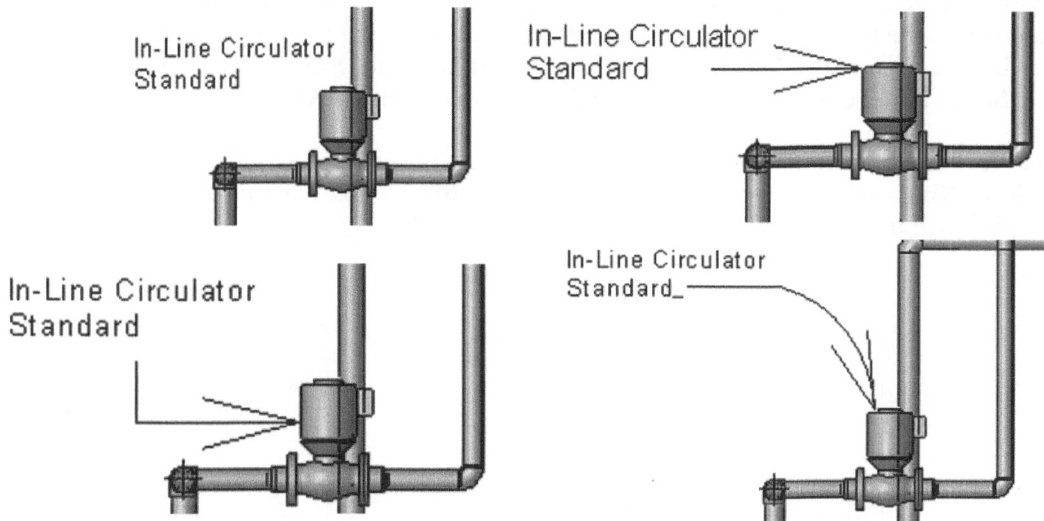

Figure 9-21 *Illustration showing various options of a leader in a text note*

After choosing the desired option for the display of the leader line, you can choose various tools from the **Leader** panel to locate the leader line in reference to the text note. For instance, you can place the leader line on the left of a text note at three different places: top left, middle left, or bottom left corner of the text note. To place the leader lines, choose the **Leader at Top Left**, **Leader at Middle Left**, or **Leader at Bottom Left** tool from the **Leader** panel. Similarly, you can place the leader line on the right of the text note. To do so, choose the **Leader at Top Right**, **Leader at Middle Right**, or **Leader at Bottom Right** tool from the **Leader** panel. By default, the **Leader at Top Left** and **Leader at Bottom Right** tools are chosen from the **Leader** panel. As a result, the leader will be attached to the text note at the top left corner or at the bottom right corner, depending on the side where the leader is placed.

After setting the options for the placement of leader, you can set the alignment of the text to be inserted. To do so, you can choose any of the three tools, namely **Align Left**, **Align Center**, or **Align Right** from the **Paragraph** panel. The **Align Left** tool is chosen by default in this panel. As a result, the text will be aligned on the left margin in the text box. You can choose the **Align Center** tool to align the text evenly between the left margin and the right margin of the text box. You can choose the **Align Right** tool to align the text to the right margin of the text box.

After setting the desired options for placing the leader line and the text alignment, move the cursor near the desired location and click to add the text note. On doing so, a leader will emerge from the location you have clicked, if the settings for the leader allow the display of leader. You may need to click once or twice depending upon the option chosen for the leader. After specifying the leader, if required, click to display a text box along with a text symbol. On doing so, the **Edit Text** contextual tab will be displayed with various options to edit the text will while inserting it.

In the **Font** panel of the **Edit Text** contextual tab, you can use the **Bold**, **Italics**, and **Underline** tools, or their combinations to format the text as required. In the Font panel, you can also use the **Subscript**, **Superscript**, **All Caps** tool, or their combination to format the text as required. In the **Paragraph** panel you can use various tools to edit the paragraph of the text that you will insert. For instance you can use the **List** tools in the **Paragraph** panel to list bullets, numbers, or alphabets in the text. You can also use the **Decrease Indent** or **Increase Indent** tool to move the paragraph to the left or right within the text note. After writing text in the text box, choose the **Close** button in the **Edit Text** panel to exit the **Edit Text** tab. Now, choose the **Modify** button in the **Select** panel of the **Modify | Place Text** tab to exit the **Text** tool.

After entering the text in the text box, you can check the spellings as well. To do so, choose the **Check Spelling** tool from the **Tools** panel of the **Modify | Place Text** tab; the **Check Spelling** dialog box will be displayed, as shown in Figure 9-22.

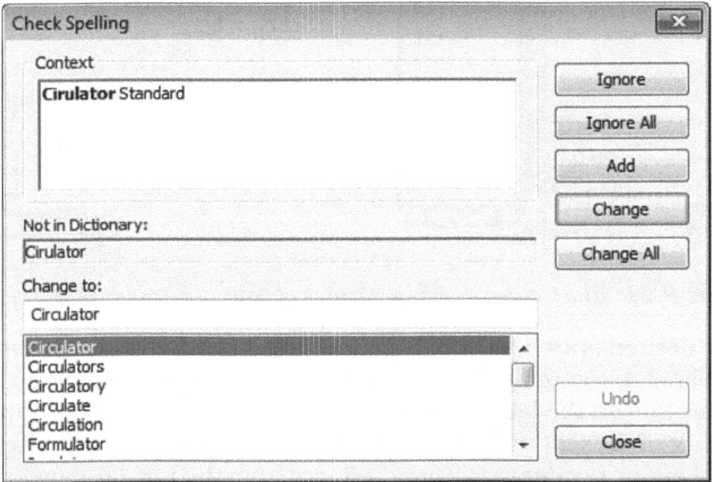

Figure 9-22 *The **Check Spelling** dialog box*

In this dialog box, the **Context** area displays the context or sentence in which the word(s) is misspelt. The **Not in Dictionary** text box displays the word that is misspelt in the context displayed in the **Context** area. The **Change to** area displays a list box containing the words suggested to replace the misspelt word. You can click on the suitable word in the list box and then choose the **Change** button to replace the misspelt word with the suggested word. On doing so, the **Revit** message box will be displayed, informing you that the spell-check operation has been completed. Choose the **Close** button and press ESC to exit the text editing option.

Note

*In the **Context** area of the **Check Spelling** dialog box, the misspelt word is displayed in boldface.*

Editing Text Notes

You can set the properties of a text note before creating it or edit it later. When you select a text note, its controls are displayed. You can use these controls to edit the text note parameters. The controls consist of one blue dot on each side of the text box that represents the stretch controls that can be used to modify the size of the text box. The rotation controls are also placed at the top right corner of the text box. You can use it to rotate the text box. The location of the leader arrow-head remains in its original position and only the text box is rotated. The leader tail automatically adjusts to the rotated text box. You can also drag the location of the leader elbow and leader head by using the drag control dots. The drag control is used to change the location of the text box.

As you select the text note, the **Modify | Text Notes** tab is displayed. In this tab, you can use various editing tools such as **Copy**, **Mirror**, **Rotate**, **Array**, and so on to edit and arrange the text note. The alignment of the text note can be modified by choosing appropriate alignment tool from the **Format** panel. In this panel, you can choose the **Add Left Side Straight Leader** or **Add Right Side Straight Leader** tool to add a leader to the left or right side of the text note. You can choose the **Remove Last Leader** tool from the **Leader** panel to remove the leader that is added last to the text note. To modify a text note, click inside the text box and then select the text note. Next, enter the new note. You can also modify the instance properties of the text note such as text font and text size. To do so, you can use various parameters in the **Properties** palette. In this palette, the value assigned to the **Horizontal Align** parameter is used to specify the horizontal text alignment of the selected text. To change the value assigned to the **Horizontal Align** parameter, click in the **Value** column corresponding to it and select the desired alignment option from the drop-down list displayed. The **Arc Leaders** instance parameter is used to specify whether or not an arc leader should be attached to a text. The check box in the **Value** field of this parameter displays a check box, which is cleared by default. You can select this check box to attach an arc leader to a text.

You can also edit the type properties of a text using the **Properties** palette. To do so, choose the **Edit Type** button from the **Properties** palette; the **Type Properties** dialog box will be displayed, as shown in Figure 9-23.

In this dialog box, you can edit the font of a text by clicking in the **Value** column corresponding to the **Text Font** parameter and then selecting the required text font from the drop-down list displayed. The **Text Size** parameter is used to specify the size of the text note. The **Tab Size** parameter is used to set the tab spacing used in text notes. The tab spacing can be inserted by pressing the TAB key. You can also select the check boxes for the **Bold**, **Italic**, and **Underline** parameters to set the format of the text note. Choose the **OK** button to close the **Type Properties** dialog box. The **Type Selector** drop-down list in the **Properties** palette of the selected text note displays the available text types. You can select the appropriate type from the available text types before creating text notes. Alternatively, you can select a text note that was created earlier and then select the new text type from the **Type Selector** drop-down list to replace the old text type. You can also use the **Copy to Clipboard** and **Paste from Clipboard** tools from the **Modify | Text Notes** tab to copy the text notes from one level to multiple levels. You can also edit the font in the text or list the text by bulleting, numbering, or adding alphabets to it. To insert the number, bullet, or alphabet before a text, click in the desired place. On doing so, the **Edit Text** contextual tab will be displayed. In this tab, you can use various options in the **Paragraph** panel to insert the list. To exit from the **Edit Text** contextual tab, choose the **Close** button from the **Edit Text** panel.

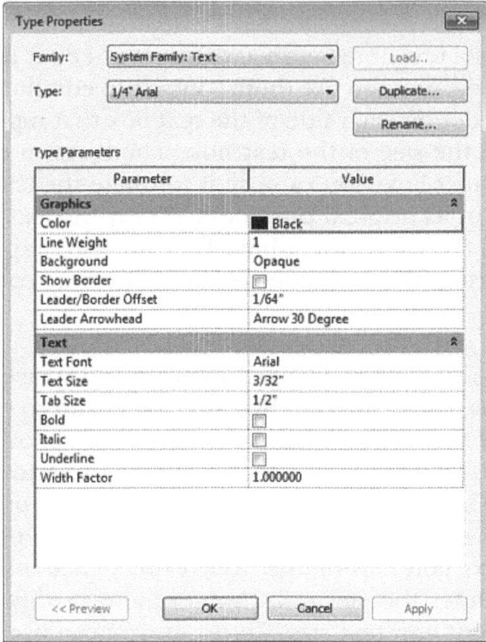

*Figure 9-23 The **Type Properties** dialog box for the selected text*

ADDING TAGS

You can easily add tag to various elements in an MEP system. A tag is a useful annotation that assists in identifying elements in a drawing. While designing complex systems using Revit, tags play an important role in arranging various elements in schedules. You can then add necessary description about each tagged element in a tabular form.

Revit provides various tools to add and edit tags. When you open a default template file, the tags of a certain category of elements are pre-loaded. Therefore, when you add the elements such as ducts, pipes, spaces, diffusers, and so on to a system, Revit automatically tags them. For other elements, you need to load their respective tags from the Revit library. Like other annotations, tags are also view-specific and therefore, they appear only in the view they have been created in. You can control the visibility of tags by choosing the **Visibility/Graphics** tool from the **Graphics** panel of the **View** tab. On doing so, the **Visibility/Graphics Overrides for <current view>** dialog box will be displayed. In this dialog box, the **Annotation Categories** tab contains the list of tag categories such as **Air Terminal Tags**, **Assembly Tags**, **Cable Tray Tags**, **Conduit Tags**, **Duct Tags**, **Electrical Equipment Tags**, **Mechanical Equipment Tags**, **Pipe Tags**, **Space Tags**, **Sprinkler Tags**, and so on. You can select appropriate check boxes to control the visibility of each category of tags. The method used for tagging an element is discussed next.

Tagging Elements by Category

Ribbon: Annotate > Tag > Tag by Category

To attach a tag to an element based on its category, choose the **Tag by Category** tool from the **Tag** panel; the **Options Bar** will display the parameters related to the placement and orientation of the tag. In the **Options Bar**, you can select the **Horizontal** or **Vertical** option from the drop-down list displayed on the left to specify the direction of the text in the tag. Select or clear the **Leader** check box to enable or disable the display of a leader line with the tag. On selecting this check box, the options in the drop-down list displayed on the right of the **Leader** check box will be enabled. You can select two options from this drop-down list: **Attached End** and **Free End**. If you select the **Attached End** option from the drop-down list, you will not be able to move the end of the leader with the tag away from the element category it is attached to. On selecting the **Attached End** option from the drop-down list, an edit box on its right will be enabled. In this edit box, you can specify the length of the leader or the distance of the tag from the attached element. Similarly, if you select the **Free End** option from the drop-down list, you can move the end of the leader away from the element it is attached to.

Loading the Tags

By default, Revit loads tags for certain categories of elements such as **Air Terminals**, **Cable Trays**, **Duct Fittings**, **Electrical Fixtures**, **Mech Equipment**, **Spaces**, and more. To display the tags that are loaded in the project, choose the **Loaded Tags And Symbols** tool from the expanded **Tag** panel of the **Annotate** tab. On doing so, the **Loaded Tags And Symbols** dialog box will be displayed. This dialog box displays the category-wise list of the tags loaded in the project, as shown in Figure 9-24.

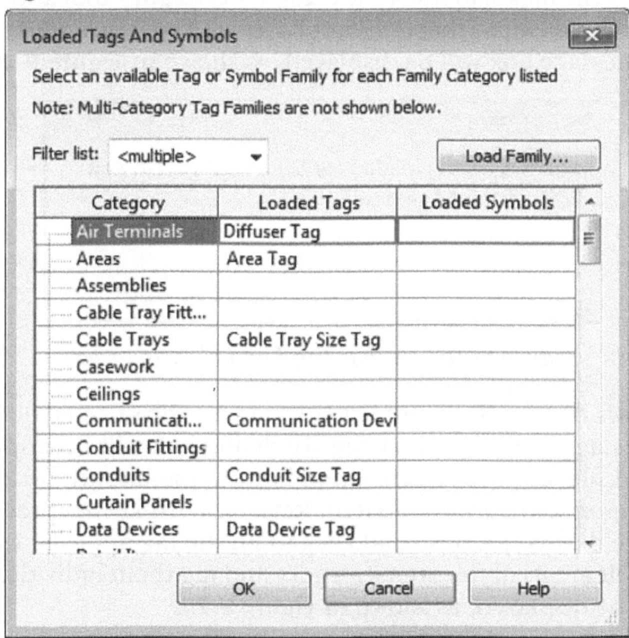

*Figure 9-24 The **Loaded Tags** dialog box*

In case the category of element to be tagged does not have its corresponding tag already loaded, choose the **Load Family** button from the **Loaded Tags And Symbols** dialog box; the **Load Family** dialog box will be displayed. You can select various categories of tags from **US Imperial > Annotations** for imperial and **US Metric > Annotations** for metric folder path based on your requirement. The **Preview** area of the **Load Family** dialog box displays the preview image of the selected tag, as shown in Figure 9-25. You can select an appropriate tag from the list and choose the **Open** button to load it into the project. On doing so, the desired tag will be added to the list of loaded tags for the corresponding element category in the **Loaded Tags And Symbols** dialog box.

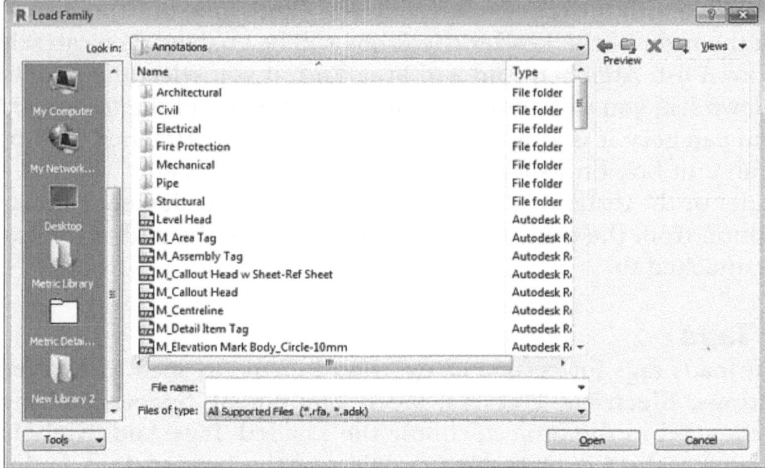

Figure 9-25 The preview of the selected tag in the ***Load Family*** *dialog box*

Another way of loading the tags is to invoke the **Tag By Category** tool and select the element to be tagged. If you select an element that does not have a tag corresponding to it already loaded, the **No Tag Loaded** message box will be displayed, as shown in Figure 9-26.

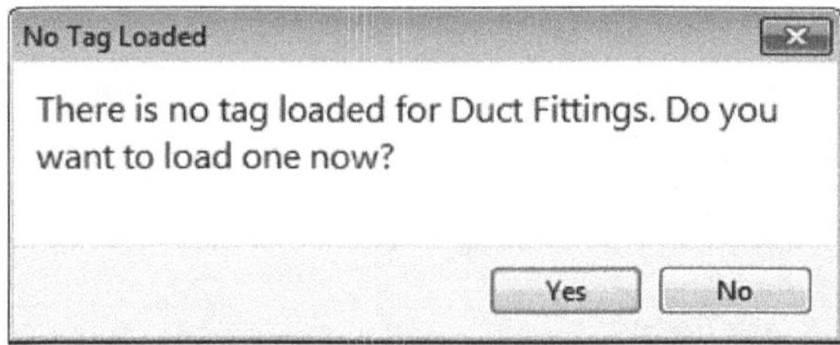

Figure 9-26 The ***No Tag Loaded*** *message box*

This message box shows that you have not loaded a tag for the selected object type. Choose the **Yes** button in this message box; the **Load Family** dialog box will be displayed. In this dialog box, select the desired file and choose the **Open** button; the tag will be loaded. After loading the tag if you move the cursor near the element, Revit will display the preview image of the tag. Move the cursor to the desired location and click when the tag appears; the tag will be placed. Next, select different elements of the same category and tag them individually. When you select a tag, its controls will be displayed, as shown in Figure 9-27.

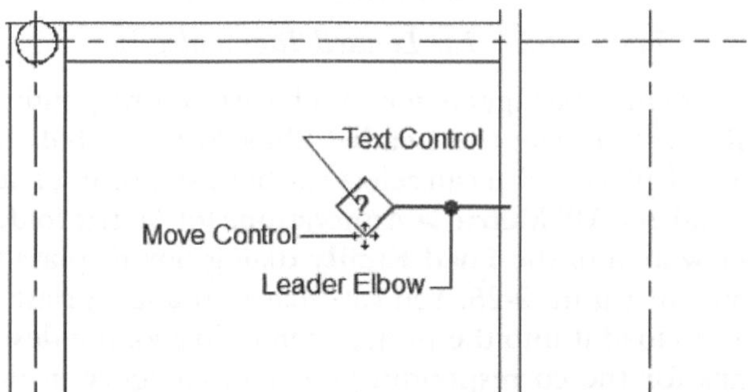

Figure 9-27 The selected tag with its controls

The move control displayed along with the tag is used to move the tag to the desired location. The leader elbow control is used to adjust the leader. The '?' control is used to enter text for the label of the tag. When you add a label, Revit displays a message box, informing you that you are changing the type parameter of the tag and that it could affect many elements. Choose **Yes** from the message box to continue working in the project; the value entered will be displayed as the label in the tag.

Tagging All Elements in a View

You can tag all elements visible in the current view by using the **Tag All** tool. On invoking this tool from the **Tag** panel, the **Tag All Not Tagged** dialog box will be displayed, as shown in Figure 9-28. This dialog box has two radio buttons: **All objects in current view** and **Only selected objects in current view**. The **Only selected objects in current view** radio button gets activated only if you select an object before invoking the **Tag All Not Tagged** dialog box. The selection of the **All objects in current view** radio button ensures that all objects present in the current view are tagged, provided their categories are selected in the **Category** column of the **Tag All Not Tagged** dialog box. The table displayed below the radio buttons shows the listing of category tags of all elements present in the current view and their corresponding loaded tags.

Tip

*You can load tags for multiple categories of components by pressing and holding the CTRL key and selecting multiple tags from the drop-down list in the **Loaded Tags** column of the **Tags** dialog box.*

***Figure 9-28** The **Tag All Not Tagged** dialog box*

Note

*If a category of elements you wish to tag does not appear in this list, you need to load the corresponding tag family and then use the **Tag All** tool.*

From the table displayed in the **Tag All Not Tagged** dialog box, select a desired category. The **Leader** check box can be used to add a leader to them. You can also select the orientation and length of the leader in this dialog box. Choose the **Apply** button to apply the settings to the current view. For example, you can tag all air diffusers in a floor plan view by using the **Tag All** tool, as shown in Figure 9-29.

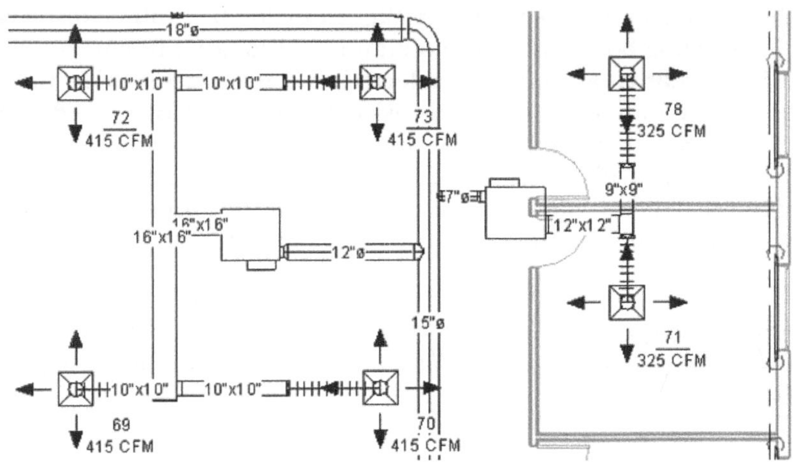

***Figure 9-29** All air diffusers tagged using the **Tag All** tool*

CALLOUT VIEWS

A callout view is an enlarged view of a part of a project model, which requires more detailing. Creating callout views is a common practice among engineers as callout views help them look at the project model more precisely and with a higher level of detail. For example, in mechanical discipline, a callout view can be used to show the details of a connection of a duct and a diffuser in the plan or an elevation view. In a project, you can create a callout view for a plan view, section view, or elevation view. In these views, the callout tag added in a view will be linked to the callout view. The view in which the callout tag is added is called the parent view of the callout view. If the parent view is deleted, the callout view will also be deleted. A callout tag, as shown in Figure 9-30, is an annotation element that represents the location of the callout in the plan, elevation, or section view.

The callout tag consists of the following parts: callout bubble, callout head, leader line, and reference labels. The callout bubble is the line drawn around that part of the structural model which you need to enlarge and view in the callout view. The callout head is a symbol that represents the callout view. When a callout view is placed on a sheet, the callout head displays a detail number and a sheet number by default. The line that connects the callout head to the callout bubble is called the leader line. The reference label in a callout tag is used for the callout views that are referenced.

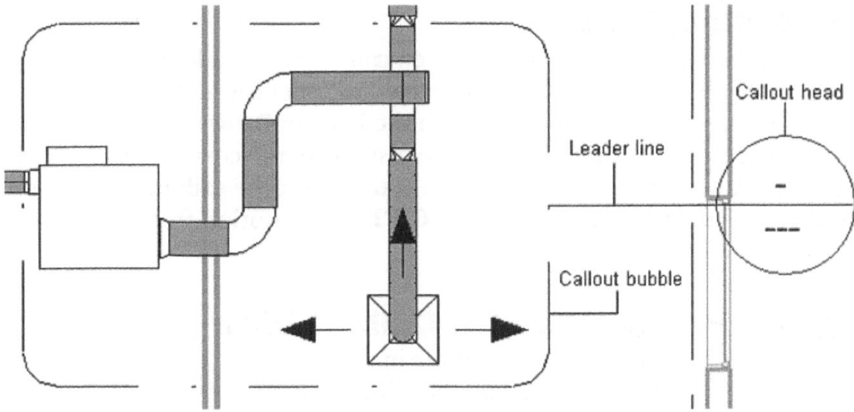

***Figure 9-30** The display of a callout tag*

Various methods for creating callout view, displaying a callout view, modifying callout view properties, and adding detail lines to a callout view are discussed in the next section.

Creating a Callout Using the Rectangle Tool

Ribbon:	View > Create > Callout drop-down > Rectangle Tool

To create a rectangular callout view, choose the **Rectangle** tool from **View > Create > Callout** drop-down; the **Modify | Callout** contextual tab will be displayed. The **Properties** palette will display the properties related to the callout view to be created. In the **Properties** palette, the **Type Selector** drop-down list displays the type of callout view to be generated. In this drop-down list, you can select any of these two types: **Detail View : Detail** and **Floor Plan : Floor Plan** (for current view). Select the **Detail View : Detail** type if you want to provide detailed information about a specific part in a model. Select the **Floor Plan : Floor Plan** (for current view) type if you want to provide more information about a part of the current view. The **Scale** pop-up in the **View Control Bar** can be used to set the view scale. In the **Options Bar**, the **Reference Other View** check box is cleared by default. You can select this check box to create a reference callout. On selecting this check box, the drop-down list next to it is activated. In this drop-down list, you can select an option to specify a view that the callout will refer to. After selecting the desired type and option, move the cursor to the top left corner of the area that you want to enlarge and then drag it toward the lower right corner to create a callout bubble, refer to Figure 9-30. Release the left mouse button when the required area is enclosed in it.

Creating a Callout Using the Sketch Tool

Ribbon:	View > Create > Callout drop-down > Sketch

In Revit, you can create a customized callout view making use of various draw tools. To do so, invoke the **Sketch** tool from **View > Create > Callout** drop-down; the **Modify| Edit Profile** contextual tab will be displayed. The **Draw** panel of this tab contains various sketching tools such as **Line, Rectangle, Pick Line,** and so on. Choose any tool from this panel to sketch the desired callout view.

Displaying Callout View

When you create a callout in the existing view, a new callout view is added to the **Project Browser** under the parent category. For example, if you create a callout view in the section view, the callout view will be added under the **Sections** heading in the **Project Browser**. In the **Project Browser**, double-click on the name of the callout view to be displayed; the corresponding callout view will be displayed in the drawing window. Alternatively, highlight the callout bubble and right-click to display the shortcut menu. Next, choose the **Go To View** option from the shortcut menu to display the callout view.

Modifying the Properties of a Callout View

You can modify the appearance of a callout bubble in the parent view by using the bubble controls displayed on selecting a callout view. You can modify the extents of a callout view by using its drag controls. The rotation control can be used to rotate the callout bubble along with its leader and tag. The leader elbow control can be dragged to the desired location.

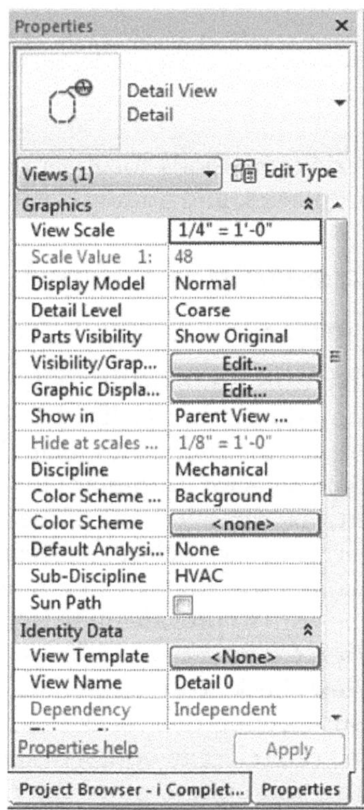

***Figure 9-31** The instance properties of the callout view in the **Properties** palette*

The instance properties of a callout view are different for different types of callouts. To modify the instance properties of a view type callout, select it from the drawing; the instance properties of the selected callout will be displayed in the **Properties** palette, as shown in Figure 9-31. The different instance properties displayed in the **Properties** palette are discussed next.

In the **Properties** palette, you can enter the name to be assigned to a new callout view in the **Value** field of the **View Name** instance parameter under the **Identity Data** head. Similarly, you can enter the title to be given on the sheet in the value field of the **Title on Sheet** parameter.

The **Display Model** parameter under the **Graphics** head is used to set the display type for the view of a building model. By default, this parameter is set to **Normal**. You can set the value of the **Display Model** parameter to **Halftone** to display the model element in the current view as a faded image. You can set the value of this parameter to the **Do not display** option to hide the model element in the current view.

The **Underlay** parameter under the **Graphics** head can be used to set the display of model elements, which are displayed in other levels and are invisible in the current view. By default, the **Underlay** parameter is set to **None**. You can select a level from the drop-down list corresponding to this parameter to make the elements of the selected level visible in the current view. The elements that are displayed as underlay appear dim.

The amount of details to be displayed in a callout view can be controlled by using the **Detail Level** parameter under the **Graphics** head. To display details, you can select any of the following three options from the drop-down list corresponding to this parameter: **Coarse**, **Medium**, and **Fine**. By default, the **Medium** option is selected in the drop-down list. As a result, model elements are displayed with fewer details in the current view. You can select the **Fine** option from this drop-down list to display the layers of various materials used in a building model. On selecting the **Fine** option, additional lines are displayed in the callout view. These lines describe composite materials.

The **Edit** button in the **Value** column for the **Visibility /Graphics Overrides** parameter can be used to control the visibility of different models and annotation elements in the callout view. The **View Scale** instance parameter is used to set the scale for a callout view. You can use the drop-down list in the Value column to select a scale for the callout view.

Creating Details in a Callout View

Ribbon:	Annotate > Detail > Detail Line

Detail Line

Revit provides various tools to create details in a callout view. You can sketch lines using the **Detail Line** tool and also add detail components provided in Revit's library.

The **Detail Lines** tool is used to create lines for a detail view. Detail lines are view-specific and appear only in the view in which they are created. You can use the callout view of a building model and trace detail lines over the image using their varying thickness.

To create detail lines for a detail view, choose the **Detail Line** tool from the **Detail** panel of the **Annotate** tab; the **Modify | Place Detail Lines** tab will be displayed. Select the type of detail lines from the **Line Style** drop-down list in the **Line Style** panel of this tab. You can select the appropriate detail line based on its usage. For example, wide lines can be used to show insulated pipe, whereas thin lines can be selected to represent normal pipe.

You can draw these lines by using the sketching tools displayed in the **Draw** panel of the **Modify | Place Detail Lines** tab. To add detail lines, you can trace over the underlay elements. On doing so, you will notice that the cursor snaps at various elements on the underlay lines. The entire detail can be sketched using a variety of line thicknesses to achieve the desired graphical representation. You can also add dimensions and symbols to details. However, after completing a detail, you can hide the underlay callout view. To do so, you need to select the callout view from the drawing and then select the **Do not Display** option from the drop-down list corresponding to the **Display Model** parameter in the **Properties** palette.

Note

*After adding the detail lines to the callout view, you can add the filled region to the drafted details by invoking the **Filled Region** tool from **Annotate > Detail > Region** drop-down.*

DRAFTING DETAILS

Drafted details are created when you want to access the details that are not referenced to the existing project views. These details are not linked to a building model and therefore, they do not update with it.

To create a drafted detail, first create a drafting view and then use the drafting tools provided in Revit to sketch the details. You can also import in-built details from Revit's detail library and use them.

After the drafted details are created, they can be used as reference details. The methods used for creating a drafting view and drafting details are discussed in the next sections.

Creating a Drafting View

Ribbon:	View > Create > Drafting View

To create a drafting view, invoke the **Drafting View** tool from the **Create** panel of the **View** tab; the **New Drafting View** dialog box will be displayed, as shown in Figure 9-32. In this dialog box, enter a name for the drafting view in the **Name** edit box. Next, select the scale for the detailing from the **Scale** drop-down list. To specify a user-defined scale, select the **Custom** option from the **Scale** drop-down list and then specify a value in the **Scale value 1** edit box. Next, choose the **OK** button; the drafting view will be created and added under the **Drafting Views** subhead of the **Mechanical** head in the **Project Browser**.

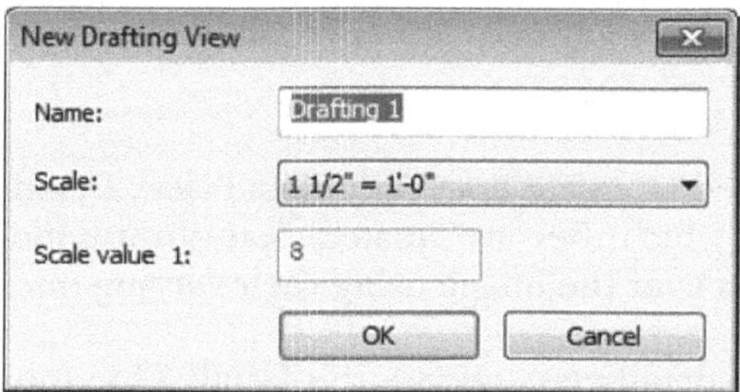

Figure 9-32 *The* ***New Drafting View*** *dialog box*

Note

In Revit, drafting views are created as independent views. As a result, when you create drafting views, project views are not displayed in the drawing window.

Drafting a Detail

The method of drafting a detail in a drafting view is similar to the one used in a callout view. In a callout view, lines are traced over an enlarged project view, whereas in a drafting view, the project view is not available and a new detail is drafted as if you are drafting on a blank sheet.

You can draft a detail by using the tools in the **Detail** panel of the **Annotate** tab. The **Detail Line** tool enables you to draw lines with varying thickness. The **Detail Component** tool in the **Component** drop-down is used to add in-built detail components from Revit's detail library. The **Insulation** tool enables you to add a graphical insulation symbol to the drafted detail. You can create graphical patterns to represent various building materials using the **Region** tool. The usage of these tools is similar to the tools in a callout view. You can also add dimensions, text notes, and break lines to complete a drafted detail.

DUPLICATING VIEWS

You can create multiple copies of a project view in Revit. These multiple views are called duplicate views. All duplicate views are dependent on the original view from which they are created. Therefore, these views are updated automatically if any changes are made in the original view. Duplicate views are useful when you want to use or place the same view on more than one sheet. These views are also useful in case of huge projects when the overall project view is too large to fit into a single sheet. In such cases, you can crop the parent view to make small segments by using the crop regions, create dependent views from them, and then place the cropped dependent views on the sheet. In Revit, you can create three types of duplicate views. The tools used for creating these duplicate views are: **Duplicate View**, **Duplicate with Detailing**, and **Duplicate as Dependent**. You can use the **Duplicate View** tool to create a view that contains only the model geometry from the current view. The **Duplicate with Detailing** tool can be used to create a view that contains view-specific elements from the current view. You can use the **Duplicate as Dependent** tool to create a view that is dependent on the current view. The method of creating duplicate view as a dependent view is discussed next.

Creating Duplicate View as Dependent View

Ribbon: View > Create > Duplicate View drop-down > Duplicate as Dependent

You can create a dependent view from a plan, elevation, section, or callout view. To create a dependent view, open the view from which you want to create duplicate views and then choose the **Duplicate as Dependent** tool from **View > Create > Duplicate View** drop-down. Alternatively, select the name of the view in the **Project Browser** and right-click; a shortcut menu will be displayed. Choose **Duplicate View > Duplicate as Dependent** from the shortcut menu; the dependent view will display a crop region boundary and will be added in the **Project Browser** as a dependent view under the primary view.

Tip

Crop regions help to exclude unwanted content from a crop view, thereby reducing the view size. In Revit, there are two types of crop regions that allow you to crop views for the model and annotation categories. You can control the visibility of a crop region by using the ***Crop View*** *or* ***Do not Crop View*** *tool from the* ***View Control Bar****.*

Next, select the crop region boundary to display drag controls. Using the drag controls, resize the primary view and then crop it to include only the required portion of the view in the dependent view. Next, select the name of the dependent view in the **Project Browser** and right-click; a shortcut menu will be displayed. Choose **Rename** from the shortcut menu; the **Rename View** dialog box will be displayed. In this dialog box, enter a name for the dependent view and choose the **OK** button; the duplicate view will be renamed. Again, open the primary view and choose the **Show Crop Region** button from the **View Control Bar** to display the crop region boundary. Similarly, create another dependent view as explained above. In this way, you can crop the primary view and create multiple dependent views. To navigate to the primary view from the dependent view, select the crop region boundary of the dependent view and right-click; a shortcut menu will be displayed. Choose **Go to Primary View** from the shortcut menu; the primary view will be displayed on the screen. You can also navigate to the dependent views from the primary view. To do so, choose the **Show Crop Region** button from the **View Control Bar** if the crop regions are not displayed in the primary view. On doing so, the crop regions for all dependent views will be displayed. Select the crop region of the required dependent view and then right-click; a shortcut menu will be displayed. Choose **Go to View** from the shortcut menu; the corresponding dependent view will open. You can display the primary or dependent views by double-clicking on their respective view names in the **Project Browser**.

Note

*The procedure to create duplicate views by using the **Duplicate View** and **Duplicate with Detailing** tools is similar to that of creating duplicate view/views as dependent views.*

SHEETS

Ribbon:	View > Sheet Composition > Sheet

In Autodesk Revit, a sheet or a drawing sheet is a document set that is used for the final working drawings in a site. A drawing sheet contains sheet views that consist of multiple drawing views or schedules added in a project. Sheets are defined by a border and a title block. To create a drawing sheet, you first need to add a sheet view to the project and then add the required project views to the added sheet views.

Adding a Drawing Sheet to a Project

To create a drawing sheet for a project, first you need to decide its title block. In Revit, title blocks are loaded as families. A title block is used to convey project information and drawing sheet title. Project information includes client name, project name, project title, project number, date of issue of drawing, drawing sheet number, scale, and so on. The project information can be added to a project by using the **Project Information** tool in the **Settings** panel of the **Manage** tab. The type of title block will decide the size of the sheet. In Revit, there are some predefined title blocks that can be used in a project. To load these title blocks so that they can be used in the sheet, choose the **Load Family** tool from the **Load from Library** panel in the **Insert** tab; the **Load Family** dialog box will be displayed, as shown in Figure 9-33. In this dialog box, browse to **US Imperial > Title blocks** (for Metric **US Metric > Title blocks**). From this location, you can select the required title block for the project.

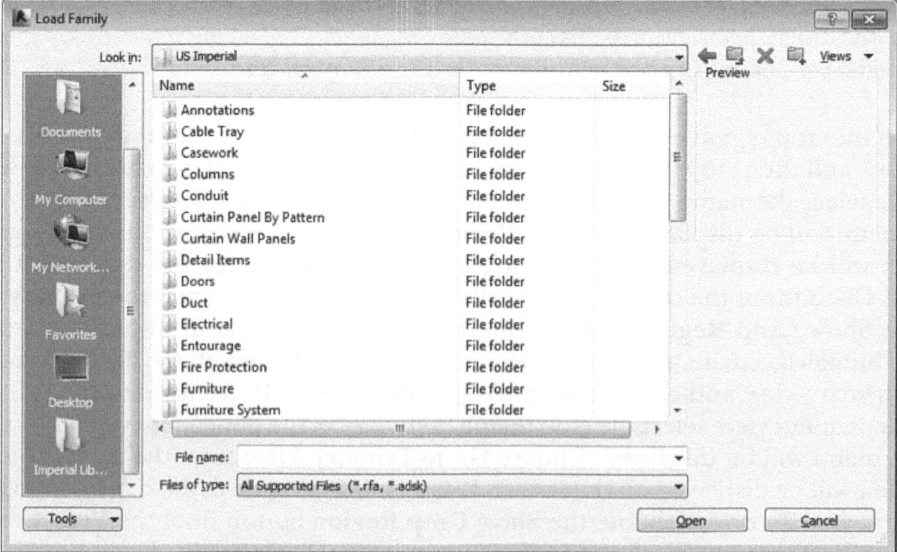

***Figure 9-33** The **Load Family** dialog box*

Note

The sizes of title blocks available in the library are based on ANSI standards for sheet size. These title blocks are available in both vertical (portrait) and horizontal (landscape) alignments.

After selecting a file for the title block from the **Load Family** dialog box, choose the **Open** button; the selected title block(s) will be loaded into the project file. Next, you need to add a drawing sheet to the project. To do so, choose the **Sheet** tool from the **Sheet Composition** panel of the **View** tab; the **New Sheet** dialog box will be displayed. This dialog box has two areas: **Select titleblocks** and **Select placeholder sheets**. Select the required title block for the drawing sheet from the list of title blocks and choose the **OK** button; the Autodesk Revit will create a sheet view and display the borders and the title block in the drawing window, as shown in Figure 9-34. As you add sheets to the project, their names and numbers will be displayed in the **Sheets** head in the **Project Browser**.

Figure 9-34 *Sheet view displayed in the drawing window*

Adding Views to a Drawing Sheet

After adding a drawing sheet to a project, you need to add project views to it. To do so, choose the **View** tool from the **Sheet Composition** panel of the **View** tab; the **Views** dialog box will be displayed, as shown in Figure 9-35.

This dialog box displays the list of project views available in a project. Select the project view that you want to add to the sheet and choose the **Add View to Sheet** button; the selected view will appear as a viewport represented by a rectangle attached to the cursor. Move the cursor to the drawing area in the sheet and click at the preferred location to add the selected view. Next, in the **Properties** palette, change the **View Scale** parameter by selecting a suitable scale from the drop-down list in its value field and choose **Apply**. The added view will adjust to the specified scale in the sheet, as shown in Figure 9-36.

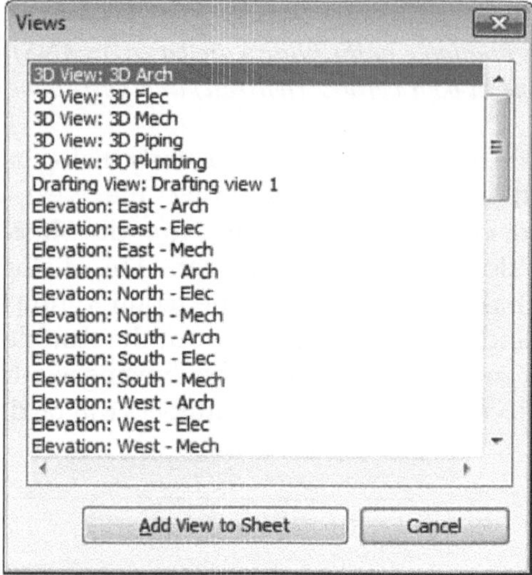

***Figure 9-35** The **Views** dialog box*

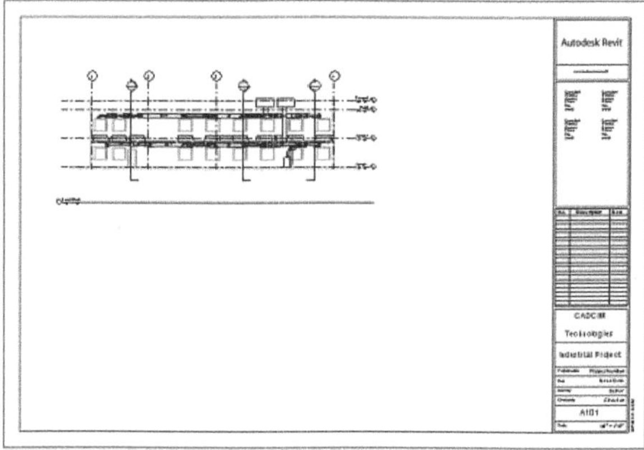

***Figure 9-36** The specified view added to the sheet*

The viewport of the inserted view will display a label line at the bottom left corner. The label line shows the view name, view scale, and view number. You can modify the properties associated with the viewport in the **Properties** palette. You can also activate the project view and then pan it to adjust the view area that you need to display in the viewport. Various options to modify the properties of the views in the viewport and to pan the view areas are discussed in the next section.

Modifying View Properties

To modify the properties of the project views added in a sheet, select the viewport associated with it; the **Properties** palette for the view will be displayed with various instance parameters associated to it. You can modify these values based on your project requirement. When you enter a new value for the **View Name** parameter, the corresponding levels and views are also renamed accordingly. You can modify the scale of a view by selecting a scale from the drop-down list in the value column of the **View Scale** parameter. When you modify the view scale of a view, the corresponding view in the viewport is scaled automatically. You can move the view to another location, if required. You can select the **Coarse, Medium,** or **Fine** option from the drop-down list corresponding to the value column of the **Detail Level** instance parameter to define the level of details to be displayed in a view. You can control the visibility of different categories of elements in each viewport. To do so, choose the **Edit** button displayed in the value field corresponding to the **Visibility/Graphics Overrides** parameter; the **Visibility/Graphics Overrides for Sheet** dialog box will be displayed. In this dialog box, you can control the visibility of various model and annotation elements. The **Rotation on Sheet** instance parameter in the **Options Bar** is used to rotate the view clockwise or counter-clockwise. You can also modify the appearance of the label line. To do so, choose the **Edit Type** button in the **Properties** palette; the **Type Properties** dialog box will be displayed, as shown in Figure 9-37. In this dialog box, the visibility of the title and extension lines can be controlled by using their respective type parameters. Some other parameters of the label line such as line weight, color, and line pattern can also be modified by using this dialog box.

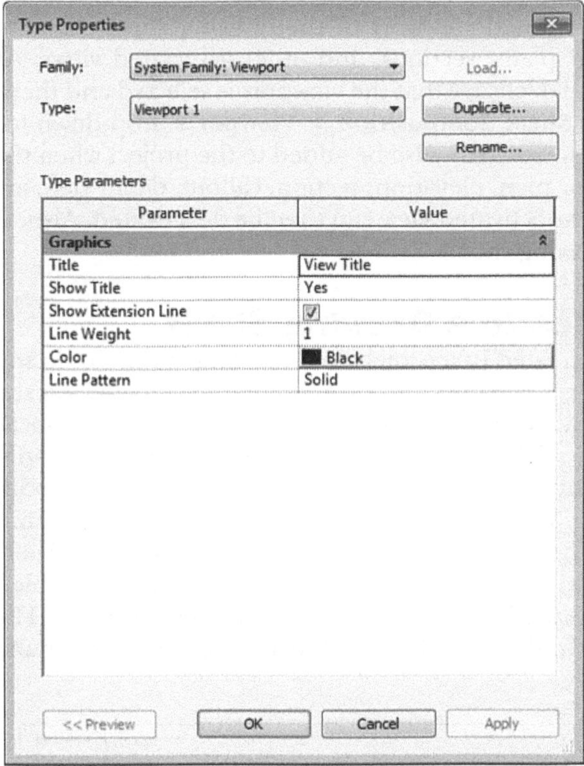

Figure 9-37 *The **Type Properties** dialog box*

Panning Views

After adding views and modifying view properties, you may need to pan the viewport to a suitable location in the sheet. To do so, first you need to activate the view in the viewport and then pan or move the views to a desired location in the sheet. To activate the view, select the viewport corresponding to it in the sheet and then right-click to display the shortcut menu. Next, choose the **Activate View** option from the shortcut menu; the view in the selected viewport will be activated. Again, right-click and choose the **Pan Active View** option from the shortcut menu displayed; the cursor will change into a symbol with four arrows. Left-click in the viewport, press and hold the left mouse button, and drag it to move entities in the viewport. Once you have panned and placed the entities at an appropriate location in the sheet, right-click and then choose **Deactivate View** from the shortcut menu to revert to the sheet.

Modifying a Building Model in Sheets

In sheets, sometimes you may need to make quick modifications in the elements of building model. To do so, you need to activate a view and make the desired modifications in it. To activate a view from a drawing sheet, select a viewport. Next, choose the **Activate View** button from the **Viewport** panel in the **Modify | Viewports** contextual tab; the view will be activated. In the activated view, you can work on the building model as in any other project view. The elements in the building model can be edited using the editing tools. When the building model is edited, the parametric change engine of Autodesk Revit modifies other project views immediately. As a result, all project views update automatically. For example, modifications made to the location of air diffuser in an activated viewport of the drawing sheet are automatically reflected in the corresponding floor plans, sections, and other associated views. After making necessary modifications in the model, ensure that the viewport is selected and then choose the **Deactivate View** tool from **View > Sheet Composition > Viewports** drop-down to return to the drawing sheet view. Note that new views can also be added to the project when the viewport is activated. You can also create a new plan, elevation, section, callout, detail view, and so on while working on the activated view. The activated view can then be deactivated. Also, the newly created views can be added to the drawing sheet.

Adding Schedules to a Drawing Sheet

You can add schedules created in a project to a drawing sheet. To do so, drag the schedules to be added from the **Project Browser** and drop them into the drawing sheet; the preview image of the schedule will be attached to the cursor. Click at the desired location in the drawing to place the schedule. The selected schedule will appear with blue triangles for each column and a break line on the right side, as shown in Figure 9-38. You can modify the appearance and properties of a schedule. The blue triangles representing the controls for the column width can be dragged to modify the width of each column in the schedule. The break line on the right border represents the split control. It is used to split the schedule table into multiple sections. When the split control is used, the schedule is split into two sections. These sections are placed adjacent to each other. In this way, the schedule can be split into a number of sections that fit into the drawing sheet.

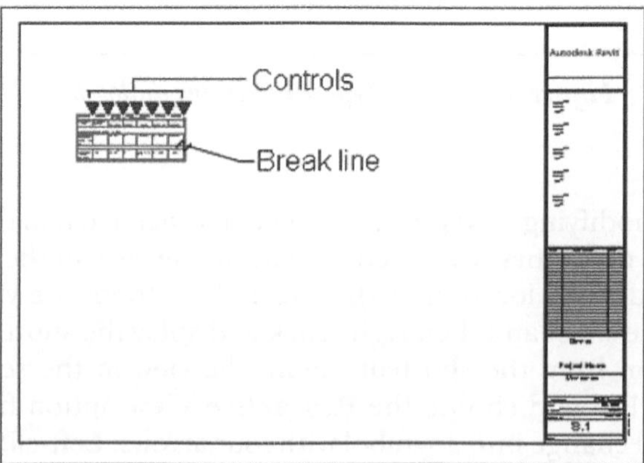

Figure 9-38 *The selected schedule with its controls*

The sections of a schedule can be moved by using the move control available at the center of the schedule section. They can also be resized by dragging the blue dot created at the schedule's end. When the schedule section is resized, the additional or reduced rows are automatically adjusted between the sections. However, the last section cannot be resized, as it contains the remaining rows. The split sections of a schedule can be rejoined. As they are sequential, a section can be joined only to its previous or next section. To join a split section, drag a section by using the move control over the previous or the next section; the two schedule sections will merge into a single schedule section.

Adding Guide Grids to a Sheet

In a sheet. you can add guide grids to a sheet. The guide grids in a sheet will help you to align the view in the sheet so that they appear in the same location from sheet to sheet. You can display the same guide grid in different sheet views. When new guide grids are created, they become available in the instance properties of sheets and can be applied to sheets. It is recommended to create only a few guide grids and then apply them to sheets. To assign a guide grid in the sheet, choose the **Guide Grid** tool in the **Sheet Composition** panel of the **View** tab. On doing so, the **Assign Guide Grid** dialog box will be displayed. In the **Name** edit box of the dialog box, enter the name of the guide grid and then choose the **OK** button; a guide grid with default spacing will be displayed on the sheet and the **Assign Guide Grid** dialog box will be closed. Now, select the guide grid that is displayed on the sheet, the **Modify | Guide Grid** contextual tab will be displayed and the properties of the guide grid will be displayed in the **Properties** Palette. In the Palette, click on the field corresponding to the **Guide Spacing** parameter and change the spacing of the guide grid to a desired spacing. In the field corresponding to the **Name** parameter you can click and change the name of the guide grid selected. Choose the **Modify** button from the **Select** panel to exit the guide grid selection.

TUTORIALS

General instructions for downloading the model file and performing the tutorials:

1. Download the *c09_rmp_2017_tut.zip* file from *www.cadcim.com*. The path of the file is as follows: *Textbooks > Civil/GIS > Revit MEP > Exploring Autodesk Revit 2017 for MEP*.

2. Next, browse to *C:\rmp_2017* and create a new folder with the name *c09_rmp_2017_tut*. Next, save and extract the file in this folder.

Tutorial 1 — Office Space-Tags

In this tutorial, you will add dimensions to a project file in different views. Further, you will annotate spaces and rooms using various annotation tools. Use the following project parameters: **(Expected time: 40 min)**

The following steps are required to complete this tutorial:

a. Open the project file.
   For Imperial *c09_Office-Space_tut1.rvt*
   For Metric *M_c09_Office-Space_tut1.rvt*
b. Dimension grid lines.
c. Add tags to the Duct and Mechanical Equipment.

d. Save the project using the **Save As** tool.
e. Close the project using the **Close** tool.

Opening the Project File

In this section, you will open the downloaded project file in Revit.

1. Choose **Open > Project** from the **Application Menu**; the **Open** dialog box is displayed.

2. In this dialog box, browse to *C:\rmp_2017\c09_rmp_2017_tut* location and choose the project file.

   For Imperial *c09_Office-Space_tut1.rvt*
   For Metric *M_c09_Office-Space_tut1.rvt*

3. Next, choose the **Open** button in this dialog box; the selected project file opens in the drawing window.

Dimensioning the Grid Line

In this section, you will add dimensions to the grid lines displayed in the **Basement** plan view.

1. Double-click on the **B1 BASEMENT** node under the **Floor Plans > Architectural** head in the **Project Browser** to open the corresponding floor plan view, if it is not selected by default.

2. Choose the **View** tab and then invoke the **Visibility/Graphics** tool from the **Graphics** panel of this tab; the **Visibility/Graphic Overrides for Floor Plan: B1 BASEMENT** dialog box is displayed.

3. In this dialog box, choose the **Annotation Categories** tab and then select the **Dimensions** check box displayed under the **Visibility** column, if it is not selected by default.

4. Choose the **Apply** button to save the changes and then choose the **OK** button; the **Visibility/ Graphic Overrides for Floor Plan: B1 BASEMENT** dialog box is closed.

5. Choose the **Annotate** tab and then choose the **Aligned** tool from the **Dimension** panel.

6. In the **Properties** palette, ensure in the imperial system the **Linear Dimension Style : Linear - 3/32" Arial** option is selected or in the Metric system the **Linear Dimension Style : Diagonal - 2.5mm Arial** option is selected from the **Type Selector** drop-down list. Next, choose the **Edit Type** button; the **Type Properties** dialog box is displayed.

7. In this dialog box, choose the **Duplicate** button; the **Name** dialog box is displayed.

8. In the **Name** edit box of the dialog box, enter **Small Dot- 3/32" Arial** (for Metric enter **Small Dot- 2.5mm Arial)** and then choose the **OK** button; the **Name** dialog box is closed.

9. In the **Type Properties** dialog box, click in the value field of the **Tick Mark** parameter; a drop-down list is displayed. Select the **Arrow Filled 15 Degree** option from this drop-down list.

10. In the **Type Properties** dialog box, click in the value field of the **Centerline Pattern** parameter; a drop-down list is displayed. Select the **Center** option from the drop-down list.

11. Choose the **OK** button in the **Type Properties** dialog box; the dialog box closes. Also, notice that in the drawing area, the dimension symbol appears with the cursor.

12. Place the cursor over grid 1a; the grid gets highlighted.

13. Click and place the cursor on grid 1 and click when grid 1 gets highlighted. Notice that a dimension is displayed between grid 1a and grid 1, as shown in Figure 9-39.

14. Move the cursor over grid 2 and click when it gets highlighted.

15. Repeat the procedure followed in step 14 and place the dimensions till grid 9. After you have clicked over the grid 9, move the cursor up and place it above the grid bubbles, as shown in Figure 9-40.

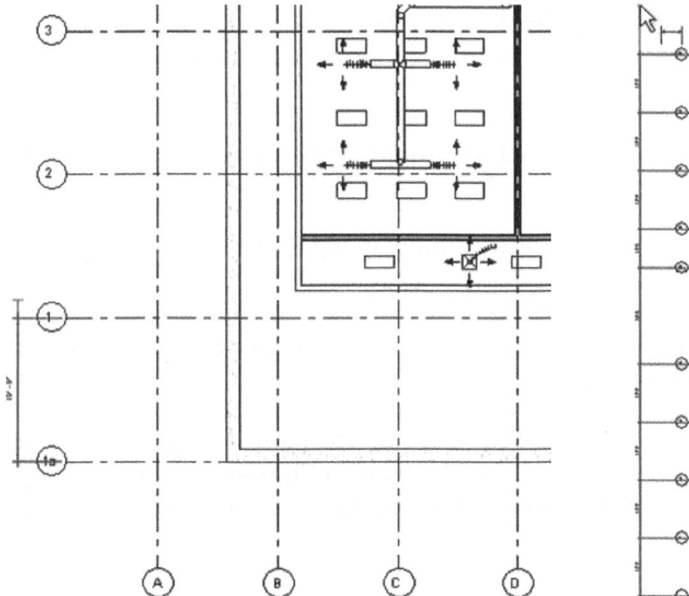

Figure 9-39 *The dimension created between grid 1a and grid 1*

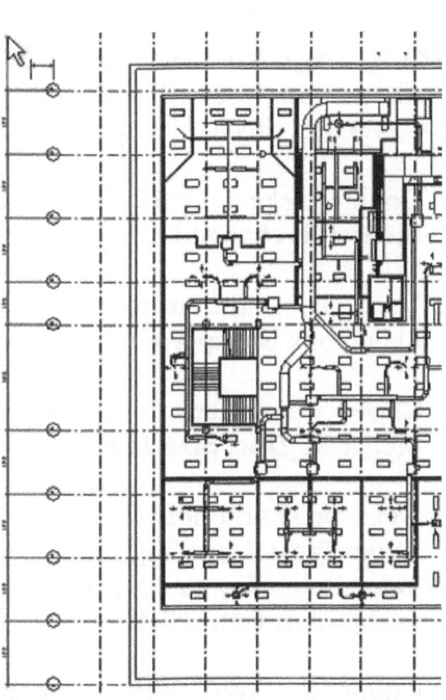

Figure 9-40 *Dimensions placed at a location above grid bubbles*

16. Now, click at the desired location, the dimensions are added. Note that you can place the dimensions based on your requirement.

17. Next, repeat the procedures followed in steps 12 to 16 and add dimensions for all vertical grids from A to T. The dimensions are placed above the structural plan view, refer to Figure 9-41.

18. Next, press ESC twice to exit the tool.

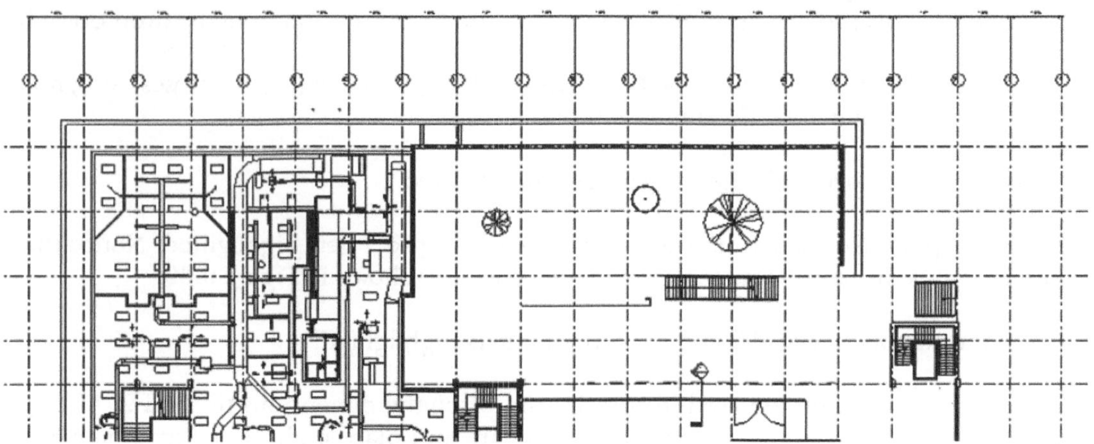

Figure 9-41 The dimensions placed at a location above the grid bubbles

Adding Tags to Duct and Mechanical Equipment

In this section, you will add tags to ducts and mechanical equipment in the **B1_HVAC DUCTWORK** Mechanical plan view.

1. Double-click on the **B1_HVAC DUCTWORK** node under **Floor Plans > Mechanical** head; the view is changed.

2. Next, choose the **Annotate** tab and then invoke the **Tag All** tool; the **Tag All Not Tagged** dialog box is displayed.

3. Click on **Duct Tags** in the **Category** column for **Duct label Rectangular** for Imperial (For Metric **M_Duct Size Tags loaded tags**).

4. Next, press and hold the CTRL key and then click on **Mechanical Equipment Tags** and **Room Tags: Room Tag** category (For Metric **M_Mechanical Equipment Tags** and **M_Room Tags: Room Tag** category) in the **Category** column; the selected categories are highlighted, as shown in Figure 9-42.

5. Choose the **Apply** button; the **Tag Visibility Enabled** message box is displayed asking to turn on the visibility of the room in the current view. Choose the **Yes** button; the message box is closed. Next, choose the **OK** button; the **Tag All Not Tagged** dialog box closes and the selected tag categories are displayed in the **B1_HVAC DUCTWORK** Mechanical plan view, as shown in Figure 9-43.

6. Next, choose the **Tag by Category** tool from the **Tag** panel and place the cursor over the diffuser; the diffuser is highlighted.

7. Click on the highlighted diffuser when the preview of the tag appears; the diffuser tag is added to the selected diffuser. Repeat this step to add tags to all diffusers in the conference rooms, refer to Figure 9-44.

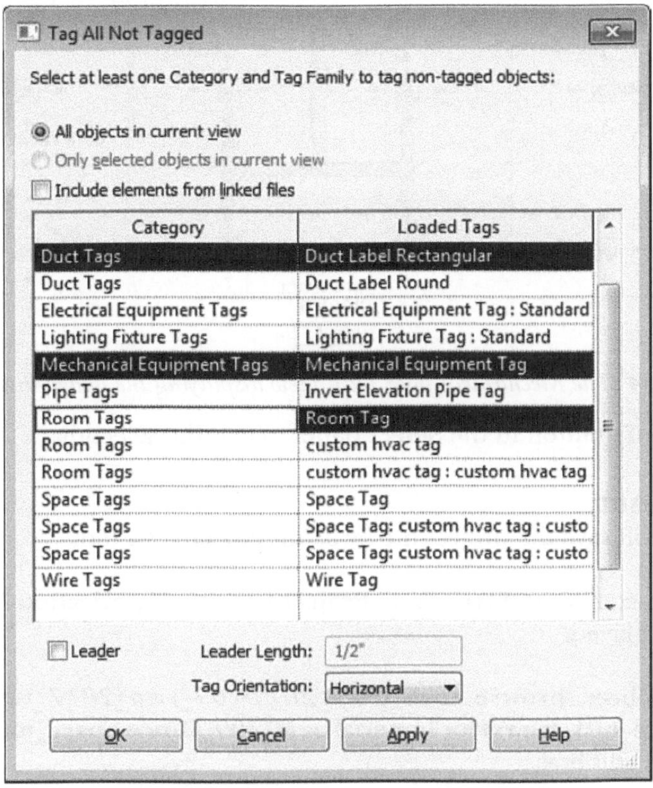

Figure 9-42 *The **Tag All Not Tagged** dialog box with selected categories highlighted*

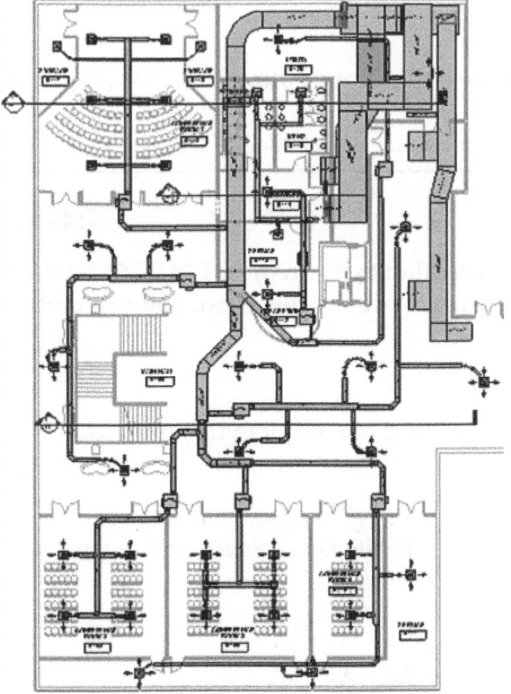

Figure 9-43 *The Mechanical plan view displaying the added tags*

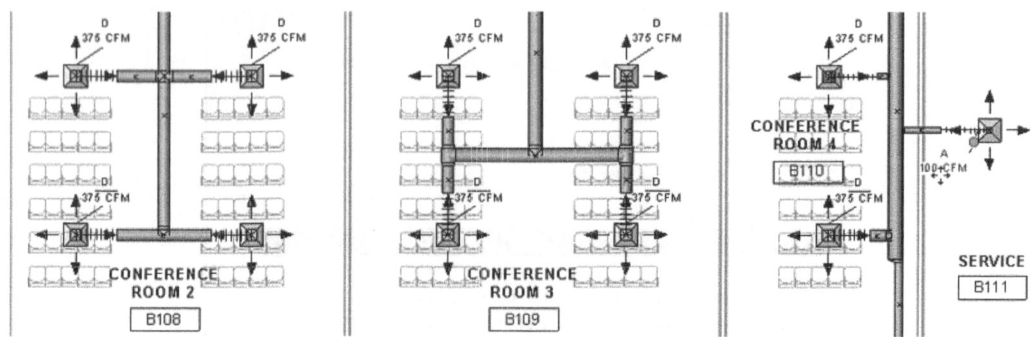

Figure 9-44 The Mechanical floor plan view displaying the added diffuser tags

8. Choose the **Modify** button in the **Select** panel to exit the selection.

Saving the Project

In this section, you will save the project file by using the **Save As** tool.

1. To save the project, choose **Save As > Project** from the **Application Menu**; the **Save As** dialog box is displayed.

2. In this dialog box, browse to *C:\rmp_2017\c09_rmp_2017_tut* and then enter **c09_Office-Space_tut1_tag.rvt** for Imperial or **M_c09_Office-Space_tut1_tag.rvt** for Metric in the **File name** edit box.

3. Now, choose the **Save** button; the **Save As** dialog box closes and the project file is saved.

Closing the Project

1. To close the project, choose the **Close** option from the **Application Menu**.

   The file is closed. This completes Tutorial 1 of Chapter 9.

Tutorial 2 — Office Space- Sheet

In this tutorial, you will create a callout view in the **B1 MEZZANINE** Architecture floor plan view of the *c09_Office-Space_tut1_tag.rvt* project file. Also, you will create a sheet and add different views in the created sheet. **(Expected time: 45 min)**

The following steps are required to complete this tutorial:

a. Open the project file.
   For Imperial *c09_Office-Space_tut1_tag.rvt*
   For Metric *M_c09_Office-Space_tut1_tag.rvt*
b. Create a callout view.
c. Create a sheet.
d. Add project views to the sheet.
e. Save the project by using the **Save As** tool.
f. Close the project by using the **Close** tool.

Opening the Project file

In this section, you will open the project file created in Tutorial 1 of Chapter 9.

1. To open the project file, choose **Open > Project** from the **Application Menu**; the **Open** dialog box is displayed.

2. In this dialog box, browse to *C:\rmp_2017\c09_rmp_2017_tut* location and choose the project file.

   For Imperial *c09_Office-Space_tut1_tag.rvt*
   For Metric *M_c09_Office-Space_tut1_tag.rvt*

3. Choose the **Open** button in this dialog box; the selected project file opens in the drawing window.

Creating a Callout View

In this section, you will create a callout view.

1. Double-click on the **B1 MEZZANINE** node under the **Floor Plans > Architectural** head of the **Project Browser**; the **B1 MEZZANINE** mechanical plan is displayed.

2. To create a callout view, invoke the **Rectangle** tool from the **Callout** drop-down in the **Create** panel of the **View** tab; the **Modify | Callout** contextual tab is displayed.

3. In the **View Control Bar**, select the **1/2" = 1'-0"** option for Imperial or select the **1: 20** option for Metric from the **Scale** drop-down list.

4. Next, select the **Detail View : Detail** option from the **Type Selector** drop-down in the **Properties** palette.

5. Now, create the callout by clicking at the first and the diagonally opposite corner, as shown in Figure 9-45; a rectangular callout is created.

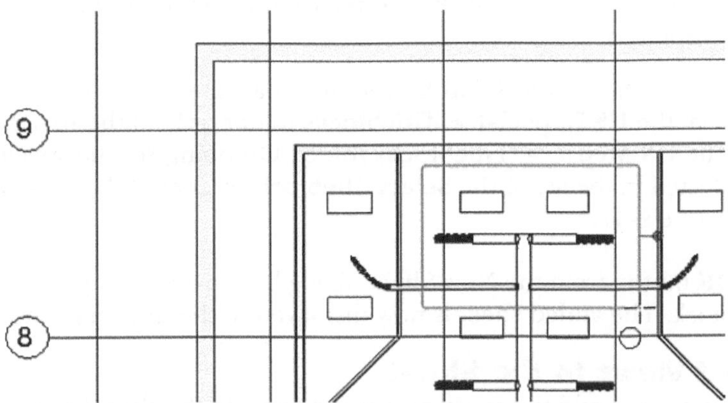

***Figure 9-45** The reference points for creating the callout*

6. After creating the rectangular callout, select it; the **Modify | Views** tab is displayed.

7. In the **Properties** palette of the selected callout, click in the value fields corresponding to the **Display Model** and **Detail Level** parameters and select the **Halftone** and **Fine** options from the drop-down lists, respectively.

8. In the **Properties** palette, click in the value field of the **View Name** parameter and enter **Duct Detail**. Next, choose the **Apply** button.

9. In the **Project Browser** double-click on the **Duct Detail** node under the **Architectural** head of the **Detail Views (Detail)** node to display the callout view, as shown in Figure 9-46.

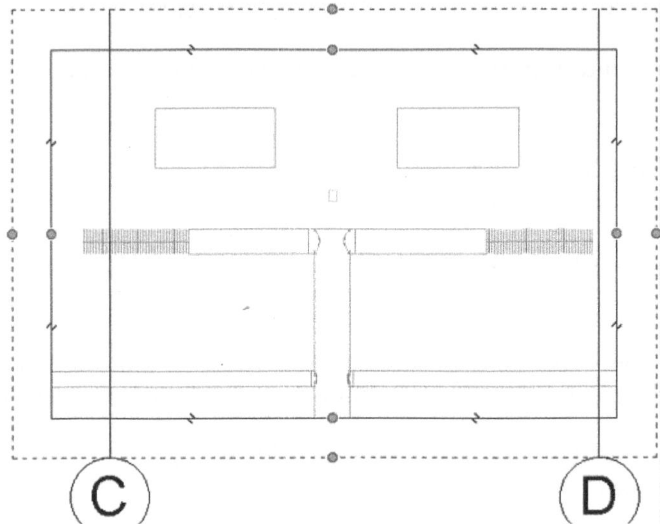

***Figure 9-46** Detailed view of the created callout view*

Creating a Sheet

In this section, you will create a sheet in the project.

1. Choose the **Sheet** tool from the **Sheet Composition** panel in the **View** tab; the **New Sheet** dialog box is displayed.

2. In this dialog box, choose the **Load** button and load the specified title block **C 17 x 22 Horizontal** from the **US Imperial > Titleblocks** folder or load the specified title block **A2 metric** from the **US Metric > Titleblocks** folder. On doing so, the specified title block is added and selected in the list of the **Select titleblocks** region of the **New Sheet** dialog box, as shown in Figure 9-47.

3. Choose the **OK** button from the **New Sheet** dialog box to create the sheet view by using the loaded title block. The added sheet is now displayed in the drawing window.

Adding Project Views to the Sheet

In this section, you need to add the specified project views to the sheet by dragging their name from the **Project Browser**. Further, based on the sheet layout, you need to place the project views at their designated place in the sheet.

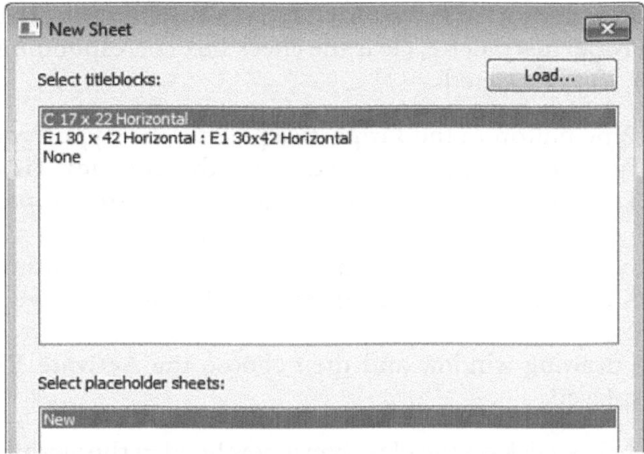

***Figure 9-47** Partial view of the **New Sheet** dialog box with the sheet loaded*

1. In the **Project Browser**, click on the **B1 MEZZANINE** node under the **Architectural** head. Next, in the **Properties** palette, click in the value field corresponding to the **View Scale** parameter and select the **1/32" = 1'-0"** option for Imperial or select the **1:500** option for Metric from the drop-down list displayed.

2. In the **Project Browser**, press and hold the left mouse button on the **B1 MEZZANINE** node and then drag the view into the drawing sheet. Release the left mouse button when the project view appears as a rectangle in the sheet.

3. Move the cursor to the lower left area of the title block such that the corner of the rectangle is close to the lower left corner of the drawing sheet. Next, click to place the view; the **B1 MEZZANINE** architectural plan view is added to the sheet and appears enclosed in a rectangle, as shown in Figure 9-48.

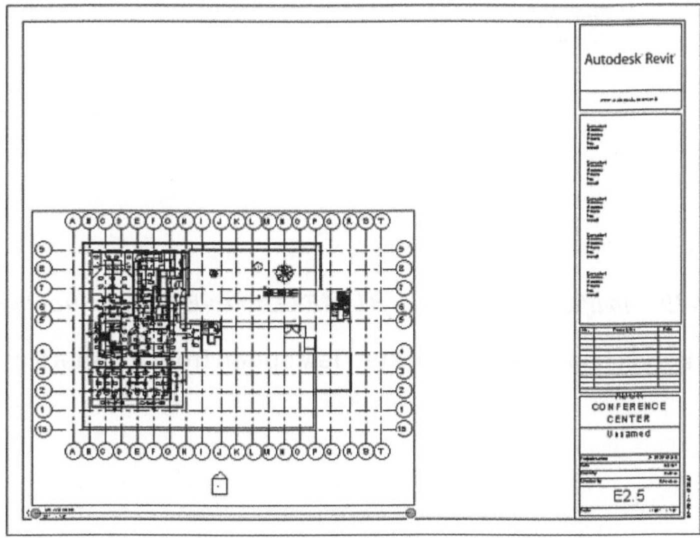

***Figure 9-48** The location of the **B1 MAZZANINE** architectural plan view in the sheet*

4. Next, ensure that the viewport of the **B1 MEZZANINE** architectural plan view is selected in the sheet. In the **Properties** palette, clear the check box corresponding to the **Crop Region Visible** parameter, if it is selected.

5. Choose the **Edit Type** button in the **Properties** palette; the **Type Properties** dialog box is displayed. In the **Type Properties** dialog box, ensure that the **View Title** option for Imperial and the **M_View Title** option for Metric is selected in the **Title** drop-down list.

6. Clear the check box corresponding to the **Show Extension Line** parameter and then choose the **Apply** and **OK** buttons; the **Type Properties** dialog box is closed.

7. Right-click in the drawing window and then choose the **Activate View** option from the shortcut menu displayed.

8. Now, in the project view, click on the elevation arrow head in the viewport below the drawing and right-click; a shortcut menu is displayed. Choose **Hide in View > Category** from the menu.

9. Again, right-click and then choose the **Pan Active View** option from the shortcut menu displayed; a move icon is displayed with the cursor.

10. In the sheet, press and drag the **B1 MEZZANINE** plan view and then place it at the location, shown in Figure 9-49.

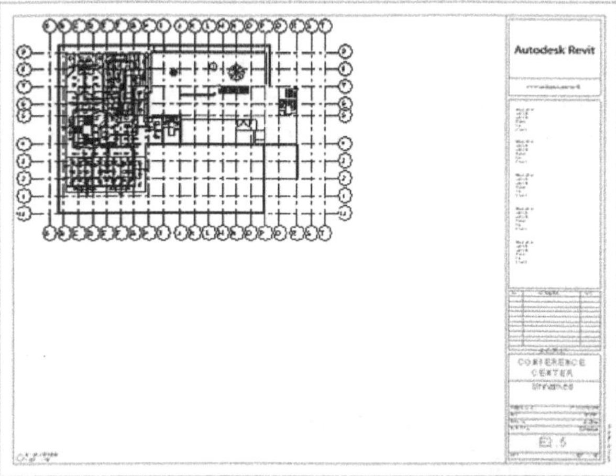

Figure 9-49 *Modified location of the **B1 MEZZANINE** architectural plan view*

11. Next, right-click and choose the **Deactivate View** option from the shortcut menu displayed.

12. Click on the **Duct Detail** node under the **Architectural** head of the **Detail Views (Detail)** node in the **Project Browser** and then drag it to the sheet. Next, in the **Properties** palette click in the value field corresponding to the **View Scale** parameter and select the **1/16"=1'** option for Imperial and **1:200** for metric from the drop-down list displayed.

13. Now, release the mouse button and click at any point to place the **Duct Detail** view, as shown in Figure 9-50.

14. Click on the **B1_HVAC DUCTWORK** node under the **Mechanical** head and then specify the value of the **View Scale** parameter as **1/32" = 1'-0"** for Imperial or **1:500** for Metric. Next, drag the **B1_HVAC DUCTWORK** node from the **Project Browser** and place it at the location shown in Figure 9-51. The three views are added to the sheet.

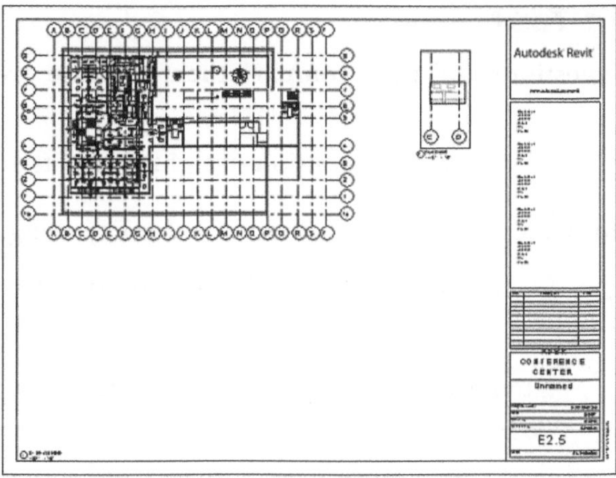

***Figure 9-50** Sheet displaying the **B1 MEZZANINE** architectural plan and callout view*

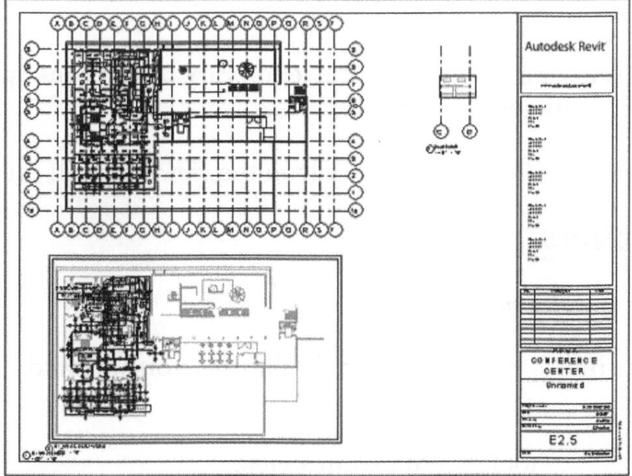

***Figure 9-51** Sheet displaying all the added plan views*

Saving the Project

In this section, you will save the project file by using the **Save As** tool.

1. Choose **Save As > Project** from the **Application Menu**; the **Save As** dialog box is displayed.
2. In this dialog box, browse to *C:\rmp_2017\c09* and then enter **c09_Office-Space_tut1_sheet.rvt** for Imperial or **M_c09_Office-Space_tut1_sheet.rvt** for Metric in the **File name** edit box.
3. Now, choose the **Save** button; the **Save As** dialog box closes and the project file is saved.

Closing the Project

1. To close the project, choose the **Close** option from the **Application Menu**.

   The file is closed. This completes the tutorial.

Self-Evaluation Test

Answer the following questions and then compare them to those given at the end of this chapter:

1. You can use the __________ tool to dimension straight elements and distances.
2. You can add the information related to a project in a sheet by using the __________tool.
3. Click on the __________ symbol to convert the temporary dimension into permanent dimension.
4. Choose the __________ tool from the **Tag** panel of the **Annotate** tab to attach a tag to an element based on its category.
5. You can activate a view from a drawing sheet by choosing the ____________option.
6. Choose the ____________ option from the shortcut menu to view the primary view of a duplicated view.
7. While creating or selecting an element, the temporary dimensions appear on it. However, they do not appear in project views. (T/F)
8. Detail lines are view-specific and appear only in the view in which they are created. (T/F)

Review Questions

Answer the following questions:

1. You need to invoke the _________ tool to display the Northing and Easting coordinates of a point in a project.
2. Choose the _________ tool to add text in a view.
3. You can tag all elements visible in a view by using the __________tool.
4. To check the spelling of the added text, you can use the __________ tool.

5. The view in which the callout tag is added is called the __________ view of the callout view.

6. To create a customized callout view using various draw tools, you can use the __________ tool from the **Callout** drop-down.

7. The Drafting Details are linked to the model and therefore are updated with the project. (T/F)

8. All duplicate views are dependent on the original view from which they are created. (T/F)

EXERCISE

Exercise 1 Conference Hall

Download the *c09_Conference-hall_exer1.rvt* file from *http://www.cadcim.com.* The path of the file is as follows: *Textbooks > Civil/GIS > Revit MEP > Exploring Autodesk Revit 2017 for MEP*. Now add callout view and add tags to ducts and diffusers at the **1ST FLOOR-HVAC DUCT** mechanical floor plan view of the downloaded file. Also add space tags to the **1ST FLOOR-HVAC DUCT** mechanical floor plan view. Refer to Figures 9-52 and 9-53 to complete the exercise.

(Expected time: 1 Hr)

1. Add callout view to the **1ST FLOOR-HVAC DUCT** mechanical plan view.
2. Add tags to round ducts in the **1ST FLOOR-HVAC DUCT** mechanical plan view.
3. Add tag to air diffusers in the **1ST FLOOR-HVAC DUCT** mechanical plan view.
4. Add space tag to **1ST FLOOR-HVAC DUCT** mechanical plan view.
5. File name to be assigned:

   For Imperial *c09_Conference-hall_exer1a.rvt*
   For Metric *M_c09_Conference-hall_exer1a.rvt*

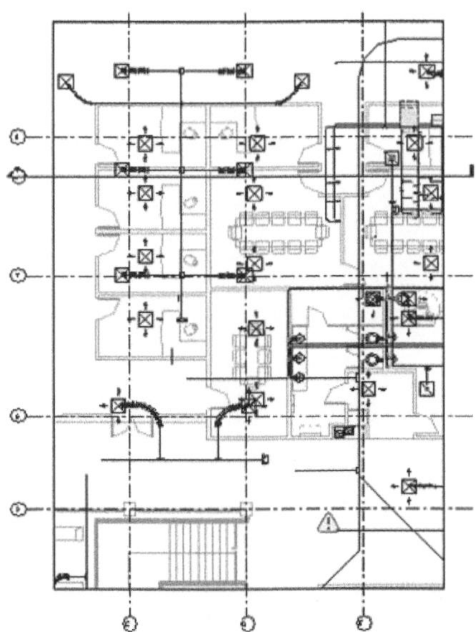

Figure 9-52 *The tags added to round ducts and air diffusers*

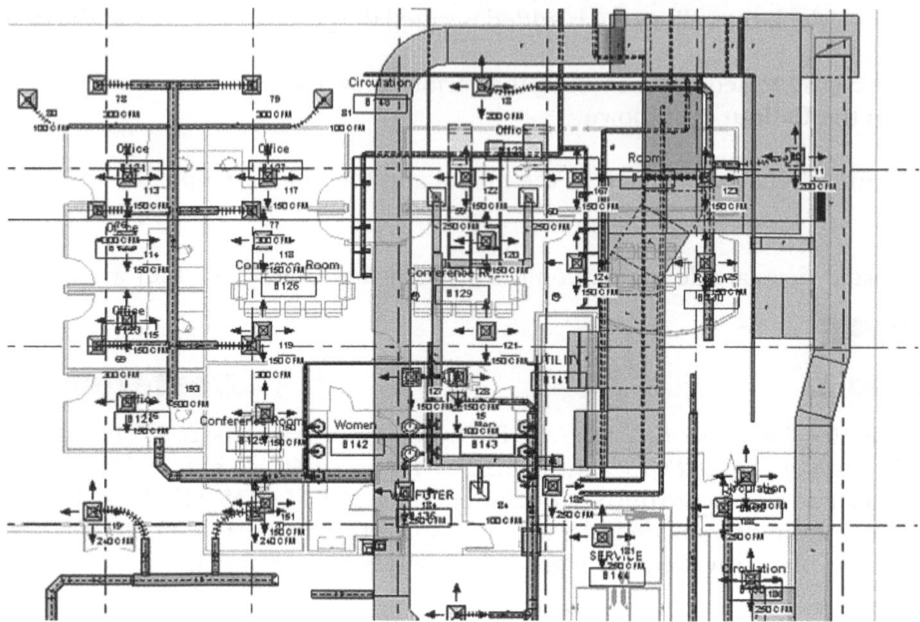

Figure 9-53 *The space tags added to the* ***1ST FLOOR-HVAC DUCTS*** *mechanical plan view*

Answers to Self-Evaluation Test

1. **Linear**, **2.** **Text** **3.** Conversion control, **4.** **Tag by Category**, **5.** **Activate View**, **6.** **Go to Primary View**, **7.** T, **8.** T

Chapter 10

Creating Families and Worksharing

Learning Objectives

After completing this chapter, you will be able to:
- *Create massing in Conceptual Mass Environment*
- *Create massing in Family Editor Environment*
- *Create massing in Project Environment*
- *Understand worksharing*

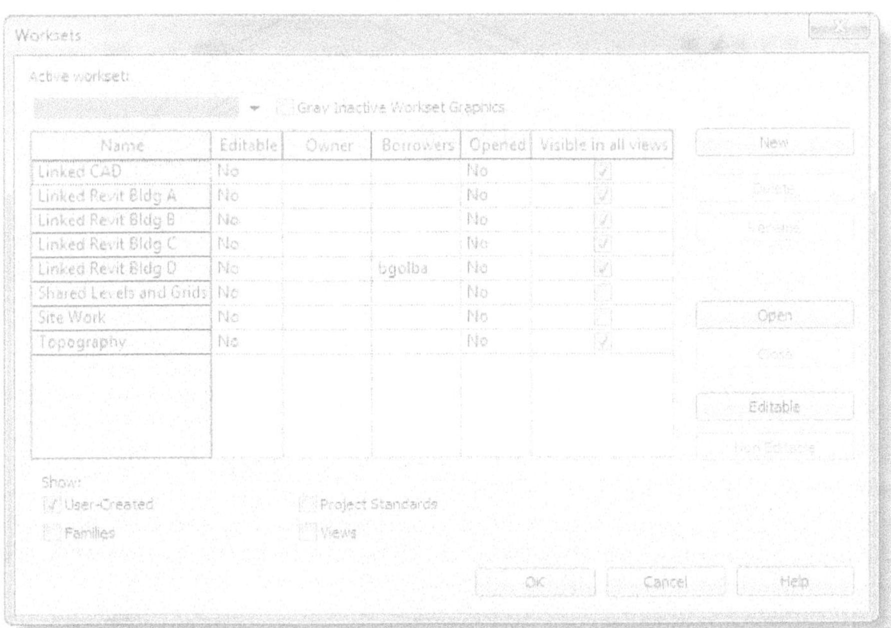

INTRODUCTION TO MASSING

In earlier chapters, you learned to use different system elements and components to create an MEP model. These system elements are parametrically associated and enable you to generate an MEP model based on specific design requirements such as duct types, cable trays, plumbing fittings, width, spaces, and so on. Each of the elements must be assigned specific properties to achieve the desired element parameters, thereby making system model accurate. Needless to say, this is a fairly time-consuming procedure. Autodesk Revit provides you an easy alternative to create system elements, known as massing.

UNDERSTANDING MASSING CONCEPTS

At the conceptualization stage of a project, you may need to study it in terms of its spaces, volumes, and shapes. You may also require to convey the basic idea of the structure of a building in a three-dimensional form without much detailing. This can be achieved using various tools which are used to create massing geometries.

The tools for creating massing geometry not only enable you to conceive and create a variety of system elements, shapes, and volumes with relative ease but also convey the potential design in terms of component masses and geometric shapes. You can create and edit geometric shapes and amalgamate them to form a complete MEP system. This process can be compared to the creation of element model using foam blocks. You have the freedom of choice to add or cut geometric shapes and join different blocks or masses to form an assembly. Figure 10-1 shows a group of volumes that can be created to represent the water closet of a plumbing fixture.

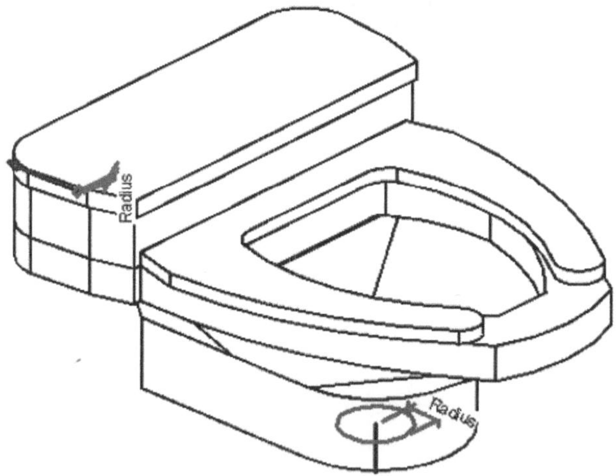

Figure 10-1 *Water closet created using the massing geometry*

Autodesk Revit provides a much-needed continuity in the design development of a project by using the same model from its conceptualization to completion. It also enables you to control the visibility of geometry between the building volumes (massing) and building elements (shell) during the initial stages of project development. Other project information such as its total area can also be extracted from the building massing.

However, it is important to understand the limitations of the massing tools. These tools are only meant for conceptual design development using simple geometric shapes. You can place the predefined massing family elements provided in additional libraries. Autodesk Revit attempts to translate the massing geometry into building elements or shell. So, it is recommended not to use massing geometry for the development of a detailed geometry such as columns, cavity walls, footing, and so on.

CREATING THE MASSING GEOMETRY

In Autodesk Revit, you can create the massing geometry in any of these three environments: Family Editor, Conceptual Design, and Project.

To create the massing geometry in the Family Editor environment, choose **New > Family** from the **Application Menu**; the **New Family - Select Template File** dialog box will be displayed. In this dialog box, choose the *Generic Model.rft* file (commonly used) from the **English_I** folder, as shown in Figure 10-2, and then choose the **Open** button; a new file will open in the Family Editor environment. In the new file, you can create the massing geometry using various tools available in the ribbon.

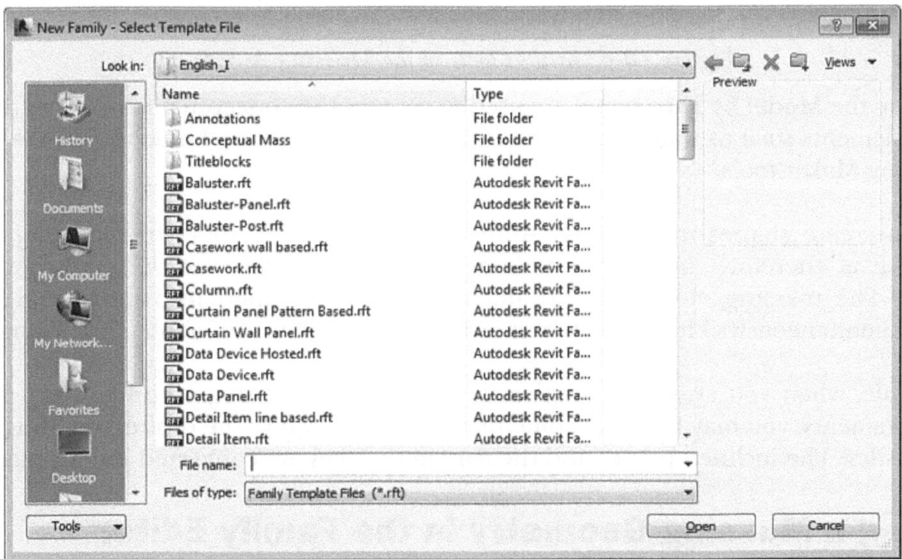

***Figure 10-2** Selecting a file from the **New Family- Select Template File** dialog box*

The Conceptual Design environment in Revit is used to create conceptual mass. In this environment the advanced modeling tools and techniques for creating massing families are provided. To start creating a conceptual mass in this environment, choose **New > Conceptual Mass** from **Application Menu**; the **New Conceptual Mass - Select Template File** dialog box will be displayed. In this dialog box, select the **Mass** template file from the **Conceptual Mass** folder and then choose **Open**; a new file in the Conceptual Design environment will open. In the new file, you can create the massing geometry using various tools available in the ribbon, as shown in Figure 10-3.

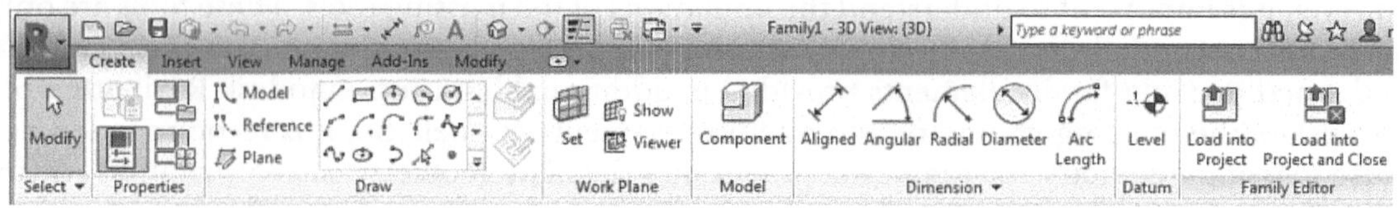

Figure 10-3 Different tools in the ribbon of the Conceptual Design Environment

The Project environment is the most common environment used in a project design. To start creating a mass in this environment, open a new file or an existing file by choosing **New > Project** or **Open > Project** from the **Application Menu**. After opening a new file or an existing file, choose the **Massing & Site** tab, as shown in Figure 10-4. In this tab, the massing tools can be accessed from the **Conceptual Mass** panel. The **Conceptual Mass** panel contains the following tools for massing: **In-Place Mass, Show Mass**, and **Place Mass.**

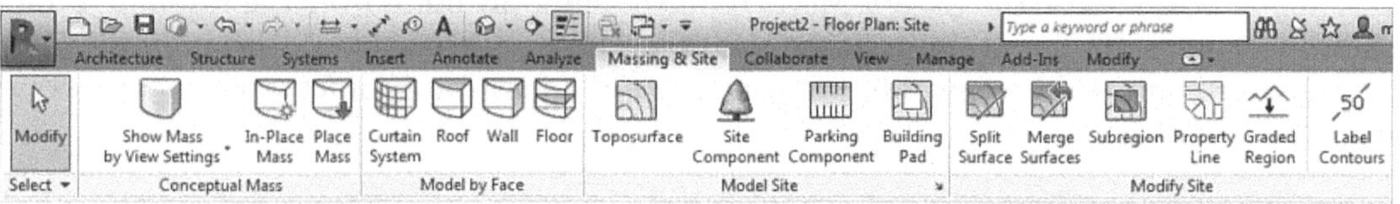

Figure 10-4 *Various tools in the* ***Massing & Site*** *tab*

The tools in the **Model by Face** panel are used to convert the conceptual mass created into real building elements such as walls, floors, roofs, and curtain systems. These tools are also called the Building Maker tools.

When you create shapes in massing, Autodesk Revit creates its corresponding building elements. It is, therefore, imperative to consider the associativity of the massing and shell elements. The massing elements may need to be transformed into individual building elements simultaneously. Therefore, the massing geometry must be created accordingly.

For example, when you create a complex geometric massing shape and convert faces into building elements, you may find that some planes do not acquire the desired building element characteristics. The inclined planes and the curved surfaces are converted into in-place roofs.

Creating a Massing Geometry in the Family Editor

As discussed earlier, the Family Editor environment provides tools to create massing geometry. To create a new mass, choose **New > Family** from **Application Menu**; the **New Family - Select Template File** dialog box will be displayed. In this dialog box, select the *Generic Model.rft* file (commonly used) from the **English_I** folder and choose **Open**; a new file will open using the selected template file.

In the Family Editor environment, the **Create** tab contains tools to create massing geometry. These tools can be used to create massing geometries in a solid or in a void form.

To create a solid form, you can use a tool depending on your requirement, such as **Extrusion / Blend / Revolve / Sweep / Swept Blend** tool from the **Forms** panel of the **Create** tab. These tools are used to create different solid forms. Similarly, to create a void form, choose the **Void Extrusion / Void Blend / Void Revolve / Void Sweep / Void Swept Blend** tool from the **Void**

Forms drop-down in the **Forms** panel. You can create a massing geometry using any of these massing tools or a combination of the **Solid** and **Void** tools. However, a designer can select the appropriate tool judiciously depending on the massing geometry to be created. The procedure of creating solid or void geometries using the tools in the Family Editor environment is discussed next.

Creating an Extrusion

Ribbon: Create > Forms > Extrusion

Extrusion

The **Extrusion** tool is used to create a massing geometry by adding height to a sketched profile. When you invoke this tool from the **Forms** panel in the **Create** tab, the **Modify | Create Extrusion** tab will be displayed. You can use different tools from this tab to sketch an extrusion profile and create a massing geometry. Figure 10-5 shows different tools in the **Modify | Create Extrusion** tab.

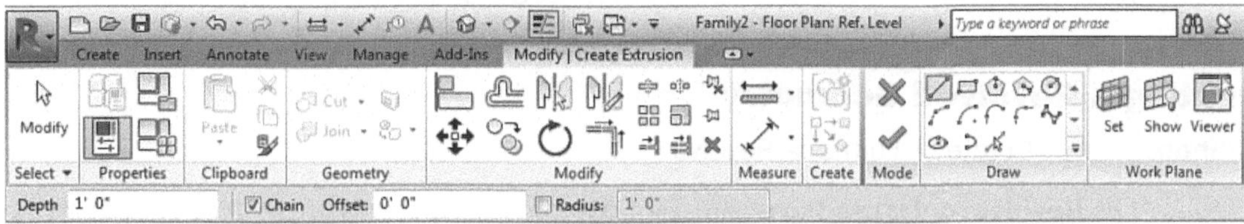

*Figure 10-5 Various tools in the **Modify / Create Extrusion** tab*

To create an extrusion, first you need to define a work plane to sketch a profile. To define a work plane, you can invoke the **Set** tool available in the **Work Plane** panel of the **Modify | Create Extrusion** tab. After specifying the work plane, you can invoke the **Reference Plane** tool from the **Datum** panel of the **Create** tab to draw reference planes for locating exact points to sketch a profile. To sketch the 2D profile to be extruded, you can invoke any of the sketching tools available in the **Draw** panel of the **Modify | Create Extrusion** tab. You can invoke the appropriate tool(s) depending on the shape of the profile that must form a closed loop. In the **Properties** panel, choose the **Properties** tool to display the **Properties** palette, if not displayed by default. In this palette, you can specify the start and end levels of extrusion and other properties. The **Extrusion Start** instance parameter in the **Properties** palette indicates the start level of extrusion from the base level. The **Extrusion End** parameter indicates the top level of extrusion. The difference between these two parameters is calculated as the depth of the extrusion. You can also enter its value in the **Depth** edit box of the **Options Bar**. Autodesk Revit assumes the depth of extrusion from the base level. After sketching the profile, choose the **Finish Edit Mode** button from the **Mode** panel to finish the sketch of the profile for extrusion.

For example to create an AHU, invoke the **Extrusion** tool from the **Forms** panel. In the **Options Bar**, you can specify the height of extrusion in the **Depth** edit box. To sketch a base profile, select the **Chain** check box, if it is not selected by default.

To create a bath tub fixture, invoke the **Void Extrusion** tool from the **Forms** panel of the **Create** tab. In the **Options Bar**, you can specify the height of extrusion in the **Depth** edit box to sketch a base profile. Next, in the **Draw** panel of the **Modify | Create Extrusion** tab, the **Line** tool (invoked by default) can be used to sketch the extrusion profile. You can also use other sketching tools available in the **Draw** panel to sketch the profile. Sketch the base of the specified dimension using temporary dimensions, as shown in Figure 10-6. After the profile is completed, choose the **Finish Edit Mode** button to extrude the sketched profile to the specified depth. The bath tub mass profile created can be viewed in the 3D view, as shown in Figure 10-7.

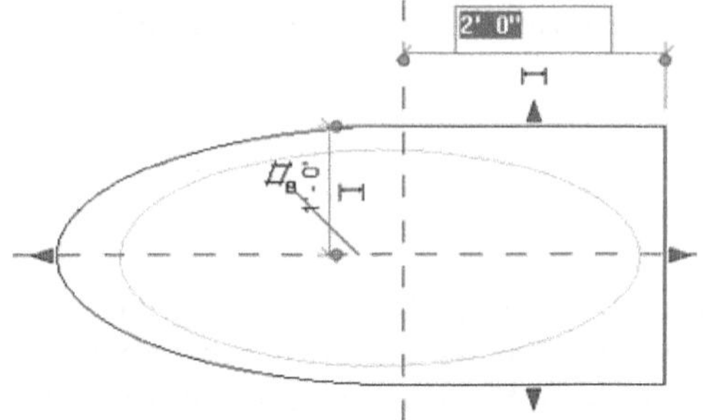

Figure 10-6 Sketch of the bath tub mass profile to be extruded

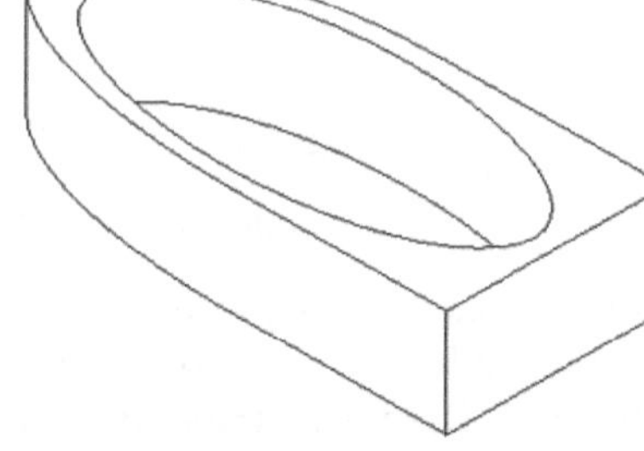

*Figure 10-7 Massing geometry created using the **Void Extrusion** tool*

Creating a Revolved Geometry

Ribbon: Create > Forms > Revolve

The **Revolve** tool is used to create a solid geometry by revolving a profile about an axis. This tool can also be used to create shapes such as domes, donuts, cylinders, and so on. To create a revolved geometry, invoke this tool from the **Forms** panel; the sketch mode is activated and the **Modify | Create Revolve** tab will be displayed, as shown in Figure 10-8.

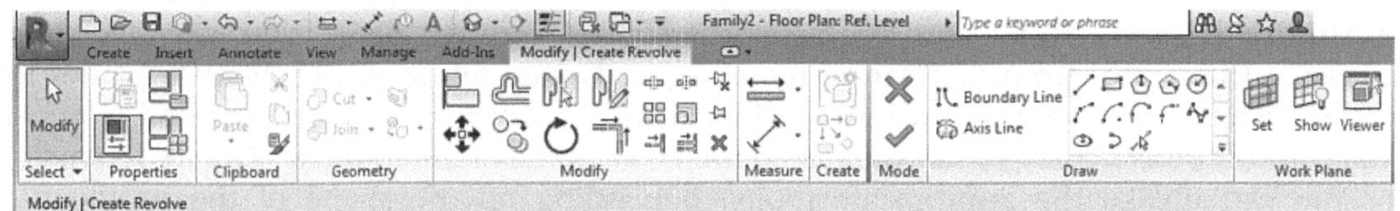

*Figure 10-8 Various options in the **Modify / Create Revolve** tab*

In the **Draw** panel, the **Boundary Lines** tool is chosen by default. As a result, various sketching tools used to sketch the profile of the revolved geometry are displayed in a list box of this panel. Before invoking any of the sketching tools, you need to set the work plane. To do so, choose the **Create** tab, and then choose the **Set** tool from the **Work Plane** panel; the **Work Plane** dialog box will be displayed. In this dialog box, you can use various options to specify the required work plane for sketching the profile of the revolved geometry. After selecting the required plane, you can sketch the profile of the revolved geometry.

To sketch the profile, choose the **Modify | Create Revolve** tab. You can use various sketching tools from the list box in the **Draw** panel of this tab. The sketched profile must be a single closed loop or multiple closed loops that do not intersect. After defining the profile, you need to define the axis about which the profile will revolve. To do so, invoke the **Axis Line** tool from the **Draw** panel; the **Line** and **Pick Lines** tools will be displayed in the list. The **Line** tool is used to draw a line that can be used as an axis and the **Pick Lines** tool is used to pick a line or an edge to define the axis of revolution. After completing the sketch and defining the axis of revolution, choose the **Finish Edit Mode** button from the **Modify | Create Revolve** tab; the **Modify | Revolve** tab will be displayed and the revolved geometry will be created.

In the **Modify | Revolve** tab, you can change the instance property of the revolved geometry. In the **Properties** palette you can set the start and end angles of revolution. The default values for these two parameters are 0° and 360°, respectively.

To create a wash basin, you can sketch the profile and define the axis for the profile, as shown in Figure 10-9. Before you start the sketch, you need to set the work plane perpendicular to the horizontal plane. The resultant revolved massing geometry with the axis and its profile is shown in Figure 10-10. Figure 10-11 shows an example of the revolved geometry in which the **End Angle** and **Start Angle** parameters in the **Properties** palette have been assigned the values 360.000° and 0.000°, respectively.

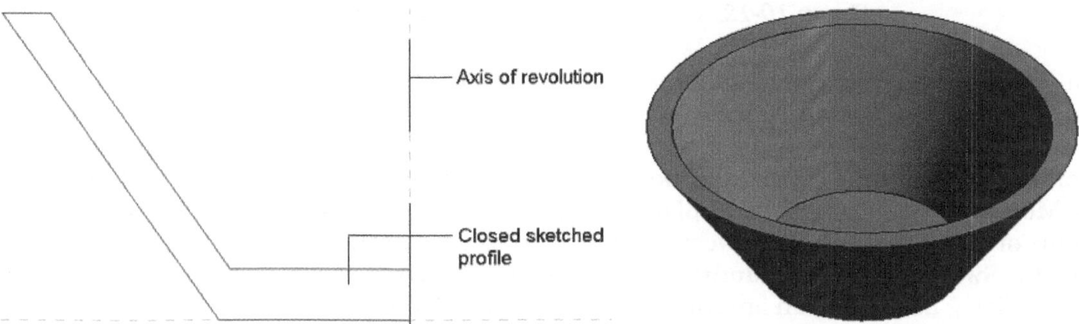

Figure 10-9 *Sketching a closed profile for a revolved geometry*

Figure 10-10 *Massing geometry created by using the* ***Revolve*** *tool*

Figure 10-11 *Revolved geometry created by revolving a profile at an angle of 180°*

Tip

In Autodesk Revit, you can quickly edit the revolve angle of a revolved geometry by selecting the geometry from the drawing and then changing the temporary angular dimension displayed in the geometry.

Creating a Sweep

Ribbon: Create > Forms > Sweep

The **Sweep** tool is used to create a massing feature by selecting a profile along a particular sketched path. To create a massing feature by sweeping a profile, invoke the **Sweep** tool from the **Forms** panel; the sketch mode will be invoked and the **Modify | Sweep** tab with its related tools will be displayed, as shown in Figure 10-12. The **Sketch Path** tool in the **Sweep** panel of the **Modify | Sweep** tab is used to sketch the path to be used for extrusion.

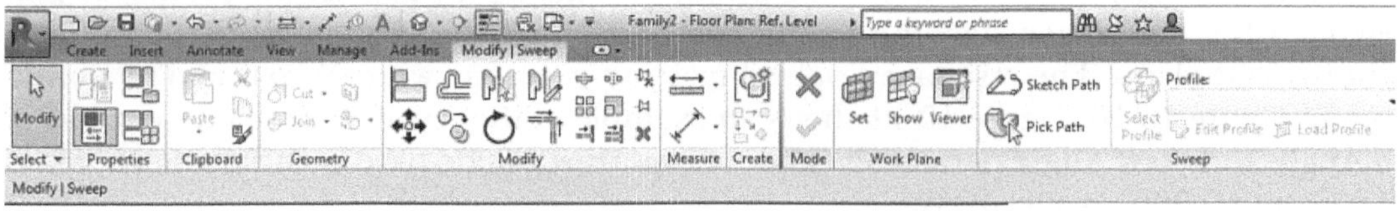

Figure 10-12 *Various options in the **Modify / Sweep** tab*

On invoking the **Sketch Path** tool, the **Modify | Sweep** tab will be replaced by **Modify | Sweep > Sketch Path** tab, which contains tools to draw path. Using the tools fromthe **Draw** panel, you can sketch the desired shape of the path, which can be an open or a closed profile. After sketching the path, choose the **Finish Edit Mode** button from the **Mode** panel; the **Modify | Sweep** tab will be displayed again. Using the options in this tab, you can sketch a profile or load a profile for the sweep geometry. To sketch a profile, choose the **Edit Profile** tool from the **Sweep** panel in the **Modify | Sweep** tab; the **Go To View** dialog box will be displayed. In this dialog box, select an appropriate view and sketch the profile using different sketching tools. After sketching the profile, choose the **Finish Edit Mode** button from the **Mode** panel; the **Modify | Sweep > Edit Profile** tab will be displayed. In this tab, choose the **Finish Edit Mode** button from the **Mode** panel; a sweep geometry will be created. Figure 10-13 shows the example of a 2D path with a sketched profile and Figure 10-14 shows the resulting massing shape.

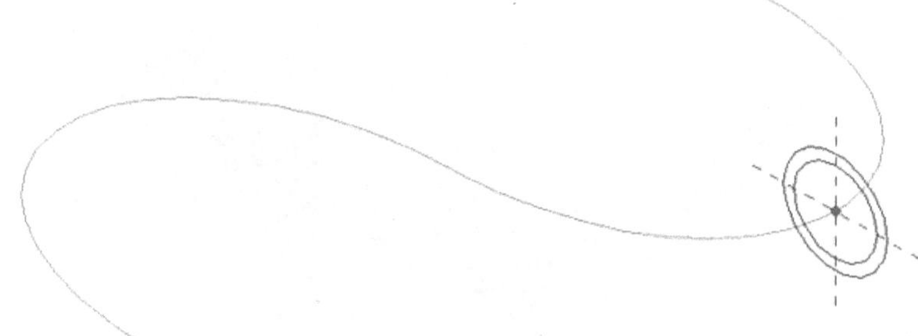

Figure 10-13 *Sketching the profile and the 2D path for creating a swept geometry*

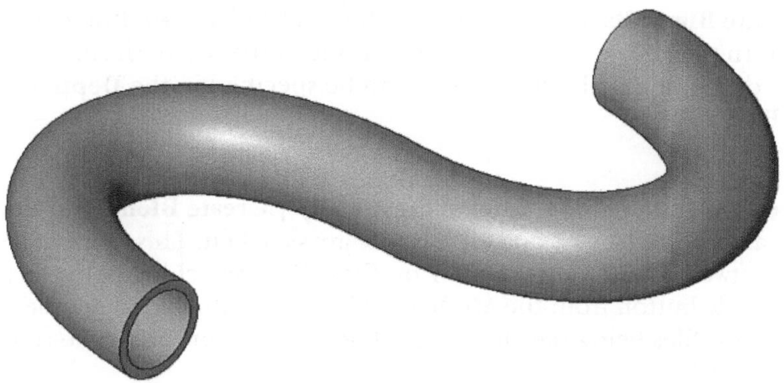

*Figure 10-14 Massing geometry created by using the **Sweep** tool*

Autodesk Revit also provides in-built profiles that can be used in projects. These profiles are available in the **Profile** drop-down list in the **Sweep** panel of the **Modify | Sweep** tab. You can also choose the **Load Profile** button from the **Sweep** panel and access the additional profiles available in the **Profiles** sub folder in the **US Imperial** folder. You can modify the **Structural, Mechanical**, and **Others** properties of the sweep profile. To do so, select the created mass by the **Sweep** tool; the **Modify | Sweep** tab will be displayed. In this tab, choose the **Edit Sweep** tool from the **Mode** panel; the properties of the sweep model will be displayed in the **Properties** palette. In this palette, click on the value field corresponding to the **Part Type** parameter under the **Mechanical** head; a drop-down list will be displayed. You can select an option from the displayed drop-down list to specify a part type to the sweep model. In the **Properties** palette, select the check box corresponding to the **Shared** parameter under the **Other** head to assign shared parameter to the sweep mass.

Creating a Blend

Ribbon: Create > Forms > Blend

Blend

Using the **Blend** tool, you can create a massing geometry by blending or linking two profiles. To create a massing geometry using this tool, invoke it from the **Forms** panel; the **Modify | Create Blend Base Boundary** contextual tab will be displayed. The tools in this tab are used to create and edit a blend. Figure 10-15 shows various tools in the **Modify | Create Blend Base Boundary** tab.

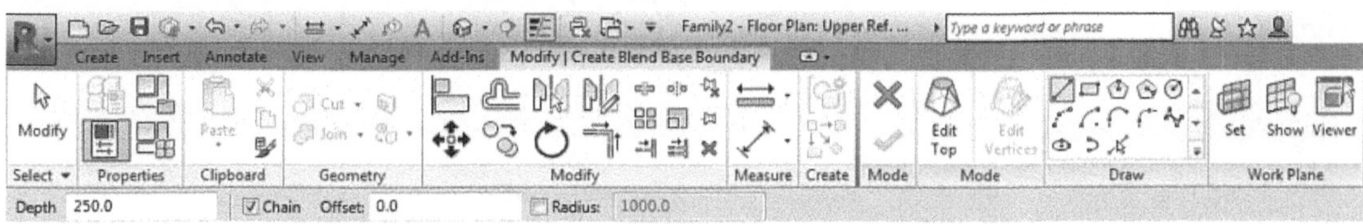

*Figure 10-15 Various tools in the **Modify / Create Blend Base Boundary** tab*

After setting the work plane, you can sketch the base profile using different sketching tools available in the **Draw** panel. In the **Properties** palette, you can specify values in the value fields of the **First End** and **Second End** instance parameters to set the height of the blend geometry. After completing the base profile, you can choose the **Edit Top** option from the **Mode** panel in the **Modify | Create Blend Base Boundary** tab; the **Modify | Create Blend Top Boundary** tab will be displayed. In this tab, you can sketch the profile of the top of the blend geometry in any work plane. The depth of the blend geometry can be specified in the **Depth** edit box available in the **Options Bar**.

The **Edit Vertices** tool in the **Mode** panel of the **Modify | Create Blend Top Boundary** tab will be available only after both the base and top profiles are sketched. This tool enables you to specify the connectivity between the vertices of their profiles. After sketching both the profiles, choose the **Finish Edit Mode** button from the **Mode** panel to create the blend geometry. Figure 10-16 shows two circular profiles being sketched as the base and top profiles. The resulting geometry is shown in Figure 10-17.

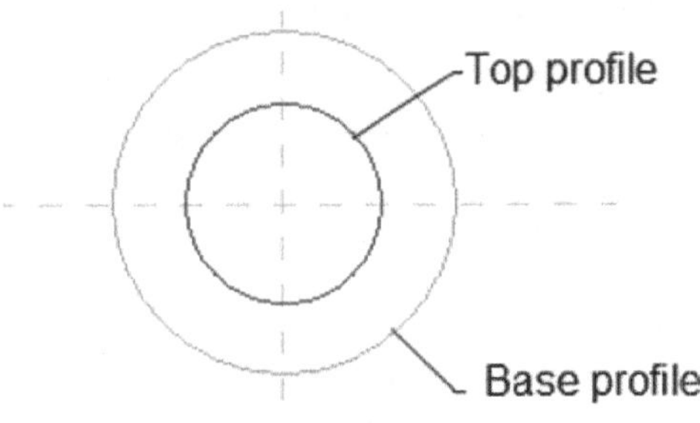

Figure 10-16 Sketching the base and top profiles to create a blend massing

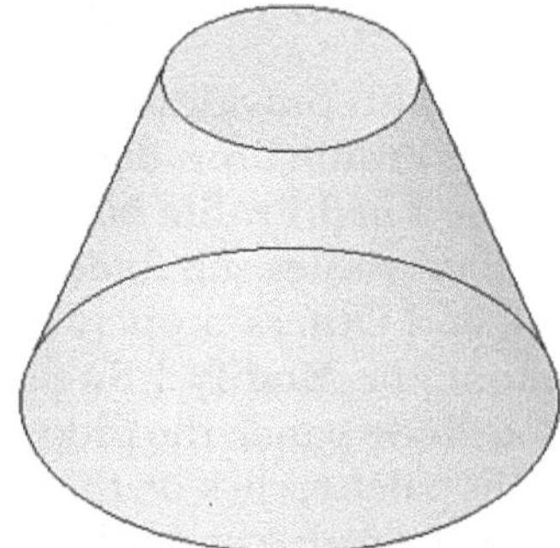

Figure 10-17 Resulting shape after blending the base and top profiles

Creating a Swept Blend

Ribbon: Create > Forms > Swept Blend

The solid swept blend geometries are created by using the **Swept Blend** tool. This tool has combined features of the **Sweep** and **Blend** tools. A geometry created using the **Swept Blend** tool consists of a path and two different profiles drawn at the either end of the path.

To create a swept blend geometry, choose the **Swept Blend** tool from the **Forms** panel; the screen will enter the sketch mode and the **Modify | Swept Blend** tab will be displayed, as shown in Figure 10-18.

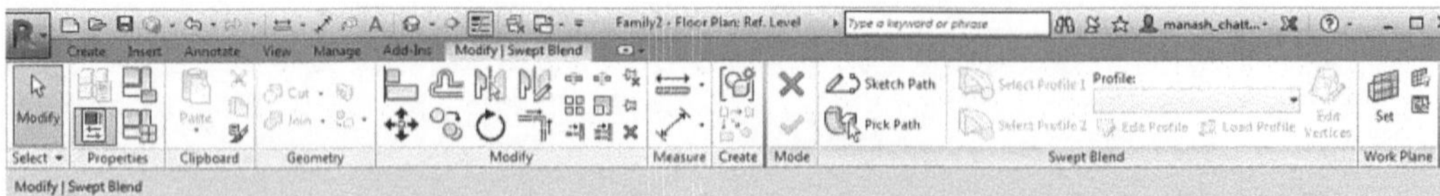

*Figure 10-18 Different options in the **Modify / Swept Blend** tab*

The **Modify | Swept Blend** tab contains various tools to sketch and edit the path and profiles of a solid swept blend geometry. Figure 10-19 shows the graphical representation of the solid swept blend geometry.

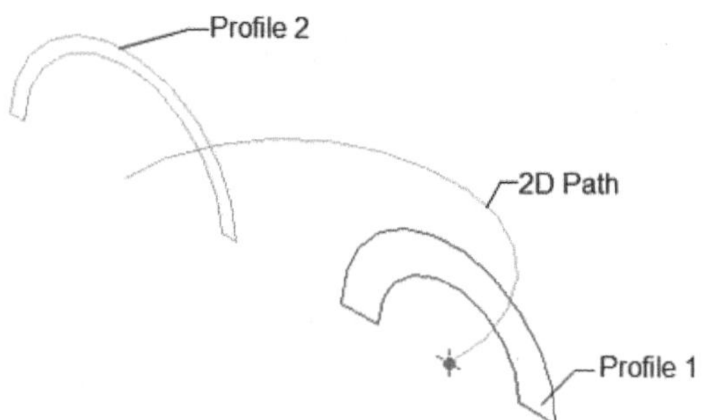

Figure 10-19 *The profiles and the 2D path for creating a swept blend geometry*

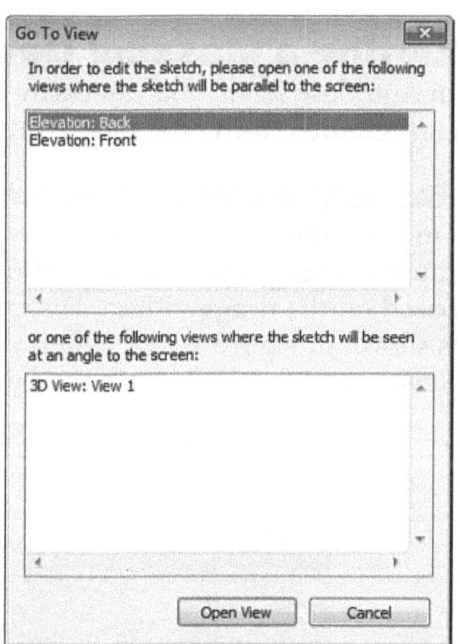

Figure 10-20 *The* ***Go To View*** *dialog box*

To create the geometry, first you need to sketch the 2D path. To do so, choose the **Sketch Path** tool from the **Swept Blend** panel; the sketch mode will be invoked. You can use various sketching tools in the **Draw** panel to sketch the 2D path. Next, choose the **Finish Edit Mode** button from the **Mode** panel of the **Modify | Swept Blend > Sketch Path** tab. Alternatively, you can define the 2D path for the solid swept blend geometry by choosing the **Pick Path** tool from the **Swept Blend** panel and then selecting an existing open curve or the edges of elements. The desired 2D path is always an open geometry composed of a single segment. Once you have sketched or picked the 2D path, you need to define a profile at either end. To define the first profile, choose the **Select Profile 1** tool from the **Swept Blend** panel and then choose the **Edit Profile** tool from the **Edit** panel; the **Go To View** dialog box will be displayed, as shown in Figure 10-20. Choose the required option from this dialog box and then choose the **Open View** button; the view will change based on the option chosen and the **Modify | Swept Blend > Edit Profile** tab will be displayed. Using the sketching tools from the **Draw** panel, sketch the first profile at the end of the 2D path, displaying a prominent red dot. Next, to finish the sketching of the first profile, choose the **Finish Edit Mode** button from the **Mode** panel of the **Modify | Swept Blend > Edit Profile** tab. Similarly, you can define the second profile. To do so, choose the **Select Profile 2** option from the **Swept Blend** panel and then choose the **Edit Profile** option from the **Mode** panel in the **Modify | Swept Blend** tab; the **Modify | Swept Blend > Edit Profile** tab will be displayed. Sketch the second profile and then choose the **Finish Edit Mode** button from the **Mode** panel; the **Modify | Swept Blend** tab will be displayed. Now, choose the **Finish Edit Mode** button from the **Mode** panel; the solid swept blend geometry will be created, as shown in Figure 10-21.

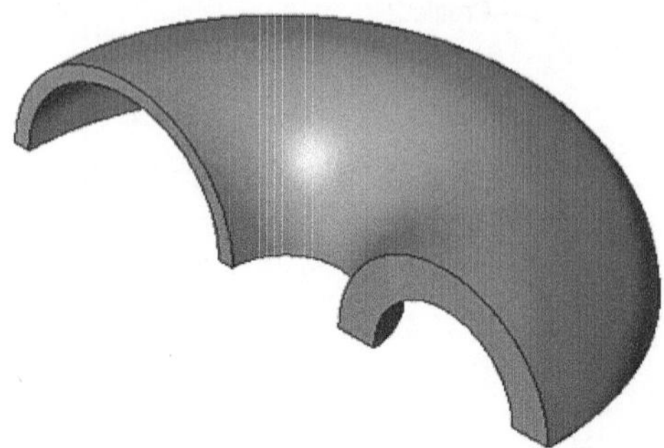

Figure 10-21 *Massing geometry created by using the **Swept Blend** tool*

Editing a Massing Geometry in the Family Editor

In Autodesk Revit, you can easily edit a massing geometry in the family editor environment. It can be edited using the drag controls or by editing the massing parameters.

Resizing a Massing Geometry Using Drag Controls

On selecting a massing geometry, a number of drag controls will be displayed as arrows. You can use a drag control to drag the face. The entire massing geometry is automatically updated, based on the dragged face. For example, a cuboid with drag controls displayed on all its faces is shown in Figure 10-22. When you drag a plane of the cuboid using drag controls, Autodesk Revit immediately updates the geometry, as shown in Figure 10-23.

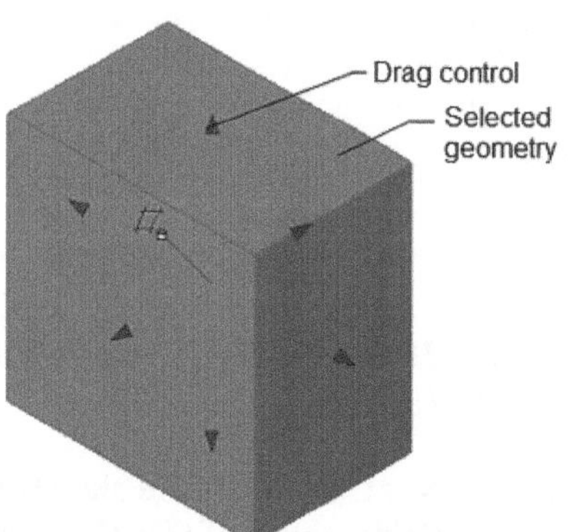

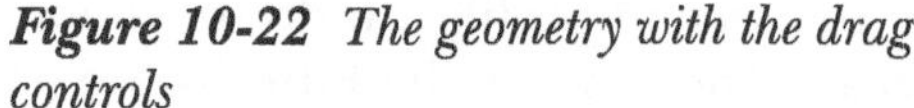

Figure 10-22 *The geometry with the drag controls*

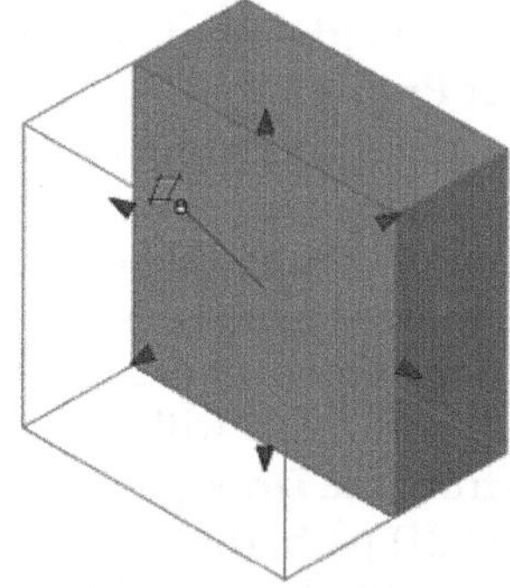

Figure 10-23 *The massing geometry resized using the drag controls*

Editing the Parameters of a Massing Geometry

The parameters of a massing geometry can be modified in the Family Editor environment. To edit the parameters, select a massing geometry created by using the **Extrusion** tool; the **Modify | Extrusion** tab will be displayed. In this tab, choose the **Edit Extrusion** tool from the **Mode** panel; the **Modify | Extrusion > Edit Extrusion** tab will be displayed. From the **Draw** panel of this tab, you can use various sketching tools to alter the sketch of the extrusion profile. You can also change the properties of extrusion such as height, material, and visibility from the **Properties** palette. For example, you can change the height of extrusion by changing the values of the **Extrusion End** and **Extrusion Start** parameters in the **Properties** palette.

To finish the editing of the selected extruded mass, choose the **Finish Edit Mode** button from the **Modify | Extrusion > Edit Extrusion** tab of the **Mode** panel; the editing of the selected extruded mass will be finished.

Similarly, you can edit other massing geometries created using the **Sweep, Swept Blend, Revolve,** and **Blend** tools.

To a certain extent, massing features can also be modified like other system elements. You can use the editing tools such as **Mirror, Copy, Group, Array,** and so on along with the massing tools to edit the massing geometry.

Creating Cuts in a Massing Geometry Using the Family Editor

You can cut a massing geometry by creating a void form in it. This void form is cut or subtracted from the massing geometry it intersects. You can create void forms by using the tools displayed in the **Void Forms** drop-down in the **Forms** panel of the **Create** tab, as shown in Figure 10-24. The **Void Forms** drop-down displays five tools: **Void Extrusion, Void Blend, Void Revolve, Void Swept Blend,** and **Void Sweep**. You can choose an appropriate tool to generate the shape and volume of the void form. The method of creating a void form using these tools is similar to that of creating a solid form.

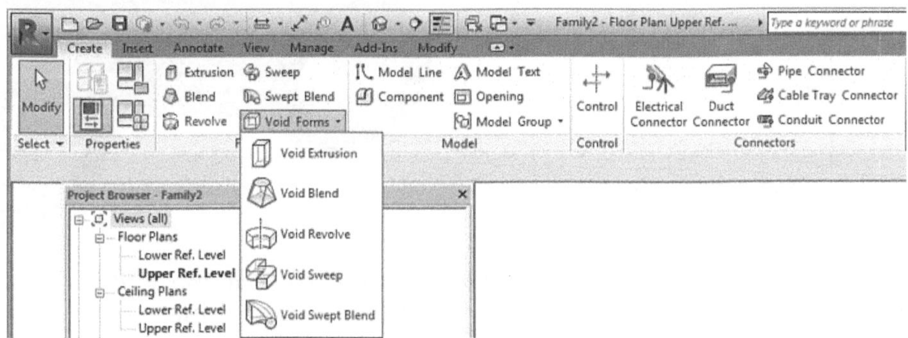

Figure 10-24 *Tools in the **Void Forms** drop-down*

When any of the tools is invoked from the **Void Forms** drop-down is invoked, the corresponding contextual tab is displayed. For example, if you invoke the **Void Extrusion** tool, the **Modify | Create Void Extrusion** tab will be displayed. You can use the options in this tab to sketch the profile for the extruded void geometry. After sketching the profile of the extruded void geometry, choose the **Finish Edit Mode** button from the **Mode** panel of the **Modify | Create Void Extrusion** tab; the **Modify | Void Extrusion** tab will be displayed. From this tab, you can use various editing options to modify the extruded void geometry. Next, click in the drawing area or press ESC; the void form will automatically cut its shape and volume from the intersecting massing geometry.

For example, Figure 10-25 shows the profile of a duct sketched using the **Void Extrusion** tool. Now, when you choose the **Finish Edit Mode** button from the **Modify | Create Void Extrusion** tab, the cutting geometry, a shaft in this case, is generated and automatically cut from the larger massing geometry. Figure 10-26 shows the resulting massing geometry.

Figure 10-25 *The profile for creating a void form using the **Void Extrusion** tool*

Figure 10-26 *The created void form using the **Void Extrusion** tool*

Similarly, you can also use the **Void Revolve, Void Sweep, Void Blend**, and **Void Swept Blend** tools from the **Void Forms** drop-down to create the void form. For example, to create a pipe bend, you can use the **Void Sweep** tool to sketch a semicircular profile and to specify its path, as shown in Figure 10-27. The resulting void form will be cut from the cuboid to create an arched opening through the building block, as shown in Figure 10-28.

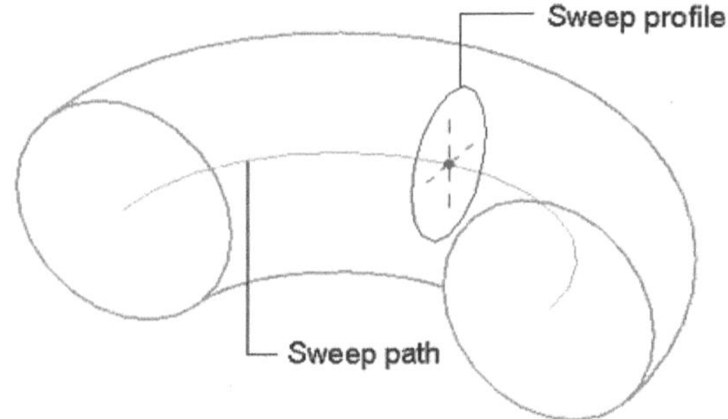

Figure 10-27 *Sketching the profile for creating a void form*

Figure 10-28 *The generated void form and the resulting massing geometry*

You can also use various editing tools such as **Copy**, **Mirror**, **Array**, and so on to create multiple copies of the void form profile of a single massing geometry. For example, a plumbing fixture has a semicircular vertical cut as the void form on one of its sides. You can select the 2D profile of the void form and use the **Copy** tool to create its duplicate.

Loading Massing Geometry into a Project

After creating massing geometries in the Family Editor, you can load them into the Project environment. To do so, choose the **Load into Project** tool from the **Family Editor** panel of the **Modify** tab; the current project file will appear, if one project file is opened on the screen. Note that if more than one project file is opened in the current session, the **Load into Projects** dialog box will be displayed, as shown in Figure 10-29. In this dialog box, you can select the check box(es) to select the project(s) in which the created mass will be loaded. After selecting the required check box(es), choose **OK**; the mass will be loaded into the selected project file(s) corresponding to the check box(es) selected. In this project file, the **Modify | Place Component** tab is chosen by default and you will notice that the mass created in the Family Editor appears in the drawing area along with the cursor.

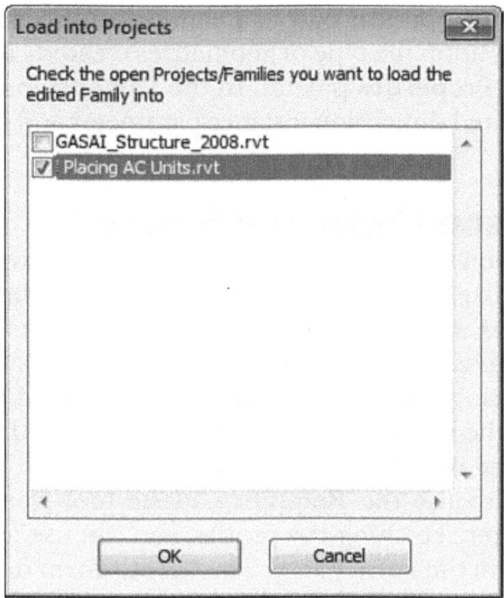

*Figure 10-29 The **Load into Projects** dialog box*

Placing the Massing Geometry in a Project

In Project environment of Autodesk Revit, you have the option to add a predefined massing geometry to the project using the **Place Mass** tool. To do so, invoke this tool from the **Conceptual Mass** panel of the **Massing & Site** tab; the **Massing - Show Mass Enabled** window will be displayed. Choose the **Close** button from the window; the **Revit** message box will be displayed. Choose the **Yes** button in this message box; the **Load Family** dialog box will be displayed. In this dialog box, browse to the **Mass** sub folder in the **US Imperial** folder and then select a massing family. After selecting the massing family, choose the **Open** button; the **Load Family** dialog box will be closed and the **Modify | Place Mass** tab will be displayed. Also, the selected family will be loaded into the project. Now, click in the drawing area to place the loaded massing geometry.

In Revit, you can either align a mass geometry with the selected faces of the components created or place it on the defined work plane based on your requirement. To place a mass geometry on a selected face, choose the **Place on Face** tool from the **Placement** panel of the **Modify | Place Mass** tab and then place the cursor on the face of the component with which you want to align the massing geometry. You will notice that the mass geometry is aligned with the face on which the cursor is placed. Now, you can click to place the mass on the plane. Similarly, while placing a mass in a drawing, you can place it at a desired level. To do so, choose the **Place on Work Plane** tool from the **Placement** panel of the **Modify | Place Mass** tab; the options for placing the mass will be displayed in the **Options Bar**. In the **Options Bar**, select the required level from the **Placement Plane** drop-down list, as shown in Figure 10-30. Click in the drawing area; a mass will be created at the selected level. Before aligning the mass geometry with the desired face or placing it in a work plane, you can also rotate it about an axis. To do so, select the **Rotate after placement** check box from the **Options Bar**. After placing the

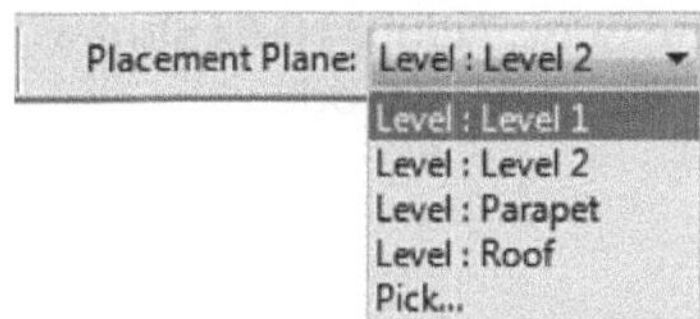

*Figure 10-30 The **Placement Plane** drop-down list*

mass geometry in the drawing, you can edit its geometrical properties such as height, width, radius, and so on, depending upon the type of geometries created. To do so, modify the instance parameters displayed in the **Properties** palette. In the **Dimensions** category of the **Properties** palette, you can select the desired dimension instance parameter and change its value in respective value field.

Creating the In-Place Mass in a Project

In the Project environment, you have the option to create an in-place massing geometry by using the **In-Place Mass** tool. Invoke this tool from the **Conceptual Mass** panel of the **Massing & Site** tab; the **Name** dialog box will be displayed. In this dialog box, enter the name of the mass in the **Name** edit box and choose **OK**; the **Create** tab will be displayed. You can use the options in this tab to sketch the massing profile and convert it into a solid or void form. To sketch the profile for the mass, choose the **Model** tool from the **Draw** panel; the **Modify | Place Lines** tab will be displayed. You can use various sketching tools available in the **Draw** panel of this tab. While sketching, you can also use the **Reference Plane** tool from the **Draw** panel to draw references for the sketch. After sketching the profile, you can use any of the tools displayed in the **Create Form** drop-down in the **Form** panel. The **Create Form** drop-down displays two tools: **Solid Form** and **Void Form**. You can use the **Solid Form** tool to create a solid form and the **Void Form** tool to create a void form. To use any of the tools from the **Create Form** drop-down, you need to select the sketched profile from the drawing and then invoke the **Solid Form** or **Void Form** tool; the **Modify | Form** tab will be displayed. Using the options in this tab, you can specify the settings to change the instance property of the mass created, divide the surfaces of the mass, and can modify the geometrical elements of the mass. You can change the instance properties of the massing geometry like material and visibility from the **Properties** palette. After changing the instance properties of the selected massing geometry, you can change the geometrical property of the surface by adding edges and profiles. The tools for changing the geometrical properties are: **X-Ray**, **Add Edge**, and **Add Profile**. You can invoke these tools from the **Form Element** panel of the **Modify | Form** (solid form) tab.

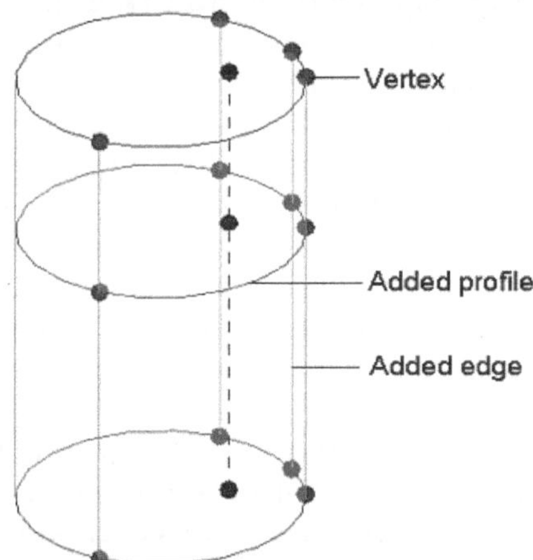

***Figure 10-31** Massing geometry with added edge and profile in the **X-Ray** mode*

The **X-Ray** tool in the **Element** panel of the **Modify | Form** tab is used to display the geometry skeleton like vertices and edges of the mass. The **Add Edge** tool can be used to add edges to the form of the mass and the **Add Profile** tool is used to add profile to the surface of the mass. Figure 10-31 shows the added edge and profile in the **X-Ray** mode.

Dividing Edges or Paths

You can divide a line or an edge of a form to define the nodes on which the components can be placed. On dividing a line or an edge, nodes are applied at the division points denoting the position of the points of placement for components. You can divide a line or an edge of a form by specifying the number of divisions, by specifying distance between the divisions, or by using the point of intersection between the line and edge with the levels, reference planes, or divided paths. To divide a path on an edge, select a form from the project view; the **Modify | Mass** tab will be displayed. In this tab, choose the **Edit In-Place** tab; the form will be displayed in the editable mode. Select an edge of the form; the **Modify | Form** tab will be displayed. In this tab, choose the **Divide Path** tool from the **Divide** panel; the properties of the path division will be displayed in the **Properties** palette. Also, the selected edges will display six nodes in equal division along its edge. You will also notice the number **6** displayed above the edge. You can click on the number and enter a different numerical value in the edit box displayed to increase the number of nodal divisions along the edge.

MASSING IN CONCEPTUAL DESIGN ENVIRONMENT

Conceptual designing is the very first phase of a design process. The primary objective of a conceptual design is to create a representation of the idea for creating the system mass of a project. For creating a building project, the conceptual design is very important for architects, engineers, and designers as it helps in finding out the final representation of the design intent. Thus, it enables them to create a more specific sets of plans.

In Revit, you can create conceptual designs in any of the following environments: Conceptual Design Environment and Revit Project Environment. The Conceptual Design Environment is used to create massing families as conceptual designs that reside outside the Project environment. These families can be loaded in the Revit Project Environment that forms the basis to create detail design by applying walls, roofs, floors, and curtain systems to them. In the Revit Project Environment, you can create conceptual designs by using the **In-Place Mass** or **Place Mass** tool from the **Conceptual Mass** panel in the **Massing & Site** tab. In this environment, you can neither create 3D reference planes nor view 3D levels.

Interface of the Conceptual Design Environment

To open the interface of the Conceptual Design Environment, choose the **Application** button and then choose **New > Conceptual Mass** from the **Application Menu**. On doing so, the **New Conceptual Mass-Select Template File** dialog box will be displayed. In this dialog box, select the *Metric Mass.rft* file in the **Conceptual Mass** folder and then choose the **Open** button; the interface of the Conceptual Design Environment along with the settings of the *Mass.rft* template file will be displayed, as shown in Figure 10-32. In the interface of the Conceptual Massing Environment, you can use various tools in the ribbon to create the conceptual mass.

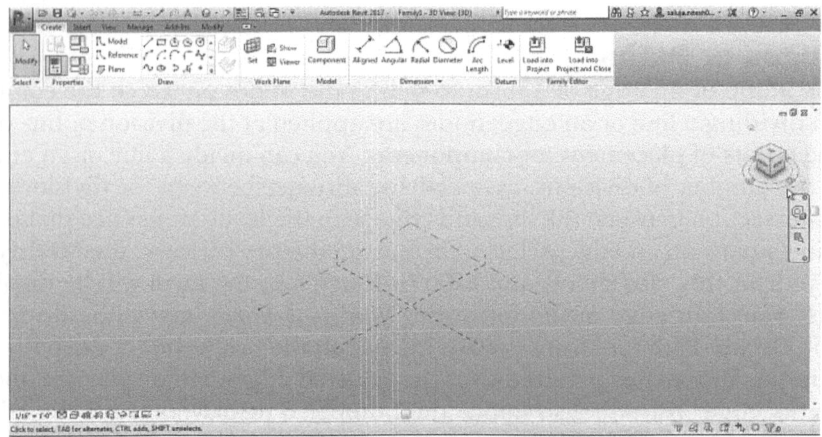

Figure 10-32 The Conceptual Design Environment interface

Creating Masses in the Conceptual Design Environment

In the Conceptual Design Environment, you can create the conceptual mass by using various tools from the ribbon. The ribbon of the Conceptual Design Environment, as shown in Figure 10-33, consists of the following tabs: **Create**, **Insert**, **View**, **Manage**, and **Modify**.

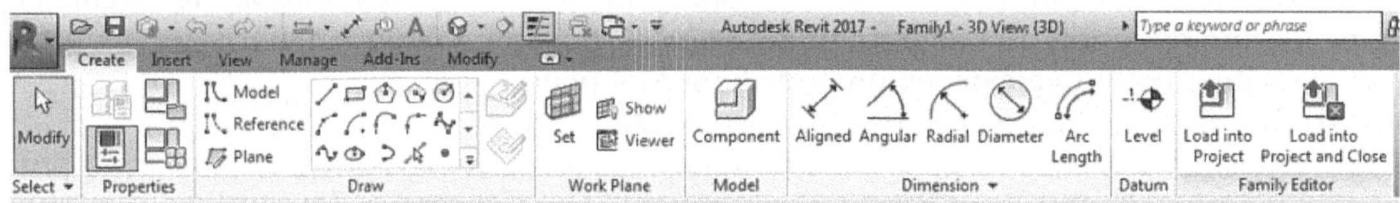

Figure 10-33 The ribbon of the Conceptual Design Environment

The **Create** tab is chosen by default. From the **Create** tab, you can access the tools required to create the Conceptual Mass. From the **Workplane** panel of the **Create** tab, you can choose any of the tools such as **Set**, **Show**, and **Viewer** that can be used for setting, showing, and viewing workplane to create the conceptual mass, respectively. You can choose the **Level** tool in the **Datum** panel to add levels that will assist in the creation of the conceptual mass. You can add levels to 3D and elevation views in the Conceptual Design Environment. The **Draw** panel of the **Create** tab contain tools that can be used to sketch the conceptual mass. In this panel, you can use the **Model**, **Reference**, and **Plane** tools to sketch the model lines, reference lines, and reference planes to create the conceptual mass. When you choose the **Model** or **Reference** tool from the **Draw** panel, the **Draw on Face** and the **Draw on Work Plane** tools will be activated. You can use any of these tools to specify the plane in which conceptual mass will be created. Also, on choosing the **Model** or **Reference** tool from the **Draw** panel, a contextual tab will be displayed along with various options in the **Options Bar**. This tab contains options that help in sketching the model or the reference line. In the **Family Editor** panel of the **Create** tab, you can choose the **Load into Project** tool to load the conceptual mass into the project file. From the **Dimension** panel of the **Create** tab, you can choose various tools to dimension the sketch of the conceptual mass. In the ribbon of the Conceptual Design Environment, the tools in the other tabs such as **Insert**, **View**, **Manage**, and **Modify** are same as those in the Project Environment. In the next sections, the method and the tools involved in the process of drawing and creating the conceptual mass are discussed.

Sketching the Conceptual Design Environment

To sketch a profile of the conceptual mass in the Conceptual Design Environment, you can use the floor plan views or the 3D views, depending upon the project requirement. You can draw a profile of the conceptual mass with or without using references. The references can be used to create constraints and reference for the conceptual mass. To draw references for a profile of the conceptual mass, you can invoke the **Reference** tool from the **Draw** panel of the **Create** tab. After invoking the **Reference** tool, you can draw the reference by using various sketching tools such as **Line**, **Rectangle**, **Circle**, **Pick Lines**, and **Point Elements** from the list box displayed next to it.

After sketching the reference, you need to sketch the model lines for the profile of the conceptual mass. To do so, choose the **Model** tool from the **Draw** panel; the **Modify | Place Lines** tab will be displayed. From the **Draw** panel of this tab, you can use the sketching tools such as **Line**, **Rectangle**, and others to sketch the profile of the conceptual mass. When you invoke a sketching tool, its corresponding options are displayed in the **Options Bar**. These options assist in sketching the profile. After you sketch the profile, you can also use various editing tools such as **Offset**, **Move**, **Copy**, and more from the **Modify** panel of the **Modify | Place Lines** tab to edit the sketch. Figure 10-34 displays the sketched profile of a conceptual mass.

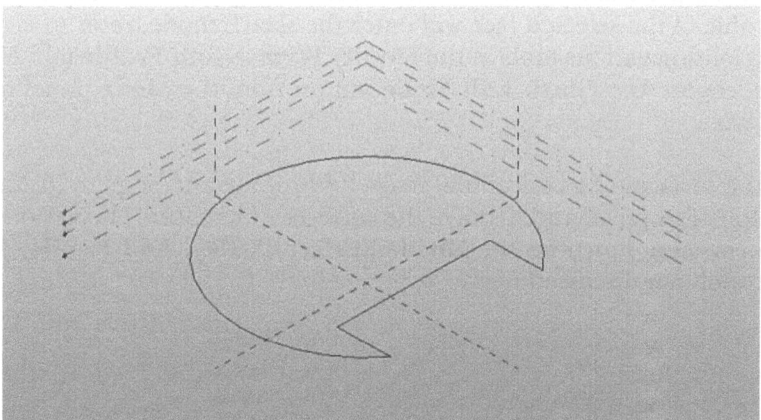

Figure 10-34 *Sketched profile of a conceptual mass*

After sketching the conceptual mass, select it; the **Modify | Line** tab will be displayed. In the **Form** panel of this tab, you can choose the **Solid Form** or the **Void Form** tool from the **Create Form** drop-down menu. You can choose the **Solid Form** tool to create a solid from the sketched lines. Alternatively, choose the **Void Form** tool to create a void or cavity in an existing solid. On choosing the **Solid Form** tool from the **Create Form** drop-down, the **Modify | Form** tab will be displayed. Also, the selected sketch line will extrude to a certain height and will appear along with its temporary dimensions. Figure 10-35 displays a solid extruded from the sketched lines.

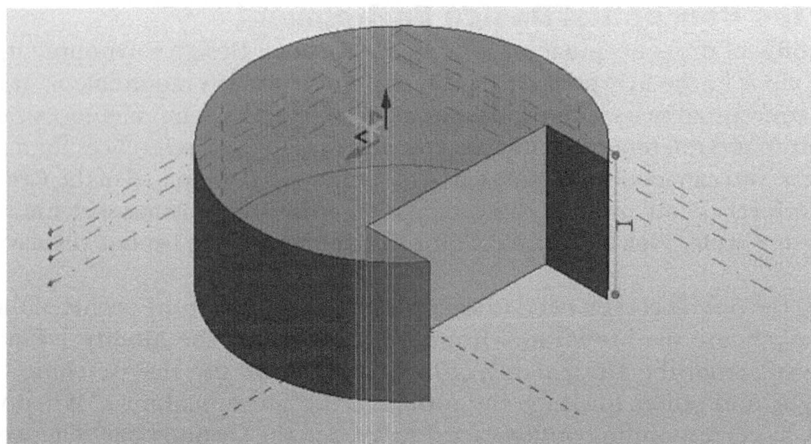

Figure 10-35 *Solid extruded from the sketched lines*

After creating a solid, you can edit its profile. To do so, select the extruded face of the solid profile and then choose the **Edit Profile** tool from the **Mode** panel of the **Modify | Form** tab. On doing so, the profile of the selected face will enter the sketch mode, refer to Figure 10-36. You can edit the sketch using various tools in the **Modify Form > Edit Profile** tab. After editing the sketched profile, choose the **Finish Edit Mode** button from the **Mode** panel to return to the **Modify | Form** tab.

You can divide the surfaces of a conceptual mass, add profile and edge to its form, display the geometric skeleton of its form, and dissolve the surfaces of its form. The various tools that you can use to perform these functions are **Divide Surface**, **X-Ray**, **Add Profile**, **Add Edge**, and **Dissolve**. These tools are discussed next.

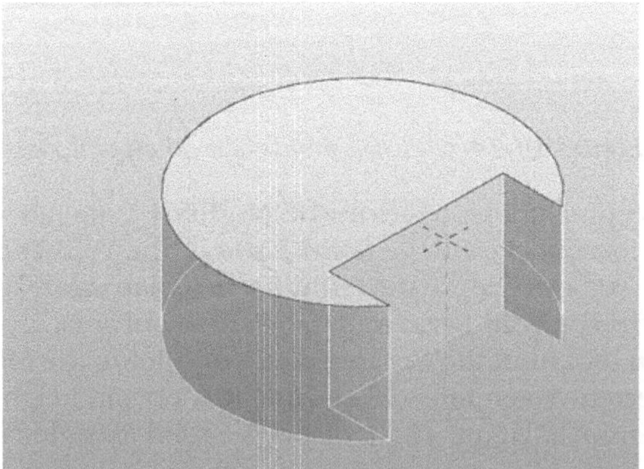

Figure 10-36 *Profile of the selected face in the editing mode*

Using X-Ray

The **X-Ray** tool is used to display the underlying geometric skeleton of a selected form. When the geometric skeleton of the selected form is displayed, it is called the X-Ray mode. This mode allows you to directly interact with the individual elements that creates the form, as the surfaces become transparent. It is to be noted that at a time only one form in all the models will be visible in the X-Ray mode. To switch the display of a form to the X-Ray mode, select it and then choose the **X-Ray** tool from the **Form Element** panel of the **Modify | Form** tab. Once you switch the form to the X-Ray mode, you can select the element again and choose the **X-Ray** tool to restore its visibility to its previous mode.

Adding Profiles

After you create a conceptual mass, you can add cross-section profiles to it. An edge is a profile that may be a single line, chain of connected lines, or a closed loop, depending upon the geometry of the form. The added profile can be used to generate a form or edit the geometry of the existing form. To add a profile to a form, select it and then choose the **Add Profile** tool from the **Form Element** panel of the **Modify | Form** tab; the cursor changes to a cross mark and you will be prompted at the **Status Bar** to insert a new profile at the cross-section of the form element. Move the cursor on the surface of the form; it will be highlighted with a blue border and a probable profile will be displayed at the position of the cursor. Click at the desired point on the surface of the form to add the profile. Note that the added profile in the form will only be visible in the X-Ray mode. Figure 10-37 displays a form with added profiles.

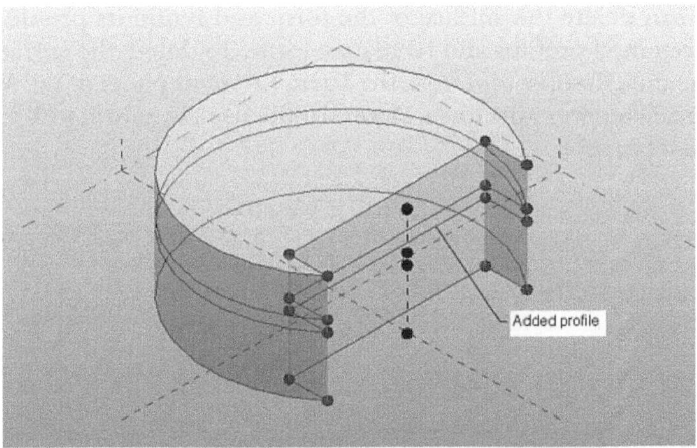

Figure 10-37 *Profiles added in the form*

Adding Edges

After you create a conceptual mass, you can add edges to it. To add an edge, select the form and then choose the **Add Edge** tool from the **Form Element** panel of the **Modify | Form** tab; the cursor will change into a cross mark. Place the cursor on the surface of the form; an edge will appear at the point of the cursor. Click at the desired point on the surface; the edge will be added to the surface of the form, as shown in Figure 10-38.

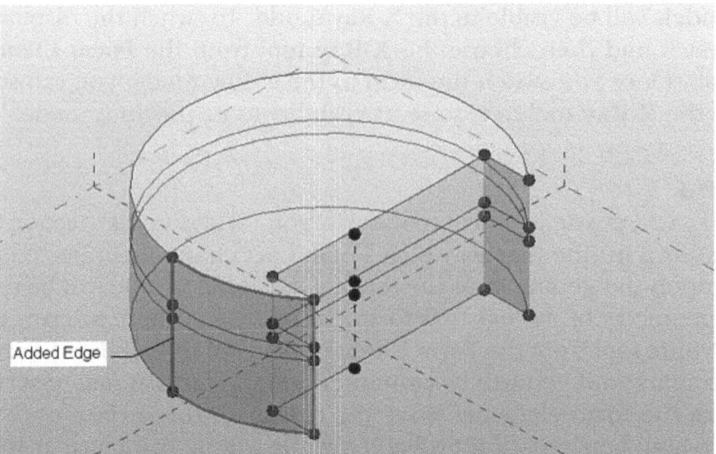

Figure 10-38 *Edge added to the form*

Dissolve

You can delete the surface of the form and retain its profile. You can also edit the retained profiles and recreate a form. To delete the surface of a form, select the form and choose the **Dissolve** tool from the **Form Element** panel of the **Modify | Form** tab; the surface(s) will be deleted from the form. Figure 10-39 displays a form with its surfaces removed on applying the **Dissolve** tool.

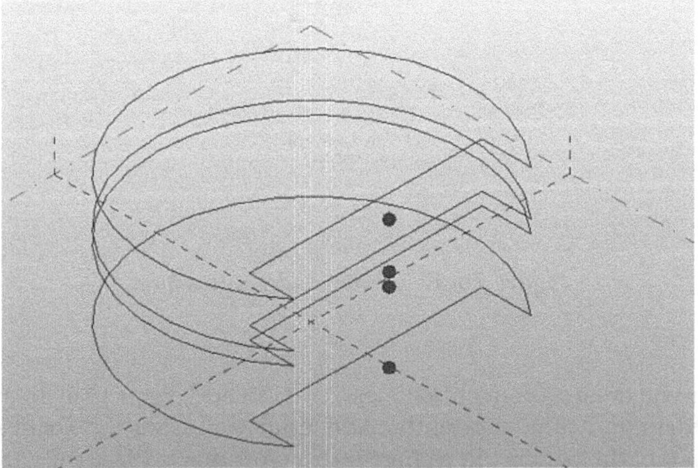

Figure 10-39 *Surfaces removed using the **Dissolve** tool*

Tip

*You can divide any face of the form. To do so, select the face and then choose the **Divide Surface** tool from the **Divide** panel of the **Modify / Form** tab; the **Modify / Divided Surface** tab will be displayed. You can use the tools from the displayed tab and the options in the **Options Bar** to divide the selected face.*

WORKSHARING CONCEPTS

Worksharing is a method of distributing work among people involved in a project to accomplish it within the stipulated period of time. In Worksharing, each person involved in the project is assigned a task that has to be accomplished through proper planning and coordination among the team members.

In a large scale project, worksharing is the most important method to finish the project in time and meet the quality requirements that are set during the process. Generally, in a large-scale building project, worksharing is based on the specialization of work. For example, professionals like Structural Engineers, Architects, Interior Architects, Electrical Engineers, Mechanical Engineers and Plumbing Engineers can contribute in their respective fields to accomplish the project. Each professional has his own set of work to perform for the accomplishment of the project. Therefore, worksharing is an important process that is needed to be implemented efficiently to complete the project in time.

Worksharing Using Workset Tools

In Autodesk Revit, you work in an integrated single file model. This implies that all the construction related information and documents are available in a single model file and this forms the basis of the worksharing process.

The process of worksharing can be implemented using the **Worksets** tool. Worksets are a collection of elements such as ducts, VAV box, AHU, diffusers and more that define the domain and the ownership of the user in a project. For example, a project may contain building elements like beams, columns, mechanical equipments, plumbing fixtures, electrical elements, architectural elements, and so on. In a worksharing environment, you can assign each element to a workset, which defines its ownership to the user, thereby restricting other users to change or modify it in the project without prior permission. Therefore, only one user can edit a workset at a time.

When you start a new Revit project, the worksharing is not activated by default because the software assumes that you are working in a single user environment. When you transform your project from a single user to a multi-tasking environment, you need to understand the concept of central file system and the utility of using the worksets. A central file is a master file of the project and stores the entire building information. This file is connected and shared by all other files representing individual users and it monitors the progress of the entire project. The files that are shared and connected to the central file are called local files. These files are a copy of the central file and are saved locally at the individual users workstation. These files can also be saved in a specified network location, thereby differentiating them from the central file. These local files act as an interfacing mechanism for working on the central file.

Process of Worksharing

With the start of a new project, you start creating the building geometry with basic detailing. But as the project progresses, you need to share the project with multiple users and speed up the process of work. To invite multiple users to work in your project, you can save the file that you have worked as a central file at a particular network location and then create copies of it in the local hard drives of individual team members. By doing so, you divide the work into different parts. Everybody will start working with the copied central file from his or her individual workstation. Before starting with the file, each member working in the project is instructed to rename the copied central file at their individual hard drive location and then open it in Revit to proceed further. The flow diagram in Figure 10-40 explains the process of worksharing in brief.

Elements in each separate file are tied to the ownership rule linked to the central file. This restricts individual team members to edit an element in his or her local file, which is owned by someone in local files. In the worksharing process, the central file behaves as the controller of all the elements that are shared by members.

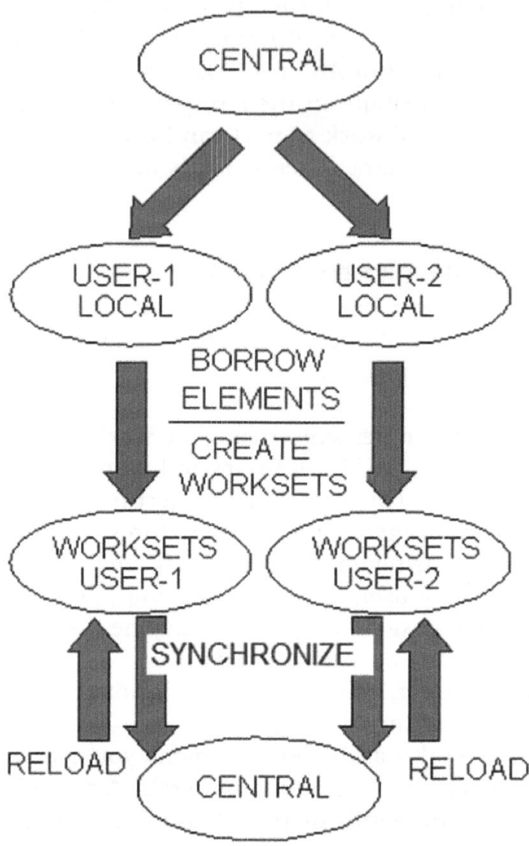

Figure 10-40 *Flow diagram explaining the Worksharing process*

Using Worksets Tool

To enable the process of worksharing, choose the Collaborate tool from the **Manage Collaboration** panel of the **Collaborate** tab; the **Collaborate** dialog box will be displayed, as shown in Figure 10-41. Ensure that the **Collaborate within your network radio** buttion is selected by default and choose **OK**; the worksharing will be enabled. Now, choose the **Worksets** tool from the **Manage Collaboration** panel of the **Collaborate** tab.

***Figure 10-41** The **Collaborate** dialog box*

In the **Worksets** dialog box, there are six different columns: **Name, Editable, Owner, Borrowers, Opened**, and **Visible in all views**, as shown in Figure 10-42. The **Name** column displays the worksets that are defined or predefined in the project. The **Editable** column shows the status of the modification of the elements and components of the workset in the project. The **Owner** column specifies the ownership of the particular workset in the project.

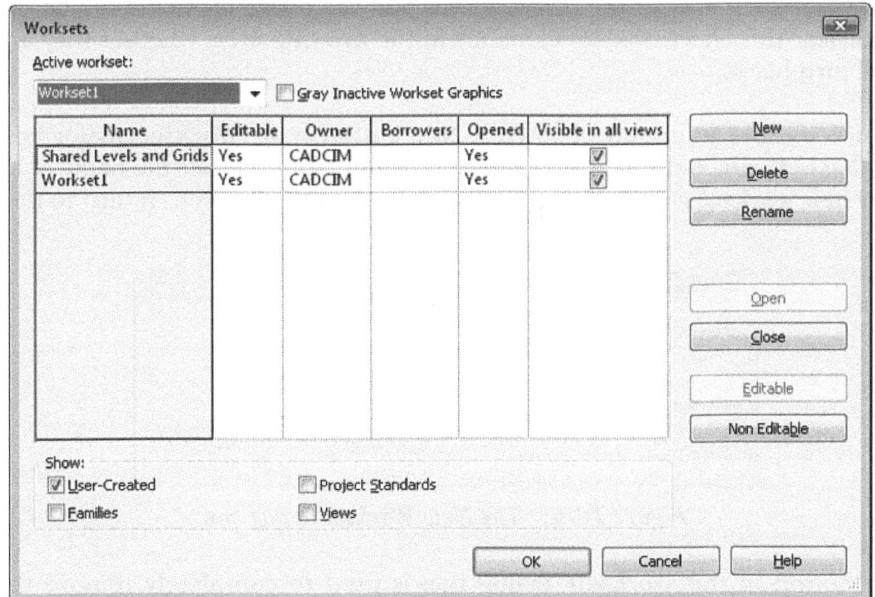

***Figure 10-42** The **Worksets** dialog box displaying different columns*

The ownership of the workset refers to the name of the user who had created it. This name refers to the user of the master file or the user of the local file. By default, Revit denotes the name of the user, which is determined by the log-on name of the operating system. In Revit, before enabling the workset, you can change the username. To do so, choose the **Options** button from the **Application Menu**; the **Options** dialog box will be displayed. In this dialog box, choose the **General** tab and specify a new name in the **Username** edit box.

The **Borrowers** column in the **Worksets** dialog box displays the name of the user currently using the elements of the worksets that do not belong to him or her. In this process, the owner or any other user can only use the borrowed worksets, if the borrower allows to do so.

The **Opened** column is used to select a workset definition. There are two options in this column: **Yes** and **No**. These options can be used to control the visibility of the elements in a group. By default, all worksets in the **Worksets** dialog box are assigned the **Yes** option. It means all the elements and components of these worksets are visible in the file. But, if you choose the **No** option, the visibility of elements and components of worksets will be disabled.

The **Visible in View** column allows you to show workset in all views. This column carries check boxes corresponding to the **Shared Level and Grids** and **Workset 1 Name** parameters. These check boxes are selected by default. On clearing these check boxes, the workset will not be displayed in any view.

You can select various options from the **Active workset** drop-down list located at the top in the **Worksets** dialog box. This drop-down list is used to select those worksets that are user defined and have the **Yes** status displayed in the **Opened** column of the **Worksets** dialog box. Select the appropriate workset available in the drop-down list to make it the current workset. If you select the **Gray Inactive Workset Graphics** check box, the elements that do not belong to the active workset will turn gray in the drawing area and the active elements will be displayed in black. If you clear this check box, all elements in the drawing area, whether they are active or inactive, will turn black.

To create a new workset definition, choose the **New** button in the **Worksets** dialog box; the **New Workset** dialog box will be displayed, as shown in Figure 10-43. Enter the name of the workset in the **Enter new workset name** edit box and choose the **OK** button to return to the **Worksets** dialog box.

New Workset

Enter new workset name:

Visible in all views

OK Cancel Help

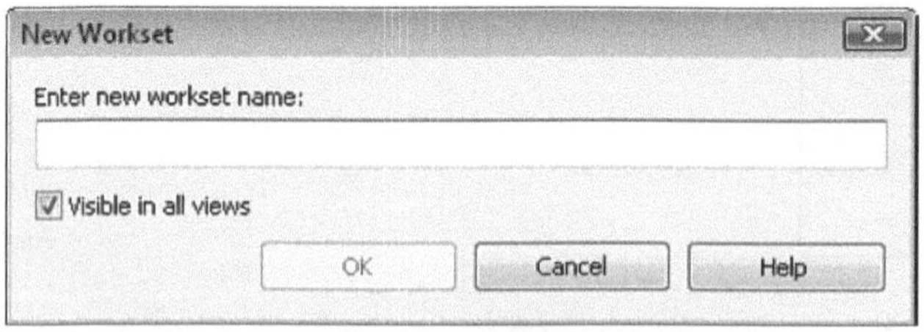

*Figure 10-43 The **New Workset** dialog box*

The **Delete** button in the **Worksets** dialog box is used to completely remove the selected workset. Note that you can delete only that workset definition which is editable. When you choose the **Delete** button, the **Delete Workset** dialog box will be displayed, as shown in Figure 10-44. This dialog box can be used to delete the elements belonging to the deleted workset or to move these elements to a different workset definition. If you select the **Deleted** radio button in this dialog box, elements that belong to the workset being deleted, will be deleted. Similarly, if you want to move these elements to a different workset, select the **Moved to** radio button and then select the appropriate workset from the **Moved to** drop-down list. Choose the **OK** button to return to the **Worksets** dialog box. You can rename the editable worksets. To do so, select the workset in the **Name** column and choose the **Rename** button; the **Rename** dialog box will be displayed. Specify a name in the **New** edit box to change the name of the selected workset. The **Open** and **Close** buttons in the **Worksets** dialog box are used to change the status of the selected workset in the **Opened** column to **Yes** and **No**, respectively. Similarly, the **Editable** and **Non Editable** buttons can also be used to change the status of the selected workset in the **Editable** column to **Yes** and **No**, respectively. While using the workset for the first time, if you choose the **Non Editable** button before saving the file to the central file, the **Revit** warning message box will be displayed. This message box warns you to save your file to the central file.

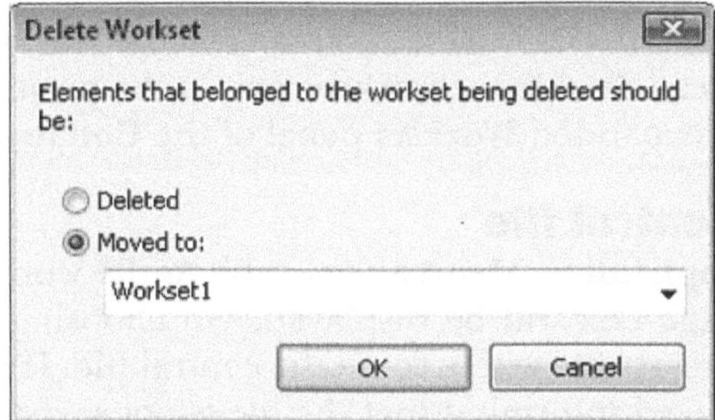

***Figure 10-44** The **Delete Workset** dialog box*

In Autodesk Revit, you can define four different types of worksets. These worksets are **User-Created**, **Families**, **Project Standards**, and **Views**. These worksets are explained next in detail.

User-Created Workset

A user can define and modify this workset as per his requirements. As a user, you can create your own workset and assign different elements and components to it. When you invoke the **Worksets** dialog box, two worksets, **Shared Levels and Grids** and **Workset1** are created by default. The **Shared Levels and Grids** workset is automatically defined for the existing levels and grids in your drawing and the **Workset1** workset is defined for all elements and components created by you.

Views Workset

In Revit, a dedicated view workset contains a dedicated view property and view-specific elements like dimensions, tags, text, and others. To display view worksets in the **Worksets** dialog box, you need to select the **Views** check box in the **Show** area of this dialog box.

The view-specific elements cannot be moved to other worksets. To own a view in a workset, select the required view from the **Project Browser** and click the right mouse button over it; a cascading menu will be displayed. Choose the **Make Workset Editable** option from it to own the view in the workset.

Families Workset

When you load a family into your project, a workset is automatically created for it. You can view the family workset by selecting the **Families** check box in the **Show** area of the **Worksets** dialog box. To own a family, select it in the **Worksets** dialog box and change the default option **No** in the **Editable** column to **Yes** by choosing the option from the available drop-down list.

Project Standards Workset

The project standards workset are used to set projects. You can view these worksets by selecting the **Project Standards** check box in the **Worksets** dialog box. In the **Worksets** dialog box, you can own a particular workset by changing the default option **No** in the **Editable** column to **Yes** by selecting the option from the available drop-down list. **Materials**, **Line Styles**, and **Callout Tags** are examples of project standard worksets.

Once you have created and edited your workset, you can exit the **Worksets** dialog box by choosing the **OK** button from it. You can disable the worksharing in the project by choosing the **Disable Worksharing** tool from the expanded **Workset** panel of the **Collaborate** tab.

Synchronizing with Central file

If you choose **Save** from **Application Menu** after enabling the worksets for the first time, the **Save File as Central** message box will be displayed. On choosing the **Yes** button from this message box, the current project file will become the central file. If you choose the **No** button, a message box will be displayed informing that the file is not saved. Choose the **Close** button from this message box to close it. To save the file as a central file, choose **Save As > Project** from **Application Menu**; the **Save As** dialog box will be displayed. Browse to a different location, specify a name in the **File name** edit box, and then choose **Save**; the file will be saved as a central file. Now, you can synchronize a project with the central file. To do so, choose the **Synchronize Now** tool from **Collaborate > Synchronize > Synchronize with Central** drop-down, as shown in Figure 10-45; the current project will be synchronized with the central file. As a result, all changes made to the current file will be reflected in the central file as well.

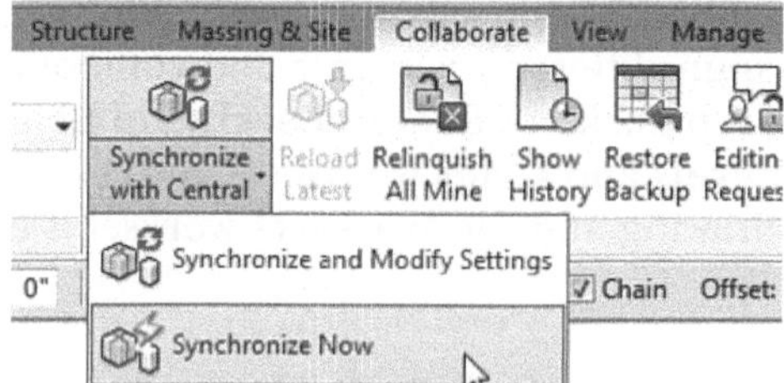

***Figure 10-45** Choosing the **Synchronize Now** tool from the **Collaborate** tab*

Note

A central file is a master project file that stores the information about the ownership of all worksets in a project. The central file should not be used for working when there is only one user.

Creating a Local File

While using a workset, you do not need to be connected to the system network to save the changes. For this, Autodesk Revit allows you to work on a local file which is the part of the building model file. A local file can be created by first opening the central file and then using the **Save As** tool to create a project file. This local file is only accessible to the user. The team member can work on the file and save it to the central file at regular intervals. The changes made to the workset are then propagated to all team members through the central file.

Saving Methodology in Worksharing

While working in a worksharing environment, it is important to learn the methods of saving your files. There are two methods of saving a file and sharing your files with others: saving a local file and synchronizing with the central file. You can save your file as a local file by choosing **Save** from **Application Menu**. The **Save** option is generally used to save the local file. Using this method, you can secure the work that you have done without affecting the worksharing process. The other method is to synchronize the file with the central file. The **Synchronize with Central** option is used to publish the work in the central file. The moment you synchronize your file to central, you acquire the changes made by other team members to their local models, provided they had also saved their files to the central file at that particular interval.

In Revit, you can synchronize a local file with the central file by choosing the **Synchronize Now** tool or the **Synchronize and Modify Settings** tool from the **Synchronize** panel. If you choose the **Synchronize Now** tool, the current project file will be saved to the central file. On choosing the **Synchronize and Modify Settings** tool, the **Synchronize with Central** dialog box will be displayed, as shown in Figure 10-46. This dialog box allows you to customize the way to save your file to central. In the **Synchronize with Central** dialog box, the **Central Model Location** text box shows the path to the central file in the network. You can then use the **Browse** button to change the path, if required. After synchronizing the required file with central, you can use various check boxes to relinquish borrowed elements and various worksets, if required. The **Comment** text box in the **Synchronize with Central** dialog box allows you to publish the message regarding the changes you made during a particular session to the team member.

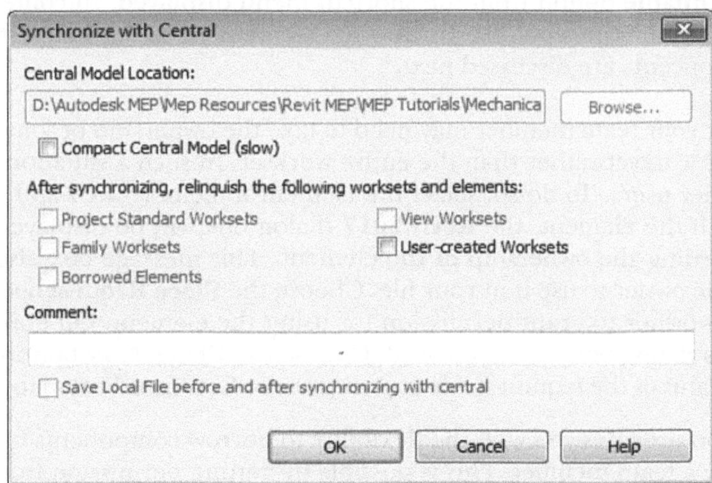

*Figure 10-46 The **Synchronize with Central** dialog box*

Reloading Files

In a worksharing environment, it is necessary to update your model corresponding to the changes made and saved to the central file by other team members. To do so, choose the **Reload Latest** tool from the **Synchronize** panel of the **Collaborate** tab. Alternatively, press RL from the keyboard to reload the file with the latest changes made in it.

Element Ownership Concepts

In a worksharing environment, you need to know about the status of ownership of a particular element or workset in the project. To check the status of ownership of an element, select it and check whether you can modify or reposition it. If you own the element, it will be highlighted in blue and can be modified and repositioned. In case, you do not own the element that you have selected, it will still be highlighted in red, and a blue icon is attached to it indicating it cannot be modified.

In Autodesk Revit, you can use color to visualize the status of workshared elements. To do so, choose the **Worksharing Display Off** option from the **View Control Bar** and then select various options from the flyout displayed, refer to Figure 10-47. You can use these options to customize the display modes to visually distinguish the following in a view: borrowed elements, current element owners, model updates, and element checkout status.

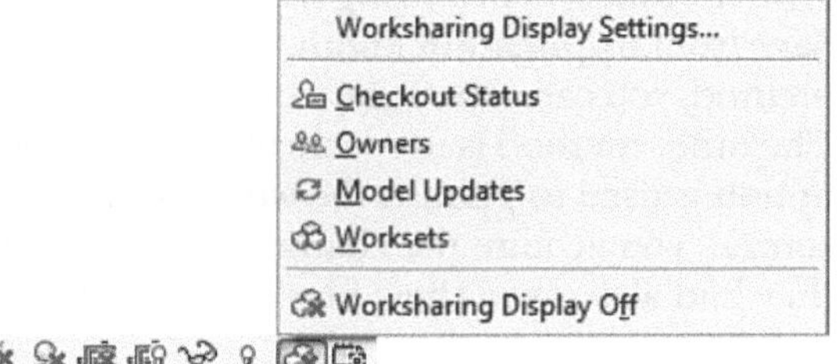

*Figure 10-47 Options in the flyout displayed upon choosing the **Worksharing Display Off** option*

In Revit, it is easy to retain the ownership status of a particular element or a component. There are several methods to get the ownership of a particular element or a workset and these are discussed next. One of the common methods of owning an element or a component is by trying to move or edit it. In this case, Autodesk Revit facilitates you to own it, provided it is not owned by anyone else in the worksharing environment. You can also get the ownership of an element by clicking the left mouse button over the blue icon that is displayed along with it. Next, to modify or edit an element, select it and click on the right mouse button and then choose the **Make Elements Editable** option from the shortcut menu displayed. In context to ownership, you need to know other concepts like Borrowing Elements, Placing Requests, and Granting Requests. These concepts are discussed next.

Sometimes, you or your team member may need to take the ownership of some of the elements within a particular workset rather than the entire workset. In such a situation, you can borrow elements from other users. To do so, select the element to be borrowed and click on the blue icon displayed with the element; the **Revit 2017** dialog box will be displayed with a warning message box regarding the ownership of the element. This message box also informs you to place request to the owner to use it in your file. Choose the **Place Request** button in the dialog box to request the owner to grant permission for using the element. On doing so, the **Check Editability Grants** dialog box will be invoked. Choose the **Check Now** button from the dialog box to check the status of the request made and choose the **Continue** button to resume the work.

Autodesk Revit also provides you with the flexibility to borrow components from worksets that are not editable by a team member. This is possible by getting permission from the user of the component, and then the borrowed elements or components can be edited, saved to central, and relinquished. In this release, the process of granting or denying permission to borrow an element or a component for editing it has been made more fast and interactive.

TUTORIAL

Tutorial 1 Dual Duct VAV box

In this tutorial, you will create a Dual Duct VAV box in the conceptual mass family environment and then set various parameters to the VAV box created.

(Expected time: 1hr 30 min)

1. File name to be assigned:

   For Imperial *Dual_Duct_VAV*
   For Metric *M_Dual_Duct_VAV*

   The following steps are required to complete this tutorial:

a. Open the Family Editor environment for massing.
b. Create the VAV box body.
c. Create the VAV box outlet sleeve.
d. Create the VAV box inlet sleeve.
e. Create the VAV box control box.
f. Attach the outlet duct connector.
g. Attach the inlet duct connector.
h. Save the project.
i. Close the project using the **Close** tool.

Opening the Family Editor Environment for Massing

In this section, you will open the Family Editor environment.

1. Choose **New > Family** from the **Application Menu**; the **New Family- Select Template File** dialog box is displayed.

2. In this dialog box, select the folder **English_I** for Imperial unit system or **English** for the Metric unit system from the **Look in:** drop-down list. Next, select the template file:

   Imperial system: *Mechanical Equipment.rft*
   Metric system: *Metric Mechanical Equipment.rft*

3. After selecting the template, choose the **Open** button. On doing so, two transverse reference planes are displayed in the working area.

Creating the VAV box Body

In this section, you will create the body of the VAV box.

1. Make sure that you are in the **Ref. Level** view, if not, then double-click on the **Ref. Level** sub node under the **Floor Plans** node in the **Project Browser**. Next, choose the **Reference Plane** tool from the **Datum** panel of the **Create** tab; the **Modify | Place Reference Plane** contextual tab is displayed.

2. In this contextual tab, choose the **Pick Lines** tool from the **Draw** panel. Next, enter the value **2' (610 mm)** in the **Offset** edit box in the **Options Bar** and press ENTER.

3. Now, pick the vertical reference plane twice to create the two reference planes at a distance of **2' (610 mm)**, one on the right and the other on the left of reference plane.

4. Next, enter the value **1' (305 mm)** in the **Offset** edit box in the **Options Bar** and press ENTER. Pick the horizontal reference plane twice to create two reference planes at a distance of **1' (305 mm)**, one above and the other below the existing reference plane.

5. Choose the **Annotate** tab and then choose the **Aligned** tool from the **Dimension** panel.

6. Next, add dimensions to the created reference planes, as shown in Figure 10-48. Choose the **Modify** button to exit the dimension tool.

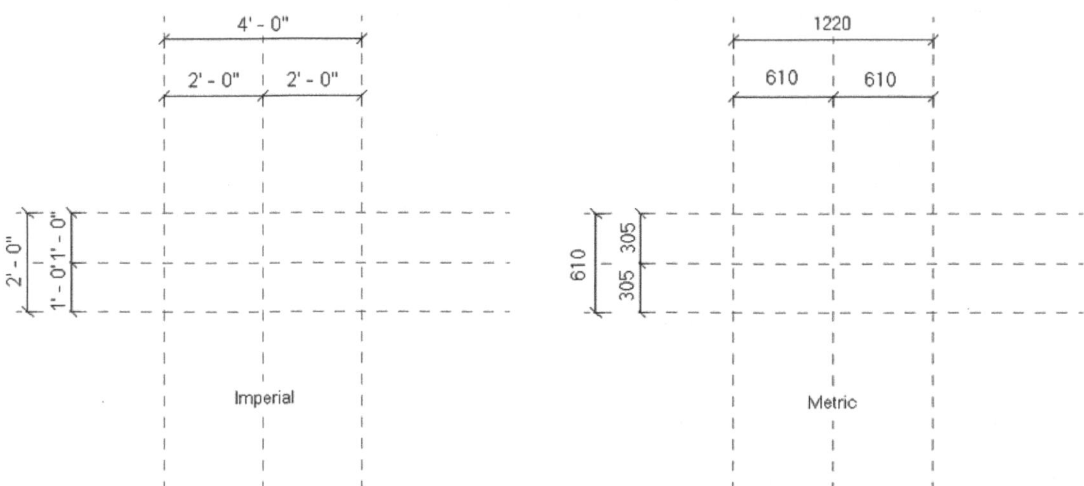

***Figure 10-48** Dimensions added to the created reference planes*

7. Select the **2' (610mm)** dimension line for the vertical reference plane; a blue **EQ** symbol appears. Click on the symbol; the dimensions are replaced by permanent **EQ** symbols.

Tip

*The **EQ** symbol ensures that whenever there is a change in the position of one of the reference planes with equality constraint, the other reference plane moves symmetrically.*

8. Next, select the **1' (305mm)** dimension line for the horizontal reference plane, and assign the equality constraint to it, as done in step 7, refer to Figure 10-49.

9. Select the **2' (610mm)** dimension line and then select the **Add parameter** option from the **Label** drop-down list in the **Options Bar**; the **Parameter Properties** dialog box is displayed, as shown in Figure 10-50.

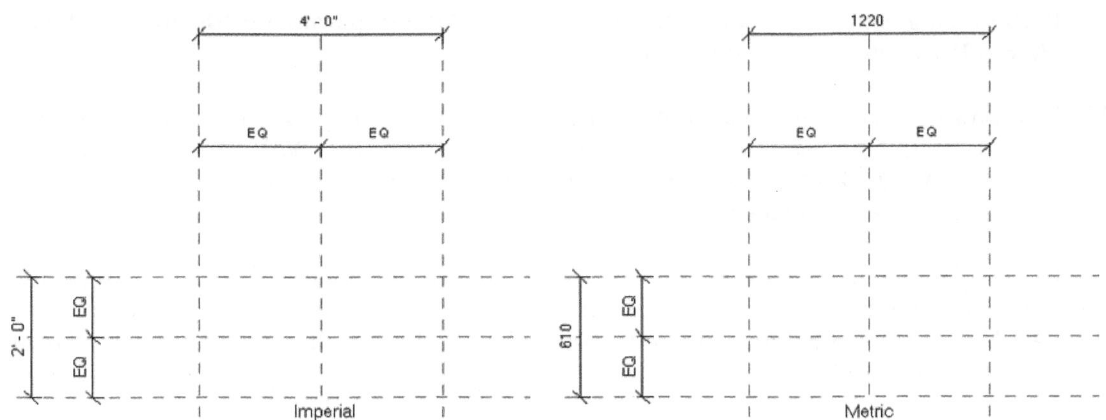

Figure 10-49 *Assigning equality constraint to the reference plane*

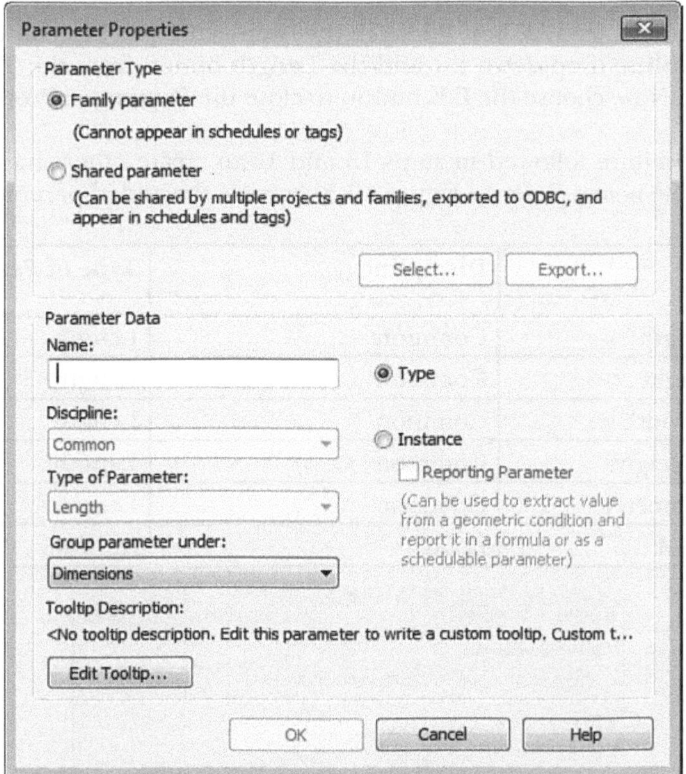

Figure 10-50 *The **Parameter Properties** dialog box*

10. In this dialog box, select the **Shared parameter** radio button in the **Parameter Type** area.

11. Next, choose the **Select** button in the **Parameter Type** area; the **Shared Parameter File Not Specified** message box is displayed, prompting you to choose one shared parameter. Choose the **Yes** button; the **Edit Shared Parameters** dialog box is displayed.

12. In this dialog box, choose the **Create** button in the **Shared parameter file** area; the **Create Shared Parameter File** dialog box is displayed.

13. Now, browse to the location **C: / rmp_2017** and create a new folder with name **c10_rmp_2017_tut**. Now, in the **File name** edit box, enter the name **Dual_Duct_VAV_box** for the Imperial system or **M_Dual_Duct_VAV_box** for the Metric system. Choose the **Save** button; the **Create Shared Parameters File** dialog box is closed.

14. In the **Edit Shared Parameters** dialog box, choose the **New** button from the **Groups** area; the **New Parameter Group** dialog box is displayed. In this dialog box, enter **Mechanical VAV box** in the **Name** edit box and choose the **OK** button; the **New Parameter Group** dialog box is closed.

15. In the **Edit Shared Parameters** dialog box, choose the **New** button from the **Parameters** area; the **Parameter Properties** dialog box is displayed.

16. In this dialog box, enter **VAV box Width** in the **Name** edit box. Select the **Common** option from the **Discipline** drop-down list and the **Length** option from the **Type of Parameter** drop-down list. Now, choose the **OK** button to close the **Parameter Properties** dialog box.

17. Repeat the procedure followed in steps 15 and 16 to create other shared parameters, as given in the table below. Refer to Figure 10-51 to view the added parameters.

Name	Discipline	Type of Parameter
VAV box Length	Common	Length
VAV box Height	Common	Length
VAV Outlet Width	Common	Length
VAV Outlet Height	Common	Length
VAV Inlet Diameter	Common	Length
VAV Max CFM	HVAC	Air Flow

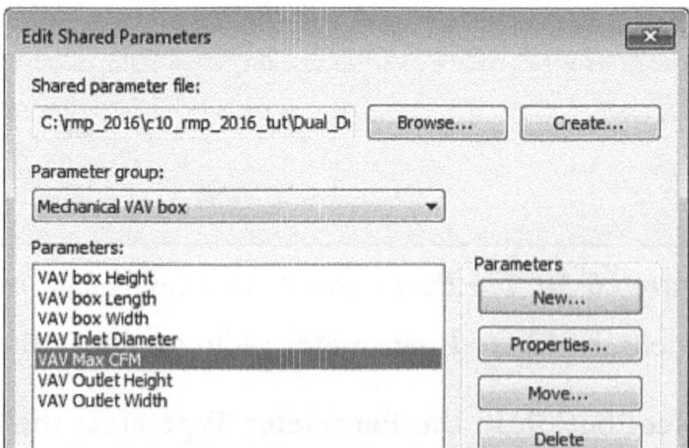

Figure 10-51 *Partial view of the* ***Edit Shared Parameters*** *dialog box displaying the created parameters*

18. Choose the **OK** button; the **Edit Shared Parameters** dialog box is closed and the **Shared Parameters** dialog box is displayed.

19. Now, select the **VAV box Width** option from the **Parameters** area of this dialog box. Choose the **OK** button in the **Shared Parameters** dialog box and then in the **Parameter Properties** dialog box to close them. Notice that the width label is assigned to the dimension line.

20. Next, select the **4'** (**1220 mm**) dimension line. Choose the **Add parameter** option in the **Label** drop-down list from the **Options Bar**; the **Parameter Properties** dialog box is displayed.

21. In this dialog box, select the **Shared parameter** radio button and then choose the **Select** button in the **Parameter Type** area; the **Shared Parameters** dialog box is displayed. In this dialog box, select the **VAV box Length** option from the **Parameters** area.

22. Now, choose the **OK** button in the **Shared Parameters** dialog box and then in the **Parameter Properties** dialog box to close them. Notice that the length label is assigned to the dimension line.

23. Double-click on the **Front** subnode under the **Elevations (Elevation 1)** head; the view is changed to Front elevation. Invoke the **Reference Plane** tool from the **Datum** panel of the **Create** tab; the **Modify | Place Reference Plane** contextual tab is displayed.

24. Choose the **Pick Lines** tool from the **Draw** panel of the **Modify | Place Reference Plane** tab. In the **Options Bar**, enter **5"** (**127 mm**) in the **Offset** edit box and press ENTER.

25. Double-click on the existing reference level to create two reference planes, one above and one below it. Choose the **Modify** button to exit the selection.

26. Choose the **Annotate** tab and then invoke the **Aligned** tool from the **Dimension** panel. Next, add dimensions to the created reference planes, as shown in Figure 10-52. Choose the **Modify** button to exit the tool.

27. Select the **5"** (**127 mm**) dimension line; the **EQ** symbol appears with the selected dimension. Click on this symbol; permanent equality constraints are assigned to the created reference planes.

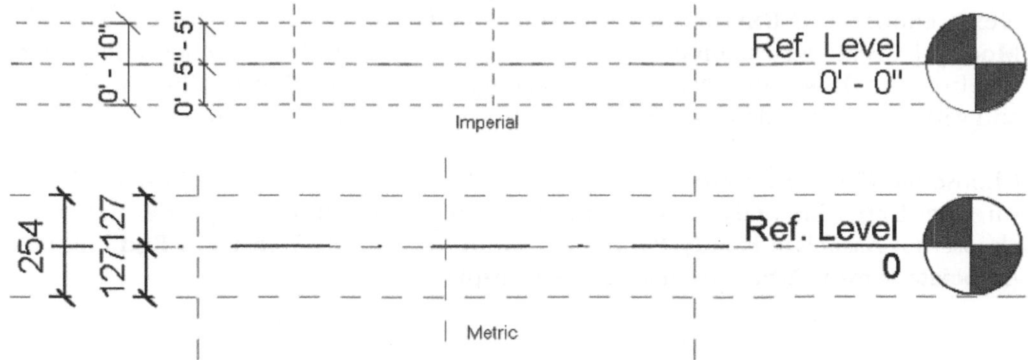

Figure 10-52 *Dimensions added to the created reference planes*

28. Next, select the **10" (254 mm)** dimension line, and then select the **Add parameter** option from the **Label** drop-down list in the **Options Bar**; the **Parameter Properties** dialog box is displayed.

29. Repeat the procedure followed in steps 21 and 22 and assign the **VAV box Height** parameter to it.

30. Select the reference plane below the reference level, and then in the **Properties** palette, enter the name **VAV box bottom** in the edit box next to **Name**.

31. Next, invoke the **Set** tool from the **Work Plane** panel of the **Create** tab; the **Work Plane** dialog box is displayed. In this dialog box, ensure that the **Name** radio button is selected. Then, choose the **Reference Plane: VAV box bottom** option from the drop-down list in the **Specify a new Work Plane** area, as shown in Figure 10-53. Choose the **OK** button; the dialog box is closed and the **Go To View** dialog box is displayed.

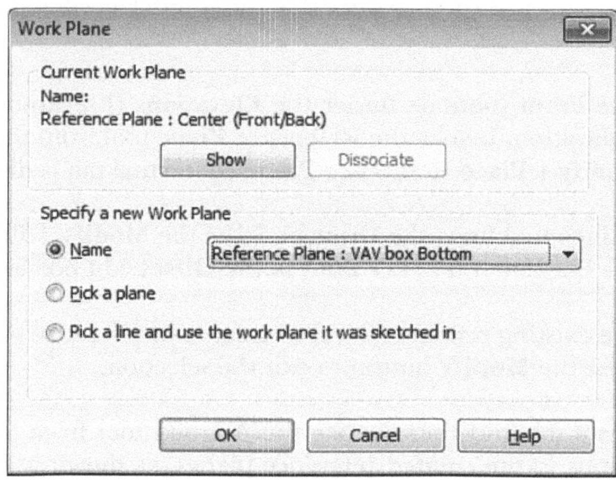

*Figure10-53 Setting reference plane from the **Work Plane** dialog box*

32. In this dialog box, select the **Floor Plan: Ref. Level** option, if it is not selected by default, and then choose the **Open View** button; the dialog box is closed and the view is changed to plan view.

33. Next, choose the **Extrusion** tool from the **Forms** panel of the **Create** tab; the **Modify | Create Extrusion** contextual tab is displayed. In this tab, choose the **Rectangle** tool from the **Draw** panel. Now, make a rectangle with **2' x 4'** (**610 x 1220** mm) dimensions, and with the already defined reference planes, as shown in Figure 10-54.

34. Choose the **Finish Edit Mode** button to exit the tool and to finish extrusion. Next, make sure that **Extrusion Start** value is set to **0' 0"** (**0.00** mm) in the **Properties** palette. Then, choose the **Associate Family Parameter** button next to the **Extrusion End** edit box; the **Associate Family Parameter** dialog box is displayed.

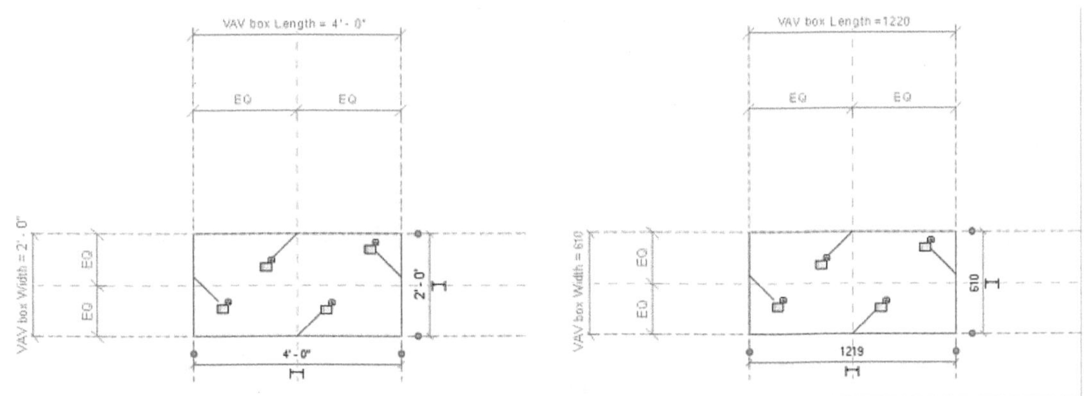

***Figure 10-54** Extrusion boundary created by using the **Rectangle** tool*

35. In this dialog box, select the **VAV box Height** option from the **Existing family parameters of compatible type** area, as shown in Figure 10-55. Next, choose the **OK** button; the **Associate Family Parameter** dialog box is closed. Notice that the end value **10" (254 mm)** is set in the **Extrusion End** edit box in the **Properties** palette. This value shows the height of the VAV box.

36. Next, double-click on the **View 1** subnode under the **3D Views** node in the **Project Browser,** the view is changed to 3D view and the model of the VAV box body is displayed, as shown in Figure 10-56.

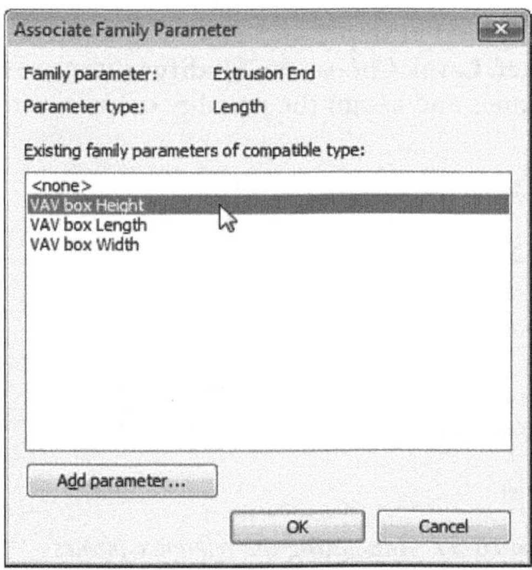

***Figure 10-55** Choosing an option from the **Associate Family Parameter** dialog box*

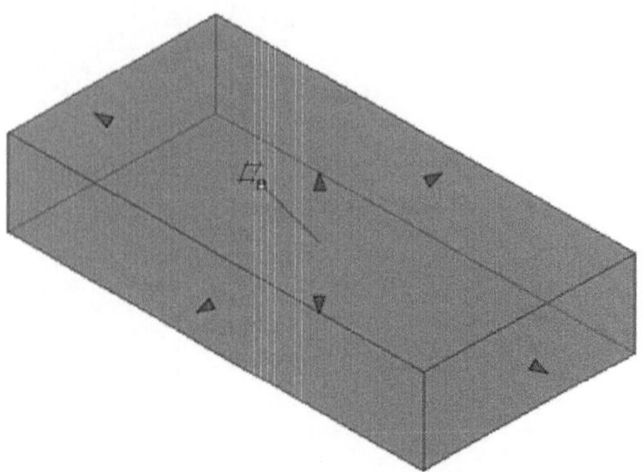

Figure 10-56 3D model of VAV box

Creating the VAV box Outlet Sleeve

In this section, you will create the sleeve for the VAV box body.

1. Double-click on the **Right** subnode under the **Elevations (Elevation 1)** node; the view is changed to Right elevation. Next, choose the **Reference Plane** tool from the **Datum** panel of the **Create** tab; the **Modify | Place Reference Plane** contextual tab is displayed.

2. In this tab, choose the **Pick Lines** tool from the **Draw** panel. Next, enter **4"** (**100 mm**) in the **Offset** edit box in the **Options Bar**. Next, pick the middle vertical reference plane twice to create one reference plane on its right, and the other on its left.

3. Repeat the procedure followed in step 2 and make two reference planes, above and below the existing horizontal **Ref. Level**. Choose the **Modify** button to exit the tool. Next, annotate the created reference planes and assign the equality constraint to it, refer to Figure 10-57.

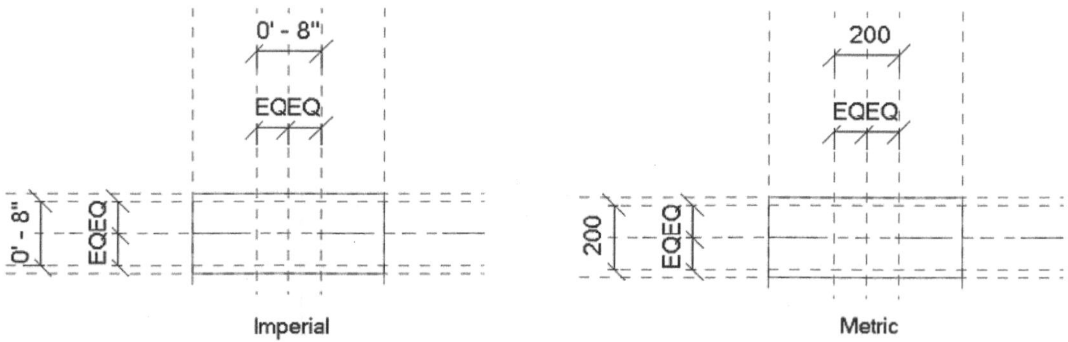

Figure 10-57 Annotating the reference planes

4. Now, assign the **VAV Outlet Width** and **VAV Outlet Height** parameters to the created reference planes following the procedure given in steps 20 through 22 of the previous section, refer to Figure 10-58.

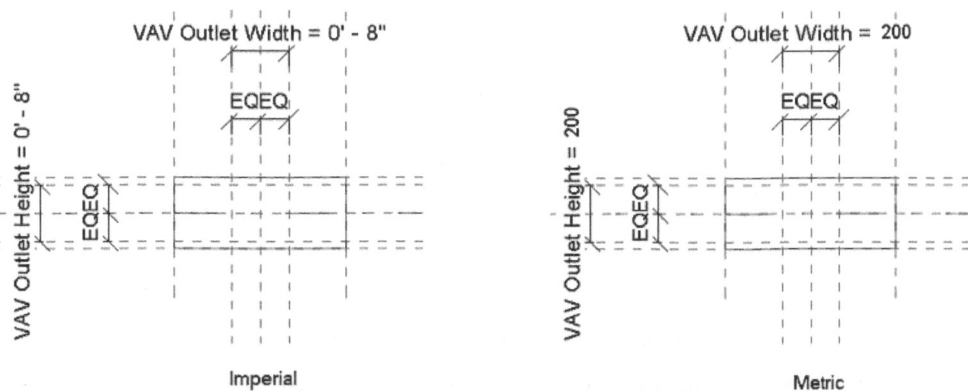

Figure 10-58 *Parameters added to the reference planes created*

5. Double-click on the **View 1** node under the **3D Views** node; the view is changed. Choose the **Set** tool from the **Work Plane** panel of the **Create** tab; the **Work Plane** dialog box is displayed. In this dialog box, choose the **Pick a plane** radio button from the **Specify a new Work plane** area and then choose the **OK** button; the dialog box is closed.

6. Move the cursor on the right face of the VAV box body and then click on the face when it is highlighted, refer to Figure 10-59.

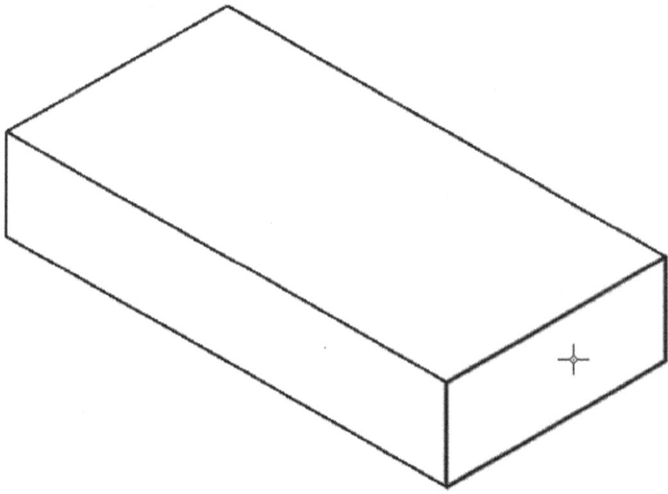

Figure 10-59 *Setting the reference plane on the face of the VAV box body*

7. Open the Right elevation from the **Project Browser**. Next, choose the **Create** tab and then choose the **Extrusion** tool from the **Forms** panel; the **Modify | Create Extrusion** contextual tab is displayed. Choose the **Rectangle** tool from the **Draw** panel of this tab.

8. Now, sketch a box with dimension **8" x 8" (200 x 200** mm) box including the boundaries of the created reference planes, as shown in Figure 10-60. Make sure in the **Properties** palette, the value for **Extrusion Start** is **2' 00" (610 mm)**. Next, enter the value **2' 2" (660 mm)** in the edit box next to **Extrusion End.** Choose the **Finish Edit Mode** button to finish sketching and exit the tool.

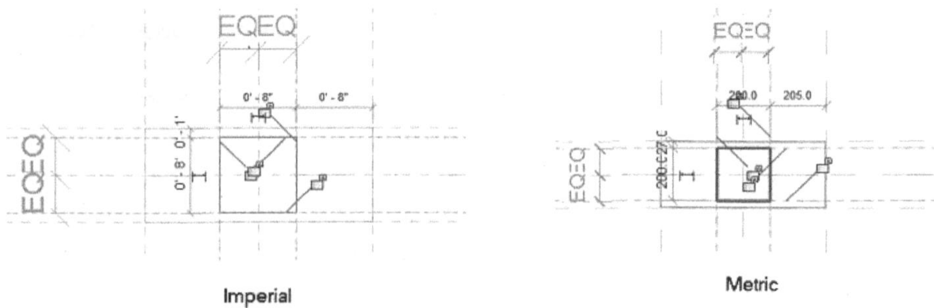

Figure 10-60 Sketching the VAV box sleeve

9. Choose the **Save As > Family** from the **Application Menu**; the **Save As** dialog box is displayed. In this dialog box, browse to *C:\rmp_2017\c10_rmp_2017_tut* and enter the name **VAV_box_Outlet_Sleeve** for Imperial system or **M_VAV_box_Outlet_Sleeve** for Metric system in the **File Name** edit box. Next, choose the **Save** button; the dialog box is closed and the file is saved.

Creating the VAV box Inlet Sleeve

In this section, you will create VAV box inlet sleeve to the previously created body.

1. Choose the **Family Types** tool from the **Properties** panel of the **Create** tab; the **Family Types** dialog box is displayed, as shown in the Figure 10-61.

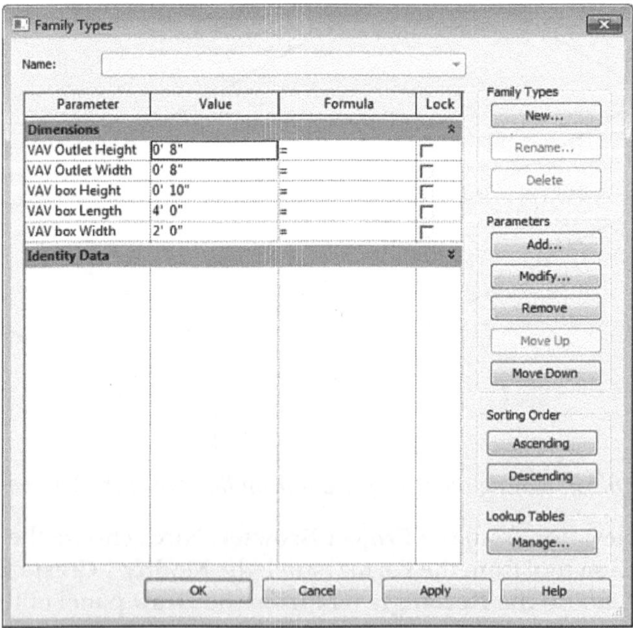

*Figure 10-61 The **Family Types** dialog box*

2. Next, choose the **Add** button in the **Parameters** area of the displayed dialog box; the **Parameter Properties** dialog box is displayed. In this dialog box, select the **Shared parameter** radio button and then choose the **Select** button from the **Parameter Type** area; the **Shared Parameters** dialog box is displayed.

3. In this dialog box, select the **VAV Inlet Diameter** option from the **Parameters** area. Choose the **OK** button in the **Shared Parameters** dialog box and then in the **Parameter Properties** dialog box to close them. Next, in the **Family Types** dialog box, enter **4"** (**100 mm**) in the **Value** field for the **VAV Inlet Diameter** option.

4. Choose the **Add** button in the **Parameters** area; the **Parameter Properties** dialog box is displayed. In this dialog box, enter **Inlet Radius** in the **Name** edit box in the **Parameter Data** area.

5. Now, select **Length** from the **Type of Parameter** drop-down list and then select the **Other** option from the **Group parameter under** drop-down list in the **Parameter Data** area. Choose the **OK** button; the **Parameter Properties** dialog box is closed.

6. Now, in the **Family Types** dialog box, click in the **Formula** field located next to the **Inlet Radius** option and then, enter **VAV Inlet Diameter / 2**, refer to Figure 10-62. Next, choose the **Apply** button and then the **OK** button; the dialog box is closed.

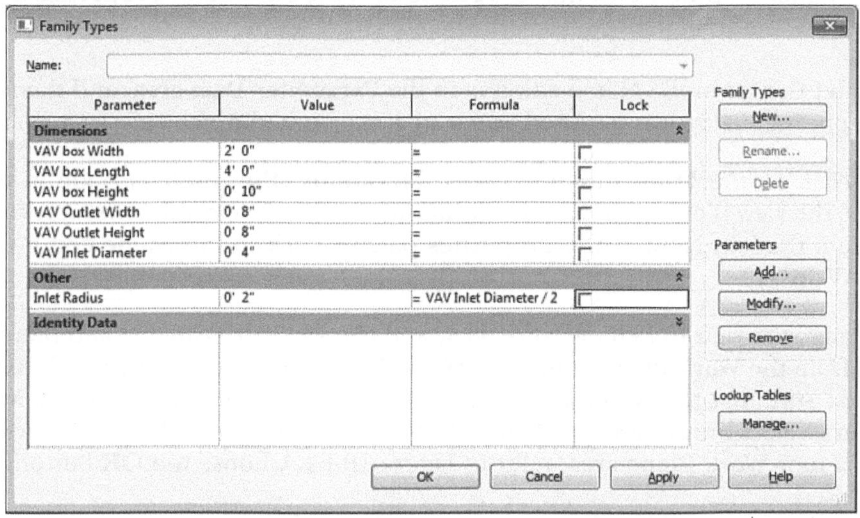

***Figure 10-62** Setting parameter values in the **Family Types** dialog box*

7. Double-click on the **Left** subnode under the **Elevations (Elevation 1)** node; the view is changed to Left elevation view. Now, choose the **Hidden Line** option from the **Visual Style** flyout in the **View Control Bar**; the VAV outlet sleeve disappears from the view.

8. Press and hold the CTRL key and select all the reference planes which define the VAV outlet sleeve. Next, choose the **Hide Element** option from the **Temporary Hide/Isolate** flyout in the **View Control Bar**.

9. Repeat the procedure followed in steps 1 and 2 of the previous section to make the two reference planes of dimension **5" (127 mm)** on either sides of the existing reference plane and assign the equality constraint to the planes created, refer to Figure 10-63.

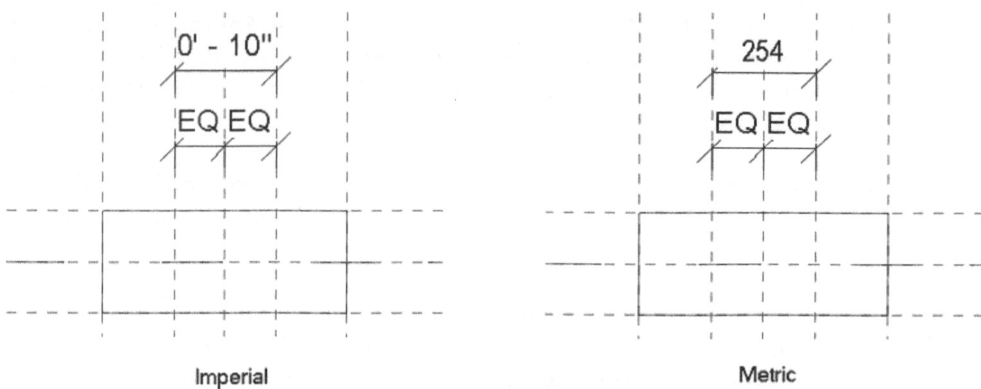

Figure 10-63 Equality constraint assigned to the created reference planes

10. Next, select the **10" (254 mm)** dimension line and then select the **Add parameter** option from the **Label** drop-down list in the **Options Bar**; the **Parameter Properties** dialog box is displayed.

11. Enter **Inlet Center** in the **Name** edit box in the **Parameter Data** area, and then choose the **OK** button; the dialog box is closed and a label is assigned to the reference planes.

12. Double-click on the **Front** subnode under **Elevations (Elevation 1)** node in the **Project Browser**; the view is changed to Front elevation view. Next, select the first vertical reference plane from the left. Now, in the **Properties** palette, click in the **Name** edit box and then enter **VAV Inlet**.

13. Now, change the view to Left elevation view and choose the **Create** tab and then invoke the **Set** tool from the **Work Plane** panel; the **Work Plane** dialog box is displayed. In this dialog box, make sure that the **Name** radio button is selected in the **Specify a new Work Plane** area. Next, select the **Reference Plane : VAV Inlet** option from the drop-down list in the **Specify a new Work Plane** area, refer to Figure 10-64. Choose the **OK** button; the dialog box is closed.

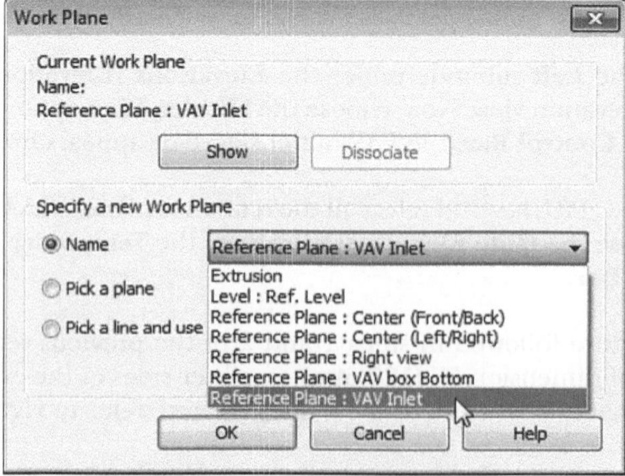

*Figure 10-64 Choosing the **Reference Plane VAV Inlet** option from the **Work Plane** dialog box*

14. Invoke the **Extrusion** tool from the **Forms** panel of the **Create** tab; the **Modify | Create Extrusion** contextual tab is displayed. Choose the **Circle** tool from the **Draw** panel of this tab. Draw two circles of **2"** (**50 mm**) radius at the intersections of the reference planes, as shown in Figure 10-65.

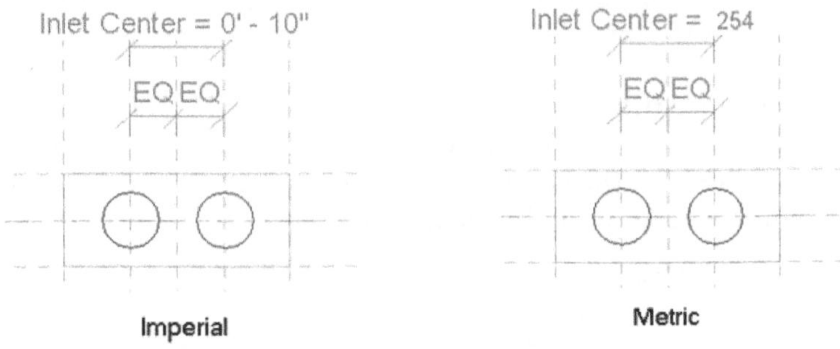

Figure 10-65 *VAV box inlet created using the* ***Circle*** *tool*

15. In the **Properties** palette, enter the value **0' 00"** (**0.00 mm**) in the **Extrusion Start** edit box and **-0' 4"** (**-100 mm**) in the **Extrusion End** edit box and then choose the **Apply** button to save changes. Next, choose the **Finish Edit Mode** button in the **Modify | Create Extrusion** contextual tab to finish the extrusion.

16. Change the view to Right elevation view and then choose the **Annotate** tab. Next, invoke the **Radial** tool from the **Dimension** panel. Next, add dimensions to the circles created and then press ESC to exit the tool.

17. Next, select both the dimension added to the circles and then choose the **Inlet Radius** option from the **Label** drop-down in the **Options Bar**. Repeat this step to assign label to both the circles, refer to Figure 10-66. Navigate to the 3D view. The geometry is created and it looks like shown in Figure 10-67.

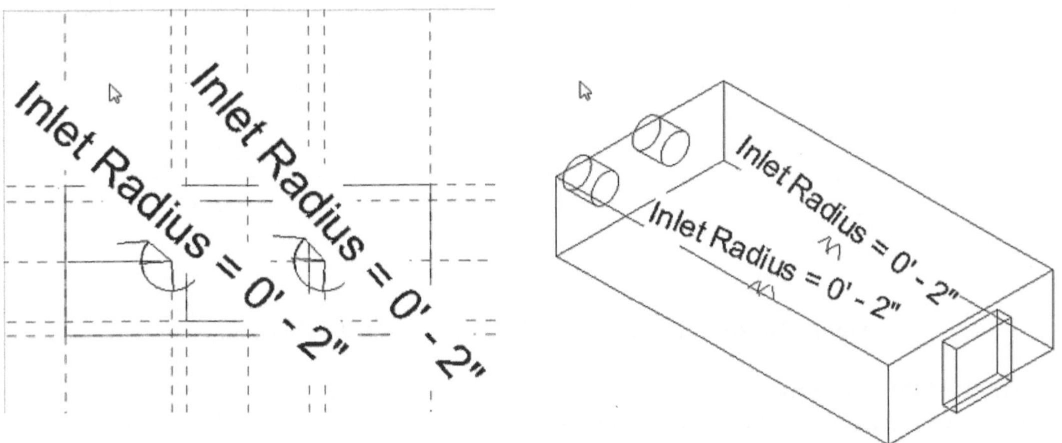

Figure 10-66 *Labels added to the created geometry*

Figure 10-67 *VAV inlet sleeve*

Creating the VAV box Control Box

In this section, you will create the control boxes to the model generated in the previous sections.

1. Invoke the **Set** tool from the **Work Plane** panel of the **Create** tab; the **Work Plane** dialog box is displayed. In this dialog box, select the **Pick a plane** radio button from the **Specify a new Work plane** area and then choose the **OK** button to close the dialog box.

2. Rotate the model and move the cursor to the Front face of the VAV box and then click when it gets highlighted, as shown in the Figure 10-68. Now, choose the **Show** tool from the **Work Plane** panel of the **Create** tab; the created workplane is highlighted, refer to Figure 10-69. Choose the **Show** button again to make the highlighted work plane disappear.

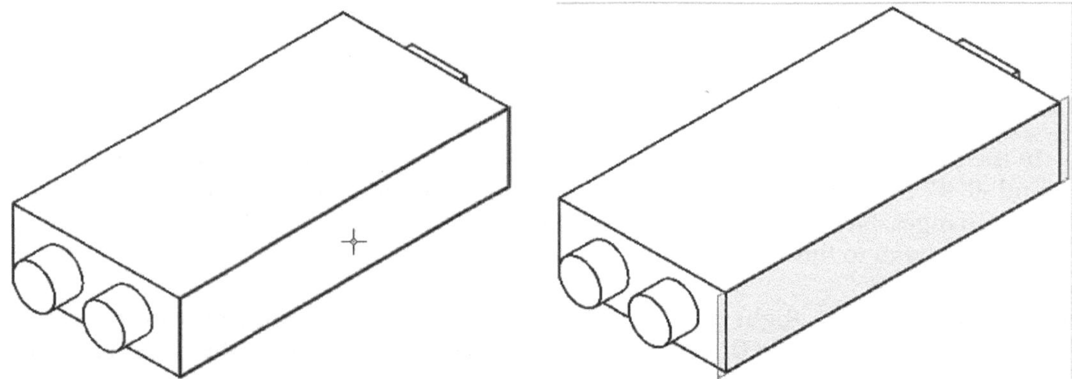

Figure 10-68 *Setting work plane to the front face* ***Figure 10-69*** *Showing the created work plane*

3. Double-click on the **Front** view and then invoke the **Reference Plane** tool from the **Datum** panel of the **Create** tab. Next, choose the **Pick Lines** tool from the **Draw** panel. Next, enter **2" (51 mm)** in the **Offset** edit box in the **Options Bar** and then press ENTER. Pick the left reference plane to create a reference plane **2" (51 mm)** to its right, as shown in Figure 10-70.

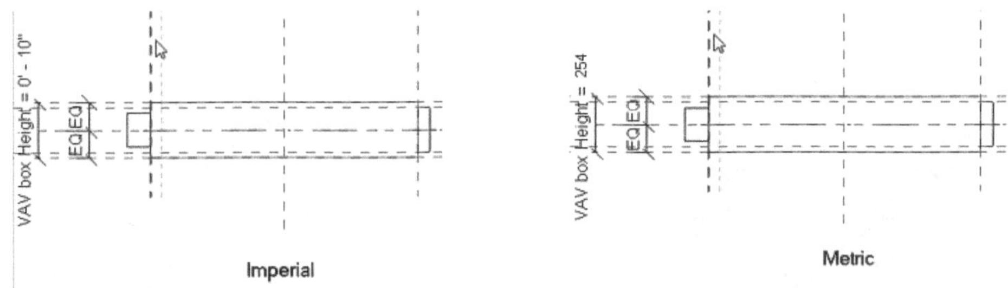

Figure 10-70 *Creating a reference plane using the* ***Pick Line*** *tool*

4. Enter **1' 00" (300 mm)** in the **Offset** edit box. Next, pick the recently created reference plane to create a reference plane on its right. Now, choose the **Modify** button to exit the tool.

5. Choose the **Create** tab and then choose the **Extrusion** tool from the **Forms** panel; the **Modify | Create Extrusion** contextual tab is displayed. Choose the **Rectangle** tool from the **Draw** panel of this tab. Now, sketch a rectangle with **1'00"x0'10" (300 x 254 mm)** dimension including the boundaries of the created reference planes, as shown in Figure 10-71.

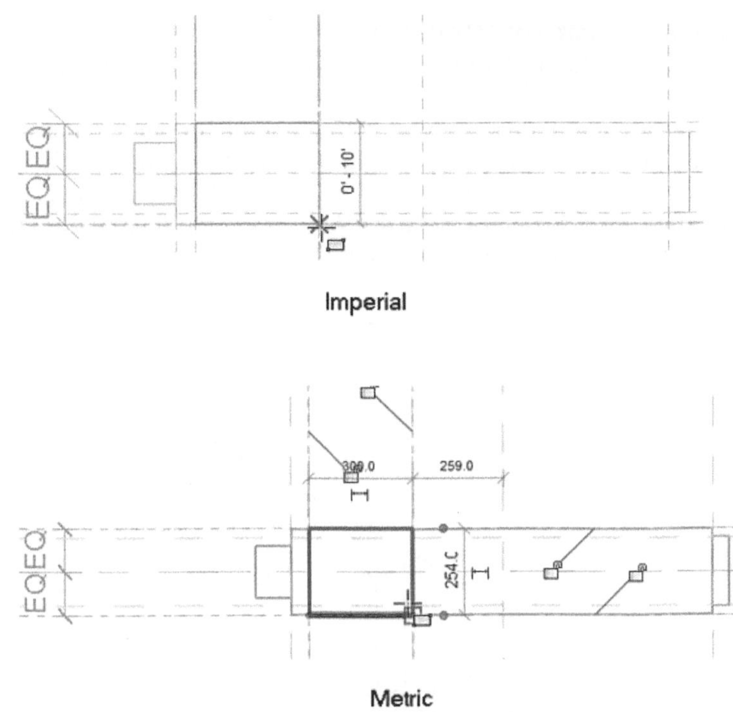

Figure 10-71 *Sketching the extrusion boundary*

6. In the **Properties** palette, click in the **Extrusion End** edit box and enter **1' 4"** (**406 mm**). Next, in the **Extrusion Start** edit box, enter **1' 00"** (**305 mm**), if it is not set by default. Next, choose the **Finish Edit Mode** button to finish sketching.

7. Repeat steps 5 and 6 to create a control box on the Back elevation with **-1' 4"** (**-406 mm**) **Extrusion End** and **-1' 00" (-305 mm) Extrusion Start** values. The final 3D view of the created geometry is shown in Figure 10-72.

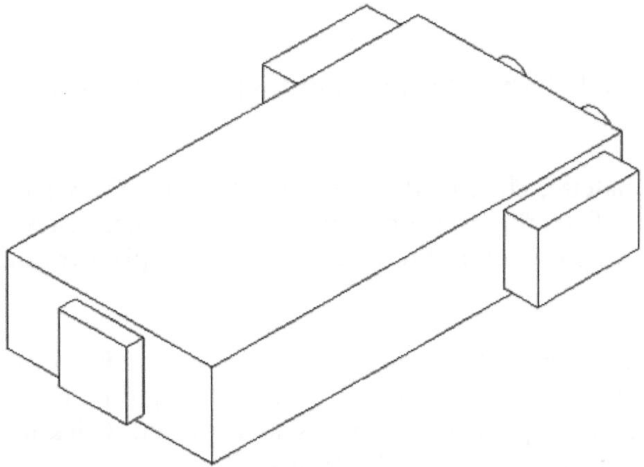

Figure 10-72 *3D view of the created control box*

Attaching the Outlet Duct Connectors

In this section, you will attach the outlet duct connector to the created geometry.

1. In the 3D view, navigate to the view in which the face of the outlet duct sleeve is visible. Next, invoke the **Duct Connector** tool from the **Connectors** panel of the **Create** tab; the **Modify | Place Duct Connector** contextual tab is displayed. Choose the **Face** tool from the **Placement** panel, if it is not chosen by default. Next, select the face of the VAV outlet sleeve to add connector to it, as shown in Figure 10-73.

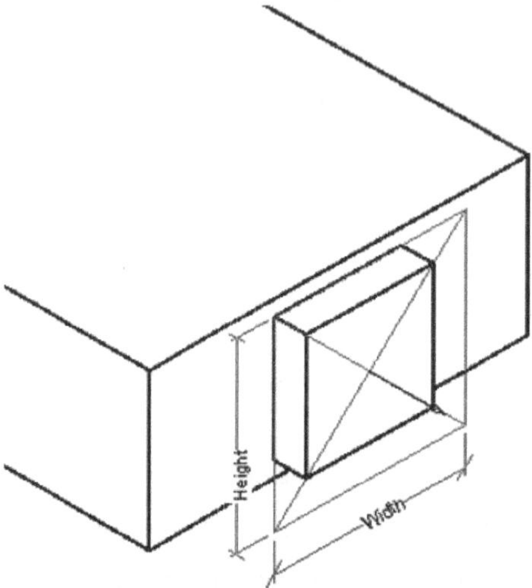

Figure 10-73 *Duct connector added to the outlet duct sleeve*

2. Choose the **Modify** button and then select the recently added duct connector. Next, click on the **+** sign next to the width dimension; the **Associate Family Parameter** dialog box is displayed. In this dialog box, select the **VAV Outlet Width** option and then choose the **OK** button; the **Associate Family Parameter** is closed and the parameter is added to the connector.

3. Repeat the procedure followed in step 2 and assign the **VAV Outlet Height** parameter to the height dimension.

4. In the **Properties** palette, click in the value field of the **Flow Direction** parameter and select the **Out** option from the drop-down list displayed. Next, click in the value field of the **System Classification** parameter and then select the **Supply Air** option, if it is not selected by default.

5. Choose the **Associate Family Parameter** button next to the **Flow** value field; the **Associate Family Parameter** dialog box is displayed. In this dialog box, choose the **Add parameter** button; the **Parameter Properties** dialog box is displayed. Click in the **Name** edit box in the **Parameter Data** area and enter **VAV Outflow**.

6. Choose the **Instance** radio button and then select the **Mechanical - Flow** option from the **Group parameter under** area, if it is not selected by default. Choose the **OK** button in the

Parameter Properties dialog box and then in the **Associate Family Parameter** dialog box to close them. Choose the **Modify** button to exit the selection.

Attaching the Inlet Duct Connectors

In this section, you will attach the inlet duct connector to the created geometry.

1. Choose the **Family Types** tool from the **Properties** panel of the **Create** tab; the **Family Types** dialog box is displayed. In this dialog box, choose the **Add** button in the **Parameters** area; the **Parameter Properties** dialog box is displayed. In this dialog box, enter **Duct Inlet Radius** in the **Name** edit box in the **Parameter Data** area.

2 Next, select the **Length** option from the **Type of Parameter** drop-down list and the **Other** option from the **Group parameter under** drop-down list in the **Parameter Data** area. Choose the **OK** button; the **Parameter Properties** dialog box is closed.

3. In the **Family Type** dialog box, click in the value field of the **Formula** column of the **Duct Inlet Radius** parameter and enter the formula **Inlet Radius + 0' 1/16" (2 mm)**, refer to Figure 10-74. Next, choose the **Apply** button and then the **OK** button to save the changes and close the dialog box.

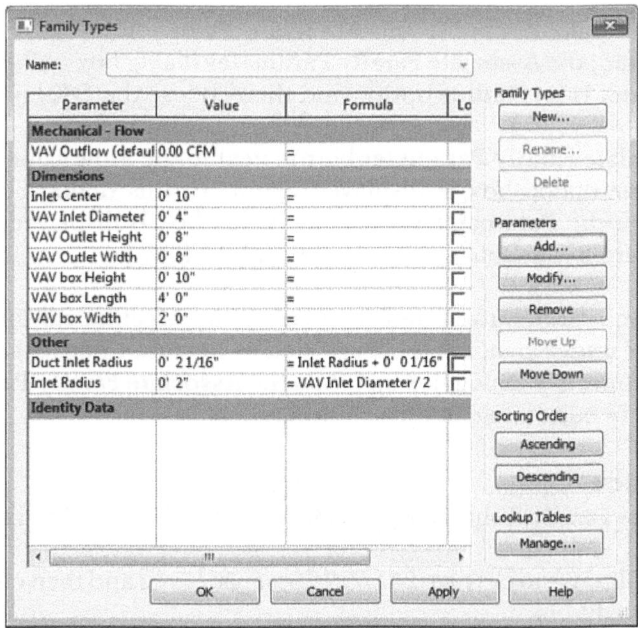

Figure 10-74 *Formulating the* ***Duct Inlet Radius*** *parameter*

4. Using the ViewCube in 3D view, navigate to the view in which the face of the inlet duct sleeve is visible, refer to Figure 10-75.

5. Next, invoke the **Duct Connector** tool from the **Connectors** panel of the **Create** tab and then choose the **Face** tool from the **Placement** panel, if it is not chosen by default. Next, select the faces of both the VAV inlet sleeves to add connectors to them, as shown in Figure 10-76.

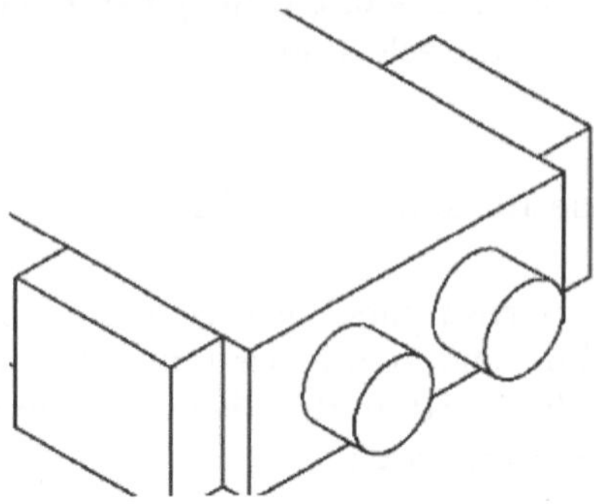

Figure 10-75 3D view of the inlet duct sleeve

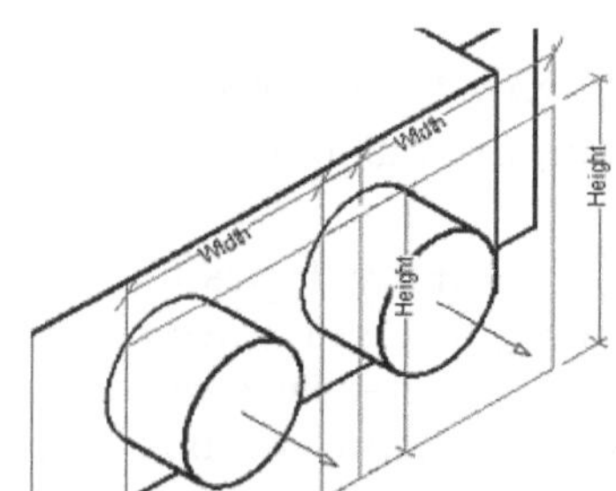

Figure 10-76 Connectors added to the inlet duct sleeves

6. Choose the **Modify** button to exit the tool and then select the recently added connectors. Now, in the **Properties** palette, click in the value field of the **Shape** parameter and then select the **Round** option from the drop-down list. In the **Flow Direction** parameter, select the **In** option from the drop-down list. Make sure that the **System Classification** parameter is set to **Supply Air**.

7. In the **Properties** palette, choose the **Associate Family Parameter** button next to the **Diameter** value field; the **Associate Family Parameter** dialog box is displayed. In this dialog box, select the **Duct Inlet Radius** option and then choose the **OK** button.

8. Choose the **Associate Family Parameter** button next to the **Flow** value field; the **Associate Family Parameter** dialog box is displayed again. In this dialog box, choose the **Add parameter** button; the **Parameter Properties** dialog box is displayed. Click in the **Name** edit box in the **Parameter Data** area and enter **Inlet Flow**.

9. Select the **Instance** radio button and then select the **Mechanical-Flow** option from the **Group parameter under** area, if it is not selected by default. Choose the **OK** button to close the **Parameter Properties** dialog box and then the **Associate Family Parameter** dialog box. Choose the **Modify** button to exit the selection.

Saving the Project

1. Choose **Save As > Family** from the **Application Menu**; the **Save As** dialog box is displayed.

2. In this dialog box, browse to *C: \ rmp_2017/\c10_rmp_2017_tut* and then enter **Dual_Duct_VAV** in the **File name** edit box.

3. Now, choose the **Save** button; the **Save As** dialog box closes and the project file is saved.

Closing the Project

1. To close the project, choose the **Close** option from the **Application Menu**.

The file is closed. This completes the tutorial.

Self-Evaluation Test

Answer the following questions and then compare them to those given at the end of this chapter:

1. To convert the created conceptual mass into real building elements such as walls, floors, roofs and so on, choose the relevant tools from the __________ panel.
2. To create a solid geometry by revolving a profile about an axis, choose the __________ tool.
3. The __________ tool is used to create a geometry with a path and two different profiles drawn at the either end of the path.
4. You can load the created massing geometry into the project by using the __________ tool.
5. You can edit the profile of a geometry by using the __________ tool from the **Mode** panel.
6. You can start the process of worksharing by using the __________ tool.
7. The added profile in a form will only be visible in the X-Ray mode. (T/F)
8. You can add levels to the 3D and elevation views in the conceptual design environment. (T/F)

Review Questions

Answer the following questions:

1. You can create a massing geometry by blending or linking two profiles using the __________ tool.
2. To add a pre-defined massing geometry in a project, you need to use the __________ tool from the **Conceptual Mass** tab.
3. You can display the geometry skeleton like vertices and edges by using the __________ tool from the **Element** panel.
4. The name of the user currently using elements in a workset can be seen under the __________ column in the **Worksets** dialog box.
5. You can synchronize a local file with the central file by choosing the __________ tool from the **Synchronize** panel.
6. You can update your model regarding the changes made and saved to the central file by other team members by using the __________ tool.
7. Once worksharing is enabled, it can be undone. (T/F)
8. The **Editable** column in the **Worksets** dialog box shows the status of the modification of elements (T/F)

EXERCISE

Exercise 1 Supply Diffusers

Create an air supply diffuser in the family editor, using the file *Mechanical Equipment.rft* for Imperial system or *Metric Mechanical Equipment.rft* for Metric system. Parameters to be used are given next. Refer to Figure 10-77 to 79 to create the model geometry.

(Expected time: 45 min)

1. Project File Parameters:
   Template File-

For Imperial	*Mechanical Equipment.rft*
For Metric	*Metric Mechanical Equipment.rft*

   File Name to be assigned-

For Imperial	*c10_Supply-Diffuser_exer1.rvt*
For Metric	*M_c10_Supply-Diffuser_exer1.rvt*

2. Dimension of the air diffuser:

Base dimensions:	2'x2' (600x600 mm)
Base geometry height:	6" (150 mm)
Top dimension:	1'6"x1'6" (450x450 mm)
Top geometry height:	3" (75 mm)
Connector radius:	6" (150 mm)
Connector height:	3" (75 mm)

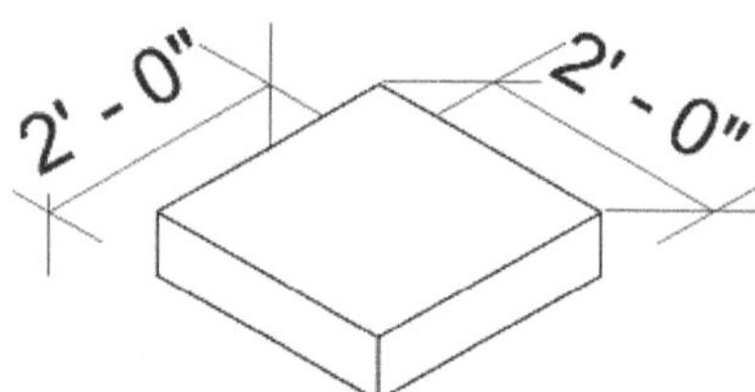

Figure 10-77 *The base geometry created*

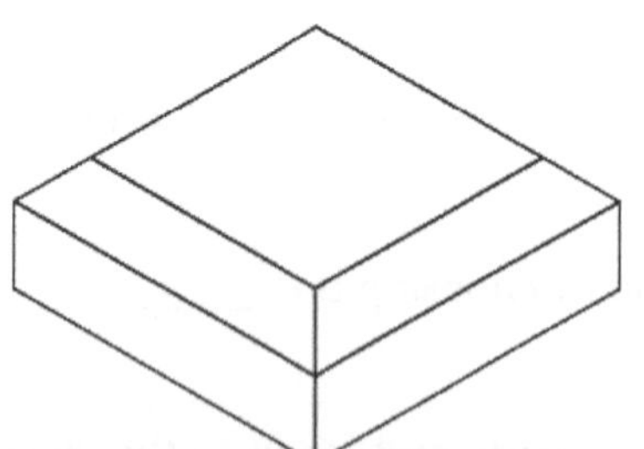

Figure 10-78 *The top geometry created on the base profile*

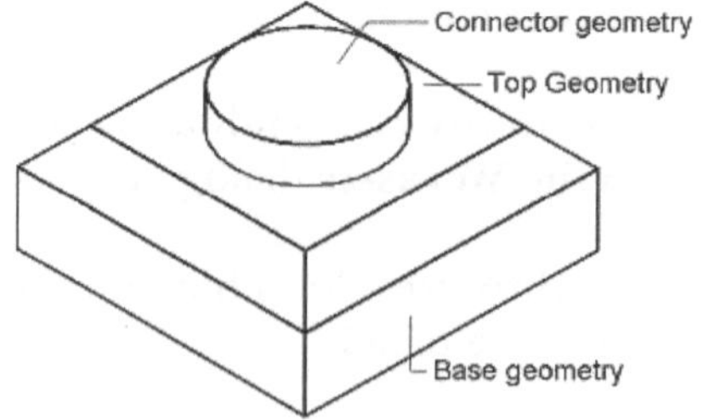

Figure 10-79 *Connector geometry created over the top profile*

Answers to Self-Evaluation Test

1. **Model by Face** **2.** **Revolve** **3.** **Swept Blend, 4. Load into Project, 5. Edit Profile, 6. Worksets, 7.** T, **8.** T

Index

A

Adding a Door to a Wall 3-43
Adding a Drawing Sheet 9-28
Adding a Plan View 3-21
Adding Doors 3-39
Adding Edges 10-21
Adding Levels 3-7
Adding Schedules to a
 Drawing Sheet 9-32
Adding Views to a Drawing Sheet 9-29
Air Flow 2-9
Aligned Tool 9-6
Angle Units 2-7
Angular Tool 9-7
Applying the Scope Box 3-29
Area and Volume Computations
 dialog box 4-14
Area and Volume
 Computations tool 4-13
Area Units 2-6
Automatically Connect tool 7-19

B

Big Steering Wheel 2-35
Binding Links 2-21
Boundary Lines tool 10-6
Browser Organization 2-18
Building Envelope 3-2
Building Model 3-39
Building Model in Sheets 9-32

C

Callout Using the Rectangle tool 9-23
Ceiling tool 3-52
Check Duct Systems tool 5-7
Color Scheme Legends 4-19
Color Schemes 4-15
Color Schemes tool 4-16
Common unit 2-5
Communication Devices 6-13
Conceptual Design environment 10-3
Controlling the Visibility of
 Scope Box 3-29
Controlling Visibility of
 Work Planes 3-16
Converting Temporary Dimensions 9-13
Creating a Blend 10-9
Creating a Custom
 Project Template 2-11
Creating a Wall Section View 3-27
Creating a Drafting View 9-26
Creating a New Template 2-11
Creating a Scope Box 3-28
Creating a Section View 3-25
Creating a Segmented Section 3-27
Creating an Automatic Ceiling 3-52
Creating an Extrusion 10-5
Creating Cuts in Massing
 Geometry 10-13
Creating the Massing Geometry 10-3
Currency Units 2-7
Curtain Walls 3-30
Cutting Openings 3-60

D

Delete Workset dialog box 10-27
Demand factor 6-25
Details in a Callout View 9-25
Dimension Line 9-4
Dimension Parameters 9-12
Dimension Text 9-4
Dimensioning 9-2
Display Model parameter 9-24
Displaying a Callout View 9-24
Dissolve tool 10-22
Dividing Edges or Paths 10-16
Dormer Opening Tool 3-62
Drafting Details 9-26
Duct Conversion Settings 5-14
Duplicate View as Dependent View 9-27
Duplicate Views 9-27

E

Electrical Equipment tool 6-27
Electrical Potential 2-9
Electrical Settings 6-18
Electrical Unit Type 2-9
Element Ownership Concepts 10-30
Elevation Views 3-23
Entities in a Dimension 9-4
Exterior Walls Type 3-30
Extrusion tool 10-5

F

Fabrication Details in Revit 5-18
Family Workset 10-28
File Locations tab 2-31
Fire protection system 8-4
Floor tool 3-49

G

Generating Solution of the Layout 7-16
Graphics Tab 2-30.
Grid Properties 3-14

H

Heating Load 2-9
HVAC Unit Type 2-8

I

Inherit Elevation button 5-15
Inspect tool 5-6

K

K Coefficient parameter 7-9
Kick-off Meeting 2-2

L

Leader Type parameter 9-12
Length Units 2-6
Level Properties 3-3
Level tool 3-7
Lighting tool 6-11
Linear tool 9-7
Linked Models in Schedules 2-24
Load Family dialog box 3-39, 9-28
Loaded Tags dialog box 6-12
Loading the Tags 9-19
Locking Permanent Dimensions 9-13
Look Tool Behavior Area 2-35
Loss Method parameter 7-9

M

Massing Concepts 10-2
Mechanical Equipment tool 5-3
Mechanical Settings dialog box 7-12
Mini Wheel Appearance 2-35
Modifying Level Parameters 3-9
Modifying the Color Scheme 4-20
Modifying the Color Scheme Legends 4-20
Modifying the Plan View Properties 3-22
Modifying the Room Properties 3-58

N

New Drafting View dialog box 9-26
Non-workshared projects 2-28

P

Panning Views 9-31
Pipe Accessories 7-22
Pipe Fittings tool 7-21
Pipe Material 7-9
Pipe Segment 7-20
Pipe Settings 7-6
Piping tool 8-3
Piping Unit Type 2-10
Place Mass tool 10-16
Place on Workplane tool 6-8
Placing the Massing Geometry 10-15
Plumbing fixtures 7-2
Power button 6-29
Process of Worksharing 10-23
Profiles 10-21
Project environment 10-4
Project Information 2-13
Project Location 2-15
Project Standards Workset 10-28
Properties of a Callout View 9-24

R

Radial tool 9-8
Reference Planes 3-15
Reloading Files in Worksets 10-29
Resizing a Massing Geometry 10-12
Revolve tool 10-6
Room Instance Parameters 3-58
Room Schedules 3-57
Room tool 3-55
Rooms 3-55
Routing Pipes 7-13
Routing Preferences dialog box 7-7

S

Saving Files 2-27
Schedule/Quantities tool 8-8
Scope Box tool 3-28
Setting the Work Plane 3-16
Shaft Opening 3-62
Sketching the Floor Boundary 3-50
Slope of the Pipe 7-11
Slope Units 2-7
Snaps tool 2-25
Spelling Checks 2-33
Spot Elevation tool 9-9
Spot Slope tool 9-11
Sprinkler head 8-8
Sprinkler tool 8-9
SteeringWheels 2-34
SteeringWheels tab 2-34
Sweep 10-08
Swept Blend tool 10-10
Synchronizing with Central file 10-28

T

Tag By Category tool 9-18
Tag on Placement 4-3
Tagging 9-18
Tags 9-18
Temporary Hide/Isolate tool 3-20

Temporary Overrides 2-27
Text Notes 9-14
Transferring Project Standards 2-17
Transformer 6-2
Types of Dimension 9-2

U

Underlay parameter 9-24
User Interface tab 2-36
User-Created Workset 10-27

V

Velocity 2-10
View Options area 2-30
View Workset 10-27
ViewCube tab 2-35
Visibility of Levels 3-9
Visibility of Linked Models 2-22
Visibility/Graphics Overrides dialog box 4-4
Void Revolve 10-14
Volume Units 2-7

W

Walk tool 2-35
Wall Openings 3-49
Wall Types 3-29
Weather Location and Site dialog box 2-16
Window Type Properties 3-46
Witness Lines 9-5
Worksets dialog box 10-25
Worksharing update frequency 2-30

X

X-Ray 10-20
X-Ray tool 10-16

Z

Zoom tool 2-35